Using Traditional Design Methods to Enhance AI–Driven Decision Making

Tien V. T. Nguyen
Industrial University of Ho Chi Minh City, Vietnam

Nhut T. M. Vo
National Kaohsiung University of Science and Technology, Taiwan

A volume in the Advances in Media,
Entertainment, and the Arts (AMEA) Book Series

Published in the United States of America by
    IGI Global
    Information Science Reference (an imprint of IGI Global)
    701 E. Chocolate Avenue
    Hershey PA, USA 17033
    Tel: 717-533-8845
    Fax: 717-533-8661
    E-mail: cust@igi-global.com
    Web site: http://www.igi-global.com

Library of Congress Cataloging-in-Publication Data

Names: Nguyen, Tien V.T., 1987- editor. | Vo, Nhut Thi Minh, 1986- editor.
Title: Using traditional design methods to enhance AI-driven decision
    making / Edited by Tien Nguyen, Nhut Vo.
Description: Hershey, PA : Information Science Reference, [2024] | Includes
    bibliographical references and index. | Summary: "Through its
    thought-provoking chapters, it aims to deepen the understanding of
    AI-Driven decision-making in higher education leadership and equip
    readers with the necessary knowledge and resources to embrace and
    leverage the potential of AI in decision-making processes"-- Provided by
    publisher.
Identifiers: LCCN 2023038664 (print) | LCCN 2023038665 (ebook) | ISBN
    9798369306390 (hardcover) | ISBN 9798369306437 (paperback) | ISBN
    9798369306406 (ebook)
Subjects: LCSH: Artificial intelligence--Educational applications. |
    Education, Higher--Decision-making. | Educational leadership.
Classification: LCC LB1028.43 .U83 2024 (print) | LCC LB1028.43 (ebook) |
    DDC 378.1/01--dc23/eng/20231023
LC record available at https://lccn.loc.gov/2023038664
LC ebook record available at https://lccn.loc.gov/2023038665

This book is published in the IGI Global book series Advances in Media, Entertainment, and the Arts (AMEA) (ISSN: 2475-6814; eISSN: 2475-6830)

British Cataloguing in Publication Data
A Cataloguing in Publication record for this book is available from the British Library.

For electronic access to this publication, please contact: eresources@igi-global.com.

Advances in Media, Entertainment, and the Arts (AMEA) Book Series

Giuseppe Amoruso
Politecnico di Milano, Italy

ISSN:2475-6814
EISSN:2475-6830

MISSION

Throughout time, technical and artistic cultures have integrated creative expression and innovation into industrial and craft processes. Art, entertainment and the media have provided means for societal self-expression and for economic and technical growth through creative processes.

The **Advances in Media, Entertainment, and the Arts (AMEA)** book series aims to explore current academic research in the field of artistic and design methodologies, applied arts, music, film, television, and news industries, as well as popular culture. Encompassing titles which focus on the latest research surrounding different design areas, services and strategies for communication and social innovation, cultural heritage, digital and print media, journalism, data visualization, gaming, design representation, television and film, as well as both the fine applied and performing arts, the AMEA book series is ideally suited for researchers, students, cultural theorists, and media professionals.

COVERAGE

- Environmental Design
- Products, Strategies and Services
- New Media Art
- Color Studies
- Geometry & Design
- Popular Culture
- Traditional Arts
- Design Tools
- Sports & Entertainment
- Cultural Heritage

IGI Global is currently accepting manuscripts for publication within this series. To submit a proposal for a volume in this series, please contact our Acquisition Editors at Acquisitions@igi-global.com or visit: http://www.igi-global.com/publish/.

Titles in this Series

For a list of additional titles in this series, please visit: www.igi-global.com/book-series/advances-media-entertainment-arts/102257

News Media and Hate Speech Promotion in Mediterranean Countries
Elias Said Hung (Universidad Internacional de la Rioja, Spain) and Julio Montero Diaz (Universidad Internacional de la Rioja, Spain)
Information Science Reference • copyright 2023 • 364pp • H/C (ISBN: 9781668484272) • US $215.00 (our price)

Examinations and Analysis of Sequels and Serials in the Film Industry
Emre Ahmet Seçmen (Beykoz University, Turkey)
Information Science Reference • copyright 2023 • 389pp • H/C (ISBN: 9781668478646) • US $215.00 (our price)

Using Innovative Literacies to Develop Leadership and Agency Inspiring Transformation and Hope
Limor Pinhasi-Vittorio (Lehman College, CUNY, USA) and Elite Ben-Yosef (The BYEZ Foundation, USA)
Information Science Reference • copyright 2023 • 287pp • H/C (ISBN: 9781668456149) • US $215.00 (our price)

Music and Engagement in the Asian Political Space
Uche Titus Onyebadi (Texas Christian University, USA) and Delaware Arif (University of South Alabama, USA)
Information Science Reference • copyright 2023 • 254pp • H/C (ISBN: 9781799858171) • US $215.00 (our price)

Handbook of Research on the Relationship Between Autobiographical Memory and Photography
Mark Bruce Nigel Ingham (London College of Communication, University of the Arts London, UK) Nela Milic (London College of Communication, University of the Arts London, UK) Vasileios Kantas (University of West Attica, Greece) Sara Andersdotter (University for the Creative Arts, Sweden) and Paul Lowe (London College of Communication, University of the Arts London, UK)
Information Science Reference • copyright 2023 • 636pp • H/C (ISBN: 9781668453377) • US $295.00 (our price)

Contemporary Manifests on Design Thinking and Practice
Gözde Zengin (Karabük University, Turkey) and Bengi Yurtsever (Mugla Sıtkı Kocman University, Turkey)
Information Science Reference • copyright 2023 • 277pp • H/C (ISBN: 9781668463765) • US $215.00 (our price)

Sustaining Creativity and the Arts in the Digital Age
Gilberto Marzano (Rezekne Academy of Technologies, Latvia)
Information Science Reference • copyright 2022 • 329pp • H/C (ISBN: 9781799878407) • US $215.00 (our price)

701 East Chocolate Avenue, Hershey, PA 17033, USA
Tel: 717-533-8845 x100 • Fax: 717-533-8661
E-Mail: cust@igi-global.com • www.igi-global.com

Table of Contents

Section 2
Intelligent Systems From Optimal-MCDM Shaping Tomorrow: An In-Depth Analysis of Decision-Making Applications in Agriculture, Judiciary, Education, and Others

Detailed Table of Contents

Section 1
AI-Driven Decision Making in Healthcare and Environmental Sciences: Nurturing Wellness, Sustaining Nature - Navigating AI Frontiers in Healthcare and Environmental Science

    Bancha Yingngam, Faculty of Pharmaceutical Sciences, Ubon Ratchathani University, Thailand
    Abhiruj Navabhatra, College of Pharmacy, Rangsit University, Thailand
    Polpan Sillapapibool, Faculty of Pharmaceutical Sciences, Ubon Ratchathani University, Thailand

This chapter explores AI's influence on pharmaceutical sciences, highlighting its enhancement of traditional design methodologies. It explores AI's transformational role in key sectors, including drug discovery, virtual screening, and drug formulation development. AI's ability to efficiently identify potential drug candidates from large chemical libraries and its use of optimization algorithms in the selection of suitable excipients and dosage forms are discussed. The chapter also emphasizes AI's significance in improving pharmaceutical manufacturing processes through parameter refinement, quality outcome prediction, and real-time anomaly detection. The integration of traditional design methods with AI ensures robust, reliable, AI-driven processes that are compliant with regulations. In conclusion, the chapter highlights the potential of AI in pharmaceutical sciences and the importance of its integration with traditional design methods. This approach empowers scientists to innovate, speed up drug development, and improve patient outcomes.

    Poomari Durga K., SRMIST, India

The AI-CDSS is a powerful tool designed to assist healthcare professionals in making informed and evidence-based decisions in patient care. It leverages artificial intelligence algorithms and data analysis techniques to provide personalized recommendations and insights. This system explores the features and benefits of the AI-CDSS, including patient data analysis, diagnostics and treatment recommendations, drug interaction and adverse event detection, predictive analytics, real-time monitoring and alerts, and continuous learning and improvement. The model also discusses the applications of AI-driven decision-making systems in healthcare, focusing on areas such as cancer diagnosis and treatment, chronic disease management, medication optimization, surgical decision support, infectious disease outbreak management, radiology and medical imaging analysis, mental health support, and clinical trials and research. Additionally, the chapter highlights existing methodologies, such as deep learning models like CNNs and RNNs, that have shown potential in cardiovascular disease prediction.

This research provides a thorough yet concise review of the opportunities and challenges for utilizing AI and IoT in the healthcare sector. Also included are an outline of AI and IoT, their applicability, certain observations on recent developments, a look at what the future holds, and difficulties facing healthcare systems. The web of things has several uses in healthcare organizations, from remote monitoring to sophisticated sensors and medical device fusion. In any event, it can help professionals communicate ideas more effectively while keeping patients safe and sound. The internet of things (IoT) for human organisations can also assist in attaining responsibility and satisfaction by promising patients to collaborate further closely with medical professionals.

Chapter 4

Alzheimer's disease is a brain disorder that slowly destroys memory and thinking skills and, eventually, the ability to carry out the simplest tasks. In most people with the disease, those with the late-onset type symptoms first appear in their mid-60s. Early-onset Alzheimer's occurs between a person's 30s and mid-60s and is very rare. Alzheimer's disease is the most common cause of dementia among older adults. Early diagnosis of Alzheimer's disease is essential for the progress of more prevailing treatments. Machine learning (ML), a branch of artificial intelligence, employs a variety of probabilistic and optimization techniques that permits PCs to gain from vast and complex datasets. As a result, researchers focus on using machine learning frequently for diagnosis of early stages of Alzheimer's disease. This project presents a review, analysis and critical evaluation of the recent work done for the early detection of Alzheimer's disease using ML techniques.

Throughout the world, diabetes is a life-threatening disease. This research study aims to develop a smart healthcare machine-learning model for diabetes prediction. The dataset is pre-processed to handle missing data and outliers, and feature selection techniques are used to identify the most relevant variables for the model. An ensemble of classifiers is built by combining logistic regression, XGBoost, random forest, and support vector machine. The performance of the proposed model is assessed using metrics such as accuracy, precision, recall, and F1-score. The results show that the random forest algorithm outperforms other models in terms of accuracy, precision, recall, and F1 score. The model achieves an accuracy of 85%, indicating that it can correctly predict diabetes in 85% of cases. In conclusion, this study demonstrates the feasibility of using machine learning models for diabetes prediction based on patient data. The model can be further improved by incorporating more extensive and diverse datasets and exploring more advanced machine-learning techniques.

Chapter 6

G. Kothai, Department of CSE, KPR Institute of Engineering and Technology, India
E. Poovammal, Department of Computing Technologies, SRM Institute of Science and Technology, India
V. Deepa, Department of Computing Technologies, SRM Institute of Science and Technology, India

Forests face several critical issues that pose significant challenges to their health and sustainability, such as deforestation, forest fires, forest fragmentation, etc. The main key issue is uncontrolled forest fires which affect both natural and human-induced and poses a significant threat to forests. Forest fires can result in the complete or partial destruction of forested areas. Addressing the damage requires a combination of effective fire management strategies, including prevention measures, early detection systems, and rapid response to wildfires. Detecting fires promptly allows authorities to issue timely evacuation orders, provide warnings to communities at risk, and deploy resources to ensure the safety of residents. However, artificial intelligence (AI) has the potential to revolutionize forest management by providing valuable insights, improving efficiency, and supporting sustainable practices. By leveraging AI technologies, forest fire management can benefit from improved situational awareness, faster response times, and optimized resource allocation.

Chapter 7

Tran Thi Hong Ngoc, An Giang University, Vietnam
Phan Truong Khanh, An Giang University, Vietnam
Sabyasachi Pramanik, Haldia Institute of Technology, India

With the fast growth of aquatic data, machine learning is essential for data analysis, categorization, and prediction. Data-driven models using machine learning may effectively handle complicated nonlinear problems in water research, unlike conventional approaches. Machine learning models and findings have been used to build, monitor, simulate, evaluate, and optimize water treatment and management systems in water environment research. Machine learning may also enhance water quality, pollution control, and watershed ecosystem security. This chapter discusses how ML approaches were used to assess water quality in surface, ground, drinking, sewage, and ocean. The authors also suggest potential machine learning applications in aquatic situations.

Chapter 8

AI-Decision Support System: Engineering, Geology, Climate, and Socioeconomic Aspects' Implications on Machine Learning 181

Phan Truong Khanh, An Giang University, Vietnam
Tran Thi Hong Ngoc, An Giang University, Vietnam
Sabyasachi Pramanik, Haldia Institute of Technology, India

From the impact of several corporeal, mechanized, ecological, and civic conditions, underground water pipelines degrade. A motivated administrative approach of the water supply network (WSN) depends on accurate pipe failure prediction that is difficult for the traditional physics-dependent model to provide. The research used data-directed machine learning approaches to forecast water pipe breakdowns using the extensive water supply network's historical maintenance data history. To include multiple contributing aspects to subterranean pipe degradation, a multi-source data-aggregation system was originally developed. The framework specified the requirements for integrating several data sources, such as the classical pipe leakage dataset, the soil category dataset, the geographic dataset, the population count dataset, and the climatic dataset. Five machine learning (ML) techniques are created for predicting pipe failure depending on the data, like LightGBM, ANN, Logistic Regression, K-NN, and SVM algorithm.

Section 2
Intelligent Systems From Optimal-MCDM Shaping Tomorrow: An In-Depth Analysis of Decision-Making Applications in Agriculture, Judiciary, Education, and Others

Chapter 9

AI-Driven Learning Analytics for Personalized Feedback and Assessment in Higher Education 206

Tarun Kumar Vashishth, IIMT University, India
Vikas Sharma, IIMT University, India
Kewal Krishan Sharma, IIMT University, India
Bhupendra Kumar, IIMT University, India
Rajneesh Panwar, IIMT University, India
Sachin Chaudhary, IIMT University, India

Advancements in artificial intelligence (AI) and learning analytics have opened up new possibilities for personalized education in higher education institutions. This chapter explores the potential of AI-driven learning analytics in higher education, focusing on its application in personalized feedback and assessment. By leveraging AI algorithms and data analytics, personalized feedback can be provided to students, targeting their specific strengths and areas for improvement. Adaptive and formative assessments can also be facilitated through AI-driven learning analytics, enabling personalized and accurate evaluation of students' knowledge and skills. However, ethical considerations, implementation challenges, and faculty training are crucial aspects that must be addressed for successful adoption. As technology continues to evolve, embracing AI-driven learning analytics can enhance student engagement, support individualized learning, and optimize educational outcomes.

Chapter 10

Integrating Artificial Intelligence in Education for Sustainable Development 231

Oluwabunmi Dorcas Bakare-Fatungase, Lead City University, Nigeria
Feranmi Emmanuel Adejuwon, Lead City University, Nigeria
Temitope Oluwatofunmi Idowu-Davies, Emmanuel Alayande University of Education, Oyo, Nigeria

A promising technology that has the potential to change many facets of the educational ecosystem is artificial intelligence (AI) which is playing a significant role in the actualization of the sustainable development goals (SDGs). The present status of AI in education was examined and identified significant areas for emerging research initiatives. Unified theory of acceptance and use of technology (UTAUT) underpinned the study to showcase ways AI technologies can be adopted and used for teaching and learning for a sustainable future. The study recommended the need for Africa as a continent to have a holistic AI ecosystem that captures our African histories, perceptions, idiosyncrasies, languages, outlooks, nuances, non-westernizations, etc., in addition to Nigeria being proactive to be the AI hub of the continent. The study is significant to educational practice, society, and policy and is theoretically based on a developing country perspective.

Retno Lestari, Universitas Brawijaya, Indonesia
Heni Dwi Windarwati, Universitas Brawijaya, Indonesia
Ridhoyanti Hidayah, Universitas Brawijaya, Indonesia

Artificial intelligence (AI) systems have become ubiquitous daily, yet many are unaware of their presence. The advancements in artificial intelligence have contributed significantly to higher education by changing how we approach problem-solving. The transformative potential of AI technology in education and training cannot be overstated. Currently, educators are utilizing AI systems to identify individual learning needs and experiences, make data-driven decisions and allocate resources more effectively. This chapter aims to equip readers with a comprehensive knowledge of the application of AI-powered decision-making in higher education. With the valuable insights and resources provided, readers can confidently integrate and leverage the potential of AI in their decision-making processes. To fully realize the potential of AI, educators, and leaders must have a fundamental understanding of its capabilities and ethical considerations. This knowledge will enable them to engage confidently and critically with AI technology and maximize its benefits.

Chapter 12

D. Joel Jebadurai, St. Joseph's College of Engineering, Chennai, India
Mary V. V. Sheela, Aarupadai Veedu Institute of Technology, Vinayaka Mission's Research
    Foundation, India
L. Rajeshkumar, St.Joseph's College of Engineering, India
M. Soundarya, Sathyabama Institute of Science and Technology, India
Rathi Meena, Dr. Umayal Ramanathan College for Women, India
Thirupathi Manickam, Christ University, India
Arul Vethamanikam G. Hudson, Ayya Nadar Janaki Ammal College, India
K. Dheenadhayalan, Mepco Schlenk Engineering College, India
M. Manikandan, SRM University, India

AI-driven decision-making tools have emerged as a novel technology poised to replace traditional agricultural practices. In this chapter, AI's pivotal role in steering the agricultural sector towards sustainability is highlighted, primarily through the utilization of AI techniques such as robotics, deep learning, the internet of things, image processing, and more. This chapter offers insights into the application of AI techniques in various functional areas of agriculture, including weed management, crop management, and soil management. Additionally, it underlines both the challenges and advantages presented by AI-driven applications in agriculture. In conclusion, the potential of AI in agriculture is vast, but it faces various impediments that, when properly identified and addressed, can expand its scope. This chapter serves as a valuable resource for government authorities, policymakers, and scientists seeking to explore the untapped potential of AI's significance in agriculture.

Chapter 13

Gowtham Rajendiran, Department of Computing Technologies, School of Computing,
    College of Engineering and Technology, SRM Institute of Science and Technology,
    Chengalpattu, India
Jebakumar Rethnaraj, Department of Computing Technologies, School of Computing,
    College of Engineering and Technology, SRM Institute of Science and Technology,
    Chengalpattu, India

Precision agriculture driven by the integration of the advanced technologies like internet of things (IoT) and machine learning (ML) is revolutionary precision agriculture, especially the indoor farming techniques. This chapter explores the comprehensive application of IoT and ML in automating indoor cultivation practices, examining their diverse benefits and practical uses in comparison with the traditional farming methodologies. IoT enables the indoor farmers to create controlled environments through interconnected sensors, monitoring crucial variables but not limited to temperature, humidity, and light intensity. Complemented by ML algorithms, data analysis becomes efficient, providing predictive models for crop growth, pest detection, and disease outbreaks. Automated environment climate control systems optimize resource utilization, while precision irrigation minimizes water usage. Real-time monitoring and early detection of plant health issues reduce crop losses, ensuring high-quality produce.

Chapter 14

R. Karthick Manoj, Academy of Maritime Education and Training, India
Aasha Nandhini S., SSN College of Engineering, India
T. Sasilatha, Academy of Maritime Education and Training, India

Early diagnosis of plant diseases is essential for successful plant disease prevention and control, as well as agricultural production management and decision-making. In this research, an efficient weighted average deep ensemble learning (EWADEL) model is used to detect plant diseases automatically. Transfer learning (TL) is a technique used to enhance existing algorithms. The performances of several pre-trained neural networks with DL such as ResNet152 DenseNet201, and InceptionV3, in addition to the usefulness of a weighted average ensemble models, are demonstrated for disease linked with leaf identification. To that aim, a EWADEL methodology is being researched in order to construct a robust network capable of predicting 12 different diseases of apple, Pomegranate, and tomato crops. Several convolutional neural network architectures were examined and ensemble to increase predictive performance using the EWADEL. In addition, the proposed approach included an examination of several deep learning models and developed EWADEL models.

Artificial intelligence (AI) has emerged as a promising technology capable of revolutionizing the judicial system by improving decision-making processes and reducing human biases. This manuscript explores the transformative potential of artificial intelligence (AI) in the judicial domain. It discusses the existing works in AI for predictive analytics, document analysis, and automated case management, in terms of methodologies and qualitative metrics used in each application. The manuscript also acknowledges the benefits, challenges, and solutions associated with incorporating AI into the judicial domain. These include the need for transparency and explainability in AI algorithms, and the ethical issues surrounding bias and privacy.

Chapter 16

The assignment problem (AP) is a well-known optimization problem that deals with the allocation of 'n' jobs to 'n' machines on a 1-to-1 basis. It minimizes the cost/time or maximizes the profit/production of the problem. Generally, the profit, sale, cost, and time are all called the parameters of the AP (in a traditional AP, out of these parameters, exactly one parameter will be considered a parameter of the problem). These are not at all crisp numbers due to several uncontrollable factors, which are in the form of uncertainty and hesitation. So, to solve the AP in this environment, the author proposes the software and ranking method-based PSK (P. Senthil Kumar) method. Here, plenty of theorems related to intuitionistic fuzzy assignment problems (IFAPs) are proposed and proved by the PSK. To show the superiority of his method, he presents 4 IFAPs. The computer programs for the proposed problems are presented precisely, and the results are verified with Matlab, RGui, etc. In addition, comparative results, discussion, merits and demerits of his method, and future studies are given.

In today's computer vision systems, the spread of object detection has been booming. Object detection in challenging conditions such as low-illumination or misty nights remains a difficult task, especially for one-stage detectors, which have limited improved solutions available. This approach improves upon existing one-stage models and excels in detecting objects in partially visible, and night environments. It segments objects using bounding boxes and tracks them in motion pictures. To detect an object in low-light environment we employ an RGB camera to generate a properly lighted image from an unilluminated image using dehazing and grayscale conversion methods. Secondly, low-illuminated images undergo dehazing and gray-scale conversion techniques to obtain a better-lighted image using the popular one-stage object detection algorithm YOLOv8. Video inputs are also taken for fast-moving vehicles; rates ranging from 5 frames per second to 160 frames per second could be efficiently predicted by YOLO-ODDT. All renowned object detectors are overshadowed in terms of speed and accuracy.

Smart speakers have taken the world by storm and have become an essential part of many households. As the use of smart speakers becomes more prevalent, the role of artificial intelligence (AI) in buying behavior has become increasingly important. With smart speakers becoming more intelligent and better integrated with AI, they have the potential to revolutionize the way consumers shop. This chapter will explore the impact of smart speakers on AI in buying behavior, the benefits and challenges of adopting this technology, and the future outlook of smart speakers and AI in commerce.

Preface

Welcome to our exploration of the symbiotic relationship between traditional design methods and the augmentation of AI-driven decision-making processes. In a world witnessing the transformative prowess of artificial intelligence (AI), the convergence of age-old design methodologies with cutting-edge AI technologies has emerged as a powerful force, redefining the landscape of decision-making and optimization across multifarious industries.

Edited by Tien V. T. Nguyen and Nhut T.M. Vo, this compendium embarks on a comprehensive journey into the realms of optimization, decision-making, and their manifold applications. We aim to scrutinize the amalgamation of optimization design strategies and decision-making frameworks within the context of artificial intelligence. We delve into the foundational bedrock, system developments, and pioneering optimization techniques that epitomize the synergy between traditional design methods and AI-driven decision-making.

This tome seeks to elucidate the pathways guiding AI-driven decision-making in the realm of higher education. Through an eclectic array of perspectives and experiences, we intend to provide a holistic view encapsulating the diverse facets surrounding AI-driven decision-making. The contributions herein expand the horizons of research pertinent to AI-driven decision-making in educational leadership, serving as a definitive reference for educational institutions seeking to fortify their AI-driven decision-making acumen and leadership development programs.

Tailored for a spectrum of leadership roles spanning from faculty members to administrative stewards, this compendium offers pragmatic implications and invaluable guidance. Each chapter is meticulously crafted to deepen comprehension of AI-driven decision-making in higher education leadership, equipping readers with the requisite knowledge and resources to harness the potential of AI in decision-making paradigms.

Catering to scholars, practitioners, and educational institutions, this book serves as an indispensable resource for comprehending and propelling the evolution of AI-driven decision-making, empowering effective leadership amidst the dynamic tapestry of education.

Intended for higher education faculty, administrators, students, librarians, researchers, graduate students, and academicians, this compendium aims to elucidate and amplify the discourse surrounding AI-driven decision-making across an extensive spectrum of domains. The thematic breadth includes, but is not confined to, elucidating the following topics:

- Role of AI-driven decision-making for leadership
- Trends of AI-driven decision-making in Industry 5.0

- AI-driven decision-making applications across various industries such as manufacturing, workforce management, smart buildings, power and grid systems, transportation, sustainable development, entertainment, tourism, forest management, smart homes, healthcare, agriculture, cultural heritage, logistics, supply chain, banking services, mechanical engineering, materials, and more.

We cordially invite contributions, encompassing research chapters and papers, to enrich the discourse encapsulated within this compendium. As we navigate through the intersections of traditional design methodologies and AI-driven decision-making, we invite you to embark on this enriching journey with us.

ORGANIZATION OF THE BOOK

Section 1: AI-Driven Decision Making in Healthcare and Environmental Sciences: Nurturing Wellness, Sustaining Nature - Navigating AI Frontiers in Healthcare and Environmental Science

In this part, we present 8 Chapters regarding decision making applications in healthcare and environmental science. An overview of the first 9 chapters will be summary in this chapter in detail.

Chapter 1: Bancha Yingngam, Abhiruj Navabhatra, and Polpan Sillapapibool discuss the impact of AI in pharmaceutical sciences in *AI-Driven Decision-Making Applications in Pharmaceutical Sciences*. They highlight AI's role in drug discovery, formulation, and manufacturing, emphasizing its compliance with traditional design methods for robust pharmaceutical processes.

Chapter 2: Poomari Durga.K explores *AI Clinical Decision Support System (AI-CDSS) For Cardiovascular Diseases*, illustrating how AI aids healthcare professionals in personalized patient care, diagnostics, treatment recommendations, and various healthcare applications.

Chapter 3: Kutubuddin Kazi's *AI Driven IoT (AIIoT) in Healthcare Monitoring* explores the opportunities and challenges of utilizing AI and IoT in healthcare, emphasizing their potential to enhance communication and patient care in the medical field.

Chapter 4: Ananya Gambhir, Ansh Bansal, Saurabh Rawat, and Anushree Sah explore the use of machine learning in the early detection of Alzheimer's disease in *Artificial Intelligence and Machine Learning Models for Alzheimer's Disease*.

Chapter 5: *A Smart Healthcare Diabetes Prediction System Using Ensemble of Classifiers* by Ayush Yadav and Bhuvaneswari Amma N G presents a machine learning model for diabetes prediction, showcasing its performance and potential in accurately predicting the disease based on patient data.

Chapter 6: *AI-Driven Powered Solution Selection: Navigating Forests and Fires for a Sustainable Future* by Kothai G, Poovammal E, and Deepa V delves into using AI to manage forest fires effectively, showcasing AI's role in forest management and fire prevention.

Chapter 7: Tran Thi Hong Ngoc, Phan Truong Khanh, and Sabyasachi Pramanik's *AI-Driven Solution Selection: Prediction of Water Quality Using Machine Learning* discusses the pivotal role of machine learning in assessing and improving water quality across various water environments.

Chapter 8: *AI-Decision Support System: Engineering, Geology, Climate, and Socioeconomic Aspects' Implications on Machine Learning Dependent* by Phan Truong Khanh, Tran Thi Hong Ngoc, Sabyasachi Pramanik explores the use of machine learning for predicting water pipe breakdowns in water supply networks. It integrates various data sources, employing five machine learning techniques to forecast pipe failure accurately.

Section 2: Intelligent Systems From Optimal-MCDM Shaping Tomorrow: An In-Depth Analysis of Decision-Making Applications in Agriculture, Judiciary, Education, and Others

In this section, we show all the rests regarding decision making applications in healthcare and environmental science. An overview of the last chapters will be summary in this chapter in detail.

Chapter 9: *AI-Driven Learning Analytics for Personalized Feedback and Assessment in Higher Education* by Tarun Vashishth, Vikas Sharma, and others investigates how AI-driven learning analytics can offer personalized feedback and assessments, enhancing student engagement and outcomes.

Chapter 10: Oluwabunmi Bakare-Fatungase, Feranmi Adejuwon, and Temitope Idowu-Davies explore *Integrating Artificial Intelligence in Education for Sustainable Development*, discussing AI's role in education for sustainable development and the need for a holistic AI ecosystem.

Chapter 11: Retno Lestari, Heni Windarwati, and Ridhoyanti Hidayah explore *AI-Driven Decision-Making Applications in Higher Education*, shedding light on AI's transformative potential in higher education and the necessity of understanding its capabilities and ethical considerations.

Chapter 12: *AI Driven Decision-Making and Optimization in Modern Agriculture Sectors* by D Joel Jebadurai, V. Sheela Mary V, and others explores AI's applications like robotics and image processing in various facets of agriculture, focusing on its potential and challenges.

Chapter 13: Gowtham Rajendiran and Jebakumar Rethnaraj explore *IoT Integrated Machine Learning Based Automated Precision Agriculture-Indoor Farming Techniques*, illustrating how IoT and ML automate indoor cultivation, optimize resource usage, and enhance crop monitoring.

Chapter 14: R.Karthick Manoj, Aasha Nandhini S, and Sasilatha T present *Automated Plant Disease Detection Using Efficient Deep Ensemble Learning Model for Smart Agriculture*, focusing on deep learning models for diagnosing and preventing plant diseases in agriculture.

Chapter 15: Anu Thomas discusses *Exploring the Power of AI-Driven Decision Making in the Judicial Domain*, examining AI's potential in revolutionizing the judicial system by improving decision-making and reducing biases.

Chapter 16: In *AI-Driven Decision Support System for Intuitionistic Fuzzy Assignment Problems* by P. Senthil Kumar, the focus is on solving assignment problems involving uncertain parameters through the proposed PSK method, offering theorems and computer programs for intuitionistic fuzzy assignment problems.

Chapter 17: Prince Sahaya Brighty S, Anuradha R, and Brindha M present *Enhanced YOLO Algorithm for Robust Object Detection*, focusing on improving object detection in challenging conditions using AI techniques, especially in low-light environments.

Chapter 18: Asi Priyanka examines *Smart Speakers: A New Normal Lifestyle*, discussing the impact of AI-powered smart speakers on consumer behavior, commerce, and their future prospects in households.

Each chapter uniquely showcases the diverse applications and implications of AI-driven decision-making across industries and domains, contributing valuable insights to the evolving landscape of AI technologies.

IN SUMMARY

As we conclude this comprehensive exploration into the realms of AI-driven decision-making, this edited reference book stands as a testament to the transformative potential and diverse applications of artificial intelligence across multifarious domains. Each chapter within this compendium represents a unique facet of AI's integration with traditional design methodologies, offering invaluable insights and pioneering contributions to the ever-evolving landscape of decision-making processes.

From predictive models forecasting water pipe breakdowns to AI's role in pharmaceutical sciences, healthcare, precision agriculture, judicial systems, and beyond, this compendium reflects the expansive influence of AI across industries. The amalgamation of AI with machine learning, IoT, deep learning, and ensemble techniques elucidates its pivotal role in revolutionizing conventional practices, optimizing resource utilization, and enhancing decision-making accuracy.

The chapters featured within this compendium not only explore the applications of AI but also emphasize the ethical considerations, challenges, and potential avenues for further research and development. They underscore the imperative need for understanding AI's capabilities, promoting transparency, and addressing biases to harness its full potential ethically and responsibly.

The collaborative efforts of esteemed researchers and authors have culminated in a compendium that serves as a rich resource for scholars, practitioners, educators, policymakers, and industry professionals. This book encapsulates the spirit of innovation, offering a holistic view of AI-driven decision-making's profound impact on various sectors and the imperative role of traditional design methods in this symbiotic relationship.

As we navigate the dynamic landscape of artificial intelligence and its intersection with decision-making paradigms, this compendium serves as a guiding light, fostering deeper understanding, critical engagement, and innovative applications of AI across industries. We extend our heartfelt gratitude to all contributors for their invaluable insights and pioneering research, shaping this compendium into an indispensable resource for navigating the AI-driven future.

In conclusion, this compendium stands as a testament to the transformative power of AI-driven decision-making, urging continuous exploration, ethical deployment, and responsible innovation to harness its full potential for the betterment of society and industries worldwide.

Warm regards,

Tien V. T. Nguyen
Industrial University of Ho Chi Minh City, Vietnam

Nhut T. M. Vo
National Kaohsiung University of Science and Technology, Taiwan

Section 1

AI–Driven Decision Making in Healthcare and Environmental Sciences: Nurturing Wellness, Sustaining Nature – Navigating AI Frontiers in Healthcare and Environmental Science

BRIEF OVERVIEW OF AI IN HEALTHCARE AND ENVIRONMENTAL SCIENCES

In the changing world of technology, artificial intelligence (AI) emerges as a force that is reshaping industries and scientific fields. This introduction acts as a guide to exploring the impact of AI on healthcare and environmental sciences.

AI is revolutionizing healthcare by bringing about new ways of diagnosing, treating, and caring for patients. Through machine learning, data analysis, and advanced computational models, medical professionals now have access to tools for precision medicine, disease detection, and personalized treatment plans. In sciences, AI goes beyond boundaries by offering innovative solutions to ecological challenges. From conserving biodiversity to mitigating climate change effects, AI enables approaches in managing ecosystems. By utilizing data analysis and predictive modeling techniques, environmental scientists can make informed decisions that contribute to the preservation of our planet.

As we delve into applications such as AI-powered decision support systems in healthcare or real-time monitoring in sciences, each chapter sheds light on a unique aspect of how AI is making an impact. Predictive algorithms assist in diagnosing diseases, while machine learning models predict water quality levels—showcasing the dimensions of AI's influence.

This overview sets the stage for an exploration of AI applications through case studies. Each chapter contributes to our knowledge and propels us forward into this era characterized by transformation driven by AI. Exploration aims to deepen our understanding of how advancements, scientific research, and environmental preservation can benefit humanity. Each chapter in this exploration contributes to the progress we are making.

In the field of healthcare, the integration of AI showcases its potential to revolutionize care and improve outcomes. AI-powered decision support systems enhance decision-making by providing timely insights into complex medical data. It also helps healthcare professionals create personalized treatment plans, optimize therapeutic interventions, and ultimately improve patient outcomes. AI's ability to analyze datasets enables it to identify patterns and correlations that may go unnoticed by humans, leading to precise and efficient healthcare delivery.

At the time, incorporating AI into environmental sciences addressed the pressing need for solutions to complex ecological challenges. The importance lies in AI's capability to process data, predict patterns, and model scenarios that assist in effective ecosystem management. This section in the book aims to cultivate an understanding of how AI plays a role in shaping a future where we prioritize well-being, sustain our natural surroundings, and achieve a shared vision of harmonious coexistence between humans and the environment. This addition is made possible by combining the fields of science and technology.

SCOPE AND OBJECTIVES

Defining the Scope of Healthcare Applications

In establishing the parameters for this exploration, our goal is to delineate the boundaries that guide the exploration of healthcare applications enhanced by artificial intelligence (AI). Within this thematic scope, each chapter aims to offer a nuanced perspective on AI's transformative influence in healthcare, encompassing advancements that balance precision with compassion.

Defining the Scope

The scope of healthcare applications covered in this book is expansive, covering a diverse range of AI-driven innovations across the entire healthcare spectrum. From precise diagnostics to personalized treatments and proactive healthcare monitoring, the chapters converge around AI's central theme: improving patient outcomes and streamlining healthcare systems.

The chapters such as "AI-Driven Decision-Making Applications in Pharmaceutical Sciences," "AI Clinical Decision Support System (AI-CDSS) For Cardiovascular Diseases," "AI Driven IoT (AIIoT) in Healthcare Monitoring," "Artificial Intelligence and Machine Learning Models for Alzheimer's Disease," and "A Smart Healthcare Diabetes Prediction System Using Ensemble of Classifiers," collectively represent the multifaceted applications of AI in healthcare.

- AI-Driven Decision-Making Applications in Pharmaceutical Sciences: Unveiling the synergy of AI and pharmaceutical sciences, this chapter explores how AI revolutionizes drug discovery, development, and manufacturing processes. From molecular data analysis to clinical trial optimization, the scope extends to an accelerated pace of drug development, foreshadowing a future where intelligent algorithms drive medical breakthroughs.

- AI Clinical Decision Support System (AI-CDSS) For Cardiovascular Diseases: Focused on cardiovascular health, this chapter delves into the realm of AI-CDSS. By assisting healthcare professionals in diagnosing and managing cardiovascular diseases, the scope extends to real-time decision support that has the potential to reshape patient care paradigms and improve cardiovascular health outcomes.
- AI-driven IoT (AIIoT) in Healthcare Monitoring: Exploring the convergence of AI and the Internet of Things (IoT) in healthcare monitoring, this chapter ventures beyond traditional healthcare settings. It showcases how interconnected devices and intelligent algorithms collaborate to monitor and manage health conditions, emphasizing the potential for proactive interventions and personalized patient care.
- Artificial Intelligence and Machine Learning Models for Alzheimer's Disease: Centered on Alzheimer's disease, this chapter expands the scope into the application of AI and machine learning models to decipher intricate patterns in data. This mention advances early diagnosis, prognosis, and potential interventions in the realm of neurodegenerative diseases.
- A Smart Healthcare Diabetes Prediction System Using Ensemble of Classifiers: Putting diabetes prediction in the spotlight, this chapter demonstrates how ensemble learning techniques enhance predictive accuracy. The scope extends to the proactive management of chronic conditions, offering insight into a future where AI aids in preventing diseases through intelligent risk prediction.

Objectives

The woven objectives within these chapters are threefold: to inform, inspire, and foster a deeper understanding of AI's transformative potential in healthcare.

- Informative Objectives: Each chapter informs readers about specific AI applications in the addressed healthcare domain, contributing to an informed perspective on the current status and future possibilities within healthcare.
- Inspirational Objectives: Beyond information, the chapters aspire to inspire curiosity and intellectual inquiry, instilling wonder about the vast possibilities ahead and encouraging readers to envision and contribute to the evolving landscape of AI in healthcare.
- Deeper Understanding Objectives: The overarching objective is to facilitate a deeper understanding of the intricate relationship between AI and healthcare. Through detailed explorations, the chapters elucidate not only technical aspects but also ethical considerations, societal impacts, and the potential for creating a more patient-centric, efficient, and accessible healthcare ecosystem.

In essence, the scope and objectives set the stage for a profound journey into the world of AI in healthcare, where innovation converges with compassion. As we explore specific applications in each chapter, the aim is to contribute to a collective understanding of AI's transformative role in shaping the future of healthcare.

Identifying the Environmental Sciences Encompassed

In defining the scope and goals within environmental sciences, we embark on a journey exploring ecological sustainability, resource management, and the symbiotic relationship between humanity and the environment. The chapters— "AI-Driven Powered Solution Selection- Navigating Forests and Fires for a Sustainable Future," "AI-Driven Solution Selection: Prediction of Water Quality Using Machine Learning," and "AI- Decision Support System: Engineering, Geology, Climate, and Socioeconomic Aspects' Implications on Machine Learning Dependent"— collectively provide a holistic view of AI's impact on environmental conservation.

Defining the Scope

The scope of environmental sciences, as outlined in these chapters, goes beyond conventional boundaries. It covers a spectrum of challenges and opportunities, with each chapter offering a unique perspective on AI's profound implications for fostering sustainability and resilience. AI-driven Powered Solution Selection- Navigating Forests and Fires for a Sustainable Future: This chapter focuses on forest ecosystems and wildfire management. It explores AI applications from early fire risk detection to sustainable forestry planning, aiming to manage forests intelligently and sustainably.

AI-Driven Solution Selection: Prediction of Water Quality Using Machine Learning: Centered on water, this chapter delves into AI's role in predicting water quality. It highlights how intelligent systems can enhance our ability to monitor and manage water resources, addressing pollution detection and resource optimization.

AI- Decision Support System: Engineering, Geology, Climate, and Socioeconomic Aspects' Implications on Machine Learning Dependent: Encompassing engineering, geology, climate, and socioeconomic dimensions, this chapter introduces a decision support system. It integrates various facets of environmental sciences, addressing connections between human activities, geological processes, and climatic factors with machine learning dependence.

Objectives

The objectives woven into these environmental science chapters are threefold—knowledge dissemination, inspiration, and fostering a deeper understanding of the relationships between AI and ecological sustainability.

- Knowledge Dissemination Objectives: The chapters aim to disseminate knowledge about practical AI applications in environmental conservation, equipping readers with insights into how AI addresses complex environmental issues.
- Inspiration Objectives: Beyond knowledge, the chapters aim to inspire readers by showcasing AI's potential to navigate and solve real-world environmental challenges. This addition sparks imagination and encourages readers to envision their roles in contributing to a more sustainable coexistence with nature.
- Deeper Understanding Objectives: The overarching objective is to foster a deeper understanding of the complex interplay between AI and environmental sciences. Each chapter elucidates broader

implications, ethical considerations, and potential societal impacts of integrating AI into ecological management.

The outlined scope and objectives form a foundation for exploring AI's transformative role in shaping the future of environmental conservation and sustainability. As readers navigate through the highlighted applications, the goal is to contribute to a collective understanding of how responsibly harnessed AI becomes a powerful ally in the global endeavor to preserve and protect our planet.

CONCLUSION

In the synthesis of AI's impact on healthcare and environmental sciences, we stand witness to a convergence of innovation and responsibility. Across diverse chapters, AI unfolds not merely as a tool but as a transformative force shaping diagnostics, treatment, and environmental conservation. In healthcare, from pharmaceutical precision to real-time cardiovascular support, each chapter showcases AI's potential to redefine healthcare. Our objectives of informing, inspiring, and fostering understanding have been met, and we envision a future where AI enhances healthcare accessibility and quality.

Simultaneously, in environmental sciences, AI emerges as a guide toward sustainability. Navigating forests, predicting water quality, and integrating decision support systems underscore AI's role in ecological safeguarding. Objectives of knowledge dissemination, inspiration, and deeper understanding pave the way for harmonious coexistence between human activities and environmental conservation. Reflecting on this journey, the symbiosis between AI, healthcare, and environmental sciences is not a trend but a necessity. Urgency in addressing global issues propels responsible AI integration, aligning innovation with ethics and compassion.

The chapters in this section encourage active participation in a transformation driven by AI, promising significant contributions to global well-being and the preservation of the environment. The journey persists, fueled by AI's potential to shape a future that prioritizes individual health and planetary sustainability.

Chapter 1
AI–Driven Decision–Making Applications in Pharmaceutical Sciences

Bancha Yingngam
https://orcid.org/0000-0001-7215-9123
Faculty of Pharmaceutical Sciences, Ubon Ratchathani University, Thailand

Abhiruj Navabhatra
https://orcid.org/0000-0003-4129-1302
College of Pharmacy, Rangsit University, Thailand

Polpan Sillapapibool
https://orcid.org/0009-0006-2306-0243
Faculty of Pharmaceutical Sciences, Ubon Ratchathani University, Thailand

ABSTRACT

This chapter explores AI's influence on pharmaceutical sciences, highlighting its enhancement of traditional design methodologies. It explores AI's transformational role in key sectors, including drug discovery, virtual screening, and drug formulation development. AI's ability to efficiently identify potential drug candidates from large chemical libraries and its use of optimization algorithms in the selection of suitable excipients and dosage forms are discussed. The chapter also emphasizes AI's significance in improving pharmaceutical manufacturing processes through parameter refinement, quality outcome prediction, and real-time anomaly detection. The integration of traditional design methods with AI ensures robust, reliable, AI-driven processes that are compliant with regulations. In conclusion, the chapter highlights the potential of AI in pharmaceutical sciences and the importance of its integration with traditional design methods. This approach empowers scientists to innovate, speed up drug development, and improve patient outcomes.

DOI: 10.4018/979-8-3693-0639-0.ch001

INTRODUCTION

The field of pharmaceutical sciences has traditionally placed great emphasis on studying decision-making processes to advance research. This promotes development and ensures the delivery of safe and effective medications to patients. However, in recent years, there has been a notable shift in this paradigm. This change is attributed to researchers integrating artificial intelligence (AI) into decision-making procedures, bringing about transformative effects not only in the pharmaceutical sector but also across various industries (Carou-Senra et al., 2023; Liu & Rudd, 2023; Malviya et al., 2023; Singh Sharma, 2023). AI-driven decision-making applications have emerged as powerful tools, enabling pharmaceutical scientists to make more informed and efficient decisions. The repercussions of this are evident in the accelerated pace of drug discovery, its optimization, and the enhancement of manufacturing processes (El-Naggar et al., 2023). Figure 1 offers a comprehensive visual representation of the key disciplines within the pharmaceutical sciences that AI-driven decision-making applications have profoundly impacted. The influence of AI is most pronounced in six primary areas: drug research and discovery, clinical development, personalized medicines, manufacturing and supply chain, launch and commercial activities, and postmarketing surveillance. AI-powered applications not only enhance decision-making but also elevate patient outcomes and improve the overall performance of the pharmaceutical industry. This highlights AI's transformative potential, positioning it as a pivotal catalyst for the future evolution of pharmaceutical sciences.

One of the foremost advantages of implementing AI in the domain of pharmaceutical sciences is its potential to expedite drug discovery and development. Traditional methods for identifying potential drug candidates have often been labor intensive, expensive, and filled with uncertainties (Khadela et al., 2023).

Figure 1. Areas of AI-driven decision-making applications in pharmaceutical sciences

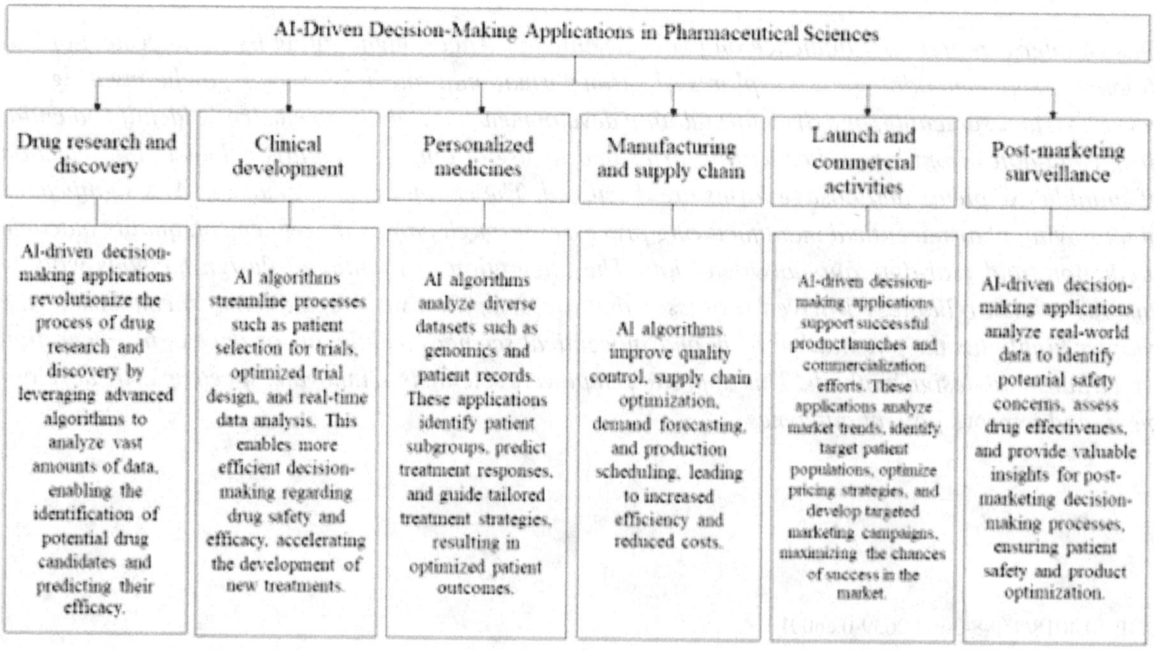

However, with the rise of AI, researchers now apply machine learning algorithms to sift through vast databases, predict molecular properties, simulate biological processes, and facilitate virtual screenings of prospective drug candidates (Bournez et al., 2023; Czub et al., 2023; Lee et al., 2023). This innovative approach reduces the time and cost of identifying drug leads, consequently accelerating the development of life-saving medications. In the field of clinical development, AI-driven decision-making applications are crucial for refining processes. Researchers utilize AI to select patients for clinical trials, design efficient trial protocols, and analyze real-time data from these trials (Aliper et al., 2023). Such evaluations are key in detecting patterns, forecasting outcomes, and guiding decisions about drug safety and effectiveness (Ranson et al., 2023). Moreover, the emergence of AI-driven decision-making applications is reshaping foundational beliefs in personalized medicine (MacMath et al., 2023). Personalized medicine tailors medical treatments to individual patients based on their unique attributes. Integrating patient-specific data, such as genomic information and electronic health records, with advanced AI algorithms provides pharmaceutical scientists with a powerful tool. They can then tailor treatments for each patient, enhancing therapeutic outcomes and reducing adverse reactions. The ability to interpret biological data, anticipate patient responses, and refine treatment plans based on individual characteristics promises to transform the pharmaceutical landscape, ushering in an age of more precise and effective healthcare (Sheng Zhang et al., 2023). In the spheres of manufacturing and supply chains, AI-driven decision-making applications are essential for refining processes and optimizing supply chains in the pharmaceutical industry (Charles et al., 2023). AI helps in quality control, supply chain management, demand forecasting, and the optimization of production schedules, resulting in increased efficiency, cost savings, and overall operational enhancement (Baviskar et al., 2023). Product launches and commercialization also benefit from AI tools, supporting successful product introductions. AI aids in pinpointing target patient populations, analyzing market trends, forecasting market demand, optimizing pricing strategies, and designing targeted marketing campaigns. Collectively, these factors lead to more successful product launches and commercialization endeavors (Lu et al., 2023). Last, postmarketing surveillance, vital for monitoring the safety and efficacy of pharmaceutical products postapproval, garners advantages from AI systems. These tools analyze real-world data, encompassing adverse event reports and patient feedback, to identify potential safety concerns, evaluate drug efficacy, and provide insights for informed postmarketing decisions (Kaku et al., 2023).

While the advantages are clear, the integration of AI systems into the pharmaceutical sciences presents challenges that demand careful consideration. An ethical dimension emerges as the adoption of AI technologies prompts deep-seated questions about the responsible and ethical handling of patient data, potential algorithmic bias, and its influence on human decision-making processes (Monteith et al., 2023). Data privacy takes center stage, as collecting, storing, and analyzing sensitive patient information necessitates stringent security measures to guard against unauthorized access or breaches (Cacciamani et al., 2023). Regulatory compliance becomes another pivotal concern when introducing AI-driven decision-making applications in the pharmaceutical industry. Regulatory bodies must provide explicit guidelines and frameworks to ensure that AI-based systems conform to rigorous safety, quality, and efficacy standards (Patil et al., 2023). The alignment of regulatory practices across different jurisdictions is essential to both foster innovation and guarantee patient safety. The interpretability of AI models also presents a significant hurdle in the pharmaceutical sciences. While AI algorithms can yield precise predictions, grasping their underlying logic is paramount for trust and acceptance (Ponzoni et al., 2023). Ensuring transparency and explainability in AI models becomes imperative, enabling researchers, clinicians, and regulators to understand, validate, and thereby reinforce confidence in the technology (Macri & Roberts,

2023). In pharmaceutical research and development, striking a balance between the benefits AI provides and essential considerations of safety, efficacy, and ethics is vital. For instance, when developing an AI system for disease diagnosis, a concerted effort is mandatory. All stakeholders, from researchers, doctors, and industry leaders to regulators and ethicists, must collaborate to devise suitable guidelines and best practices. Such collaboration ensures that the AI system prioritizes patient welfare, maintains privacy standards, and upholds the highest ethical tenets. It is also pivotal to consistently monitor AI-driven systems, pinpointing and rectifying unforeseen consequences or biases that might surface over time. Continuous refinement of algorithms, supported by rigorous validation and clinical trials, contributes to the ongoing advancement of AI in the pharmaceutical field. Addressing these challenges and ensuring the trust of patients, healthcare professionals, and regulators is paramount. Striking the right balance between nurturing innovation and ensuring accountability is vital for the responsible and effective integration of AI tools. The overarching aim of such integration is to enhance patient outcomes, accelerate drug discovery, and elevate the overall quality of health care delivery.

This chapter provides an in-depth exploration of the various facets of pharmaceutical sciences, with the following primary objectives:

1. Understanding AI's role in pharmaceutical sciences: This section explores the diverse roles AI occupies in drug discovery, formulation development, and manufacturing. It further probes the interplay between AI and traditional design techniques.
2. Exploring advanced technologies, methodologies, and challenges: Here, the author discusses the latest AI technologies relevant to pharmaceutical sciences, elucidates the methodologies in use, and highlights the challenges encountered when integrating AI systems.
3. Presenting practical case studies: This segment shows successful applications of AI in pharmaceutical research and development, thereby grounding theoretical discussions with real-world examples.
4. Anticipating future trends in AI for pharmaceutical sciences: This section offers insights into the future trajectory of AI within the pharmaceutical domain, highlighting potential opportunities and challenges as the technology matures.
5. Deepening the understanding of AI and traditional design method integration: Dedicated to give readers a comprehensive perspective, this section bridges the gap between traditional methods and recent AI innovations in pharmaceutical sciences.
6. Highlighting benefits for patients and the global healthcare ecosystem: In the concluding segment, the author emphasizes the transformative potential of melding AI with traditional design techniques in the pharmaceutical sciences. This synthesis promises to enhance patient outcomes and amplify the efficiency of the entire pharmaceutical industry.

This chapter is organized as follows: Section 2 explores AI's utility in drug discovery, highlighting its efficiency in virtual screening and predictive modeling. Section 3 focuses on AI's role in drug formulation, detailing its contributions to selection, delivery optimization, and stability enhancement. Section 4 covers AI's importance in pharmaceutical manufacturing, quality assurance, and regulatory compliance. In Section 5, the blend of traditional design methodologies with AI approaches is explored, addressing challenges inherent to AI's "black box" nature and discussing alignment strategies. Section 6 shows practical AI applications through case studies. Section 7 critically evaluates the challenges and ethics of AI integration, while Section 8 projects future trends. The chapter culminates with Section 9, summarizing insights and reflecting on AI's potential trajectory in the field.

AI APPLICATIONS IN DRUG DISCOVERY AND VIRTUAL SCREENING

Traditional drug discovery methods are characteristically lengthy and intricate, often spanning over a decade and costing billions of dollars. A significant portion of this duration and expense arises from the reliance on manual data analysis, which is labor intensive, time consuming, and susceptible to human error (Yingngam, 2023). One of AI's distinguishing attributes in drug discovery is its proficiency in deploying complex neural network architectures. For instance, convolutional neural networks (CNNs) are designed to process structured grid data such as images, rendering them particularly suitable for analyzing molecular structures and identifying patterns critical for drug efficacy (Chen et al., 2023b; Lv et al., 2023). Recurrent neural networks (RNNs) and long short-term memory networks (LSTMs) excel at analyzing sequential data, making them prime candidates for examining amino acid sequences in proteins or nucleotide sequences in DNA and RNA. Transformer architectures, especially those with self-attention mechanisms, have proven invaluable in sequence alignment and predicting protein structures, as exemplified by models such as DeepMind's AlphaFold (Ren et al., 2023).

Table 1 delineates a comparison between conventional methodologies and emergent AI-driven techniques in drug discovery. AI-enhanced methods promise a stark contrast to their traditional counterparts, offering substantial reductions in both time and cost. AI, especially when applying machine learning algorithms, can optimize every step of the drug discovery pipeline. Such optimization accelerates the process and reduces expenses. AI's prowess lies in guiding researchers to viable drug leads based on predictive analyses. The efficacy of AI models in drug discovery is intimately tied to the quality and depth of their input data. Raw biological data, whether genomic sequences or protein structures, require thorough preprocessing. This entails embedding transformations, data normalization, and resorting to augmentation techniques for limited datasets (Albahra et al., 2023).

Additionally, AI's capacity to sift through vast datasets unveils valuable insights swiftly and accurately that might otherwise remain obscured. By capitalizing on machine learning, AI can adeptly predict the efficacy, potential toxicity, and possible interactions of compounds in proposed drugs. This predictive capability can assist in developing safer and more effective medications (Andrianov et al., 2023). Another salient aspect of AI algorithms is their inherent ability for continuous learning and adaptability to new data. Such adaptability ensures that AI's predictive models and methodologies evolve, reinforcing AI's growing significance in drug discovery. This continuous learning aspect accentuates the transformative role of AI in the field of drug discovery (Askr et al., 2023).

While AI holds the promise to transform drug discovery, it also presents its own set of challenges. Ensuring model generalization, offering model interpretability—particularly in high-stakes drug discovery scenarios—and upholding data privacy, especially when dealing with patient-specific data, are of utmost importance (Jariwala et al., 2023). As illustrated in Table 2, this chapter juxtaposes the success rates of traditional drug discovery against those facilitated by AI. Conventional drug discovery methods entail a meticulous and iterative procedure to develop potential drug compounds, which then proceed to rigorous in vitro and in vivo testing. Despite its widespread use, this method demands significant resources and frequently results in high attrition rates; only a small fraction of the tested compounds eventually gain market approval (Yingngam, 2023). Cheminformatics represents a domain where AI is making impressive strides. AI tools aid in molecular docking, predicting how drugs will interact with their target proteins. Quantitative structure-activity relationship (QSAR) models, notably tree-based iterations, forecast the biological activity of molecules based on their chemical constituents (Hadap et al., 2023). Conversely, AI-driven drug discovery leverages sophisticated algorithms and vast databases, significantly accel-

5

Table 1. Comparison of traditional and AI-driven methods in drug discovery

Process Step	Traditional Method	AI-Driven Method
Target identification	Based on expert knowledge and analysis of biomedical literature	Using machine learning to analyze large volumes of data, predict protein functions, and identify potential targets
Lead identification	High-throughput screening of compounds against the target	Using AI to predict potential lead compounds based on structural and functional similarities
Lead optimization	Iterative chemical modifications and testing for improved efficacy and reduced toxicity	Using AI to predict the impact of chemical modifications on efficacy and toxicity
Preclinical testing	In vitro and in vivo studies to evaluate safety and efficacy	Use of AI models to predict outcomes of preclinical studies, reducing the number of experiments needed
Clinical trial design	Trial design based on previous similar trials and expert knowledge	AI models can predict optimal trial design based on historical data, improving efficiency and success rates
Data analysis	Manual analysis of clinical trial data	Machine learning algorithms can analyze large volumes of data quickly and identify patterns and correlations

erating the drug discovery journey. Deep learning, a subset of machine learning, is utilized to predict drug-target interactions, assess compound toxicity, and optimize chemical structures. These techniques frequently surpass human capabilities in terms of both precision and efficiency, enhancing the efficacy and potential success rate of drug development (Nguyen & Patuwo, 2023).

The ever-evolving landscape of drug discovery, constantly enriched by new research, demands adaptive AI models. Approaches such as online learning, where models are continuously updated with new data without discarding prior knowledge, are essential (Sarkar et al., 2023). However, drawing a direct comparison between the success rates of traditional drug discovery and its AI-enhanced counterpart is intricate. While AI-driven techniques show a marked rise in both efficiency and precision, their adoption is still in the early stages. By the mid-2020s, only a handful of AI-formulated drugs had traversed the entire spectrum of clinical trials. The intrinsic differences in the methodologies and timelines between traditional and AI-driven processes further muddle this comparison (Yingngam, 2023). While awaiting more comprehensive data, the potential of AI to revolutionize drug discovery remains evident. As AI methodologies mature and integrate smoothly with traditional processes, there is an expectation of a notable increase in drug development success rates. This progression could hasten the introduction of more effective treatments to patients, ensuring that they are available more promptly and at more affordable costs.

Recent studies underscore the escalating importance of AI in drug discovery and virtual screening (Liu et al., 2023). Deep learning algorithms are pivotal in identifying and refining potential drug candidates due to their capabilities in predicting bioactivity, pharmacokinetics, and toxicity. Moreover, AI finds increasing utility in de novo drug design, where generative models such as variational autoencoders (VAEs) and generative adversarial networks (GANs) are employed to concoct novel drug candidates with desired attributes (Feng & Wei, 2023). Machine learning, another dimension of AI, amplifies the virtual screening of vast chemical compound libraries, foresees drug-target interactions, predicts potential side effects, and paves the way for precision medicine, customizing treatments based on individual patient

Table 2. Success rates of AI-aided drug discovery versus traditional methods

Aspect	Traditional Methods	AI-Aided Methods
Time to discover a new drug	Typically, takes 10-15 years	Can potentially reduce the time to a few years, or even months for certain stages of discovery
Cost of drug discovery	Estimated at around $2.6 billion per new drug (including the cost of failed trials)	AI has the potential to significantly reduce costs by improving efficiency and reducing failure rates
Drug candidates tested to get one approved drug	Thousands to millions of compounds	AI methods can potentially reduce the number of compounds that need to be synthesized and tested
Rate of success in clinical trials	Historically low, with approximately 10% of drugs entering Phase I trials eventually being approved	AI has the potential to increase success rates by predicting efficacy and toxicity more accurately, and by optimizing clinical trial design
Lead optimization	Iterative, time-consuming process	AI can expedite lead optimization by predicting the impact of modifications on drug properties

data (Andrianov et al., 2023). AI data mining accelerates knowledge discovery, aiding drug repurposing by unveiling novel applications for existing medications (Feng & Wei, 2023; Sarkar et al., 2023).

Figure 2 portrays the AI-enhanced drug discovery pipeline, spanning from the inception of target identification to the culmination of candidate selection. This pipeline demarcates the varied drug discovery stages, clarifying how AI can bolster both the process's efficiency and its end results. The drug discovery journey begins with target identification, where a biological entity linked to a disease, such as a specific protein or gene, is spotlighted as a potential target for drug intervention. AI refines this phase, allowing for the rapid and precise pinpointing of prospective targets by analyzing copious biological datasets. Once potential targets emerge, target validation ensues. This step validates the target's involvement in the disease mechanism and assesses its "druggability". AI accelerates this validation by parsing through existing target data and forecasting its likely disease association. This is followed by hit identification, where potential hits or compounds that could engage with the target are detected. AI enhances the efficiency of chemical database screening to identify these potential hits. Progressing from here, the hits transition to the hit-to-lead optimization phase, where they mature into "lead" compounds characterized by enhanced potency, selectivity, and drug-resembling traits. AI propels this optimization, projecting the ramifications of chemical alterations on compound properties. In lead optimization, these lead compounds are further honed to augment their drug-like attributes while curbing potential adverse effects. Here, AI becomes indispensable, forecasting the probable outcomes of subsequent modifications. In the final candidate selection phase, the most promising drug candidates are earmarked for deeper development based on projected efficacy, safety, and manufacturability. AI becomes instrumental at this juncture, facilitating decision-making by synthesizing and analyzing multisource data (Yingngam, 2023). The following section delves into the fascinating realm of AI applications in drug discovery and virtual screening, transforming facets of pharmaceutical sciences traditionally perceived as intricate and time-consuming.

Furthermore, one of the standout algorithms in this domain is deep learning, particularly convolutional neural networks (CNNs) and recurrent neural networks (RNNs). CNNs have shown exceptional promise

Figure 2. AI-driven drug discovery pipeline: from target identification to candidate selection

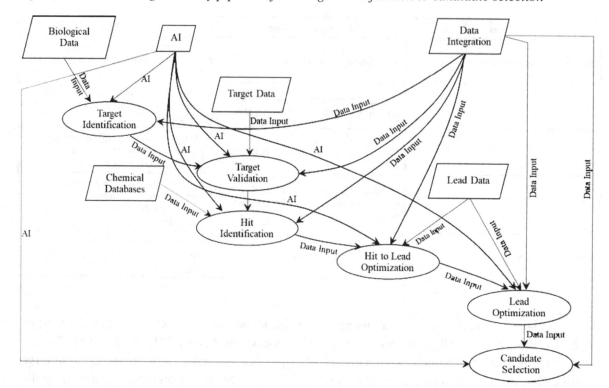

in analyzing molecular structures and predicting drug interactions by processing drug compound images. By recognizing patterns and structures within these images, CNNs can predict how a potential drug might interact with targeted biological pathways. RNNs, on the other hand, have been effectively employed to analyze sequential data such as time-series drug reaction data, enabling researchers to predict potential side effects or the drug's efficacy over time. Additionally, reinforcement learning, a subset of machine learning, has been gaining traction. Algorithms under this umbrella work by continuously refining their predictions based on feedback and optimizing the drug discovery process through iterative improvement. In addition, generative adversarial networks (GANs) and variational autoencoders (VAEs) play pivotal roles in de novo drug design. These algorithms generate novel molecular structures that can be potential new drugs. GANs operate by having two networks, a generator and a discriminator, contesting each other. In the context of drug discovery, the generator tries to create authentic-looking molecular structures, while the discriminator attempts to differentiate between real and generated structures. This process results in the production of novel and viable molecular compounds. VAEs, on the other hand, encode known molecular structures into a latent space and can then decode this space to generate new potential drug molecules. The advantage is that VAEs can generate molecular structures in regions of latent space where data might be sparse, leading to the discovery of novel drug candidates. Through a deeper exploration of these specific algorithms and methodologies, the chapter can shed light on the technical intricacies and groundbreaking potential of AI-driven processes in drug discovery within the pharmaceutical sciences.

Role of AI Algorithms in Identifying Potential Drug Candidates

Before exploring the intricacies of the topic at hand, it is essential to delineate the relationship between AI, machine learning, and deep learning. These interconnected domains profoundly influence drug development processes, as shown in Figure 3. AI, the overarching term, denotes the ability of machines to perform tasks typically requiring human intelligence. In drug development, AI automates processes, sifts through extensive datasets, and pinpoints potential drug candidates. Machine learning, a subset of AI, empowers machines to learn and adapt from experience. It leverages statistical techniques to discern patterns in data, facilitating decision-making or inferences without being explicitly programmed. Within drug development, machine learning is pivotal for predicting drug candidate properties, identifying prospective drug-target interactions, and virtually screening expansive compound libraries. Deep learning, a more specialized branch of machine learning, harnesses intricate, multilayered artificial neural networks to analyze vast and complex datasets. In the realm of drug development, deep learning is instrumental in forecasting compound bioactivity, crafting new potential drug molecules through de novo drug design, and personalizing medicine based on individual patient data (Sarkar et al., 2023).

AI algorithms, fortified by machine learning and deep learning, are exceptionally adept at identifying potential drug candidates—a task historically time-consuming, resource-intensive, and susceptible to error. These algorithms distinguish themselves with their capability to sift through expansive datasets, discern patterns, and make accurate predictions, thereby revolutionizing the preliminary stages of drug discovery. Traditionally, potential drug candidates have been pinpointed by screening vast libraries of chemical compounds against a biological target, such as a protein or enzyme associated with a disease (Yingngam, 2023). This method, while comprehensive, is both resource-draining and time-consuming. Additionally, it often lacks the finesse to address the multifaceted biological systems and intricate networks underlying disease mechanisms. In contrast, AI algorithms can significantly enhance this process with a technique termed in silico screening. Fueled by machine learning and deep learning, these algorithms can forecast compound-target interactions rooted in historical data patterns and a comprehensive grasp of biological systems. Consequently, they are equipped to prioritize compounds with the highest likelihood of achieving the intended effects, thus diminishing the reliance on extensive physical screening. Furthermore, AI algorithms offer an integrated perspective grounded in systems biology, moving beyond isolated target-centric strategies to encompass the entire breadth of disease networks. These algorithms harbor the potential to explore novel drug candidates by anticipating off-target effects, decoding intricate disease networks, and identifying drugs optimized to modulate these networks effectively (Sadri, 2023). The following subsections delve into machine learning algorithms for predictive modeling and the integration of AI-driven methodologies in virtual screening.

Machine Learning Algorithms for Predictive Modeling

Machine learning algorithms, fundamental to AI, utilize historical data to make predictions, identify patterns, and guide decision-making. These algorithms are garnering increasing accolades for their prowess in processing and analyzing vast chemical libraries to identify potential drug compounds—a feat traditionally much more challenging and protracted. Figure 4 offers a clear depiction of how these algorithms leverage data to forecast interactions between drugs and their respective targets. The process begins with data collection, a phase that amasses information on known drug-target interactions, the structures of drugs and targets, and other relevant biological and chemical information. The volume and

Figure 3. Hierarchical relationship of artificial intelligence (AI), machine learning (ML), and deep learning (DL) in drug development

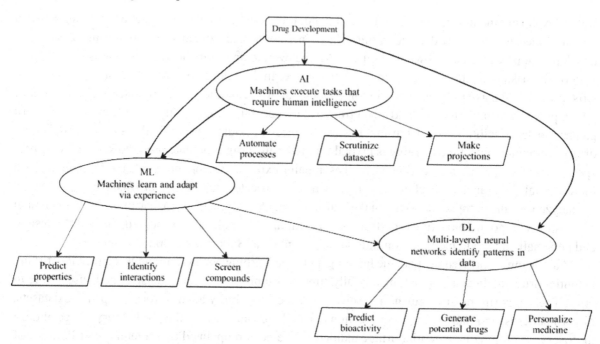

veracity of the data gathered during this phase play a pivotal role in shaping the efficacy of the subsequent machine-learning model. This is followed by data preprocessing, a stage dedicated to cleansing the data, addressing missing values, and converting the data into a format amenable to machine learning algorithms. For instance, chemical structures might be transmuted into molecular descriptors. Furthermore, this stage might involve balancing the dataset, especially if the number of noninteractions dramatically outweighs recorded interactions. Subsequent to preprocessing is feature selection, which zeroes in on the most salient features or variables for the model. These features might be delineated on the basis of domain-specific knowledge (such as the essential properties of drugs and targets), statistical scrutiny or automated feature selection techniques. The next phase, model training, is where the algorithm immerses itself in the data. Here, the characteristics of each drug-target duo are fed into the algorithm, refining the model's parameters to narrow the gap between its predictions and the authenticated interactions. After training, the focus shifts to model validation, wherein the model's competence is gauged on a separate dataset that remained untouched during the training. This evaluation ensures the model's robustness when faced with novel, unexplored data. Once the model successfully navigates the validation process, it can predict potential interactions between novel drugs and targets (Yingngam, 2023).

Various machine learning algorithms, including decision trees, random forests, support vector machines, and deep learning models, are employed in drug discovery. Table 3 provides specific instances of their application. These advanced tools shine when analyzing an eclectic mix of data related to chemical structures and associated biological activities (Bannigan et al., 2023). The standout feature of machine learning algorithms, setting them apart from conventional methods, is their unparalleled prowess in discerning intricate relationships between a prospective drug candidate's chemical architecture and its potential therapeutic impact. This profound analysis stems from machine learning's adeptness

Figure 4. Workflow of machine learning algorithms in predicting drug-target interactions

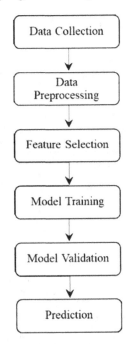

at navigating multidimensional data and capturing the minute intricacies and interplay that determine a compound's efficacy and safety. Furthermore, machine learning algorithms are adept at projecting pivotal pharmacokinetic and pharmacodynamic traits of prospective drug candidates. This encompasses the absorption, distribution, metabolism, excretion, and toxicity—often abbreviated as ADME/T—of a specific compound. Such foresight is invaluable during the incipient phases of drug discovery and development, empowering researchers to sideline candidates possessing unfavorable ADME/T characteristics (Di Lascio et al., 2023). By facilitating the early elimination of unsuitable candidates, machine learning algorithms contribute to considerable savings in subsequent drug development stages, both temporally and financially. As a result, these algorithms are instrumental in refining and amplifying the efficiency of the drug discovery trajectory, underscoring their revolutionary potential within the pharmaceutical sciences.

For illustration, a study spearheaded by Wang et al. (2023) highlighted molecular toxicity prediction's pivotal role in drug discovery as a determinant directly influencing human well-being and decisively shaping a drug's trajectory. The researchers accentuated the merits of pinpointing molecular toxicity with precision in drug discovery's embryonic stages. Such early detection facilitates the removal of suboptimal molecules, curbing the squandering of resources in subsequent phases. While they recognized the escalating trend of machine learning deployment for molecular toxicity prediction, they noted a lacuna: existing models often bypass the comprehensive 3-dimensional (3D) data of molecules. As a remedial measure, they introduced QuantumTox—a pioneering strategy employing quantum chemistry to envisage drug molecule toxicity, adeptly harnessing molecules' stereostructural nuances. To further elevate the model's precision and versatility, they incorporated gradient-boosting decision trees coupled with bagging ensemble learning techniques. Empirical analyses spanning diverse tasks underscored their model's superior performance over baseline models, even in scenarios with more limited datasets.

Table 3. Overview of machine learning algorithms utilized in drug discovery and their specific applications

Machine Learning Algorithm	Applications in Drug Discovery	Examples	Reference
Supervised learning (e.g., Decision trees, support vector machines, linear regression)	Predictive modeling of drug efficacy and toxicity, Quantitative structure-activity relationship (QSAR) modeling	Predicting drug-protein interactions, Forecasting drug absorption, distribution, metabolism, and excretion (ADME) properties	Fang et al. (2023)
Unsupervised learning (e.g., clustering, principal component analysis)	Pattern recognition, Drug clustering based on chemical properties	Identifying subgroups of compounds with similar characteristics, Drug repositioning	Murali and Karuppasamy (2023)
Deep learning (e.g., convolutional neural networks, recurrent neural networks)	Predicting molecular properties, Drug-target interaction prediction, Generating novel drug candidates	Predicting binding affinity of drug-target pairs, Drug design	Kyro et al. (2023)
Reinforcement learning (e.g., Q-Learning)	Optimizing chemical structures, Multiobjective optimization	Designing novel compounds with desired properties	Noaro et al. (2023)
Transfer learning	Applying models trained on one task to a related task	Using a model trained to predict binding affinity for one target to predict binding affinity for a related target	Suhartono et al. (2023)
Graph neural networks	Drug design, Drug-target interaction prediction	Modeling chemical structures as graphs and predicting their properties	Abate et al. (2023)

Virtual Screening Using AI-Driven Approaches

Virtual screening—a crucial drug discovery procedure that involves searching molecular databases for compounds likely to bind to drug targets—is undergoing a revolutionary shift catalyzed by advancements in AI (Chen et al., 2023a). While traditionally a labor-intensive and time-consuming endeavor, the incorporation of AI-driven methods has streamlined and accelerated the procedure, heightening both the precision and efficiency of virtual screening (Sarkar et al., 2023). Deep learning algorithms, with their capacity to analyze intricate, nonlinear relationships between molecular configurations and biological activity, are becoming indispensable in virtual screening, granting unparalleled insights for the identification of promising drug candidates (Neelakandan & Rajanikant, 2023). Among these, CNNs stand out for their proficiency in predicting the binding affinities of molecules to target proteins—a pivotal metric in evaluating a compound's therapeutic potential. CNNs, with their adeptness at discerning complex patterns directly from unprocessed data, including the 3D molecular structure, further refine the accuracy of virtual screening (Johannsen et al., 2023). Additionally, in silico drug discovery, which replaces labor-intensive lab work with computational models and simulations, has been substantially enhanced by AI integration. Cutting-edge AI algorithms empower researchers with the tools to virtually sift through expansive chemical realms—spanning millions or even billions of molecules—to foresee their interactions with biological targets and gauge their drug-like characteristics. These AI-enhanced methods optimize the virtual screening procedure and amplify its predictive precision (Feng & Wei, 2023). The implications are substantial, as improved early predictions can significantly expedite the overall drug development pipeline, conserve resources and ultimately accelerate the delivery of effective therapeutics to the market.

Deep learning, especially CNNs, has transformed the realm of virtual screening. CNNs, originally designed for image recognition tasks, have been adapted to analyze molecular structures, thus facilitating the prediction of potential bioactive compounds. These networks dissect compound images layer by layer, capturing intricate molecular features that can bind to target proteins. Moreover, graph neural networks (GNNs) have also been at the forefront in recent years. GNNs represent molecules as graphs, where atoms are nodes and bonds are edges. This approach is especially adept at capturing the relational information between atoms in a molecule, making GNNs particularly effective in predicting drug properties and interactions directly from molecular structures without the need for manual feature extraction. Another noteworthy algorithm is GANs in the realm of structure-based drug design within virtual screening. GANs consist of two neural networks: a generator that creates molecular structures and a discriminator that evaluates them. The generator crafts novel molecular structures, while the discriminator assesses these structures against known bioactive compounds. This iterative competitive process fine-tunes the generator's capability, leading to the creation of potential drug candidates that are likely to have high bioactivity. Additionally, reinforcement learning has been introduced into the GAN framework, where the generator is rewarded for producing molecules that meet certain criteria, further refining the drug candidate search. Through an in-depth exploration of these specific algorithms and methodologies, the chapter can elucidate the technical underpinnings and the transformative potential of AI-driven processes in virtual screening within the pharmaceutical sciences.

Reduction of Time and Cost Through Virtual Screening

AI drives a transformative shift in the field of drug discovery, particularly through the application of virtual screening (Clyde et al., 2023). This technology has emerged as a powerful tool that significantly reduces the time and cost of drug discovery processes (Sarkar et al., 2023). This section underscores how AI-driven virtual screening can streamline and expedite pharmaceutical research and development.

Expediting Lead Identification

Identifying lead compounds is a crucial step in drug discovery, involving the recognition and enhancement of biologically active compounds that could be developed into therapeutic drugs. Historically, this process relied greatly on high-throughput screening, a method that demands much time and resources. However, AI has revolutionized this field by using machine learning and deep learning algorithms to speed up the identification of lead compounds (Chatterjee et al., 2023). These algorithms leverage vast amounts of biochemical data to predict and optimize the bioactivity of potential lead compounds (Ranson et al., 2023). Through learning from these extensive datasets, AI algorithms can discern patterns and make predictions far beyond human capability (Ranjan et al., 2023). For example, predictive models can be trained on molecular descriptors and biological activity data, facilitating the rapid identification of potential lead compounds (Clyde et al., 2023). This not only accelerates the drug discovery timeline but also improves predictor accuracy, thereby reducing the likelihood of failure in subsequent stages. Through the implementation of AI-driven techniques, researchers anticipate a significant reduction in the time needed to identify promising drug candidates, leading to a concurrent decrease in associated costs (Czub et al., 2023).

Exploration of Chemical Space

The term "chemical space" refers to the enormous multidimensional realm encompassing all conceivable molecules, estimated to number approximately 10^{60} (Fallani et al., 2023). The sheer size and complexity of this space render it virtually impossible to explore fully using traditional techniques. However, AI has introduced new possibilities in this regard. AI-powered algorithms, particularly those based on deep generative models, are now capable of exploring the chemical space more effectively (Vogt, 2023). These algorithms can be trained to generate novel molecules with desirable properties, continually improving their ability to produce increasingly promising molecular structures through iterative feedback and reinforcement learning. For instance, (Ståhl et al., 2019) developed a fragment-based reinforcement learning approach to optimize the design of novel molecules with desirable properties, a critical step in medicinal chemistry programs. Their method, based on an actor-critic model built using bidirectional LSTM networks, learns to generate new compounds with desired properties starting from an initial set of lead molecules. It then iteratively improves these molecules by substituting some of their fragments. The generative process uses a balanced binary tree, formed based on the similarity of the fragments, to bias the output toward generating structurally similar molecules. They validated their method with a case study that yielded promising results, demonstrating the method's potential for facilitating the design of efficacious and safe compounds in medicinal chemistry.

These generative AI models can produce an array of diverse and novel molecular structures, potentially beyond human consideration, thus enabling a broader exploration of the chemical space (Vogt, 2023). This innovation not only minimizes the time needed for the exploration process but also substantially cuts the costs associated with the synthesis and testing of numerous molecular structures. Furthermore, AI allows for the integration of drug-likeness, synthetic feasibility, and predicted bioactivity into the exploration process (Gautam et al., 2023). This comprehensive approach ensures that the generated compounds are not only potentially active but also practically viable as drug candidates, reducing the likelihood of failure in the later stages of drug development (Sadybekov & Katritch, 2023).

Utilizing Machine Learning for Predictive Modeling in Drug Discovery

The integration of machine learning into drug discovery has spurred significant advancements in the field, notably in predictive modeling. Two key areas—the prediction of pharmacokinetic properties and toxicity risk assessment—have particularly benefited from the impact of machine learning. Due to its sophisticated computational capabilities, machine learning can analyze and extract useful information from vast, complex datasets—a critical aspect of these applications. As a result, significant improvements have been observed in the accuracy and speed of predicting properties such as pharmacokinetics and toxicity risks. Therefore, machine learning offers an innovative avenue for enhancing efficacy and accelerating drug discovery processes.

Predicting Pharmacokinetic Properties

Pharmacokinetics, encompassing the absorption, distribution, metabolism, and excretion (ADME) properties of a compound, plays a critical role in the drug discovery process (Tran et al., 2023). The accurate prediction of these properties is crucial because they determine a drug's behavior in the body and, subsequently, its efficacy and safety. Machine learning algorithms provide a more efficient approach for predicting the pharmacokinetic properties of potential drug candidates (Sobhia et al., 2023). These algorithms, trained on extensive datasets comprising the structural and physicochemical properties of molecules and their corresponding pharmacokinetic parameters, can predict how new compounds might behave within a biological system (Fernández-Quintero et al., 2023). Predictive models relying on machine learning methods such as decision trees, random forests, and deep learning networks are increasingly being employed. They can offer early and rapid predictions about a drug candidate's pharmacokinetic profiles, helping to mitigate the risk of failure in later stages of drug development (Tran et al., 2023). This leads to significant savings in time and cost, thereby accelerating the process of bringing effective and safe drugs to market (Sobhia et al., 2023).

Toxicity Prediction and Risk Assessment

Toxicity prediction and risk assessment are further areas that can benefit from AI-driven decision-making algorithms. Neural networks, for instance, are frequently used for these purposes. Figure 5 illustrates the typical architecture of a neural network designed to predict drug toxicity. This network takes into account input features such as the drug's chemical structure, pharmacokinetics, and potential drug–drug interactions.

1. Input layer: This layer consists of nodes that correspond to the features of the drug under analysis. Each feature—for example, a particular aspect of the drug's chemical structure or a pharmacokinetic parameter—is represented by one or more nodes.
2. Hidden layers: Following the input layer, the network comprises one or more hidden layers. These layers include nodes (also known as neurons) that perform transformations on the inputs they receive and convey the results to the next layer. The transformations of each node are governed by the weights and biases of connections from nodes in the preceding layer, which are learned during the training phase.
3. Activation functions: Every node within the hidden layers applies an activation function to the weighted sum of its inputs. This function introduces nonlinearity into the model, thereby enabling it to detect complex patterns in the data.
4. Output layer: The output layer represents the model's prediction. For instance, in predictive toxicology, it could be a single node that displays the predicted toxicity level of the drug.
5. Backpropagation and adjustment: During the neural network training process, the backpropagation algorithm is used to tweak the weights and biases of the nodes. These adjustments are made based on the difference between the network's output and the known toxicity levels from the training examples.

A considerable number of drug candidates falter during clinical trials due to toxicity issues. Predicting drug-induced toxicity early on is crucial for increasing both the safety and success rate of drug development. As per a study by Wong et al. (2019), approximately 13.8% of drugs make it from Phase 1 to Food and Drug Administration (FDA) approval. One of the main reasons clinical trials fail is due to safety issues, frequently caused by drug-induced toxicity. This study offers a comprehensive analysis of clinical trial success rates, although it does not specify the percentage of failures attributed to toxicity. A widely referenced report published in 2011 by Arrowsmith discovered that 30% of drug failures in phases II and III are due to safety concerns, including toxicity (Arrowsmith, 2011). Nonetheless, this

Figure 5. Neural network architecture for predictive toxicology in drug development

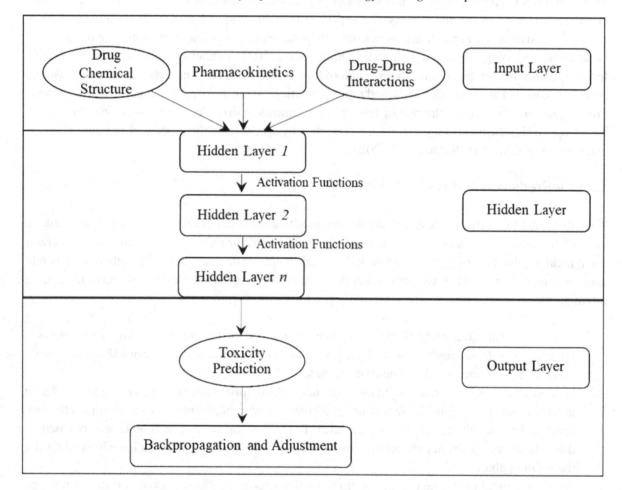

figure also encapsulates other safety issues alongside toxicity. A paper issued by Cook et al. in 2014 titled "Lessons Learned from the Fate of AstraZeneca's Drug Pipeline: A Five-Dimensional Framework" suggests that between 2005 and 2010, roughly one-fifth of drug failures during the preclinical phase at AstraZeneca were related to safety issues, including toxicity (Cook et al., 2014). Machine learning has shown considerable effectiveness in predicting toxicity and assessing risk (Singh Sharma, 2023). Predictive models are trained on diverse datasets, encompassing chemical structures, toxicological data, and associated biological endpoints (Mo et al., 2023). By discerning patterns within these datasets, machine learning models can anticipate the toxic effects of new compounds. Different machine learning methods, such as support vector machines, neural networks, and gradient boosting models, are used to anticipate various types of toxicity, including liver, heart, and kidney toxicity, among others (Badwan et al., 2023; Chandrasekar et al., 2023; Tran et al., 2023). This approach facilitates an early evaluation of a drug candidate's safety and helps determine which compounds to focus on for further development. Consequently, it aids in mitigating potential risks, costs, and failures during the later stages of drug discovery and development (Tran et al., 2023).

AI-DRIVEN DECISION-MAKING IN DRUG FORMULATION DEVELOPMENT

The integration of AI has revolutionized various facets of pharmaceutical sciences, particularly drug formulation development. Traditionally, formulation development has been a complex, labor-intensive process primarily reliant on trial-and-error methods, necessitating considerable resources and time. However, the emergence of AI-driven decision-making tools has markedly increased the efficiency of this process. These sophisticated AI algorithms are currently employed for formulation selection, thereby enhancing the accuracy and speed at which optimal drug combinations and ratios are determined. Moreover, AI-driven strategies are instigating breakthroughs in drug delivery systems, offering personalized solutions that optimize drug release kinetics. Notably, AI also paves the way for enhancing drug stability and bioavailability, significantly bolstering therapeutic effectiveness while mitigating side effects. The incorporation of AI into drug formulation development marks a transformative shift in the paradigm, promising significant potential for the future of pharmaceutical sciences. The following sections provide a comprehensive exploration of these groundbreaking advancements.

AI-Powered Optimization Algorithms for Formulation Selection

The formulation development phase, a critical and intricate stage in pharmaceutical sciences, necessitates the identification of the optimal composition and production processes. In this context, emerging AI-driven optimization algorithms prove instrumental in streamlining the formulation and selection of drugs and expediting the development process.

AI Implementation in Optimization Algorithms for Decision-Making

Formulation selection involves a comprehensive evaluation of numerous elements, including drug stability, solubility, bioavailability, patient acceptability, and manufacturability. Traditional approaches largely rely on labor-intensive trial-and-error experiments. However, AI-driven optimization algorithms provide a groundbreaking alternative (Navabhatra et al., 2022). Employing methods such as genetic algorithms, swarm intelligence, and gradient-based optimization, these AI tools identify the best formulation given the needed characteristics. They frame the drug formulation process as an optimization problem with an objective function defined by the crucial quality attributes of the drug product. Advanced AI algorithms, such as DNNs, CNNs, and reinforcement learning, are emerging as formidable tools in formulation development. While DNNs delve deep into multilayered data for intricate insights, CNNs have shown potential in microscopic analysis of formulations, especially in recognizing patterns in particle size, shape, and distribution. Reinforcement learning, on the other hand, iteratively refines formulations based on continuous feedback loops, fostering dynamic optimization (Vora et al., 2023). By assessing the interactions between the formulation's components, these algorithms predict and select the optimal formulation (Carou-Senra et al., 2023). AI applications thus streamline the formulation selection process by focusing on the most promising formulations, eliminating the need for exhaustive trial-and-error tests, and consequently reducing costs and time.

In the noteworthy research study titled "Artificial neural network modeling of nanostructured lipid carriers containing 5-*O*-caffeoylquinic acid-rich *Cratoxylum formosum* leaf extract for skin application", the in vitro antiaging properties of *C. formosum* extract for potential dermal applications were explored (Navabhatra et al., 2022). The plant extract was encapsulated in nanostructured lipid carriers

(CFE-NLCs), and their biological properties, such as enhancement of type I procollagen synthesis and inhibition of matrix metalloproteinase (MMP) activity, were analyzed to understand potential benefits. An artificial neural network (ANN) integrated with K-fold cross-validation was utilized to examine the impacts of formulation constituents and optimize the CFE-NLCs. The physicochemical attributes, skin absorption capabilities, and potential irritation of these carriers were evaluated. Analysis using liquid chromatography with tandem mass spectrometry (LC–MS/MS) provided compelling evidence that 5-*O*-caffeoylquinic acid plays a crucial role as the key component in CFE. Our research revealed that the extract possesses a notable capability to boost the production of type I procollagen, a crucial protein that helps retain skin elasticity and firmness. In addition, the extract has shown a significant capacity to restrain specific enzymes, notably MMP-1, MMP-3, and MMP-9. These enzymes have a reputation for degrading collagen, a fundamental substance that contributes to youthful and healthy skin appearance, and thus, they are implicated in the skin aging process. The extract, by suppressing these MMPs, shows the potential for shielding and preserving skin collagen levels, a feature that would be advantageous for maintaining a youthful look. These compelling results were observed in primary human dermal fibroblasts, which adds credibility to the findings and suggests that the extract may have practical applications in promoting skin health and counteracting the visible signs of aging. The optimized CFE-NLCs demonstrated superior skin absorption, enhanced biocompatibility, and reduced irritation potential compared to the free botanical extract solution. The findings suggest that CFE-NLCs hold potential as skincare ingredients due to their advantageous properties.

As exemplified in the aforementioned study, ANNs integrated with K-fold cross-validation serve as powerful tools often employed in pharmaceutical product optimization. ANNs excel at modeling complex nonlinear relationships between inputs and outputs, which are commonly encountered in pharmaceutical formulation development. This capability allows them to accurately depict the intricate interdependencies among formulation constituents. Moreover, ANNs function without the need for explicit programming or rule-based instructions to learn from data, a vital feature in formulation optimization where associations between variables are complex, multidimensional, and often not fully understood. ANNs are exceptional at recognizing patterns and making predictions, which makes them incredibly useful in forecasting the effects of changes in formulation constituents on the overall properties of pharmaceutical products. Coupling ANNs with K-fold cross-validation ensures the model's applicability to a wider range of situations. In this process, the dataset is divided into 'K' subsets. The model is then trained on 'K-1' subsets, while the remaining subset is used for validation. This procedure is repeated K times, with each subset being used for validation exactly once. This approach helps prevent overfitting, a situation where the model becomes excessively attuned to the training data and performs poorly when presented with new data. K-fold cross-validation provides an estimate of how the model would perform with an independent dataset, and it also reveals the variability of the model's performance. This insight helps evaluate the robustness of the ANN model. Moreover, in pharmaceutical development, where gathering data can be costly and time-consuming, K-fold cross-validation promotes optimal data use by employing all the data for both training and validation, ensuring that there is no waste of data. Thus, using ANNs in tandem with K-fold cross-validation results in a robust, adaptable, and predictive tool for studying and optimizing pharmaceutical products.

Fast-Tracking Formulation Development With AI

One significant advantage of AI-driven optimization algorithms is their ability to expedite formulation development timelines. These tools can swiftly analyze a vast array of possible formulations and manufacturing processes, outpacing conventional methods. AI algorithms possess iterative learning capabilities, improving their predictions with each optimization cycle. This continuous refinement allows the algorithm to enhance its efficiency over time, leading to faster formulation development. Furthermore, AI models are adept at integrating complex, multifaceted data such as physicochemical properties, manufacturing parameters, and even patient-specific information. Incorporating this information might be challenging in traditional formulation development processes. Evidence of the significant impact of AI on the speed and efficiency of drug formulation development can be found in future research studies.

For instance, Jiang et al. (2023), in their article published in the "International Journal of Pharmaceutics: X", reported how machine learning methods contribute significantly to the acceleration of formulation development, especially in forming chemically stable amorphous solid dispersions prepared by hot-melt extrusion. The authors specifically discussed how AI can expedite formulation development by predicting the physicochemical properties of various formulations. Abdalla et al. (2023), in their study published in the "International Journal of Pharmaceutics", detailed the use of machine learning to predict the production of selective laser-sintered 3D-printed drug products. The study emphasized the benefits of AI in rapidly narrowing down the most effective formulations, thereby saving both time and resources. Another pivotal AI tool in the QSAR model forecasts the behavior of molecules in drug formulations based on their inherent chemical structures. QSAR models, integrated with AI, can predict molecular interactions, stability, and potential degradation routes, thereby facilitating robust formulation strategies (Kasture & Shende, 2023). Moreover, Yacoub et al. (2022), in their article published in "Drug Delivery", used an AI-based model to predict the in situ formation of nanoparticles for arthritis therapy via intra-articular delivery. The AI model significantly accelerated the development process by enabling the prediction of suitable formulations. The use of the developed products for intra-articular injection demonstrated their effectiveness in piroxicam delivery for rheumatoid arthritis treatment. GANs, a class of machine learning models, are also making strides in drug formulation. By simulating and predicting the outcomes of countless drug formulations, GANs aid in determining the most efficacious drug combinations, thereby streamlining the formulation process (Bao et al., 2023). As a result, these AI tools deliver a more comprehensive and personalized formulation development process, potentially boosting the success rate and productivity of drug products.

Machine learning, particularly regression models and decision trees, has been invaluable in predicting the behavior of complex formulations. Regression models, given their predictive nature, are adept at estimating the physical and chemical stability of new formulations based on historical data. Such models can predict how various ingredients in a formulation might interact over time, facilitating the identification of the most stable and effective combinations. Decision trees, on the other hand, offer a more visual approach, breaking down formulation decisions into a series of binary choices. This method is particularly useful for determining ingredient proportions and sequencing in the formulation process, allowing scientists to visually trace the decisions leading to an optimal formulation. Neural networks, particularly deep learning models, have made strides in the realm of complex drug formulations, such as those involving controlled release. These models can process a vast amount of data, from ingredient properties to manufacturing conditions, to predict how a drug will release over time in various environments. The attraction of deep learning lies in its ability to recognize intricate patterns across vast datasets, enabling it to anticipate potential formulation challenges or innovations that might not be immediately apparent to human researchers. Additionally, reinforcement learning models have been introduced to optimize the formulation process. In this approach, an AI agent iteratively adjusts formulations, receives feedback on the formulation's effectiveness, and refines the process in real time, speeding up the traditionally time-intensive research and development phase. A more profound exploration of these algorithms can provide readers with insights into the intricacies and transformative potential of AI-driven processes in formulation development within the pharmaceutical sciences.

Enhancing Drug Delivery With AI-Driven Approaches

Over the years, drug delivery has become increasingly complex, necessitating precise control over several factors, such as the drug release rate, site-specific targeting, and overcoming biological barriers. Traditional methods of optimizing drug delivery systems often rely on labor-intensive, iterative processes of formulation development and testing. However, these conventional approaches are gradually being supplanted by AI-driven methodologies, promising to introduce a new level of precision, speed, and efficacy to drug delivery. The integration of AI-driven approaches into drug delivery development is more than a theoretical proposition. Numerous studies have already demonstrated the utility of these approaches in a variety of applications, ranging from optimizing nanoparticle formulations for targeted drug delivery to predicting the behavior of transdermal patches and designing controlled-release oral dosage forms. Nevertheless, the potential of AI in this area remains largely untapped, and its full realization necessitates concerted efforts in research and development, standardization, and validation. In the upcoming subsections, we delve deeper into the role of AI in drug delivery, specifically focusing on drug release kinetics and drug delivery optimization.

Predictive Modeling for Drug Release Kinetics

Drug release kinetics are of paramount importance in determining a drug's therapeutic efficacy, as they describe the rate at which the drug is released from the delivery system and becomes available at the intended site of action. The emergence of AI-driven predictive models, notably machine learning and deep learning algorithms, has revolutionized the anticipation of drug release kinetics. Factors that these models consider include the properties of the drug, the composition and structure of the delivery system, and environmental conditions. Training these models on extensive datasets enables the identification of intricate patterns and correlations, which may prove challenging through traditional methodologies. In predictive modeling, key optimization techniques such as backpropagation and gradient descent play pivotal roles. The choice of an appropriate loss function, such as the mean squared error or cross-entropy, ensures effective training of the AI model, optimizing its predictive accuracy (Navabhatra et al., 2022). Consequently, predictive modeling of drug release kinetics can enhance control over drug release rates, optimize therapeutic efficacy, and minimize side effects. This approach also reduces the necessity for exhaustive in vitro and in vivo testing, conserving both time and resources in the drug development process.

A compelling example of this application is demonstrated in the research conducted by S. Wang et al. (2022). In their study, they applied ANNs, a form of machine learning, to predict drug release profiles from two dosage forms, namely, quercetin solid dispersions and apigenin nanoparticles. Their focus was primarily on poorly soluble drugs, a frequent challenge in pharmaceutical science, and they developed a model trained with experimental data to predict release profiles. This innovative approach negates the need for labor-intensive testing, saving considerable time and resources during the drug development process. In another remarkable study, Borjigin et al. (2023) employed a deep learning algorithm to predict the dissolution performance of mini-tablets from sustained-release formulations. Mini tablets have been increasingly adopted as an alternative to monolithic tablets due to their ease of use for pediatric populations, dose flexibility, and ability to tailor drug release profiles. Drawing inspiration from the human brain's architecture, this machine learning approach models complex, nonlinear relationships. In this context, the deep learning model was trained on a dataset encompassing diverse formulation factors and environmental conditions. This research exemplifies the potential of deep learning in predicting how variations in formulation and conditions can influence drug dissolution, thereby facilitating better control over this critical process. Further expanding the scope of AI in this field, Deng et al. (2023) utilized machine learning to model drug release from a sustained-release microsphere formulation. Their predictive model was trained on a multitude of data points, including drug properties and formulation composition. They showed that machine learning could accurately predict drug release kinetics, thereby enhancing control over drug release rates.

Personalized Drug Delivery Optimization

Personalized medicine is revolutionizing modern healthcare, with AI playing a substantial role, particularly in optimizing drug delivery for individual patients. AI algorithms can process and analyze vast amounts of data, including genomic information, patient medical histories, and lifestyle factors, to make personalized predictions. This data-driven approach aids in designing drug delivery systems tailored to the individual needs of patients. By predicting the optimal drug dosage, release rate, and administration route, AI significantly contributes to personalized drug delivery optimization. This not only enhances therapeutic effectiveness and reduces side effects but also improves patient compliance, leading to better treatment outcomes. In certain instances, AI algorithms can help in the real-time adjustment of drug delivery based on continuous monitoring of patient responses, further enhancing the personalization of therapy.

The advent of personalized medicine, largely facilitated by the integration of AI technologies, is undoubtedly redefining modern healthcare. AI's contribution to personalized drug delivery is a prime example of this transformative innovation. AI algorithms' ability to process and analyze an extensive amount of data—encompassing genomic information, patient medical history, and lifestyle factors—allows these technologies to make personalized predictions that can inform the design of drug delivery systems catering specifically to an individual's needs.

Several studies have illustrated the role of AI in predicting optimal drug dosages. One example is the study conducted by (Z. Wang et al., 2022), in which the authors developed a pharmacokinetic model for individualized dosing of vancomycin, a commonly used antibiotic, using AI. This model considered patient-specific factors such as age, weight, renal function, and previous exposure to the drug. The AI model accurately predicted the proper dosage, improving therapeutic effectiveness and minimizing side effects. AI algorithms can also predict the optimal drug release rate and administration route. A study conducted by Lu et al. (2022) employed a machine learning approach to optimize the release rate of drugs from 3D-printed tablets. The machine learning model predicted the best tablet design parameters to achieve the desired release rate. Furthermore, He et al. (2021) utilized AI to predict the most efficient administration route (oral, injection, or topical) for different drugs based on the patient's condition and drug properties. Moreover, AI technologies can assist in the real-time adjustment of drug delivery based on continuous monitoring of patient responses. In a study by Rashid et al. (2022), an AI-based closed-loop system was used for insulin delivery in patients with type 1 diabetes. The system monitored the patient's glucose levels in real time and adjusted the insulin delivery accordingly, thereby demonstrating improved glucose control.

Improving Drug Stability and Bioavailability With AI-Based Formulation Design

The development and optimization of drug formulations are vital processes that directly influence the stability and bioavailability of therapeutic agents. Interpretable machine learning is gaining traction in the pharmaceutical sciences. While AI models provide predictions, it is equally crucial to glean insights into why these predictions are made. Tools such as SHAP (Shapley Additive exPlanations) and LIME (Local Interpretable Model-Agnostic Explanations) have been instrumental in providing this interpretability, ensuring that the scientific community can trust and understand AI-driving decisions in drug formulation (Jiang et al., 2023). This section investigates the potential applications of AI and related technologies in augmenting drug stability and bioavailability, addressing the hurdles encountered in conventional formulation design. The discussion covers the role of AI in forecasting drug–drug and drug-excipient interactions, overseeing the stability of drugs under varying conditions and bolstering drug solubility and permeability, all of which critically influence their bioavailability.

Prediction of Formulation Stability

Stability is a key attribute of pharmaceutical formulations. It refers to the extent to which a product retains, within specified limits, the same properties and characteristics throughout its period of storage and use. Unstable formulations can lead to drug degradation, compromising the efficacy and safety of the product. Predicting the stability of a formulation is a complex task due to the multifactorial nature of the process. However, machine learning algorithms are well suited to handle this complexity. They can process large datasets containing myriad variables such as the properties of the drug and its excipients, the manufacturing process, and storage conditions. By training on historical stability data, AI models can learn to identify patterns and correlations that affect stability. Once trained, these models can predict the stability of new formulations, assisting formulation scientists in designing more stable drug products. This predictive ability can lead to substantial cost and time savings by minimizing stability-related failures.

Several instances of AI-driven approaches showing promise in predicting pharmaceutical formulation stability include the following: Han et al. (2019) described a deep learning model in a publication in the Journal of Controlled Release that predicts the stability of pharmaceutical solid forms under various storage conditions. This model was trained on a large stability dataset and provided predictions with significantly higher accuracy than traditional computational methods, demonstrating the potential of deep learning in predicting pharmaceutical stability and reducing the need for costly stability testing. Another study focused on the use of AI to predict the stability of protein formulations. Proteins are highly sensitive to storage and environmental conditions, making their stability prediction crucial for biopharmaceutical development. AI models, specifically machine learning and deep learning algorithms, were used to predict the stability of protein formulations based on factors such as pH, ionic strength, and excipient concentrations. These AI models, trained on experimental stability data, were able to predict the stability of proteins in new formulations with high accuracy (Fanjin Wang et al., 2023). Machine learning algorithms have also been applied to predict degradation pathways. This is critical, as impurities can form due to these pathways, affecting drug stability. Machine learning models have been used to predict these degradation pathways based on the structure of the drug molecule and storage conditions. These models can aid scientists in anticipating potential stability issues and designing more stable formulations (Liu et al., 2022). Moreover, a machine-learning-based predictive tool, DE-Interact, has been developed for studying drug-excipient interactions during product development. The results suggest that the developed AI model offers a reliable tool for quick referencing during the selection of excipients in formulation design (S. Patel et al., 2023). In conclusion, while these studies demonstrate promising advances, they represent the early stages of applying AI in this field. Further research is necessary to improve the accuracy of these models and validate them under a wider range of conditions and formulations.

Optimization of Bioavailability-Enhancing Strategies

Bioavailability is a critical parameter in the pharmaceutical sciences. It determines the fraction of the administered dose of a drug that reaches the systemic circulation and the rate at which this occurs. A well-designed formulation ensures optimal bioavailability, thereby maximizing the drug's therapeutic effect. AI is paving the way for more efficient optimization of bioavailability. Machine learning models can be trained on diverse datasets that include the physicochemical properties of the drug, formulation characteristics, and even patient-specific factors. By identifying the key features influencing bioavailability, these models can provide valuable insights for the design of optimal drug delivery systems. Furthermore, AI algorithms can support the design of advanced drug delivery systems, such as nanoparticle-based or targeted delivery systems, which can significantly enhance the bioavailability of poorly soluble or permeable drugs.

AI and machine learning techniques have shown significant potential for enhancing bioavailability in drug delivery systems, especially in the development of advanced delivery systems such as nanoparticle-based systems or in predicting the attributes of modern drug datasets. A 2023 study by Fargerholm et al. (Fagerholm et al., 2023) emphasized the creation and validation of an in silico system named ANDROMEDA, designed for predicting human clinical pharmacokinetics. ANDROMEDA seamlessly integrates machine learning and conformal prediction into a novel physiologically based pharmacokinetic model. The study had three key objectives: evaluating ANDROMEDA's predictive capabilities, comparing its performance with traditional lab methods, and exploring the pharmacokinetic properties of modern drugs. The evaluation leveraged two distinct datasets: a benchmark set of 24 drugs displaying diverse physicochemical properties and a group of 28 novel small drug molecules launched in 2021. The prediction errors for crucial parameters ranged from approximately 1.2- to 2.5-fold at the median and peaked at 16-fold for both datasets. Notably, ANDROMEDA's predictive accuracy was comparable to, or even surpassed, the top-performing lab-based prediction methods, offering a significantly broader prediction range. The modern drugs were found to possess a higher average molecular weight than the benchmark set 15 years ago, reflecting an increase of approximately 200 g/mol. They were generally anticipated to exhibit complex pharmacokinetics, encompassing permeability and dissolution challenges and significant renal, biliary and/or gut wall elimination. In conclusion, ANDROMEDA outperformed traditional laboratory methods in predicting the pharmacokinetics of modern and physicochemically diverse drugs, underscoring its value as an in silico system in human clinical pharmacokinetic studies.

AI-DRIVEN DECISION-MAKING IN PHARMACEUTICAL MANUFACTURING

In the dynamic landscape of pharmaceutical sciences, the infusion of AI technologies has marked a new era in pharmaceutical manufacturing. Traditionally, this sector has been plagued by process inefficiencies, variability, and quality control issues. However, AI-driven decision-making tools are increasingly being employed to mitigate these challenges and optimize the manufacturing process. Through the application of AI algorithms, manufacturers can now predict, monitor, and fine-tune processes in real time, leading to increased efficiency and cost-effectiveness. AI-driven monitoring tools also facilitate real-time quality assurance, significantly minimizing the risk of errors and improving product consistency. Additionally, the role of AI in enhancing regulatory compliance and data integrity cannot be understated. AI provides the necessary tools to maintain stringent regulatory standards while ensuring the security and integrity of manufacturing data.

The success of AI implementation in pharmaceutical manufacturing can be gauged using various key performance indicators (KPIs), as summarized in Table 4. These include production efficiency, gauging increased production rates or yields; quality control, focusing on the number of detected and resolved defects; predictive maintenance, assessing reductions in unplanned downtime or increases in equipment lifespan; supply chain optimization, documenting reductions in stockouts or improvements in demand forecast accuracy; cost efficiency, monitoring overall reductions in manufacturing costs; compliance and regulatory adherence, tracking the reduction in regulatory violations or the time taken to prepare for audits; safety, quantifying a reduction in the number of safety incidents; and innovation, highlighting the number of new processes or improvements instigated by AI insights. It is important to remember that the relevance of each KPI will largely depend on the specific goals set for AI implementation.

The following sections explore the exciting potential of AI to transform pharmaceutical manufacturing, highlighting its expanding impact on the industry.

Table 4. Key performance indicators (KPIs) for AI implementation in pharmaceutical manufacturing

KPI	Description
Production efficiency	Measures the output of the manufacturing process per unit of input. AI can help optimize manufacturing processes to maximize efficiency.
Quality compliance Rate	Measures the percentage of products that meet quality standards. AI can help improve quality control and reduce the rate of defects or noncompliance.
Waste reduction	Measures the amount of waste generated by the manufacturing process. AI can help optimize processes to minimize waste.
Predictive maintenance	Measures the effectiveness of predictive maintenance in reducing equipment downtime. AI can predict when maintenance is needed based on patterns in the data.
Inventory turnover Ratio	Measures how often inventory is sold and replaced over a certain period. AI can help optimize inventory management and supply chain logistics.
Energy efficiency	Measures the energy consumption of the manufacturing process. AI can optimize processes to reduce energy use.
Production lead time	Measures the time from the start of the production process to the completion of the finished product. AI can help reduce lead time by optimizing various stages of the production process.
Product customization	Measures the ability to customize products to meet specific customer needs. AI can enable more efficient customization by predicting customer requirements and optimizing production processes.

Figure 6. Process flow diagram for AI integration in pharmaceutical manufacturing

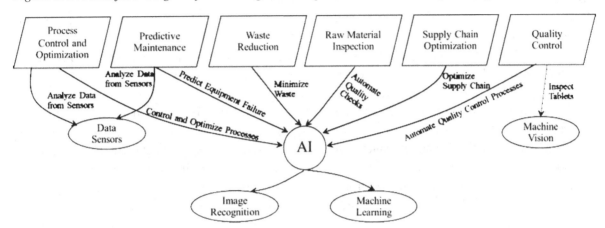

Process Optimization Using AI Algorithms

The application of AI in pharmaceutical manufacturing opens new avenues for process optimization. Advanced algorithms enable more precise parameter tuning, improve manufacturing efficiency, and facilitate the implementation of quality by design (QbD) principles. Figure 6 highlights the multiple stages in the pharmaceutical manufacturing process, underscoring how AI can be utilized at each juncture to augment efficiency, safety, and product quality. The initial step, raw material inspection, begins with the examination and validation of raw materials. At this point, AI can be harnessed to automate quality inspections, possibly utilizing techniques such as image recognition to pinpoint anomalies. Next are process control and optimization. Here, AI algorithms can be used to regulate and enhance manufacturing processes such as mixing, granulation, and tablet pressing. For instance, AI can analyze sensor data in real time to modify process parameters and maintain optimal conditions. The third phase is predictive maintenance. By employing AI, companies can anticipate when equipment might malfunction or require servicing, consequently reducing downtime and augmenting efficiency. This anticipation is achieved by examining equipment sensor data and using machine learning algorithms to discern patterns that precede failure. Quality control follows, where AI can be engaged to automate quality control processes. This automation could include inspecting final products for flaws or inconsistencies. Machine vision systems, for example, could inspect tablets and identify any that deviate from the standard size or shape. The penultimate stage is supply chain optimization. At this juncture, AI can be used to optimize the supply chain by predicting product demand and adjusting production schedules accordingly. This optimization can curtail inventory costs and help ensure that demand is met. Finally, waste reduction involves employing AI to minimize waste. This reduction can be achieved by optimizing processes to consume fewer resources and by predicting and averting issues that might result in product loss.

Intelligent Parameter Optimization

In pharmaceutical manufacturing, fine-tuning process parameters is paramount to ensuring product quality, consistency, and efficiency. AI algorithms offer a promising approach for intelligent parameter optimization, contributing to substantial improvements in the manufacturing process. AI-powered optimization techniques, such as deep learning, reinforcement learning, and swarm intelligence, facilitate the identification of optimal process parameters based on complex relationships within manufacturing data. For instance, in a study by Ficzere et al. (2022), a deep learning model incorporating machine vision was utilized to optimize the process parameters during the crucial phase of tablet coating in pharmaceutical manufacturing. The researchers deployed a YOLOv5 model specifically for defect recognition. The YOLO (You Only Look Once) algorithms used in the study enabled the network to process the entire image as input and predict the location and category of object-bounding boxes based on the entire image's characteristics. YOLOv5, part of the YOLO family, was initially trained on the comprehensive Common Objects in Context (COCO) dataset, which features 80 diverse classes and over 200,000 labeled images. This specific algorithm considerably enhanced both training and processing times, outperforming other object recognition algorithms. The constructed model effectively predicted the optimal settings for achieving a uniform tablet coating and proved itself to be a proficient tool for real-time defect detection and classification with remarkable accuracy. In another study, Oh et al. (2022) applied reinforcement learning to biopharmaceutical production. The researchers utilized an integrated algorithm combining the double-deep Q-network and model predictive control to optimize fermentation process parameters in a semibatch bioreactor. This reinforcement learning approach resulted in an increased yield of the target antibiotic and a reduction in production time, with successful application in an industrial-scale penicillin production process. These examples underscore the potential of AI algorithms to make substantial contributions to pharmaceutical manufacturing by intelligently optimizing process parameters. These algorithms can analyze vast datasets encompassing a variety of parameters, such as temperature, pressure, pH, and mixing speed, to find the optimal settings that maximize manufacturing efficiency and product quality. The application of AI for parameter optimization enables manufacturers to rapidly adjust and optimize process parameters in response to changes in raw materials, environmental conditions, or product specifications. This significantly reduces the need for time-consuming and costly trial-and-error methods, leading to more efficient operations, cost savings, and improved product quality.

QbD Implementation

QbD is a systematic approach to pharmaceutical development that begins with predefined objectives and emphasizes product and process understanding and control. Implementing QbD principles necessitates understanding the intricate interactions between raw materials, process parameters, and product quality attributes (Lagare et al., 2023). AI algorithms, especially machine learning models, play a pivotal role in facilitating QbD implementation. By extracting insights from large and complex datasets, these models can pinpoint key variables affecting product quality and establish the design space, a fundamental concept in QbD. The design space is a multidimensional range of input variables and process parameters that ensures the production of products with the desired quality attributes. AI models aid in defining and optimizing this space, guaranteeing that the manufacturing process operates within a controlled state, thereby delivering consistent quality.

For instance, a study conducted by Manzano et al. (2021) illustrated the use of AI models, specifically deep learning algorithms, in defining and optimizing the design space in pharmaceutical development. The researchers used a deep learning model to analyze vast and complex datasets, capturing the interaction between various input variables and process parameters in drug manufacturing. Based on the insights from the analysis, the model identified the key variables impacting product quality and established the optimal range of these variables (the design space), which ensured the production of drugs with desired quality attributes. This optimized design space allowed the manufacturing process to operate within a state of control, thus ensuring consistent product quality, a key aspect of the QbD approach.

Furthermore, AI models can also be utilized to develop robust control strategies for real-time monitoring and adjustment of process parameters, further enhancing process control and product consistency in line with QbD principles. A recent study by Puranik et al. (2022) showcased the potential of AI models for developing robust control strategies for pharmaceutical manufacturing. The researchers used reinforcement learning, a type of machine learning, to monitor process parameters in real time and adjust them as necessary. The model was trained to recognize deviations from optimal process conditions and make necessary adjustments to correct them, thereby maintaining a state of control and ensuring consistent product quality. This study further emphasized the alignment of AI models with QbD principles and their potential to enhance process control and product consistency in pharmaceutical manufacturing.

Real-Time Monitoring and Quality Assurance

The proliferation of digital technology and data in the pharmaceutical industry has paved the way for the deployment of advanced tools and methodologies that can significantly enhance operational efficiency and product quality. Among these, real-time monitoring and quality assurance have emerged as vital applications. As part of the broader landscape of AI-driven decision-making in the pharmaceutical sciences, this subsection investigates the transformative potential of real-time monitoring and quality assurance systems. Harnessing the power of AI, these systems not only streamline process monitoring but also facilitate instant decision-making and corrective actions, thereby ensuring optimal manufacturing conditions and superior product quality. Utilizing vast and complex data generated during pharmaceutical manufacturing, AI algorithms can detect subtle deviations in process parameters, accurately predict potential quality issues, and initiate prompt corrective measures. These capabilities have profound implications for maintaining the integrity of pharmaceutical production processes and achieving the stringent quality standards that characterize the pharmaceutical industry.

AI-Driven Process Monitoring

AI-driven process monitoring signifies a significant advancement in pharmaceutical manufacturing, allowing manufacturers to augment process control, enhance product quality, and boost manufacturing efficiency. This approach utilizes cutting-edge AI algorithms to analyze real-time manufacturing data, capturing intricate relationships and patterns that traditional methods might overlook. A study conducted by Obeid et al. (2021) demonstrated the application of machine learning algorithms for process monitoring in pharmaceutical manufacturing. The researchers trained a machine learning model on a large dataset of process parameters and corresponding quality metrics from a tablet manufacturing process. The trained model could predict quality outcomes based on real-time process data and effectively monitor production parameters.

AI models' ability to instantly identify deviations from optimal manufacturing conditions is another crucial aspect. Upon detecting variations, these models can either alert operators or autonomously adjust process parameters to realign the process within the optimal range. An exemplifying research study by Szlęk et al. (2022) used a deep learning model for real-time monitoring of a drug formulation process. The model could immediately detect anomalies in the process parameters, and it was integrated with the control system to autonomously adjust these parameters and bring the process back to its optimal state. This capability ensures consistency and adherence to quality standards, thus minimizing the risk of product defects and waste. Such real-world applications underscore the potential of AI to revolutionize process monitoring in pharmaceutical manufacturing.

Predictive Maintenance and Fault Detection

AI-driven predictive maintenance and fault detection hold significant importance in pharmaceutical manufacturing. Employing these techniques allows manufacturers to foresee equipment failures and perform maintenance procedures before a failure transpires, thereby minimizing downtime and averting potential product quality issues. The review article by Mourtzis et al. (2020) provides an in-depth analysis of the practical application of AI algorithms in the maintenance of industrial equipment, which accounts for 60–70% of total manufacturing production costs. In their comprehensive review, they examined various AI algorithms that had been trained on a vast collection of historical equipment data. These AI algorithms demonstrated an ability to discern patterns and trends associated with equipment failures by meticulously analyzing a multitude of parameters, such as vibration, temperature, pressure, and operational cycles. Due to this predictive capability, researchers have been able to transition from reactive to proactive maintenance strategies, marking a significant enhancement in operational efficiency.

AI models are not only capable of predicting equipment failures but also excel in real-time fault detection in process data, which may indicate issues such as equipment malfunctions, process deviations, or quality defects. Timely detection of these issues allows for quick corrective measures, thereby reducing the impact on product quality and manufacturing efficiency. Rathore et al. (2023) provide a compelling illustration of how AI models can be harnessed for fault detection in biopharmaceutical production processes. The researchers described their utilization of a deep learning model trained on real-time process data, which demonstrated a robust capacity for recognizing anomalies suggestive of potential equipment malfunctions or deviations in the process. The immediacy of this detection enabled rapid corrective measures, thereby curtailing any potential adverse effects on product quality and operational efficiency. Such investigations highlight the transformative potential of AI in elevating predictive maintenance and fault detection approaches within the realm of pharmaceutical manufacturing.

Regulatory Compliance and Data Integrity

Regulatory compliance and data integrity serve as fundamental pillars in pharmaceutical manufacturing, directly influencing the quality, safety, and efficacy of the end product. The diverse and intricate nature of worldwide regulatory guidelines calls for innovative tools to ensure sustained compliance. Concurrently, maintaining the integrity of manufacturing data is crucial for effective quality control, traceability, and compliance reporting. With the progressive digital transformation within the pharmaceutical industry, AI has emerged as a vital player in these sectors. This section delves into the growing influence of AI on boosting compliance and securing data integrity. It explores how AI-powered systems are revolutionizing regulatory compliance activities by enabling real-time monitoring, efficient interpretation, and automated reporting in alignment with regulatory standards.

AI-Enabled Compliance Systems

Regulatory compliance in the pharmaceutical industry can be challenging due to the multitude of guidelines and standards set by global regulatory bodies. AI-enabled systems are emerging as potent tools to manage this complexity and streamline compliance activities. For instance, a study by Batanova et al. (2023) used machine learning algorithms to analyze a vast amount of regulatory data to identify applicable compliance requirements for drug manufacturing. The developed system continuously monitored the manufacturing processes, alerting operators to potential deviations and suggesting corrective actions to maintain compliance.

AI-enabled systems can also expedite regulatory reporting by automatically generating reports that adhere to the specific requirements of different regulatory bodies. Thakkar et al. (2023) conducted a study that showcased the use of AI in facilitating regulatory reporting. They developed an AI system that automatically compiled and formatted data into reports that met the requirements of the Food and Drug Administration (FDA), the European Medicines Agency (EMA), and other regulatory bodies. The automation of this process reduced the risk of human error, enhanced reporting efficiency, and ensured consistent compliance. This study highlights the ability of AI to revolutionize regulatory compliance in the pharmaceutical industry, improving efficiency and accuracy.

Risk Assessment and Mitigation

Risk assessment and mitigation are essential components of the pharmaceutical manufacturing process, and the utilization of AI in these areas is growing. AI algorithms are capable of processing large datasets to identify and prioritize potential risks, be they related to product quality, process performance, equipment reliability, or compliance. In an illustrative review by Dedeloudi et al. (2023), a machine learning algorithm was employed to scrutinize both historical and real-time data derived from the manufacturing process. The algorithm successfully discerned patterns and trends indicating potential risks and ranked them based on their implications for product quality and manufacturing efficiency.

Predictive analytics can also forecast future risks, enabling proactive actions to prevent these risks from becoming a reality. A study by Kulkov (2021) demonstrated the power of predictive analytics in pharmaceutical manufacturing. They developed an AI model that predicted the risk of equipment failure based on historical performance data and real-time operational parameters. This allowed the manufacturer to take preemptive action, preventing costly downtime and potential product quality issues.

AI can also contribute to the development of effective risk mitigation strategies. Saha et al. (2022) conducted a study in which they used AI to model the complex interactions between various process parameters and outcomes. The AI model helped identify optimal risk mitigation actions, for instance, determining the best course of action to mitigate the risk of a potential equipment failure or quality defect. This aligns with the principles of QbD and good manufacturing practices (GMPs), demonstrating how AI-driven risk assessment and mitigation tools provide a systematic and transparent approach to ensuring product quality and manufacturing efficiency.

INTEGRATING TRADITIONAL DESIGN METHODS WITH AI-DRIVEN APPROACHES

This section explores a compelling convergence—the amalgamation of traditional design methodologies with AI-driven strategies in the pharmaceutical sciences. This synergistic blend is emerging as an innovative pathway, fortifying established techniques with predictive power and sophisticated algorithms of artificial intelligence. The approach is not just about what has been known and practiced for years; it is about augmenting this knowledge with the rapidly evolving capabilities of AI. This synthesis provides unparalleled opportunities for more precise, more efficient, and, ultimately, more effective solutions in pharmaceutical development and manufacturing. As this section unfolds, readers will glean insights into how this fusion of traditional and avant-garde strategies is reshaping the landscape of pharmaceutical sciences, heralding an era of AI-driven decision-making applications.

Leveraging the Expertise of Traditional Design Methods

In the pursuit of innovative solutions in the pharmaceutical sciences, it is crucial to acknowledge and harness the expertise of traditional design methods. Combining these time-tested techniques with state-of-the-art AI-driven approaches can yield more efficient and robust design solutions.

Experimental Design Principles

Traditional design methods in the pharmaceutical sciences have been refined over decades of research and practice. These methods encompass drug discovery techniques, formulation development, process design, and quality control. Each of these methods carries a wealth of empirical knowledge and expert intuition, serving as a valuable guide in the AI-driven design process. For instance, traditional drug design methods, such as structure-activity relationship (SAR) studies, have long informed the design of new drug molecules. An example of integrating these insights with AI-driven drug discovery is seen in a study by L. Wang et al. (2022), where a deep learning model was used in combination with SAR studies to design novel SARS-CoV-2 3CL protease covalent inhibitors. This approach can steer AI models toward areas of the chemical space likely to yield promising drug candidates. Similarly, in formulation design, traditional methods such as experimental design and QbD principles can be used in conjunction with AI models. The empirical rules and guidelines from these methods can guide the AI-driven design process, increasing the chances of successful formulation development. Bagde et al. (2023), for instance, demonstrated this application by using AI models along with QbD principles for optimizing a complex drug formulation composition.

Process Understanding and Knowledge Integration

Understanding the underlying processes is a critical prerequisite for successful AI implementation. Without a sound understanding of the involved processes, AI models risk becoming "black boxes," generating predictions without clear insights into the reasons behind those predictions. AI-driven methods in the pharmaceutical sciences should be developed to facilitate process understanding and integrate knowledge from traditional design methods. This integration involves translating the empirical knowledge and expert intuition from traditional methods into quantifiable variables that AI models can use. For example, in drug discovery, molecular descriptors derived from traditional medicinal chemistry can serve as input features for AI models, thus integrating expert knowledge into the AI-driven drug discovery process. A study conducted by Shi et al. (2023) utilized this approach. They incorporated traditional molecular descriptors into their deep learning model, which was used for predicting the bioactivity of anti-breast cancer drugs. Similarly, in the context of pharmaceutical manufacturing, process variables and quality attributes, as defined by traditional process understanding and QbD principles, can serve as input and output variables for AI models. A relevant application of this approach was demonstrated by Destro et al. (2022), where AI models were trained on process variables and quality attributes to optimize a pharmaceutical manufacturing process. This knowledge integration ensures that the AI model's predictions align with our understanding of the manufacturing process, thereby enhancing trust in the model's predictions.

Addressing Interpretability and Transparency

While AI brings numerous advantages to the pharmaceutical sciences, it also presents challenges, particularly in terms of interpretability and the maintenance of quality standards. Addressing the black box nature of AI algorithms and ensuring rigorous validation of AI predictions are paramount for the successful integration of AI in this field.

The Black Box Nature of AI Algorithms

In the context of AI, the term "black box" refers to systems or models that function opaquely, providing little to no understanding of their internal workings. It primarily pertains to complex machine learning models, especially deep learning models, which can make accurate predictions but are difficult to interpret. The "black box" metaphor signifies that inputs and outputs are visible, but the internal decision-making process of the model is obscured or not readily understandable. This makes it hard to interpret why the model made a specific prediction or decision. In the pharmaceutical field, for instance, a deep learning model could be developed to predict the viability of potential drug compounds using various molecular and biological features. The features of a specific compound are input, and the model outputs a prediction indicating the potential success of the compound as a therapeutic drug. While the prediction may be accurate, the model does not offer a clear explanation or line of reasoning as to why it deems this particular compound potentially successful. This so-called 'black box' nature of AI models can present considerable challenges in sensitive sectors such as pharmaceuticals.

Addressing the Black Box Nature of AI Algorithms

AI algorithms, particularly complex algorithms such as deep learning models, are often considered "black boxes" due to their lack of interpretability. That is, they can make accurate predictions but cannot easily explain the reasoning behind those predictions. This can be problematic in the pharmaceutical sciences, where understanding the rationale behind predictions is essential for trust, decision-making, and regulatory approval. To counter this issue, several strategies are in place. One such method is the application of interpretable machine learning models, such as decision trees or linear models, which offer more transparent and intelligible predictions. A study by Dandolo et al. (2023) introduces accelerated model-agnostic explanations (AcMEs), a model-agnostic interpretation technique that can provide insights into the contribution of each feature to a prediction, thereby demystifying the black box nature of complex AI models.

Another approach is the use of Shapley Additive Explanations (SHAP) for interpreting the output of machine learning models. Zou et al. (2022) provide an exhaustive study on SHAP, showing its effectiveness in providing fair and accurate interpretations. Moreover, integrating expert knowledge from traditional design methods into the AI model can enhance its interpretability. A study by Pornaroontham et al. (2023) showcases the success of this approach, where a machine learning model was trained using molecular descriptors based on medicinal chemistry principles. This allowed the model's predictions to be linked back to these principles, providing a chemically interpretable rationale for the predictions.

Validating AI Predictions Through Experimentation

Quality standards in pharmaceutical sciences require rigorous validation of any new methods or predictions, and AI is no exception (Madarász et al., 2023). AI predictions need to be validated experimentally to ensure that they are reliable and accurate (Ma et al., 2023). Experimental validation involves comparing the AI predictions with experimental data. For instance, if an AI model predicts the activity of a new drug molecule, this prediction can be validated by synthesizing the molecule and testing its activity in the laboratory (Lin et al., 2022). This process can also inform the iterative refinement of AI models. Discrepancies between AI predictions and experimental results can highlight areas where the AI model may need to be improved (Yingngam et al., 2021). This feedback loop between AI predictions and experimental validation ensures that AI models continue to learn and improve over time (Navabhatra et al., 2022). Furthermore, experimental validation is essential for the regulatory approval of AI-driven methods in the pharmaceutical sciences. Regulatory bodies such as the US FDA require robust validation of AI models to ensure that they meet the rigorous quality standards of the pharmaceutical industry (US FDA, 2019).

Ensuring Regulatory Compliance and Quality Standards

The implementation of AI in the pharmaceutical sciences must adhere to established regulatory compliance and quality standards. Leveraging traditional methods and confronting biases and ethical considerations are paramount to ensuring the appropriate use of AI.

Regulatory Compliance Through Traditional Methods

The pharmaceutical industry is heavily regulated to guarantee the safety, efficacy, and quality of drugs (Ackley et al., 2023). The application of AI should align with these regulatory frameworks to ensure compliance (U.S. FDA, 2019). Traditional methods often serve as the foundation for regulatory standards, incorporating years of established scientific understanding and practice. They are typically transparent, reproducible, and well understood, making them compliant with regulations (Fisher et al., 2022). To ensure that AI methodologies meet these standards, it is crucial to integrate and validate AI models against these traditional methods. An example is the integration of QbD principles into AI models used in drug manufacturing. By designing AI models that consider critical quality attributes and process parameters, defined traditionally through QbD, we can ensure that AI-driven methodologies are compliant with existing regulatory frameworks (Chaudhary et al., 2023). Moreover, regulatory bodies worldwide, such as the FDA and the European Medicines Agency (EMA), are working on guidelines for the use of AI in pharmaceutical sciences (EMA, 2021). Compliance with these evolving regulations is crucial for the widespread acceptance and use of AI in this industry.

Mitigating Biases and Ethical Considerations

As AI continues to demonstrate remarkable potential, it is imperative to carefully consider and address the biases and ethical implications intrinsically associated with AI models. By their nature, these models are trained on vast datasets, and as a result, they may unwittingly reflect and even intensify the biases inherent within these data. Such bias has the potential to skew predictions, raising serious questions regarding ethics and fairness (Martin et al., 2022). One effective strategy to counteract this bias is to ensure that the training data for AI models are diverse and representative. To illustrate, in the realm of drug discovery, the training data should encompass a wide range of chemical structures and biological targets, thereby precluding bias toward specific molecules or targets (Yoo et al., 2023). Furthermore, the development and deployment of AI models should be governed by ethical guidelines. This encompasses respect for the privacy and confidentiality of data, a commitment to transparency and interpretability of models, and the inclusion of human oversight in AI decision-making (Kelly et al., 2023). Detailed ethical considerations for AI application in the pharmaceutical sciences are outlined in Table 5. Integrating traditional design methodologies can further bolster these ethical safeguards. The proven principles and empirical guidelines inherent in traditional methods can serve as a robust framework for AI models, promoting their ethical and responsible use (Khan et al., 2021).

Table 5. Ethical and regulatory considerations for AI in pharmaceutical sciences

Ethical and Regulatory Considerations	Description
Data privacy	AI often relies on large amounts of data, including sensitive health data. Protecting patient privacy and ensuring data is used in a way that respects individual rights is crucial.
Transparency and interpretability	AI models, particularly deep learning models, can be opaque or 'black boxes'. Ensuring there's enough transparency and interpretability to validate the decisions made by AI is important.
Regulatory approval of AI-driven treatments	The regulatory pathway for AI-driven treatments can be unclear and ensuring that these treatments meet the same safety and efficacy standards as traditional treatments is essential.
Bias	AI models can be biased based on the data they're trained on. Ensuring that AI does not perpetuate or exacerbate health disparities is important.
Responsibility and liability	If an AI model makes a decision that leads to a negative outcome, determining who is responsible can be challenging.
Data quality	AI models are only as good as the data they are trained on, and ensuring the data is accurate, representative, and high-quality is crucial.
Security	AI models and data can be targeted by cyber-attacks. Ensuring robust security measures are in place is important.
Consent	Ensuring patients have given informed consent for their data to be used, particularly in the context of AI, is an important ethical consideration.
Job displacement	AI has the potential to automate some roles in pharmaceutical sciences, leading to job displacement. Considering the potential social impacts of this is important.

CASE STUDIES AND SUCCESS STORIES

This section presents a series of compelling case studies and success stories illustrating the practical impacts of AI-driven decision-making in the pharmaceutical sciences. These narratives underscore the transformative power of artificial intelligence in real-world applications, showcasing how AI can enhance efficiencies, improve accuracy, and propel innovation in this crucial field. Instances of successful AI implementation provide tangible evidence of abstract concepts, transitioning theoretical ideas into the vivid realm of practicality. Delving into these engaging stories offers a deeper understanding of the true potential of AI in the pharmaceutical sciences, inspiring readers with tangible results already achieved in this cutting-edge field.

As shown in Table 6, several pharmaceutical companies have already made significant strides in leveraging AI for various applications. AstraZeneca collaborated with BenevolentAI to use AI for drug discovery, focusing on identifying potential therapeutic drugs for idiopathic pulmonary fibrosis and chronic kidney disease. Pfizer teamed up with IBM Watson to accelerate drug discovery in immuno-oncology. Novartis, in collaboration with Microsoft, launched the Novartis AI Innovation Lab to apply AI across various research and business activities, including drug discovery and commercialization. Meanwhile, Sanofi partnered with Google to establish a virtual innovation lab that employs AI to understand key diseases and extract related patient insights. Exscientia, a biotech company, pioneers the use of AI in automated drug design, having already progressed AI-designed drugs into clinical trials. These

Table 6. Real-world examples of AI in pharmaceutical sciences: Companies and their AI initiatives

Company	AI Initiatives	Source
AstraZeneca	Collaborated with BenevolentAI to use AI for drug discovery and uses AI in areas like predictive modeling and digital health solutions.	https://www.astrazeneca.com/
BenevolentAI	Uses AI to improve drug discovery and development, including target identification, lead optimization, and clinical trial design.	https://www.benevolent.com/
Pfizer	Uses AI in several areas including drug discovery, clinical trials, manufacturing optimization, and real-world evidence.	https://www.pfizer.com/
IBM Watson Health	Applies AI in various areas of healthcare and pharmaceutical sciences, including drug discovery, personalized medicine, and clinical trial optimization.	https://www.ibm.com/watson-health
Novartis	Collaborated with Microsoft to create an AI innovation lab to revolutionize medicine with AI.	https://www.novartis.com/
DeepMind (Alphabet)	Developed AlphaFold, an AI tool for predicting protein structure with unprecedented accuracy, greatly benefiting drug discovery.	https://www.deepmind.com/
Exscientia	Specializes in AI-driven drug discovery, and notably advanced the first AI-designed drug into clinical trials.	https://www.exscientia.ai/
Insilico Medicine	Uses AI for drug discovery and aging research, with a focus on deep learning and reinforcement learning.	https://insilico.com/
Recursion Pharmaceuticals	Applies AI and machine learning to automate experimental biology and generate drugs for a wide range of diseases.	https://www.recursion.com/

real-world examples depict the growing intersection of AI and pharmaceutical sciences, with promising results already being reported.

AI can significantly enhance the efficiency of the drug development process, thereby reducing both the time and costs involved. This is visually depicted in Figure 7, which conveniently segments the process into several stages. For instance, during the discovery and preclinical research phases, AI has the capacity to accelerate target identification, lead discovery, and preclinical testing. It achieves this by analyzing copious amounts of data and predicting outcomes more accurately than traditional methods. Consequently, there is a reduction in the pursuit of unsuccessful leads, which results in considerable time and resource savings. Moving on to clinical trials, AI proves instrumental in designing more streamlined trials. It assists in the accurate selection of potential participants, offers predictions on outcomes, and monitors results in real time. The outcome is a decrease in the number of trials needed, the time taken, and the costs involved. In regard to regulatory approval, AI aids in forecasting regulatory outcomes based on prior decisions and assists in the preparation of regulatory submissions, thereby accelerating the approval process. Finally, in the manufacturing and supply chain phases, AI serves to optimize manufacturing processes and the supply chain, which results in cost reduction and a shorter time to market. Overall, AI's benefits for drug development are profound and wide-ranging, marking a significant evolution in pharmaceutical research and production.

Figure 7. The impact of AI on reducing drug development time and costs

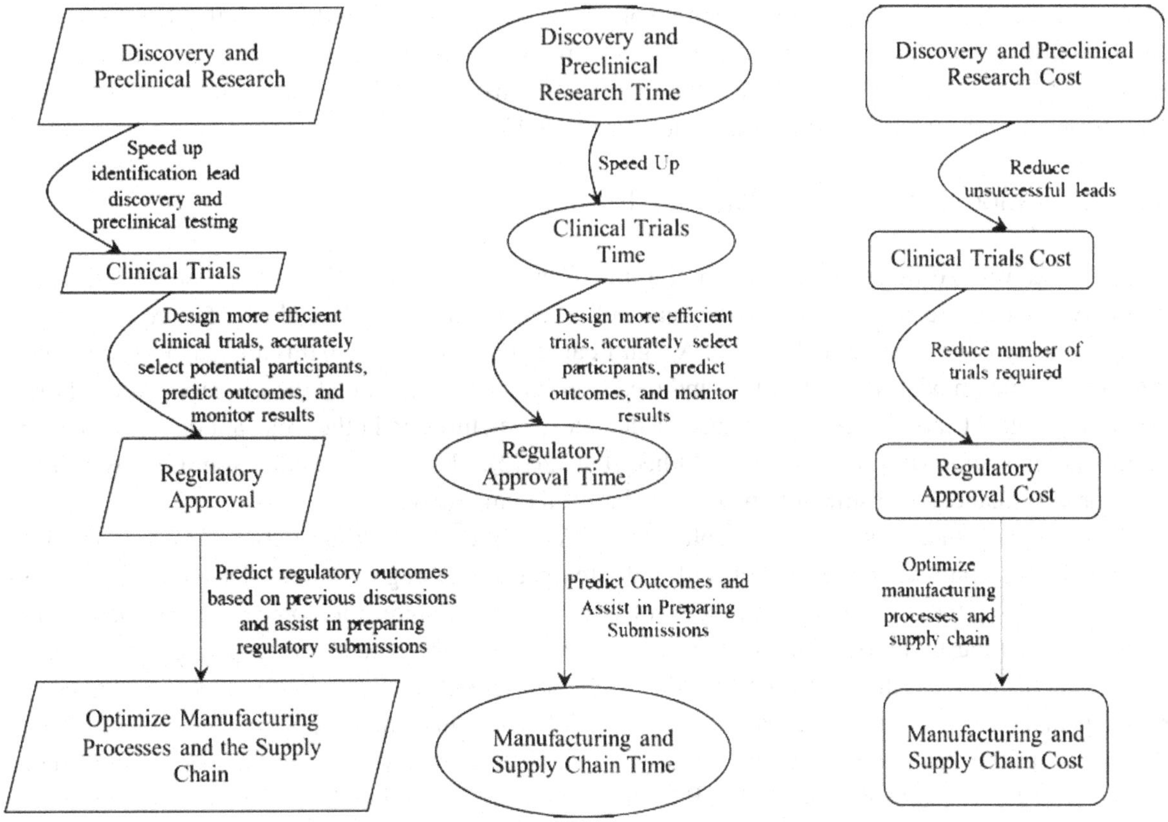

Accelerating Drug Discovery and Repurposing

AI has shown promising results in accelerating drug discovery and repurposing, transforming the landscape of pharmaceutical research. These developments revolve around virtual screening and molecular design, as well as predictive models for drug safety and toxicity.

Virtual Screening and Molecular Design

The deployment of AI in virtual screening and molecular design has remarkably expedited the drug discovery process. AI-driven virtual screening can analyze vast libraries of chemical compounds, identifying those with the potential to become effective drugs. It does this by predicting how well a compound will bind to a target, such as a protein associated with a disease (C. N. Patel et al., 2023). A striking example of the power of AI in this context is the discovery of Halicin, a novel antibiotic (Stokes et al., 2020). Machine learning models were used to screen over a hundred million chemical compounds, leading to the discovery of halicin, which demonstrated broad-spectrum antibacterial activity. Furthermore, AI can aid in designing new molecules with desired properties, an approach often termed de novo drug design (Grisoni, 2023). This process, which is traditionally laborious and time-consuming, has been made efficient with AI. A success story in this domain is the development of DSP-1181, a molecule for the treatment of obsessive-compulsive disorder (Exscientia, 2023). Created through the combined efforts of Exscientia and Sumitomo Dainippon Pharma, DSP-1181 was the first drug molecule designed entirely by AI to enter clinical trials. Another example of AI's power in molecular design is the development of RO-6889450, a potential treatment for Parkinson's disease. Atomwise and Collaborations Pharmaceuticals used AI to identify a molecule that could act on the enzyme DJ-1, implicated in the early onset of Parkinson's disease (Collaborations Pharmaceuticals, 2023).

Predictive Models for Drug Safety and Toxicity

AI has demonstrated its promise in predicting the safety and toxicity of new drug candidates. These predictive models are crucial because they can help prevent late-stage clinical trial failures due to unforeseen safety issues (Delso et al., 2021). A significant application of AI in this area involves the use of machine learning models to predict drug-induced liver injury (DILI), one of the primary causes of drug failure in clinical trials. These models analyze chemical structures and other relevant data to assess the likelihood of a compound causing DILI (Rathee et al., 2022). This early detection significantly reduces the time and financial investment in potentially harmful compounds.

An exemplary success story in the application of AI for predicting drug safety and toxicity involves BenevolentAI, a pioneer in the field of artificial intelligence for drug discovery. The company has developed a state-of-the-art AI platform capable of analyzing vast amounts of biomedical information, and it utilized this robust tool to make a significant discovery about the potential therapeutic application of an existing drug. Amid the COVID-19 pandemic, BenevolentAI applied its AI model to a plethora of biomedical databases. The model searched for potential treatments among approved and investigational drugs. One of the standout results was baricitinib, a drug initially developed for the treatment of rheumatoid arthritis (Richardson et al., 2020). Baricitinib works by inhibiting the activity of certain proteins involved in causing inflammation in the body, a mechanism that was originally proven effective in controlling the symptoms of rheumatoid arthritis. However, the AI platform from BenevolentAI identified that the anti-inflammatory properties of baricitinib could also be useful in reducing lung inflammation commonly observed in severe cases of COVID-19. Subsequent to Benevolent AI's discovery, Novartis (2023) conducted further studies on baricitinib. Intriguingly, their investigations revealed that the drug also showed potential for mitigating heart cell damage, a common and severe complication associated with COVID-19. This implies that baricitinib might not only help to manage the primary respiratory symptoms of the virus but also reduce the risk of cardiac complications in patients. This case study illustrates the power of AI in identifying new uses for existing drugs and predicting potential safety and toxicity issues. Such AI-driven predictive models could lead to significant improvements in the drug development process, saving time, money, and potentially lives.

Precision Medicine and Personalized Treatment

AI holds immense potential in the realm of precision medicine and personalized treatment. By driving advancements in genomic analysis, patient stratification and the development of predictive models for treatment response, AI has been instrumental in promoting individualized, patient-centric care. Figure 8 typically illustrates the sequential process of deploying AI to scrutinize patient data and formulate personalized treatments. The first phase, data collection, involves the accumulation of a myriad of patient-specific data. This could encompass genetic data (obtained by sequencing the patient's genome), clinical data (including medical history and current health status), and lifestyle data (encompassing elements such as diet and exercise habits). Following data collection, the subsequent step is data preprocessing. At this juncture, the accumulated data are cleansed and processed, which may involve addressing missing values, normalizing variables, and converting the data into a format suitable for the AI algorithm. The next step is data integration, which requires amalgamating diverse types of data to construct a comprehensive patient profile. Given that different types of data (such as genetic and lifestyle data) are often present in

Figure 8. The role of AI in precision medicine: From patient data to tailored therapies

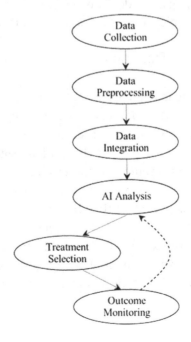

varied formats, this integration can be a complex process. Following data integration, AI algorithms can proceed with the analysis of consolidated patient data. This analysis might involve identifying patterns and relationships within the data, estimating disease risk based on genetic and lifestyle factors, and proposing potential treatment strategies. Once the AI completes its analysis, healthcare providers can move toward treatment selection. With AI analysis as a guide, a treatment strategy can be chosen that aligns with the patient's unique profile. This could involve the selection of a specific drug that the AI predicts the patient will respond favorably to or suggest lifestyle changes that could mitigate disease risk. The final step is outcome monitoring. After treatment administration, patient outcomes can be observed and fed back into the AI system. This feedback loop can enhance AI learning and improvement over time and permit further customization of the patient's treatment plan.

Genomic Analysis and Patient Stratification

The advent of AI-based genomic analysis has truly transformed the realm of precision medicine, enabling the deciphering of vast genomic data. This analysis brings forth a valuable understanding of genetic variations that play a part in disease development, which in turn helps to customize treatments based on the unique genetic profiles of individual patients. Table 7 summarizes case studies of precision medicine aided by AI. A significant success story in this area is the use of AI by Tempus, a technology company aiming to personalize cancer care. An important study in the field of AI-driven genomic analysis was conducted by DeGroat et al., who used deep learning to call genetic variants from sequencing data, aiding in the identification of genetic markers for disease (DeGroat et al., 2023). Tempus, a health technology company, successfully uses AI to personalize cancer care. They launched a series of clinical trials called TIME Trials that leveraged their vast clinical and molecular database to design more effective and personalized cancer therapies (TEMPUS, 2023). Deep Genomics, a biotechnology company, uses AI for patient stratification by identifying genetic biomarkers associated with specific disease states. A relevant case study involves their AI platform, which identified a novel therapeutic target for Wilson disease, a rare genetic disorder, leading to the development of DG12P1, a novel oligonucleotide therapy that is currently being tested in preclinical trials (Weiskirchen & Penning, 2021).

Predictive Models for Treatment Response

AI is also making strides in predicting individual patients' responses to treatments. By integrating clinical, genomic, and even lifestyle data, AI models can provide highly individualized predictions about a patient's likely response to a given treatment. For instance, In Silico Medicine (https://insilico.com/), a company focused on drug discovery, aging research, and longevity, uses AI to predict responses to anti-aging drugs. One of their major achievements is the development of an AI system called GENTRL, which designed novel molecules for fibrosis treatment in just 46 days, showcasing the capability of AI to predict drug responses (Zhavoronkov et al., 2019). In the field of mental healthcare, GeneSight developed by Myriad Genetics (https://genesight.com/) uses genetic data to guide antidepressant selection for patients with major depressive disorder (MDD). A significant study validating the GeneSight tool is the GUIDED trial (Greden et al., 2019). The trial demonstrated that patients whose treatment was guided by GeneSight experienced significantly better outcomes than those receiving standard treatment.

Table 7. Case studies of precision medicine aided by AI

Case Study	Description	Source
Tempus Labs	Tempus Labs uses AI to analyze clinical and genomic data to help doctors make more personalized treatment decisions for cancer patients.	https://www.tempus.com/
Deep Genomics	Deep Genomics uses AI to predict the impact of genetic variations on disease, enabling more personalized treatments for genetic disorders.	https://www.deepgenomics.com/
Google's DeepVariant	DeepVariant is an AI tool developed by Google that uses deep learning to generate more accurate genomic variants from sequencing data, improving the ability to diagnose and treat genetic diseases.	https://github.com/google/deepvariant
Color Genomics	Color uses AI and machine learning to interpret genetic data and provide personalized health recommendations.	https://www.color.com/
IBM Watson for Oncology	IBM Watson for Oncology uses AI to analyze a patient's medical information and provide personalized treatment recommendations based on the latest research.	https://www.ibm.com/
Microsoft's InnerEye	InnerEye is an AI tool developed by Microsoft that uses machine learning to analyze medical images and assist in planning treatment for cancer patients.	https://www.microsoft.com/en-us/research/project/medical-image-analysis/
Flatiron Health	Flatiron Health uses AI to analyze real-world data from electronic health records to improve cancer treatments and patient outcomes.	https://flatiron.com/

Pharmaceutical Manufacturing Optimization

AI is exerting a profound impact on pharmaceutical manufacturing by promising improved efficiencies and cost savings. It has found extensive applications in areas such as process control and optimization, predictive maintenance, and quality assurance.

Process Control and Optimization

AI-driven process control and optimization hold the potential to enhance manufacturing efficiency and consistency while reducing waste and downtime. AI models can analyze process variables in real time, automatically adjusting parameters to optimize production and maintain product quality. A notable example of this application is Siemens's use of AI in its Process Control System, Simatic PCS 7 (Kazemi et al., 2019). The system optimizes pharmaceutical manufacturing processes, resulting in reduced energy consumption and waste production using AI. AI algorithms analyze real-time data to manage and control manufacturing parameters, adjusting them as needed to achieve optimal efficiency. Another success story involves AstraZeneca, which leveraged AI to optimize the manufacturing process for a specific drug product (Jarrahi et al., 2023). Through machine learning algorithms, they successfully identified process parameters affecting product yield, enabling the optimization of these parameters to maximize output.

Predictive Maintenance and Quality Assurance

Predictive maintenance powered by AI can prevent equipment failures before they occur, thus reducing downtime and maintenance costs. A study conducted by Chen in 2017 highlighted how such an approach could save pharmaceutical companies up to 20% of maintenance costs. General Electric's Predix platform stands out in this regard, using AI to predict potential equipment failures in manufacturing processes, including those in the pharmaceutical industry (Chen, 2017). AI also plays an integral role in enhancing quality assurance in pharmaceutical manufacturing. An illustrative case study is Novartis's deployment of AI in their production lines. Novartis partnered with Microsoft in 2019 to develop an AI system that continuously assesses images of tablets, identifying any deviations from their standard appearance, thereby ensuring the quality of the product and eliminating potentially defective tablets before they reach the market (Microsoft, 2023).

Clinical Trial Design and Optimization

AI is emerging as a powerful tool in the conceptualization and optimization of clinical trials. As summarized in Table 8, it offers enhanced capabilities for patient selection and recruitment, refinement of trial design, and improvement of endpoints. This heralds a significant shift in the way clinical trials are conducted. Figure 9 portrays various stages of the clinical trial process, highlighting how AI can be leveraged to enhance each stage. The trial design stage involves defining the trial's objectives, determining the patients to be included (based on inclusion and exclusion criteria), and establishing the sample size and trial duration. AI proves instrumental in this stage by predicting the likely outcomes of diverse trial designs using historical data, thereby enabling researchers to select the most effective and efficient design. The next stage, patient recruitment, often poses substantial challenges during a clinical trial. Here, AI can process patient data to pinpoint individuals likely to meet the trial's criteria and respond affirmatively to recruitment initiatives. Once the trial commences, the data collection stage begins, where patient responses to the treatment are compiled. AI can expedite this process by automating the collection of specific types of data, such as those gathered from wearable devices. After data collection, the data

Table 8. Summary of AI applications in various stages of clinical trials

Stages of Clinical Trials	Applications of AI
Designing clinical trials	AI can help in identifying the right criteria for patient selection, choosing optimal sample sizes, and predicting outcomes.
Patient recruitment	AI can analyze electronic health records (EHRs), genetic data, and social media to identify potential participants more efficiently.
Data collection	AI can enhance the capture of real-time data via wearable devices and apps, improving adherence to protocols and capturing more detailed patient responses.
Data analysis	Machine learning algorithms can analyze large volumes of data to identify patterns, correlations, and predictive factors more quickly and accurately than traditional statistical methods.
Monitoring trial progress	AI can help monitor patient compliance, detect adverse events in real time, and identify any issues that might jeopardize the integrity of the trial.
Posttrial analysis	AI can support the interpretation of trial results, identify subgroups of patients who responded particularly well (or poorly) to the treatment, and predict long-term outcomes and side effects.

Figure 9. The application of AI in designing and optimizing clinical trials

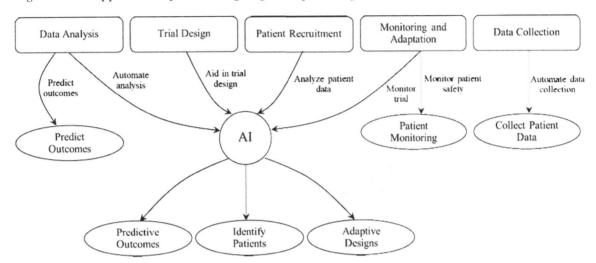

analysis stage involves examining the data gathered during the trial to ascertain the treatment's effectiveness. AI can automate portions of this analysis, recognize patterns and correlations within the data, and even forecast future outcomes based on preliminary data. Last, during the monitoring and adaptation stage, AI can oversee the ongoing trial for any potential concerns or notable results. This might entail real-time monitoring of patient safety data or the use of adaptive trial designs where the trial protocol is adjusted on the basis of early findings. The subsequent subsections delve into patient selection and recruitment and optimization of trial design and endpoints in greater detail.

Patient Selection and Recruitment

Patient selection and recruitment are critical steps in clinical trials. AI can streamline these processes, identifying potential participants rapidly, accurately, and efficiently. Figure 10 provides a visual illustration of how AI can boost patient recruitment for clinical trials, elucidated with a specific example or case study. The process begins with the establishment of recruitment criteria for the trial, which include essential patient demographics, disease stage, and prior treatments, among others. Subsequently, the data collection stage is set in motion. AI can access and analyze a wide range of data sources, such as electronic health records, genomic databases, and patient registries, to pinpoint potential participants. This process might involve leveraging natural language processing to interpret clinical notes and machine learning algorithms to predict which patients are likely to meet the trial criteria based on their data profiles. Upon data analysis, the AI system curates a list of potential patients who potentially align with the recruitment criteria for the trial, a step known as potential patient identification. Next, the process of patient contact is embarked upon. Here, the AI system assists in connecting with these potential participants. This assistance can encompass providing contact lists to human recruiters or automating the initial contact through methods such as emails or text messages. The subsequent stage involves screening and enrollment. Once potential participants have demonstrated interest, the AI further assists in the screening process, facilitating the confirmation of whether the patient indeed satisfies all the trial criteria. Candidates who pass this stage are then enrolled in the clinical trial. Finally, AI can also play a

Figure 10. Case study of AI-driven patient recruitment for clinical trials

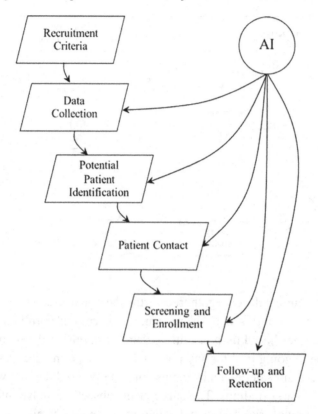

crucial role in patient follow-up and retention efforts. It does this by predicting which patients are likely to drop out and proposing personalized strategies to sustain their engagement.

For instance, Deep 6 AI, a healthcare AI firm, uses natural language processing and machine learning to scan medical records for suitable trial participants (https://deep6.ai/). A 2022 review study published in Frontiers in Public Health demonstrated the effectiveness of this approach, showing that it can significantly reduce the time needed for patient recruitment (Cascini et al., 2022). Another instance is the startup Mendel.ai, which has developed an AI-powered engine that sifts through vast amounts of clinical data to match patients with suitable clinical trials (https://www.mendel.ai/). A 2018 pilot study involving Mendel.ai and the Stanford Cancer Institute found that this system could increase patient recruitment by 30% (Businessware, 2018). This approach ensures that the right patients gain access to potentially life-saving treatments while aiding researchers in finding the participants they need for their studies.

Optimization Trial Design and Endpoints

AI has brought revolutionary changes to clinical trial design and endpoint selection. It enables the creation of adaptive trial designs that can be adjusted based on real-time data, enhancing efficiency and potentially increasing the likelihood of trial success. For example, PROCOVA+ employs AI to generate digital twins of patients participating in trials. A paper published in Alzheimer's & Dementia in 2021 demonstrated how this approach allowed trials to be conducted with fewer participants while still maintaining statistical power. Digital twins act as control factors, enabling trials to swiftly adapt to new data, potentially expediting more efficient trials (Walsh et al., 2021). Furthermore, AI proves valuable in identifying the most appropriate trial endpoints. Digital health companies such as Antidote (https://www.antidote.me/), Deep 6 AI (https://deep6.ai/), Mendel. AI (https://www.mendel.ai/), Smart Patients (https://www.smartpatients.com/), and Synergy (https://www.synergyai.co/) leverage AI to analyze unstructured data from trial protocols. This allows them to align these protocols with suitable endpoints, thereby enhancing the probability of positive outcomes. In a separate study, an AI-driven system for matching clinical trials demonstrated its ability to effectively and reliably screen cancer patients for trial eligibility. The results displayed an accuracy rate of 95.7% for exclusion criteria and 91.6% for the overall eligibility assessment in Australian lung cancer patients (Alexander et al., 2020).

Overall, as summarized in Table 9, AI brings both remarkable advantages and significant challenges to the field of pharmaceutical sciences. Positively, AI has the potential to accelerate drug discovery by analyzing vast quantities of data to identify promising drug candidates. It can promote precision medicine by using patient data to predict individual responses to drugs, and it can improve clinical trials by enhancing patient recruitment and monitoring. AI can also optimize manufacturing processes, boost efficiency, and reduce waste. However, the use of AI is not without potential pitfalls. These include data privacy and security concerns, given the large amounts of data needed for AI training and operation. There may also be issues with the interpretability of AI models, which often operate as "black boxes", obscuring the reasoning behind certain predictions or decisions. The integration of AI technologies with existing systems and workflows can prove challenging and resource intensive. Last, the fact that regulatory guidelines for AI in healthcare are still in development adds an additional layer of complexity to its application.

Table 9. Pros and cons of AI application in pharmaceutical sciences

Pros	Cons
Improved Efficiency: AI can greatly speed up the drug discovery process, reduce the time for clinical trials, and increase efficiency in manufacturing.	Data Quality: AI models are only as good as the data they are trained on. Poor quality data can lead to inaccurate predictions.
Cost Reduction: AI has the potential to significantly reduce the costs associated with drug discovery, clinical trials, and manufacturing.	Interpretability: It can be challenging to understand and interpret the predictions made by complex AI models, particularly deep learning models.
Personalized Medicine: AI can analyze large amounts of patient data to enable more personalized treatments.	Regulatory Challenges: There can be significant regulatory hurdles associated with using AI in pharmaceutical sciences, particularly in areas like patient data privacy and the approval of AI-driven treatments.
Predictive Capabilities: AI can predict outcomes such as drug efficacy, toxicity, and patient responses, which can lead to better decision-making.	Ethical Considerations: There are ethical issues associated with the use of AI, particularly in areas like patient data privacy and bias in AI models.
Data Analysis: AI can analyze large amounts of complex data more quickly and accurately than humans.	Dependence on AI: Overreliance on AI models may lead to overlooking critical human judgment and intuition.
Drug Repurposing: AI can help identify new uses for existing drugs, which can be a more efficient way to find new treatments.	Job Displacement: While AI can create new opportunities, it can also displace jobs, particularly those involving routine tasks.

CHALLENGES AND ETHICAL CONSIDERATIONS

This section explores the multifaceted challenges and ethical considerations that come with utilizing AI in the pharmaceutical sciences. These are significant and complex aspects that must not be ignored while advancing in this technologically sophisticated realm. Topics range from data security and privacy concerns to potential biases in machine learning models and from transparency requirements to the ethical implications of automated decision-making. These issues stimulate crucial debates about the responsible application of AI. In highlighting these challenges, the later sections strive to promote an insightful discussion, not only about the opportunities but also about the responsibilities linked with the implementation of AI-based decision-making in pharmaceutical sciences. This serves as a reminder of the overarching goal: to use AI for the good of humanity while upholding fairness, transparency, and individual rights.

Data Quality and Availability

Data quality and availability are paramount in harnessing the potential of AI within the pharmaceutical sciences. The validity of AI predictions and their ethical implications are heavily dependent on these aspects. This encompasses considerations of data reliability, representativeness, and the pressing matters of data privacy and security.

Data Reliability and Representativeness

The reliability and representativeness of data substantially determine the effectiveness and validity of AI models deployed in pharmaceutical settings. 'Reliability' pertains to the consistency and accuracy of data over repeated measurements, while representativeness refers to how well data samples reflect the broader population or the intended phenomenon. Unreliable or unrepresentative data can generate misleading predictions or biased outcomes, posing risks, particularly in critical areas such as drug discovery and patient treatment. Furthermore, it may magnify existing health disparities if the data predominantly represent certain demographic groups. For example, machine learning models developed to predict drug responses might be less accurate for individuals from diverse ethnicities if they are trained on a dataset predominantly comprising individuals from a particular ethnic group. This requires comprehensive and diverse data collection that encompasses various populations, conditions, and variables to ensure fairness and accuracy.

Data Privacy and Protection

The use of AI in pharmaceutical sciences often requires handling sensitive health data, raising significant concerns about data privacy and protection. It is crucial to maintain the confidentiality of patient data by adhering to ethical standards and legal regulations such as the Health Insurance Portability and Accountability Act (HIPAA) and the General Data Protection Regulation (GDPR). The risk of reidentification from deidentified data is heightened with the escalating use of AI, as shown by the case of the AI company DeepMind, which faced scrutiny over its handling of patient data from the UK National Health Service. This incident underscores the urgency of implementing robust data governance and security protocols, including encryption, anonymization techniques, and stringent access controls. Moreover, transparency about how data are used, shared, and stored is vital to maintaining public trust in AI applications within the pharmaceutical sciences.

Interpretability and Explainability of AI Models

As AI increasingly permeates the pharmaceutical sciences, the issues of interpretability and explainability of AI models become more pressing. These challenges pertain to the transparency and accountability of AI systems, as well as the fairness and potential biases inherent in these models.

Transparency and Accountability

Many AI algorithms, including those based on deep learning, are complex and not easily explainable, giving rise to the well-known "black box" problem. This lack of clarity can obstruct trust in AI models, particularly when their predictions bear significant consequences for human lives, as is the case in the pharmaceutical sciences. Simultaneously, accountability involves addressing the responsibility and liability for AI-driven outcomes. In the absence of transparency and an explicit understanding of a model's functioning, pinpointing accountability becomes convoluted. For instance, if an AI model predicts a potentially dangerous side effect of a drug, who bears responsibility if this prediction is incorrect? Enhancing transparency and reinforcing accountability can be eased by documenting the AI development process, conducting regular audits, and using interpretable machine learning models or explainability techniques such as LIME (Local Interpretable Model-agnostic Explanations) (Garreau, 2023) or SHAP (SHapley Additive exPlanations) (Shujia Zhang et al., 2023).

Bias and Fairness

While AI harbors enormous potential to transform pharmaceutical sciences, it also poses the risk of perpetuating, or even amplifying, existing biases. Biases in AI can originate from various sources, such as biased training data or inherent algorithmic bias. For example, if training data for an AI model lack representation from certain demographic groups, the model's performance may be suboptimal for these groups, potentially leading to unfair outcomes. In the pharmaceutical context, this could result in specific drugs being less effective for certain demographics simply because the AI models were not sufficiently trained to account for their characteristics. To counteract this, it is vital to ensure diversity and representativeness in training data, employ techniques to find and rectify bias in AI algorithms, and incorporate fairness considerations throughout the model development process.

Regulation and Legal Considerations

As the implications of AI continue to expand, the focus on regulation and legal liability becomes increasingly significant (Čartolovni et al., 2022). Adherence to regulatory compliance and judicious management of intellectual property rights and liabilities appear to be indispensable tasks in this rapidly transforming field.

Regulatory Compliance

AI applications within the pharmaceutical sciences are governed by an extensive array of regulations aimed at ensuring safety, efficacy, and adherence to ethical norms. These regulations encompass local, national, and international authorities and involve authorities such as the FDA in the U.S., the EMA in Europe, and others across the globe. Ensuring regulatory compliance requires rigorous control over data privacy, validation of AI algorithms' reliability and safety, and verification of their outputs. For example, a clinical decision-support system must ensure the secure handling of patient data and that the system's recommendations are in line with validated medical guidelines. In a time when the regulatory landscape for AI is under continual evolution, persistent monitoring of regulatory changes and active engagement with regulatory bodies will appear to be vital strategies for organizations and researchers alike.

Intellectual Property and Liability

As AI systems gain complexity, fresh queries appear around intellectual property (IP) rights and liabilities. For instance, if an AI system finds a novel molecule with potential pharmaceutical applications, who holds the right to this discovery? Would it be the developers of the AI system, the owners of the data used to train the system, or the AI system itself? When considering liability, if an AI-driven system incurs harm, such as erroneously predicting drug interactions, who bears the liability? Developers, users, or manufacturers of the AI system? These questions lack clear-cut answers and remain the subject of ongoing legal and ethical discussions. As legal systems worldwide wrestle with these issues, companies and researchers must stay informed about emerging legal precedents and regulations. Additionally, setting up robust IP strategies and clarifying terms and conditions can aid in mitigating potential disputes and liabilities.

Ethical Considerations and Societal Impact

The progression of AI in the pharmaceutical sciences starts with a spectrum of ethical considerations and societal impacts that demand careful and thoughtful resolution. These issues include the necessity of human oversight and accountability, along with the broader societal influence and accessibility of these novel technologies.

Data Privacy and Protection

In the age of data-driven pharmaceutical research, protecting patient and proprietary data is paramount. AI models often require vast datasets, which may sometimes contain sensitive patient information. It is essential to ensure that the data used to train these models are anonymized and protected from breaches. Regulatory standards, such as the General Data Protection Regulation (GDPR) in Europe (https://gdpr-info.eu/), offer guidelines for data handling and protection, which AI implementations in pharmaceutical sciences must adhere to.

Bias in AI Models

AI models are only as unbiased as the data they are trained on. If training datasets in the pharmaceutical sciences are unrepresentative or biased, the AI model can produce skewed or unfair outcomes. It is essential to ensure that datasets are diverse and representative of real-world populations to avoid such biases. Regular audits and evaluations of AI models against diverse datasets can help in detecting and rectifying these biases.

Human Oversight and Accountability

As AI solidifies its role in the pharmaceutical sciences, the importance of human oversight and accountability escalates. Maintaining substantial human control over AI applications is indispensable for preserving ethical integrity, building public trust, and maintaining accountability. This oversight encompasses human engagement in the creation and deployment of AI models through their ongoing management and decision-making within AI-enabled systems. Accountability is intrinsically connected to oversight. Humans must always be accountable for the results produced by AI systems within the pharmaceutical sciences. This includes clarity about AI-driven decisions, the ability to contest these decisions, and the assignment of responsibility when errors occur. It is also crucial to prevent complex AI algorithms from creating "responsibility gaps", where accountability for a specific outcome is still ambiguous.

Regulatory Guidelines

As AI technologies proliferate in the pharmaceutical sciences, they must align with established regulatory guidelines. These guidelines ensure that AI-driven innovations meet safety, efficacy, and ethical standards. For instance, AI models predicting drug toxicity or potential side effects must undergo stringent validation before being widely adopted.

Societal Impact and Accessibility

AI-driven innovations within the pharmaceutical sciences have the potential to dramatically enhance health outcomes and transform the delivery of healthcare. However, if not carefully managed, these advancements can also intensify societal disparities. It is critical to contemplate who receives help from these AI advancements and who may be adversely affected. For instance, if AI-improved pharmaceutical services are exclusively available to specific demographics or populations, they can worsen existing health inequities. Therefore, an ethically compliant deployment of AI should ensure fair accessibility and prevent discrimination based on economic status, geographical location, or other determinants. Furthermore, societal impact also includes potential job displacement due to AI automation. While AI can streamline operations and boost efficiency, it may also make certain roles obsolete. Balancing these technological advancements with their human implications will be a significant ethical consideration. In conclusion, as AI's role within the pharmaceutical sciences broadens, the requirement for thorough ethical scrutiny and consideration of its societal impact grows in tandem. Harmonizing technological potential with ethical obligations and societal benefits is the cornerstone of a sustainable and fair AI-driven future in the pharmaceutical sciences.

In the authors' prospective, the integration of AI into pharmaceutical research and development opens up a vast frontier of opportunities, but with it comes a myriad of ethical and regulatory considerations that need deeper exploration in the chapter. At the core of these considerations is the assurance of data integrity and the transparency of AI-driven processes. Ethical dilemmas arise when AI models trained on vast datasets inadvertently use biased or unrepresentative data, potentially leading to skewed results or misleading predictions. Moreover, patient data, which are a pivotal component in many AI pharmaceutical applications, have stringent privacy concerns. Addressing these concerns means delving into data anonymization techniques, the principle of informed consent, and the potential ramifications of data breaches. On the regulatory front, pharmaceuticals are already subjected to rigorous validation and approval processes. When AI-driven methods are employed, ensuring that these models are interpretable, reproducible, and adhere to established guidelines is paramount.

To ensure responsible and compliant AI-driven processes in pharmaceutical research and development, several strategies can be employed. First, continuous monitoring and auditing of AI algorithms should be institutionalized to detect and rectify biases and validate their predictions against real-world outcomes. Second, cross-disciplinary collaboration between AI experts, ethicists, and regulatory authorities can help in crafting guidelines tailored for AI in pharmaceuticals, bridging the gap between rapid technological advancements and regulatory frameworks. Furthermore, ensuring transparency in AI processes by adopting explainable AI (XAI) techniques can make AI decisions understandable to stakeholders and regulators, aiding in accountability. Last, establishing dedicated ethical committees within pharmaceutical organizations can oversee AI integrations, ensuring that they remain within ethical boundaries and adhere to both existing and emerging regulatory standards. By proactively addressing these ethical and regulatory challenges, the pharmaceutical industry can harness the power of AI while upholding its commitment to patient safety, data integrity, and societal trust.

PREDICTED TRENDS IN AI APPLICATION IN PHARMACEUTICAL SCIENCES

As we gaze into the next decade, the influence of AI in the pharmaceutical sciences is poised not only to broaden but also to evolve in complexity. Highlighted in Table 10, one of the most transformative trends is the projected mass implementation of personalized medicine, empowered by AI's extraordinary ability to parse through and analyze voluminous datasets tied to individual patients. This advancement promises the dawn of precision-based treatments and medication regimens tailored uniquely to each patient.

Furthermore, the process of drug discovery is set for a change in thinking, with AI leading the charge. The author expects rapid progress in the creation of AI-driven pharmaceuticals, leading to a surge of these personalized treatments in clinical trials and, ultimately, their market debut. AI is also predicted to drastically alter the landscape of clinical trials. With improvements in participant recruitment approaches and a more streamlined process for data gathering and analysis, AI is expected to markedly increase the speed and efficiency of these trials. By enhancing participant recruitment strategies and refining the process of data collection and analysis, AI is projected to significantly enhance the speed and efficacy of trials. Another promising area of AI deployment is in the sphere of pharmaceutical manufacturing. AI, with its ability to perfect processes and strengthen quality control, redefines the standards of manufacturing practices.

Table 10. Predicted trends in AI application in pharmaceutical sciences for the next decade

Trend	Description	Potential Impact
Increased use of AI in drug discovery	AI will be more often used in the first stages of drug discovery, including target identification, lead optimization, and preclinical testing.	This will likely speed up the drug discovery process and reduce costs.
AI-powered personalized medicine	With more data available and more powerful AI models, personalized medicine will become increasingly possible.	This could significantly improve patient outcomes and allow for more effective treatment plans.
AI in clinical trials	AI will be used to design more efficient clinical trials, predict outcomes, and monitor participant health.	This could make clinical trials faster, cheaper, and more effective.
AI in manufacturing and supply chain	The use of AI in manufacturing processes and supply chain management will likely increase.	This could reduce waste, increase efficiency, and lower costs.
AI in regulatory compliance and postmarket surveillance	AI will be increasingly used to ensure compliance with complex regulations and to check the safety of drugs after they are on the market.	This could help reduce the risk of regulatory issues and adverse events.
Integration of AI and advanced technologies	AI will be integrated with other technologies like IoT, blockchain, and 5G to enhance data collection, processing, and security.	This could lead to more data-driven and secure practices in the pharmaceutical industry.
Ethics, privacy, and regulation of AI	As AI becomes more prevalent, there will be an increased focus on ethical issues, data privacy, and the regulation of AI.	This could shape the way AI is used and could lead to new regulatory frameworks.
AI and real-world evidence	AI will play a crucial role in analyzing real-world data for drug development and pharmacovigilance.	This could enhance our understanding of drug safety and efficacy in diverse populations.

However, parallel to these promising advancements, there is a critical need to address the inherent challenges associated with AI. Paramount among these are issues related to data privacy and security, model interpretability, and the seamless integration of AI into existing workflows. Additionally, the development of comprehensive regulatory frameworks to govern AI applications in healthcare will be of key importance. Navigating these challenges successfully will be crucial in ensuring the safe and responsible deployment of AI, ultimately enabling us to reap the full benefits of this technology within the pharmaceutical sciences.

CONCLUSION AND FUTURE SCOPE

The integration of AI has had a transformative effect on many industries, notably the pharmaceutical sector. This chapter investigates the profound influence of AI-driven decision-making applications on various dimensions of the pharmaceutical sciences. From accelerating drug discovery to perfecting manufacturing processes, AI has appeared to be a potent tool, displaying its capabilities in streamlining processes, finding patterns, predicting outcomes, and boosting the overall efficiency of the pharmaceutical industry. Merging conventional design strategies with AI-powered decision-making holds considerable promise for enhancing the strength, dependability, and regulatory conformity of these advanced technologies. By using the advantages of both techniques, we can forge a more solid, dependable, and efficient route for pharmaceutical research and development. It becomes indispensable to balance the innovative capabilities of AI with the established principles and methodologies of traditional design methods to spearhead an innovative, effective, and responsible future for pharmaceutical sciences.

In the future, AI-driven decision-making applications will harbor immense transformative potential in the realm of pharmaceutical sciences. The continuous evolution of AI technologies, such as machine learning and data analytics, in tandem with advances in related fields such as genomics, is expected to engender increasingly nuanced and effective decision-making in pharmaceutical research and development. As the field expands, AI implementation is expected to become more refined, leading to more correct predictions, improved patient outcomes, and more efficient processes. One noteworthy direction for future exploration rests in personalized medicine, where AI can be employed to tailor treatments to individual patients based on their unique genetic makeup and health profiles. This level of personalization holds the potential to revolutionize patient care and outcomes. Moreover, there is an urgent necessity for more extensive research and discussion surrounding the ethical, privacy, and regulatory considerations tied to AI in the pharmaceutical industry. As AI systems amplify complexity, it is still paramount to ensure transparency, fairness, and the protection of patient data. Establishing guidelines and frameworks that encourage ethical and responsible use of AI appears to be a critical area for future investigation and policymaking. Finally, the potential of AI-driven decision-making in pharmaceutical sciences to help global health is immense. By easing more efficient drug development processes, enhancing patient outcomes, and curbing healthcare costs, AI holds the potential to bring about significant advancements in healthcare delivery. In summary, the upcoming trajectory of the pharmaceutical sciences hinges on the smart integration of AI-guided decision-making and classic design approaches. Harnessing the benefits of both methodologies will allow for an extended exploration of possibilities in pharmaceutical research and development, helping the delivery of safer and more efficient treatments to patients more swiftly and economically than ever. The journey toward fully actualizing the transformative potential of AI in the pharmaceutical sciences is still ongoing. However, with each forward stride, the pharmaceutical field moves closer to a future where AI-driven decision-making, integrated with traditional design methods, enhances the ability to discover, develop, and deliver life-saving medicines to those who need them most.

ABBREVIATIONS

AI Artificial intelligence
ANN Artificial neural network
CNNs Convolutional neural networks
EMA European Medicines Agency
FDA Food and Drug Administration
GANs Generative adversarial networks
QbD Quality by Design
QSAR Quantitative structure-activity relationship
VAEs Variational autoencoders
US FDA US Food and Drug Administration

REFERENCES

Abate, C., Decherchi, S., & Cavalli, A. (2023). Graph neural networks for conditional de novo drug design. *Wiley Interdisciplinary Reviews. Computational Molecular Science*, *13*(4), e1651. doi:10.1002/wcms.1651

Abdalla, Y., Elbadawi, M., Ji, M., Alkahtani, M., Awad, A., Orlu, M., Gaisford, S., & Basit, A. W. (2023). Machine learning using multimodal data predicts the production of selective laser sintered 3D printed drug products. *International Journal of Pharmaceutics*, *633*, 122628. doi:10.1016/j.ijpharm.2023.122628 PMID:36682506

Ackley, D., Birkebak, J., Blumel, J., Bourcier, T., de Zafra, C., Goodwin, A., Halpern, W., Herzyk, D., Kronenberg, S., Mauthe, R., Shenton, J., Shuey, D., & Wange, R. L. (2023). FDA and industry collaboration: Identifying opportunities to further reduce reliance on nonhuman primates for nonclinical safety evaluations. *Regulatory Toxicology and Pharmacology*, *138*, 105327. doi:10.1016/j.yrtph.2022.105327 PMID:36586472

Albahra, S., Gorbett, T., Robertson, S., D'Aleo, G., Kumar, S. V. S., Ockunzzi, S., Lallo, D., Hu, B., & Rashidi, H. H. (2023). Artificial intelligence and machine learning overview in pathology & laboratory medicine: A general review of data preprocessing and basic supervised concepts. *Seminars in Diagnostic Pathology*, *40*(2), 71–87. doi:10.1053/j.semdp.2023.02.002 PMID:36870825

Alexander, M., Solomon, B., Ball, D. L., Sheerin, M., Dankwa-Mullan, I., Preininger, A. M., Jackson, G. P., & Herath, D. M. (2020). Evaluation of an artificial intelligence clinical trial matching system in Australian lung cancer patients. *JAMIA Open*, *3*(2), 209–215. doi:10.1093/jamiaopen/ooaa002 PMID:32734161

Aliper, A., Kudrin, R., Polykovskiy, D., Kamya, P., Tutubalina, E., Chen, S., Ren, F., & Zhavoronkov, A. (2023). Prediction of clinical trials outcomes based on target choice and clinical trial design with multimodal artificial intelligence. *Clinical Pharmacology and Therapeutics*, *114*(5), 972–980. doi:10.1002/cpt.3008 PMID:37483175

Andrianov, A. M., Shuldau, M. A., Furs, K. V., Yushkevich, A. M., & Tuzikov, A. V. (2023). AI-driven de novo design and molecular modeling for discovery of small-molecule compounds as potential drug candidates targeting SARS-CoV-2 main protease. *International Journal of Molecular Sciences*, *24*(9), 8083. doi:10.3390/ijms24098083 PMID:37175788

Arrowsmith, J. (2011). Trial watch: Phase II failures: 2008-2010. *Nature Reviews. Drug Discovery*, *10*(5), 328–329. doi:10.1038/nrd3439 PMID:21532551

Askr, H., Elgeldawi, E., Aboul Ella, H., Elshaier, Y. A. M. M., Gomaa, M. M., & Hassanien, A. E. (2023). Deep learning in drug discovery: An integrative review and future challenges. *Artificial Intelligence Review*, *56*(7), 5975–6037. doi:10.100710462-022-10306-1 PMID:36415536

Badwan, B. A., Liaropoulos, G., Kyrodimos, E., Skaltsas, D., Tsirigos, A., & Gorgoulis, V. G. (2023). Machine learning approaches to predict drug efficacy and toxicity in oncology. *Cell Reports Methods*, *3*(2), 100413. doi:10.1016/j.crmeth.2023.100413 PMID:36936080

Bagde, A., Dev, S., Madhavi, K., Sriram, L., Spencer, S. D., Kalvala, A., Nathani, A., & Singh, M. (2023). Biphasic burst and sustained transdermal delivery in vivo using an AI-optimized 3D-printed MN patch. *International Journal of Pharmaceutics, 636*, 122647. doi:10.1016/j.ijpharm.2023.122647 PMID:36754185

Bannigan, P., Bao, Z., Hickman, R. J., Aldeghi, M., Häse, F., Aspuru-Guzik, A., & Allen, C. (2023). Machine learning models to accelerate the design of polymeric long-acting injectables. *Nature Communications, 14*(1), 35. doi:10.103841467-022-35343-w PMID:36627280

Bao, Z., Bufton, J., Hickman, R. J., Aspuru-Guzik, A., Bannigan, P., & Allen, C. (2023). Revolutionizing drug formulation development: The increasing impact of machine learning. *Advanced Drug Delivery Reviews, 202*, 115108. doi:10.1016/j.addr.2023.115108 PMID:37774977

Batanova, E., Birmpa, I., & Meisser, G. (2023). Use of Machine Learning to classify clinical research to identify applicable compliance requirements. *Informatics in Medicine Unlocked, 39*, 101255. doi:10.1016/j.imu.2023.101255

Baviskar, K., Bedse, A., Raut, S., & Darapaneni, N. (2023). Artificial intelligence and machine learning-based manufacturing and drug product marketing. In Bioinformatics Tools for Pharmaceutical Drug Product Development (pp. 197-231). Wiley. doi:10.1002/9781119865728.ch10

Borjigin, T., Zhan, X., Li, J., Meda, A., & Tran, K. K. (2023). Predicting mini-tablet dissolution performance utilizing X-ray computed tomography. *European Journal of Pharmaceutical Sciences, 181*, 106346. doi:10.1016/j.ejps.2022.106346 PMID:36494000

Bournez, C., Riool, M., de Boer, L., Cordfunke, R. A., de Best, L., van Leeuwen, R., Drijfhout, J. W., Zaat, S. A. J., & van Westen, G. J. P. (2023). CalcAMP: A new machine learning model for the accurate prediction of antimicrobial activity of peptides. *Antibiotics (Basel, Switzerland), 12*(4), 725. doi:10.3390/antibiotics12040725 PMID:37107088

Businessware. (2023, October 15). Life image and mendel.ai partner to bring the power of ai to accelerate clinical trial process for life sciences and academic medical facilities. *BuisnessWire.* https://www.businesswire.com/news/home/20181106005630/en/life-image-and-mendel.ai-partner-to-bring-the-power-of-ai-to-accelerate-clinical-trial-process-for-life-sciences-and-academic-medical-facilities

Cacciamani, G. E., Chen, A., Gill, I. S., & Hung, A. J. (2023). Artificial intelligence and urology: Ethical considerations for urologists and patients. *Nature Reviews. Urology.* doi:10.103841585-023-00796-1 PMID:37524914

Carou-Senra, P., Ong, J. J., Castro, B. M., Seoane-Viaño, I., Rodríguez-Pombo, L., Cabalar, P., Alvarez-Lorenzo, C., Basit, A. W., Pérez, G., & Goyanes, A. (2023). Predicting pharmaceutical inkjet printing outcomes using machine learning. *International Journal of Pharmaceutics: X, 5*, 100181. doi:10.1016/j.ijpx.2023.100181 PMID:37143957

Čartolovni, A., Tomičić, A., & Lazić Mosler, E. (2022). Ethical, legal, and social considerations of AI-based medical decision-support tools: A scoping review. *International Journal of Medical Informatics, 161*, 104738. doi:10.1016/j.ijmedinf.2022.104738 PMID:35299098

Cascini, F., Beccia, F., Causio, F. A., Melnyk, A., Zaino, A., & Ricciardi, W. (2022). Scoping review of the current landscape of AI-based applications in clinical trials. *Frontiers in Public Health*, *10*, 949377. doi:10.3389/fpubh.2022.949377 PMID:36033816

Chandrasekar, V., Ansari, M. Y., Singh, A. V., Uddin, S., Prabhu, K. S., Dash, S., Khodor, S. A., Terranegra, A., Avella, M., & Dakua, S. P. (2023). Investigating the use of machine learning models to understand the drugs permeability across placenta. *IEEE Access : Practical Innovations, Open Solutions*, *11*, 52726–52739. doi:10.1109/ACCESS.2023.3272987

Charles, V., Emrouznejad, A., & Gherman, T. (2023). A critical analysis of the integration of blockchain and artificial intelligence for supply chain. *Annals of Operations Research*, *327*(1), 7–47. doi:10.100710479-023-05169-w PMID:36718465

Chatterjee, A., Walters, R., Shafi, Z., Ahmed, O. S., Sebek, M., Gysi, D., Yu, R., Eliassi-Rad, T., Barabási, A.-L., & Menichetti, G. (2023). Improving the generalizability of protein–ligand binding predictions with AI-Bind. *Nature Communications*, *14*(1), 1989. doi:10.103841467-023-37572-z PMID:37031187

Chaudhary, S., Muthudoss, P., Madheswaran, T., Paudel, A., & Gaikwad, V. (2023). Artificial intelligence (AI) in drug product designing, development, and manufacturing. In A. Philip, A. Shahiwala, M. Rashid, & M. Faiyazuddin (Eds.), *A Handbook of Artificial Intelligence in Drug Delivery* (pp. 395–442). Academic Press. doi:10.1016/B978-0-323-89925-3.00015-0

Chen, S., Gao, J., Chen, J., Xie, Y., Shen, Z., Xu, L., Che, J., Wu, J., & Dong, X. (2023a). ClusterX: A novel representation learning-based deep clustering framework for accurate visual inspection in virtual screening. *Briefings in Bioinformatics*, *24*(3), bbad126. Advance online publication. doi:10.1093/bib/bbad126 PMID:37020333

Chen, W., Liu, X., Zhang, S., & Chen, S. (2023b). Artificial intelligence for drug discovery: Resources, methods, and applications. *Molecular Therapy. Nucleic Acids*, *31*, 691–702. doi:10.1016/j.omtn.2023.02.019 PMID:36923950

Chen, Y. (2017). Integrated and intelligent manufacturing: Perspectives and enablers. *Engineering (Beijing)*, *3*(5), 588–595. doi:10.1016/J.ENG.2017.04.009

Clyde, A., Liu, X., Brettin, T., Yoo, H., Partin, A., Babuji, Y., Blaiszik, B., Mohd-Yusof, J., Merzky, A., Turilli, M., Jha, S., Ramanathan, A., & Stevens, R. (2023). AI-accelerated protein–ligand docking for SARS-CoV-2 is 100-fold faster with no significant change in detection. *Scientific Reports*, *13*(1), 2105. doi:10.103841598-023-28785-9 PMID:36747041

Collaborations Pharmaceuticals. (2023, June 3). Collaborations Pharmaceuticals, Inc. Collaborations Pharmaceuticals, Inc. and Atomwise Try to Beat Parkinson's Disease Using Artificial Intelligence. *PR Newswire*. https://www.prnewswire.com/news-releases/collaborations-pharmaceuticals-inc-and-atomwise-try-to-beat-parkinsons-disease-using-artificial-intelligence-300724633.html

Cook, D., Brown, D., Alexander, R., March, R., Morgan, P., Satterthwaite, G., & Pangalos, M. N. (2014). Lessons learned from the fate of AstraZeneca's drug pipeline: A five-dimensional framework. *Nature Reviews. Drug Discovery*, *13*(6), 419–431. doi:10.1038/nrd4309 PMID:24833294

Czub, N., Szlęk, J., Pacławski, A., Klimończyk, K., Puccetti, M., & Mendyk, A. (2023). Artificial intelligence-based quantitative structure-property relationship model for predicting human intestinal absorption of compounds with serotonergic activity. *Molecular Pharmaceutics*, *20*(5), 2545–2555. doi:10.1021/acs.molpharmaceut.2c01117 PMID:37070956

Dandolo, D., Masiero, C., Carletti, M., Dalle Pezze, D., & Susto, G. A. (2023). AcME—Accelerated model-agnostic explanations: Fast whitening of the machine-learning black box. *Expert Systems with Applications*, *214*, 119115. doi:10.1016/j.eswa.2022.119115

Dedeloudi, A., Weaver, E., & Lamprou, D. A. (2023). Machine learning in additive manufacturing & Microfluidics for smarter and safer drug delivery systems. *International Journal of Pharmaceutics*, *636*, 122818. doi:10.1016/j.ijpharm.2023.122818 PMID:36907280

DeGroat, W., Venkat, V., Pierre-Louis, W., Abdelhalim, H., & Ahmed, Z. (2023). Hygieia: AI/ML pipeline integrating healthcare and genomics data to investigate genes associated with targeted disorders and predict disease. *Software Impacts*, *16*, 100493. doi:10.1016/j.simpa.2023.100493

Delso, G., Cirillo, D., Kaggie, J. D., Valencia, A., Metser, U., & Veit-Haibach, P. (2021). How to Design AI-Driven Clinical Trials in Nuclear Medicine. *Seminars in Nuclear Medicine*, *51*(2), 112–119. doi:10.1053/j.semnuclmed.2020.09.003 PMID:33509367

Deng, J., Ye, Z., Zheng, W., Chen, J., Gao, H., Wu, Z., Chan, G., Wang, Y., Cao, D., Wang, Y., Lee, S. M.-Y., & Ouyang, D. (2023). Machine learning in accelerating microsphere formulation development. *Drug Delivery and Translational Research*, *13*(4), 966–982. doi:10.100713346-022-01253-z PMID:36454434

Destro, F., Nagy, Z. K., & Barolo, M. (2022). A benchmark simulator for quality-by-design and quality-by-control studies in continuous pharmaceutical manufacturing – Intensified filtration-drying of crystallization slurries. *Computers & Chemical Engineering*, *163*, 107809. doi:10.1016/j.compchemeng.2022.107809

Di Lascio, E., Gerebtzoff, G., & Rodríguez-Pérez, R. (2023). Systematic evaluation of local and global machine learning models for the prediction of adme properties. *Molecular Pharmaceutics*, *20*(3), 1758–1767. doi:10.1021/acs.molpharmaceut.2c00962 PMID:36745394

El-Naggar, N. E.-A., Dalal, S. R., Zweil, A. M., & Eltarahony, M. (2023). Artificial intelligence-based optimization for chitosan nanoparticles biosynthesis, characterization and in-vitro assessment of its antibiofilm potentiality. *Scientific Reports*, *13*(1), 4401. doi:10.103841598-023-30911-6 PMID:36928367

EMA. (2021). *Guidelines on Good Manufacturing Practice specific to Advanced Therapy Medicinal Products*. EMA.

Exscientia. (2023, June 3). *World-first as AI-designed drug for OCD proceeds to clinical trials*. Exscientia. https://www.exscientia.ai/news-insights/world-first-as-ai-designed-drug-for-ocd-proceeds-to-clinical-trials

Fagerholm, U., Hellberg, S., Alvarsson, J., & Spjuth, O. (2023). In silico prediction of human clinical pharmacokinetics with ANDROMEDA by prosilico: Predictions for an established benchmarking dataset, a modern small drug dataset, and a comparison with laboratory methods. *Alternatives to Laboratory Animals*, *51*(1), 39–54. doi:10.1177/02611929221148447 PMID:36572567

Fallani, A., Sandonas, L. M., & Tkatchenko, A. (2023). Enabling inverse design in chemical compound space: Mapping quantum properties to structures for small organic molecules. *arXiv preprint arXiv:2309.00506*. doi:/arXiv.2309.00506 doi:10.48550

Fang, C., Wang, Y., Grater, R., Kapadnis, S., Black, C., Trapa, P., & Sciabola, S. (2023). Prospective validation of machine learning algorithms for absorption, distribution, metabolism, and excretion prediction: An industrial perspective. *Journal of Chemical Information and Modeling, 63*(11), 3263–3274. doi:10.1021/acs.jcim.3c00160 PMID:37216672

Feng, H., & Wei, G. W. (2023). Virtual screening of DrugBank database for hERG blockers using topological Laplacian-assisted AI models. *Computers in Biology and Medicine, 153*, 106491. doi:10.1016/j.compbiomed.2022.106491 PMID:36599209

Fernández-Quintero, M. L., Ljungars, A., Waibl, F., Greiff, V., Andersen, J. T., Gjølberg, T. T., Jenkins, T. P., Voldborg, B. G., Grav, L. M., Kumar, S., Georges, G., Kettenberger, H., Liedl, K. R., Tessier, P. M., McCafferty, J., & Laustsen, A. H. (2023). Assessing developability early in the discovery process for novel biologics. *mAbs, 15*(1), 2171248. doi:10.1080/19420862.2023.2171248 PMID:36823021

Ficzere, M., Mészáros, L. A., Kállai-Szabó, N., Kovács, A., Antal, I., Nagy, Z. K., & Galata, D. L. (2022). Real-time coating thickness measurement and defect recognition of film coated tablets with machine vision and deep learning. *International Journal of Pharmaceutics, 623*, 121957. doi:10.1016/j.ijpharm.2022.121957 PMID:35760260

Fisher, A. C., Liu, W., Schick, A., Ramanadham, M., Chatterjee, S., Brykman, R., Lee, S. L., Kozlowski, S., Boam, A. B., Tsinontides, S. C., & Kopcha, M. (2022). An audit of pharmaceutical continuous manufacturing regulatory submissions and outcomes in the US. *International Journal of Pharmaceutics, 622*, 121778. doi:10.1016/j.ijpharm.2022.121778 PMID:35500688

Garreau, D. (2023). Theoretical analysis of LIME. In J. Benois-Pineau, R. Bourqui, D. Petkovic, & G. Quénot (Eds.), *Explainable Deep Learning AI* (pp. 293–316). Academic Press. doi:10.1016/B978-0-32-396098-4.00020-X

Gautam, V., Gaurav, A., Masand, N., Lee, V. S., & Patil, V. M. (2023). Artificial intelligence and machine-learning approaches in structure and ligand-based discovery of drugs affecting central nervous system. *Molecular Diversity, 27*(2), 959–985. doi:10.100711030-022-10489-3 PMID:35819579

Greden, J. F., Parikh, S. V., Rothschild, A. J., Thase, M. E., Dunlop, B. W., DeBattista, C., Conway, C. R., Forester, B. P., Mondimore, F. M., Shelton, R. C., Macaluso, M., Li, J., Brown, K., Gilbert, A., Burns, L., Jablonski, M. R., & Dechairo, B. (2019). Impact of pharmacogenomics on clinical outcomes in major depressive disorder in the GUIDED trial: A large, patient- and rater-blinded, randomized, controlled study. *Journal of Psychiatric Research, 111*, 59–67. doi:10.1016/j.jpsychires.2019.01.003 PMID:30677646

Grisoni, F. (2023). Chemical language models for de novo drug design: Challenges and opportunities. *Current Opinion in Structural Biology, 79*, 102527. doi:10.1016/j.sbi.2023.102527 PMID:36738564

Hadap, A., Pandey, A., Jain, B., & Rawat, R. (2023). Theories methods and the parameters of quantitative structure–activity relationships and artificial neural network. In D. K. Verma, C. Verma, & J. Aslam (Eds.), *Computational Modeling and Simulations for Designing of Corrosion Inhibitors* (pp. 319–335)., doi:10.1016/B978-0-323-95161-6.00019-9

Han, R., Xiong, H., Ye, Z., Yang, Y., Huang, T., Jing, Q., Lu, J., Pan, H., Ren, F., & Ouyang, D. (2019). Predicting physical stability of solid dispersions by machine learning techniques. *Journal of Controlled Release, 311-312*, 16–25. doi:10.1016/j.jconrel.2019.08.030 PMID:31465824

He, S., Leanse, L. G., & Feng, Y. (2021). Artificial intelligence and machine learning assisted drug delivery for effective treatment of infectious diseases. *Advanced Drug Delivery Reviews, 178*, 113922. doi:10.1016/j.addr.2021.113922 PMID:34461198

Jariwala, N., Putta, C. L., Gatade, K., Umarji, M., Ruhina Rahman, S. N., Pawde, D. M., Sree, A., Kamble, A. S., Goswami, A., Chakraborty, P., & Shunmugaperumal, T. (2023). Intriguing of pharmaceutical product development processes with the help of artificial intelligence and deep/machine learning or artificial neural network. *Journal of Drug Delivery Science and Technology, 87*, 104751. doi:10.1016/j.jddst.2023.104751

Jarrahi, M. H., Askay, D., Eshraghi, A., & Smith, P. (2023). Artificial intelligence and knowledge management: A partnership between human and AI. *Business Horizons, 66*(1), 87–99. doi:10.1016/j.bushor.2022.03.002

Jiang, J., Lu, A., Ma, X., Ouyang, D., & Williams, R. O. III. (2023). The applications of machine learning to predict the forming of chemically stable amorphous solid dispersions prepared by hot-melt extrusion. *International Journal of Pharmaceutics: X, 5*, 100164. doi:10.1016/j.ijpx.2023.100164 PMID:36798832

Johannsen, S., Gierse, R. M., Olshanova, A., Smerznak, E., Laggner, C., Eschweiler, L., & Reiling, N. (2023). Not every hit-identification technique works on 1-deoxy-d-xylulose 5-phosphate synthase (DXPS): Making the most of a virtual screening campaign. *ChemMedChem, 202200590*(11), e202200590. doi:10.1002/cmdc.202200590 PMID:36896721

Kaku, K., Nakayama, Y., Yabuuchi, J., Naito, Y., & Kanasaki, K. (2023). Safety and effectiveness of empagliflozin in clinical practice as monotherapy or with other glucose-lowering drugs in Japanese patients with type 2 diabetes: Subgroup analysis of a 3-year postmarketing surveillance study. *Expert Opinion on Drug Safety, 22*(9), 819–832. doi:10.1080/14740338.2023.2213477 PMID:37194266

Kasture, K., & Shende, P. (2023). Amalgamation of artificial intelligence with nanoscience for biomedical applications. *Archives of Computational Methods in Engineering, 30*(8), 4667–4685. doi:10.100711831-023-09948-3

Kazemi, Z., Safavi, A. A., Pouresmaeeli, S., & Naseri, F. (2019). A practical framework for implementing multivariate monitoring techniques into distributed control system. *Control Engineering Practice, 82*, 118–129. doi:10.1016/j.conengprac.2018.10.003

Kelly, B. S., Kirwan, A., Quinn, M. S., Kelly, A. M., Mathur, P., Lawlor, A., & Killeen, R. P. (2023). The ethical matrix as a method for involving people living with disease and the wider public (PPI) in near-term artificial intelligence research. *Radiography*, 29, S103–S111. doi:10.1016/j.radi.2023.03.009 PMID:37062673

Khadela, A., Popat, S., Ajabiya, J., Valu, D., Savale, S., & Chavda, V. P. (2023). AI, ML and other bio-informatics tools for preclinical and clinical development of drug products. In Bioinformatics Tools for Pharmaceutical Drug Product Development (pp. 255-284). Wiley. doi:10.1002/9781119865728.ch12

Khan, S. R., Al Rijjal, D., Piro, A., & Wheeler, M. B. (2021). Integration of AI and traditional medicine in drug discovery. *Drug Discovery Today*, 26(4), 982–992. doi:10.1016/j.drudis.2021.01.008 PMID:33476566

Kulkov, I. (2021). The role of artificial intelligence in business transformation: A case of pharmaceutical companies. *Technology in Society*, 66, 101629. doi:10.1016/j.techsoc.2021.101629

Kyro, G. W., Brent, R. I., & Batista, V. S. (2023). HAC-Net: A hybrid attention-based convolutional neural network for highly accurate protein–ligand binding affinity prediction. *Journal of Chemical Information and Modeling*, 63(7), 1947–1960. doi:10.1021/acs.jcim.3c00251 PMID:36988912

Lagare, R. B., Huang, Y. S., Bush, C. O. J., Young, K. L., Rosario, A. C. A., Gonzalez, M., Mort, P., Nagy, Z. K., & Reklaitis, G. V. (2023). Developing a virtual flowability sensor for monitoring a pharmaceutical dry granulation line. *Journal of Pharmaceutical Sciences*, 112(5), 1427–1439. doi:10.1016/j.xphs.2023.01.009 PMID:36649791

Lee, J., Yoon, H., Lee, Y. J., Kim, T. Y., Bahn, G., Kim, Y. H., Lim, J.-M., Park, S.-W., Song, Y.-S., Kim, M.-S., & Beck, B. R. (2023). Drug–target interaction deep learning-based model identifies the flavonoid troxerutin as a candidate TRPV1 antagonist. *Applied Sciences (Basel, Switzerland)*, 13(9), 5617. doi:10.3390/app13095617

Lin, Y., Zhang, Y., Wang, D., Yang, B., & Shen, Y.-Q. (2022). Computer especially AI-assisted drug virtual screening and design in traditional Chinese medicine. *Phytomedicine*, 107, 154481. doi:10.1016/j.phymed.2022.154481 PMID:36215788

Liu, J., Jia, H., Mei, M., Wang, T., Chen, S., & Li, J. (2022). Efficient degradation of diclofenac by digestate-derived biochar catalyzed peroxymonosulfate oxidation: Performance, machine learning prediction, and mechanism. *Process Safety and Environmental Protection*, 167, 77–88. doi:10.1016/j.psep.2022.09.007

Liu, J. Y. H., & Rudd, J. A. (2023). Predicting drug adverse effects using a new gastro-intestinal pace-maker activity drug database (GIPADD). *Scientific Reports*, 13(1), 6935. doi:10.103841598-023-33655-5 PMID:37117211

Liu, X., Zhang, W., Tong, X., Zhong, F., Li, Z., Xiong, Z., Xiong, J., Wu, X., Fu, Z., Tan, X., Liu, Z., Zhang, S., Jiang, H., Li, X., & Zheng, M. (2023). MolFilterGAN: A progressively augmented generative adversarial network for triaging AI-designed molecules. *Journal of Cheminformatics*, 15(1), 42. doi:10.118613321-023-00711-1 PMID:37031191

Lu, A., Zhang, J., Jiang, J., Zhang, Y., Giri, B. R., Kulkarni, V. R., Aghda, N. H., Wang, J., & Maniruzzaman, M. (2022). Novel 3d printed modular tablets containing multiple anti-viral drugs: A case of high precision drop-on-demand drug deposition. *Pharmaceutical Research*, *39*(11), 2905–2918. doi:10.100711095-022-03378-9 PMID:36109460

Lu, M., Yin, J., Zhu, Q., Lin, G., Mou, M., Liu, F., Pan, Z., You, N., Lian, X., Li, F., Zhang, H., Zheng, L., Zhang, W., Zhang, H., Shen, Z., Gu, Z., Li, H., & Zhu, F. (2023). Artificial Intelligence in Pharmaceutical Sciences. *Engineering (Beijing)*. Advance online publication. doi:10.1016/j.eng.2023.01.014

Lv, Q., Zhou, F., Liu, X., & Zhi, L. (2023). Artificial intelligence in small molecule drug discovery from 2018 to 2023: Does it really work? *Bioorganic Chemistry*, *141*, 106894. doi:10.1016/j.bioorg.2023.106894 PMID:37776682

Ma, L., Zhang, J., Lin, L., Wang, T., Ma, C., Wang, X., Li, M., Qiao, Y., Wang, Y., Zhang, G., & Wu, Z. (2023). Data-driven engineering framework with AI algorithm of Ginkgo Folium tablets manufacturing. *Acta Pharmaceutica Sinica. B*, *13*(5), 2188–2201. doi:10.1016/j.apsb.2022.08.011 PMID:37250167

MacMath, D., Chen, M., & Khoury, P. (2023). Artificial Intelligence: Exploring the Future of Innovation in Allergy Immunology. *Current Allergy and Asthma Reports*, *23*(6), 351–362. doi:10.100711882-023-01084-z PMID:37160554

Macri, R., & Roberts, S. L. (2023). The use of artificial intelligence in clinical care: A values-based guide for shared decision making. *Current Oncology (Toronto, Ont.)*, *30*(2), 2178–2186. doi:10.3390/curroncol30020168 PMID:36826129

Madarász, L., Mészáros, L. A., Köte, Á., Farkas, A., & Nagy, Z. K. (2023). AI-based analysis of in-line process endoscope images for real-time particle size measurement in a continuous pharmaceutical milling process. *International Journal of Pharmaceutics*, *641*, 123060. doi:10.1016/j.ijpharm.2023.123060 PMID:37209791

Malviya, N., Malviya, S., & Dhere, M. (2023). Transformation of pharma curriculum as per the anticipation of pharma industries-need to empower fresh breeds with globally accepted pharma syllabus, soft skills, ai and hands-on training. *Indian Journal of Pharmaceutical Education and Research*, *57*(2), 320–328. doi:10.5530/ijper.57.2.41

Manzano, T., Fernàndez, C., Ruiz, T., & Richard, H. (2021). Artificial Intelligence Algorithm Qualification: A Quality by Design Approach to Apply Artificial Intelligence in Pharma. *PDA Journal of Pharmaceutical Science and Technology*, *75*(1), 100–118. doi:10.5731/pdajpst.2019.011338 PMID:32817323

Martin, C., DeStefano, K., Haran, H., Zink, S., Dai, J., Ahmed, D., Razzak, A., Lin, K., Kogler, A., Waller, J., Kazmi, K., & Umair, M. (2022). The ethical considerations including inclusion and biases, data protection, and proper implementation among AI in radiology and potential implications. *Intelligence-Based Medicine*, *6*, 100073. doi:10.1016/j.ibmed.2022.100073

Microsoft. (2023). *Novartis empowers scientists with AI to speed the discovery and development of breakthrough medicines*. Microsoft. https://news.microsoft.com/source/features/digital-transformation/novartis-empowers-scientists-ai-speed-discovery-development-breakthrough-medicines/

Mo, Q., Zhang, T., Wu, J., Wang, L., & Luo, J. (2023). Identification of thrombopoiesis inducer based on a hybrid deep neural network model. *Thrombosis Research, 226*, 36–50. doi:10.1016/j.thromres.2023.04.011 PMID:37119555

Monteith, S., Glenn, T., Geddes, J. R., Achtyes, E. D., Whybrow, P. C., & Bauer, M. (2023). Challenges and ethical considerations to successfully implement artificial intelligence in clinical medicine and neuroscience: A narrative review. *Pharmacopsychiatry, 56*(6), 209–213. doi:10.1055/a-2142-9325 PMID:37643732

Mourtzis, D., Angelopoulos, J., & Panopoulos, N. (2020). Intelligent predictive maintenance and remote monitoring framework for industrial equipment based on mixed reality. *Frontiers of Mechanical Engineering, 6*, 578379. doi:10.3389/fmech.2020.578379

Murali, P., & Karuppasamy, R. (2023). Imidazole and biphenyl derivatives as anticancer agents for glioma therapeutics: Computational drug repurposing strategy. *Anti-cancer Agents in Medicinal Chemistry, 23*(9), 1085–1101. doi:10.2174/1871520623666230125090815 PMID:36698225

Navabhatra, A., Brantner, A., & Yingngam, B. (2022). Artificial neural network modeling of nanostructured lipid carriers containing 5-*O*-caffeoylquinic acid-rich cratoxylum formosum leaf extract for skin application. *Advanced Pharmaceutical Bulletin, 12*(4), 801–817. doi:10.34172/apb.2022.082 PMID:36415630

Neelakandan, A. R., & Rajanikant, G. K. (2023). A deep learning and docking simulation-based virtual screening strategy enables the rapid identification of HIF-1α pathway activators from a marine natural product database. *Journal of Biomolecular Structure & Dynamics*. doi:10.1080/07391102.2023.2194997

Nguyen, H. N. B., & Patuwo, M. Y. (2023). Quantitative structure-activity relationship (QSAR) modeling of the activity of anti-colorectal cancer agents featuring quantum chemical predictors and interaction terms. *Results in Chemistry, 5*, 100888. doi:10.1016/j.rechem.2023.100888

Noaro, G., Zhu, T., Cappon, G., Facchinetti, A., & Georgiou, P. (2023). A personalized and adaptive insulin bolus calculator based on double deep q- learning to improve type 1 diabetes management. *IEEE Journal of Biomedical and Health Informatics, 27*(5), 2536–2544. doi:10.1109/JBHI.2023.3249571 PMID:37027579

Novartis. (2023, October 15). *Novartis Institutes for Biomedical Research, AI predicts heart cell damage.* Novartis. https://www.novartis.com/stories/discovery/ai-predicts-heart-cell-damage

Obeid, S., Madžarević, M., Krkobabić, M., & Ibrić, S. (2021). Predicting drug release from diazepam FDM printed tablets using deep learning approach: Influence of process parameters and tablet surface/volume ratio. *International Journal of Pharmaceutics, 601*, 120507. doi:10.1016/j.ijpharm.2021.120507 PMID:33766640

Oh, T. H., Park, H. M., Kim, J. W., & Lee, J. M. (2022). Integration of reinforcement learning and model predictive control to optimize semi-batch bioreactor. *AIChE Journal. American Institute of Chemical Engineers, 68*(6), e17658. doi:10.1002/aic.17658

Patel, C. N., Mall, R., & Bensmail, H. (2023). AI-driven drug repurposing and binding pose meta dynamics identifies novel targets for monkeypox virus. *Journal of Infection and Public Health, 16*(5), 799–807. doi:10.1016/j.jiph.2023.03.007 PMID:36966703

Patel, S., Patel, M., Kulkarni, M., & Patel, M. S. (2023). DE-INTERACT: A machine-learning-based predictive tool for the drug-excipient interaction study during product development—Validation through paracetamol and vanillin as a case study. *International Journal of Pharmaceutics, 637*, 122839. doi:10.1016/j.ijpharm.2023.122839 PMID:36931538

Patil, R. S., Kulkarni, S. B., & Gaikwad, V. L. (2023). Artificial intelligence in pharmaceutical regulatory affairs. *Drug Discovery Today, 28*(9), 103700. doi:/ doi:10.1016/j.drudis.2023.103700

Ponzoni, I., Páez Prosper, J. A., & Campillo, N. E. (2023). Explainable artificial intelligence: A taxonomy and guidelines for its application to drug discovery. *Wiley Interdisciplinary Reviews. Computational Molecular Science, 13*(6), e1681. doi:10.1002/wcms.1681

Pornaroontham, P., Kim, K., Kulprathipanja, S., & Rangsunvigit, P. (2023). Water-soluble organic former selection for methane hydrates by supervised machine learning. *Energy Reports, 9*, 2935–2946. doi:10.1016/j.egyr.2023.01.118

Puranik, A., Dandekar, P., & Jain, R. (2022). Exploring the potential of machine learning for more efficient development and production of biopharmaceuticals. *Biotechnology Progress, 38*(6), e3291. doi:10.1002/btpr.3291 PMID:35918873

Ranjan, A., Kumar, H., Kumari, D., Anand, A., & Misra, R. (2023). Molecule generation toward target protein (SARS-CoV-2) using reinforcement learning-based graph neural network via knowledge graph. *Network Modeling and Analysis in Health Informatics and Bioinformatics, 12*(1), 13. doi:10.100713721-023-00409-2 PMID:36627927

Ranson, J. M., Bucholc, M., Lyall, D., Newby, D., Winchester, L., Oxtoby, N. P., Veldsman, M., Rittman, T., Marzi, S., Skene, N., Al Khleifat, A., Foote, I. F., Orgeta, V., Kormilitzin, A., Lourida, I., & Llewellyn, D. J. (2023). Harnessing the potential of machine learning and artificial intelligence for dementia research. *Brain Informatics, 10*(1), 6. doi:10.118640708-022-00183-3 PMID:36829050

Rashid, M. M., Askari, M. R., Chen, C., Liang, Y., Shu, K., & Cinar, A. (2022). Artificial intelligence algorithms for treatment of diabetes. *Algorithms, 15*(9), 299. doi:10.3390/a15090299

Rathee, S., MacMahon, M., Liu, A., Katritsis, N. M., Youssef, G., Hwang, W., Wollman, L., & Han, N. (2022). DILI C: An AI-based classifier to search for drug-induced liver injury literature. *Frontiers in Genetics, 13*, 867946. doi:10.3389/fgene.2022.867946 PMID:35846129

Rathore, A. S., Nikita, S., Thakur, G., & Mishra, S. (2023). Artificial intelligence and machine learning applications in biopharmaceutical manufacturing. *Trends in Biotechnology, 41*(4), 497–510. doi:10.1016/j.tibtech.2022.08.007 PMID:36117026

Ren, F., Ding, X., Zheng, M., Korzinkin, M., Cai, X., Zhu, W., Mantsyzov, A., Aliper, A., Aladinskiy, V., Cao, Z., Kong, S., Long, X., Man Liu, B. H., Liu, Y., Naumov, V., Shneyderman, A., Ozerov, I. V., Wang, J., Pun, F. W., & Zhavoronkov, A. (2023). AlphaFold accelerates artificial intelligence powered drug discovery: Efficient discovery of a novel CDK20 small molecule inhibitor. *Chemical Science (Cambridge), 14*(6), 1443–1452. doi:10.1039/D2SC05709C PMID:36794205

Richardson, P., Griffin, I., Tucker, C., Smith, D., Oechsle, O., Phelan, A., & Stebbing, J. (2020). Baricitinib as potential treatment for 2019-nCoV acute respiratory disease. *Lancet*, *395*(10223), e30–e31. doi:10.1016/S0140-6736(20)30304-4 PMID:32032529

Sadri, A. (2023). Is target-based drug discovery efficient? Discovery and "off-target" mechanisms of all drugs. *Journal of Medicinal Chemistry*, *66*(18), 12651–12677. doi:10.1021/acs.jmedchem.2c01737 PMID:37672650

Sadybekov, A. V., & Katritch, V. (2023). Computational approaches streamlining drug discovery. *Nature*, *616*(7958), 673–685. doi:10.103841586-023-05905-z PMID:37100941

Saha, E., Rathore, P., Parida, R., & Rana, N. P. (2022). The interplay of emerging technologies in pharmaceutical supply chain performance: An empirical investigation for the rise of Pharma 4.0. *Technological Forecasting and Social Change*, *181*, 121768. doi:10.1016/j.techfore.2022.121768

Sarkar, C., Das, B., Rawat, V. S., Wahlang, J. B., Nongpiur, A., Tiewsoh, I., Lyngdoh, N. M., Das, D., Bidarolli, M., & Sony, H. T. (2023). Artificial intelligence and machine learning technology driven modern drug discovery and development. *International Journal of Molecular Sciences*, *24*(3), 2026. doi:10.3390/ijms24032026 PMID:36768346

Shi, L., Yan, F., & Liu, H. (2023). Screening model of candidate drugs for breast cancer based on ensemble learning algorithm and molecular descriptor. *Expert Systems with Applications*, *213*, 119185. doi:10.1016/j.eswa.2022.119185

Singh Sharma, K. (2023). Artificial intelligence assisted fabrication of 3D, 4D and 5D printed formulations or devices for drug delivery. *Current Drug Delivery*, *20*(6), 752–769. doi:10.2174/15672018206 66221207140956 PMID:36503474

Sobhia, M. E., Kumar, H., & Kumari, S. (2023). Bifunctional robots inducing targeted protein degradation. *European Journal of Medicinal Chemistry*, *255*, 115384. doi:10.1016/j.ejmech.2023.115384 PMID:37119667

Ståhl, N., Falkman, G., Karlsson, A., Mathiason, G., & Boström, J. (2019). Deep reinforcement learning for multiparameter optimization in de novo drug design. *Journal of Chemical Information and Modeling*, *59*(7), 3166–3176. doi:10.1021/acs.jcim.9b00325 PMID:31273995

Stokes, J. M., Yang, K., Swanson, K., Jin, W., Cubillos-Ruiz, A., Donghia, N. M., MacNair, C. R., French, S., Carfrae, L. A., Bloom-Ackermann, Z., Tran, V. M., Chiappino-Pepe, A., Badran, A. H., Andrews, I. W., Chory, E. J., Church, G. M., Brown, E. D., Jaakkola, T. S., Barzilay, R., & Collins, J. J. (2020). A deep learning approach to antibiotic discovery. *Cell*, *180*(4), 688–702.e613. doi:10.1016/j. cell.2020.01.021 PMID:32084340

Suhartono, D., Majiid, M. R. N., Handoyo, A. T., Wicaksono, P., & Lucky, H. (2023). Toward a more general drug target interaction prediction model using transfer learning. *Procedia Computer Science*, *216*, 370–376. doi:10.1016/j.procs.2022.12.148 PMID:36643181

Szlęk, J., Khalid, M. H., Pacławski, A., Czub, N., & Mendyk, A. (2022). Puzzle Out Machine Learning Model-Explaining Disintegration Process in ODTs. *Pharmaceutics*, *14*(4), 859. doi:10.3390/pharmaceutics14040859 PMID:35456693

TEMPUS. (2023, October 15). *Tempus Announces Real-World Data-Driven Program to Accelerate Precision Oncology Research.* TEMPUS. https://www.tempus.com/news/tempus-announces-real-world-data-driven-program-to-accelerate-precision-oncology-research/

Thakkar, S., Slikker, W. Jr, Yiannas, F., Silva, P., Blais, B., Chng, K. R., Liu, Z., Adholeya, A., Pappalardo, F., Soares, M. L. C., Beeler, P. E., Whelan, M., Roberts, R., Borlak, J., Hugas, M., Torrecilla-Salinas, C., Girard, P., Diamond, M. C., Verloo, D., & Tong, W. (2023). Artificial intelligence and real-world data for drug and food safety – A regulatory science perspective. *Regulatory Toxicology and Pharmacology, 140*, 105388. doi:10.1016/j.yrtph.2023.105388 PMID:37061083

Tran, T. T. V., Tayara, H., & Chong, K. T. (2023). Recent studies of artificial intelligence on in silico drug distribution prediction. *International Journal of Molecular Sciences, 24*(3), 1815. doi:10.3390/ijms24031815 PMID:36768139

U.S. Food and Drug Administration (U.S. FDA). (2019). *Proposed regulatory framework for modifications to artificial intelligence/machine learning (ai/ml)-based software as a medical device (SAMD) - discussion paper and request for feedback.* US FDA.

Vogt, M. (2023). Exploring chemical space — Generative models and their evaluation. *Artificial Intelligence in the Life Sciences, 3*, 100064. doi:10.1016/j.ailsci.2023.100064

Vora, L. K., Gholap, A. D., Jetha, K., Thakur, R. R. S., Solanki, H. K., & Chavda, V. P. (2023). Artificial intelligence in pharmaceutical technology and drug delivery design. *Pharmaceutics, 15*(7), 1916. doi:10.3390/pharmaceutics15071916 PMID:37514102

Walsh, D., Schuler, A. M., Hall, D., Walsh, J. R., & Fisher, C. K. (2021). Using digital twins to reduce sample sizes while maintaining power and statistical accuracy. *Alzheimer's & Dementia, 17*(S9), e054657. doi:10.1002/alz.054657

Wang, F., Sangfuang, N., McCoubrey, L. E., Yadav, V., Elbadawi, M., Orlu, M., Gaisford, S., & Basit, A. W. (2023). Advancing oral delivery of biologics: Machine learning predicts peptide stability in the gastrointestinal tract. *International Journal of Pharmaceutics, 634*, 122643. doi:10.1016/j.ijpharm.2023.122643 PMID:36709014

Wang, L., Yu, Z., Wang, S., Guo, Z., Sun, Q., & Lai, L. (2022). Discovery of novel SARS-CoV-2 3CL protease covalent inhibitors using deep learning-based screen. *European Journal of Medicinal Chemistry, 244*, 114803. doi:10.1016/j.ejmech.2022.114803 PMID:36209629

Wang, S., Yang, J., Chen, H., Chu, K., Yu, X., Wei, Y., Zhang, H., Rui, M., & Feng, C. (2022). A strategy for the effective optimization of pharmaceutical formulations based on parameter-optimized support vector machine model. *AAPS PharmSciTech, 23*(1), 66. doi:10.120812249-022-02210-2 PMID:35102463

Wang, Z., Ong, C. L. J., & Fu, Z. (2022). AI models to assist vancomycin dosage titration. *Frontiers in Pharmacology, 13*, 801928. doi:10.3389/fphar.2022.801928 PMID:35211014

Weiskirchen, R., & Penning, L. C. (2021). COMMD1, a multipotent intracellular protein involved in copper homeostasis, protein trafficking, inflammation, and cancer. *Journal of Trace Elements in Medicine and Biology, 65*, 126712. doi:10.1016/j.jtemb.2021.126712 PMID:33482423

Wong, C. H., Siah, K. W., & Lo, A. W. (2019). Corrigendum: Estimation of clinical trial success rates and related parameters. *Biostatistics (Oxford, England)*, *20*(2), 366. doi:10.1093/biostatistics/kxy072 PMID:30445524

Yacoub, A. S., Ammar, H. O., Ibrahim, M., Mansour, S. M., & El Hoffy, N. M. (2022). Artificial intelligence-assisted development of in situ forming nanoparticles for arthritis therapy via intra-articular delivery. *Drug Delivery*, *29*(1), 1423–1436. doi:10.1080/10717544.2022.2069882 PMID:35532141

Yingngam, B. (2023). New drug discovery. In Multidisciplinary Applications of Natural Science for Drug Discovery and Integrative Medicine (pp. 134-184). IGI Global. doi:10.4018/978-1-6684-9463-9.ch005

Yingngam, B., Navabhatra, A., Rungseevijitprapa, W., Prasitpuriprecha, C., & Brantner, A. (2021). Comparative study of response surface methodology and artificial neural network in the optimization of the ultrasound-assisted extraction of diarylheptanoid phytoestrogens from *Curcuma comosa* rhizomes. *Chemical Engineering and Processing*, *165*, 108461. doi:10.1016/j.cep.2021.108461

Yoo, J., Kim, T. Y., Joung, I., & Song, S. O. (2023). Industrializing AI/ML during the end-to-end drug discovery process. *Current Opinion in Structural Biology*, *79*, 102528. doi:10.1016/j.sbi.2023.102528 PMID:36736243

Zhang, S., Lei, H., Zhou, Z., Wang, G., & Qiu, B. (2023). Fatigue life analysis of high-strength bolts based on machine learning method and SHapley Additive exPlanations (SHAP) approach. *Structures*, *51*, 275–287. doi:10.1016/j.istruc.2023.03.060

Zhang, S., Zhang, X., Du, J., Wang, W., & Pi, X. (2023). Multitarget meridians classification based on the topological structure of anticancer phytochemicals using deep learning. *Journal of Ethnopharmacology*, *117244*. doi:10.1016/j.jep.2023.117244 PMID:37777031

Zhavoronkov, A., Ivanenkov, Y. A., Aliper, A., Veselov, M. S., Aladinskiy, V. A., Aladinskaya, A. V., Terentiev, V. A., Polykovskiy, D. A., Kuznetsov, M. D., Asadulaev, A., Volkov, Y., Zholus, A., Shayakhmetov, R. R., Zhebrak, A., Minaeva, L. I., Zagribelnyy, B. A., Lee, L. H., Soll, R., Madge, D., & Aspuru-Guzik, A. (2019). Deep learning enables rapid identification of potent DDR1 kinase inhibitors. *Nature Biotechnology*, *37*(9), 1038–1040. doi:10.103841587-019-0224-x PMID:31477924

Zou, Y., Shi, Y., Sun, F., Liu, J., Guo, Y., Zhang, H., Lu, X., Gong, Y., & Xia, S. (2022). Extreme gradient boosting model to assess risk of central cervical lymph node metastasis in patients with papillary thyroid carcinoma: Individual prediction using SHapley Additive exPlanations. *Computer Methods and Programs in Biomedicine*, *225*, 107038. doi:10.1016/j.cmpb.2022.107038 PMID:35930861

Chapter 2
Intelligent Support for Cardiovascular Diagnosis:
The AI-CDSS Approach

Poomari Durga K.
SRMIST, India

ABSTRACT

The AI-CDSS is a powerful tool designed to assist healthcare professionals in making informed and evidence-based decisions in patient care. It leverages artificial intelligence algorithms and data analysis techniques to provide personalized recommendations and insights. This system explores the features and benefits of the AI-CDSS, including patient data analysis, diagnostics and treatment recommendations, drug interaction and adverse event detection, predictive analytics, real-time monitoring and alerts, and continuous learning and improvement. The model also discusses the applications of AI-driven decision-making systems in healthcare, focusing on areas such as cancer diagnosis and treatment, chronic disease management, medication optimization, surgical decision support, infectious disease outbreak management, radiology and medical imaging analysis, mental health support, and clinical trials and research. Additionally, the chapter highlights existing methodologies, such as deep learning models like CNNs and RNNs, that have shown potential in cardiovascular disease prediction.

INTRODUCTION

The AI-CDSS is considered to assist healthcare professionals in making well-informed and evidence-based decisions in patient attention. It utilizes artificial intelligence algorithms and data analysis techniques to provide personalized recommendations and insights.

DOI: 10.4018/979-8-3693-0639-0.ch002

Features

1. Patient Data Analysis: The AI-CDSS can process and analyses large amounts of patient information, including medical records, lab results, imaging reports, and hereditary information. It can extract relevant information, identify patterns, and detect potential risks or abnormalities.

2. Diagnostics and Treatment Recommendations: Based on the analysis of patient data, the AI-CDSS can generate diagnostic suggestions and treatment recommendations. It can compare the patient's data with a vast database of medical knowledge, clinical guidelines, and research papers to provide the most relevant and up-to-date information.

3. Drug Interaction and Adverse Event Detection: The AI-CDSS can help identify potential drug interactions and adverse events by analysing the patient's medication history and known side effects. It can alert healthcare professionals to potential risks and suggest alternative medications or dosage adjustments.

4. Predictive Analytics: By leveraging machine learning and predictive modelling techniques, the AI-CDSS can forecast disease progression, estimate treatment outcomes, and classify patients at risk of emerging certain conditions. This can aid in early intervention and defensive care strategies.

5. Real-time Monitoring and Alerts: The AI-CDSS can integrate with monitoring devices and electronic health records to provide real-time alerts and notifications. It can detect critical changes in vital signs, lab values, or other health indicators, ensuring timely intervention and reducing the risk of adverse events.

6. Continuous Learning and Improvement: The AI-CDSS can continuously learn from new data, patient outcomes, and feedback from healthcare professionals. It can adapt and update its algorithms to improve accuracy and relevance over time.

Benefits

1. Enhanced Decision-Making: The AI-CDSS provides healthcare professionals with valuable insights, recommendations, and access to a wealth of medical knowledge. It helps improve diagnostic accuracy, treatment selection, and patient outcomes.

2. Time and Cost Efficiency: By automating data analysis and providing instant recommendations, the AI-CDSS saves time for healthcare professionals. It streamlines workflows, reduces errors, and optimizes resource allocation.

3. Improved Patient Safety: The AI-CDSS helps identify potential risks, drug interactions, and adverse events, enhancing patient safety and reducing medical errors.

4. Personalized Care: The AI-CDSS takes into account individual patient data and characteristics, providing personalized recommendations tailored to each patient's specific needs.

5. Research and Population Health Insights: Aggregated and anonymized data from the AI-CDSS can contribute to research efforts, population health management, and the identification of disease trends and patterns.

Applications for an AI-Driven Decision-Making System in Healthcare

1. Cancer Diagnosis and Treatment: The AI-CDSS can assist oncologists in diagnosing and treating cancer patients. By analysing medical imaging data, genetic profiles, and patient records, it can provide insights on tumour detection, subtype classification, treatment options, and personalized therapy recommendations.
2. Chronic Disease Management: The AI-CDSS can aid in the management of chronic conditions such as diabetes, CVD, and respiratory disorders. It can monitor patients' vital signs, lab results, and lifestyle data to provide real-time feedback, medication adjustments, and lifestyle recommendations to optimize disease control.
3. Medication Optimization and Adverse Event Prevention: The AI-CDSS can analyse a patient's medication history, genetic profile, and health data to optimize medication regimens, identify potential drug interactions, and minimize the risk of adverse drug events. It can alert healthcare professionals to potential risks and suggest alternative medications or dosages.
4. Surgical Decision Support: Surgeons can benefit from AI-CDSS in surgical planning and decision-making. By integrating preoperative imaging, patient characteristics, and surgical outcomes data, the system can provide guidance on optimal surgical approaches, potential complications, and postoperative care, aiding in improving surgical precision and patient outcomes.
5. Infectious Disease Outbreak Management: During infectious disease outbreaks, the AI-CDSS can analyse epidemiological data, patient symptoms, and demographic information to predict disease spread, identify high-risk populations, and guide public health interventions. It can assist in contact tracing, resource allocation, and vaccination strategies.
6. Radiology and Medical Imaging Analysis: The AI-CDSS can analyses medical images such as CT scans, and MRIs to assist radiologists in detecting abnormalities, identifying specific conditions, and providing quantitative assessments. It can help improve diagnostic accuracy and reduce the time required for image interpretation.
7. Mental Health Support: The AI-CDSS can support mental health professionals in diagnosing and treating mental health conditions. By analysing patient-reported symptoms, behavioural patterns, and treatment response data, it can provide recommendations for personalized treatment plans, therapy options, and mental health support resources.
8. Clinical Trials and Research: The AI-CDSS can contribute to clinical trials by analysing patient data, identifying suitable candidates, and predicting treatment response. It can assist researchers in identifying new patterns, risk factors, and potential therapeutic targets by analysing large-scale patient datasets, accelerating medical research and drug discovery.

Chronic disease management is an essential aspect of healthcare that focuses on providing effective care and support to people with long-term conditions. Chronic diseases, also known as non-communicable diseases, have a lasting impact on an individual's health and well-being, requiring ongoing management and attention. Conditions such as diabetes, cardiovascular diseases, respiratory disorders, and certain cancers fall under the umbrella of chronic diseases. The management of these conditions involves a multidimensional approach that encompasses medical interventions, lifestyle modifications, patient education, and continuous healthcare provider support.

Effectively managing chronic diseases entails more than just addressing symptoms; it requires comprehensive strategies to minimize complications and optimize the overall quality of life for patients. Recent advancements in healthcare technologies, including the integration of AI-driven decision-making systems, have greatly improved the precision, personalization, and efficiency of chronic disease management.

Central to chronic disease management is accurate diagnosis and regular monitoring to assess the progression of the condition and evaluate the effectiveness of treatment. Diagnostic tools, such as medical tests and imaging, play a vital role in gathering relevant data to inform healthcare decisions. Medication optimization is another crucial aspect, ensuring that patients receive the right medications, dosages, and combinations to control symptoms, prevent complications, and minimize adverse effects.

In addition to medical interventions, lifestyle modifications form a fundamental component of chronic disease management. These modifications may include dietary adjustments, regular physical activity, smoking cessation, stress management, and weight control. By adopting healthier behaviours, individuals can improve their overall health, manage symptoms, and reduce the risk of complications associated with chronic diseases.

Patient education and empowerment are integral to successful chronic disease management. By providing individuals with information about their condition, treatment options, and self-care techniques, they are empowered to actively participate in managing their health. This includes educating patients on medication adherence, recognizing warning signs, self-monitoring techniques, and accessing appropriate support networks.

The integration of AI-driven decision-making systems has revolutionized the field of chronic disease management. These systems can analyse vast amounts of patient data, including medical records, and hereditary information, to provide personalized recommendations, predictive analytics, and real-time monitoring. By leveraging AI technologies, healthcare professionals can make evidence-based decisions, detect potential risks, optimize treatment plans, and improve patient outcomes.

RELATED WORKS

S. I. Joy et al (2003) explores the transformative role of AI, ML and deep learning-based CNN, in revolutionizing cardiology through improved diagnostics and analysis of electrocardiogram (ECG) data. With the ever-increasing volume of ECG big data, the need for automatic analysis and interpretation has become crucial for enhanced diagnosis and personalized patient care. The article highlights the significance of curated clinical ECG datasets, both private and publicly accessible, in facilitating the detection and management of cardiac and extra-cardiac diseases. By leveraging AI techniques, the integration of human intelligence with ML algorithms offers a promising avenue for more accurate cardiac anomaly detection, moving modern medicine towards advanced cardiology practices. The review emphasizes the importance of addressing gaps and challenges in implementing AI-driven ECG analysis while exploring the vast clinical and research possibilities for transforming cardiology.

K. Karboub et al. (2021) conducted a study on various AI approaches to enhance the accurateness of cardiovascular disease diagnosis. Trained on MIT-BIH arrhythmia dataset, normal sinus rhythm, and BIDMC congestive heart failure dataset, these models are tested on a dataset comprising over 72,000 samples from patients with similar pathologies.

W. Jiang et al. (2022) examines the effects of COVID-19 on cardiovascular, respiratory, and mental health, while exploring various patient monitoring systems. The research identifies limitations in existing systems and proposes a wearable telehealth solution capable of monitoring crucial physiological parameters such asp, body temperature, heart rate, blood oxygen saturation, respiratory rate, and cough. By leveraging AI and sensor techniques, this system has the potential to estimate lung function.

J. Morales et al. seven state-of-the-art methods for quantifying RSA using a simulation model and real-life application data. The methods evaluated include cross entropy, time-frequency coherence, and subspace projections, which perform well in capturing changes in cardiorespiratory coupling during sleep. The study provides an objective comparison of RSA quantification methods to guide future analyses. Additionally, the researchers introduce a freely accessible online simulation model that can be used to compare existing and newly proposed RSA estimation approaches. This research contributes to the understanding and application of RSA as a biomarker in various conditions and diseases.

M. Opoku Agyeman et al., (2022) reviews recent contributions in heart beat acquisition, arrhythmia diagnosis, IoT, and visualization. By analysing the relevant literature on CNN and IoT devices in heart disease diagnostics, the review identifies research gaps and provides suggestions for future research directions.

Y. Jiang et al. (2022) reviews recent contributions in heart beat acquisition, arrhythmia detection, visualization and IOT. By analysing the relevant literature on CNN and IoT devices in heart disease diagnostics, the review identifies research gaps and provides suggestions for future research directions.

Y. Li et al. (2023) proposes a novel deep-learning approach for noncontact and continuous BP measurement using camera-based image sequences of the forehead. The proposed model, called Hybrid D1DCnet, combines deep 1-D convolutions, attention-based LSTM units, and multilayer perceptron (MLP) to predict systolic BP (SBP) and diastolic BP (DBP) from forehead imaging photoplethysmography (iPPG) waveforms.

G. M., V. Ravi et al., (2023) presents a deep learning-based method for multilabel ECG signal classification, accurately identifying up to two labels representing eight heart abnormalities and the normal condition. To address the black-box nature of deep learning models, an XAI framework is established using class activation maps obtained from the Grad-CAM technique. The proposed methodology trains a CNN and achieves high performance in multilabel classification.

S. K. Zhou et al. (2021) outline the characteristics of medical imaging, identify clinical needs and explore how developing trends in DL are addressing these issues. We delve into topics such as network architecture, handling sparse and noisy labels, federated learning, interpretability, quantification. Additionally, we provide case studies on digital pathology and imaging of the chest, brain, cardiovascular system, and abdomen to highlight notable research advancements in these areas. While not an exhaustive literature survey, we emphasize significant breakthroughs and conclude by discussing promising future directions in medical imaging research.

E. Brophy et al. (2022) aims to explore the use of electrocardiogram (ECG) as a standard for recording the cardiac status and monitoring key metrics such as heart rate inconsistency. Due to the impracticality of long-term ECG monitoring, remote data collection by patients has become crucial. However, ECG signals often get contaminated with noise during collection of data. This survey introduces a novel approach using a custom loss function in a CNN to denoise motion artifact in ECG data, surpassing the performance of more common loss functions. The proposed model significantly improves the signal-to-noise ratio of ECG signals and preserves the structure of R waves, resulting in previously unobtainable high-quality ECG

W. Ai et al. (2020) addresses the challenges posed by the complex and heterogeneous dynamics of patients during device development and validation. Our proposed framework involves the integration of a high-level physiologically computational based heart model into an automated system for closed-loop validation of CIEDs. This framework encompasses test generation, execution, and evaluation, utilizing an integrated optimization algorithm to explore physiological conditions. The results indicate that the heart model framework achieves high system test coverage while providing clinically relevant responses.

R. F. Mansour et al. (2021) have developed an automated framework that utilizes a high-level based computational heart model to validate CIEDs in a closed-loop fashion. This framework encompasses test generation, execution, and valuation, with the aid of an integrated stochastic optimization algorithm that explores various physical conditions. The obtained results demonstrate that employing a heart model framework enables high system coverage while generating clinically relevant responses.

C. Chakraborty et al. (2022) utilized machine learning (ML) classification algorithms to predict heart disease by leveraging IoMT-based cloud-fog diagnostics. The fog layer, integrated into the system, enables swift analysis of patient data using ML classification techniques. The performance of the proposed healthcare model is evaluated through different mockups, aiming to achieve improved accuracy and overall performance compared to previous models.

B. Zhang et al. (2019) introduces a specialized framework tailored for monitoring and managing the care of elderly adults receiving home care. The framework adopts a comprising IoT-Intelligent Terminal (IT)-Cloud, which facilitates acquisition, signal transmission, remote interaction, and diagnosis. In order to assess the risk of heart disease, the study implements five diagnosis methods: DT,RF, SVM, KNN, and BPNN. The experimental results demonstrate an accuracy rate exceeding 95%, validating the efficacy of the primary diagnosis and the efficiency of data flow and remote interaction within the system.

O. Cheikhrouhou et al. (2021) presents a Fog-enabled ECG analysis approach leveraging wearable IoT devices for cardiovascular disease detection. The proposed modular 1D-CNN approach allows for real-time analysis and prompt initiation of emergency countermeasures. By deploying the inference module over the Fog infrastructure, lower latency and enhanced quality of service can be achieved. The experimental results, including an F1-measure score of approximately 1 on the MIT-BIH Arrhythmia database and a 25% improvement in response time, validate the effectiveness of the proposed approach. This research contributes to the advancement of Fog computing and its application in remote patient monitoring systems, addressing the limitations for ECG analysis.

J. Chen et al. (2019) presents a novel predictive framework for ECG signal processing in remote heart monitoring systems. The framework addresses the limitations of current technologies by enabling predictive analysis and capturing inter-patient variability. The proposed methodology achieves high accuracy in detecting heart abnormalities and generates precautionary warnings for preventive actions. While the primary focus is on providing quality healthcare for elderly and heart patients, the developed approach is also applicable to other biomedical signals. This research contributes to the advancement of remote heart monitoring and holds potential for improving healthcare outcomes in various settings.

G. Wang et al. (2019) developed stretchable optical sensing patch system offers a versatile solution for real-time monitoring of key physiological parameters, including HR, SpO2, and sweat pH. The system's ability to simultaneously measure these parameters using a single optical sensor on a flexible substrate demonstrates its potential for applications in fitness guidance, skin disease detection, and wound management. The sensor patch system provides a noninvasive and convenient solution for continuous monitoring, enhancing the quality of healthcare and promoting personal well-being.

S. -Y. Lee et al. (2019) presents a monitoring system for heart sound auscultation using a combination of phonocardiogram and electrocardiogram. The integration of chip implementation and a smartphone application enables efficient signal processing and facilitates the visualization and identification of heart-related physiological signals. The proposed wavelet-based QRS complex detection algorithm achieves high accuracy, enhancing the performance of the system. By combining signal visualization with traditional auscultation, the monitoring system eliminates uncertainty in heart sounds and reduces the training period required to acquire auscultation skills. This research contributes to improving the diagnostic accuracy and efficiency of heart sound auscultation.

G. Yang et al. (2019) presented here showcases the applications of wearable sensors in disease care and explores the requirements for flexibility and stretchability. The investigation of nano-based enhancements and progress in different types of sensors highlight the continuous advancements in the field. However, research challenges still need to be addressed, and future directions must be pursued to further enhance the capabilities of flexible and stretchable sensors in chronic disease care.

D. Biswas et al. (2019) deliver a thorough and in-depth review of recent research concerning heart rate estimation from PPG signals. The review not only covers the theoretical aspects of PPG sensing but also explores other potential applications, such as biometric identification and disease diagnosis utilizing PPG. The primary objective of this article is to establish a solid foundation for forthcoming research in the domain of pervasive monitoring through wrist PPG.

C. Liu et al (2019) introduces an innovative IoT-based wearable 12-lead ECG system designed to facilitate early detection of CVD. The system is built upon four key components: 1) a sensing layer featuring textile dry ECG electrodes, 2) a network layer integrating technologies such as Bluetooth and WiFi, 3) a cloud-based platform for data storage and computation, and 4) an application layer dedicated to analysis of signal and decision-making. The primary objective of their research is to tackle real-time signal quality assessment (SQA) and lightweight QRS detection challenges for wearable ECG applications. The proposed approach combines multiple signal quality indices and ML techniques to classify 10-second single-channel ECG segments as either satisfactory or unacceptable. Additionally, the study develops a lightweight QRS detector to precisely locate QRS complexes in the ECG signal.

S. Shah et al. (2019) present a physical-computation-electronics system that combines mixed-signal components to enable real-time monitoring of three vital signs: heart rate and blood oxygen saturation. This system employs signals from electrocardiography (ECG), arterial blood pressure, and photoplethysmography. To achieve its functionality, the design utilizes the field-programmable analog array (FPAA), a reconfigurable and programmable signal-processing platform. The FPAA's core technology, floating-gate CMOS devices, plays a key role in the implementation. Additionally, the system incorporates an on-chip low-power microcontroller, ensuring efficiency without compromising accuracy.

B. S. Chandra et al. (2019) enhanced the robustness and accuracy of detection, especially in critical-care scenarios, there has been a recent suggestion to incorporate additional signals such as BP. Consequently, estimating the location of heartbeats requires the fusion of information from multiple signals. However, existing approaches often indirectly obtain multimodal estimates by combining separate signal-specific intermediate estimates through voting mechanisms. In contrast, we propose a direct fusion approach that combines information from multiple signals without relying on intermediate estimates, enabling robust estimation of heartbeat location.

Our proposed method employs a CNN as a heartbeat detector, which learns fused features from multiple physiological signals. This approach eliminates the need for manually selecting signal-specific features and ad hoc fusion schemes. Additionally, being data-driven, the algorithm can learn suitable features from any arbitrary set of signals.

O. S. Albahri et al. (2019) explores the potential of IoT in healthcare services and presents a fault-tolerant framework, FTF-mHealth-IoT, to address telemedicine architecture failures. It introduces the risk local triage algorithm (RLLT) for emergency case detection and healthcare service identification.

The study uses two datasets, evaluating triage levels in patients and assessing healthcare service availability in distributed hospitals. The analytic hierarchy process (AHP) effectively solves hospital selection challenges within mHealth. The paper's implications support modern healthcare practices and highlight the benefits of IoT technology in improving patient monitoring and resource management.

L. Sun et al. (2022) proposes BeatClass, a sustainable deep learning-based system for heart beat classification in IoT-based eHealth. It utilizes stacked Bi-LSTMs and a GAN to address challenges in classifying interpatient electrocardiograms, especially the difficult classification of Supraventricular ectopic beats (S). BeatClass achieves higher F1-scores compared to state-of-the-art methods for classifying N, S, and V heartbeats. The step-by-step approach of using multiple classification models enhances overall classification performance. The paper highlights the adaptability of BeatClass to different physical signal datasets and varying sampling rates, supporting sustainable IoT-based eHealth applications.

These studies collectively contribute to the advancement of AI in cardiovascular health, ECG analysis, device testing, and wearable technologies, offering promising directions for future research in these areas.

METHODOLOGY

Existing Methodology

The utilization of artificial intelligence (AI) techniques in cardiovascular disease (CVD) prediction has witnessed significant advancements. AI has the potential to enhance risk assessment models by leveraging large-scale data and advanced algorithms, through the use of deep learning models such as CNNs and RNNs

Deep learning models, including CNNs and RNNs, have demonstrated promise in analysing complex medical data for accurate CVD prediction. These models are trained using extensive datasets that encompass patient records, medical imaging data, laboratory results, genetic information, and lifestyle factors.

CNNs are specifically adept at image analysis, enabling them to analyse medical images like cardiac MRI or CT scans. They can detect anatomical abnormalities, identify plaque buildup, and evaluate cardiac function, all of which contribute to CVD risk assessment. Additionally, CNNs can extract pertinent features from medical images K. Karboub and provide quantitative assessments, aiding in risk prediction.

RNNs, on the other hand, excel in analysing sequential data such as longitudinal patient records or time-series physiological measurements. By capturing temporal dependencies, RNNs can identify patterns and trends relevant to CVD risk. For instance, they can examine blood pressure readings, cholesterol levels, or electrocardiogram (ECG) data over time to predict the probability of future cardiovascular events.

To develop AI models, large-scale datasets are employed for training and validation. These datasets comprise electronic health records, population-wide health surveys, genetic databases, and longitudinal studies. The models are trained using supervised learning techniques, mapping input features to CVD outcomes based on known cases within the dataset. Subsequently, the models are evaluated and fine-tuned using various performance metrics to optimize their predictive accuracy.

The integration of AI models in CVD prediction has the potential to enhance risk stratification, early detection, and personalized treatment strategies. By harnessing AI's capabilities, these models can process extensive patient data, identify intricate patterns, and provide risk estimates with improved accuracy and efficiency. Furthermore, AI models can incorporate a broad range of risk factors beyond traditional ones, including genetic markers, environmental factors, and social determinants of health.

However, it is essential to acknowledge that the deployment of AI models in clinical practice necessitates rigorous validation, thorough evaluation, and consideration of ethical and regulatory aspects. Models need to be tested on diverse populations, external datasets, and real-world clinical settings to ensure their generalizability and reliability.

Proposed Methodology

An AI clinical decision support system (CDSS) for cardiovascular disease (CVD) can be developed using the following methodology:

Collect data from a variety of sources, such as electronic health records (EHRs), clinical trials, and population studies. The data should include features that are relevant to CVD, such as age, sex, blood pressure, cholesterol levels, and smoking status.

Clean and preprocess the data to remove errors and inconsistencies, and to normalize the data so that all the features are on the same scale.

Choose an AI algorithm to train on the data. Some popular algorithms include logistic regression, decision trees, random forests, and SVM.

Train the AI algorithm on the data. This involves feeding the algorithm the data and letting it learn the patterns in the data.

Evaluate the AI algorithm on a test set to get an idea of how well it will perform on new data.

Deploy the AI algorithm in a cloud environment so that it can be accessed by healthcare professionals from anywhere in the world.

Figure 1. Block diagram of the proposed AI-CDSS

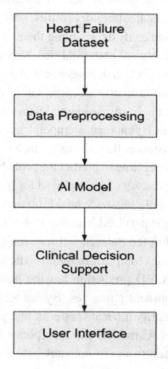

The AI CDSS can be used to generate risk scores for patients, which can help healthcare professionals make decisions about patient care. The CDSS can also be used to provide clinical decision support, such as suggesting preventive measures or treatment options

Some of the Challenges in Developing an AI-Driven Model for CVDs

Data scarcity: There is a lack of large, comprehensive datasets of CVD data. This makes it difficult to train machine learning algorithms that can make accurate predictions.

Data heterogeneity: The data that is available for CVDs is often heterogeneous. This means that the data is collected from different sources and in different formats. This can make it difficult to clean and preprocess the data.

Data bias: The data that is available for CVDs may be biased. This means that the data may not be representative of the general population. This can lead to machine learning algorithms that make biased predictions.

Despite these challenges, there is great potential for AI-driven models to improve the early detection and prevention of CVDs. By developing accurate and robust AI-driven models, we can help to save lives and improve the quality of life for people with CVDs.

RESULTS AND ANALYSIS

Dataset Details

For the proposed work, a dataset consisting of 303 cases is utilized, with each row representing the health records of different patients. These records include attributes such as sex, target, restecg, exang, slope, thalach, thal, fbs, chol, trestbps, ca,age, and oldpeak,chestpain.

Figure 2. Gender and heart disease parameter chart

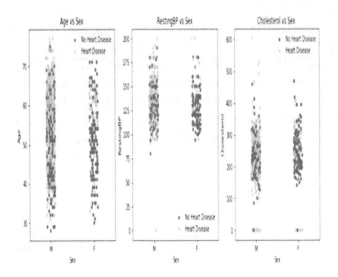

Figure 3. Gender and heart disease parameter chart

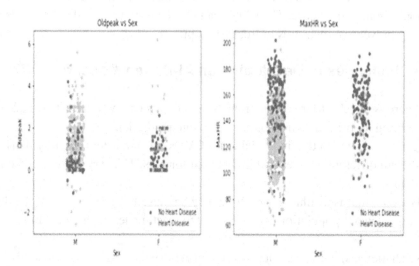

The analysis reveals that heart diseases are prevalent among the male population, showing connections to various numerical features. Particularly, in males aged 50 and above, cases of heart diseases tend to be more frequent when positive old peak values and maximum heart rates below 140 are observed. However, due to the limited number of data points for females compared to males, it remains difficult to identify specific ranges or values indicating heart disease cases in the female population.

CONCLUSION

Chronic disease management is a comprehensive approach aimed at empowering individuals to effectively manage their long-term health conditions. Through the integration of AI-driven decision-making systems, healthcare providers gain access to powerful tools that enhance diagnosis, treatment, monitoring, and patient education. By utilizing these technologies, we can improve the quality of care, optimize outcomes, and ultimately enhance the lives of individuals living with chronic diseases.

AI methodologies, particularly deep learning models like CNNs and RNNs, have significant potential in enhancing cardiovascular disease prediction. These models can analyse diverse data sources, extract relevant features, and provide accurate risk estimates. As AI technology continues to progress and more comprehensive datasets become available, AI-driven CVD prediction models are poised to play an increasingly pivotal role in clinical practice. They can assist healthcare professionals in identifying high-risk individuals, tailoring interventions, and improving patient outcomes.

REFERENCES

Ai, W., Patel, N. D., Roop, P. S., Malik, A., & Trew, M. L. (2020, June). Closing the Loop: Validation of Implantable Cardiac Devices With Computational Heart Models. *IEEE Journal of Biomedical and Health Informatics, 24*(6), 1579–1588. doi:10.1109/JBHI.2019.2947007 PMID:31613786

Albahri, O. S. (2019). Fault-Tolerant mHealth Framework in the Context of IoT-Based Real-Time Wearable Health Data Sensors. *IEEE Access : Practical Innovations, Open Solutions*, 7, 50052–50080. doi:10.1109/ACCESS.2019.2910411

Biswas, Simões-Capela, Van Hoof, & Van Helleputte. (2019). Heart Rate Estimation From Wrist-Worn Photoplethysmography: A Review. *IEEE Sensors Journal, 19*(16), 6560-6570. . doi:10.1109/JSEN.2019.2914166

Brophy, E., Hennelly, B., De Vos, M., Boylan, G., & Ward, T. (2022). Improved Electrode Motion Artefact Denoising in ECG Using Convolutional Neural Networks and a Custom Loss Function. *IEEE Access : Practical Innovations, Open Solutions, 10*, 54891–54898. doi:10.1109/ACCESS.2022.3176971

Chakraborty, C., & Kishor, A. (2022, December). Real-Time Cloud-Based Patient-Centric Monitoring Using Computational Health Systems. *IEEE Transactions on Computational Social Systems, 9*(6), 1613–1623. doi:10.1109/TCSS.2022.3170375

Chandra, B. S., Sastry, C. S., & Jana, S. (2019, March). Robust Heartbeat Detection From Multimodal Data via CNN-Based Generalizable Information Fusion. *IEEE Transactions on Biomedical Engineering, 66*(3), 710–717. doi:10.1109/TBME.2018.2854899 PMID:30004868

Cheikhrouhou, O., Mahmud, R., Zouari, R., Ibrahim, M., Zaguia, A., & Gia, T. N. (2021). One-Dimensional CNN Approach for ECG Arrhythmia Analysis in Fog-Cloud Environments. *IEEE Access : Practical Innovations, Open Solutions, 9*, 103513–103523. doi:10.1109/ACCESS.2021.3097751

Chen, J., Valehi, A., & Razi, A. (2019). Smart Heart Monitoring: Early Prediction of Heart Problems Through Predictive Analysis of ECG Signals. *IEEE Access : Practical Innovations, Open Solutions, 7*, 120831–120839. doi:10.1109/ACCESS.2019.2937875

G. M., V., Ravi, S., V., G. E. A. & S., K.P. (2023, August). Explainable Deep Learning-Based Approach for Multilabel Classification of Electrocardiogram. *IEEE Transactions on Engineering Management, 70*(8), 2787–2799. doi:10.1109/TEM.2021.3104751

Jiang, W., Majumder, S., Kumar, S., Subramaniam, S., Li, X., Khedri, R., Mondal, T., Abolghasemian, M., Satia, I., & Deen, M. J. (2022). A Wearable Tele-Health System towards Monitoring COVID-19 and Chronic Diseases. *IEEE Reviews in Biomedical Engineering, 15*, 61–84. doi:10.1109/RBME.2021.3069815 PMID:33784625

Jiang Y. (2023). IEMS: An IoT-Empowered Wearable Multimodal Monitoring System in Neurocritical Care. *IEEE Internet of Things Journal, 10*(2), 1860-1875. . doi:10.1109/JIOT.2022.3210930

Joy, S. I., Kumar, K. S., Palanivelan, M., & Lakshmi, D. (2023). Review on Advent of Artificial Intelligence in Electrocardiogram for the Detection of Extra-Cardiac and Cardiovascular Disease. *Canadian Journal of Electrical and Computer Engineering, 46*(2), 99–106. doi:10.1109/ICJECE.2022.3228588

Karboub, K., Tabaa, M., Monteiro, F., Dellagi, S., Moutaouakkil, F., & Dandache, A. (2021). Automated Diagnosis System for Outpatients and Inpatients with Cardiovascular Diseases. *IEEE Sensors Journal, 21*(2), 1935-1946. . doi:10.1109/JSEN.2020.3019668

Lee, S.-Y., Huang, P.-W., Chiou, J.-R., Tsou, C., Liao, Y.-Y., & Chen, J.-Y. (2019, December). Electro-cardiogram and Phonocardiogram Monitoring System for Cardiac Auscultation. *IEEE Transactions on Biomedical Circuits and Systems*, *13*(6), 1471–1482. doi:10.1109/TBCAS.2019.2947694 PMID:31634841

Li, Y. (2023). Hybrid D1DCnet Using Forehead iPPG for Continuous and Noncontact Blood Pressure Measurement. *IEEE Sensors Journal, 23*(3), 2727-2736. . doi:10.1109/JSEN.2022.3230210

Liu, C., Zhang, X., Zhao, L., Liu, F., Chen, X., Yao, Y., & Li, J. (2019, April). Signal Quality Assessment and Lightweight QRS Detection for Wearable ECG SmartVest System. *IEEE Internet of Things Journal*, *6*(2), 1363–1374. doi:10.1109/JIOT.2018.2844090

Mansour, R. F., Amraoui, A. E., Nouaouri, I., Díaz, V. G., Gupta, D., & Kumar, S. (2021). Artificial Intelligence and Internet of Things Enabled Disease Diagnosis Model for Smart Healthcare Systems. *IEEE Access : Practical Innovations, Open Solutions*, *9*, 45137–45146. doi:10.1109/ACCESS.2021.3066365

Morales, J., Moeyersons, J., Armanac, P., Orini, M., Faes, L., Overeem, S., Van Gilst, M., Van Dijk, J., Van Huffel, S., Bailon, R., & Varon, C. (2021, June). Model-Based Evaluation of Methods for Respiratory Sinus Arrhythmia Estimation. *IEEE Transactions on Biomedical Engineering*, *68*(6), 1882–1893. doi:10.1109/TBME.2020.3028204 PMID:33001798

Opoku Agyeman, M., Guerrero, A. F., & Vien, Q.-T. (2022). Classification Techniques for Arrhythmia Patterns Using Convolutional Neural Networks and Internet of Things (IoT) Devices. *IEEE Access : Practical Innovations, Open Solutions*, *10*, 87387–87403. doi:10.1109/ACCESS.2022.3192390

Shah, S., Töreyin, H., Güngör, C. B., & Hasler, J. (2019, December). A Real-Time Vital-Sign Monitoring in the Physical Domain on a Mixed-Signal Reconfigurable Platform. *IEEE Transactions on Biomedical Circuits and Systems*, *13*(6), 1690–1699. doi:10.1109/TBCAS.2019.2949778 PMID:31670678

Sun, Wang, Qu, & Xiong. (2022). BeatClass: A Sustainable ECG Classification System in IoT-Based eHealth. *IEEE Internet of Things Journal, 9*(10), 7178-7195. . doi:10.1109/JIOT.2021.3108792

Wang, G., Zhang, S., Dong, S., Lou, D., Ma, L., Pei, X., Xu, H., Farooq, U., Guo, W., & Luo, J. (2019, April). Stretchable Optical Sensing Patch System Integrated Heart Rate, Pulse Oxygen Saturation, and Sweat pH Detection. *IEEE Transactions on Biomedical Engineering*, *66*(4), 1000–1005. doi:10.1109/TBME.2018.2866151 PMID:30130170

Yang, G., Pang, G., Pang, Z., Gu, Y., Mäntysalo, M., & Yang, H. (2019). Non-Invasive Flexible and Stretchable Wearable Sensors With Nano-Based Enhancement for Chronic Disease Care. *IEEE Reviews in Biomedical Engineering*, *12*, 34–71. doi:10.1109/RBME.2018.2887301 PMID:30571646

Zhang, B. (2022). A Framework for Remote Interaction and Management of Home Care Elderly Adults. IEEE Sensors Journal, 22(11). . doi:10.1109/JSEN.2022.3170295

Zhou, S. K., Greenspan, H., Davatzikos, C., Duncan, J. S., Van Ginneken, B., Madabhushi, A., Prince, J. L., Rueckert, D., & Summers, R. M. (2021, May). A Review of Deep Learning in Medical Imaging: Imaging Traits, Technology Trends, Case Studies With Progress Highlights, and Future Promises. *Proceedings of the IEEE*, *109*(5), 820–838. doi:10.1109/JPROC.2021.3054390 PMID:37786449

Chapter 3
AI–Driven IoT (AIIoT) in Healthcare Monitoring

Kutubuddin Kazi

iD https://orcid.org/0000-0001-5623-9211

Brahmdevdada Mane Institute of Technology, Solapur, India

ABSTRACT

This research provides a thorough yet concise review of the opportunities and challenges for utilizing AI and IoT in the healthcare sector. Also included are an outline of AI and IoT, their applicability, certain observations on recent developments, a look at what the future holds, and difficulties facing healthcare systems. The web of things has several uses in healthcare organizations, from remote monitoring to sophisticated sensors and medical device fusion. In any event, it can help professionals communicate ideas more effectively while keeping patients safe and sound. The internet of things (IoT) for human organisations can also assist in attaining responsibility and satisfaction by promising patients to collaborate further closely with medical professionals.

INTRODUCTION

Due to the current popularity of both Artificial Intelligence(AI) and the Internet of Things(IoT), it is currently normal practice to incorporate these two technologies. Everyone has a stake in the healthcare system, so everyone needs to know how to navigate it. But remembering every little thing is a difficult chore. Humans can only perform at a certain level mentally and physically. As a result, exceeding one's maximum can only be done by technologies like IoT and AI. No matter what industry the technologies are used in, using innovative solutions in healthcare is always a smart idea(Mazin,2022). IoT and AI are also powerful drivers behind the digital revolution. The full digital ecosystem, an IoT ecosystem(Javaid,2021) of connected gadgets, has been built and is getting stronger every day. It includes smart homes, municipal infrastructure, supply chain, retailing, manufacturing, healthcare, education, and life sciences. IoT is utilized to give individuals intelligent help because it is equipped with AI and machine learning, among other things. It is gradually replacing both minor and significant processes in a variety of sectors. There is no exception in healthcare as discussed by Raza(2017).

DOI: 10.4018/979-8-3693-0639-0.ch003

IoT and AI reciprocally depend on one another. IoT calls for processing extremely huge quantities of data which must be analysed and set to use.

Therefore, AI procedures may and ought to be employed to improve IoT-related functions in order to give users and/or consumers really meaningful experiences. What type of meaning does AI give the IoT?(Dziak,2017)

IoT, which connects zillions of smarter gadgets, is a nascent technology and as such does have flaws. For instance, there is still room for improvement in terms of IoT data transfer accuracy and speed. Additionally, the AI system learns from what it models itself after in addition to mimicking how humans accomplish jobs. The core of AI is this system of self-improvement. IoT can benefit greatly from AI, to put it generally. To provide intelligence to IoT, it is implemented as AI software that is integrated within IoT gadgets and enhanced by fog or edge computing solutions. Because of the enormous volume of quickly analysed sensor data that smart devices produce, machine learning(ML) explained by Kazi(2023) & Kazi(2022) must be used to increase the intelligence of physical objects.

The emphasis of AI in healthcare could be on disease diagnosis and therapy for the last 50 years as discussed by Pradeepa(2022), Pardeshi (2022) & Waghmare(2022). Primarily rule-based systems are capable of diagnosing and treating disease, but clinical practises could not fully adopt them. They did not pointedly outperform individuals in diagnosis, and there was deprived interoperability with workflows for doctors and medical record systems by Nagare(2014), Nagare(2015) & Kazi(2022). However, integrating medical procedures and EHR systems alongside the application of AI in healthcare by Tadlagi(2022), Kazi(2022) & Vinay(2022) for diagnostic and treatment plans can frequently be difficult, whether it is rules-based or algorithmic. The majority of AI and healthcare features offered by medical software suppliers for clinical trials, diagnosis, and treatment are stand-alone and focus on just one aspect of care. Certain EHR software providers have launched to incorporate fundamental powered by AI (Babitha,2022, & Devi,2022) healthcare analytics features into their range of services. To be able to benefit from the deployment of AI inside healthcare effectively, healthcare providers who utilise solitary EHR systems would likely need to undertake considerable integration efforts themselves or make use of other suppliers who possess AI capabilities that are able to interact with their EHR by Dixit(2014) & Kazi(2022).

It is likely that when AI and IoT are combined in the healthcare industry, operational efficiency will increase. The fundamental processes that enable the intelligent and effective deployment of AI algorithms in IoT devices are tracking (gathering)(Nikita(2020), monitoring (analysing)(Halli, 2022), controlling, optimising (training)(Kazi,2017,2018), and automation (modelling, predicting)(Kazi,2022 & Kazi,2022).

When they operate together, they help lighten the administrative load on clinical staff. Medical staff will be enabled to devote more time to interacting with clients thanks to enhanced clinical workflows, which will inevitably result in a more patient-centric approach to the administration of healthcare services discussed by Pardeshi(2022). Consequently, the following are the primary application cases for AI-enabled IoT shown in Figure 1.

AI has meaningfully altered the way doctors recognise, track and treat, patients in healthcare sector. Medical staff might otherwise miss disease indications and trends, but AI in healthcare's ability to quickly assess enormous quantities of clinical records helps identify them discussed by Wale(2019). AI applications in healthcare extend widely, from projecting outcomes using electronic health records to radiological image analysis for earlier detection. By employing AI in hospital/clinic settings, healthcare systems may grow smarter, quicker, and further effective in treating billions of patients worldwide. AI, which will alter how patients receive high-quality care while lowering expenses for carers and improving health outcomes, seems to be the probable future for healthcare as discussed by Ayala(2014).

Figure 1. AI enabled IoT in healthcare

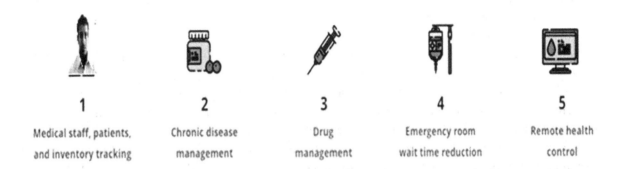

1	2	3	4	5
Medical staff, patients, and inventory tracking	Chronic disease management	Drug management	Emergency room wait time reduction	Remote health control

It all began using IBM's Watson AI system, which was developed to offer accurate and timely responses to inquiries. Natural language processing(NLP), a technique used to understand and interpret human speech, was the focus of IBM's 2011 Watson for Healthcare introduction. This event is mentioned in articles on artificial intelligence in healthcare. Along with IBM, other tech behemoths like Apple, are now investing more and more in AI-based healthcare technologies as discussed by Almotiri(2016).

In the area of healthcare, AI offers truly incredible potential. AI is expected to drastically change our ability to assess healthcare data, diagnose diseases, improve treatments for them, and perchance preclude individuals. AI in healthcare makes it possible for healthcare professionals to make better judgments using exact/precise information that reduces costs, saves period, and generally enhances the administration of health data. AI can transform healthcare sector, opening the way towards an era in which patients can get superior care and treatment more quickly than any time before, including finding new cancer treatments to improve individuals experiences(Ayala,2014).

ML has become one of the most often used forms of AI in healthcare(Veenis2020).

This extensive approach, which forms the basis of diverse perspectives on AI and healthcare technology, has several variations. The manner that the healthcare system functions has altered as a result of ML, which made it possible to apply AI to medical diagnosis and treatment(Dixit,2015). ML algorithms discussed by Sreenivasulu(2022) can swiftly assess the huge amount of clinical documentation, identify trends, and forecast medical outcomes with greater accuracy than ever before. By examining patient information and medical imaging along with creating new medicines, the statistical science underlying ML is helping healthcare professionals improve their treatments and reduce costs(Aavula, 2022). Medics can correctly detect disorders and adapt remedies to the needs of specific patients by utilising AI technology like ML for activities like disease diagnostics or medication research and development. Additionally, the use of AI in healthcare, especially ML, enables professionals to find previously unknown associations between diseases in medical records or identify minor variations in vital signs which could point to a potential issue.

Precision medicine is where typical machine learning is most commonly used. It is a significant advancement for data scientists of many healthcare organizations to be able to anticipate which treatment procedures would be beneficial for individuals according to their characteristics and their medical framework. Medical imaging as discussed by Kazi(2022) and clinical data are required for instruction for the majority of ML and precision medicine applications used in healthcare when the outcome is known. This is what directed learning is. NLP-based speech recognition is also used in healthcare AI which is based on deep learning (DL). The lack of elements in a DL model which are important to human reviewers makes it challenging to assess the model's output. As DL technology discussed by Vahida(2023) advances, healthcare professionals will find it increasingly important to understand how it works and how to apply it effectively in clinical settings.

For many years, some hospitals have adopted AI-driven IoT(AIIoT). AI-powered IoT devices are frequently seen in patient rooms, health information systems, as well as cloud-based services. By improving accessibility to diagnosis, preventative care, and therapies while significantly reducing the associated costs, researchers anticipate that digital healthcare will help to revolutionize the entire healthcare business. Keeping track of patients who are deemed to be high-risk is difficult when trying to control the expense of medical care. In the USA, managing chronic diseases accounts for around 30% of total healthcare spending, with heart disease, diabetes, and asthma accounting for a larger share of these costs(Patil(2023).

Healthcare practitioners will be able to routinely monitor high-risk patients thanks to AI-powered IoT devices like remote monitoring. The experts predict that digital health care might result in savings of up to 350 billion USD, with the handling of chronic pathogens expected to account for over 200 billion of those savings. An Internet of Medical Things(IoMT) powered by AI is another name for the AIIoT. In this scenario, any medical devices including the corresponding apps that frequently link to healthcare information technology systems across a computer network would be included in the IoMT. In this context, the IoMT refers to medical devices having Wi-Fi connectivity that frequently interact with one another. Such a collection of devices can connect to Amazon AWS's cloud storage to save data that has been gathered and can be analysed later.

The body of research shows that the AIIoT can be quite useful in several different sectors of healthcare. Elder care is one example of this, which entails monitoring older patients' stay in hospitals and nursing facilities and acquiring pertinent information. It covers a variety of medical devices, such as EKG monitors, that are used at the bedside in hospitals. With current breakthroughs taking place across the IoT powered by AI, this field has continued to grow. Both healthcare professionals and specific patients are anticipated to gain from the growing use of AIIoT in the healthcare industry. Remote tracking and communication, areas whereby the AIIoT may have a very important role, improve the quality of the remedies patients receive. Mobile medical apps or wearables discussed by Waghmare et al(2022) that enable patients to collect their unique health information are another usage powered by AI-IoT in healthcare. The technology revolution, that enables the general public to cultivate healthier lifestyles by making optimal use of associated gadgets like wearables, tablets, and handheld devices, is largely responsible for this element.

The ability to make decisions is generally strengthened by analysis of data gathered through electronic healthcare records, individual clinical information gathered from imaging equipment, and specific handheld devices. Patients themselves may be able to manage their health quite actively thanks to this feature. These data-rich, individualised analyses of health will constitute the gold standard for the future. Patients are to be given individualised treatment plans to combat disease discussed by Pradeepa et al(2023). People learn how to improve their wellness from what is produced, and they will also be strongly inspired to take charge of their own life. The purpose of the connected equipment is improved by employing their apps more effectively in clinical decisions, according to academics, who assert that there's a new business inside Clinical Decision Support-CDS software. This sector is expanding notably concerning AIIoT.

The field of pharmaceutical sciences has traditionally placed great emphasis on studying decision-making processes to advance research. This promotes development and ensures the delivery of safe and effective medications to patients. However, in recent years, there has been a notable shift in this paradigm. This change is attributed to researchers integrating artificial intelligence (AI) into decision-making procedures, bringing about transformative effects not only in the pharmaceutical sector but also across various industries (Carou-Senra,2023; Liu, 2023; Malviya, 2023; Singh, 2023). AI-driven decision-making applications have emerged as powerful tools, enabling pharmaceutical scientists to make more informed and efficient decisions. The repercussions of this are evident in the accelerated pace of drug discovery, its optimization, and the enhancement of manufacturing processes (El-Naggar, 2023). Figure 1 offers a comprehensive visual representation of the key disciplines within the pharmaceutical sciences that AI-driven decision-making applications have profoundly impacted. The influence of AI is most pronounced in six primary areas: drug research and discovery, clinical development, personalized medicines, manufacturing and supply chain, launch and commercial activities, and postmarketing surveillance. AI-powered applications not only enhance decision-making but also elevate patient outcomes and improve the overall performance of the pharmaceutical industry. This highlights AI's transformative potential, positioning it as a pivotal catalyst for the future evolution of pharmaceutical sciences.

One of the foremost advantages of implementing AI in the domain of pharmaceutical sciences is its potential to expedite drug discovery and development. Traditional methods for identifying potential drug candidates have often been labor intensive, expensive, and filled with uncertainties (Khadela., 2023). However, with the rise of AI, researchers now apply machine learning algorithms to sift through vast databases, predict molecular properties, simulate biological processes, and facilitate virtual screenings of prospective drug candidates (Bournez, 2023; Czub, 2023; Lee, 2023). This innovative approach reduces the time and cost of identifying drug leads, consequently accelerating the development of life-saving medications. In the field of clinical development, AI-driven decision-making applications are crucial for refining processes. Researchers utilize AI to select patients for clinical trials, design efficient trial protocols, and analyze real-time data from these trials (Aliper, 2023). Such evaluations are key in detecting patterns, forecasting outcomes, and guiding decisions about drug safety and effectiveness (Ranson,2023). Moreover, the emergence of AI-driven decision-making applications is reshaping foundational beliefs in personalized medicine (MacMath., 2023). Personalized medicine tailors medical treatments to individual patients based on their unique attributes. Integrating patient-specific data, such as genomic information and electronic health records, with advanced AI algorithms provides pharmaceutical scientists with a powerful tool. They can then tailor treatments for each patient, enhancing therapeutic outcomes and reducing adverse reactions. The ability to interpret biological data, anticipate patient responses, and refine treatment plans based on individual characteristics promises to transform the pharmaceutical landscape, ushering in an age of more precise and effective healthcare (Sheng, 2023). In the spheres of manufacturing and supply chains, AI-driven decision-making applications are essential for refining processes and optimizing supply chains in the pharmaceutical industry (Charles., 2023). AI helps in quality control, supply chain management, demand forecasting, and the optimization of production schedules, resulting in increased efficiency, cost savings, and overall operational enhancement (Baviskar,2023). Product launches and commercialization also benefit from AI tools, supporting successful product introductions. AI aids in pinpointing target patient populations, analyzing market trends, forecasting market demand, optimizing pricing strategies, and designing targeted marketing campaigns. Collectively, these factors lead to more successful product launches and commercialization endeavors (Lu., 2023). Last, postmarketing surveillance, vital for monitoring the safety and efficacy of pharmaceutical products postapproval, garners advantages from AI systems. These tools analyze real-world data, encompassing adverse event reports and patient feedback, to identify potential safety concerns, evaluate drug efficacy, and provide insights for informed postmarketing decisions (Kaku, 2023).

HEALTHCARE HISTORY WITH AI

A fundamental change in healthcare is being brought about by AI, which seeks to replicate how humans think. Future healthcare will demand more AI applications due to the intricacy and growth of data. Healthcare organisations and biological businesses are already using a variety of AI technologies discussed by Devi(2022). The origins of AI can be found in the 1950s when British mathematician Alan Turing questioned if machines could reason. The life sciences didn't adopt AI until more than ten years later, and the 1970s saw its introduction into the healthcare industry. ANN(Shirgan,2010), Bayesian networks (Kamuni,2022), and hybrid intelligence systems were used in more clinical contexts beginning in the 1980s and continuing into the present. However, AI for healthcare has not yet developed into a prominent industrial application in collective equity finance. AI is now employed to help patients and clinicians in virtual as well as real life.

AI could combine cognitive ability with physical talent, displaying its full capabilities when it is paired with other technologies like robotics. For instance, Genki Kanda created a robotic AI system that could enhance the usage of stem cells in regenerative medicine processes.

AI IN HEALTHCARE: TYPES

AI isn't a singular technology; it's a collection of innovations with specialised procedures and jobs to assist healthcare objectives. These technologies can be used to support a wide range of activities, some of which are crucial to raising the standard of healthcare (Figure 2).

Machine Learning

Arguably most prevalent type of AI in the workplace and the foundation of several AI applications is machine learning. ML is frequently applied to healthcare to estimate the efficacy of treatment procedures in precise medical applications. Neural networks(NN), a sophisticated type of ML that may be used for categorization, are also applied in the healthcare industry. NN, for instance, can decide whether a patient can contract a disease. To identify possibly malignant lesions in radiographs or find pertinent aspects that humans are unable to see, DL, a NN model having degrees of characteristics of parameters that imply outcomes, is frequently utilized and discussed by Kosgiker (2018).

Natural Language Processing (NLP)

NLP, which comprises tools for text analysis, speech recognition, and translation, may be used in AI. NLP is mostly utilised in healthcare for the development, comprehension, and organisation of documents and research. It is possible to create reports, record patient contacts, and other things by analysing this unorganised data. Additionally, it can improve triage systems, help forecast patient outcomes, and create diagnostic models as discussed by Kazi (2017).

Figure 2. Different standards of healthcare

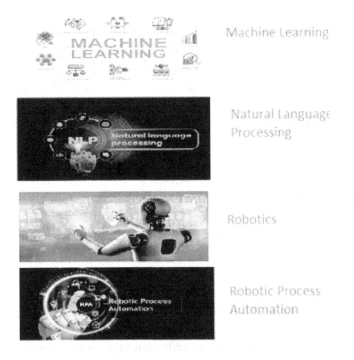

Robotics

One of the most well-known uses of AI in healthcare and various other industries is physical robots. Advanced robotics work in conjunction with people and can be applied to more complex tasks, like surgery. Since about 2000, surgical robots have been approved in the US. With the use of this technology, surgeons will be able to see more clearly and make more accurate, less-invasive incisions and stitches. Robots discussed by Kumtole(2022) serve as a companion of the surgeon yet do not perform surgery; decision-making was still left to the actual surgeon.

Robotic Process Automation

Robotic process automation carries out duties to reduce the administrative hassle, which may be significant, for medical facilities. This technology stands out from other forms of AI since it is less expensive and simpler to use, but it can also dramatically increase productivity and cost-effectiveness. Robotic process automation is utilised in healthcare for routine tasks including updating patient data, billing patients, and authorising. To extract data and enter it into systems, it can be used in conjunction with technology such as image recognition as discussed by Nikita (2022).

AI FOR TREATMENT AND DIAGNOSIS

Since its first applications in medicine, AI has placed a lot of emphasis on diagnostic and therapeutic applications. Although they were unable to compete against human diagnosticians, rule-based systems were only partially adopted for the diagnosis and treatment of disease. Precision medicine using AI is now employed for cancer detection and therapy, together with ML and NLP. Precision medicine is a capable application with the potential for better diagnosis and treatment in the future, despite some challenges, such as treating certain kinds of cancer.

Cancer

Utilising AI technology for the treatment of cancer may enhance the rapidity and precision of diagnosis, support decision-making, and provide improved health outcomes. This depends on AI's capacity to process massive amounts of data, extract links, and recognise traits that are invisible to humans.

Neurology

In neurology, AI is utilised to aid in the diagnosis and management of neurodegenerative illnesses like Parkinson's, Alzheimer's, and Amyotrophic Lateral Sclerosis(ALS). AI is used to analyse speech recordings, neuroimaging, & cognitive test data to understand the biomarkers of various disorders while comparing findings to expected ranges.

Cardiology

AI Supporting improved outcomes from therapy for cardiac patients. The main applications include treating strokes, identifying heart illness, improving diagnostic imaging capabilities, forecasting cardiac risk, and employing biomedical devices for monitoring heart rhythms.

TECHNOLOGY AND RHM (REMOTE HEALTHCARE MONITORING) ARCHITECTURE

The wellness monitoring platform is an algorithm that collects data from the custodian's smart device, as well as medical sensors, affixed onto the the individual's body. The controller is a health monitoring server (HMS), which analyses the past medical history and present health to produce an Individualised Healthcare Plan (IHP) in real-time. During times when there are important conditions, it produces signal notifications, alerts, and exceptions. The hospital service for obtaining health problem detection, health monitoring operation for review and oversight, and fast response are the key components of the smart service. The PRMC handles storing and using information concurrently. The IHP receives real-time service from the health monitoring system. The healthcare system allows doctors to conclude a health status based on the written report provided by HMS and the prior medical information retrieved from the PRMC, which houses all personal records discussed by Akansha (2022).

Figure 3. Technology design for intelligent healthcare services

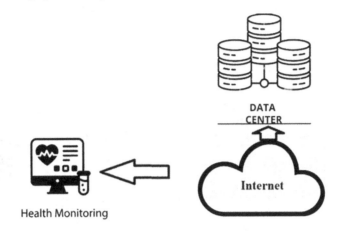

The PRMC serves as a central repository for all patient health information, including electronic records of patients' current ailments. Additionally, it transmits to all systems linked to it the headers of limitations and protocols that carry the required data. Additionally, a medical monitoring service provides on-site storage. The primary necessity for a condensed technology framework for smarter healthcare services, as depicted in Fig. 3, is that storage stores an individual's medical record and health statistics as discussed by Afrin (2022). The Patient-Central Electronic Health Record (PC-EHR) is a flexible data repository that houses patients' past medical histories as well as their specific personal data, including their names, addresses, and contact information.

USE OF AI-DRIVEN IOT (AIIoT) FOR CONVERGENCE SMART HEALTHCARE INFRASTRUCTURES

The adoption of AIIoT continues to be one of the quickest in the healthcare industry. Specific patients having any type of chronic condition, elderly people, and those who need ongoing care tend to greatly benefit from this approach. It is prone to boost the efficacy and quality of the particular service offered by integrating AI-driven IoT(AIIoT) including through one's own medical devices. By 2025, investment in healthcare AIIoT products will total one trillion US dollars, according to a report. It's feasible that this circumstance will pave the way for everyone to receive extremely accessible, individualised, and prompt healthcare. An illustration of a sophisticated healthcare system is shown in Figure 4.

AI IN COVID-19 CLINICAL DECISION BASED X-RAY

As seen in Figure 5 below, the Chest Radiographs (CR) dataset contains 150 frontal CXR(X-ray) images that are examined posterior-anterior and collected from various hospitals at Solapur(MS). For CXR-based COVID-19 identification, deep network graph diffusion pseudo-labeling is demonstrated. A deep semi-supervised architecture is used to identify COVID-19 using GraphXCovid in Figure 6. It uses a cutting-edge optimisation algorithm to generate pseudo-labeling using Dirichlet energy. Thus,

Figure 4. Illustration of an intelligent healthcare system

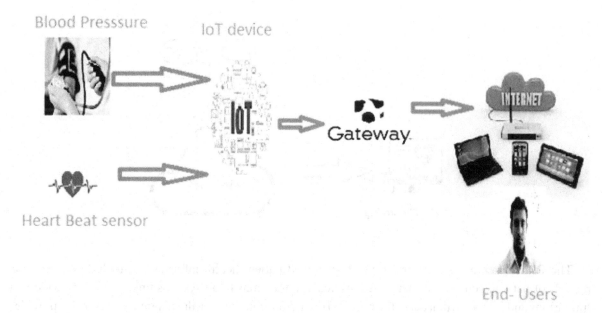

Figure 5. XAI in (COVID -19) clinical decisions based on x-ray

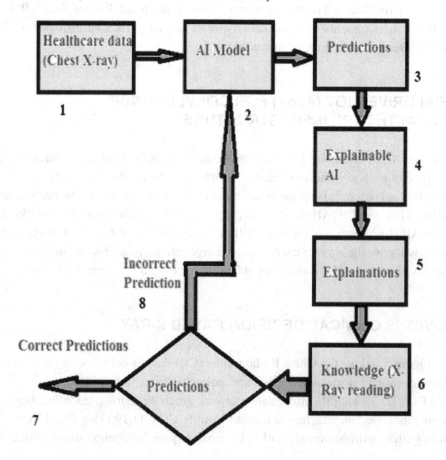

Figure 6. CXR result

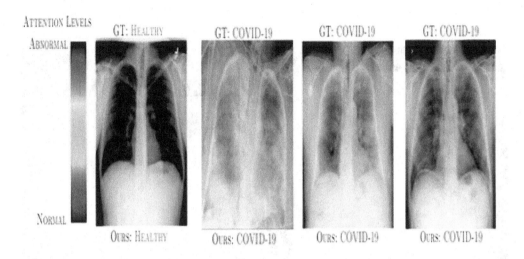

high sensitivity in illness, i.e., COVID-19, is produced with few labels discussed by Kazi(2023). The key features of this approach include attention maps and an iterative deep-net scheme. The research is regarded as the deep SSL technique's replacement because it combines deep neural network generalisation and feature extraction. The procedure can be described in more detail as optimising epochs for Deep-net extraction for graph building and diffusing labelled sets to unlabeled data. Pseudo-labels are created as a result, which optimise the model parameter through frequent changes and are then iterated until finished. The imbalance in the medical data issue is addressed in this instance during the diffusion. The characteristic most in charge of this prediction, according to an XAI model, is intake. Then, after examining the characteristics, doctors can suggest the best treatments or exercises.

Figure 7. I-Score model with top features for CXR

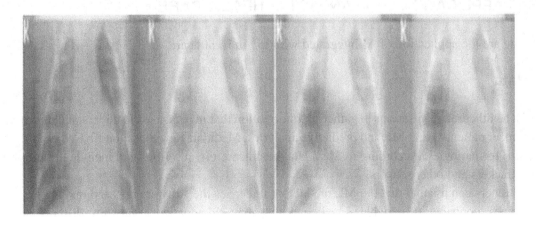

Figure 8. COVID-19 pneumonia identification

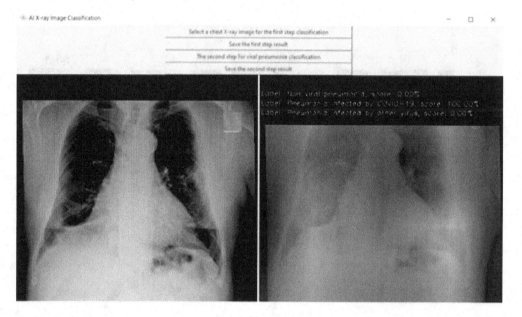

Getting an influential score(I-score) for those with pneumonia, as shown in Figure 7, will be made easier by reading the talk that follows. EHR data is known to have several difficulties, which would make for very intriguing predictions if the supporting choices made for them could be explained.

The basic framework is based on VGG-19, whose convolution kernel has been adjusted to meet the needs. Bright colors are used to establish the final values and designate the area of interest for medical analysis. To discover the ideal settings, the hyper-parameters are trained using grid search. Two distinct CNN models are CNN1 for the output of virus infection, test samples to divide the standard set, and training samples with category labels. Finally, CNN2 produces the result by precisely categorising the infection shown in Figure 8.

From the chest radiographs (SCR) dataset X-ray images, one can also identify Pneumonia. For that one can use the same database as has previously used for COVID-19 case.

OTHER APPLICATION OF AI AND IOT IN HEALTHCARE

Following are the application of AI integrated with IoT in Healthcare.

Medidata

To assist healthcare organisations in gathering information that may be used to understand the quality of life of cancer patients using ML and predictive analytics, Medidata develops cloud-based mobile health (mHealth) technologies. According to Medidata, healthcare organisations can include the program in activity trackers and other sensors.

Researchers can assume that the ML model that underlies the software is based on data on various cancer types, contributing variables, medicines that may aid inpatient treatment, different kinds of physical activity, and diet, among other things. The ML algorithm within the software is then put into the data. As a result, the algorithm would have discovered what information may link to treatments that could or might not improve the standard of life for cancer patients.

The programme would therefore be able to anticipate the best course of action for each patient. Users might or might not require to upload data about their new therapies beforehand into the application itself.

In 2016, Memorial Sloan Kettering Cancer Centre (MSK) conducted a study on cancer therapy adopting mHealth technology, according to Medidata, which claims to have assisted MSK in compiling the data into the Medidata Cloud. The purpose of the study was to measure the standard of life for individuals receiving induction chemotherapy in multiple myeloma using sensor devices and cellphones. To monitor patterns in clients, MSK deployed activity trackers, smartphone App, with Medidata's cloud computing platform. Researchers planned to use fitness tracker info that was gathered through the Medidata Cloud to find multiple myeloma medicines that extend life expectancy while enhancing the standard of life. Patterns of physical activity and other motions, as well as sleep quality, were among the variables that MSK would monitor. Patients were instructed to wear the trackers constantly for four chemotherapy cycles after putting them on for 1 to 7 days to establish a baseline. The visualisation and analytics dashboard from Medidata was to be used by MSK researchers to track how well patients were following treatment guidelines and to spot trends and anomalies.

Senseonics

Eversense, a continuous glucose monitoring (CGM) device made by Senseonics, employs a sensor implanted beneath the individual's skin to record information about the blood sugar level for ninety days. According to the manufacturer, the gadget uses predictive machine learning and analytics to assist people with diabetes in taking control of their health. According to Senseonics, a qualified doctor implants the sensor under the individual's armpit skin. No sensor component pokes through the skin in any way. The author can assume that this software's ML models were trained using information on fluctuating glucose levels. ML algorithm of the software is then put into the data. As a result, the algorithm would have learned which numbers correspond to typical glucose levels. In that case, the programme would be able to foretell whether the user's blood glucose level is headed for an elevated or depressed point. The user may or may not need to upload into the app beforehand details on their prescriptions, diet, and physical activity, among other things. The patient is then alerted every five minutes via their mobile device via a transmitter, which can also vibrate the patient's body to warn them when their phone is out of reach. Additionally, the patient will have access to information that will help them comprehend their glucose patterns and history.

Propeller Health

To assist those sufferings from asthma in apprising their medication use, identifying triggers, overseeing symptoms, and gaining a greater grasp over their illness via machine learning, Propeller Health offers the Propeller, a device via sensors that includes asthma inhalers. The device, formerly known as Asthmapolis, is said to be compatible with the majority of inhalers and Bluetooth spirometers, according to Propeller Health. According to the manufacturer, the software's machine learning model was trained using data on the patient's inhaler usage as well as information on air quality, temperature, wind speed, and humidity. The ML algorithm of the software would then be applied to the data. The algorithm would have learned from this that this information corresponds to asthma attacks or COPD attacks.According to symptoms and other criteria, the programme would then eventually be able to anticipate when asthma or COPD incident is about to occur. The user may or may not need to submit data into the software beforehand on their degree of weariness, diet, immune system health, and sleep quality. To assist the patient in tracking and managing the disease, the data is also available to the patient's healthcare professional.

Microsoft Azure

Microsoft provides Azure IoT, which it says may assist healthcare organisations in tracking usage of technology to enhance patient well-being, maintain essential equipment, and lower readmissions using machine learning. Other industries, including manufacturing, transportation, retail, smart cities, and natural resources, can also use the technology. The software, according to Microsoft, can be included in patient monitoring and tracking equipment used by healthcare organisations.

The Researchers can assume that the ML model underlying the software was trained on a variety of health and medical data, including BP readings, compliance with the patient's personal goals, admission, discharge, and transfer (ADT) events, and patient-generated data such as assessment-based depression indicators, among others, to learn about and lower the risk of patient readmission. The ML algorithm of the software is then put into the data.

This could have taught an algorithm to identify information points that link to a particular patient group's physiological readings, adherence to the doctor's post-release instructions, wellness and daily practises, and assistance upon discharge, amongst other factors. The software would thus be able to forecast the likelihood of readmission for a certain risk group.

Microsoft says it has assisted Roche Diagnostics in providing services to its clients more affordably. The business required the capacity to use analytics to:

- Manage the in-vitro diagnostic (IVD) equipment remotely like fixed assets,
- Estimate the likelihood of any IVD solutions being down while being used in the client's clinical environment.
- Provide a customer with the ideal IVD option for their requirements.
- Offer data analytics and visualisation for enhanced decision-making
- Lay the groundwork for future upkeep.

The software was installed onto the patient's equipment by Cleidon International, a Microsoft IT partner after Roche Diagnostics approached them. As a result, the client is now able to review the system's health data, troubleshoot problems, and dispatch support teams for assistance while also gathering operational data from the IVDs in close to real-time, such as location.

CONCERNS ABOUT SECURITY IN THE AIIOT

There are a tonne of devices linked to the web due to the rapid adoption of AIIoT. Such intelligent things continue to be targeted regularly for their risks regarding data security. For instance, two security researchers found more than 68,000 medical systems online that were vulnerable towards the end of 2018, with more than 12,000 of those belonging to a particular healthcare provider. The fact that the equipment was linked via the internet using computers running an extremely outdated rendition of XP, which is an operating system known to include numerous vulnerabilities that may be exploited, was a significant concern surrounding this discovery. Shodan, a search engine that can locate AIIoT gadgets online, was used to find such devices. By using hard-coded access and a technique known as brute force, these are incredibly simple to hack.

The two researchers made anesthesia paraphernalia, infusion systems, and straightforward Shodan queries public. In this instance, according to the researchers, the attackers succeeded in authenticating through SSH on such phony medical devices over many hundreds times and even left behind multiple malware payloads. In this instance, the researchers discovered that most of the time, the hackers did not know what they'd just hijacked and left the device contaminated as a component of their botnets discussed by Chinthamu(2023).

IoT PRIVACY RISKS IN THE AI DRIVEN HEALTHCARE INDUSTRY

It is extremely challenging to evaluate possible risks in the AIIoT considering the considerable ambiguity surrounding whether or not the IoT will affect the community as an entire entity. We can currently observe the effects of the growing data gathering from cellular service providers, social media, and cellphone sensors on a related topic. The simplest method to research the broad privacy consequences of the IoT's AI-driven innovation is to examine how confidentiality has historically impacted earlier technologies. A conclusion generally could be derived from this parallel is that, although the data broadcast by a particular endpoint device itself may not generate any privacy-related issues, the volume of data collected from various devices may. Furthermore, several characteristics make it more challenging to protect the AIIoT from privacy issues. Users barely even realise they are being tracked because almost all data collecting is passive, less obtrusive, and more pervasive. Some of these main dangers or vulnerabilities of IoT elements include assaults physical, RFID integration, WSN's integration, DOS/DDOS, and unauthorized data access as discussed by Kazi(2023).

The research has accepted how AIIoT is widespread, so which case various devices tend to detect and gather information about individuals and surroundings to provide a certain sort of services. Healthcare providers, who are located under the users' authority, process the data that has been acquired in this scenario. The case for a collection of policy commissions for Massachusetts, which purchased medical insurance for state staff and provided free access to any researcher interested in such information, serves as a good illustration of these privacy violations. Though PIN code, gender, and DOB were ever removed, information was explicitly anonymized by removing variables like address, name, and social security number to safeguard the patient's privacy as discussed by Pardeshi(2022).

According to the literature, even though obvious identifiers were removed from existing health records, the remaining information (such as PIN codes, DOB, and sex) was typically enough to help reidentify people when attempting to connect them to the general voter database. A bit more precise, Sweeney might divulge or even provide the governor's medical records, complete with diagnoses and prescriptions, into the governor's office. They gave the public their word that the privacy of the patient wouldn't be explicitly jeopardised by such a publication of GIC data. It's critical to show that AOL released over 20 million searches to attract additional academic researchers, which constituted a severe privacy breach of AOL search data.

HOW AI AND IOT COULD TRANSFORMING DAY-TO-DAY HOSPITAL OPERATIONS

Naturally, hospitals generate a tonne of data. While medical professionals provide visual information in the manner of X-rays or CT scans, individual monitors capture vital signs like heartrate, blood pressure(BP), and temperature. Each of these data has the potential to be extremely important, but only when organisations can see it as the appropriate moment and the resources to analyse it in an emergency.

Newer AI and IoMT technology may offer clinicians the best possible access to this information. As a consequence, they are changing how hospitals operate where they have been implemented. Here are six ways that AI and IoT are starting to alter hospital operations now.

Improving Diagnostic Accuracy

Even some pandanmic or common diseases, such as breast and lung cancer, may prove challenging to detect. Using imaging with CT scanner, clinicians must properly identify possible tumours in patients with these illnesses. False both positive and negative results are still frequent even though this method of diagnosis is the most reliable one. AI also analyses the scans and enhances their quality by stitching together images and eliminating visual distortion for an improved and easy-to-read scan. These AI systems have proven to be more accurate even radiologists in a number of tests in spotting cancer signals on CT scan.

Remote Patient Monitoring

In order to give healthcare professionals updated on vital signs, remote patient monitoring systems make use of the internet availability of IoT devices. With the use of such remote sensors, healthcare professionals can monitor a patient's wellbeing from any location around the clinic and be made aware of important health developments. The labour required to monitor the wellness of patients when they are in a hospital is decreased through the use of IoT healthcare networks. According to the patient's health, nurses usually need to physically record and log their vital signs periodically. These vital signs are instantly recorded and logged by an electronic monitoring system, freeing up workers for other important duties. These solutions are probably going to be increasingly typical as medical IoT technology advances.

Reducing Need of Follow-Ups Visits

Similar IoT applications can monitor patients' health after they depart the hospital and eliminate the requirement for subsequent visits. Healthcare professionals employ IoT devices, for instance, at the Even while folks who have the problem note it frequently goes better after birth, an issue like this typically requires follow-up appointments. 57% of patients might avoid their initial follow-up appointment by having an IoT system in situ.

Decreased Wait Times

In modern hospitals, IoT technology additionally cuts down on wait times. When a room becomes available, automated bed monitoring devices alert hospital employees, enabling administrators to receive emergencies as soon as feasible.

How to Recognise Critical Patients

Finding patients that require immediate attention while hospitals are under pressure along with capacity is essential to giving patients superior care. It is a difficult process. Healthcare professionals are under a lot of stress to quickly analyse a huge amount of clinical data and make choices. Fortunately, in these circumstances, AI and IoT devices offer assistance. To save their sickest patients, hospitals are turning to novel AI-powered virtual helpers. These systems analyse patients' vital signs and health status and notify clinicians when an individual's health starts to deteriorate. Such medical AI systems have occasionally been able to identify issues that doctors overlooked. The mortality rate for patients in the intensive care unit was reduced by 13% as a result of these AI programmes in several different hospitals.

Tracking Medical Equipment

Hospitals may incur enormous costs as a result of lost medical devices. For instance, hospitals frequently lose between three and seven of the healing pumps they use for low-pressure wound care each year. These can be replaced for between $20,000 and $30,000 each. The danger of missing medical devices can be significantly reduced for organisations with the correct tracking solutions in place, which also helps to control expenses and ensure that devices are accessible when needed. In order to be tracked while in hospital in addition to if someone is discharged home accompanied a patient, newer mobile pump units now have GPS, RFID, and other systems integrated in. When pumps is taken off the rack for an individual, the RFID scanner also immediately asks insurance for clearance. A person gets pre-approved to bring their equipment home whether necessary thanks to this procedure.

APPLICATION OF AI IN IOT-BASED LOGISTICS FOR HEALTHCARE

IoT healthcare solution is designed for sick commercial truck drivers. The business proprietor's staff wellness and expenditure control programme includes preventing emergency cases. InData Labs team got began by carefully examining the current solution. Its AI specialists examined the abilities of the current app to identify the most effective ways to improve it. Researchers gathered the following kinds of data(from Driver)(Figure 9) in addition to the wristbands data to feed into the algorithm as input:

Gathered Info be fed into the Client's record for further processing. So, the subsequent data sources are used to get the input for the ML-model:

The Researchers trained the model to carry out a couple of tasks using the extensive input data:

- Examine the state of drivers' health
- Recognise health issues
- Produce a push notification system

Figure 9. Driver's data

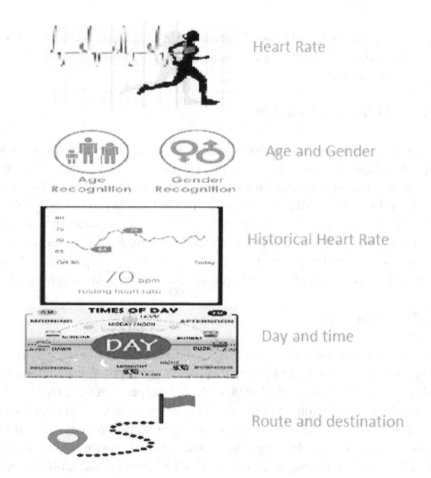

Figure 10. Data sources for input to logistics system

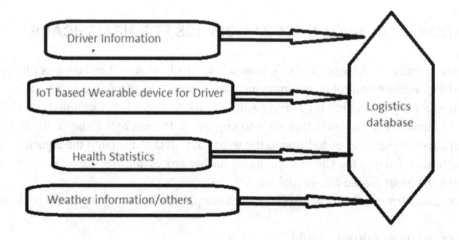

Figure 11. Fitness zones

- Send drivers notifications and advice

Figure 10 shows the information available at logistics server for health monitoring of driver's. The algorithm divides the output into three zones or groups (Figure 11). Green Zone, Yellow Zone, and Red Zone are typical symbols for these zones. Different push messages and suggestions are provided to vehicles from a server based on one or more categories. Here are some examples:

The team from InData Labs utilised the ApplePush Notification service(APNs) to activate the distant notifications capability and finish the work. The researchers processed and stored data using a client's service as well.

AI'S POTENTIAL IN HEALTHCARE

The Author is sure you are aware of ChatGPT and its application as an AI system unless you have been living in a community in the mountains of India for the past few months. The truth is that artificial intelligence, or at least the concept, has been available for quite a while. However, up until recently, it was more of a number-crunching technique that went through all possible combinations of reactions until it found one that matched. As opposed to the genuine intelligence and reasoning that are traditionally associated with AI. All things considered, AI has quickly entered mainstream society, changing the way we perceive innovation and the future of our planet. Healthcare is undoubtedly one field where this is the subject of heated debate and continued discussion.

AI in the medical field has the potential to revolutionize how we identify, treat, and avoid diseases. The use of technology might enhance patient outcomes, lower costs, and boost the effectiveness of the healthcare system. These are the five greatest ways that AI can improve healthcare (Figure 12), in author's opinion, along with five obstacles that must be solved before the technology can be used to its full potential.

While there is little doubt that AI has the potential to improve healthcare, there are also huge obstacles that must be solved. Here are the top five, in author's opinion shown in Figure 13:

DISCUSSION

Errors in the healthcare system can be dangerous as well as expensive. According to the literature, medical mistakes cause numerous deaths worldwide each year, in developed as well as emerging economies.

Figure 12. Ways AI improve healthcare system

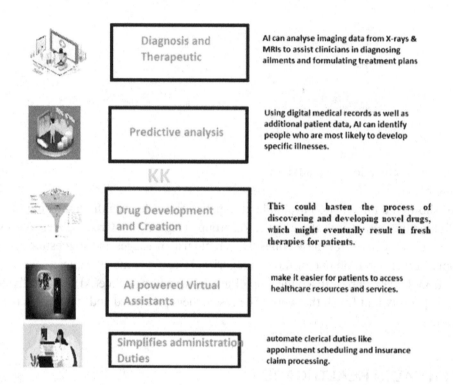

Figure 13. Obstacles that must solved

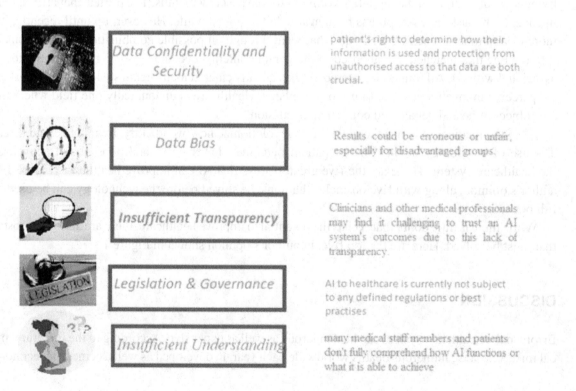

According to a study based on 37 million medical records, roughly 1,95,000 individuals every year in the USA pass away as a consequence of clinical errors that could have been easily avoided. It is significantly worse in developing African nations, where the number occasionally triples. Therefore, it is abundantly obvious that robust clinical decision-support tools are required to shorten diagnostic times and improve illness diagnosis accuracy. AI-driven Traditional statistical methods have given way in the IoT to artificially complicated neural networks. To make healthcare choices more effective, data mining & IoT solutions are now often used in clinical applications. Decision trees, ANN, SVM, Bayesian networks, and bagging algorithms are only a few methods of data mining that are currently widely applied in clinical support systems to assist with health-related choices. Because they can find concealed relationships and patterns in medical data, ANN and data mining have drawn a lot of interest in building therapeutic support.

It is prudent to keep in mind that privacy and security concerns related to AIIoT must be resolved permanently to realise its development and expansion. First, it's critical to recognise that AIIoT frequently employs a variety of hardware, software, and services to achieve its objectives. There's an enormous demand for the creation of a set of standards that should be accompanied correctly through the micro and macro levels of realising IoT to incorporate networks for IoT frameworks to achieve an expanded framework, for example, to create a smart healthcare system by combining several innovative hospitals. The present demands for IoTs are to have clearly defined architectural standards that involve user interfaces, data models, and pertinent protocols that can handle a greater range of hardware, people, OSes, and languages.

Second, identity management is required to address safety and privacy threats related to AIIoT. By attempting to share identifying information amongst the devices for all first connections, managing identities in a network of devices can easily be accomplished. Such a procedure may be extremely vulnerable to eavesdropping, which may then lead to a man-in-the-middle assault and potentially jeopardise the entire architecture of AIIoT. To aid in preventing identity theft, there's consequently some significant need for a certain kind of preset management institution of identity or hubs that could track the whole connection between the necessary devices via the software's use of cryptography along with additional relevant techniques. The three-layer framework of AI-driven Internet of items, as described by the majority of authors, is never able to handle the real opening, closing, and proper administration of exchange between both existing items. Therefore, there is a huge demand for protocols that can deal with all of these problems and finally make communication between the required devices easier. An additional layer that can manage the protocols, connections, and pertinent sessions that are present among the communications across the pertinent heterogeneous devices must be accommodated as part of the framework of AIIoT.

As a result, AIIoT structures that are used for connected medical equipment and smart homes are highly vulnerable to various security and privacy risks. As a result, there are several security and privacy issues along with pertinent needs that need to be handled. With the development of today's technology, it's crucial to include additional novel network protocols, like IPv6, etc, to realise an evolving mashup of IoT topology. At the moment, most research on the issues of AIIoT focuses mainly on accessibility and authorization control protocols. The primary advancements in AIIoT have mainly occurred on smaller scales, like in little hospitals. Several security and privacy issues need to be properly addressed before AI-driven IoT can be expanded. Indeed, AIIoT will significantly change how we live today.

CONCLUSION

By enhancing detection and therapy, forecasting, developing and discovering drugs, automated assistants and Chatbots, and simplifying administrative processes, AI has the potential to advance health care greatly. To fully reap those benefits, however, significant issues like data privacy and its security, bias in the information, a lack of honesty and regulations, and a shortage of knowledge must be resolved. The author believes organisations in healthcare, authorities, and experts must work together to ensure that technology is used in an ethical, practical, and beneficial way. Hospitals can now fully utilise data from sources such as CT scanning and medical records thanks to novel AI and IoT developments. Even when they are not at the facility, these tools enable doctors to perform remote assessments of individuals' health and determine which ones require urgent care. Additionally, they can improve the precision of diagnoses for several disorders, including cancer of the breast and lungs.

ABBREVIATION

AI Artificial intelligence
IoT Internet of Things
ANN Artificial neural network
CNNs Convolutional neural networks
RHM Remote Healthcare Monitoring
HMS Healthcare Monitoring Services
6LoWPAN Low Power Wireless Area Network
WSN Wireless Sensor Network
NLP Natural Language Processing
ML Machine Learning
DL Deep Learning

REFERENCES

Aayula. (2022). Design and Implementation of sensor and IoT based Remembrance system for closed one. *Telematique, 21*(1), 2769–2778.

Akansha, K. (2022). Email Security. *Journal of Image Processing and Intelligent remote sensing, 2*(6).

Almotiri. S. (2016). Mobile health system in the context of IoT. *2016 IEEE 4th International Conference on Future Internet of Things and Cloud Workshops*. IEEE. doi:10.1109/W-FiCloud.2016.24

Babitha, M. (2022). Trends of Artificial Intelligence for online exams in education. *International journal of Early Childhood special. Education, 14*(01), 2457–2463.

Chinthamu. (2023). Self-Secure firmware model for Blockchain-Enabled IOT environment to Embedded system. *European Chemical Bulletin, 12*(S3), 653–660. 10.31838/ecb/2023.12.s3.075

Devi, S. (2022). A path towards child-centric Artificial Intelligence based Education. *International Journal of Early Childhood special. Education, 14*(03), 9915–9922.

Dixit. (2014). A Review paper on Iris Recognition. *Journal GSD International society for green. Sustainable Engineering and Management, 1*(14), 71–81.

Dixit. (2015). Iris Recognition by Daugman's Algorithm – an Efficient Approach. *Journal of applied Research and Social Sciences,* 2(14), 1 - 4.

Dziak, D. (2017). IoT-based information system for healthcare application: design methodology approach. *mdpi.com.* doi:10.3390/app7060596

(2022). Halli. Nanotechnology in IoT Security. *Journal of Nanoscience. Nanoengineering & Applications, 12*(3), 11–16.

Javaid, M., & Khan, I. H. (2021). Internet of Things (IoT) enabled healthcare helps to take the challenges of COVID-19 Pandemic. *Journal of Oral Biology and Craniofacial Research, 11*(2), 209–214. doi:10.1016/j.jobcr.2021.01.015 PMID:33665069

(2023). K S. Detection of Malicious Nodes in IoT Networks based on Throughput and ML. *Journal of Electrical and Power System Engineering, 9*(1), 22–29.

Kalmkar, S., Mujawar, A., & Liyakat, D. K. K. S. (2022). 3D E-Commers using AR. *International Journal of Information Technology & Computer Engineering, 2*(6), 18–27. doi:10.55529/ijitc.26.18.27

Kamuni. (2022). Fruit Quality Detection using Thermometer. *Journal of Image Processing and Intelligent Remote Sensing, 2*(5).

K. Kazi. Lassar Methodology for Network Intrusion Detection. *Scholarly Research Journal for Humanity science and English Language,* 2017, Vol 4, Issue 24, pp.6853 - 6861.

Kazi, K. (2022). Smart Grid energy saving technique using Machine Learning. *Journal of Instrumentation Technology and Innovations, 12*(3), 1–10.

Kazi, K. (2022). *Systematic Survey on Alzheimer (AD).* Diseases Detection.

Kazi, K. S. (2023). IoT based Healthcare system for Home Quarantine People. *Journal of Instrumentation and Innovation Sciences, 8*(1), 1–8.

Kazi, S. L. (2018). Significance of Projection and Rotation of Image in Color Matching for High-Quality Panoramic Images used for Aquatic study. *International Journal of Aquatic Science, 09*(02), 130–145.

(2022). Kazi. IoT-Based Healthcare Monitoring for COVID-19 Home Quarantined Patients. *Recent Trends in Sensor Research & Technology, 9*(3), 26–32.

Kazi. Model for Agricultural Information system to improve crop yield using IoT. *Journal of open Source Development,* 2022, Vol 9, Issue 2, pp. 16 – 24.

(2022). Kazi. Reverse Engineering's Neural Network Approach to human brain. *Journal of Communication Engineering & Systems, 12*(2), 17–24.

(2017). Kazi. S. Significance And Usage Of Face Recognition System. *Scholarly Journal For Humanity Science and English Language, 4*(20), 4764–4772.

(2018). Kosgiker. Machine Learning- Based System, Food Quality Inspection and Grading in Food industry. *International Journal of Food and Nutritional Sciences, 11*(10), 723–730.

Kumtole, S. (2022). Automatic wall painting robot Automatic wall painting robot. *Journal of Image Processing and Intelligent remote sensing, 2*(6).

Mazin. (2022). IoT and artificial intelligence implementations for remote healthcare monitoring systems: A survey. *Computer and Information Sciences, 34*(8), 4687-4701

Nagare, S. (2014). Different Segmentation Techniques for brain tumor detection: A Survey. *MM- International society for green. Sustainable Engineering and Management, 1*(14), 29–35.

Nagare, S. (2015). An Efficient Algorithm brain tumor detection based on Segmentation and Thresholding. Journal of Management in Manufacturing and services, 2.

Nikita, K. (2020). Design of Vehicle system using CAN Protocol. *International Journal for Research in Applied Science and Engineering Technology, 8*(V), 1978–1983. doi:10.22214/ijraset.2020.5321

Nikita, S. (2022). Announcement system in Bus. *Journal of Image Processing and Intelligent remote sensing, 2*(6).

Pardeshi. (2022). Development of Machine Learning based Epileptic Seizureprediction using Web of Things (WoT). *NeuroQuantology : An Interdisciplinary Journal of Neuroscience and Quantum Physics, 20*(8), 9394–9409.

Pardeshi. (2022). Implementation of Fault Detection Framework for Healthcare Monitoring System Using IoT, Sensors in Wireless Environment. *Telematique, 21*(1), 5451–5460.

Peña. (2014). *Ontology agents and their applications in the web-based education systems: towards an adaptive and intelligent service artificial intelligence on education view project.* Springer. doi:10.1007/978-3-540-88071-4_11

Pradeepa, M. (2022). Student Health Detection using a Machine Learning Approach and IoT. *2022 IEEE 2nd Mysore sub section International Conference (MysuruCon).* IEEE.

Rahman. (2020). Intelligent waste management system using deep learning with IoT. *Journal of King Saud University. Computer and Information Sciences.* doi:10.1016/j.jksuci.2020.08.016

(2023). Rajesh. Modelo De Apariencia Discriminatorio Para Un Sólido Seguimiento En Línea De Múltiples Objetivos. *Telematique, 22*(1), 24–43.

Ravi. (2012). *Pattern Recognition- An Approach towards Machine Learning.* Lambert Publications.

Raza, U., Kulkarni, P., & Sooriyabandara, M. (2017). Low power wide area networks: An overview. *IEEE Communications Surveys and Tutorials, 19*(2), 855–873. doi:10.1109/COMST.2017.2652320

(2022). S. L. Predict the Severity of Diabetes cases, using K-Means and Decision Tree Approach. *Journal of Advances in Shell Programming, 9*(2), 24–31.

Shirgan. (2010). Face Recognition based on Principal Component Analysis and Feed Forward Neural Network. *National Conference on Emerging trends in Engineering, Technology, Architecture*. IEEE.

Sreenivasulu. (2022). Implementation of Latest machine learning approaches for students Grade Prediction. *International Journal of Early Childhood special. Education, 14*(03), 9887–9894.

Tadlagi. (2022). Depression Detection. [JHMIB]. *Journal of Mental Health Issues and Behavior, 2*(6), 1–7.

Tanaka, Y., Minet, P., & Watteyne, T. (2019). Tanaka. 6LoWPAN fragment forwarding. *IEEE Commun. Stand. Mag, 3*(1), 35–39. doi:10.1109/MCOMSTD.2019.1800029

Vahida. (2023). Deep Learning, YOLO and RFID based smart Billing Handcart. *Journal of Communication Engineering & Systems, 13*(1), 1–8.

Veenis, J. F., & Brugts, J. J. (2020). Remote monitoring of chronic heart failure patients: Invasive versus non-invasive tools for optimising patient management. Netherlands. *The Hearing Journal, 28*(1), 3–13. doi:10.100712471-019-01342-8 PMID:31745814

Vinay. (2022). *Multiple object detection and classification based on Pruning using YOLO*. Lambart Publications.

Waghmare. (2022). Smart watch system. [IJITC]. *International Journal of Information Technology and Computer Engineering, 2*(6), 1–9.

Wale. (2019). Smart Agriculture System using IoT. *International Journal of Innovative Research In Technology, 5*(10), 493–497.

Chapter 4
Artificial Intelligence and Machine Learning Models for Alzheimer's Disease

Ananya Gambhir
University of Petroleum and Energy Studies, India

Ansh Bansal
University of Petroleum and Energy Studies, India

Saurabh Rawat
Graphic Era University, India

Anushree Sah
 https://orcid.org/0000-0003-3444-5860
University of Petroleum and Energy Studies, India

ABSTRACT

Alzheimer's disease is a brain disorder that slowly destroys memory and thinking skills and, eventually, the ability to carry out the simplest tasks. In most people with the disease, those with the late-onset type symptoms first appear in their mid-60s. Early-onset Alzheimer's occurs between a person's 30s and mid-60s and is very rare. Alzheimer's disease is the most common cause of dementia among older adults. Early diagnosis of Alzheimer's disease is essential for the progress of more prevailing treatments. Machine learning (ML), a branch of artificial intelligence, employs a variety of probabilistic and optimization techniques that permits PCs to gain from vast and complex datasets. As a result, researchers focus on using machine learning frequently for diagnosis of early stages of Alzheimer's disease. This project presents a review, analysis and critical evaluation of the recent work done for the early detection of Alzheimer's disease using ML techniques.

DOI: 10.4018/979-8-3693-0639-0.ch004

INTRODUCTION

Background on Alzheimer's Disease

Alzheimer's is a neurological disorder that is responsible for the gradual damage of the brain cells which leads to serious issues like memory loss, low functioning, and behavioural changes. This condition leads to the most frequent cause of dementia, which is a term that describes a decrease in mental ability affecting daily life routine. This disease was first discovered by Doctor Alois Alzheimer, in 1906, who identified several abnormal clumps along with tangled bundles of fibres in the brain tissue of a human who then died due to an unknown mental illness. These clumps and tangles, which are the primary indicators of this disease are now known as amyloid plaques and neurofibrillary tangles. Further adding, the lost connections found between neurons in the brain is another significant characteristic leading this disorder. Neurons are responsible to carry these messages and signals to different parts of the body from our human brain.

Alzheimer's disease has affected 5 million people and more according to recent researches in the United States yearly and it is expected to increase with the growth in the population. Though the main cause of this ailment is yet to be fully understood, according to the researches it is thought to result from a combination of factors including genetics, environment, along with lifestyle. Development of Alzheimer's disease is associated with age, congenital genes, high blood pressure, cholesterol, as well as head injury. Alzheimer's progression is basically classified into three stages: mild, moderate, and excess. Memory loss as well as difficulty with language and problem-solving are usual in the mild stage, while trouble with daily activities, personality, and behaviour changes may occur in the moderate stage. Lastly, in the severe or excess stage, patients tend to require complete care from others i.e. they become dependent on others and may even lose the ability to do basic things (Boschetti et al., 2018).

Alzheimer's disease, a state where abnormal proteins get assembled up in the brain, causing damage to brain cells, which in due course results in cognitive function loss and in worst cases death also. The initial symptoms of Alzheimer's include inconvenience in recalling recent events, language impairment, mood and behaviour changes, and may even face problems in performing one's basic duties like eating or dressing (Jain et al., 2018). In the far stages of this disease, one may experience more severe memory loss, confusion, and may feel hard to do daily activities. Although a cure for Alzheimer's is not yet available, but there exists treatments and medications from the latest research that can help manage symptoms and slow down the progression of this disease. To investigate the root causes of Alzheimer's with a view to add to more effective treatments and eventually finding a cure we have several studies ongoing. (Sah, Bhadula, et al., 2018).

Overview of AI and ML Models

Alzheimer's disease is degenerative and irreversible brain condition that impacts memory, cognition, and conduct. At present, there is no definitive recognition or remedy available for this disease. Artificial intelligence and machine learning models are being utilized by the researchers which will help to create new diagnostic tools and improve their understanding of the disease. AI by helping with analysis and research has altered the way data is analysed and utilized, and it keeps the potential to bring a big and a benefitable revolution in medical care by advancing and giving fast, low-cost, and accurate automation (Sah et al., 2021). Various studies have been conducted and are conducting to improve and upgrade data along with information on these complicated diseases such as Alzheimer's using AI algorithms that exploit the features of Machine(Gupta & Kumar, 2023). Machine Learning (ML) and Deep Learning (DL) techniques are mainly used by AI to create these algorithms which are further applied in the bio-medical and clinical fields. These algorithms integrate and process a large amount of data sources, which includes neuroimaging, biochemical markers, clinical data, and neuropsychological (NPS) data from both patients and controls. The primary applications of AI in the biomedical field includes Computer-Aided Diagnosis (CAD), which then automates the diagnostic process and supports and assists in early and differential diagnosis of AD or dementia of various aetiology. Unfortunately, despite this substantial exploration, there is still no cure for these diseases. Yet, some clinical trials are at present underway, by using monoclonal antibodies which target different Aβ species, including monomeric and aggregated oligomers (Sah, Dumka, et al., 2018). Research has indicated that some treatments are both safe and effective for Alzheimer's patients. However, artificial intelligence (AI) can be leveraged to automate the synthesis of compounds by analysing literature and screening data. By updating the AI model based on cell-based or organoid-based experiments, the technology can suggest a plan for molecular optimization and perform bioassays to assess the after effects. This automated drug development cycle based on AI design can expedite the creation of new drugs. Additionally, AI can be utilized to repurpose existing drugs for Alzheimer's treatment through the analysis of huge scale metabolome, molecular structure data, and clinical databases. This approach offers a cost-effective and rapid pathway to drug development (Finney et al., 2023). AI technology can be utilized to streamline clinical trials in both the planning and execution stages. By analyzing various data through AI algorithms, participant selection can be optimized to determine which population subset may respond positively to new drugs. If wearable data is coupled with AI, real-time non-invasive diagnostics can be provided, which may prevent subject drop-out. Although not many AI applications have been implemented in clinical trials, this technology shows potential to aid research and create new effective therapies. In Alzheimer's disease research, various AI and ML models have been developed (Rawat & Sah, 2013).

The different models used for predicting Alzheimer's disease include predictive models, image analysis models, and natural language processing models. Predictive models use patient data to predict the possibility of developing AD and to predict the advancement of the disease in already diagnosed patients. Image analysis models utilize imaging techniques like MRI and PET to analyse brain scans for AD signs and track changes over time (Rawat & Sah, 2012)(Sah et al., 2020). NLP models analyse written or spoken language to identify patterns or markers that may indicate AD, such as changes in vocabulary or syntax in speech patterns or written language(Tăuţan et al., 2021).

To recognize this disease (AD) and track its progression, cognitive testing models that involve memory or reasoning tests are employed. There are models that aims to develop biomarkers for AD through a combination of predictive models, image analysis models, and cognitive testing models they are called the neuroimaging initiative in short term also called ADNI. Another AI and ML model, the DeepAD, uses deep learning techniques to analyse MRI scans and predict the progression of AD with high accuracy. These models are providing valuable insights into AD diagnosis and progression, which can improve early detection, monitor treatment effectiveness, and lead to better treatments and a cure for this disease(Rawat & Kumar, 2020)(Muhammed Niyas & Thiyagarajan, 2023).

LITERATURE REVIEW ON AI AND ML MODELS FOR ALZHEIMER'S DIAGNOSIS

Introduction to AI and ML Models for Alzheimer's Diagnosis

Alzheimer's disease is a forging ahead brain condition which proceeds to negatively affect our memory, reasoning, behaviour adding up to overall brain related activities. Unfortunately, there is currently no medication known to eliminate and cure this degenerative illness. Nonetheless, early detection and proper treatment can help delay the disease's progression and improve and extend the overall life quality. Artificial intelligence (AI) and machine learning (ML) models can help assist in the timely detection of Alzheimer's by analysing vast amounts of data to collect new patterns and relationships that are invisible to our human naked eye. By inspecting brain scans, for instance, these models can look over and examine changes in brain structure and activity that are indicative of the disease. Additionally, they can also survey cognitive tests and genetic markers to detect early signs of the illness. One way to use these models for Alzheimer's diagnosis is to train them using large sets of brain scans and cognitive tests(Shirbandi et al., 2021).

The probability of developing Alzheimer's disease is predicted by the use of different models in analysis of the new patient data. This prediction can assist doctors in making early diagnoses and promptly initiating treatment. Additionally, AI and ML models may be adopted to monitor the progression of the disease over time by examining changes in brain activity and structure. By doing so, doctors can adjust treatment plans accordingly to slow down disease progression. In general, the use of advanced AI and ML technologies has the power to significantly transform the diagnosis and effective treatment of Alzheimer's disease by enabling early detection and providing more effective treatments (García-Garví et al., 2023).

Review of Current Research on AI and ML Models for Alzheimer's Diagnosis

Alzheimer's disease is a widespread neurodegenerative condition impacting numerous individuals globally. Scientists are investigating the use of AI and ML to assist in the early diagnosis of Alzheimer's disease due to advancements in technology. Studies have analyzed the research literature on the implementation of AI models in the early detection of dementia in grownups. The review of outcome data has demonstrated that AI or ML structure can have a significant impact on any minor specialty within AOCD during every treatment stage. For prediction of dementia types ahead of time, ANN, MRI data, and labelling segments have been the most often used. Many studies have established the potential of AI and ML models to accurately detect Alzheimer's disease and anticipate its progression. There are several notable research studies in this area(Ammour et al., 2020).

- According to a report in the Journal of Alzheimer's Disease, a research study utilized machine learning methods to examine MRI scans of patients who had Alzheimer's disease and individuals who were healthy. This model has successfully predicted the disease status of people with a high level of accuracy(Yu et al., 2023).
- A research published in the Journal of Alzheimer's Disease utilized machine learning to scrutinize PET scans of both Alzheimer's disease patients and healthy individuals. The model was capable of detecting slight alterations in brain metabolism that are related to the illness.
- The Journal of Medical Systems published a study that utilized a deep learning method to examine medical images of individuals who have Alzheimer's disease. The results stated that the model iden-

tified the disease with great accuracy, demonstrating strong sensitivity and specificity(Parimbelli et al., 2021).

- A group of experts at the University of California, Berkeley has created an AI system that can predict Alzheimer's disease with great accuracy by examining speech patterns. The model examines various linguistic traits, such as fillers, pauses, and grammatical mistakes, to make its predictions.
- A study that was recently published in Nature Communications utilized both AI and traditional statistical methods to examine extensive genetic information in order to discover new genetic risk factors for Alzheimer's disease. No information has been left out in the paraphrased text(Pereira et al., 2019).

Deep learning, a type of ML, uses a hierarchical learning process to learn features. It has been used in different fields including AI & ML for classification or prediction. Deep learning is considered an advanced pioneering approach for machine learning which has shown impressive performance in identifying complex structures in high-dimensional data, especially in computer future vision. Recently, there has been considerable attention in this field for timely perception and preprogrammed classification of this disease. This is due to the availability of large-scale multimodal neuroimaging datasets generated by rapid progress in neuroimaging techniques. For the identification of deep learning papers which were between Jan 2013 and July 2018 were published, a structured analysis of issuing was then made using deep structured learning undertaking with neuroimaging data for diagnostic classification of AD was performed, using a PubMed and Google Scholar search engine. The algorithm and neuroimaging type were used to review, evaluate, and classify papers, and the results were summarized. Out of the 16 studies that met the inclusion criteria, less than 5 used a combination of traditional intelligent retrieval and deep learning, while the remaining 12 used only deep learning methods (Abood & Abdul-Majeed, 2023). The accuracy of AD classification and the prediction of conversion from MCI to AD was up to 98.8% and 83.7%, respectively, when traditional machine learning was combined with stacked auto-encoder for feature selection. Deep learning approaches such as CNN and RNN, which used neuroimaging data, with perfect accuracies up to 96.0% for categorization and 84.2% for MCI conversion projection. The highest categorization interpretation was achieved on the combination of multimodal neuroimaging and fluid biomarkers. The use of deep learning techniques is becoming more advanced and seems to show potential for accurately diagnosing Alzheimer's disease through a combination of different types of neuroimaging data. The use of deep structured learning in Alzheimer's research is still developing, with efforts to incorporate new types of data, such as omics data, and to increase the transparency of the diagnostic process. Overall, studies indicate that AI and machine learning models have the potential to make early diagnosis and prediction of Alzheimer's disease possible, but more research is necessary to verify their effectiveness and make them a part of clinical practice (Khojaste-Sarakhsi et al., 2022).

Discussion of Benefits and Limitations of Using AI and ML Models for Alzheimer's Diagnosis

Millions of people worldwide are affected by Alzheimer's which is a disorder damaging our brain, its early diagnosis can be difficult. However, AI and ML models are capable to transform the diagnosis and treatment of Alzheimer's disease. Despite their advantages, AI and ML models also have drawbacks:

- Increased accuracy: AI and ML models can analyse large datasets and detect patterns which are many often missed by human experts.
- Early detection: AI and ML models can identify subtle changes in brain structure and function that may indicate Alzheimer's disease, allowing for earlier detection and intervention intervention thus improving the overall life quality.
- Cost-effective: AI and ML models can reduce the cost of Alzheimer's diagnosis and treatment by automating tasks that would otherwise require human expertise.
- Customizable: AI and ML models can be customized to fit the specific needs of specific group of individuals, taking into account factors such as age, gender, and medical history resulting in faster results.
- Improved patient outcomes: The detections made by the use of AI & ML models are more accurate resulting in earlier detection and personalized treatment plans can lead to improved patient outcomes and quality of life for those with Alzheimer's disease (Xu et al., 2023).

Limitations of using AI and ML models for Alzheimer's diagnosis:

- Data bias:: AI and ML models rely on large datasets to train and learn from, and if these datasets are biased or incomplete, the models may produce inaccurate or discriminatory results and leading to more miserable conditions of the patients suffering from it.
- Lack of transparency: AI and ML models can be complex, and it can be challenging to understand how they make their decisions, making it difficult to identify potential errors or biases(Veverka et al., 2023).
- Limited availability: AI and ML models require significant computational resources, making them less accessible to smaller healthcare providers and low-income patients.
- Ethical concerns: The use of AI and ML models raises ethical concerns around privacy, data security, and the potential misuse of patient data.
- Legal and regulatory challenges: The use of AI and ML models in healthcare is subject to legal and regulatory challenges, and there is a need for clear guidelines and regulations to ensure patient safety and privacy(Liu et al., 2023).

To add up, using AI & ML models for diagnosis of Alzheimer's disease shows various notable changes and advancements, better precision early detection of the disease therefore resulting in better treatment and results for patient. Though these models have their limitations and ethical consideration that need to be resolved before these models are put in extensive use everywhere.

AI AND ML MODELS FOR ALZHEIMER'S TREATMENT AND MANAGEMENT

Introduction to AI and ML Models for Alzheimer's Treatment and Management

Alzheimer's is a degenerative mind problem that influences memory, thinking and conduct. As of now there no remedy for Alzheimer's infection, and treatment centres around overseeing side effects and lessening the progression of the illness.AI and ML have the potential to help develop more effective treatments for dementia by providing insights into disease mechanisms and facilitating the identification of potential therapeutic goals.

One potential application of AI and ML in the research of this disease research is the discovery of biomarkers. Biomarkers are measurable markers of disease that can be used to diagnose and track disease progression. AI and ML algorithms can be used on large datasets of patient profiles and biomarker data to get a hold of the patterns and relationships that may predict Alzheimer's disease.

Another potential application of AI and ML in Alzheimer's disease research is to find new and more efficient drugs for the treatment of the disease. AI and ML algorithms can be used to analyse large databases of drug compounds and predict their potential efficacy in the treatment of Alzheimer's.

Concluding, AI and ML significantly influences the advancement of Alzheimer's related treatments. Through the advancement in this technology, researchers can get new insights of the disease mechanisms, identify biomarkers, discover new drugs, and personalised treatment regimens for patients.

Review of Current Research on AI and ML Models for Alzheimer's Treatment and Management

There is a growing body of researchers focusing on the application of AI and ML in Alzheimer's disease research. Here are some recent examples of research in this area:

Deep learning algorithms to identify biomarkers: A study published in the journal Alzheimer's & Dementia used a deep learning algorithm to analyse MRI images and identify brain atrophy that may indicate Alzheimer's disease the. The researchers found that their deep learning algorithms were able to accurately predict which patients would develop Alzheimer's over the next two years(Nadda et al., 2023).

Predictive models for drug discovery: A study published in the Journal of Chemical Information and Modelling used machine learning to analyse large databases of chemical compounds and determine their potential performance effectively for the treatment of Alzheimer's disease. The researchers found several promising compounds that could be tested further in clinical trials(Muniraj et al., 2023).

Personalized treatment planning: A study published in the Journal of Alzheimer's Disease used machine learning to analyse patient data and identify subgroups of patients with different disease trajectories. Research has found that patients of different subgroups are responding differently to different treatments thus lowering the trust, the power of personalized treatments planned for Alzheimer's disease for different patients through AI & ML models. (Fanourgakis et al., 2023).

AI-powered virtual assistants for dementia patients are being researched at the University of Waterloo where researchers have developed an AI-powered virtual assistant which then helps patients with dementia to perform their everyday tasks such as reminding appointments and taking medication so as for their speedy recovery. Natural language is being used the virtual assistant to process machine learning algorithms to understand the patient's needs and provide personalized assistance for each patient using this service.

In conclusion, these studies are demonstrating the potential of AI and ML in the recognition, detection and treatment of Alzheimer's disease. However, more research is needed to validate these findings and the researchers ae on it to determine how to integrate this technology into clinical practice in the best way. (Yang et al., 2023).

Discussion of Benefits and Limitations of Using AI and ML Models for Alzheimer's Treatment and Management

There are several benefits for using AI and ML models for the treatment of this ailment, which include:

Improved correctness along with performance: AI and ML algorithms can analyze vast patient datasets and discover various patterns and relationships useful that might not be readily apparent to human researchers. This can lead to more accurate diagnosis, appropriate treatment, and effective medications.

Personalized treatment plans: AI and ML algorithms are helpful in analysing patient data to identify individual characteristics of each patient and treatment preferences, resulting in more personalized, perfect and effective treatments along with better plans(Singh et al., 2016).

Cost savings: By identifying more effective treatments using these techniques, AI and ML algorithms can lower the cost of drug development and healthcare delivery for Alzheimer's patients.

However, there also include many limitations as well as challenges associated with the use of AI and ML models for the medical care and management of Alzheimer's disease, including:

Data quality along with bias: Large datasets to identify patterns and correlations are in use by AI and ML. If by chance the data is of poor quality or biased in some way (e.g., include only a limited number of patients), the results will not be accurate or representative(Chen et al., 2023).

Ethical concerns: There are various ethical concerns surrounding the use of AI and ML algorithms in healthcare, which includes different concerns regarding data privacy, algorithmic bias, along with the potential for AI to replace human clinics.

Lack of insight: Some AI and ML algorithms are difficult to interpret as well as understand therefore making it difficult to know how a particular diagnosis or recommendation was arrived at.

Limited resources: While AI and ML algorithms have shown promise in Alzheimer's research, they are not yet widely available for clinical use, and more research is needed to prove their efficacy and safety.

Overall, while AI and ML models have the potential to revolutionize the treatment and management of Alzheimer's disease, it is important to carefully consider the benefits and limitations and ensure their use in morally and responsibly(Leela et al., 2023).

RESULTS AND DISCUSSION OF AI AND ML MODELS FOR ALZHEIMER'S

Datasets

A Dataset containing almost 2 Lakh 14 thousand entries has been pick from the official site of U.S Department of Health And Human Services.
https://catalog.data.gov/dataset/alzheimers-disease-and-heal
thy-aging-data

Graphs and Reports

The above Figure 1 shows the pandas generated report from Year start to Year end. From the year 2015-2020.

The above Figure 2 depicts the locations where the disease has been detected, where the research was conducted, in the form of location abbreviation and location description.

Figure 1. Research articles trend for AI in Alzheimer disease from Elsvier

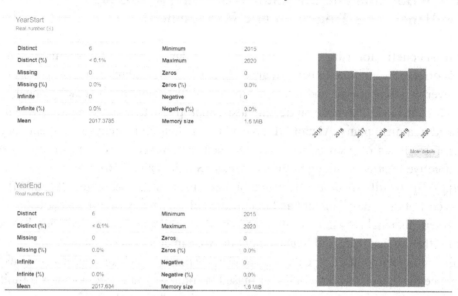

Figure 2. Locations where disease been detected

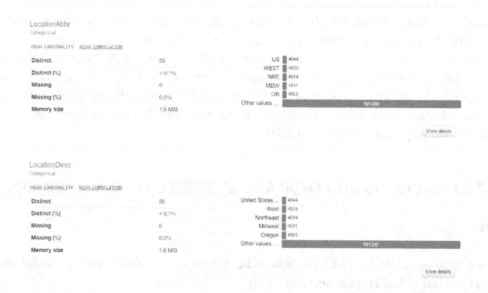

The above Figure 3 depicts the Alzheimer's affected areas in the body i.e., affected mental health along with overall health.

The above Figure 4 shows the causes of the disease.

The above Figure 5 shows the age group of the affected disease.

The above graph shows the affected regions Figure 6.

The above Figure 7 depicts the correlation Heatmap.

Figure 3. Alzheimer's affected areas i.e., affected mental health along with overall health

Figure 4. Causes of the disease

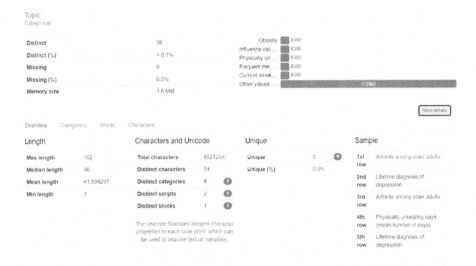

Code

```
import pandas as pd
from pandas_profiling import ProfileReport
df=pd.read_csv('Alzheimer_s_Disease_and_Healthy_Aging_Data.csv')
print(df)
profile=ProfileReport(df)
```

Figure 5. Age group of the affected disease

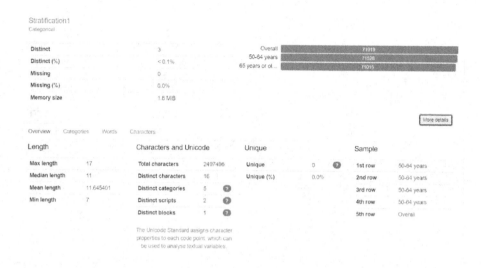

Figure 6. Affected regions

```
profile.to_file(output_file="Alzheimer_s_Disease_and_Healthy_Aging_Data.html")
sorted_dataset=df.sort_values('YearStart')
print(sorted_dataset)
sorted_dataset=df.sort_values('LocationDesc')
print(sorted_dataset)
sorted_dataset=df.sort_values('LocationID')
print(sorted_dataset)
```

Figure 7. Correlation Heatmap

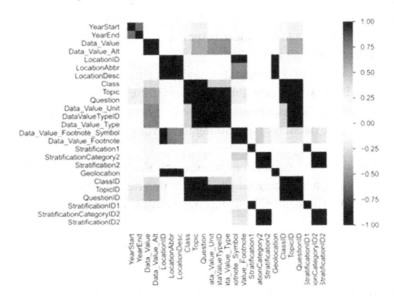

FUTURE DIRECTIONS AND CONCLUSION

Discussion of Likely Future Directions for Research and Development of AI and ML Models for Alzheimer's

The evolution and implementation of AI and ML models for the analysis of Alzheimer's treatment is an ongoing area of investigation, and there are several potential future directions for research and growth in this field:

1. Integration with other mechanisms: Wearables and sensors can lay out precious data on a patient's activity level, sleep patterns, with several other physiological measures which are then merged with clinical data for the better accuracy of diagnoses and treatment plans(Yin et al., 2023). The examples include, wearable devices could be used to track changes in a patient's gait, which has been shown to be a predictor of the decay in Alzheimer's disease.

2. Longitudinal studies: Longitudinal studies are used to track patients over time are important for understanding the procedure of Alzheimer's disease and the potency of treatments. AI and ML models analyses large amounts of longitudinal data and get a hold of the patterns and correlations that may be prophetic of disease continuation. For example, researchers could use AI algorithms to analyse brain imaging data to recognize changes in brain structure and function that may indicate the onset of Alzheimer's disease.

3. Multi-modal data analysis: The data analysis here involves combining data from various sources, like brain imaging, genetic data, and patient's records to provide a more comprehensive understanding of Alzheimer's disease. AI and ML models can be used to identify biomarkers and possibility for the disease, which could help identify patients at high risk for developing Alzheimer's.

4. Clinical verdict: AI and ML models can provide clinical decision support for healthcare providers treating patients with Alzheimer's disease. For example, visionary models that use patient data to predict disease progression and treatment response can be made, which could inform treatment decisions and better the patient results.

5. Cooperation and data allocation: Cooperation and data allocation are essential for the development and validation of AI and ML models for Alzheimer's research and treatment. Open data sharing creativity and partnership between public and private operations can help speeding in this field by providing access to large datasets and enabling the development of sturdy AI and ML models.

In conclusion, the potential future directions for research along with growth of AI and ML models for Alzheimer's disease are huge, and continued progress in this field by our researchers has the potential to transfigure the diagnosis, treatment, and management of this devastating disease.

REFERENCES

Abood, M. J. K., & Abdul-Majeed, G. H. (2023). Classification of network slicing threats based on slicing enablers: A survey. *International Journal of Intelligent Networks*, *4*(April), 103–112. doi:10.1016/j.ijin.2023.04.002

Ammour, A., Aouraghe, I., Khaissidi, G., Mrabti, M., Aboulem, G., & Belahsen, F. (2020). A new semi-supervised approach for characterizing the Arabic on-line handwriting of Parkinson's disease patients. *Computer Methods and Programs in Biomedicine*, *183*, 104979. doi:10.1016/j.cmpb.2019.07.007 PMID:31542687

Boschetti, E., D'Amato, A., Candiano, G., & Righetti, P. G. (2018). Protein biomarkers for early detection of diseases: The decisive contribution of combinatorial peptide ligand libraries. *Journal of Proteomics*, *188*, 1–14. doi:10.1016/j.jprot.2017.08.009 PMID:28882677

Chen, R., Cai, N., Luo, Z., Wang, H., Liu, X., & Li, J. (2023). Multi-task banded regression model: A novel individual survival analysis model for breast cancer. *Computers in Biology and Medicine*, *162*(April), 107080. doi:10.1016/j.compbiomed.2023.107080 PMID:37271111

Fanourgakis, S., Synacheri, A. C., Lavigne, M. D., Konstantopoulos, D., & Fousteri, M. (2023). Histone H2Bub dynamics in the 5′ region of active genes are tightly linked to the UV-induced transcriptional response. *Computational and Structural Biotechnology Journal*, *21*, 614–629. doi:10.1016/j.csbj.2022.12.013 PMID:36659919

Finney, C. A., Delerue, F., Gold, W. A., Brown, D. A., & Shvetcov, A. (2023). Artificial intelligence-driven meta-analysis of brain gene expression identifies novel gene candidates and a role for mitochondria in Alzheimer's disease. *Computational and Structural Biotechnology Journal*, *21*, 388–400. doi:10.1016/j.csbj.2022.12.018 PMID:36618979

García-Garví, A., Layana-Castro, P. E., & Sánchez-Salmerón, A. J. (2023). Analysis of a C. elegans lifespan prediction method based on a bimodal neural network and uncertainty estimation. *Computational and Structural Biotechnology Journal*, *21*, 655–664. doi:10.1016/j.csbj.2022.12.033 PMID:36659931

Gupta, N. S., & Kumar, P. (2023). Perspective of artificial intelligence in healthcare data management: A journey towards precision medicine. *Computers in Biology and Medicine, 162*(April), 107051. doi:10.1016/j.compbiomed.2023.107051 PMID:37271113

Jain, I., Jain, V. K., & Jain, R. (2018). Correlation feature selection based improved-Binary Particle Swarm Optimization for gene selection and cancer classification. *Applied Soft Computing, 62*, 203–215. doi:10.1016/j.asoc.2017.09.038

Khojaste-Sarakhsi, M., Haghighi, S. S., Ghomi, S. M. T. F., & Marchiori, E. (2022). Deep learning for Alzheimer's disease diagnosis: A survey. *Artificial Intelligence in Medicine, 130*(June), 102332. doi:10.1016/j.artmed.2022.102332 PMID:35809971

Leela, M., Helenprabha, K., & Sharmila, L. (2023). Prediction and classification of Alzheimer Disease categories using Integrated Deep Transfer Learning Approach. *Measurement. Sensors, 27*(March), 100749. doi:10.1016/j.measen.2023.100749

Liu, Q., Gao, C., Zhao, Y., Huang, S., Zhang, Y., Dong, X., & Lu, Z. (2023). Health warning based on 3R ECG Sample's combined features and LSTM. *Computers in Biology and Medicine, 162*(April), 107082. doi:10.1016/j.compbiomed.2023.107082 PMID:37290388

Muhammed Niyas, K. P., & Thiyagarajan, P. (2023). A systematic review on early prediction of Mild cognitive impairment to alzheimers using machine learning algorithms. *International Journal of Intelligent Networks, 4*(April), 74–88. doi:10.1016/j.ijin.2023.03.004

Muniraj, P., Sabarmathi, K. R., Leelavathi, R., & Balaji, B. S. (2023). HNTSumm: Hybrid text summarization of transliterated news articles. *International Journal of Intelligent Networks, 4*(March), 53–61. doi:10.1016/j.ijin.2023.03.001

Nadda, R., Repaka, R., & Sahani, A. K. (2023). Honeybee stinger-based biopsy needle and influence of the barbs on needle forces during insertion/extraction into the iliac crest: A multilayer finite element approach. *Computers in Biology and Medicine, 162*(May), 107125. doi:10.1016/j.compbiomed.2023.107125 PMID:37290393

Parimbelli, E., Wilk, S., Cornet, R., Sniatala, P., Sniatala, K., Glaser, S. L. C., Fraterman, I., Boekhout, A. H., Ottaviano, M., & Peleg, M. (2021). A review of AI and Data Science support for cancer management. *Artificial Intelligence in Medicine, 117*(August 2020), 102111. doi:10.1016/j.artmed.2021.102111

Pereira, C. R., Pereira, D. R., Weber, S. A. T., Hook, C., de Albuquerque, V. H. C., & Papa, J. P. (2019). A survey on computer-assisted Parkinson's Disease diagnosis. *Artificial Intelligence in Medicine, 95*(August 2018), 48–63. doi:10.1016/j.artmed.2018.08.007

Rawat, S., & Kumar, R. (2020). Direct-Indirect Link Matrix: A Black Box Testing Technique for Component-Based Software. *International Journal of Information Technology Project Management, 11*(4), 56–69. doi:10.4018/IJITPM.2020100105

Rawat, S., & Sah, A. (2012). An approach to Enhance the software and services of Health care centre. *AHA Journals, 3*(7), 126–137.

Rawat, S., & Sah, A. (2013). An Approach to Integrate Heterogeneous Web Applications. *International Journal of Computer Applications, 70*(23), 7–12. doi:10.5120/12205-7639

Roshini, A., & Kiran, K. V.D. (2023). Hierarchical energy efficient secure routing protocol for optimal route selection in wireless body area networks. *International Journal of Intelligent Networks, 4*, 19–28. doi:10.1016/j.ijin.2022.11.006

Sah, A., Bhadula, S. J., Dumka, A., & Rawat, S. (2018). A software engineering perspective for development of enterprise applications. Handbook of Research on Contemporary Perspectives on Web-Based Systems, (pp. 1–23). IGI Global. doi:10.4018/978-1-5225-5384-7.ch001

Sah, A., Choudhury, T., Rawat, S., & Tripathi, A. (2020). A Proposed Gene Selection Approach for Disease Detection. *Advances in Intelligent Systems and Computing, 1120*, 199–206. doi:10.1007/978-981-15-2449-3_16

Sah, A., Dumka, A., & Rawat, S. (2018). Web technology systems integration using SOA and web services. Handbook of Research on Contemporary Perspectives on Web-Based Systems, (pp. 24–45). IGI Global. doi:10.4018/978-1-5225-5384-7.ch002

Sah, A., Studies, E., Rawat, S., Choudhury, T., Studies, E., Dewangan, B. K., & Studies, E. (2021). An extensive Review of Web-Based Multi Granularity Service Composition. *International Journal of Web-Based Learning and Teaching Technologies, 17*(4), 0–0. doi:10.4018/IJWLTT.285570

Shirbandi, K., Khalafi, M., Mirza-Aghazadeh-Attari, M., Tahmasbi, M., Kiani Shahvandi, H., Javanmardi, P., & Rahim, F. (2021). Accuracy of deep learning model-assisted amyloid positron emission tomography scan in predicting Alzheimer's disease: A Systematic Review and meta-analysis. *Informatics in Medicine Unlocked, 25*(August), 100710. doi:10.1016/j.imu.2021.100710

Singh, G., Vadera, M., Samavedham, L., & Lim, E. C. H. (2016). Machine Learning-Based Framework for Multi-Class Diagnosis of Neurodegenerative Diseases: A Study on Parkinson's Disease. *IFAC-PapersOnLine, 49*(7), 990–995. doi:10.1016/j.ifacol.2016.07.331

Tăuţan, A. M., Ionescu, B., & Santarnecchi, E. (2021). Artificial intelligence in neurodegenerative diseases: A review of available tools with a focus on machine learning techniques. *Artificial Intelligence in Medicine, 117*(July 2020). doi:10.1016/j.artmed.2021.102081

Veverka, P., Brom, T., Janovič, T., Stojaspal, M., Pinkas, M., Nováček, J., & Hofr, C. (2023). Electron microscopy reveals toroidal shape of master neuronal cell differentiator REST – RE1-silencing transcription factor. *Computational and Structural Biotechnology Journal, 21*, 731–741. doi:10.1016/j.csbj.2022.12.026 PMID:36698979

Xu, J., Wang, Y., Zhang, J., Abdelmoneim, A. A., Liang, Z., Wang, L., Jin, J., Dai, Q., & Ye, F. (2023). Elastic network models and molecular dynamic simulations reveal the molecular basis of allosteric regulation in ubiquitin-specific protease 7 (USP7). *Computers in Biology and Medicine, 162*(March), 107068. doi:10.1016/j.compbiomed.2023.107068 PMID:37290391

Yang, M. J., Song, H., Shi, P., Liang, J., Hu, Z., Zhou, C., Hu, P. P., Yu, Z. L., & Zhang, T. (2023). Integrated mRNA and miRNA transcriptomic analysis reveals the response of Rapana venosa to the metamorphic inducer (juvenile oysters). *Computational and Structural Biotechnology Journal, 21,* 702–715. doi:10.1016/j.csbj.2022.12.047 PMID:36659925

Yin, B. K., Lázaro, D., & Wang, Z. Q. (2023). TRRAP-mediated acetylation on Sp1 regulates adult neurogenesis. *Computational and Structural Biotechnology Journal, 21,* 472–484. doi:10.1016/j. csbj.2022.12.024 PMID:36618986

Yu, H., Liu, C., Zhang, L., Wu, C., Liang, G., Escorcia-Gutierrez, J., & Ghoneim, O. A. (2023). An intent classification method for questions in "Treatise on Febrile diseases" based on TinyBERT-CNN fusion model. *Computers in Biology and Medicine, 162*(May), 107075. doi:10.1016/j.compbiomed.2023.107075 PMID:37276755

Chapter 5
A Smart Healthcare Diabetes Prediction System Using Ensemble of Classifiers

Ayush Yadav
Vellore Institute of Technology, Chennai, India

Bhuvaneswari Amma N. G.
https://orcid.org/0000-0003-3660-380X
Vellore Institute of Technology, Chennai, India

ABSTRACT

Throughout the world, diabetes is a life-threatening disease. This research study aims to develop a smart healthcare machine-learning model for diabetes prediction. The dataset is pre-processed to handle missing data and outliers, and feature selection techniques are used to identify the most relevant variables for the model. An ensemble of classifiers is built by combining logistic regression, XGBoost, random forest, and support vector machine. The performance of the proposed model is assessed using metrics such as accuracy, precision, recall, and F1-score. The results show that the random forest algorithm outperforms other models in terms of accuracy, precision, recall, and F1 score. The model achieves an accuracy of 85%, indicating that it can correctly predict diabetes in 85% of cases. In conclusion, this study demonstrates the feasibility of using machine learning models for diabetes prediction based on patient data. The model can be further improved by incorporating more extensive and diverse datasets and exploring more advanced machine-learning techniques.

INTRODUCTION

Recent research by the World Health Organization (WHO) shows that the number of people with diabetes is rising worldwide, as is their death rate. Based on these trends, the World Health Organization projected that diabetes will be the sixth major cause of death by 2030. One of the illnesses with the fastest global growth rates is diabetes (Ihnaini et al., 2021). Diabetes is characterized as a group of metabolic

DOI: 10.4018/979-8-3693-0639-0.ch005

disorders that raise blood glucose levels in people. The following are the two underlying causes of elevated glucose levels: (1) insufficient insulin production by the human body, and (2) inadequate insulin response by the body's cells. The hormone released by the pancreas, insulin, aids in controlling blood sugar levels. The blood sugar level should remain within the recommended range (3.6–6.9 mmol/l or 70–120 mg/dl). Hypoglycemia is defined as glucose levels below 50 mg/dl, which can cause increased thirst, perspiration, seizures, and diabetic coma. Clinically relevant tasks in diabetes treatment include hypoglycemic prediction. As hypoglycemia can cause dangerous side effects including seizures and coma, it is important to detect it early on and take precautions. There is evidence that higher glucose levels (>200 mg/dl) represent hyperglycemia, which can cause long-term vascular problems such as diabetic retinopathy, neuropathy, and nephropathy (El-Sappagh et al., 2019).

To improve the quality of life, appropriate glucose regulation requires supervision. Type-1, Type-2, and gestational diabetes are the three subtypes of diabetes (Kibria et al., 2022). When the beta cells that produce insulin in the pancreas are destroyed by the immune system, type 1 diabetes results. Approximately 10% of people have type 1 diabetes. While it is challenging to prevent, a therapy that involves giving the body insulin externally is an option. type 2 diabetes, on the other hand, results from improper utilization of the insulin produced by the pancreas. Diabetes type 2 is the most prevalent and affects people older than 45 years in about 90% of instances. Patients with type 2 diabetes have a 2 to 4 times higher risk of developing heart disease. Gestational diabetes is a type of diabetes that affects pregnant women. Blood glucometers are employed to measure diabetes throughout certain periods. Continuous glucose monitoring devices, which offer a less intrusive way to record the patient's current glycemic level, are used to test diabetes continually. The majority of the body's organs, such as the kidneys, eyes, heart, and nerves, among others, are impacted by delayed diabetes identification. Consequently, getting a precise and timely diagnosis of diabetes is essential. Appropriate data analysis becomes essential for the diagnosis and interpretation of diabetes when handling data as a classification problem for machine learning (ML). Therefore, it is very valuable to employ artificial intelligence to accurately anticipate diabetes.

Consequently, getting a precise and timely diagnosis of diabetes is essential. Appropriate data analysis becomes essential for the diagnosis and interpretation of diabetes when handling data as a classification problem for ML. Therefore, it is very valuable to employ artificial intelligence to accurately anticipate diabetes. To estimate a patient's risk of acquiring diabetes, machine learning algorithms can examine their genetic predispositions, lifestyle choices, and medical history. Patients can better manage their diabetes by using machine learning algorithms to monitor glucose levels in real-time and send alarms when levels are outside of the usual range. ML models can be used to identify the most effective treatment strategies for individual patients based on their unique medical history and other factors. ML and AI can help healthcare professionals make more informed decisions about diabetes prevention, management, and treatment, which can improve patient outcomes and reduce healthcare costs. With the use of machine learning, patients may easily confirm their health in the early stages, and it will also help practitioners with future research. It can be applied to problems with both regression and classification (Ganie & Malik, 2022). Due to the classification challenge nature of diabetes prediction, we group individuals according to their diabetes status. Numerous ML techniques are useful for evaluating and synthesizing the data into pertinent knowledge from various perspectives. As a part of ML datasets must be prepared features must be selected and extracted, training and testing, and additional assessment. Clinical data, text data, and sensor data are just a few examples of the several types of data that are gathered utilizing various wearable technology, most of which is in raw form. Preprocessing, which includes managing missing values in the dataset and imputing missing values to enable accurate predictions, is necessary to convert this data into a usable format. The dataset has a wide range of features; selecting the most important attributes from the feature space is essential to producing the most accurate forecast. ML techniques including support vector machines (SVM), decision trees (DT), neural networks (NN), and random forests (RF) can be applied to effectively predict diabetes. These models are tested using the test dataset after training to see if they are functioning as intended. Researchers can also more precisely forecast diabetes by employing ensemble algorithms, which classify the dataset using bagging, boosting, and stacking techniques based on majority vote. The models with the highest number of votes are chosen as the ultimate result of majority voting, which combines the best model outcomes (Abnoosian et al., 2023). The outcome of this project will be an ML-based tool that can assist healthcare providers in diagnosing diabetes early and accurately. Using this tool, diabetes healthcare costs can be reduced and patient outcomes can be improved.

RELATED WORK

Using machine learning models and data mining techniques, there has been a great deal of enthusiastic study on the subject of diagnosing diabetes patients in recent years. The machine learning approach, which integrates many models to achieve greater predicted outcomes, has been used by researchers. A sample from the PIMA dataset was used in the experiment. Tuppad and Patil released an assessment of machine learning for clinical decision support in diabetes in 2022 (Tuppad & Patil, 2022). This study emphasizes the many features of machine learning-based diabetes applications and highlights the gaps in technology and medicine. It also describes the breadth of machine learning-based diabetes clinical decision support applications.

A comparative research of machine learning algorithms for the early detection of diabetes mellitus in women was carried out by Sumbal Malik and S. Harous (Malik et al., 2022). To predict diabetes in women, this study evaluates the effectiveness and performance of various machine learning algorithms. Meenakshi used machine learning classifiers and methods to predict Type-2 Diabetes Mellitus (Shamreen et al., 2022). The algorithm's objective is to produce a prediction model that can precisely determine if an individual has diabetes. Shafi and Ansari performed comparative research on early diabetes prediction using machine learning methods (Shafi & Ansari, 2021). Using direct surveys, this study developed a prediction model for early diabetes mellitus in a Bangladeshi tertiary hospital. A potent hybrid prediction model for early Type 2 diabetes detection was created (Albahli, 2020). Machine learning-based diabetes prediction was the main focus of Rani's research (Rani, 2020). Fregoso et al. conducted a systematic review in 2021 that looked at 90 articles to pinpoint important potential areas for machine learning-based diabetes prediction (Fregoso et al., 2021). This systematic review looked over 90 articles to determine the main promising areas for diabetes prediction using machine learning techniques. To forecast diabetes using the PIMA dataset, an alternative method was presented using Artificial Neural Network (ANN) (Jian et al., 2021). A trial was carried out, and the results showed that the recommended approach worked with 90% accuracy.

Using the feature selection process, Hamza proposed a hybrid approach called k-means clustering mixed with SVM (K-SVM) (Osman, 2017). The PIMA dataset was used to assess the model to obtain experimental results. ANN is applied in the diabetes prediction process by multiple research associates. With the PIMA dataset, the accuracy of the model is 77.85%. For the diagnosis and prognosis of diabetes mellitus, a study employed several machine learning methods, such as AdaBoost with Decision Stump, DT, SVM, and Naive Bayes (NB) (Vijayan & Anjali, 2015). The experiment was carried out using a sample that was taken from the PIMA dataset. The results showed that AdaBoost with DT outperformed the others, with an accuracy of 80.72%.

An ensemble technique based on a voting system was proposed (Khan et al., 2023). They made use of an NHANES dataset from 2013 and 2014 that included 54 characteristics and 10,172 patients. An experiment's results showed that the recommended approach was successful, with an area under the curve value of 75%. The dataset was subjected to several machine learning techniques for categorization, with logistic regression achieving the highest accuracy rate at 96%. With a 98.8% accuracy rate, the AdaBoost classifier emerged as the top model following the pipeline application.

A diabetes prediction model utilizing machine learning techniques, such as Naive Bayes, Decision Trees, Random Forests, and Support Vector Machines, was presented (Soni & Verma, 2020). With an accuracy score of 86.67%, Random Forest was shown to have the best performance.

In 2021, "Lakshmi and Shanthi's Diabetes Prediction Using Ensemble Learning and Feature Selection Techniques" presented a diabetes prediction model using feature selection techniques like Relief and Chi-Square and ensemble learning techniques including AdaBoost, Bagging, and Random Forest (Mujumdar & Vaidehi, 2020). The ensemble strategy, which combined Bagging and Relief, was shown to have the best accuracy (92.86%) based on the results.

Research offers a thorough analysis of the several machine learning techniques—such as logistic regression, decision trees, artificial neural networks, support vector machines, and deep learning—that are used to predict diabetes. All things considered, this research shows how machine learning methods may accurately predict diabetes and have the potential to enhance diabetes prevention and care.

Improving the integration between clustering and classification algorithms is crucial to support early diabetes identification while handling data with missing values. This paper offers an improved approach that makes use of machine learning methods. To meet the goals, results have been compared and examined. The objectives of the study are summed up as follows:

- Classification of positive and negative diabetes using machine learning algorithms.
- Experiments were conducted on the PIMA dataset.
- To verify the robustness of the suggested technique, the following assessment criteria were used: accuracy, precision, recall, F1-score, and AUC curve.
- The suggested methodology produces better outcomes when compared to existing methodologies with the same stated parameters.
- The suggested technique has been empirically evaluated using basic classifiers typically used, including Logistic Regression, Support Vector Machine, Random Forest, and XGBoost.

PROPOSED METHODOLOGY

To improve the results and accuracy of diabetes detection was the aim of this investigation. Authors have proposed using a set of machine learning techniques to binary categorize illnesses as either positive or negative. Data preprocessing and data augmentation were done before the data was fed into the model. The suggested model's flowchart is shown in Figure 1.

Figure 1. Flow diagram of proposed approach

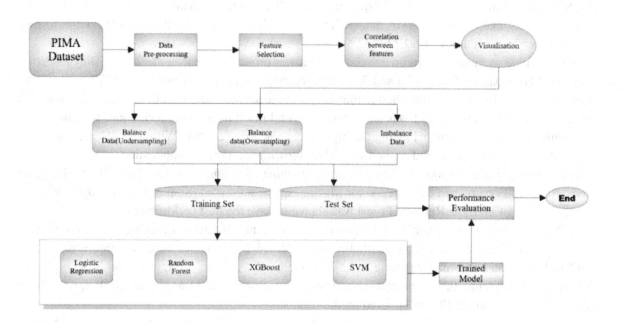

Data Description

For this research effort, the Pima Indians Diabetes dataset, May 2008, which is available on Kaggle, was selected for experimentation. The dataset includes multiple medical analysis variables in addition to one target variable. Determining if a patient has diabetes is the dataset's main goal. All other elements in the dataset are independent, except the outcome variable. The patient's age, number of pregnancies, BMI, insulin level, and other variables are among the independent variables.

Data Preprocessing

For the machine learning algorithm to use the data, data preparation is an essential step that converts the data into a practical and efficient format. The first step in preparing data is data normalization. With this approach, data translation into linear form is achieved. Another name for it is min-max normalization, in which each attribute's value falls between [0,1]. The subsequent preprocessing technique used is label encoding. The dependent variable in this approach is whether or not a person has diabetes. Consequently, all of the string values in the output variable are replaced with 0 and 1 to determine the output class. Numerous variables in the dataset contained missing values, such as the skin thickness parameter, the insulin attribute, and the pregnancy parameter. All of the missing values were filled in using the median value for a particular characteristic. Another name for this data preparation technique is replacement by median.

MODEL ARCHITECTURE

We have integrated several machine learning techniques, such as logistic regression, random forest, and support vector machines, in the proposed method. A few algorithms are briefly examined in this section.

Logistic Regression

Such a statistical model, sometimes known as a logit model, is widely used in categorization and predictive analytics. Logistic regression determines the probability that an event, like voting or not, will occur based on a dataset of independent variables. Within the Supervised Learning category, logistic regression is one of the most often used machine learning algorithms. It is used to predict the categorical dependent variable using a predefined set of independent factors.

- Logistic regression is used to predict the output when the dependent variable is categorical. The outcome must therefore be a discrete or categorical value. It can be anything from true or false, yes or no, 0 or 1, etc., however probabilistic values between 0 and 1 are presented rather than a specific value like 0 or 1.
- Logistic regression and linear regression are quite similar, except for the way they are used. Logistic regression is utilized to address classification challenges, whereas linear regression is employed to address regression issues.
- Instead of fitting a regression line, we fit a "S" shaped logistic function in logistic regression, which predicts two maximum values (0 or 1).
- The logistic function's curve indicates a number of potential outcomes, including the presence of disease.
- Among the most important machine learning techniques is logistic regression, which can classify new data using both continuous and discrete datasets and provide probabilities.

Random Forest

Using different subsets of the dataset to build several decision trees, the well-known ML method Random Forest makes predictions using the results from all the trees. It is a classifier that can address both classification and regression issues. Regression uses the average of all decision tree results, while classification uses the total of all the decision tree votes to obtain the final result. RF is viewed as an ensemble of different straightforward decision trees. The whole dataset is gathered and divided into k bootstrap samples, or "bags", for the current study. The DT algorithm is used for each bootstrap sample. Voting is performed once each decision tree's results have been compiled.

XGBoost

A popular and highly effective open-source implementation of the gradient boosted tree technique is known as XGBoost (extreme gradient boosting). Gradient boosting is a supervised learning approach that combines an ensemble of predictions from various weaker and simpler models to accurately predict a target variable. XGBoost stands out in machine learning competitions due to its ability to handle diverse data types, relationships, distributions, and customizable hyperparameters. It can be used to address problems related to regression, classification (both binary and multiclass), and ranking.

Performance

XGBoost has a solid history of delivering high-calibre outcomes in a variety of machine learning tasks, particularly in Kaggle contests where it has been a favorite choice for successful solutions.

Scalability

XGBoost is ideal for enormous datasets since it is made for scalable and effective machine learning model training.

Customizability

XGBoost is quite flexible since it offers a large selection of hyperparameters that may be changed to maximize performance.

Managing Missing Values

Working with real-world data, which frequently involves missing values, is made simple by XGBoost's built-in support for handling missing values.

Interpretability

XGBoost gives feature importance, giving for a clearer grasp of which factors are most crucial when producing predictions, in contrast to certain machine learning algorithms that can be challenging to read.

Support Vector Machine

One of the most well-liked supervised learning algorithms, Support Vector Machine, or SVM, is used to solve classification and regression issues. Nevertheless, it is largely employed in machine learning classification issues. The SVM algorithm's objective is to establish the optimal line or decision boundary that can divide n-dimensional space into classes, allowing us to quickly classify fresh data points in the future. A hyperplane is the name given to this optimal decision boundary. SVM selects the extreme vectors and points that aid in the creation of the hyperplane. Support vectors, which are used to represent these extreme instances, form the basis for SVM.

SVM can be of two types:

- **Linear SVM:** Linear SVM is used for data that can be divided into two classes using a single straight line. This type of data is called linearly separable data, and the classifier employed is known as a linear SVM classifier.

- **Nonlinear SVM:** Nonlinear SVM is used for nonlinearly separated data. If a dataset cannot be classified using a straight line, it is considered nonlinear data, and the classifier employed is referred to as a Nonlinear SVM classifier.

Feature Selection

The process of picking a subset of pertinent features (variables, predictors) for use in model creation is known as feature selection. Features are the input variables that we provide to our machine learning models. Our dataset's columns each represent a feature. We must make sure to employ only the necessary features to train an ideal model. When there are too many characteristics, the model may pick up on noise and uninteresting patterns. The process of selecting the crucial aspects of our data is known as feature selection. We gather vast amounts of data to train a model to improve machine learning. Typically, a sizeable amount of the data obtained is noise, and some of the columns in our dataset may not have a major impact on how well our model performs. The removal of unnecessary characteristics that could impair model performance and increase model interpretability are three reasons why feature selection is crucial in machine learning. It can also assist in lowering the dimensionality of the data. There are several techniques for feature selection in machine learning, including the following:

- **Filter Methods:** These strategies rank the significance of characteristics according to their connection with the desired variable. Examples include mutual information, the chi-square test, and the Pearson correlation coefficient.
- **Wrapper Techniques:** Using each subset as input to train and test a model, these techniques assess subsets of characteristics. The effectiveness of the model is assessed in order to determine the significance of the feature subset. Example include forward selection and backward selection.
- **Embedded Methods:** These techniques include feature selection as a step in the model-training procedure. For ex. Lasso regression and decision trees
- **Dimensionality Reduction Techniques:** Techniques for reducing the dimensions of a feature space while retaining the most crucial data are known as dimensionality reduction approaches. Examples include linear discriminant analysis (LDA) and principal component analysis (PCA) (LDA).

To guarantee that the chosen features are generalizable to fresh data, feature selection should be carried out on a different validation set or by cross-validation. While choosing features, it's also crucial to carefully analyze the problem's context and domain knowledge since some characteristics could be crucial for the model's performance even if they are not highly associated with the target variable.

Data Balancing

The balancing of data in machine learning refers to the process of ensuring that the data used to train a model have an equal representation of each class or category. In other words, balancing the data involves adjusting the frequency of each class so that the model can learn from an unbiased dataset.

Imbalanced data can result in a biased model that performs poorly on the underrepresented class, as the model may have learned to prioritize the overrepresented class. To avoid this, balancing techniques are used to equalize the number of samples in each class or to generate synthetic samples for the under-represented class.

Some common techniques used for balancing data include:

Using Undersampling

By maintaining all the data in the minority class and reducing the size of the majority class, undersampling is a strategy for balancing imbalanced datasets. It is one of several methods data scientists may employ to obtain out more accurate information from datasets that were initially unbalanced.

Using Oversampling

A single instance may be chosen more than once because random oversampling involves choosing random instances from the minority class with replacement and augmenting the training data with multiple copies of this instance.

Training and Testing of Dataset

Training and testing are two essential steps in machine learning that use labeled data to build and assess a prediction model.

A machine learning algorithm is trained using a labeled dataset to discover patterns and connections between the input characteristics and the associated output labels. The algorithm's parameters are modified during training until they can correctly predict the output label for a particular input characteristic.

Testing is the process of assessing a trained model's performance and accuracy on a different dataset than the one it was exposed to during training. The generalization performance of the model, which assesses how effectively the model can predict new data, is commonly evaluated using the testing dataset.

When machine learning algorithms are used to generate predictions on data that were not used to train the model, their performance is estimated using the train-test split technique. It is a quick and simple process to carry out, and the outcomes let you evaluate the effectiveness of machine learning algorithms for your particular predictive modeling issue. While being straightforward to use and understand, there are some circumstances in which the method should not be used, such as when the dataset is tiny and further setup is needed, as when it is used for classification and the dataset is unbalanced.

Performance Evaluation

Classification Matrix

There are four possible outcomes when making categorization predictions.

- **True Positives:** When you correctly anticipate that an observation belongs to a class and it truly does.
- **True Negatives:** When you forecast that an observation doesn't belong to a class and it truly does not.
- **False Positives:** When you assume an observation belongs to a class when it does not.

- **False Negatives:** When you assume an observation doesn't belong to a class when it actually does.

An ROC curve (receiver operating characteristic curve) is a graph showing the performance of a classification model at all classification thresholds. This curve plots two parameters:

- True Positive Rate
- False Positive Rate

RESULTS AND DISCUSSION

In this section, we delve into the key findings and implications of our research on diabetes prediction using machine learning. Our primary objective was to predict diabetes at early-stage, and we applied a range of machine learning algorithms to the Pima Indian Diabetes dataset. Our results demonstrated varying levels of accuracy across the different machine learning algorithms applied in this study. Notably, random forest, achieved the highest accuracy in predicting early-stage diabetes. This algorithm's robust performance suggests its potential utility in clinical practice for early diagnosis.

Feature Importance

Understanding the factors contributing to accurate predictions is crucial for both clinicians and data scientists. Our analysis of feature importance revealed that variables such as glucose, Insulin exhibited a strong influence on the prediction models. These findings offer valuable insights into the risk factors associated with diabetes, which can inform more targeted prevention and intervention strategies.

Clinical Relevance

The application of machine learning in early-stage diabetes prediction holds significant promise for improving patient care. Timely diagnosis is a critical factor in managing the disease effectively. Our research highlights the potential for leveraging machine learning in clinical settings to assist healthcare professionals in identifying high-risk individuals and initiating early interventions.

Limitations and Future Directions

It is important to acknowledge the limitations of this study. One limitation is the reliance on a single dataset, which may not capture the full spectrum of diabetes-related factors. Future research can benefit from incorporating a wider range of datasets and exploring the use of more advanced algorithms. Additionally, incorporating more diverse datasets may enhance the generalizability of our findings.

Performance Analysis

The proposed methodology used four machine learning algorithms viz., logistic regression, random forest XGBoost and support vector machine. Experiments were conducted using the PIMA diabetes dataset. The dataset has 768 data points and 9 feature columns where zero has been replaced with their median

Figure 2. Diabetes dataset statistical description

	Pregnancies	Glucose	BloodPressure	SkinThickness	Insulin	BMI	DiabetesPedigreeFunction	Age	Outcome
count	768.000000	768.000000	768.000000	768.000000	768.000000	768.000000	768.000000	768.000000	768.000000
mean	3.845052	120.894531	69.105469	20.536458	79.799479	31.992578	0.471876	33.240885	0.348958
std	3.369578	31.972618	19.355807	15.952218	115.244002	7.884160	0.331329	11.760232	0.476951
min	0.000000	0.000000	0.000000	0.000000	0.000000	0.000000	0.078000	21.000000	0.000000
25%	1.000000	99.000000	62.000000	0.000000	0.000000	27.300000	0.243750	24.000000	0.000000
50%	3.000000	117.000000	72.000000	23.000000	30.500000	32.000000	0.372500	29.000000	0.000000
75%	6.000000	140.250000	80.000000	32.000000	127.250000	36.600000	0.626250	41.000000	1.000000
max	17.000000	199.000000	122.000000	99.000000	846.000000	67.100000	2.420000	81.000000	1.000000

values. Figure 2 depicts the statistical description of diabetes dataset. The dataset has been divided into testing and training datasets. Accuracy, precision, recall and F1 score are the most common evaluation metrics adopted for checking the robustness and efficiency of the algorithms. True positive (TP) refers to situations where the predicted class value and the actual class value are both 1. True negative (TN) indicates that both the expected and actual classes have a value of zero. When your anticipated class differs from the actual class, false negatives (FNs) and false positives (FPs) occur. The most crucial metric is accuracy, which is calculated as the ratio of all properly predicted observations to all observations. Getting statistical measures of the data: A crucial part of data analytics and machine learning is statistics. Finding hidden patterns through data analysis and visualization is made easier.

Figure 3 depicts the correlation between features. A correlation matrix is a table that shows the correlation coefficients for various variables. The correlation between all potential pairings of values in a table is shown in the matrix. It is an effective tool for compiling a sizeable dataset and for locating and displaying data patterns. The variables are shown in rows and columns of a correlation matrix. The correlation coefficient is contained in each cell of a table. This section compares all of the traditional machine learning algorithms for identifying diabetes. It has been done to evaluate and compare the accuracy of all traditional methods. For the experiment, the PIMA diabetic dataset, has two classes: positive and negative. The outcomes of multiple machine learning models employing the PIMA dataset are compared using the following performance metrics:

- **Accuracy:** It is the proportion of correct predictions made by the model out of the total number of predictions. In other words, it measures how well the model correctly predicts the correct class labels. It is calculated as: Accuracy = (True Positives + True Negatives) / (True Positives + False Positives + True Negatives + False Negatives)
- **Precision:** It measures the proportion of true positives (correctly predicted positive instances) out of all the instances that the model predicted as positive. It indicates how confident the model is when it makes a positive prediction. It is calculated as: Precision = True Positives / (True Positives + False Positives)
- **Recall:** It measures the proportion of true positives out of all the actual positive instances in the dataset. It indicates how well the model can find all positive instances. It is calculated as: Recall = True Positives / (True Positives + False Negatives)

Figure 3. Correlation between diabetic features

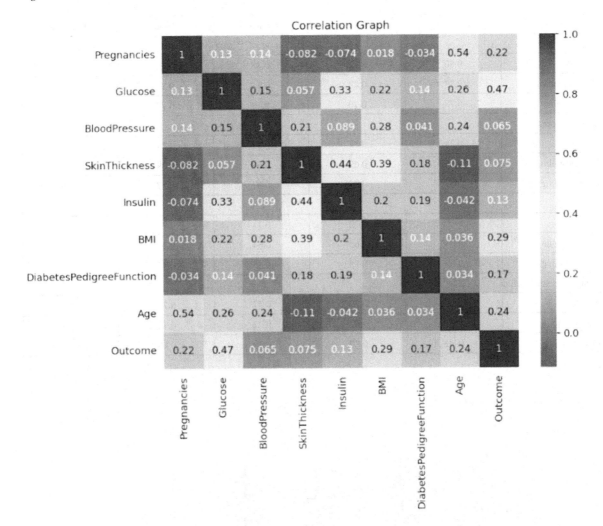

- **F1-score:** It is the harmonic mean of precision and recall, and is used to balance between precision and recall. It provides a single score that combines both precision and recall and is often used when both measures are important. It is calculated as: F1-score = 2 x (Precision x Recall) / (Precision + Recall)
- **AUC (area under the curve):** This is a measure of the model's ability to distinguish between positive and negative instances. It is calculated by plotting the true positive Rate (TPR) against the false positive rate (FPR) at different probability thresholds. AUC ranges from 0 to 1, with higher values indicating better performance

Table 1 shows the accuracy, precision, F1_score, recall and AUC value for all the machine learning algorithms in both balanced and imbalanced data. We balanced the data using two methods i.e. undersampling and oversampling. Accuracy, precision, recall, F1-score, and AUC value are commonly used performance metrics to evaluate the performance of machine learning models. As shown in Table 1,

Table 1. Comparison of classifiers concerning the performance metrics

Algorithm	Accuracy	Precision	F1-Score	Recall	AUC Value
Logistic Regression					
Normal	0.80	0.77	0.75	0.75	0.85
Undersampling	0.73	0.74	0.73	0.74	0.82
Oversampling	0.78	0.79	0.79	0.77	0.88
Random Forest					
Normal	0.78	0.74	0.75	0.74	0.86
Undersampling	0.68	0.69	0.69	0.69	0.78
Oversampling	0.87	0.87	0.87	0.87	0.95
XGBoost					
Normal	0.75	0.72	0.71	0.73	0.82
Undersampling	0.64	0.65	0.64	0.64	0.73
Oversampling	0.85	0.85	0.85	0.85	0.93
Support Vector Machine					
Normal	0.81	0.79	0.77	0.75	0.86
Undersampling	0.72	0.62	0.72	0.72	0.82
Oversampling	0.80	0.80	0.80	0.80	0.89

Figure 4. Performance analysis

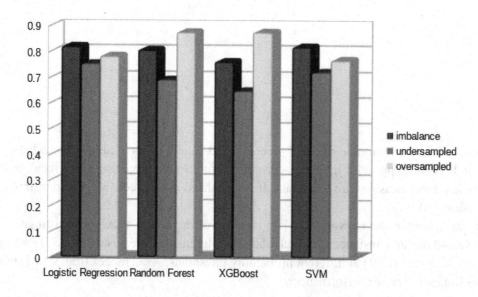

oversampling of data gives better results in terms of accuracy and AUC value than undersampling and imbalanced data and the oversampling. RF algorithm has the highest accuracy of 87% and an AUC value of 0.95. Figure 4 shows the comparison of different types of data with all algorithms that we are studying in this paper and the oversampling of RF is the best algorithm in terms of accuracy and AUC value.

The receiver operating characteristic (ROC) curves for machine learning models compare the true positive rate to the false positive rate at various thresholds (TPR vs. FPR). Using Table 1, the values for the covered surface under ROC curves are calculated. The suggested model has a larger covered area percentage of 95% (diabetes dataset), according to an analysis of the ROC curve of the diabetes datasets. As shown none of the other basic classifiers, including XGBoost, logistic regression, and support vector machine, have an area under the curve greater than 93%. AUC calculates the performance of the binary classifier over several thresholds and offers an aggregate metric in the ROC curve. The AUC's value runs from 0 to 1, therefore a successful model will have an AUC close to 1 and hence have a strong degree of separability.

Figure 5 depicts the ROC analysis. The classifier is represented by the red dotted line, which plots as a diagonal line and is no better than random guessing. A perfect classifier would have a true positive rate of 100% and a false positive rate of 0%. Although not perfectly accurate, most real-world instances will fall somewhere between these two lines; this has a higher predictive potential than guessing at random. The ideal classifier would "hug" the top left corner of Figure 5 like the blue line, maintaining a high true positive rate while simultaneously having a low false positive rate. This is often what we're going for.

One benefit offered by ROC curves is that they make it easier for us to identify a categorization threshold that is appropriate for our particular scenario. For instance, we would want the false positive rate to be extremely low if we were testing an email spam classifier. We would not want someone to miss an essential email because our system was too aggressively removing spam. To ensure that no crucial emails were missed, we would probably even let a significant number of genuine spam emails (true positives) pass the filter. However, if our classifier is determining if a person has a fatal condition, we could be willing to accept a greater percentage of false positives (misdiagnosing the sickness) to ensure that we do not miss any real positives (people who have the illness).

Figure 5. ROC analysis

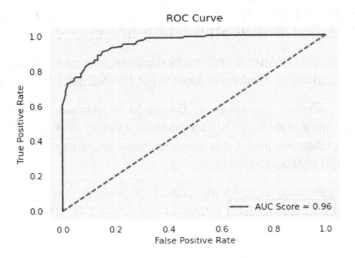

CONCLUSION

Based on the study, it can be concluded that machine learning algorithms such as logistic regression, random forest, support vector machine, and XGBoost can be effectively used for predicting diabetes. The study involved the analysis of several parameters such as glucose levels, BMI, age, blood pressure, and skin thickness, among others, to predict the likelihood of diabetes in individuals. The study found that random forest was the most accurate algorithm with an accuracy rate of 87%, followed by XGBoost with 85%, support vector machine with 81%, and logistic regression with 80%. This indicates that random forest can be considered as a suitable algorithm for diabetes prediction. However, it is important to note that the accuracy of the algorithm depends on the quality of the dataset used. The study also highlighted the importance of feature selection and data preprocessing in improving the accuracy of the models. In conclusion, the study demonstrates the potential of machine learning algorithms for predicting diabetes and highlights the need for further research to improve the accuracy of the models. The findings of this study can be used to develop more accurate and efficient predictive models for diabetes diagnosis and management.

REFERENCES

Abnoosian, K., Farnoosh, R., & Behzadi, M. H. (2023). Prediction of diabetes disease using an ensemble of machine learning multi-classifier models. *BMC Bioinformatics*, 24(1), 337. doi:10.118612859-023-05465-z PMID:37697283

Albahli, S. (2020). Type 2 machine learning: An effective hybrid prediction model for early type 2 diabetes detection. *Journal of Medical Imaging and Health Informatics*, 10(5), 1069–1075. doi:10.1166/jmihi.2020.3000

El-Sappagh, S., Elmogy, M., Ali, F., Abuhmed, T., Islam, S. R., & Kwak, K. S. (2019). A comprehensive medical decision–support framework based on a heterogeneous ensemble classifier for diabetes prediction. *Electronics (Basel)*, 8(6), 635. doi:10.3390/electronics8060635

Fregoso-Aparicio, L., Noguez, J., Montesinos, L., & García-García, J. A. (2021). Machine learning and deep learning predictive models for type 2 diabetes: A systematic review. *Diabetology & Metabolic Syndrome*, 13(1), 1–22. doi:10.118613098-021-00767-9 PMID:34930452

Ganie, S. M., & Malik, M. B. (2022). An ensemble machine learning approach for predicting type-II diabetes mellitus based on lifestyle indicators. *Healthcare Analytics*, 2, 100092. doi:10.1016/j.health.2022.100092

Ihnaini, B., Khan, M. A., Khan, T. A., Abbas, S., Daoud, M. S., Ahmad, M., & Khan, M. A. (2021). A smart healthcare recommendation system for multidisciplinary diabetes patients with data fusion based on deep ensemble learning. *Computational Intelligence and Neuroscience*, 2021, 2021. doi:10.1155/2021/4243700 PMID:34567101

Jian, Y., Pasquier, M., Sagahyroon, A., & Aloul, F. (2021, December). A machine learning approach to predicting diabetes complications. []. MDPI.]. *Health Care*, 9(12), 1712. PMID:34946438

Khan, M. A., Iqbal, N., Jamil, H., & Kim, D. H. (2023). An optimized ensemble prediction model using AutoML based on soft voting classifier for network intrusion detection. *Journal of Network and Computer Applications, 212*, 103560. doi:10.1016/j.jnca.2022.103560

Kibria, H. B., Nahiduzzaman, M., Goni, M. O. F., Ahsan, M., & Haider, J. (2022). An ensemble approach for the prediction of diabetes mellitus using a soft voting classifier with an explainable AI. *Sensors (Basel), 22*(19), 7268. doi:10.339022197268 PMID:36236367

Malik, S., Harous, S., & El-Sayed, H. (2020, September). Comparative analysis of machine learning algorithms for early prediction of diabetes mellitus in women. In *International Symposium on Modelling and Implementation of Complex Systems* (pp. 95-106). Cham: Springer International Publishing.

Mujumdar, A., & Vaidehi, V. (2019). Diabetes prediction using machine learning algorithms. *Procedia Computer Science, 165*, 292–299. doi:10.1016/j.procs.2020.01.047

Osman, A. H., & Aljahdali, H. M. (2017). Diabetes disease diagnosis method based on feature extraction using K-SVM. *International Journal of Advanced Computer Science and Applications, 8*(1).

Rani, K. J. (2020). Diabetes prediction using machine learning. *International Journal of Scientific Research in Computer Science Engineering and Information Technology, 6*, 294–305. doi:10.32628/CSEIT206463

Shafi, S., & Ansari, G. A. (2021, May). Early prediction of diabetes disease & classification of algorithms using machine learning approach. In *Proceedings of the International Conference on Smart Data Intelligence (ICSMDI 2021)*. SSRN. 10.2139srn.3852590

Shamreen Ahamed, B., Arya, M. S., & Nancy, A. O. (2022). Diabetes Mellitus Disease Prediction Using Machine Learning Classifiers and Techniques Using the Concept of Data Augmentation and Sampling. In *ICT Systems and Sustainability: Proceedings of ICT4SD 2022* (pp. 401–413). Springer Nature Singapore.

Soni, M., & Varma, S. (2020). *Diabetes prediction using machine learning techniques. International Journal of Engineering Research & Technology* (Vol. 9). Ijert.

Tuppad, A., & Patil, S. D. (2022). Machine learning for diabetes clinical decision support: A review. *Advances in Computational Intelligence, 2*(2), 22. doi:10.100743674-022-00034-y PMID:35434723

Vijayan, V. V., & Anjali, C. (2015, December). Prediction and diagnosis of diabetes mellitus—A machine learning approach. In *2015 IEEE Recent Advances in Intelligent Computational Systems (RAICS)* (pp. 122-127). IEEE.

Chapter 6
AI–Driven Powered Solution Selection:
Navigating Forests and Fires for a Sustainable Future

G. Kothai

Department of CSE, KPR Institute of Engineering and Technology, India

E. Poovammal

Department of Computing Technologies, SRM Institute of Science and Technology, India

V. Deepa

iD https://orcid.org/0000-0001-8028-5429

Department of Computing Technologies, SRM Institute of Science and Technology, India

ABSTRACT

Forests face several critical issues that pose significant challenges to their health and sustainability, such as deforestation, forest fires, forest fragmentation, etc. The main key issue is uncontrolled forest fires which affect both natural and human-induced and poses a significant threat to forests. Forest fires can result in the complete or partial destruction of forested areas. Addressing the damage requires a combination of effective fire management strategies, including prevention measures, early detection systems, and rapid response to wildfires. Detecting fires promptly allows authorities to issue timely evacuation orders, provide warnings to communities at risk, and deploy resources to ensure the safety of residents. However, artificial intelligence (AI) has the potential to revolutionize forest management by providing valuable insights, improving efficiency, and supporting sustainable practices. By leveraging AI technologies, forest fire management can benefit from improved situational awareness, faster response times, and optimized resource allocation.

DOI: 10.4018/979-8-3693-0639-0.ch006

INTRODUCTION

A forest is a complex and diverse ecosystem characterized by a dense collection of trees, shrubs, plants, and various forms of wildlife that interact within a specific geographic area. Forests can vary widely in terms of their composition, structure, and ecological functions, but they generally consist of a significant number of trees that grow closely together, creating a canopy that shades the ground beneath (Abedi2019). Forests play a vital role in maintaining the health of the planet's ecosystems. They provide habitat and sustenance for a vast array of plant and animal species, many of which are uniquely adapted to these environments. Forests also contribute to global ecological processes such as carbon sequestration, oxygen production through photosynthesis, regulation of water cycles, and the preservation of soil quality. Forests can be categorized into different types based on factors like climate, location, and dominant tree species. These types include tropical rainforests, temperate forests, boreal forests, and more.

The sustainable use, conservation, and protection of forest ecosystems need to be ensured which can be done by forest management. Biodiversity Conservation, Ecosystem Health, Resource Sustainability, Carbon Sequestration and Climate Change Mitigation, Preventing Deforestation and Degradation, Habitat Preservation, Disaster Risk Reduction, Cultural and Societal Values, Economic Opportunities, Invasive Species and Disease Control, Research and Education, Legal and Policy Frameworks and Long-Term Planning are the significant factors that leads to the requirement of forest management.

The Biodiversity Conservation provides an incredibly biodiverse ecosystems of a forest, where a variety of plant and animal species are accommodated (Cardille 2001). Proper management will help in preserving and protecting the biodiversity with healthy habitats and ecosystem functions. The Ecosystem Health in forests provides a crucial ecosystem service such as carbon sequestration, oxygen production, water regulation, and soil stabilization. Effective management helps in maintaining these services to ensure the overall health and stability of ecosystems.

The Resource Sustainability furnishes the sources of valuable resources like timber, non-timber forest products such as fruits, nuts, medicinal plants, and freshwater. Managing these resources sustainably ensures that they are available for current and future generations. Figure 1 demonstrates the sustainable provision of forest ecosystem.Forests play a significant role in capturing and storing carbon dioxide from the atmosphere, helping to mitigate climate change which leads to Carbon Sequestration and Climate Change Mitigation. Proper management practices can enhance this capacity and contribute to global climate goals.

Unplanned deforestation and forest degradation can lead to loss of biodiversity, disruption of ecosystems, and increased greenhouse gas emissions. Forest management aims to prevent these negative impacts through responsible land use planning. Many species, including endangered ones, rely on forests for their habitat. Proper forest management helps conserve these habitats, preventing species decline and promoting ecosystem resilience.

Well-managed forests can reduce the risk of natural disasters like landslides, floods, and wildfires (Belgherbi, 2018). Healthy forests with intact root systems stabilize soil, reduce erosion, and provide natural buffers against such events. Forests hold cultural, spiritual, and recreational value for many communities. Responsible management respects these values while ensuring that forests remain accessible and beneficial to society. Sustainable forest management supports industries such as forestry, tourism, and recreation, contributing to local and national economies.

Effective forest management strategies can help prevent the spread of invasive species and manage disease outbreaks, which can have devastating impacts on forest ecosystems. Managed forests provide

Figure 1. Sustainable provision of forest ecosystem
(Hernández 2022)

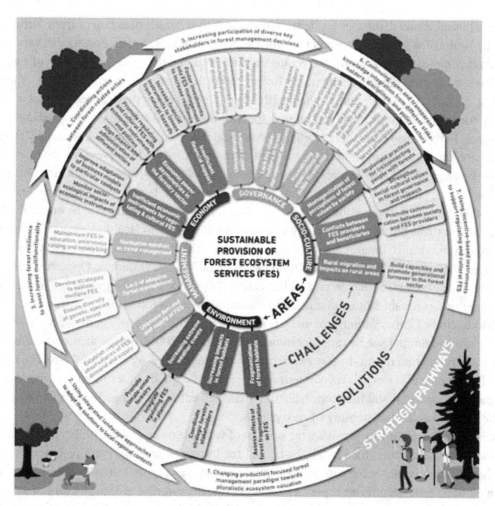

opportunities for scientific research and education, leading to a better understanding of ecosystems, biodiversity, and natural processes. Forest management ensures compliance with environmental laws and regulations, promoting responsible land use and minimizing conflicts between different land uses. By managing forests, we can plan for the long term, ensuring that future generations can enjoy the benefits of healthy and productive ecosystems.

In summary, forest management is crucial for maintaining the delicate balance between human needs and the health of ecosystems. It addresses challenges such as resource exploitation, habitat loss, climate change, and biodiversity decline, while also enabling sustainable development and the continued provision of vital ecosystem services. This paper squarely fractionalized into several segments. The issues in forest have been elaborated in section 2. The section 3 describes the forest fire along with factors that contribute to the perception of forest fires as being more perilous in nature. The various effects of forest fire are discussed in section 4. The section 5 elaborates the beyond the flames: unraveling the multi-faceted threats of forest fires. The aftermath of destruction: understanding the damages caused by forest fires are described in section 6. The section 7 describes safeguarding ecosystems and communities: the imperative for effective fire management strategies. Navigating the flames: exploring effective fire management strategies is elaborated in section 8. The section 9 describes the alerting nature's fury: vigilance and alerts for forest fire awareness. The section 10 describes the Tech-infused woodlands: the role of artificial intelligence in forest management. The section 11 elaborates the Elevating Forest management: the transformative role of ai in conservation and sustainability. Unveiling the power of ai algorithms for advancing forest and forest fire management are described in section 12.Harnessing the power of ai algorithms for advanced forest management are elaborated in section 13. AI algorithms revolutionizing forest fire management: insights and innovations are described in section 13. Section 14 concludes with the Conclusion.

ISSUES IN FOREST

Forests around the world face a range of issues that impact their health, biodiversity, and ecological balance. Some of the key issues affecting forests include:

- **Deforestation:** Deforestation (Drüke, 2023), the permanent removal of trees and forests (Hansen 2013), is a critical issue. It leads to habitat loss, disrupts ecosystems, contributes to climate change, and reduces biodiversity.
- **Illegal Logging:** Illegal logging is a significant problem, contributing to deforestation and habitat destruction. It also undermines sustainable forest management and can have negative social and economic impacts.
- **Habitat Loss:** Forests provide habitats for countless species, and their destruction leads to loss of biodiversity. This affects not only animals and plants but also ecosystems and the services they provide to humans.
- **Climate Change:** Forests play a crucial role in carbon sequestration, helping to mitigate climate change by absorbing carbon dioxide. Deforestation and degradation release stored carbon, contributing to global warming.
- **Forest Degradation:** Forest degradation refers to the deterioration of forest quality due to factors like pollution, overgrazing, and invasive species. This compromises biodiversity and ecosystem services.
- **Invasive Species:** Invasive species can outcompete native species, disrupt ecosystems, and lead to the decline of vulnerable species. They can affect the composition and health of forest ecosystems.
- **Wildfires/ Forest Fire:** Uncontrolled wildfires can devastate forests, leading to habitat loss, releasing large amounts of carbon into the atmosphere, and posing threats to nearby communities (Gugliette2011).
- **Fragmentation:** Habitat fragmentation due to roads, agriculture, and urbanization can isolate populations of plants and animals, reducing genetic diversity and making it harder for species to thrive.
- **Illegal Wildlife Trade:** The trade in illegal wildlife products (Norouzzadeh2018)(Miao 2019), including plants and animals from forests, threatens species and can lead to overexploitation and habitat destruction.
- **Monoculture Plantations:** Some forests are converted into monoculture plantations for commercial purposes. These lack biodiversity and can harm local ecosystems.

- **Lack of Sustainable Management:** Unsustainable logging practices and inadequate forest management can lead to ecological imbalances, soil erosion, and degradation.
- **Indigenous and Local Community Rights:** Many forests are home to indigenous and local communities whose rights to land and resources are often not respected, leading to conflicts and social challenges.

Efforts are being made globally to address these issues through sustainable forest management, conservation initiatives, policy changes, and international agreements. Collaborative approaches involving governments, NGOs, local communities, and industries are crucial to ensure the protection and restoration of forest ecosystems.

Uncontrolled forest fires are a key challenge due to their capacity to rapidly spread, causing extensive ecological damage, endangering lives, and overwhelming firefighting efforts, often exacerbated by factors like dry conditions, strong winds, and limited resources.

FOREST FIRE

Forest fires, also known as wildfires, are destructive and often devastating natural phenomena that have profound impacts on ecosystems, communities, and the environment. These fires result from the rapid combustion of vegetation, fueled by a combination of dry conditions, high temperatures, and strong winds. While some wildfires are ignited by natural factors such as lightning strikes, many are caused by human activities, such as discarded cigarettes, campfires, or power lines.

The occurrence of forest fires (Goparaju L, 2023) is a complex interplay of ecological, climatic, and human factors. They have been a natural part of many ecosystems for millennia, playing a role in clearing dead vegetation, rejuvenating soil, and promoting new growth. However, the increasing frequency and intensity of modern forest fires have been linked to climate change, land use changes, and human encroachment into wild areas.

Forest fires pose significant challenges due to their potential to cause widespread destruction. The flames can spread rapidly, consuming vast areas of forests, grasslands, and shrublands. Beyond the immediate threat to human lives and property, forest fires have far-reaching consequences. They release enormous amounts of smoke and pollutants into the air (Kumari 2020), affecting air quality and posing health risks. The destruction of habitats threatens biodiversity and disrupts ecosystems, with long-lasting ecological and environmental impacts.

Efforts to manage and mitigate the impacts of forest fires include fire prevention strategies, early detection and rapid response systems, controlled burns to reduce fuel buildup, and community education about responsible land management practices (Malik 2013). Effective firefighting involves the coordination of resources, including specialized teams, equipment, aircraft, and technology.

As global temperatures rise and weather patterns become more unpredictable, the challenge of forest fires intensifies (Martínez 2013). Balancing the ecological role of fires with the need to protect human lives and safeguard ecosystems remains a critical task for governments, environmental organizations, and communities around the world.

The wildfires are particularly dangerous and concerning issue due to their far-reaching ecological, environmental, economic, and social impacts. There are many factors that contribute to the perception of forest fires as being more perilous in nature.

- **Ecosystem Destruction:** Forest fires can cause severe damage to ecosystems, destroying habitats for various plant and animal species. This can lead to loss of biodiversity, disrupt food chains, and negatively impact ecosystem services.
- **Air Quality:** Forest fires release large amounts of smoke, particulate matter, and pollutants into the air, affecting air quality and posing health risks to people, especially those with respiratory issues.
- **Climate Change:** Forest fires release substantial amounts of carbon dioxide into the atmosphere, contributing to greenhouse gas emissions and exacerbating climate change. This can create a feedback loop, as warmer temperatures and drier conditions can lead to more frequent and intense fires.
- **Loss of Carbon Sink:** Forests act as carbon sinks, absorbing and storing carbon dioxide from the atmosphere. When forests burn, this stored carbon is released back into the air, further contributing to climate change.
- **Water Quality:** Intense fires can lead to soil erosion and runoff, affecting water quality in rivers, lakes, and other water bodies. Ash and debris can contaminate water sources and disrupt aquatic ecosystems.
- **Habitat Fragmentation:** Fires can create fragmented landscapes (Anderson 2016), isolating species and preventing natural migration patterns. This can lead to genetic isolation and reduced biodiversity.
- **Economic Loss:** Forest fires can result in substantial economic losses due to damage to timber resources, infrastructure, and property. Costs also include firefighting efforts, rehabilitation, and recovery.
- **Human Health:** Smoke and air pollutants from fires can pose serious health risks to people, causing respiratory problems and exacerbating preexisting conditions.
- **Human Safety:** Forest fires can threaten human lives and property, especially in communities located near or within forested areas. Evacuations and firefighting efforts can put lives at risk.
- **Cultural Significance:** Many forests hold cultural and historical significance for indigenous and local communities. Fires can destroy cultural heritage sites and disrupt traditional practices.
- **Long-Term Impact:** Recovery and regeneration after a major forest fire can take years or even decades. The loss of mature trees and disruption of ecosystems can have long-lasting effects.

Addressing the issue of forest fires requires a comprehensive approach, including effective firefighting strategies, fire prevention measures, land management practices, community engagement, and policies to mitigate climate change and promote sustainable land use.

EFFECTS OF FOREST FIRE

Forest fires have a range of effects that can profoundly impact ecosystems, communities, and the environment (Karabulut 2013). Some of the effects are:

- **Habitat Destruction:** Forest fires destroy habitats for countless plant and animal species, leading to loss of biodiversity and disrupting ecosystems.

- **Loss of Biodiversity:** Fires can lead to the loss of plant and animal species, altering the composition and structure of ecosystems.
- **Air Quality Degradation:** Fires release smoke, particulate matter, and pollutants into the air, affecting air quality and posing health risks to humans and wildlife.
- **Carbon Emissions:** Burning vegetation releases carbon dioxide, contributing to greenhouse gas emissions and climate change.
- **Soil Degradation:** Intense fires can cause soil erosion, stripping away protective vegetation and affecting soil structure and quality.
- **Water Contamination:** Ash runoff from fires can contaminate water sources, affecting aquatic ecosystems and water quality.
- **Climate Feedback:** Carbon released by fires contributes to climate change, creating a feedback loop that leads to more frequent and severe fires.
- **Loss of Timber Resources:** Forest fires damage valuable timber resources, impacting industries and economies reliant on forestry.
- **Property Damage:** Fires threaten homes, infrastructure, and communities, leading to property damage and economic loss.
- **Community Disruption:** Evacuations and firefighting efforts can disrupt communities, leading to displacement and social challenges.
- **Long-Term Recovery:** Ecosystems may take years or decades to recover, affecting ecosystem services and human livelihoods.
- **Wildlife Displacement:** Many animals lose their habitats, leading to shifts in animal populations and potential endangerment.

Addressing the effects of forest fires requires a multi-pronged approach, including fire prevention, responsible land management, early detection, effective firefighting strategies, and policies to mitigate climate change and promote sustainable practices.

In addition to the immediate and direct ramifications of forest fires, a multitude of additional hazards and repercussions emerges as a consequence of these deleterious occurrences (Karabulut 2013)(Roy 2003) and they are are Smoke Inhalation, Human Health, Displacement and migration, Infrastructure damage, loss of livelihoods, tourism impact, water supply contamination, secondary erosion and landslides, hazardous materials release, loss of cultural heritage, social stress and post-fire invasive species

THE AFTERMATH OF DESTRUCTION: UNDERSTANDING THE DAMAGES CAUSED BY FOREST FIRES

Forest fires inflict a wide array of damages that reverberate through ecosystems, communities, and the environment (Kuter 2011). These damages encompass ecological, environmental, economic, and social aspects:

Ecological Damages

- *Habitat Loss:* Forest fires obliterate habitats for numerous plant and animal species, disrupting ecosystems and causing irreparable damage to biodiversity.

- *Species Extinction:* Many species unable to escape the flames face extinction, leading to the loss of genetic diversity and weakening ecosystem resilience.
- *Food Chain Disruption:* Fire alters the availability of food sources, affecting predator-prey relationships and disrupting the balance of ecosystems.
- *Invasive Species:* Post-fire environments are vulnerable to colonization by invasive species, which can outcompete native plants and further degrade ecosystems.
- *Erosion and Soil Degradation:* Burned landscapes are prone to erosion, with soil becoming less stable and susceptible to degradation.

Environmental Damages

- *Air Pollution:* Fires release smoke, particulates, and pollutants, deteriorating air quality and posing health risks to humans and wildlife.
- *Carbon Emissions:* Burning vegetation releases carbon dioxide, contributing to greenhouse gas emissions and accelerating climate change.
- *Water Contamination:* Ash runoff can contaminate water sources, harming aquatic life and affecting water quality.

Economic Damages

- *Timber Resource Loss:* Forest fires damage valuable timber resources, impacting industries dependent on forestry and causing economic losses.
- *Property Damage:* Fires threaten homes, infrastructure, and communities, resulting in property destruction, displacing communities, and causing economic strain.
- *Tourism Impact:* Tourism and outdoor recreation decline in affected areas, leading to economic losses for local economies.

Social Damages

- *Human Health:* Smoke inhalation from fires can lead to respiratory and cardiovascular issues, increasing hospital admissions and impacting human health.
- *Displacement:* Communities near fire-affected areas may need to evacuate, leading to temporary or permanent displacement.
- *Emotional Stress:* Fire impacts can cause emotional distress and psychological stress among affected individuals and communities.

Climate Impact

- *Climate Feedback:* Carbon emissions from fires contribute to climate change, potentially intensifying fire frequency and severity in the future.

Long-Term Recovery

- *Ecosystem Regeneration*: Ecosystems may require extensive time to recover, affecting ecosystem services and the well-being of surrounding areas.

Cultural and Historical Losses

- *Cultural Heritage:* Fires can destroy cultural heritage sites, artifacts, and traditional knowledge held by indigenous and local communities.

Understanding these damages underscores the urgency of fire prevention, responsible land management, and the implementation of strategies to mitigate the far-reaching and often irreversible consequences of forest fires.

SAFEGUARDING ECOSYSTEMS AND COMMUNITIES: THE IMPERATIVE FOR EFFECTIVE FIRE MANAGEMENT STRATEGIES

Fire management strategies are essential for several critical reasons (Karabulut 2013)(Martínez 2013) (Malik 2013) such as to Prevent Loss of Lives and Property, Protect Ecosystems, Mitigate Air Quality Issues, Carbon Sequestration, Preserve Cultural and Historical Sites, Promote Controlled Burns, Maintain Ecosystem Balance, Reduce Economic Losses, Enhance Resilience, Promote Sustainability, Facilitate Collaboration and Adapt to Changing Conditions.

- **Prevent Loss of Lives and Property:** Effective fire management helps prevent the loss of human lives, homes, and infrastructure by controlling and mitigating the spread of fires.
- **Protect Ecosystems:** Fire management strategies aim to minimize the ecological impacts of fires, preserving habitats, biodiversity, and the health of ecosystems.
- **Mitigate Air Quality Issues:** Managed fires can reduce the release of harmful pollutants and smoke, improving air quality and reducing health risks for humans and wildlife.
- **Carbon Sequestration:** Controlled burning can help manage carbon emissions, contributing to efforts to mitigate climate change by maintaining carbon sinks.
- **Preserve Cultural and Historical Sites:** Fire management helps protect cultural heritage sites, artifacts, and traditional knowledge held by indigenous and local communities.
- **Promote Controlled Burns:** Managed fires, or prescribed burns, can reduce the buildup of flammable materials, preventing more destructive and uncontrollable wildfires.
- **Maintain Ecosystem Balance:** Certain ecosystems, like fire-dependent ecosystems, require periodic burning for regeneration, seed germination, and overall health.
- **Reduce Economic Losses:** Fire management minimizes economic losses by preventing damage to timber resources, infrastructure, and industries dependent on forests.
- **Enhance Resilience:** Implementing fire management strategies builds resilience in communities, ecosystems, and landscapes, making them better prepared for future fire events.

- **Promote Sustainability:** Sustainable fire management integrates ecological, social, and economic considerations, ensuring a balance between human needs and environmental health.
- **Facilitate Collaboration:** Fire management involves coordination among agencies, communities, and stakeholders, fostering cooperation and effective response.
- **Adapt to Changing Conditions:** As climates change and fire risks increase, adaptive fire management strategies are crucial to address evolving challenges.

By implementing well-designed fire management strategies, there is higher possibility to reduce the devastating impacts of uncontrolled wildfires and promote the health and sustainability of ecosystems, communities, and the environment.

NAVIGATING THE FLAMES: EXPLORING EFFECTIVE FIRE MANAGEMENT STRATEGIES

Fire management strategies encompass a range of proactive approaches aimed at preventing, controlling, and mitigating the impacts of wildfires (Kuter 2011)(Sowmya 2010). These strategies include:

Fire Prevention

- *Public Education:* Raising awareness about fire risks, responsible behavior in fire-prone areas, and the importance of fire safety.
- *Regulations and Policies:* Implementing regulations on activities that can trigger fires, such as campfires or discarded cigarette butts.
- *Firebreaks:* Creating cleared areas or natural barriers to halt the spread of fires.

Fire Suppression and Control

- *Early Detection:* Utilizing technology, surveillance, and community reporting to quickly identify and respond to wildfires.
- *Firefighting Crews:* Employing trained firefighting personnel, equipment, and aircraft to extinguish and contain fires.
- *Aerial Resources:* Deploying helicopters and airplanes to drop water or fire retardant on active fires.

Prescribed Burns (Controlled Burns)

- *Planning:* Strategically conducting intentional fires during favorable conditions to reduce excess vegetation, prevent larger fires, and rejuvenate ecosystems.
- *Ecosystem Health:* Mimicking natural fire cycles to promote ecological balance, stimulate seed germination, and clear underbrush.

Fuel Management

- *Thinning:* Removing excess vegetation and trees to decrease fuel loads and reduce fire intensity.
- *Fuel Breaks:* Creating strips of cleared land to interrupt fire spread and slow its progress.

Community Preparedness

- *Evacuation Plans:* Developing and practicing evacuation plans for communities at risk, ensuring safe and efficient evacuation in emergencies.
- *Defensible Space:* Clearing vegetation and debris around homes to create a buffer zone that reduces fire risk.

Early Warning Systems

- *Monitoring and Prediction:* Using weather forecasts, historical data, and fire behavior modeling to predict fire conditions and potential risks.
- *Alert Systems:* Notifying communities and individuals about fire risks through alarms, apps, and communication channels.

Collaboration and Partnerships

- *Interagency Cooperation:* Coordinating efforts among different agencies, organizations, and stakeholders involved in fire management.
- *Community Engagement:* Involving local communities, indigenous groups, and landowners in planning and implementing fire management strategies.

Research and Innovation

- *Technological Advances:* Utilizing drones, satellite imagery, and fire behavior models to improve firefighting and decision-making.
- *Climate Adaptation:* Developing strategies that account for changing climate conditions and their impact on fire risks.

Post-Fire Recovery

- *Rehabilitation:* Implementing strategies to restore ecosystems, prevent erosion, and promote natural regeneration after fires.
- *Community Support:* Providing assistance and resources to communities affected by fires for rebuilding and recovery.

By combining these diverse fire management strategies, authorities can enhance their ability to prevent, control, and manage wildfires, minimizing their ecological, environmental, economic, and social impacts.

FLAME FIGHTERS: THE CRUCIAL ROLE OF EARLY FOREST FIRE DETECTION

Detecting forest fires promptly is vital for swift intervention and mitigation. Rapid detection allows firefighting teams to respond quickly, preventing fires from spreading uncontrollably. This minimizes ecological damage, protects human lives, property, and wildlife, and reduces the release of harmful pollutants. Early detection also optimizes resource allocation, aids in preserving ecosystems, and supports climate change mitigation by curbing carbon emissions(Pratihast 2016). Overall, timely fire detection is essential for effective fire management and minimizing the devastating impacts of wildfires.

The early detection of forest fires is of utmost importance for a variety of convincing rationales.

Early Intervention

Early detection enables swift response, allowing firefighting teams to contain and extinguish fires before they escalate into large, uncontrollable infernos. It also refers to swift and proactive action taken in the initial stages of a situation. In the context of forest fires, early intervention means detecting and responding to fires as soon as they ignite. This is crucial because addressing fires in their early stages prevents them from spreading and becoming uncontrollable. Swift intervention by firefighting teams, equipped with the right resources, can contain fires, reducing their size, impact, and potential damage to ecosystems, property, and lives.

Risk Mitigation

Identifying fires in their early stages reduces the potential for them to spread, minimizing the risk to communities, ecosystems, and property. Risk mitigation in the context of forest fires involves taking proactive measures to reduce the potential negative impacts and consequences of fires. This includes strategies to prevent fires from spreading uncontrollably, minimizing their destructive effects. By identifying and addressing fire risks early, such as through fuel management, creating firebreaks, and implementing responsible land practices, the likelihood of large-scale devastation to ecosystems, communities, and property is reduced. Risk mitigation strategies aim to safeguard lives, biodiversity, and valuable resources by taking preventive actions that lessen the overall impact of forest fires.

Resource Allocation

Efficient detection enables the allocation of firefighting resources where they are most needed, optimizing response efforts and minimizing resource wastage. Resource allocation in the context of forest fires refers to the strategic distribution of firefighting personnel, equipment, and tools to efficiently combat and manage fire incidents. Effective resource allocation ensures that the right resources are deployed to the right places at the right time, maximizing the impact of firefighting efforts. This includes identifying priority areas, assessing the scale and intensity of fires, and coordinating the deployment of resources to contain and extinguish fires swiftly. Proper resource allocation is crucial for minimizing fire spread, protecting communities, and optimizing firefighting strategies for the best possible outcomes.

Ecosystem Preservation

Swift intervention limits the ecological damage caused by fires, preserving habitats, biodiversity, and the health of ecosystems. Ecosystem preservation in the context of forest fires involves strategies to minimize the ecological impacts of fires on natural habitats and biodiversity. It includes measures to protect and conserve plant and animal species, maintain ecological balance, and promote the health of ecosystems. Through methods such as controlled burns, fuel management, and post-fire rehabilitation, ecosystems can be managed to mimic natural fire regimes, stimulate regeneration, and prevent the dominance of invasive species. Ecosystem preservation aims to sustain the integrity and resilience of ecosystems, ensuring their long-term health and functionality even in the face of fire disturbances.

Air Quality

Rapid detection aids in minimizing the release of harmful pollutants and smoke, improving air quality and safeguarding human and animal health. Air quality in the context of forest fires refers to the condition of the atmosphere in areas affected by smoke and pollutants generated by fires. When forest fires occur, they release smoke, particulates, and harmful gases into the air, which can degrade air quality and pose health risks to both humans and wildlife. Monitoring and managing air quality during fires is crucial to protect respiratory health, especially for vulnerable populations. Implementing measures such as public health advisories, air quality monitoring stations, and timely evacuation alerts helps mitigate the adverse effects of poor air quality caused by forest fires.

Carbon Emissions

Quicker fire response can help reduce the carbon emissions produced by fires, contributing to efforts to combat climate change. Carbon emissions in the context of forest fires refer to the release of carbon dioxide (CO_2) and other greenhouse gases into the atmosphere when vegetation and organic matter burn. Forest fires can contribute significantly to carbon emissions, which are a major driver of climate change. The burning of trees, plants, and other organic materials releases stored carbon back into the atmosphere, intensifying the greenhouse effect and warming the planet. Managing forest fires to minimize carbon emissions is crucial for mitigating climate change impacts. Strategies such as controlled burns, carbon offset programs, and reforestation efforts aim to reduce the carbon footprint associated with forest fires and promote long-term environmental sustainability.

Community Safety

Early detection enhances the safety of communities by allowing timely evacuation and alerting residents to potential dangers. Community safety in the context of forest fires focuses on protecting the well-being and lives of residents living in fire-prone areas. It involves implementing measures to prepare, inform, and evacuate communities at risk of fire incidents. Community safety strategies include creating defensible spaces around homes, developing and practicing evacuation plans, and establishing early warning systems to alert residents about fire threats. By prioritizing community safety, authorities aim to minimize the risk of injuries, fatalities, and property damage during fire emergencies, ensuring that residents have the information and resources they need to make informed decisions and take necessary actions to stay safe.

Economic Impact

Detecting fires early can reduce economic losses by preventing damage to timber resources, infrastructure, and industries reliant on forests. Economic impact in the context of forest fires refers to the financial consequences and losses incurred due to fire-related damages. Forest fires can have far-reaching economic effects, including the destruction of timber resources, damage to infrastructure, property loss, and reduced economic activities in affected areas. Industries reliant on forestry, such as logging and tourism, may suffer significant setbacks. Additionally, firefighting efforts and recovery expenses can strain local and regional budgets. Managing the economic impact of forest fires involves implementing fire prevention measures, allocating resources for firefighting and recovery, and fostering sustainable land management practices to mitigate losses and ensure long-term economic resilience in fire-prone regions.

Technological Advances

Leveraging modern technologies, such as satellites, drones, and fire behavior modeling, enhances the accuracy and speed of fire detection. Technological advances in the context of forest fires refer to the innovative tools, methods, and solutions that enhance fire detection, management, and response. Modern technologies like satellites, drones, geographic information systems (GIS), and advanced fire behavior models have revolutionized firefighting efforts. These technologies enable real-time fire monitoring, accurate mapping of fire perimeters, and predictive modeling of fire behavior. Such advancements aid

Figure 2. Technology advancement in forest management
(Shivaprakash 2022)

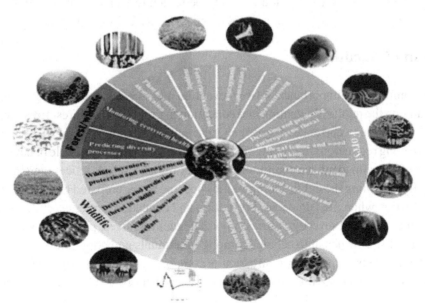

in early detection, rapid response coordination, and informed decision-making for firefighting teams. By leveraging these technologies, authorities can improve the efficiency and effectiveness of their fire management strategies, leading to better outcomes in terms of fire control, ecosystem preservation, and community safety. The figure 2 represents the distinct technology advancement in forest management.

Collaborative Efforts

Early detection fosters collaboration among agencies, organizations, and communities, facilitating coordinated response actions. Collaborative efforts in the context of forest fires involve the coordination and cooperation among various stakeholders, organizations, and agencies to collectively address fire-related challenges. Effective fire management requires collaboration between local, regional, and national entities, including fire departments, emergency services, government agencies, non-governmental organizations, and communities. Collaborative efforts enhance information sharing, resource allocation, and response strategies, leading to a more comprehensive and coordinated approach to fire prevention, detection, suppression, and recovery. By working together, stakeholders can pool their expertise, resources, and knowledge, ultimately improving the overall effectiveness of fire management and ensuring a more resilient and adaptive response to fire incidents.

Adaptive Planning

Identifying patterns in fire occurrence helps authorities develop adaptive fire management plans to address changing conditions and risks. Adaptive planning in the context of forest fires refers to the flexible and responsive approach to fire management strategies in light of changing conditions, risks, and circumstances. As fire dynamics, weather patterns, and ecosystems evolve, adaptive planning allows authorities to adjust their strategies and tactics accordingly. This involves continuously monitoring and assessing fire trends, learning from past experiences, and incorporating new information and technologies to enhance preparedness and response. Adaptive planning ensures that fire management strategies remain relevant and effective, enabling authorities to better address emerging challenges and optimize their efforts to mitigate the impacts of forest fires on ecosystems, communities, and the environment.

Prevention and Education

Early detection reinforces the importance of fire prevention measures, encouraging responsible behavior and awareness among the public. Prevention and education in the context of forest fires involve proactive measures to minimize the occurrence of fires and raise public awareness about fire safety. Prevention includes implementing regulations, enforcing fire bans, and promoting responsible behavior in fire-prone areas. Education efforts aim to inform communities about fire risks, safe practices, and the importance of early reporting. By educating the public, communities become better prepared to prevent accidental fires and take prompt action when fires do occur. Prevention and education strategies collectively contribute to reducing the frequency and severity of forest fires, safeguarding lives, property, and ecosystems, and fostering a culture of fire-responsible behavior among individuals and communities.

In essence, detecting forest fires early is an essential component of effective fire management, enabling timely and well-coordinated responses that protect lives, ecosystems, and the environment. The numerous advantages associated with the detection of forest fires are: Early Intervention where Swift detection allows firefighting teams to respond quickly, containing fires in their early stages before they escalate into larger, more destructive incidents. Minimized Spread where timely detection helps prevent fires from spreading uncontrollably, reducing the extent of damage and the resources needed for suppression.

In Ecosystem Preservation, the Early response minimizes ecological damage, preserving habitats, biodiversity, and the health of ecosystems. Reduced Air Pollution Prompts detection reduces the release of harmful pollutants and smoke, improving air quality and minimizing health risks. Carbon Emission Mitigation Swifts intervention which helps to manage carbon emissions by preventing prolonged burning and the release of stored carbon. Community Safety that detects fires early enables timely evacuation alerts, protecting residents and preventing loss of life.

The Optimized Resource Allocation occurs when Early detection ensures firefighting resources are deployed where needed, maximizing the effectiveness of response efforts. In Financial Savings, Quicker containment reduces firefighting costs and economic losses due to property damage and disruptions. The Climate Resilience helps in Managing fires promptly aids in adapting to changing climate conditions, mitigating the impact of fire-induced carbon emissions. Enhanced Planning occurs when Early detection data informs adaptive fire management plans, improving preparedness for future fire events. The Public Awareness helps in Highlighting the importance of early detection fosters public vigilance and cooperation in reporting fires. Collaboration with Rapid detection encourages agencies, communities, and stakeholders to collaborate effectively in firefighting efforts. By reaping these advantages, early detection plays a pivotal role in minimizing the devastating impacts of forest fires on ecosystems, communities, and the environment.

SAFEGUARDING THE WILDERNESS: EFFECTIVE PREVENTION STRATEGIES FOR FOREST FIRES

Prevention mechanisms for forest fires encompass a range of proactive strategies aimed at reducing the likelihood of fires and their potential to escalate. These mechanisms include enforcing regulations to curb fire-prone activities, educating the public about responsible behavior, and managing vegetation to limit fuel sources. Creating firebreaks and defensible spaces, practicing safe campfire practices, and employing early detection systems are also part of prevention efforts. By adopting these measures, communities and authorities work to minimize human-caused fire ignitions, protect natural landscapes, and enhance overall fire safety. The figure 3 represents the study on forest fire with the area and location for the year 2017 to 2019.

Prevention mechanisms for forest fires involve a range of strategies aimed at reducing the likelihood of fires starting and spreading. Some key prevention mechanisms include:

Regulations and Policies

Implementing and enforcing laws that restrict activities with a high potential to cause fires, such as campfires, fireworks, and open burning.

Figure 3. Study on forest fire
(Ban 2020)

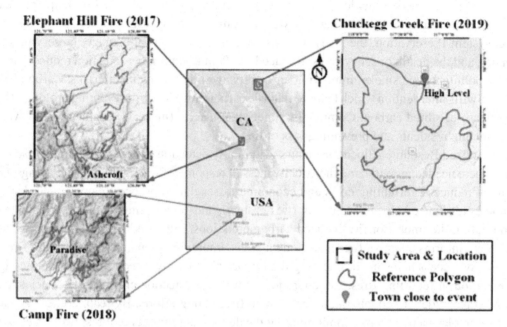

Public Education and Awareness

Raising awareness among the public about fire risks, responsible behavior in fire-prone areas, and the importance of fire safety.

Fuel Management

Thinning forests and removing excess vegetation to reduce fuel loads and limit the intensity of potential fires.

Firebreaks and Defensible Space

Creating cleared areas or natural barriers that prevent the spread of fires and establishing defensible spaces around homes to protect against approaching fires.

Vegetation Management

Pruning trees, removing dead or dry vegetation, and maintaining landscaping in a way that minimizes fire risk.

Campfire Safety

Educating campers and outdoor enthusiasts about proper campfire practices, including choosing safe locations, keeping fires small, and ensuring fires are completely extinguished.

Cigarette Disposal

Educating individuals about proper cigarette disposal to prevent accidental fires caused by discarded cigarette butts.

Early Detection Systems

Implementing fire detection technologies, such as surveillance cameras, satellite monitoring, and sensors, to quickly identify fire ignitions.

Fire Bans and Restrictions

Imposing temporary fire bans or restrictions during periods of high fire danger to prevent human-caused ignitions.

Community Planning

Designing communities with fire-resistant materials, proper spacing between structures, and evacuation routes in mind.

Wildland-Urban Interface Management

Managing the interface between developed areas and natural landscapes to reduce fire risk and protect both human and natural assets.

Firewise Communities

Encouraging communities to adopt Firewise principles, which involve creating defensible spaces, using fire-resistant materials, and promoting fire-safe practices.

By implementing a combination of these prevention mechanisms, will significantly reduce the occurrence of forest fires and minimizes the risks they pose to ecosystems, communities, and the environment.

ALERTING NATURE'S FURY: VIGILANCE AND ALERTS FOR FOREST FIRE AWARENESS

Warning systems for forest fires involve the establishment of mechanisms to alert communities, authorities, and relevant stakeholders about the potential or actual occurrence of fires. These systems rely on a combination of technologies such as weather monitoring, satellite imagery, sensors, and surveillance cameras to detect fire ignitions. Once a fire is detected, timely alerts are disseminated through various channels, including mobile apps, text messages, sirens, and public announcements. These warnings enable residents to take immediate action, evacuate if necessary, and inform firefighting teams for swift response. Warning systems play a critical role in minimizing fire-related risks, protecting lives, and allowing communities to prepare and respond effectively to the threat of forest fires.

Warning techniques for forest fires involve a variety of strategies to notify and prepare communities for fire-related threats:

Sensors and Surveillance

Using advanced sensors and cameras to detect smoke or heat signatures, triggering alerts to authorities and residents.

Satellite Monitoring

Utilizing satellite imagery to identify fire hotspots and communicate potential risks in remote areas.

Weather Forecasting

Monitoring weather conditions that contribute to fire risk and issuing warnings during periods of elevated danger.

Automated Alerts

Sending automated messages, texts, or app notifications to residents, providing real-time updates on fire conditions.

Sirens and Public Address Systems

Employing audible warnings like sirens or loudspeakers to alert communities and prompt action.

Emergency Services Coordination

Collaborating with fire departments, police, and emergency services to ensure effective communication during fire incidents.

Community Education

Educating residents about warning signs, response procedures, and evacuation plans through workshops and outreach programs.

Mobile Apps

Developing smartphone apps that deliver instant fire alerts, evacuation routes, and safety instructions.

Radio and Television Broadcasts

Broadcasting fire-related information through local radio and television stations to reach a wider audience.

Social Media Platforms

Utilizing social media platforms to disseminate timely information, encourage preparedness, and answer questions from the public.

By employing a combination of these techniques, the ability to warn communities about impending forest fires, empowered residents to take proactive steps for safeguarding lives and property.

TECH-INFUSED WOODLANDS: THE ROLE OF ARTIFICIAL INTELLIGENCE IN FOREST MANAGEMENT

AI in forest management involves the application of artificial intelligence techniques to enhance the monitoring, conservation, and sustainable use of forests. Machine learning algorithms, data analysis, and remote sensing technologies are used to analyze vast amounts of data from various sources, such as satellite imagery, weather data, and sensor networks. AI assists in tasks like early detection of forest fires, predicting disease outbreaks in trees, monitoring wildlife habitats, and optimizing timber harvesting practices. By providing insights and predictions, AI contributes to making informed decisions for preserving biodiversity, mitigating climate change, and ensuring the long-term health and productivity of forests.

AI techniques play a pivotal role in modern forest management, offering innovative solutions for various challenges such as

Forest Monitoring and Analysis

- *Satellite Imagery:* AI processes satellite data to monitor forest health, track deforestation, and assess land cover changes.
- *Remote Sensing:* AI helps analyze remote sensing data to estimate tree density, detect disease outbreaks, and map forest attributes.

Fire Detection and Management

- *Image Analysis:* AI algorithms analyze images to detect smoke, fire fronts, and hotspot anomalies, enabling early fire detection.
- *Predictive Models:* AI models forecast fire behavior, aiding firefighting strategies and evacuation planning.

Wildlife Conservation

- *Camera Traps:* AI identifies and classifies species in camera trap images, aiding wildlife monitoring and conservation efforts.
- *Sound Analysis:* AI can recognize animal sounds, helping identify species presence and migration patterns.

Disease and Pest Detection

- *Image Recognition:* AI identifies disease symptoms in tree leaves or pests on plants, assisting in early intervention.

Forest Planning and Optimization

- *Decision Support Systems:* AI aids in optimizing timber harvesting schedules, considering factors like ecological impact and economic viability.
- *Spatial Analysis:* AI helps determine optimal locations for new plantations, considering soil quality and biodiversity.

Carbon Sequestration and Climate Change Mitigation

- *Carbon Accounting:* AI estimates carbon sequestration and tracks changes in forest carbon stocks, aiding climate change mitigation efforts.

Risk Assessment and Adaptation Planning

- *Data Analysis:* AI processes historical data to assess past fire behavior, aiding in modeling future fire risks and adapting management strategies.

Automated Data Collection

- *Drones and Sensors:* AI-powered drones and sensors collect data on forest conditions, enabling efficient monitoring.

Predictive Modeling

- *Machine Learning*: AI models predict forest growth, biodiversity changes, and future ecosystem dynamics.

Resource Allocation

- *Optimization Algorithms:* AI optimizes allocation of resources like firefighting crews, equipment, and supplies during fire emergencies.

AI techniques in forest management empower decision-makers with accurate insights, enhance efficiency, and contribute to sustainable practices for conserving and managing forests for future generations.

ELEVATING FOREST MANAGEMENT: THE TRANSFORMATIVE ROLE OF AI IN CONSERVATION AND SUSTAINABILITY

AI revolutionizes forest management by leveraging advanced technologies to enhance monitoring, prediction, and decision-making. It aids early fire detection through image analysis and sensors, models fire behavior, optimizes resource allocation during emergencies, and predicts disease outbreaks in trees. AI processes camera trap images and acoustic data to monitor wildlife and assess ecosystem health. It estimates carbon sequestration, tracks deforestation, and aids optimal timber harvesting schedules. By analyzing vast datasets, AI assists in adaptive planning, informs decisions for sustainable practices, and empowers forest managers to protect ecosystems and mitigate climate change impacts effectively.AI in forest management are as follows

- **Early Fire Detection:** AI-powered image analysis and sensors can quickly identify smoke or fire hotspots, enabling early fire detection and swift intervention.
- **Fire Behavior Modeling:** AI algorithms predict fire behavior based on factors like weather, terrain, and vegetation, aiding firefighting strategies.
- **Wildlife Monitoring:** AI processes camera trap images and acoustic data to identify species, track migration patterns, and assess wildlife health.
- **Disease Detection:** AI analyzes images of tree leaves to detect disease symptoms early, allowing for timely interventions.
- **Carbon Accounting:** AI estimates carbon sequestration in forests, helping in climate change mitigation efforts and carbon offset programs.
- **Deforestation Tracking:** AI processes satellite data to monitor deforestation and illegal logging activities, supporting conservation efforts.
- **Resource Allocation:** AI optimizes the allocation of firefighting resources, ensuring efficient deployment during fire emergencies.
- **Timber Harvesting Optimization:** AI assists in planning optimal timber harvesting schedules while considering ecological and economic factors.
- **Ecosystem Modeling:** AI-driven predictive models simulate ecosystem dynamics, aiding in understanding long-term impacts of management decisions.
- **Data Collection:** Drones and sensors equipped with AI collect real-time data on forest conditions, aiding in monitoring and assessment.
- **Spatial Analysis:** AI helps in identifying suitable locations for new plantations, taking into account soil quality and biodiversity.

Figure 4. Artificial intelligence in forest management

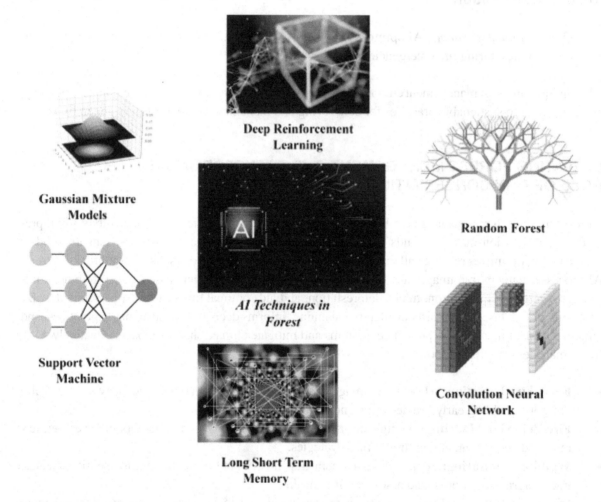

- **Adaptive Planning:** AI enables adaptive forest management strategies by analyzing historical data and predicting future risks and conditions.
- **Decision Support:** AI provides decision-makers with insights from complex data sets, aiding in informed choices for sustainable forest management.

By harnessing the power of AI, forest managers can make more accurate predictions, optimize resource utilization, respond effectively to emergencies, and implement strategies that contribute to the long-term health and sustainability of forests.

UNVEILING THE POWER OF AI ALGORITHMS FOR ADVANCING FOREST AND FOREST FIRE MANAGEMENT

AI algorithms have emerged as indispensable tools in the domains of forest and forest fire management. With their ability to process vast amounts of data, extract meaningful patterns, and make predictions, these algorithms are transforming the way we understand, protect, and sustain our natural environments. In this context, AI algorithms offer sophisticated solutions for forest management, ranging from species identification and growth prediction to disease detection and carbon accounting. Similarly, in the realm of forest fire management, these algorithms contribute by enabling early fire detection, modeling fire behavior, optimizing resource allocation, and enhancing decision-making for effective firefighting strategies. Figure 4 explores the pivotal role AI algorithms play in revolutionizing our approach to preserving forests and mitigating the impact of forest fires.

Forest Management

- *Image Analysis:* AI processes satellite and drone images to monitor forest health, detect changes in vegetation, and assess tree density.
- *Species Identification:* AI identifies plant and animal species through image analysis and sound recognition, aiding biodiversity monitoring.
- *Disease Detection:* AI analyzes leaf images to detect signs of diseases in trees, enabling early intervention to prevent outbreaks.
- *Growth Prediction*: AI models predict forest growth and dynamics based on historical data, aiding sustainable timber harvesting and planning.
- *Carbon Sequestration:* AI estimates carbon sequestration in forests, contributing to climate change mitigation efforts.
- *Deforestation Tracking:* AI processes satellite imagery to detect deforestation and illegal logging, supporting conservation efforts.
- *Spatial Analysis:* AI assists in selecting optimal sites for reforestation, considering factors like soil quality and ecosystem suitability.

Forest Fire Management

- *Fire Detection*: AI analyzes satellite imagery, sensor data, and drone footage to detect fire hotspots and smoke, enabling early detection.
- *Fire Behavior Modeling:* AI predicts fire spread based on factors like weather, topography, and vegetation, aiding firefighting strategies.
- *Risk Assessment:* AI models assess fire risks by analyzing historical fire data and environmental conditions, informing preparedness efforts.
- *Resource Allocation:* AI optimizes the allocation of firefighting resources, such as crews and equipment, during fire emergencies.
- *Evacuation Planning:* AI helps plan efficient evacuation routes and strategies, ensuring the safety of residents in fire-prone areas.
- *Real-time Monitoring:* AI-powered sensors and cameras provide real-time updates on fire behavior, aiding real-time decision-making.
- *Predictive Analysis:* AI-driven models forecast fire behavior based on changing conditions, assisting in adapting firefighting strategies.

AI algorithms empower forest and fire managers with accurate insights, predictive capabilities, and informed decisions, contributing to effective and sustainable forest management while mitigating the impact of forest fires on ecosystems and communities.

HARNESSING THE POWER OF AI ALGORITHMS FOR ADVANCED FOREST MANAGEMENT

In the realm of forest management, the integration of Artificial Intelligence (AI) algorithms has ushered in a new era of precision and efficiency. These algorithms, powered by advanced data analysis and machine learning techniques, have the remarkable ability to unravel intricate patterns within forests, enabling us to understand ecosystems on a deeper level. This introduction delves into the intricate workings of AI algorithms in forest management, exploring how they process diverse datasets, uncover insights into species distribution, growth trends, and health assessments, and ultimately empower us to make informed decisions that ensure the sustainable preservation of our forests.

Random Forest

Random Forest is an ensemble learning algorithm that constructs multiple decision trees and combines their outputs. In the context of forest management, it processes image data from cameras or drones. Each decision tree independently analyzes patches of the image to predict the species present in those areas. The algorithm aggregates these predictions from all trees to create a comprehensive species classification map of the entire forest.

Random Forest is employed for species classification based on image data from cameras or drones. It can accurately identify various plant and animal species, aiding biodiversity monitoring. Random Forest operates by creating multiple decision trees and aggregating their outputs. In forest management, it analyzes image data from cameras or drones (Rangelov 2023). Each decision tree processes a subset of the data and predicts the species present in a given image patch. The algorithm then combines the predictions from all trees to provide accurate species classification across the entire image.

Convolutional Neural Networks (CNNs)

CNNs process satellite or drone images to detect changes in forest cover, monitor deforestation, and assess tree health. They identify patterns and anomalies in imagery that might indicate disease outbreaks or illegal activities.

CNNs are deep learning models designed to process visual data like images. In forest management, they take satellite or drone images as input. CNNs automatically learn to extract relevant features like textures, patterns, and shapes from these images. By passing the images through multiple convolutional and pooling layers, CNNs can detect changes in forest cover, monitor deforestation, and assess tree health based on patterns and anomalies in the data.

Long Short-Term Memory (LSTM) Networks

LSTM networks are a type of recurrent neural network (RNN) designed to process sequential data. In forest management, they analyze time-series data from weather stations. LSTM cells possess memory capabilities, allowing them to capture dependencies over time. They learn from historical weather patterns to predict forest growth, disease outbreaks, and ecosystem changes. By factoring in variables like temperature, rainfall, and sunlight, LSTM networks offer insights into the impact of climate variations on forests.

LSTM (Rangelov 2023) networks are applied to time-series data from weather stations to predict forest growth and ecosystem changes over time. They can estimate the impact of climate variations on forest health.

Support Vector Machines (SVM)

SVMs are machine learning models used for classification tasks. In forest management, they process spectral data collected by remote sensing devices. These devices capture the reflectance of various wavelengths of light, which corresponds to different vegetation types. SVMs analyze this data and create a boundary that separates different types of forests. This enables accurate classification of different forest covers.

SVM is used for forest classification based on spectral data from remote sensing devices. It helps distinguish different forest types, aiding land management and conservation efforts.

Gaussian Mixture Models (GMM)

GMMs are statistical models used for clustering data into different components. In forest management, GMMs cluster satellite images into different vegetation types. By analyzing the spectral information in these images, GMMs can identify areas with different levels of biodiversity, or even areas where certain plant species dominate. GMMs are applied to cluster satellite images into vegetation types. They help identify areas of high biodiversity or areas susceptible to pests, facilitating targeted management.

AI ALGORITHMS REVOLUTIONIZING FOREST FIRE MANAGEMENT: INSIGHTS AND INNOVATIONS

The relentless threat of forest fires demands a proactive and data-driven approach to management. This is where Artificial Intelligence (AI) algorithms step in, reshaping the landscape of forest fire management. By harnessing the power of AI, we can not only detect fires early but also predict their behavior and strategize effective responses. This introduction delves into the mechanics of AI algorithms in forest fire management, illuminating how these algorithms analyze diverse data sources, model fire dynamics, optimize resource allocation, and ultimately empower us to safeguard both ecosystems and communities against the devastating impact of forest fires.

Random Forest

Random Forest is used to predict fire risk. It learns from historical fire data and environmental factors such as temperature, humidity, wind speed, and vegetation density. The algorithm evaluates the relationships between these variables and fire occurrences. By assessing various combinations, it estimates the likelihood of fires breaking out in specific regions, aiding fire prevention strategies.

Random Forest can predict fire risk by analyzing historical fire data and environmental factors such as temperature, humidity, and wind speed. It assists in assessing the likelihood of fire occurrences in specific areas. For forest fire management, Random Forest is utilized for fire risk assessment. It analyzes historical fire data and environmental factors such as temperature, humidity, wind speed, and vegetation density. The algorithm trains on past fire incidents and their associated conditions, allowing it to predict the likelihood of fire occurrence in specific areas.

Convolutional Neural Networks

In forest fire management, CNNs are employed for early fire detection. Cameras or drones capture real-time images of forested areas. These images are fed into the CNN, which can identify visual cues like smoke plumes, fire fronts, or anomalous heat signatures. The CNN's ability to recognize these patterns enables rapid detection and timely response. CNNs are used for early fire detection by analyzing real-time images from cameras or drones. They identify smoke plumes or fire fronts, enabling swift response.

Long Short-Term Memory (LSTM) Networks

LSTM models predict fire behavior by examining historical weather data and predicting how changing conditions might affect fire spread. By analyzing factors like wind speed, humidity, and temperature, LSTM networks provide valuable insights into fire dynamics and help firefighting teams anticipate fire movements. LSTM models can predict fire behavior by analyzing historical weather data and predicting how changing conditions might influence fire spread.

Support Vector Machines (SVM)

SVMs are applied to predict fire perimeters by analyzing satellite imagery and topographical data. By learning from past fire incidents, SVMs create a boundary that separates burned areas from unburned ones. This helps predict how fires might spread based on terrain characteristics and vegetation density. SVMs assist in predicting fire perimeters by analyzing satellite imagery and topographical data. They estimate how fires might progress based on terrain characteristics.

Gaussian Mixture Models (GMM)

In the context of forest fire management, GMMs are utilized for smoke detection. They learn the color distribution of smoke plumes in images captured by cameras or drones. GMMs can then identify unusual color patterns that indicate the presence of smoke, enabling early fire detection.

These AI algorithms showcase the diverse ways technology can be harnessed for effective forest management and forest fire management. They contribute to informed decision-making, early detection, efficient resource allocation, and sustainable practices in preserving natural ecosystems and safeguarding against fire hazards.

AI IN FOREST FIRE DETECTION AND MANAGEMENT

Background

In a vast forest region, the threat of wildfires is a constant concern due to dry weather conditions and human activities. Traditional methods of fire detection, primarily reliant on manual surveillance and occasional aerial monitoring, are limited in their efficiency and speed. The local authorities seek more advanced and proactive measures to detect, monitor, and manage forest fires.

The implementation of AI involves various techniques to address different stages of forest fire management. The stages are early detection, predictive analytics, rapid response, resource allocation and forest fire analysis.

Early Detection

A system powered by AI algorithms, such as machine learning and computer vision, is deployed to analyze live feeds from cameras strategically positioned throughout the forest. These cameras utilize image recognition to identify smoke, flame patterns, and other indicators of potential fires. Machine learning models continuously analyze these images, learning to distinguish between normal activities and potential fire outbreaks.

Predictive Analytics

AI is used to analyze historical data, including weather patterns, vegetation health, and human activity in the region. Predictive analytics help in forecasting the likelihood of a fire outbreak in specific areas, allowing proactive measures to be taken before a fire occurs.

Rapid Response

Upon fire detection, AI-powered systems trigger immediate alerts to the fire department and relevant authorities. Drones equipped with infrared cameras and AI are deployed to provide real-time updates on the fire's movement, intensity, and direction, aiding firefighters in strategizing their response.

Resource Allocation

AI assists in optimizing resource allocation by suggesting the most effective deployment of firefighting teams and equipment based on the fire's predicted path and intensity.

Post-Fire Analysis

After the fire is contained, AI is used to assess the damage, calculate the affected area, and plan rehabilitation efforts. It helps in understanding the fire's impact on the ecosystem and in devising strategies for reforestation and habitat restoration.

Resolution and Impact

The integration of AI in forest fire management significantly improves response time, accuracy in detection, and resource allocation. By detecting fires at their early stages, authorities can contain them before they spread extensively, reducing environmental and economic damage. The use of predictive analytics minimizes the occurrence of wildfires by allowing preemptive actions.

Challenges and Future Developments

While AI has shown immense potential in forest fire management, there are ongoing challenges, including the need for continuous system improvement, better integration of data sources, and ensuring the accessibility of AI-driven systems in remote forest areas.

Future developments may involve advancements in AI models that can handle diverse environmental conditions and further integration of technologies like satellite imaging, Internet of Things (IoT), and unmanned aerial systems to enhance the efficiency of fire detection and response.

This case study highlights the significant role AI can play in early detection, rapid response, and efficient management of forest fires, mitigating their devastating impact on ecosystems and communities.

CONCLUSION

Forests are incredibly diverse ecosystems, housing a wide array of plant and animal species. When a forest fire occurs, it can lead to the loss of biodiversity. Species that are unable to flee or find refuge in unburned areas may perish, leading to declines in populations and potential extinctions. The loss of biodiversity has cascading effects on ecosystem functioning and resilience. Forest fires can cause soil degradation and erosion.

In conclusion, the integration of AI algorithms in forest and forest fire management represents a transformative leap towards more effective, informed, and sustainable practices. These algorithms have proven their prowess in deciphering complex patterns, predicting outcomes, and optimizing resource allocation. From accurate species identification and growth predictions in forest management to early fire detection, behavior modeling, and real-time decision-making in fire management, AI algorithms have emerged as indispensable tools.The potential implications of integrating AI in forest fire management are immense. This technology not only minimizes the environmental and economic impact of wildfires but also enhances the safety of wildlife and communities residing in these areas. Furthermore, it allows for efficient resource allocation, reducing response time and, consequently, minimizing the extent of devastation caused by these natural disasters.

The potential benefits are vast which incurs from preserving biodiversity and optimizing timber harvesting to mitigating the devastating effects of forest fires on ecosystems and communities. By embracing

AI algorithms, we stand on the cusp of a new era in which data-driven insights drive conservation efforts and ensure the well-being of the environment. The ongoing development of AI-driven models and the integration of additional technologies like IoT and satellite imaging hold promise for further enhancing the efficacy and reach of these systems. With continuous advancements, AI in forest fire management stands as a critical tool for safeguarding our natural landscapes and communities, offering a proactive and data-driven approach to mitigate the destructive consequences of wildfires.

REFERENCES

Abedi Gheshlaghi, H., Feizizadeh, B., & Blaschke, T. (2019). GIS-based forest fire risk mapping using the analytical networkprocess and fuzzy logic. *Journal of Environmental Planning and Management*, *63*(3), 481–499. doi:10.1080/09640568.2019.1594726

Anderson, T. M., White, S., Davis, B., Erhardt, R., Palmer, M., Swanson, A., Kosmala, M., & Packer, C. (2016). The spatial distribution of African savannah herbivores: Species associations and habitat occupancy in a landscape context. *Philosophical Transactions of the Royal Society of London. Series B, Biological Sciences*, *371*(1703), 20150314. doi:10.1098/rstb.2015.0314 PMID:27502379

Ban, Y., Zhang, P., Nascetti, A., Bevington, A. R., & Wulder, M. A. (2020). Near Real-Time Wildfire Progression Monitoring with Sentinel-1 SAR Time Series and Deep Learning. *Scientific Reports*, *10*(1), 1322. doi:10.103841598-019-56967-x PMID:31992723

Belgherbi, B., Benabdeli, K., & Mostefai, K. (2018). Mapping the riskforest fires in Algeria: Application of the forest of Guetarnia in Western Algeria. *Ekologia (Bratislava)*, *37*(3), 289–300. doi:10.2478/eko-2018-0022

Cardille, J. A., & Ventura, S. J. (2001). Occurrence of wildfire in thenorthern Great Lakes Region: Effects of land cover and landownership assessed at multiple scales. *International Journal of Wildland Fire*, *10*(2), 145–154. doi:10.1071/WF01010

Drüke, M., Sakschewski, B., von Bloh, W., Billing, M., Lucht, W., & Thonicke, K. (2023). Fire may prevent future Amazon forest recovery after large-scale deforestation. *Communications Earth & Environment*, *4*(1), 248. doi:10.103843247-023-00911-5

Goparaju, L., Prasad, R. C. P., Babu Suresh, K. V., & Tecimen, H. B. (2023). Editorial: Forest fire emissions and their impact on global climate change. *Frontiers in Forests and Global Change*, *6*, 1188632. doi:10.3389/ffgc.2023.1188632

Gugliette, D., Conedera, M., Mazzolenıs, S., & Ricotta, C. (2011). Mapping fire ignition risk in a complex anthropogeniclandscape. *Remote Sensing Letters*, *2*(3), 213–219. doi:10.1080/01431161.2010.512927

Hansen, M. C., Potapov, P. V., Moore, R., Hancher, M., Turubanova, S. A., Tyukavina, A., Thau, D., Stehman, S. V., Goetz, S. J., Loveland, T. R., Kommareddy, A., Egorov, A., Chini, L., Justice, C. O., & Townshend, J. R. G. (2013). High-Resolution Global Maps of 21st-Century Forest Cover Change. *Science*, *342*(6160), 850–853. doi:10.1126cience.1244693 PMID:24233722

Hernández-Morcillo, M., Torralba, M., Baiges, T., Bernasconi, A., Bottaro, G., Brogaard, S., Bussola, F., Díaz-Varela, E., Geneletti, D., Grossmann, C. M., Kister, J., Klingler, M., Loft, L., Lovric, M., Mann, C., Pipart, N., Roces-Díaz, J. V., Sorge, S., Tiebel, M., & Plieninger, T. (2022). Scanning the solutions for the sustainable supply of forest ecosystem services in Europe. *Sustainability Science, 17*(5), 2013–2029. doi:10.100711625-022-01111-4 PMID:35340343

Karabulut, M., Karakoc, A., Gurbuz, M., & Kizilelma, Y. (2013). Determination of forest fire risk areas using geographicalinformation systems in Baskonus Mountain (Kahramanmaras). *The Journal of International Social Research, 6*(24), 171–179.

Kumari, B., & Pandey, A. C. (2020). MODIS based forest fire hotspot analysis and its relationship with climatic variables. *Spatial Information Research, 28*(1), 87–99. doi:10.100741324-019-00275-z

Kuter, S., Usul, N., & Kuter, N. (2011). Bandwidth determination forkernel density analysis of wildfire events at forest sub-districtscale. *Ecological Modelling, 222*(17), 3033–3040. doi:10.1016/j.ecolmodel.2011.06.006

Malik, T., Rabbani, G., & Farooq, M. (2013). Forest fire risk zonation using remote sensing and GIS technology in Kansrao ForestRange of Rajaji National Park, Uttarakhand, India. India. *International Journal of Advanced RS and GIS, 2*(1), 86–95.

Martínez-Fernández, J., Chuvieco, E., & Koutsias, N. (2013). Modelling long-term fire occurrence factors in Spain byaccounting for local variations with geographically weightedregression. *Natural Hazards and Earth System Sciences, 13*(2), 311–327. doi:10.5194/nhess-13-311-2013

Miao, Z., Gaynor, K. M., Wang, J., Liu, Z., Muellerklein, O., Norouzzadeh, M. S., McInturff, A., Bowie, R. C. K., Nathan, R., Yu, S. X., & Getz, W. M. (2019). Insights and approaches using deep learning to classify wildlife. *Scientific Reports, 9*(1), 8137. doi:10.103841598-019-44565-w PMID:31148564

Norouzzadeh, M. S., Nguyen, A., Kosmala, M., Swanson, A., Palmer, M. S., Packer, C., & Clune, J. (2018). Automatically identifying, counting, and describing wild animals in camera-trap images with deep learning. *Proceedings of the National Academy of Sciences of the United States of America, 115*(25), E5716–E5725. doi:10.1073/pnas.1719367115 PMID:29871948

Pratihast, A. K., De Vries, B., Avitabile, V., De Bruin, S., Herold, M., & Bergsma, A. (2016). Design and implementation of an interactive web-based near real-time forest monitoring system. *PLoS One, 11*(3), e0150935. doi:10.1371/journal.pone.0150935 PMID:27031694

Rangelov, D., Boerger, M., Tcholtchev, N., Lämmel, P., & Hauswirth, M. (2023). Design and Development of a Short-Term Photovoltaic Power Output Forecasting Method Based on Random Forest, Deep Neural Network and LSTM Using Readily Available Weather Features. *IEEE Access : Practical Innovations, Open Solutions, 11*, 41578–41595. doi:10.1109/ACCESS.2023.3270714

Roy, P.S. (2003). Forest fire and degradation assessment usingsatellite remote sensing and geographic information system. *Satellite Remote Sensing and GIS Applications in Agricultural Meteorology*, 361-400.

Shivaprakash, K. N., Swami, N., Mysorekar, S., Arora, R., Gangadharan, A., Vohra, K., Jadeyegowda, M., & Kiesecker, J. M. (2022). Potential for Artificial Intelligence (AI) and Machine Learning (ML) Applications in Biodiversity Conservation, Managing Forests, and Related Services in India. *Sustainability (Basel)*, *14*(12), 7154. doi:10.3390u14127154

Sowmya, S. V., & Somashekar, R. K. (2010). Application of remotesensing and geographical information system in mapping forestfire risk zone at Bhadra wildlife sanctuary, India. *Journal of Environmental Biology*, *31*(6), 969. PMID:21506484

Chapter 7
AI–Driven Solution Selection:
Prediction of Water Quality Using Machine Learning

Tran Thi Hong Ngoc
An Giang University, Vietnam

Phan Truong Khanh
An Giang University, Vietnam

Sabyasachi Pramanik
ⓘ https://orcid.org/0000-0002-9431-8751
Haldia Institute of Technology, India

ABSTRACT

With the fast growth of aquatic data, machine learning is essential for data analysis, categorization, and prediction. Data-driven models using machine learning may effectively handle complicated nonlinear problems in water research, unlike conventional approaches. Machine learning models and findings have been used to build, monitor, simulate, evaluate, and optimize water treatment and management systems in water environment research. Machine learning may also enhance water quality, pollution control, and watershed ecosystem security. This chapter discusses how ML approaches were used to assess water quality in surface, ground, drinking, sewage, and ocean. The authors also suggest potential machine learning applications in aquatic situations.

INTRODUCTION

Wastewater carrying toxins from fast economic growth threatens natural water ecology. So, several water pollution management methods evolved. Water quality analysis and assessment have greatly enhanced water pollution control efficiency. The multivariate statistical approach, fuzzy inference, and water quality index (WQI) are among the various methods used to monitor and measure water quality globally. While many water quality metrics may be traced in accordance with regulations, the final findings may vary

DOI: 10.4018/979-8-3693-0639-0.ch007

according to parameter selection. Taking into account that all water quality metrics is impractical due to cost, technical difficulty, and inability to account for variability. Recently, developments in machine learning have led academics to anticipate that huge volumes of data may be achieved and assessed to accomplish complex and large-scale water quality monitoring needs.

Machine Learning (ML) algorithms are used in artificial intelligence to examine data and find patterns to forecast future information. With its accuracy, flexibility, and extensibility, machine learning has become a popular data analysis and processing tool in several fields. Machine learning simplifies the finding of underlying mechanisms for complex nonlinear relational data. Recently, ML showed a huge potential as a tool in ecological science and engineering due to its versatility. In spite of the difficulty of ML for water quality measurement and assessment, much precise results are predicted.

Complex water kinds include drinking, wastewater, and groundwater, surface, marine, and fresh. These water kinds have varied qualities, making quality study difficult. Previous research suggests that machine learning may effectively handle these difficulties. In this study, we address the pros and cons of typical ML approaches and their implementations and performance in surface water, groundwater, drinking water, wastewater, and ocean water (Figure 1).

ML is commonly utilized to find insights or predictions from vast data from many contexts. Prior to using ML, data collecting, algorithm selection, model training, and validation are needed. Among these methods, selecting an algorithm is the key aspect.

Figure 1. Water systems employ machine learning extensively. WWTP, wastewater treatment facility (Zhu et al. 2022)

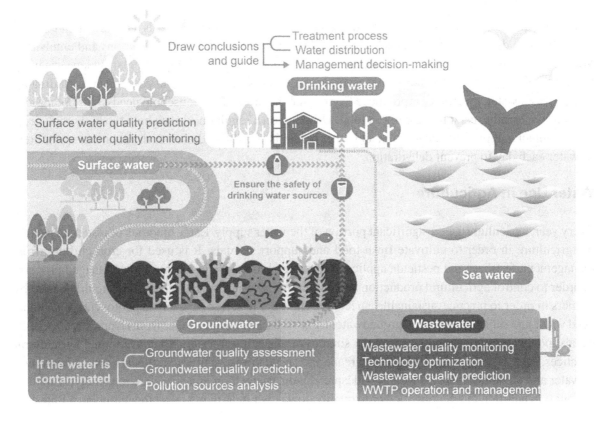

Machine learning has two primary classes: supervised and unsupervised. Labels in datasets distinguish these two kinds. Supervised learning predicts from labeled training datasets. Input and anticipated output values are included in each training instance. Supervised learning algorithms discover input-output correlations and create a predictive model to estimate the outcome from the I/P data. Supervised learning methods, such as LR, ANN, decision trees, SVM, Naive Bayes, KNN, and random forests are designed for data classification and regression.

In contrast, unsupervised learning handles data generally without labels, addressing pattern recognition problems using unlabeled training datasets. Unsupervised learning classifies training data depending on features, primarily via dimensionality reduction and grouping. But, the quantity and significance of categories are unknown. Thus, unsupervised learning is often employed for classification and association mining. PCA, K-means, and other unsupervised machine learning methods are popular. Reinforcement learning, which allows machines to generalize and solve unlearned problem is a different kind of ML method. In contrast to the other 2 ML classes, it is sometimes used in the aquatic aspect.

Section 3 consists of the methodology used, section 4 is the conclusion.

WHAT PURPOSES DOES WATER SERVE?

Water is a resource that is essential to life and may be used for a wide range of tasks, from everyday household tasks to supporting the operations of whole enterprises.

Domestic Water Uses

Cooking requires water to assist bring food to a boil, steam, or simmer. Water is a useful agent to assist wash clothing, dishes, and food items because of its special ability to generate solutions and emulsions. Water washing aids in the removal of pollutants. It is necessary for maintaining personal hygiene, cleaning teeth, and having showers. At home, it's used for gardening. Many household equipment, including air coolers, need water. Electricity is produced from water and utilized for household needs. Our bodies lose water as we breathe, perspire, and digest food. Drinking on a regular basis can help the body replace its water content and prevent dehydration and other health issues. It is advised to drink one to seven liters of water each day to prevent dehydration.

Water Use in Agriculture

Every year, agriculture uses a significant portion of the water supply. Large amounts of water are needed in agriculture in order to cultivate fresh food and support animals. It is used for crop chilling, frost management, fertilizer and pesticide application, and irrigation. Water use has to be managed properly in order to control agricultural production and output. Many water-saving techniques should be used by farmers in order to practice sustainable agriculture. In order to create oxygen via photosynthesis, plants need water and sunshine. Rainfall, groundwater from wells, and surface water from rivers, streams, open canals, ponds, reservoirs, and lakes are the sources of agricultural water. All conventional agricultural practices, such as growing rice, wheat, sugarcane, etc., need the usage of water. Illegal chemical dumping in water and the atmosphere, as well as widespread industrialization, may have an impact on the quality of water. In addition to affecting food crop quality, low water quality may lead to a number of illnesses.

Food contamination and accompanying diseases are mostly caused by water pollution. A reliable supply of high-quality water is groundwater. Fish farms, dairy farms, and cattle farms all utilize water.

Water's Industrial Uses

Hotels, hostels, dining establishments, workplaces, and other commercial buildings all utilize water. It is necessary for the manufacture and production of steel, food, chemicals, paper, cars, textiles, dying, and other items. A substantial volume of water is required by power plants for cooling. Since water is a universal solvent, it is employed in industrial manufacturing to dissolve a variety of substances. It is less often used as a catalyst and more frequently utilized as a solvent. Additionally, a number of industrial operations make use of water vapor. Petroleum refineries and smelting plants both utilize water. Water is used in industry to fabricate, dilute, and process goods. There are easy ways to go about thanks to rivers, canals, seas, and oceans. When compared to land transportation without any obstructions, there won't be as much friction in the water. It provides economical options together with a cargo-transporting method that works. One source of hydroelectricity is water. To hold water that is later used to power turbines, dams are built across rivers and lakes. Worldwide, hydroelectricity is a renewable energy source that is in use. It has reduced reliance on fossil fuels as a source of energy. Gases, minerals, and oil are extracted with the help of water. It is necessary for a number of important mining tasks. Water is utilized in heat exchangers and steam turbines in addition to being a solvent.

Water's Medicinal Properties

Water is used in medicine for a variety of purposes, including in dentistry and hemodialysis. It is used to clean surgical instruments and supplies. It is necessary for hydrotherapy as well. Since some patients have compromised immune systems; water contamination by bacteria is a serious problem in the hospital context. Direct touch, ingestion, inadvertent contact, aspiration of water, and blood contact are all possible ways for the waterborne illness to spread. Hospitals and clinics should not utilize water unless it has undergone extensive treatment. In order to prevent contaminating water that the patient will consume, clinicians should take the necessary precautions.

METHODOLOGY (MACHINE LEARNING IN VARIOUS WATER APPLICATIONS)

Various researchers have utilized ML to solve water treatment and management system problems (Fig. 2), like real-time tracking, estimation, pollutant source estimating, concentration prediction, water resource allotment, and technology optimization.

To improve water management and pollution control, accurate prediction of water quality is crucial. For predicting total dissolved solids (TDS), salt absorption ratio (SAR), and total hardness (TH) content in aquatic environments with limited data, machine learning models have been effectively used. However, it is still uncertain how well these models forecast the levels of TDS, SAR, and TH in the Karun River system because of the many sources of pollution and the intricate behaviors of pollutants. To solve this challenge, the following models were employed to predict TDS, SAR, and TH variables in the four Karun River stations for the years 1999–2019: multiple linear regression (MLR), M5P model tree, support vector regression (SVR), and random forest regression (RFR). Initially, the principal component analysis

(PCA) method was used in order to decrease the quantity of input variables. The root mean square error (RMSE) and coefficient of determination (R2) are used to evaluate the created models.

Based on PCA, it was shown that the most significant inputs on TDS and SAR are sodium (Na), chloride (Cl), and TH, respectively, whereas calcium (Ca) and magnesium (Mg) are the most efficient on TH. According to the findings, the models with the lowest prediction errors across all stations were the RFR, SVR, and MLR ones for TDS, SAR, and TH, respectively. In Darkhovin station, the RFR model performed best for TDS prediction (R2 = 0.98, RMSE = 70.50 mg l−1), SVR model for SAR prediction (R2 = 0.99, RMSE = 0.04), and MLR model for TH prediction (R2 = 0.99, RMSE = 1.54 mg l−1). The results of the comparison showed that the TDS, SAR, and TH could be correctly estimated for all stations by the machine learning models.

Implementations in Surface Water

Civic and industry wastewater from human actions is the principal cause of urban water quality degradation. ML in surface water quality analysis is trendy. Several surface water quality estimation and assessment techniques exist. Various attempts were made to optimize ML models and improve estimation accuracy.

Data collecting is essential to machine learning model development. Additionally, aggregated and periodic water quality estimating findings may be benchmarked in water system management. Conventional environmental tracking approaches are used by agents. But, established approaches for in situ tracking have challenges. Remote sensing technologies provide real-time, huge-scale water quality tracking and show pollution movement and dispersion patterns that traditional approaches cannot identify. (Khanh, P. T. et al. 2023) saw that experiment-dependent ML let advanced optimization using real-time sensor data and satellite data, and the partial least squares (PLS), support vector regression, and DNN approaches were more accurate than conventional models. Since certain water quality variables, like pathogen concentrations, aren't optically active or need high-spatial-resolution hyperspectral data, remote sensing cannot directly detect them, but it may estimate those utilizing different measurable data. Wu et al. built a CNN model which can distinguish clean and dirty water from photos. Multiple comparison studies on a sea surface picture dataset confirmed the efficiency of this CNN. The benefit of CNN is that it uses the reflection picture as input without requiring feature engineering or parameter modification. Because of equipment or human error, few data will be missing, inaccurate, or destroyed, creating a sparse matrix and poor model application performance.

Data cleansing, another crucial ML stage, becomes necessary. Data cleaning may be done by not utilizing the raw data, utilizing averages or medians, or utilizing ML and matrix completion. (Ngọc, T. H. et al. 2023) used Deep Neural Network and deep matrix factorization to estimate organic O_2 requirement. The rationality and dependability of the technique were verified utilizing California Harbor waters as a case history. Data cleaning enhances machine learning model accuracy by improving data quality.

Machine learning prediction accuracy depends on model selection and training dataset quality. ANN and SVM predict water quality components well. SVM may outperform ANN in prediction and generalization. One explanation is because neural network model parameter tuning is unstable; therefore nonlinear disturbances greatly impair ANN accuracy. SVM minimizes generalization error better than ANN because it limits it rather than training error. Effective river management requires real-time monitoring of water quality or relying on other data while monitoring circumstances are insufficient due to complicated dynamic changes over time. Researchers have confirmed that LSTM (Long Short-Term Memory) and BWNN (Biased Wavelet Neural Network) networks can manage fluctuating and

Figure 2. Various ML methods in water treatment and management systems. SVM, RF, ANN, Decision Tree, PCA, XGBoost, DO, and MP are used in the analysis
(Zhu et al. 2022)

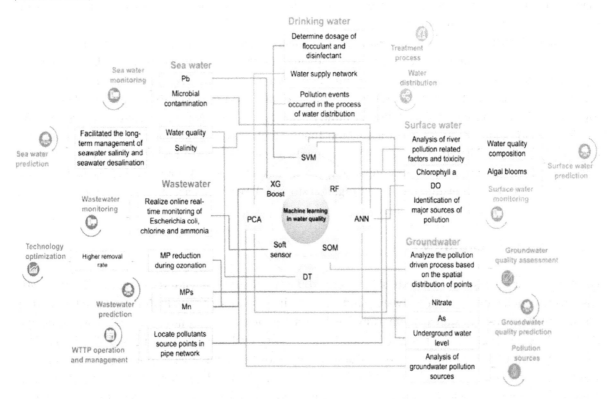

non-seasonal water-quality data. Traditional linear statistical models like the autoregressive integrated moving average (ARIMA) model may estimate time series. It is substandard to the BWNN model that is motivated by the self-adaption of the ANN and the time-frequency features of wavelet basis functions, and the Long Short Term Memory technique that masters straightway from time-series data. Long Short Term Memory and BWNN recognize nicely the nonlinear connection between variables and their projected variables, and utilize past data to forecast the future.

The characteristics used to train machine learning models affect prediction accuracy. Redundant variables increase model complexity and decrease inverse power and accuracy. A most important surface water quality measures is dissolved oxygen (DO), which reflects the water environment and its capacity to support water life. The linear polynomial neural network approach predicted Danube River DO concentration. The forecast accuracy was most affected by temperature, pH, BOD, and phosphorus content among 17 water quality factors. For prediction of DO accumulation in Columbia River, USA, among 5 variables chloride, NO_x, cumulative dissolved solids, pH, and water temperature are closely associated with dissolved oxygen and may impact forecast accuracy. These findings align with (Roy, A. et al. 2023), who found that I/P parameters impact model estimation achievement. Furthermore to water parameters, eutrophication affects surface water quality forecast. (Ngoc, T. T. H. et al. 2023) discovered that nutrients, organic matter, and environmental factors generated algal blooms using the adaptive neuro-fuzzy inference system technique. (Jayasingh, R. et al. 2022) utilized meteorological and weekly water quality data to forecast chlorophyll-a concentrations in two U.S. locations. SVM and ANN showed equal accuracy. The incorporation of meteorological parameters greatly enhanced forecast accuracy. The machine learning model may also include regional hydrological and socioeconomic elements to provide complete regional water environment management.

ML model performance relies on its architecture, hence understanding algorithm logical structure is crucial to machine learning effectiveness. PNN's advantage over other neural network models in identifying crucial model parameters is that the quantity of hidden neurons and PNN layers is selected by data, preserving trial time. The Deep Neural Network model utilized to predict BOD has 19.20%–25.16% lower RMSE than conventional machine learning. Because there are DNN has numerous layers between its I/P and O/P, and it requires latest activation functions improve model convergence and minimize training difficulty compared to classic ANNs (sigmoid). Time series-based LSTM predicts water quality effectively. It has 3 information gates: input, forget, and output gate, cell state, and hidden state govern sequential information transmission, forgetting, and storage. BWNN can accomplish this aim, but needs enough input characteristics for accuracy.

Applications in Groundwater

Drinking water comes from groundwater. Thus, groundwater safety is vital to human well-being. ML has several applications in groundwater study, which includes quality evaluation and contamination estimation. Multivariate statistical analysis has become popular for groundwater quality assessments. PCA and cluster analysis are popular. Groundwater quality evaluation has been used SVM, DT, RF, and ANN algorithms. Studies on groundwater quality mostly examine ML approaches to determine viable solutions for certain challenges. In Tabriz City, Iran, (Pramanik, S. et al. 2021) compared 5 data mining techniques: normal DT, Random Forest, chi-square automatic interaction detector, and iterative dichotomizer to spot semiarid groundwater parameters and their impact on high-quality groundwater. (Pramanik, S. et al. 2022) calculated Seoul's urban groundwater quality spatial pattern using a self-organizing neural network and fuzzy c-means clustering. The researchers used a self-organizing map approach to classify groundwater samples into three categories by contamination degree and examined the pollution-directed technique dependent on geographic distribution. GIS methods were utilized to create groundwater quality maps to better detect contamination.

The intricate hydrogeology of groundwater contrasted predicting quality change trends is more challenging when dealing with surface water. Machine learning has been used to analyze regional data on a big scale and forecast water quality. PSO and SVM were used to assess and forecast groundwater WQI by (Samanta, D. et al. 2021) demonstrating its feasibility. A single groundwater contaminant, like nitrate and arsenic, may be estimated. (Pramanik, S et al. 2023) predicted groundwater nitrate constituent and distribution using an SVM. (Pramanik, S. et al. 2023) assessed groundwater nitrate contamination risk utilizing enhanced regression tree, multivariate discriminant analysis, and Support Vector Machine, and found that India's Khadar Plain is at higher risk of nitrate contamination. (Andrushia et al. 2023) utilized ML to forecast US groundwater nitrate levels and discovered that it can also predict national groundwater quality.

(Vidya Chellam, V. et al. 2023) predicted groundwater arsenic contamination in Ohio, and Japan utilizing an ANN. Additionally, groundwater levels may be forecast. In a study by (Praveenkumar, S. et al. 2023), DNN was shown to be the most accurate and efficient machine learning approach for predicting groundwater levels throughout the season, compared to ANFIS and SVM. (Pramanik, S. 2023) used ensemble modeling to estimate Indian city groundwater levels with 85% accuracy.

The investigation of contamination sources is crucial for groundwater safety. Studies employ PCA and clustering extensively. After PCA reduced dimensionality and K-means grouped data, (Veeraiah, V. et al. 2023) examined natural and anthropogenic hydro-geochemistry sources. (Pramanik, S. and Bandyopadhyay, S. 2023) used multivariate statistical analysis and Principal Component Analysis to discover ground-water quality parameters.

Groundwater quality and resources are frequently examined using a data mining decision tree. This algorithm can identify and describe connections between input and output variables using certain criteria. Performance and capacity to generalize rules to detect drinking-quality groundwater are benefits of RF. Since continuous data sets are better for groundwater law induction than discrete data sets, RF's greatest performance (accuracy of 97.10%) gives effective groundwater resource planning and management judgments. Current groundwater quality index prediction research uses the integrated model that may merge numerous weak learners into a lone strong learner and increase estimation performance. Integration is fantastic with boosting. To create models with lower variance, it is important to reduce over fitting when merging excellent models.

Drinking Water Application

In drinking water source operation, analysis, distribution, and decision making, machine learning is frequently used. Drinking water is usually surface or groundwater. The examination and estimation of source water quality using ML may help reduce pollution early. (Bansal, R. et al. 2022) investigated multisensor-dependent Artificial Neural Network and Support Vector Machine approaches for dynamic water quality tracking in 2022. The models generate satisfactory identification rates for the two water groups. Support Vector Machine was more stable than ANN. (Dushyant, K. et al. 2022) used drinking water quality information from 4 Norwegian metropolitans to suggest adaptive frequency analysis. Their findings supported early drinking water quality threat cautioning, administration, and decision-taking. Moreover, (Gupta, A. et al. 2022) combined LSTM and Deep Neural Network to forecast time series data and created a water quality estimation approach which can accurately estimate water quality in the following 6 months. (K.aushik, D. et al. 2022) employed a Support Vector Machine to forecast pollution episodes under unknown circumstances using UV absorption. All four SVM datasets have good detection rates and low error rates. Most investigations have used chemical or physical measures, while microbiological factors, notably for E. coli, have seldom been studied. Machine learning can estimate drinking water plant coagulant and disinfectant levels. SVM algorithms are prominent in occlusion and disinfection construction because to their simple structure and resilience. (Bhattacharya, A. et al. 2021) suggested a predictive chemical dose control technique that was more successful than proportional-integral-derivative feedback control based on SVM-predicted residual free chlorine.

The necessity of drinking water has motivated researchers to concentrate on typical metropolitan water supply framework functioning, fault tracking, and catastrophe estimation. Due to the intricacy of water supply networks, drinking water therapy facilities which satisfy regulations can be re-polluted in transportation that may be monitored utilizing biological stability measures and purified. Cluster analysis may show water quality differences between networks. Furthermore, (Mandal, A. et al. 2021) employed cluster analysis to determine how mixed water sources, including Al migration and seasonal fluctuations, affect aluminum remnants in urban drinking water supply frameworks. (Meslie, Y. et al. 2021) correctly casts water quality utilizing an RF technique. Burst water supply pipelines cause massive water loss and microbiological and chemical contamination. DL algorithms may forecast bursting locations with high uncertainty. (Pramanik, S. 2022) introduced a water leakage detection method using a random DT bagging classifier with shuffled frog-leaping optimization and minimal sensors at ideal locations in a WSN (water supply network). Pipe longevity matters in water-supply management. A sophisticated meta-learning framework dependent on a neural network by (Taviti Naidu, G. et al. 2023) demonstrated that residual chlorine affects pipeline service life. An SVM method may also forecast water distribution system contamination. (Chandan, R. R. et al. 2023) used PCA, the analytic hierarchy process, Random Forest and XGBoost frameworks to quantify catastrophe effects on water supply systems. However, real-time data collecting challenges restrict the practicality of this strategy.

Regional development and population growth are limited by water production capacity. (Mondal, D. et al. 2023) created a hybrid ANN-genetic algorithm weighted variables. The test findings indicate that this system effectively monitors water quality, having a strong correlation between projected and real values.

Machine learning can enhance wastewater treatment systems by analyzing historical data. (Ghosh, R. et al. 2023) used an SVM and adaptive evolutionary algorithm to mimic anaerobic, anoxic, and toxic conditions to reduce the anoxic tank capacity and conserve land area. Additionally, machine learning optimizes tertiary wastewater treatment methods including RO, NF, ozonize, and absorption. According to (Mall, P. K. et al. 2023) using an RF to anticipate micro pollutant decrease in ozone led to improved removal efficiency. Using a high-resolution fluorescence excitation-emission matrix for machine learning may improve accuracy by computing the complicated nonlinear connection between statistical models for drinking water performance prediction.

The hybrid statistical model accurately predicts water production responses to different parameter variations, making it a valuable tool for changing water treatment systems rapidly and effectively. (Pandey, B. K. et al. 2023) suggested a time-series clustering-based autonomous tracking system for urban water administration and discovered significant water demand from 6 to 9 AM summertime owing to civic and public garden watering. (Pandey, B. K. et al. 2023) used a gated RNN and a 20-minute time step to forecast short-term water consumption for 15 and 24 hours. (Ahamad, S. et al. 2023) utilized DAN2 and KNN to anticipate every day, every week and every month water consumptions in Iraq. DAN2 performed best of the three models. Every day, every week, and every month models predicted 97%, 98%, and 99% accurately. Machine learning can balance water-supply systems. Using accurate water demand predictions to allocate water resources is promising.

In conclusion, Artificial Neural Network and Support Vector Machine are often used in the area of drinking water, particularly in big quantities. The training phase's few seconds of computer time allows dynamic tracking frameworks to check drinking water grade and safeness in real time. Increased training strategies have significantly increased ANN recognition rates, regardless of their effectiveness with susceptible to noise.

Utilizations in Wastewater

ML is frequently utilized in water quality tracking and estimation, technological improvement, and WWTP operation and administration. Industrial and domestic wastewater includes contaminants, requiring water quality testing before therapy. Multiresolution analysis with Principal Component Analysis gave (Veeraiah, V. et al. 2023) a much sensitive method for tracking sewage measures at different scales than PCA. Big data collection, processing, and analysis depend on real-time internet tracking. A black box-based soft sensor was suggested for online, real-time E-monitoring. (Dhamodaran, S. et al. 2023) indicated that E. coli rose significantly after high rains, presumably owing to urban runoff resuspending sewer silt. Soft sensors and ANNs may reduce the expenditure and complexity of WWTP action and ailment and provide real-time chlorine and ammonia monitoring. The boosting-iterative predictor weighting-partial least squares approach and several sensors were used to create a water quality tracking system with a UV spectrometer and turbidimeter to measure COD and cumulative suspended solids. Boosting-IPW-PLS subdued factors irrelevant to water quality by allocating tiny weights and created a wastewater quality estimation framework.

(Dhamodaran, S. et al. 2023) employed Decision Tree to identify the specific sequence of MP removal by RO and NF, revealing particle dimension elimination, electrostatic repulsion, and adsorption as the primary separating processes. Additionally, XGBoost predicts MP removal efficiency in RO and NF. Two neural-network-based models by () helped practitioners choose the right adsorbent for a contaminant. According to the preceding situations, machine learning approaches may be extensively used in the future to treat wastewater with MPs and new contaminants.

Machine learning has improved water treatment analysis by providing predicted data. ANN solves difficult nonlinear environmental issues, including pollution elimination. (Veeraiah, V. et al. 2023) developed an Artificial Neural Network model to estimate COD and BOD levels in wastewater. Currently, water quality estimation algorithms focus on identifying specific pollutant levels. (Pandey, B. K. et al. 2022) developed CatBoost to reliably anticipate tetracycline (TC) elimination using a photodegradation rate under varied realistic settings.

Metal–organic system (Pramanik, S. 2023) used 3 models (RF, SVM, and ANN) to estimate the elimination of 5 variables. RF provided the most accurate findings after verifying all models. Machine learning can predict biological signs. Bayes methods, such as naive and semi Naïve Bayes networks, were used to forecast pathogen elimination capability and reflect the relationship between pathogen minimization, operational circumstances, and tracking parameters. RF predicted wastewater Clostridiales and Bacteroidales by (Pramanik, S. and Bandyopadhyay, S. 2023). Comprehensive assessment and computation techniques for estimating excrement contamination sources have been developed using RF, reducing the spread of water-borne illnesses.

Many variables may impact the effluent quality of WWTPs. WWTP operation and maintenance might be difficult when expenses must be managed. Thus, machine learning may help WWTP managers save expenses and enhance operations. Toxic contaminants in sewage networks may disrupt WWTP functioning. XGBoost and RF identified contaminants and their source sites in a wastewater network to avoid such situations. Sensors for flow measurement are often put in sewage pipelines. However, contaminants rust, and excessive turbidity may cause measurement instability and erroneous results. Deep learning may increase sensor accuracy in numerous situations. (Anand, R. et al. 2022) utilized previous sensor settings to explain common failures. Once a defect was found, the model could adapt the process to maintain WWTP functioning.

Machine Learning in Aquatic Settings

Seawater contamination is threatening Earth's ecosystems. Machine learning can monitor marine pollution to solve these problems. The lead-prediction algorithm was trained utilizing past tracking data from Queensland's Simon stations using XGBoost. The researchers discovered the framework selected I/P parameters and predicted water quality effectively. (Choudhary, S. et al. 2022) presented an RF and

UAV trash mapping program to track seaside plastic garbage. An ensemble ML system with a 2-layered learning framework predicted beach water coastal microbial contamination concentration. (Sinha, M. et al. 2021) used an LSTM-CNN framework to predict a single antibiotic resistance gene (ARG) in beach water to enhance accuracy. Using machine learning classification techniques, (Reepu, et al. 2023) recognized differentially indicated genes in dolphins revealed to seawater contaminants. Many researchers have also developed monitoring devices for algal blooms that might cause serious pollution. (Bansal, R. et al. 2021) trained the XGBoost framework using water type and algal bloom spectral properties to recognize and classify algal bloom algae. (Dutta, S. et al. 2021) used Mahalanobis distance-based hierarchical cluster analysis to assess the North Yellow and Bohai Seas' water quality. In conclusion, machine learning can detect seawater contaminants, quantify their quantity and distribution, and analyze marine creature state.

Protecting marine life requires monitoring seawater quality ecosystems. Many researchers assess seawater quality using machine learning. (Pramanik, S. and Raja, S. S. 2020) suggested a KNN-based near-shore water quality prediction model in 2022. BPNN, SVR, and Long Short Term Memory frameworks were used to create a water quality prediction technique that significantly enhanced accuracy. (Pramanik, S. et al. 2020) suggested a water quality estimation approach using an upgraded grey regression analysis algorithm and Long Short Term Memory based on multivariate correlation and time-series features. (Pramanik, S. 2023) used a geographic-based water quality assessment approach to evaluate geosynchronous ocean color image data and 1240 water quality sample stations in Zhe-jiang's coast.

Moreover, 80% of the earth's population will experience a freshwater catastrophe by 2040. In locations with severe water shortages, desalinated saltwater provides freshwater. However, seawater desalination still faces challenges such as poor efficiency and dependability.

(Apostolopoulos, I.D. et al. 2020) utilized a Convolutional Neural Network approach with transfer learning to categorize saline molecules in water at various concentrations to enhance water treatment facility saltwater treatment attainment. (Boussouf, S. et al. 2023) used regression and ML methods such logistic regression, RF, SVM, and LSTM to anticipate the Salton Sea's salinity and development tendency, enabling prolonged control of seawater saltness and salt removal.

The single water estimation framework was extensively explored, and the integrated model has emerged recently. Distinct models have distinct methods for different input characteristics, resulting in varying predicted performance. The aggregation model of (Guardieiro, V. et al. 2023) favors classifier selection. Upon entering fresh data, the most suitable prediction model is chosen before generating predictions. This method selects models using input characteristics, while (Aydin, H.E. et al. 2023) XGBoost approach can cover I/P features and pick 7–10 out of 25 to integrate with Artificial Neural Network and various implementation techniques without losing information during model training. A potential modeling algorithm is XGBoost. XGBoost is a quick, accurate feature selection technique that relies on sample size.

Because it can forecast water gradations, improve water resource management, manage water resource deficiencies, and more, machine learning is frequently utilized to handle water environment issues. There are also hurdles in employing machine learning to assess water quality, including the need for vast volumes of high-quality data. Accurate data collection in water treatment and administration systems is challenging due to expenditure or technical constraints. Due to the complexity of actual water treatment and management systems, present algorithms are limited to specific systems, limiting the widespread use of ML techniques. Practical use of machine learning approaches needs researchers to have professional expertise.

The following factors may help overcome the aforesaid challenges: (1) In future research and engineering, explore developing sophisticated sensors, such as soft sensors, for water quality monitoring to acquire correct data for ML algorithms. (2) Improve the feasibility and reliability of techniques and design more general techniques and models for water treatment and management. (3) Train diverse personnel to create sophisticated ML methods and use them in technical procedures.

CONCLUSION

River management requires the precise prediction of water quality parameters for drinking, residential, agricultural, and aquaculture applications as well as for pollution monitoring. Four machine learning techniques (MLR, M5P, RBFSVR, and RFR) were used in this study to estimate TDS, SAR, and TH parameters during a 20-year period at the four stations along the Karun River. The PCA approach was used for input variable preprocessing in the MLR, M5P, and RBF-SVR models as the choice of input parameters had a substantial influence on the performance of machine learning models. Additionally, the relative relevance of the input parameters was used to estimate the effective parameters in the RFR model. Based on the aforementioned research, it can be said that the most accurate models for forecasting TDS, SAR, and TH at each station were the RFR, RBF-SVR, and MLR models. Furthermore, in comparison to the other models, the M5P model's performance in forecasting the water quality parameters of the Karaun River was subpar at all stations. The findings demonstrate that the proposed modeling process may provide highly generalized formulations. As a result, under predicted circumstances, machine learning-based models are a suitable substitute for physically based modeling. They can thus somewhat save time and lower the expense of checking the quality of the water. It is feasible to extrapolate the findings to rivers with comparable water quality, particularly in dry regions, since the models of this study primarily used water quality criteria for prediction rather than river morphology. Additionally, it may provide a basis upon which managers, engineers, and politicians can plan, oversee, and decide on important matters pertaining to various rivers. Future research suggests modeling and estimating river water quality using hybrid machine learning and deep learning approaches, then comparing the outcomes with the findings of this work.

REFERENCES

Ahamad, S., Veeraiah, V., Ramesh, J. V. N., Rajadevi, R., Reeja, S. R., Pramanik, S., & Gupta, A. (2023). *Deep Learning based Cancer Detection Technique, Thrust Technologies' Effect on Image Processing.* IGI Global.

Anand, R., Singh, J., Pandey, D. K., Pandey, B., Nassa, V. K., & Pramanik, S. (2022). Modern Technique for Interactive Communication in LEACH-Based Ad Hoc Wireless Sensor Network. In M. M. Ghonge, S. Pramanik, & A. D. Potgantwar (Eds.), *Software Defined Networking for Ad Hoc Networks.* Springer., doi:10.1007/978-3-030-91149-2_3

Andrushia, A. D., Neebha, T. M., Patricia, A. T., Sagayam, K. M., & Pramanik, S. (2023). Capsule Network based Disease Classification for VitisVinifera Leaves. *Neural Computing & Applications.* doi:10.100700521-023-09058-y

Apostolopoulos, I. D., & Mpesiana, T. A. (2020). Covid-19: Automatic detection from X-ray images utilizing transfer learning with convolutional neural networks. *Physical and Engineering Sciences in Medicine, 43*(2), 635–640. doi:10.100713246-020-00865-4 PMID:32524445

Aydin, H. E., & Iban, M. C. (2023). Predicting and analyzing flood susceptibility using boosting-based ensemble machine learning algorithms with SHapley Additive exPlanations. *Natural Hazards, 116*(3), 2957–2991. doi:10.100711069-022-05793-y

Bhattacharya, A., Ghosal, A., Obaid, A. J., Krit, S., Shukla, V. K., Mandal, K., & Pramanik, S. (2021). Unsupervised Summarization Approach with Computational Statistics of Microblog Data. In D. Samanta, R. R. Althar, S. Pramanik, & S. Dutta (Eds.), *Methodologies and Applications of Computational Statistics for Machine Learning* (pp. 23–37). IGI Global. doi:10.4018/978-1-7998-7701-1.ch002

Boussouf, S., Fernández, T., & Hart, A. B. (2023). Landslide susceptibility mapping using maximum entropy (MaxEnt) and geographically weighted logistic regression (GWLR) models in the Río Aguas catchment (Almería, SE Spain). *Natural Hazards, 117*(1), 207–235. doi:10.100711069-023-05857-7

Chandan, R. R., Soni, S., Raj, A., Veeraiah, V., Dhabliya, D., Pramanik, S., & Gupta, A. (2023). Genetic Algorithm and Machine Learning. Advanced Bioinspiration Methods for Healthcare Standards, Policies, and Reform. IGI Global. doi:10.4018/978-1-6684-5656-9

Choudhary, S., Narayan, V., Faiz, M., & Pramanik, S. (2022). Fuzzy Approach-Based Stable Energy-Efficient AODV Routing Protocol in Mobile Ad hoc Networks. In M. M. Ghonge, S. Pramanik, & A. D. Potgantwar (Eds.), *Software Defined Networking for Ad Hoc Networks*. Springer. doi:10.1007/978-3-030-91149-2_6

Dhamodaran, S., Ahamad, S., Ramesh, J. V. N., Muthugurunathan, G., Manikandan, K., Pramanik, S., & Pandey, D. (2023). Food Quality Assessment using Image Processing Technique. Thrust Technologies' Effect on Image Processing. IGI Global.

Dhamodaran, S., Ahamad, S., Ramesh, J. V. N., Sathappan, S., Namdev, A., Kanse, R. R., & Pramanik, S. (2023). *Fire Detection System Utilizing an Aggregate Technique in UAV and Cloud Computing, Thrust Technologies' Effect on Image Processing*. IGI Global.

Dushyant, K., Muskan, G., Gupta, A., & Pramanik, S. (2022). Utilizing Machine Learning and Deep Learning in Cyber security: An Innovative Approach. In M. M. Ghonge, S. Pramanik, R. Mangrulkar, & D. N. Le (Eds.), *Cyber security and Digital Forensics*. Wiley. doi:10.1002/9781119795667.ch12

Dutta, S., Pramanik, S., & Bandyopadhyay, S. K. (2021). Prediction of Weight Gain during COVID-19 for Avoiding Complication in Health. *International Journal of Medical Science and Current Research, 4*(3), 1042–1052.

Guardieiro, V., Raimundo, M. M., & Poco, J. (2023). Enforcing fairness using ensemble of diverse Pareto-optimal models. *Data Mining and Knowledge Discovery, 37*(5), 1930–1958. doi:10.100710618-023-00922-y

Gupta, A., Verma, A., & Pramanik, S. (2022). Security Aspects in Advanced Image Processing Techniques for COVID-19. In S. Pramanik, A. Sharma, S. Bhatia, & D. N. Le (Eds.), *An Interdisciplinary Approach to Modern Network Security*. CRC Press.

Khanh, P. T., Ngọc, T. H., & Pramanik, S. (2023). Future of Smart Agriculture Techniques and Applications. In A. Khang & I. G. I. Global (Eds.), *Advanced Technologies and AI-Equipped IoT Applications in High Tech Agriculture*. doi:10.4018/978-1-6684-9231-4.ch021

Ngọc, T. H., Khanh, P. T., & Pramanik, S. (2023). Smart Agriculture using a Soil Monitoring System. In A. Khang & I. G. I. Global (Eds.), *Advanced Technologies and AI-Equipped IoT Applications in High Tech Agriculture*. doi:10.4018/978-1-6684-9231-4.ch011

Ngoc, T. T. H., Pramanik, S., & Khanh, P. T. (2023). The Relationship between Gender and Climate Change in Vietnam. *The Seybold Report*. 10.17605/OSF.IO/KJBPT

Pandey, B. K., Pandey, D., Nassa, V. K., George, A. S., Pramanik, S., & Dadheech, P. (2023). Applications for the Text Extraction Method of Complex Degraded Images. The Impact of Thrust Technologies on Image Processing. Nova Publishers.

Pandey, B. K., Pandey, D., Nassa, V. K., Hameed, A. S., George, A. S., Dadheech, P., & Pramanik, S. (2023). A Review of Various Text Extraction Algorithms for Images. In *The Impact of Thrust Technologies on Image Processing*. Nova Publishers. doi:10.52305/ATJL4552

Pandey, B. K., Pandey, D., Wairya, S., Agarwal, G., Dadeech, P., Dogiwal, S. R., & Pramanik, S. (2022). Application of Integrated Steganography and Image Compressing Techniques for Confidential Information Transmission. Cyber Security and Network Security. Wiley. . doi:10.1002/9781119812555.ch8

Praveenkumar, S., Veeraiah, V., Pramanik, S., Basha, S. M., Lira Neto, A. V., De Albuquerque, V. H. C., & Gupta, A. (2023). *Prediction of Patients' Incurable Diseases Utilizing Deep Learning Approaches, ICICC 2023*. Springer. doi:10.1007/978-981-99-3315-0_4

Reepu, S. Kumar, Chaudhary, M. G., Gupta, K. G., Pramanik, S., & Gupta, A. (2023). Information Security and Privacy in IoT. J. Zhao, V. V. Kumar, R. Natarajan and T. R. Mahesh, (eds.) Handbook of Research in Advancements in AI and IoT Convergence Technologies. IGI Global.

Roy, A., & Pramanik, S. (2023). A Review of the Hydrogen Fuel Path to Emission Reduction in the Surface Transport Industry. *International Journal of Hydrogen Energy*.

Samanta, D., Dutta, S., Galety, M. G., & Pramanik, S. (2021). A Novel Approach for Web Mining Taxonomy for High-Performance Computing. *The 4th International Conference of Computer Science and Renewable Energies (ICCSRE'2021)*. IEEE. 10.1051/e3sconf/202129701073

Sinha, M., Chacko, E., Makhija, P., & Pramanik, S. (2021). Energy Efficient Smart Cities with Green IoT. In C. Chakrabarty (Ed.), *Green Technological Innovation for Sustainable Smart Societies: Post Pandemic Era*. Springer. doi:10.1007/978-3-030-73295-0_16

Taviti Naidu, G., Ganesh, K. V. B., Vidya Chellam, V., Praveenkumar, S., Dhabliya, D., Pramanik, S., & Gupta, A. (2023). Technological Innovation Driven by Big Data. In *Advanced Bioinspiration Methods for Healthcare Standards, Policies, and Reform*. IGI Global. doi:10.4018/978-1-6684-5656-9

Veeraiah, V., Shiju, D. J., Ramesh, J. V. N., Ganesh, K. R., Pramanik, S., & Pandey, D. (2023). *A, Gupta, Healthcare Cloud Services in Image Processing, Thrust Technologies' Effect on Image Processing*. IGI Global.

Vidya Chellam, V., Veeraiah, V., Khanna, A., Sheikh, T. H., Pramanik, S., & Dhabliya, D. (2023). *A Machine Vision-based Approach for Tuberculosis Identification in Chest X-Rays Images of Patients, ICICC 2023*. Springer. doi:10.1007/978-981-99-3315-0_3

Zhu, M., Wang, J., Yang, X., Zhang, Y., Zhang, L., Ren, H., Wu, B., & Ye, L. (2022). A review of the application of machine learning in water quality evaluation. *Eco-Environment & Health, 1*(2). doi:10.1016/j.eehl.2022.06.001

Chapter 8
AI–Decision Support System:
Engineering, Geology, Climate, and Socioeconomic Aspects' Implications on Machine Learning

Phan Truong Khanh
An Giang University, Vietnam

Tran Thi Hong Ngoc
An Giang University, Vietnam

Sabyasachi Pramanik
https://orcid.org/0000-0002-9431-8751
Haldia Institute of Technology, India

ABSTRACT

From the impact of several corporeal, mechanized, ecological, and civic conditions, underground water pipelines degrade. A motivated administrative approach of the water supply network (WSN) depends on accurate pipe failure prediction that is difficult for the traditional physics-dependent model to provide. The research used data-directed machine learning approaches to forecast water pipe breakdowns using the extensive water supply network's historical maintenance data history. To include multiple contributing aspects to subterranean pipe degradation, a multi-source data-aggregation system was originally developed. The framework specified the requirements for integrating several data sources, such as the classical pipe leakage dataset, the soil category dataset, the geographic dataset, the population count dataset, and the climatic dataset. Five machine learning (ML) techniques are created for predicting pipe failure depending on the data, like LightGBM, ANN, Logistic Regression, K-NN, and SVM algorithm.

DOI: 10.4018/979-8-3693-0639-0.ch008

INTRODUCTION

The management of the WSN depends on providing a consistent and secure water supply. The main parts of a WSN are water distribution pipelines, which transport water from water treatment facilities to users. Since some of the subterranean water pipes in US metropolitan communities were installed in the 19th century, this corrosion is particularly severe for those pipelines. Each year, over 2 trillion gallons of potable water are lost due to the more than 700 water main breaks that occur daily in Canada and the United States. Water pipe breakdown may result in huge financial losses and have a negative effect on society or the environment. The US Water Service Agency estimates that the substitution expenditures of the US's current WSNs and their expected expansions would total more than \$1 trillion over the next twenty years. These terrible problems put pressure on management to adopt management practices for long-term improvement and credible pipe failure estimation models to implement preventive support for loss minimization.

In order to create accurate prediction models, it is essential to identify the important variables (also known as input variables) that affect pipe failure. Experimental testing, finite element models, and historical data analysis have all been used in the last several decades to evaluate numerous elements that might cause pipe breakage. These elements can be extensively divided into 3 categories, such as physical, operational, and environmental, according to a recent assessment. The pipe's age, length, material, and diameter are among the physical parameters that are most often taken into account. For instance, Kettle and Goulter used statistical methods to determine the connection between pipe diameters and break probability.

Longer pipes are more likely to fail, as established by (Tai. P. et al. 2023). The frequency of prior failures is the operational component that has been studied the most. These studies show that a pipe's likelihood of failure is often correlated with the frequency of prior failures along the line. Another typical operating component for pipes in the WSNs is water pressure. Inside H_2O pressure and the likelihood of breakage in cement and metal pipes are shown to be positively correlated. Environmental elements may also be a role in pipe malfunctions. The variables consist of soil categories, climate, and traffic volumes. Additionally, a lot of these aspects are often much unknown. Previous research has shown the impact of many climatic variables, including temperature and rainfall, on pipe malfunctions. The findings suggested that the likelihood of pipe failure might rise with greater temperature swings. It is important to comprehend how these three different kinds of contributing elements interact with the likelihood of pipe failure. In addition to the components listed above, it is becoming clearer that cooperation with various sorts of conditions, like social and economic issues, must also be taken into account in performing forecast for WSNs. For instance, current research on the dependability and flexibility of communities took into account the impact of configuration collapse and population-related data. But, the current pipe failure prediction model has only seldom taken these considerations into account. Meanwhile, shareholders are keenly focused in interpreting the processes of the key contributing causes to pipe failures in order to implement informed resource allocation choices. This is in addition to establishing reliable and effective techniques for pipe failure assessment. Although earlier research looked at the effects of several parameters on the likelihood of pipe collapse, the comparative relevance (i.e., level of the effect) is still not properly known. So, while creating a pipe collapse prediction model, the interpretability factor is equally crucial.

The current approaches for predicting pipe collapse often fall into models that are based on physics, mathematical models, and ML models fall under these three groups. Here, the benefits and drawbacks of every approach are concisely discussed. Physical-dependent approaches compare the allowed toughness of a pipe to the actual capacity by using experimental or semi-empirical feature equations which take physical elements into account. Following that, a sampling approach, like the Monte Carlo simulation, may be used to compare the pipe's prevailing robustness and its piling in order to calculate the failure probability of the pipe. Physics-dependent models might easily show the various inputs of the components taken into account, but this approach is often computationally expensive for the whole system. This is because a WSN has many pipes (thousands), and estimating the failure risk of each needs a huge number of samplings. Additionally, several favored physics-dependent models like the B31G model, are too cautious. Comparatively, statistical models are more affordable, especially for niches with ample historical recording data. Previous investigations have revealed that several statistical models may be used to pipe failure forecasting. Statistical models often use statistical equations to describe time-dependent breakage prediction models, including the time-exponential technique, LR model, and Poisson process model. The inference of pipe failure in recent research has employed Bayesian networks. These models may also be used to failure prediction with the presumption that the collapse design won't change in time to come. The statistical models, however, may only take a limited number of physical variables into account without disclosing how those parameters physically relate to pipe failures. Utilizing the growing quantity of data available, data-directed ML models have recently been a developed technique for the prediction of pipe collapse. The most well-liked methods for determining the intricate association between pipe failure and other factors include ANN, neuro-fuzzy systems, LR, and GAs. Despite the fact that many times these ML-dependent techniques might provide good computing capability and as 'black boxes' with little or no interpretability, they are often attacked for their accuracy. Some research utilized better explicable machine learning approaches, such as tree-dependent approaches and the LR technique, to get around this issue. Based on the authors' expertise and understanding, these approaches may not attain a level of accuracy for water pipe failure prediction that is sufficient. Additionally, despite the fact that certain machine learning approaches was employed to forecast pipe collapse, there is currently no systematic comparison of the various ML techniques in this application area. In conclusion, reliable prediction and fair interpretation of pipe failure probably remain difficult and so need more effort even with the important datasets kept by water organizations along with the WSN administration.

Given the aforementioned research gaps, the intent of this study is to interpret ML model which enables high-fidelity and effective estimation of pipe collapse in WSNs, we offer a multi-source data aggregation system. The suggested approach was tested on a sizable WSN dataset which encompasses greater than 6400 miles of water pipe, making it the biggest dataset that have been examined so far.

In the data preparation step, ecological, geographical, and population-based data are taken into account. The findings of the clarification besides being lining up with other research also highlight the significant influence of socioeconomic conditions. The suggested analytical paradigm may be simply used by various WSN management agencies, despite the fact that the effects of the elements may differ in different WSNs. Section 2 consists of the literature review of ML algorithms for predicting pipe collapse, section 3 discusses the Framework for multi-source data accumulation for a vast WSN, section 4 consists of the methodology used, and section 5 concludes the chapter.

HISTORY OF ML ALGORITHMS FOR PREDICTING PIPE COLLAPSE

A popular strategy for predicting pipe breakdown is to treat the issue as a classification problem, i.e., categorizes a pipe as intact or crushed using the provided characteristics. The 5 primary categories of the present supervised machine learning techniques for classification problems include logic-dependent approaches, perceptron-dependent methods, statistical learning approaches, instance-dependent learning approaches, and SVMs. While prior research had employed several machine learning approaches to predict whether or not a pipe would break depending on the variety of pipe input circumstances, there is a shortage of a thorough comparison between various machine learning approaches. To effectively compare the effectiveness of these machine learning classes for predicting pipe breaks, 5 well-known machine learning approaches —the LightGBM technique, the ANN, LR, KNN, and SVC—are chosen as the representative of each category. Based on the observed input variables, the machine learning model's goal is to categorize every pipe as either intact or collapsed. Below is a basic explanation of various ML algorithms.

LightGBM

A gradient boosting system which is a part of logic-based classification methods is called LightGBM. GOSS, EFB, and Histogram and Leaf-wise Tree Growth Strategy are the three characteristics that make up the LightGBM. To put it more precisely, the GOSS is a sampling process which keeps all events having big gradients and performs random sampling on the events having minor gradients. To account for the data distribution shifting throughout the sampling technique, a constant multiplier is employed for data events having minor gradients. Thus, using these two tactics improves overall performance. The EFB approach divides the features into fewer bundles in order to maximize computational performance. EFB and histogram techniques are used by LightGBM to effectively handle category information. As a result, the typical one-hot encoding is not required to encode categorical features, which is a considerable advantage, particularly when the categorical feature comprises a large number of unique values. (Chen, Y. et al. 2023) contains extensive ideas and information.

ANN: Artificial Neural Network

The commonly used perceptron known as the ANN (Pramanik, S. and Bandyopadhyay, S. 2023) imitates how the human brain processes a variety of inputs to produce an output. The I/P layer, hidden layers, and O/P layer are the main elements of an ANN architecture. To reduce the error between the O/P and goal estimates in training, the weight coefficients for the neurons in every layer are repeatedly adjusted. It calculates the weighted total of each neuron's I/Ps and produces an O/P having an activation function. Every neuron's interaction between I/Ps and O/Ps may be mathematically expressed by Eq. (1).

$$\partial = x(\sum_{j=1}^{m} y_r z_r + c) \tag{1}$$

∂ is the O/P of every neuron, f is its activation function, y_r is the weight of z_r and c is its bias.

Figure 1. Confusion matrix for classifying pipe state

		Predicted results	
		Predicted condition **break**	Predicted condition **intact**
True condition	Condition **break**	True break (TB)	False intact (FI)
	Condition **intact**	False break (FB)	True intact (TI)

Linear Regression

By fitting sample data into a logistic function, LR (Dhamodaran S, et al. 2023) is one of the statistical learning techniques. Because of this, LR has been frequently used in engineering. Given that each factor's weight is known after training, the ML (Ahamad, S. et al. 2023) method in question is (1) explicable, and (2) it awarded each sample for a classification issue a value between 0 and 1 that can be understood as the classification probability (Pandey, B. K. et al. 2023). The formula for linear regression in mathematics is Eq. (2).

$$j = \frac{1}{1 + e^{-(y0 + \sum_{j=1}^{k} y_j z_j)}} \tag{2}$$

where j is the O/P of every specimen, y_j is the vector sample having the ith feature, and y_j represents its weight feature to be tweaked during training method; w0 represents constant bias. As seen in equation LR is unable to manage categorical variables. Thus, conversion approaches like one-hot-encoder are needed. Fig 1 portrays the confusion matrix in classifying pipe state.

KNN

One of the most basic and fundamental algorithms for pattern categorization is kNN (Bhattacharya, A. et al. 2021). The assumption is that instances of the same class are near together. The effectiveness of kNN relies on how distances are calculated between instances. The often utilized distance measure is Euclidean distance. The Euclidean distance between specimen y_i and y_j is defined as Eq. (3).

$$l(y_i, y_j) = \sqrt{(y_{i1} - y_{j1})^2 (y_{i2} - y_{j2})^2 (y_{i3} - y_{j3})^2 + \ldots\ldots + (y_{im} - y_{jm})^2} \tag{3}$$

yi_m represents the mth feature of the ith sample.

To calculate the distance between a sample y_i in the test dataset and every specimen in the training database, kNN moves over the entire database. The top k points closest to y_i would be jot down (like Set A) for classification.

Support Vector Classification

Support vector classification is a SVM that uses the best vector of hyperplane to do classification jobs. A plane known as the hyperplane (Mandal, A. et al. 2021) has the ability to split the n-dimensional data points into 2 halves. For example, the hyperplane is a line on a 2D plane when the events are a 2D dataset. Finding the hyperplane that might maximize margins (the cumulative of distances from the hyperplane to the closest training specimens from every class) is the goal of SVC. SVC resolves the following optimization equations mathematically.

Metrics for Evaluating ML Models

The 5 machine learning approaches provide a continuous value between as their output. 0 and 1 that represents the likelihood that a pipe will be collapsed? This certainty rating frequently translated as the likelihood of collapse. Provided that the test dataset's ground certainty is a binary class (either absolutely fine or collapsed), a typical method of analyzing the estimation outcomes is to split them into every class according to a threshold, in this case, 0.5. On the contrary, if the output is more than 0.5, the sample is projected to be broken; otherwise, it is 'intact'. A confused matrix may be created using the projected outcomes and the actual data, as illustrated in Fig. 'True Break' and 'True Intact' refer to the properly categorized samples in Figure 1. 'False Intact' refers to pipes that are supposed to be intact but end up breaking. The pipes that are anticipated by the term "False break"

This research quantifies ML model performance using accuracy, recall, and precision based on categorized prediction outcomes.

$$Accuracy = \frac{TC + TF}{TC + TF + FC + FF} \tag{4}$$

$$Re\,call = \frac{TC}{TC + TF} \tag{5}$$

$$Pr\,ecision = \frac{TC}{TC + FC} \tag{6}$$

Here TC indicates True Collapse, TF stands for True Fine, FC stands for False Collapse and FF stands for False Fine.

Figure 2 portrays the Outline of the Cleveland Wireless Develop Network.

Figure 2. Outline of the Cleveland Wireless Develop Network network (a) showing the pipes under the control of the Cleveland Water Division, (b) showing an instance of repair records, (c) showing the dispersal of pipe assistance in years, and (d) showing the expected yearly maintenance cost ($)

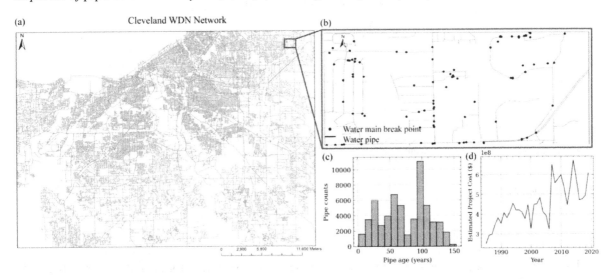

Three metrics—accuracy, recall, and precision—are utilized in the work to significantly evaluate the performance of ML approaches depending on the classified estimation outcomes. These metrics are provided in Eqs. (4)–(6).

FRAMEWORK FOR MULTI-SOURCE DATA ACCUMULATION FOR A VAST WSN

In data-driven ML techniques, the preprocessing of the data is a crucial stage. The Cleveland Water Firm that oversees a big WSN in the country gathered the pipe related dataset and past repairs records utilized in this research. The Cleveland Water Department is in charge of providing water to 520,000 working user accounts across 6500 miles of water main pipes in Allen County, the 2nd-most populated county in the US province of Ohio. One of the major cities in North America's Great Lakes region is located in the study area.

The ratio between True Collapses and every Real Breaks is the recall. More specifically, a higher recall value indicates that the model correctly detects more break examples in the testing dataset. More projected break samples that are actual break samples are indicated by a higher precision value. In actuality, a low recall value might result in the failure pipes being missed, while a low accuracy value could result in undamaged pipes being incorrectly replaced, raising unnecessary maintenance expenses.

This region's soil often freezes and thaws throughout the winter months as a result of its unusual geology. Fig. 2 shows the Cleveland Water Department's system overview. The dispersion of the pipe network that has a sum of 55,945 pipes is shown in 2(a). The data record contains information about each pipe's physical characteristics, such as its age, material, diameter, and length. Fig. A record of pipe repair in one of the WSN's locations is shown in 2(b). The points represent the places that have undergone maintenance. The Cleveland Water Department (CWD) also keeps track of the maintenance date.

Figure 3. Schema for assembling datasets from many sources

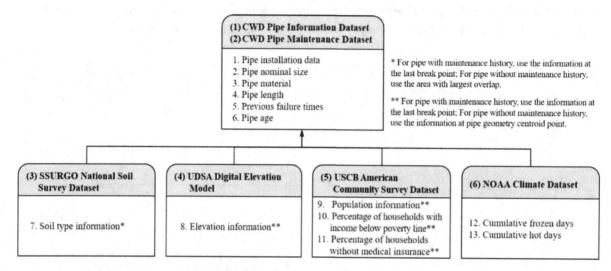

The distribution of pipe ages in the water supply network is shown in fig 2(c). As can be observed, several pipes have been in service for more than a century. The expected yearly cost, assuming all the broken pipes were completely rebuilt, is shown in 2(d). The estimate is dependent on the Cleveland Water Agency's experience, where the price to replace a pipe is anticipated to be roughly $483.74/foot. The actual total cost, however, could be less than the predicted amount because: 1) Multiple damages might be fixed simultaneously; and 2) The care may merely arrange the collapse rather than entirely restore the pipe. The ability to accurately estimate when a water pipe will burst will be very helpful when creating a maintenance budget.

Data from numerous sources are first pooled to offer a thorough knowledge of probable causes for WSN failures and related maintenance. Despite the fact that more and more data are now available in the public domain, it may be challenging to merge data from many sources since they are sometimes provided by different organizations and kept in various configurations. The absence of best practices for efficiently assembling datasets from multiple sources has been identified as a limitation in the present implementation of data-directed techniques. Additionally, the purpose of this section is for providing a numerous-source data-aggregation system as an addition to the creation of these recommendations. In this research, six datasets are explicitly taken into account, including: (1) the WSN pipe related database (2) previous pipe collapse database (1) and (2) are from the Cleveland Water Agency, (3) is from the National Cooperative Soil Survey's SSURGO soil type dataset.

Figure 3 shows the schema for assembling datasets from many sources. Fig 4 portrays the examples of assumptions made during the data aggregation.

The US Communal Analysis 5-Year Data received from the US Population Agency, the geographical dataset from the Digital Elevation Technique by the US Agency of Farming, the climate dataset from the Central Oceanic and Weather Agency. The last four datasets, which are all available to the general public, are combined with the 2 datasets supplied by the Cleveland Water Agency to provide the entire training and datasets for testing. Fig. presents the data aggregation framework. 3. The following provides further detail on the assumptions and requirements for data aggregation.

Figure 4. Examples of assumptions made during the data aggregation (Ngọc, T. H. et al. 2023) technique for various datasets include (a) the pipe collapse dataset (Reepu, et al. 2023), which was dependent on the proximity of the collapse level to the pipe, (b) the soil category database, which was dependent on geological data, (c) the geographical dataset, which was dependent on coordinates in the digital advancement technique and (d) the population database, which was dependent on the coordinate of the pipe

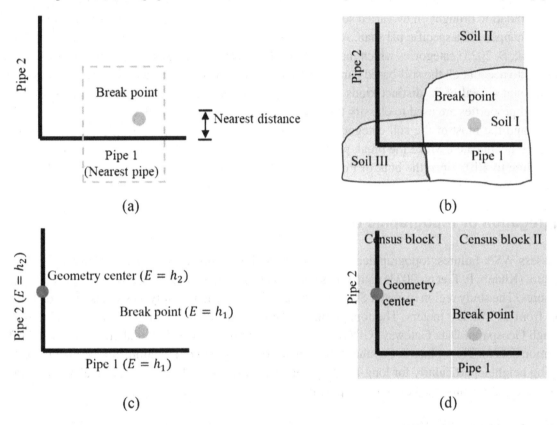

Streamline Information Gathering and Record-Breaking

CWD offers two separate layer formats for pipe information and break data in Geographic Information System (Chandan, R. R. et al. 2023). As seen in Fig 2 (b). The break-records database is denoted by "points," whereas the pipe-information dataset is denoted by "lines."

Analysis revealed that there is some overlap between these two categories of data, but not much. The reason is that although break sites are taped manually or by Global Positioning System sensors that dosen't matches up with the water pipes, pipelines are based on real laydown. As shown in Fig. 4 (a), the break points are presumed to locate at the closest pipe for data aggregation if the interval is smaller than 1 m that is the standard resolution for Global Positioning Services devices. This enables the appropriate water pipelines to be linked to the break records. The physical characteristics of each pipe may be acquired by allocating the failure records to the relevant pipe (i.e., Table 1) that may be immediately derived from the actual pipe information database consists of the pipe size, pipe constituents, and pipe distance.

Aggregation of Soil Types

Since water pipelines are often buried underground, earlier research has shown the critical significance of the interaction between soil and pipes in pipe failures. The unequal ground settling may cause failures in the pipelines in particular. The likelihood of a pipe failure may also be impacted by the process of pipe degradation brought on by varied soil corrosivity. Previous research revealed that the pipe decomposition happens in a specific pH span. A more realistic approach would be to take into account the soil (Pramanik, S. 2023) categories which may be derived from the open dataset, since it is almost difficult to take into account all the soil-based parameters which can affect the pipe leakage. This research takes into account a total of 72 distinct kinds of soil. The slope, primary constituents, surface texture, and other soil properties are used to classify these soil types. In accordance with the primary site of failure records and the most of the soil category where the pipe is buried, the soil category information for each pipe is allocated. Since the break point is located there, Pipe 1 has been given the soil type Soil I according to 4(b). Since the bulk of Pipe 2 is located in Soil II and has no break records, Soil II has been given as the soil type.

Aggregation of Topographic Data

To assess WSN failures, topographical data can be used to compensate for missing operational water pressure (Khanh, P. T. et al. 2023) data. Pipes situated at more elevations typically experience low water pressures. The study region of Water Supply Network pipes in Allen County, USA, has a broad elevation span from 240 to 410 meters. The topographical dataset, collected from the USDA elevation dataset through Geospatial Data Gateway (GDG), has a resolution of 40 m. The digital elevation model offers elevation data for every place in Cuyahoga. Similar to soil category combination, pipe segments can have varying heights, particularly for long-length pipelines. As shown in Fig. 4(c), the breakpoint elevation is utilized to determine the height of the pipe having break records, such as Pipe 1.

Census Data Collection

Given that WSN is virtually always run for localities, it becomes sense to assume that community parameters (like user habits, census) can have an impact on the likelihood that pipes may fail. Public census statistics which include community characteristics are used in the research to demonstrate this conclusion. Huge variables that characterize each community block are included in the census dataset that was received from the US Census Bureau. The census information breaks down Cuyahoga County into 2952 community blocks. Based on the dataset's availability, the census, poverty rate, and non-healthcare insurance rate given in Table 2 are chosen in order to take the community aspects into account from many angles. As a lone pipe can pass through numerous census blocks, the population data for every pipe is assigned to a representative location determined in this research. As seen in Fig. In 4(d), the representative point for the pipe without break records is selected as the pipe geometry center while the breakpoint in the pipe having failure evidence is utilized as the indicative point.

Figure 5. Training and interpretation process for ML

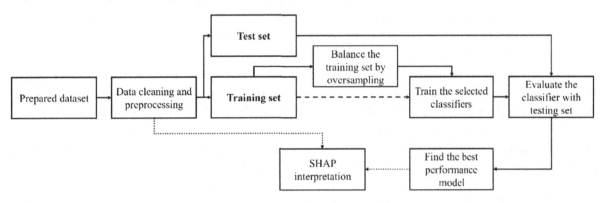

Data Accumulation for Climate

Previous research has shown that the pipe's break is significantly influenced by the seasons (e.g., atmospheric temperature, rainfall). The results suggest that the soil-pipe interaction may have contributed to the increased frequency of pipe breakage on particularly cold or hot days. The temperature data for predicting yearly pipe breaks, however, were not taken into consideration in earlier investigations. The aggregate number of colder and hotter days is employed in the research to represent the environment each pipe experienced throughout the course of its service life in order to get around this constraint in taking climate impacts into account. The term "cold days" refers to days with lower temperature below 32 °F. The term "hot days" refers to days with greatest temperature over 90 F. The total of the days is taken from a dataset made available by climate agent providers. Each pipe utilized in this research experienced a total number of cold and hot days from the time of installation until the chosen study year.

Water pressures are often lower at higher altitudes. Allen County, Cleveland, Ohio, which is the location of the WSN pipes under study, has a wide variety of elevations, from 240m to 410 m. The topographical dataset is derived from the USDA elevation dataset's Geospatial Data Gateway (GDG), which has a 30 m resolution. Any place in the Cuyahoga region may have its height determined using the digital elevation model (DEM).

A comprehensive dataset which integrates the physical features of water pipelines, operating circumstances, geological situations, community socioeconomic features, and climatic conditions is created using the established data aggregation framework and will be employed. Fig 5 depicts the training and interpretation process for machine learning.

RESEARCH CASE

Workflow of machine learning modeling for machine learning-based pipe failure prediction is shown in Fig 5. The established methodology for the prediction of water pipe breaks is shown in overview in Figure 5. The combined dataset determined by criterion are chosen and cleansed by excluding the specimens having a missing components and outliers indicated in Section 3.

The assembled dataset was divided into a training set and a test set at random by the 8:2 ratios, which is a standard method for determining the capacity of the model to forecast. As seen in Fig. 5. To train the model, both balanced and unbalanced training datasets are employed. This research utilized the oversampling approach that randomly repeats the minor class of pipes, to balance the dataset until the amount of break specimens matches the number of intact specimens. The testing dataset remains the same. As a result, the same testing dataset was used to assess the models that were trained on both balanced and unbalanced datasets. The entire dataset is utilized further for machine learning approaches through the utilization of an explanation procedure called SHAP to comprehend the effect of providing components on the pipe collapse after the best performing ML model has been found. As the chosen model is fitted once again in accordance with the entire dataset, it must be highlighted that the model analysis findings are not dependent on the train-test splitting approach. Below are descriptions of data preparation and machine learning model performance estimation.

Preparing Data and Evaluating Its Features

Setting Up the Dataset and Assigning Labels

The machine learning model is specified as a classification issue since the goal of the research is to estimate the pipe state at a particular time period, where the pipe status is either broken or working fine. It is impractical to create a dataset which covers every year of every pipe, and doing so might produce a very unbalanced dataset. The succeeding steps were used to construct the ultimate dataset for machine learning training and testing in order to reduce the degree of imbalance and fully use the break records.

1. For every pipe, a year at random between the time of installation and the last updation made prior to this research (Aug 2023) is chosen. Time-Dependent variables (i.e., prior collapse instances, pipe age, total number of frigid and hot days encountered) are identified during this time.
2. The pipe status noted for the chosen year is denoted by the numbers 0 for fine status or 1 for collapse status.
3. The data from the most recent break year for any pipe having a break record (or breaks) is attached to the dataset established in the older stages in order to totally use the pipe collapse history.
4. The final created dataset is split into a training dataset and a testing dataset in a 8:2 ratio.

The data aggregation procedure outlined in the previous section of this study is applied to the chosen data. The next step is data cleaning, which involves removing data points with missing information. 40,236 pipe data specimens, comprising 32,436 fine samples and 7354 break samples, are acquired after data cleaning.

Given that Step 1's random year selection may have an impact on the model's prediction outcomes. For evaluating the performance of the model, 10 random choices are made, and the average estimates of the evaluation metrics are utilized.

There are 13 elements in total, including two categorical variables and 11 continuous variables. The four basic categories of these elements are physical, operational, environmental, and sociological.

In both the training and testing datasets, factor histograms are depicted in Figure 6. In general, the training dataset adequately covers the testing dataset's characteristics. Dispersal of the physical variables is depicted in more detail in Fig 6(a) to (d). The most common materials in WSN systems are cast iron and ductile iron, although there exist a lot of pipes whose composition is unknown. The features of two operational variables are shown in figures 6(e) and (f). The four environmental variables are shown in

Figure 6a. Histograms of the variables taken into account for the training and test sets

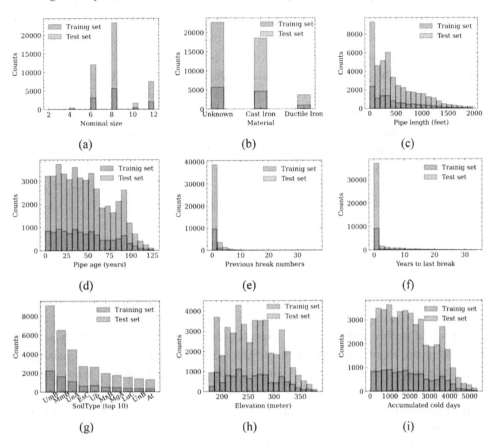

Figure 6b. Histograms of the variables taken into account for the training and test sets

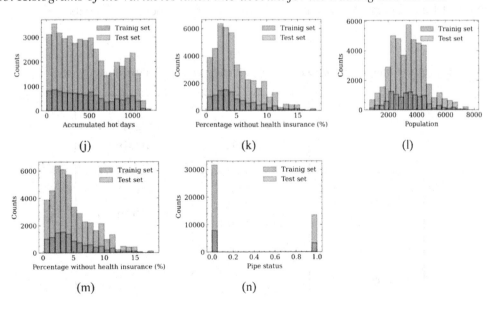

6(g) to (j). The pipes are allocated to 72 distinct soil types, although for ease of viewing. The number of hot and cold days over time is one of the climatic elements taken into account. It is intriguing to learn that they exhibit the same characteristics as the pipe age distribution, which shows that the importance of the climatic variables in pipe failures. As seen in Fig. 6(k) to (m), the census, the proportion of person living in poverty, and the proportion of families without access to health insurance are selected to reflect the socioeconomic characteristics of each pipe for the community they serve. The poverty rate for the majority of community blocks is under 40%. The most impoverished block, however, has more than 90% of its families with yearly earnings below the poverty line. The percentage of residents without health insurance in community blocks varies from 0.2% to 18%, mirroring the reported poor status. The outcomes are shown in Fig. 6. (n).

Connection Between Internal Variables and Failure State

The correlation matrix may be utilized to demonstrate both the external relationships between each component and the goal as well as the internal relationships among the elements thought to lead to pipe collapses. Various correlation indicators are utilized to assess the variables' correlation since the datasets include both category and numeric variables.

The fact that several of the socioeconomic variables under consideration (such as population, poverty rate, and proportion of people without health insurance) are connected but not firmly suggests that the ML model should regard them as independent variables. Furthermore, there is no association between any one I/P variable and the dominating O/P variable, suggesting that the pipe failure is a complicated issue that depends on many different factors.

Figure 1 illustrates how to find the correlations between several sorts of data. 7. In particular, Pearson correlation (Samanta, D. et al. 2021) is used to express the correlation between two numerical variables, while Cramer's V coefficient is used to quantify the connection between two categorical variables. Additionally, between category and numerical data, the correlation ratio is employed. These indicators range from 0 to 1 for category components and from 1 to 1 for numerical elements (1 or 1 signifies an

Figure 7. The correlation metrics used to categorical and numerical variables

	Continuous variable	Categorical variable
Continuous variable	Pearson correlation	Correlation ratio
Categorical variable	Correlation ratio	Cramér's V

entirely positive or negatively associated relationship, whereas 0 denotes no relationship). Due to the article length restriction, a thorough explanation of the correlation calculations is not included here. Readers who are interested might consult the Supplementary file (Algorithm I).

The pipe failure state (designated as "target" in the picture) and the final correlation matrix among the 13 variables taken into account are shown in picture 8. The hotter days, colder days, and pipe ages are the elements with the strongest correlation amounts to the aim (pipe failure condition). These suggest that among the most crucial elements affecting pipe conditions are the weather and pipe service age. The subsequent features also include the pipe length, interval year, and the preceding break number, among others. All of these are taken into account in the current study's observation of their actions in the machine learning model and model clarification.

Prediction of Pipe Failure Based on L

Results of Predictions

The average ROC, PRC, AUC and average training time of 10 selected datasets are computed and shown in Fig. to show the overall performance of various models. In spite of unbalanced or balanced training sets, the LightGBM model outperformed all other models under consideration in terms of ROC and PRC values as well as training time.

Figure 8. Map showing the correlation between the forecast objective and the variables under consideration

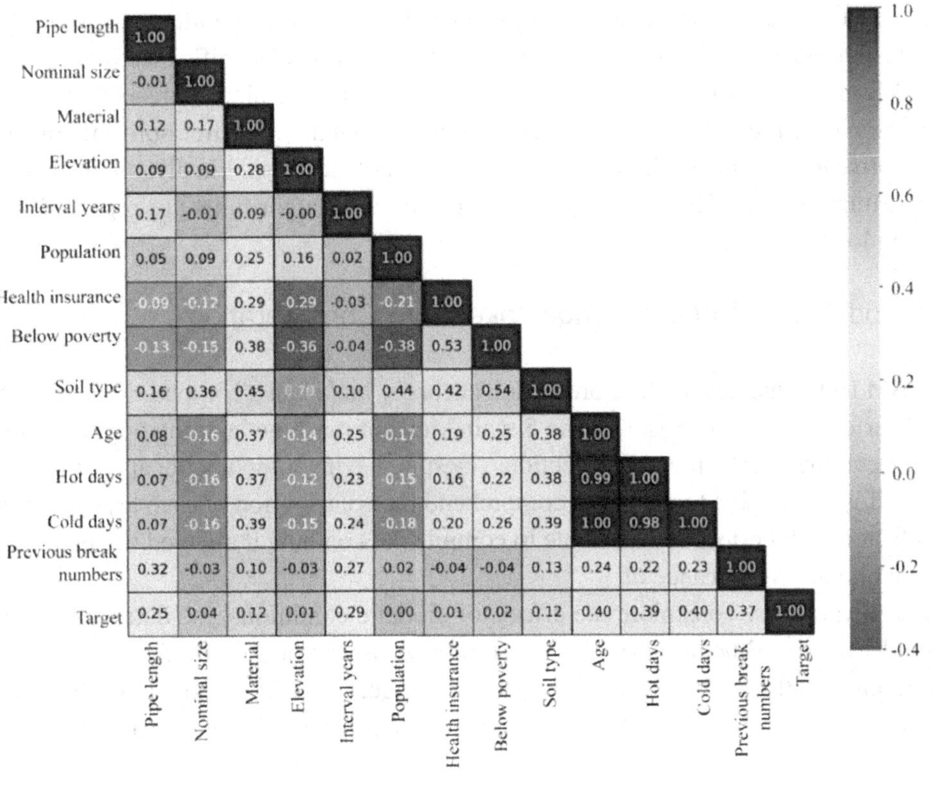

As a result of encoding, the I/P database is lesser sparse than for different frameworks. It may be shown that the LightGBM, ANN, LR, and kNN produced comparable ROC estimates while contrasting the ROC matrix and PRC matrix, which is in disagreement with the previously noted findings (in Fig. 9). The PRC matrix displays better evident differences between estimates for several models, demonstrating a superior recognition of the most effective models. According to the PRC findings, the balanced training LightGBM framework surpassed the unbalanced training model with respect to AUC of PRC estimate.

The outcomes of employing train-test splitting that is based randomly are shown in Figs. 8, 9, and 10. However, whether a machine learning model developed using information from past occurrences can accurately predict future events is a crucial challenge in engineering applications. The aforesaid procedures are once again computed using a time-line-based train-test splitting approach to allay this worry. Due to the identical findings, the results are not covered in this article. Readers who are interested might consult Fig. to Fig. S1. In the supporting information, it is S3.

The performance of these machine learning models is compared under several indicators based on the accuracy, training time, handling of categorical variables, and intrinsic model interpretability in order to well analyze the performance of utilizing various machine learning approaches for pipe failure estimation. It is clear that the LightGBM has the highest accuracy on the present dataset based on the classification results using balanced and unbalanced training datasets. When trained with the balanced dataset, the areas under PRC for the test dataset are around 0.86. The ANN, LR, SVC, and kNN models came next. The learning process was completed by the LR model, chased by the LightGBM approach and ANN approach, in terms of computing efficiency, in a matter of seconds. Among these models, the kNN and SVC models took the highest time. Because of its histogram and leaf-wise tree development method, the LightGBM approach is the only technique which can analyze the categorical data without any encoding. Despite the objective of this research is not the intrinsic explanatory capacity of various models; rather, they are addressed here for completeness based on earlier studies. As the weights of every element are visible and may be evaluated depending on their physical significance, statistical algorithms (such as the LR model) are often seen to be the most understandable algorithms. The relative relevance of components may be measured based on their functions throughout the tree splitting, making logistic-dependent approaches like the LightGBM model fairly simple to grasp. Finally, the instance-dependent learning algorithms (e.g., kNN), SVM, and perceptron-based algorithms are regarded as black box models having low interpretability.

SHAP Method Analysis of the Things Taken Into Consideration

The LightGBM technique has the best prediction accuracy and is also computationally competent, according to a performance comparison of the 5 main kinds of machine learning approaches for classification tasks mentioned in the preceding sections. Despite having a moderate capacity for explanation, the model itself is still unable to explicitly comprehend the contribution of each aspect to the result. To assess each factor's total effect, it is possible to compile data on how it affected the pipe break. Fig. 11 highlights the broader significance of

the analyzed variables. To explore the effects of climatic conditions, the dataset is stored with the Pipe age, colder days, and hotter days. The outcome reveals that out of all of them, "Cold days" have the most influence, followed by "Hot days." and "Pipe age." The three most important variables end up being pipe length, last break interval, and cold days. The nominal pipe size and the pipe's material

Figure 9. Prediction outcomes using training datasets that are unbalanced and balanced ('I' stands for fine and 'B' stands for collapse)

		Predicted results		
		I	B	Recall
True condition	I	6023	489	0.925
	B	694	1293	0.651
Precision		0.897	0.726	0.861

LightGBM model

		Predicted results		
		I	B	Recall
True condition	I	5681	831	0.872
	B	585	1402	0.705
Precision		0.906	0.628	0.833

ANN model

		Predicted results		
		I	B	Recall
True condition	I	5032	1480	0.773
	B	381	1606	0.808
Precision		0.929	0.520	0.781

LR model

		Predicted results		
		I	B	Recall
True condition	I	5992	520	0.920
	B	934	1053	0.530
Precision		0.865	0.669	0.828

kNN model

		Predicted results		
		I	B	Recall
True condition	I	5975	537	0.918
	B	890	1097	0.552
Precision		0.870	0.671	0.832

SVC model

a) Test set prediction results by model trained with imbalanced data

		Predicted results		
		I	B	Recall
True condition	I	5390	1082	0.833
	B	473	1591	0.771
Precision		0.919	0.595	0.818

LightGBM model

		Predicted results		
		I	B	Recall
True condition	I	4849	1623	0.749
	B	332	1732	0.839
Precision		0.935	0.516	0.771

ANN model

		Predicted results		
		I	B	Recall
True condition	I	5027	1445	0.776
	B	458	1606	0.778
Precision		0.916	0.526	0.777

LR model

		Predicted results		
		I	B	Recall
True condition	I	4803	1669	0.742
	B	399	1665	0.807
Precision		0.923	0.500	0.757

kNN model

		Predicted results		
		I	B	Recall
True condition	I	4994	1478	0.772
	B	447	1617	0.783
Precision		0.917	0.522	0.774

SVC model

b) Test set prediction results by model trained with balanced data

Figure 10. Evaluation of implemented ML models utilizing various metrics comparison

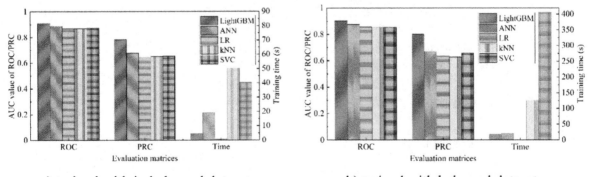

a) trained with imbalanced dataset

b) trained with balanced dataset

Table 1. Summary of the model for predicting pipe breaks

	LightGBM	Artificial Neural Network	Logistic Regression	KNN	SVC
Accuracy	○ ○ ○	○ ○	○	○	○
Learning technique speed	○ ○	○ ○	○ ○ ○	○	○
Dealing categorical values	○ ○ ○	○	○	○	○
Model Interpretability	○ ○	○	○ ○ ○	○	○

○ ○ ○ indicates a job well done.
○ Indicates the poorest effort.

have considerably less of an impact on the pipe break likelihood. Table 1 summarizing the model for predicting pipe breaks

The impacts of each element on the likelihood of a pipe breaking are shown in detail in the following figures. Each variable's effect value for each sample is calculated using the SHAP approach. The impact values of each element are taken from all pipe samples in order to indicate the total influence of the variables taken into consideration on the risk of a pipe breaking. Continuous variables' effects are colorized according to their magnitudes. The mean values of the impact variables serve as a representation. Based on the observations, it is possible to deduce the following conclusions. Numerous of these findings are in line with earlier research, proving the validity of the framework explanation findings.

1) The effect of physical elements is seen in Figure 12. All of these variables all have a positive impact on the likelihood of a pipe failing, meaning that the higher the factor's value, the higher the SHAP value. According to the dispersal of pipe length estimates, lengthy pipes posses a greater likelihood of failure

Figure 11. The total ranking of variables taken into account for pipe failure likelihood

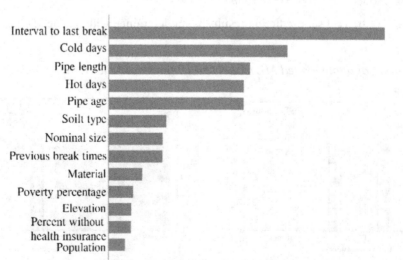

Figure 12. Effects of physical elements

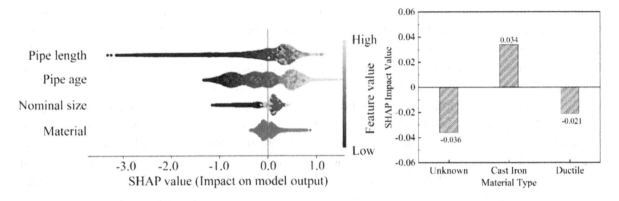

Figure 13. SHAP values shown to demonstrate how operational variables have an influence

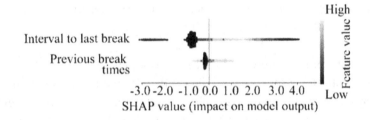

Figure14. Influenced by environmental influences

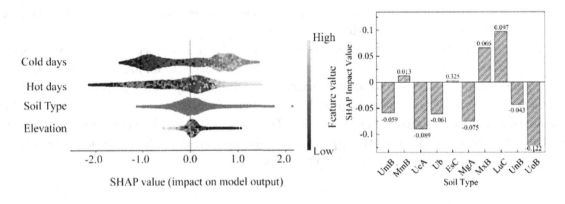

Figure 15. Impacting factors are local

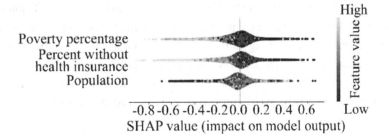

than smaller pipes. On pipe age, same observations may be made. Greater SHAP values for older pipes indicate that they are more prone to failure than newer pipes. Additionally, there is a positive association between the nominal size and the SHAP estimate, indicating that pipes having bigger nominal diameters are more likely to fail. On the right side of Fig 12, the effect of the pipe material is shown individually. Cast iron has a +ve SHAP effect value whereas ductile iron has a -ve SHAP impact value, despite both having low SHAP values. This shows that pipes constructed of cast iron have a larger break probability than pipes made of ductile iron. Ductile iron is less brittle than cast iron, which contributes to this in part.

2) Fig. 13 displays the results of operational service factors. The time since the most recent break has a greater influence on the likelihood of a pipe collapse than the durations of earlier breaks. The failure probability is observed to grow with a longer period since the previous break in the pipe, but a shorter time gap exhibits both positive and negative effects on the failure probability. This suggests that several pipes were damaged shortly after installation or repair. This finding is consistent with earlier research, which showed that a pipe's failure rate follows a bathtub curve, with large failure probability occurring either early in a pipe's life or as it begins to wear down. In addition, the SHAP values in Fig. 13 demonstrate that a higher rupture probability at the pipe correlates to a greater quantity of prior fails at the pipe. This is in line with empirical findings from practitioner interviews, according to which pipe failures tend to happen more often in the same places.

For the environmental elements shown in Fig. 14, the findings showed that the likelihood that a pipe would break increased with the number of cold days it had. It could be brought on by the effect of soil settling brought on by the freezing and thawing of the soil. On the RHS Fig 14, the effect of soil categories is shown. The LuC soil has the greatest pipe rupture probability among the top 10 soil types where the majority of pipes are hidden, while the UoB soil has the lowest rupture rate. Last but not least, the outcome shows that pipes placed at higher altitudes are less likely to burst, which makes sense given that pipelines at higher altitudes encounter low service water pressure. As a result, the pipe is subjected to reduced internal stress from the service water pressure.

4) With respect to the socio cultural elements shown in Fig. 15, it is unexpected to learn those populations with lower socioeconomic status or less access to health care had a lower likelihood of experiencing a water pipe break. The fact that the poverty-stricken neighborhoods get fewer inspections or typically consume less water may have contributed to the pipe's longer lifespan. Additional research based on additional data is needed for in-depth justifications. The chance of pipe failure is not consistently influenced by a community block's density, despite this in most pipe samples; a highly populated location is associated with a considerably greater water pipe break risk.

CONCLUSION

In order to understand the consequences of contributing elements, this research intends to investigate the use of ML approaches to forecast water pipe failures dependent on data from a large water supply network. A crucial step that enables taking into account contributing reasons for pipe collapses, such as the geology, climate, and socioeconomic aspects, is the proposal of a design which combines water supply network maintenance records with many public databases. Five separate machine learning models, each from the 5 main categories of ML classification frameworks, are created for pipe collapse estimation using the aggregated data. Both an unbalanced training dataset, where the bulk of the data come from intact pipes, and a balanced training database, which uses the oversampling approach to achieve balance, are utilized to train the models. The outcomes of several training datasets are contrasted. The SHAP interpolation technique then interprets the learned ML model. This study's major contributions include:

1. It offers a cutting-edge framework for data aggregation that integrates many publicly available datasets, producing the biggest real-field dataset (in terms of size and chronology) and correspondingly the highest amount of I/P parameters for ML modeling in water supply network. As a result, this research greatly broadens and digs in at the grasp of the communities about the influences of technology, geology, weather, and socio-economical issues. This is the first study that, to the best of our knowledge, evaluates how socioeconomic characteristics affect the collapse of water delivery networks.

2. Five common ML algorithms are investigated and thoroughly contrasted by 5 criteria (accuracy, computing time, effect of categorical variables, interpretation) for the purpose of implementation. The maximum performance was attained by the LightGBM framework having the second lowest training time. However, it has been shown that the ROC is very confident regarding the dataset is severely skewed; use the PRC measure.

3. The SHAP's capacity to understand the effect of the contributing components was shown by the interpretation findings' consistency with earlier research. The findings show that pipe buried time, in particular the time since the previous failure, encountered colder days, hotter days, and pipe age, have a substantial impact. The contribution of the pipe's physical characteristics and the environment are consistent with the findings of other investigations. According to the contribution of community factors, places with high poverty have a reduced likelihood of pipe breakage (or are maintained less often), but locations with high population density have a greater likelihood of water pipe breakage. These show that socioeconomic considerations show a significant impact on the circumstances of pipe service.

Moreover, complicated nonlinear interactions between varieties of elements lead to water pipe failure. Due to the model's capacity and the availability of data, previous research often streamlined the analysis process by taking a limited number of elements into account. Future research should think about including more sophisticated ML approaches and a larger dataset to increase the accuracy of pipe failure prediction. The change of decision-taking approach for ardent management of water supply network to meet sustainability objective may be catalyzed by advancements in several areas.

REFERENCES

Ahamad, S., Veeraiah, V., Ramesh, J. V. N., Rajadevi, R., Reeja, S. R., Pramanik, S., & Gupta, A. (2023). Deep Learning based Cancer Detection Technique. Thrust Technologies' Effect on Image Processing. IGI Global.

Bhattacharya, A., Ghosal, A., Obaid, A. J., Krit, S., Shukla, V. K., Mandal, K., & Pramanik, S. (2021). Unsupervised Summarization Approach with Computational Statistics of Microblog Data. In D. Samanta, R. R. Althar, S. Pramanik, & S. Dutta (Eds.), *Methodologies and Applications of Computational Statistics for Machine Learning* (pp. 23–37). IGI Global., doi:10.4018/978-1-7998-7701-1.ch002

Chandan, R. R., Soni, S., Raj, A., Veeraiah, V., Dhabliya, D., Pramanik, S., & Gupta, A. (2023). Genetic Algorithm and Machine Learning. Advanced Bioinspiration Methods for Healthcare Standards, Policies, and Reform.IGI Global. doi:10.4018/978-1-6684-5656-9

Chen, Y., Jia, J., Wu, C., Ramirez-Granada, L., & Li, G. (2023). Estimation on total phosphorus of agriculture soil in China: A new sight with comparison of model learning methods. *Journal of Soils and Sediments*, *23*(2), 998–1007. doi:10.100711368-022-03374-x

Dhamodaran, S., Ahamad, S., Ramesh, J. V. N., Sathappan, S., Namdev, A., Kanse, R. R., & Pramanik, S. (2023). *Fire Detection System Utilizing an Aggregate Technique in UAV and Cloud Computing, Thrust Technologies' Effect on Image Processing*. IGI Global.

Jayasingh, R. (2022). Speckle noise removal by SORAMA segmentation in Digital Image Processing to facilitate precise robotic surgery. *International Journal of Reliable and Quality E-Healthcare*, *11*(1), 1–19. doi:10.4018/IJRQEH.295083

Mondal, D., Ratnaparkhi, A., Deshpande, A., Deshpande, V., Kshirsagar, A. P., & Pramanik, S. (2023). Applications, Modern Trends and Challenges of Multiscale Modelling in Smart Cities. In *Data-Driven Mathematical Modeling in Smart Cities*. IGI Global., doi:10.4018/978-1-6684-6408-3.ch001

Ngọc, T. H., Khanh, P. T., & Pramanik, S. (2023). Smart Agriculture using a Soil Monitoring System. In A. Khang & I. G. I. Global (Eds.), *Advanced Technologies and AI-Equipped IoT Applications in High Tech Agriculture*. doi:10.4018/978-1-6684-9231-4.ch011

Pandey, B. K., Pandey, D., Nassa, V. K., Hameed, A. S., George, A. S., Dadheech, P., & Pramanik, S. (2023). A Review of Various Text Extraction Algorithms for Images. In *The Impact of Thrust Technologies on Image Processing*. Nova Publishers. doi:10.52305/ATJL4552

Pramanik, S. (2023). Intelligent Farming Utilizing a Soil Tracking Device. In A. K. Sharma, N. Chanderwal, R. Khan, & I. G. I. Global (Eds.), *Convergence of Cloud Computing, AI and Agricultural Science*. doi:10.4018/979-8-3693-0200-2.ch009

Pramanik, S. (2023). An Adaptive Image Steganography Approach depending on Integer Wavelet Transform and Genetic Algorithm. *Multimedia Tools and Applications*, *82*(22), 34287–34319. Advance online publication. doi:10.100711042-023-14505-y

Pramanik, S., & Bandyopadhyay, S. (2023). Identifying Disease and Diagnosis in Females using Machine Learning. In I. G. I. John Wang (Ed.), *Encyclopedia of Data Science and Machine Learning*. Global., doi:10.4018/978-1-7998-9220-5.ch187

Reepu, K. S., Chaudhary, M. G., Gupta, K. G., Pramanik, S. & Gupta, A. (2023). Information Security and Privacy in IoT. Handbook of Research in Advancements in AI and IoT Convergence Technologies. IGI Global.

Tai, P., Wu, F., Chen, R., Zhu, J., Wang, X., & Zhang, M. (2023). Effect of herbaceous plants on the response of loose silty sand slope under rainfall. *Bulletin of Engineering Geology and the Environment*, *82*(1), 42. doi:10.100710064-023-03066-x

Section 2

Intelligent Systems From Optimal–MCDM Shaping Tomorrow: An In–Depth Analysis of Decision–Making Applications in Agriculture, Judiciary, Education, and Others

INTRODUCTION

The journey commences by reflecting on the enormous influence that AI has on decision-making procedures. As we explore the complexities of AI applications, we are specifically interested in the field of agriculture. Here, precision farming and the integration of IoT are being used to develop innovative farming practices for the future. Next, we explore the legal realm, unraveling the complex aspects of AI's involvement in predictive analytics, document analysis, and automated case management. Furthermore, the exploration also encompasses the field of education, where the utilization of AI-driven decision-making and learning analytics enhances cognitive abilities and maximizes educational results.

AI-DRIVEN LEARNING ANALYTICS FOR PERSONALIZED EDUCATION

Artificial intelligence (AI) and learning analytics are powerful agents of change in the ever-changing field of higher education. This chapter examines the use of AI-driven learning analytics in tailored feedback and assessment in higher education institutions. The incorporation of AI algorithms and data analytics enables the customized delivery of feedback, precisely identifying individual strengths and areas for enhancement. The chapter explores how AI-driven learning analytics might facilitate adaptive and formative assessments, providing individualized and precise evaluations of students' knowledge and skills. AI-driven decision-making in education, ranging from personalized learning to adaptive assessments, catalyzes improved student engagement and maximized outcomes. Nevertheless, ethical considerations, implementation challenges, and the imperative for faculty training are crucial aspects that need to be tackled. In this part, we have introduced 3 full chapters regarding applications of decision-making in chapters 9-11.

AGRICULTURE: CULTIVATING TOMORROW WITH AI

In the realm of agriculture, the combination of the Internet of Things (IoT) and precision farming enables a novel strategy to be implemented. By harnessing the power of interconnected sensors, automated precision agriculture practices maximize the usage of available resources while simultaneously reducing their impact on the environment. This chapter on artificial intelligence-driven decision-making in modern agriculture sectors reveals a wide range of applications in the management of weeds, crops, and soil, highlighting both the obstacles and the opportunities that are present in this journey toward transformation. For more details, please read Chapters 12-14.

JUDICIARY: DECODING JUSTICE WITH ARTIFICIAL INTELLIGENCE

Our investigation next leads us to the judicial system, where artificial intelligence serves as a guiding light for the enhancement of decision-making procedures. Within the realms of predictive analytics and document analysis, case studies provide light on the incorporation of artificial intelligence, providing insights into approaches, obstacles, and potential solutions. In this section, we dig into the ethical considerations concerning transparency, bias, and privacy, keeping in mind the complexities that arise when artificial intelligence is introduced into a sector that is based on human judgment, see Chapter 15.

ADDITIONAL TOPICS OF INTELLIGENT SYSTEMS IN OPTIMIZATION, OBJECT DETECTION, AND CONSUMER BEHAVIOR

Chapter 16 explores the boundaries of intelligent systems, addressing a wide range of obstacles and opportunities along the way. A novel strategy, known as the PSK (P. Senthil Kumar) method, is utilized to investigate the Assignment Problem (AP), which is widely recognized as a task that requires optimization. Solutions for Intuitionistic Fuzzy Assignment Problems (IFAPs) are pioneered by this method, which is based on software and a ranking mechanism. The PSK technique demonstrates its superiority by utilizing formal theorems and practical examples on four different IFAPs. The findings are validated by computer programs that have been presented with great care, which also helps to generate a comprehensive comparative study and discussions on the merits, demerits, and potential routes for further research.

In Chapter 17, the focus shifts to computer vision, where the author discusses the difficulties associated with object recognition, particularly in challenging environments such as low illumination and misty evenings. The current generation of one-stage detectors is struggling with restrictions, which has led to the development of an innovative technique. This method that has been proposed not only performs exceptionally well in detecting objects in difficult circumstances, but it also considerably improves both speed and accuracy. Through the utilization of cutting-edge techniques, including dehazing and grayscale conversion, as well as the utilization of YOLOv8 and YOLO-ODDT algorithms, the proposed method surpasses the capabilities of established object detectors.

For the purpose of highlighting the revolutionary influence of smart speakers that are seamlessly connected with artificial intelligence (AI), the investigation extends beyond the sphere of consumer behavior. As smart speakers grow more commonplace in homes, they are having a significant impact on shoppers' decisions that are guided by artificial intelligence. The purpose of this article is to provide a thorough vision of the future of artificial intelligence and smart speakers in the context of the commercial environment by navigating through the strengths and weaknesses of this mutually beneficial partnership, as shown in Chapter 18.

An enlightening tour of intelligent systems is provided in this article. It covers a wide range of topics, including optimization methods, cutting-edge object identification methodologies, and the changing landscape of AI-infused consumer behavior.

CONCLUSION

As we come to the end of this investigation, we will review the most important discoveries from each domain, with a particular focus on the overarching impact that AI will have on the future. Because of the dynamic nature of artificial intelligence, it is guaranteed to undergo continual change, which has prompted a call to action for additional research and investigation in these always-shifting settings.

CLOSING STATEMENT

This part initiates an exciting investigation into intelligent systems that are powered by artificial intelligence. As the readers embark on this voyage, they are filled with anticipation for the disclosures that are contained within the in-depth investigation of the uses of artificial intelligence in the fields of agriculture, the court, education, and others.

Chapter 9
AI–Driven Learning Analytics for Personalized Feedback and Assessment in Higher Education

Tarun Kumar Vashishth

iD https://orcid.org/0000-0001-9916-9575

IIMT University, India

Vikas Sharma

iD https://orcid.org/0000-0001-8173-4548

IIMT University, India

Kewal Krishan Sharma

IIMT University, India

Bhupendra Kumar

IIMT University, India

Rajneesh Panwar

IIMT University, India

Sachin Chaudhary

iD https://orcid.org/0000-0002-8415-0043

IIMT University, India

ABSTRACT

Advancements in artificial intelligence (AI) and learning analytics have opened up new possibilities for personalized education in higher education institutions. This chapter explores the potential of AI-driven learning analytics in higher education, focusing on its application in personalized feedback and assessment. By leveraging AI algorithms and data analytics, personalized feedback can be provided to students, targeting their specific strengths and areas for improvement. Adaptive and formative assessments can also be facilitated through AI-driven learning analytics, enabling personalized and accurate evaluation of students' knowledge and skills. However, ethical considerations, implementation challenges, and faculty training are crucial aspects that must be addressed for successful adoption. As technology continues to evolve, embracing AI-driven learning analytics can enhance student engagement, support individualized learning, and optimize educational outcomes.

DOI: 10.4018/979-8-3693-0639-0.ch009

Figure 1. AI-driven learning analytics in higher education

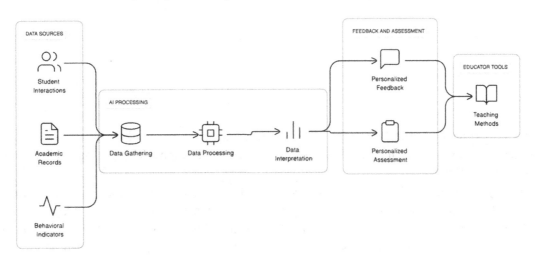

INTRODUCTION

In the rapidly evolving landscape of higher education, the integration of Artificial Intelligence (AI) and learning analytics has emerged as a transformative force. This introduction sets the stage by defining key concepts and highlighting their significance.

Definition and Significance

Definition: AI-driven Learning Analytics in higher education refers to the utilization of artificial intelligence and data analytics techniques to gather, process, and interpret educational data. It aims to provide personalized feedback and assessment to students and educators. This multidimensional approach harnesses data from various sources, including student interactions with digital learning platforms, academic performance records, and behavioral indicators.

Significance: The significance of AI-driven Learning Analytics in higher education is profound. It represents a convergence of advanced technologies that has the potential to revolutionize teaching and learning. By offering personalized insights and feedback, it enhances student engagement, learning outcomes, and the overall educational experience. Moreover, it empowers educators with data-driven tools to tailor their teaching methods effectively.

Evolution of AI in Higher Education

The introduction sets the stage for the exploration of AI in higher education by tracing its evolutionary journey.

Historical Context: The journey of AI in higher education is rooted in the broader evolution of artificial intelligence. It began in the mid-20th century with early experiments in computer-assisted instruction.

Figure 2. Tracing the evolutionary journey of AI in higher education

| Historical Context | Early Experiments | Expert Systems | Online Learning Platforms | Data-Driven AI | Current Landscape |

Early Experiments: In the 1960s and 1970s, AI was employed for simple tasks in education, such as programmed instruction and automated testing. These initial forays laid the foundation for more advanced applications.

Expert Systems: In the 1980s and 1990s, expert systems were introduced, enabling AI to provide personalized tutoring and guidance to students. This era marked a significant shift towards adaptive learning.

Online Learning Platforms: With the advent of online learning platforms and digital educational resources in the 2000s, AI found a broader range of applications. These platforms utilized AI for content recommendation, adaptive assessments, and intelligent analytics.

Data-Driven AI: The recent years have witnessed a proliferation of data-driven AI applications in higher education. Machine learning, predictive analytics, and natural language processing are being used to personalize learning experiences, predict student outcomes, and automate administrative tasks.

Current Landscape: Today, AI in higher education has reached a stage where it not only enhances teaching and learning but also plays a pivotal role in institutional decision-making. It leverages big data, advanced algorithms, and cloud computing to create a dynamic and adaptive educational ecosystem.

As we embark on this exploration, it is crucial to recognize the rich history and ongoing evolution of AI in higher education. This journey underscores the transformative potential of AI to shape the future of learning and academia.

GOALS AND OBJECTIVES

Goals

Comprehensive Understanding: To provide readers with a comprehensive understanding of AI-driven Learning Analytics and its applications in higher education.

Practical Insights: To offer practical insights into how AI can be leveraged to enhance personalized feedback and assessment in higher education settings.

Ethical Awareness: To raise awareness about the ethical considerations and challenges associated with AI-driven Learning Analytics in higher education.

Future Prospects: To discuss the prospects and trends in AI-driven Learning Analytics, considering emerging technologies and potential advancements.

Objectives

Define AI-driven Learning Analytics: To define and explain the concept of AI-driven Learning Analytics, including its components and methodologies.

Highlight Significance: To emphasize the significance of AI-driven Learning Analytics in improving personalized feedback and assessment in higher education.

Explore Applications: To explore various applications and use cases of AI-driven Learning Analytics, illustrating how it can benefit both educators and students.

Examine Ethical Concerns: To critically examine the ethical concerns related to data privacy, fairness, and transparency when implementing AI-driven Learning Analytics.

Provide Practical Examples: To provide practical examples and case studies of institutions or systems successfully utilizing AI for personalized feedback and assessment.

Offer Implementation Guidance: To offer guidance on how educators and institutions can effectively implement AI-driven Learning Analytics, including considerations for data collection and algorithmic decision-making.

Discuss Future Trends: To discuss emerging trends and future directions in AI-driven Learning Analytics, considering the evolving landscape of technology and education.

STRUCTURE OF THE CHAPTER

This chapter is meticulously structured to offer readers a comprehensive exploration of the intersection of AI and learning analytics in higher education.

The introduction provides an overview of the chapter's objectives and the significance of AI-driven learning analytics in higher education. The fundamentals of learning analytics are discussed, covering key concepts, terminology, and the role of learning analytics in higher education. The chapter delves into the integration of AI and learning analytics, examining the benefits and challenges and assessing the current state of AI in higher education. Data collection and processing are explored, emphasizing data sources, preprocessing techniques, and ethical considerations in data collection. AI-driven personalization in education is discussed, including personalized learning approaches, adaptive learning systems, and the benefits for both students and educators. The generation of feedback is a critical component, detailing automated feedback mechanisms, personalized feedback strategies, and the use of AI in grading and assessment.

Predictive analytics for student success examines early warning systems, identifying at-risk students, and strategies for intervention. Real-world case studies and practical applications are presented, showcasing AI-driven learning analytics in action, highlighting successes, and lessons learned. Ethical and privacy considerations emphasize data security and privacy issues, fairness, transparency, and compliance with regulations. Future trends and directions provide insights into emerging technologies, their potential impact on higher education, and recommendations for educators and institutions. The chapter concludes with a summary of key takeaways, offering insights into the future of AI-driven learning analytics and closing remarks.

Figure 3. Learning analytics and its components

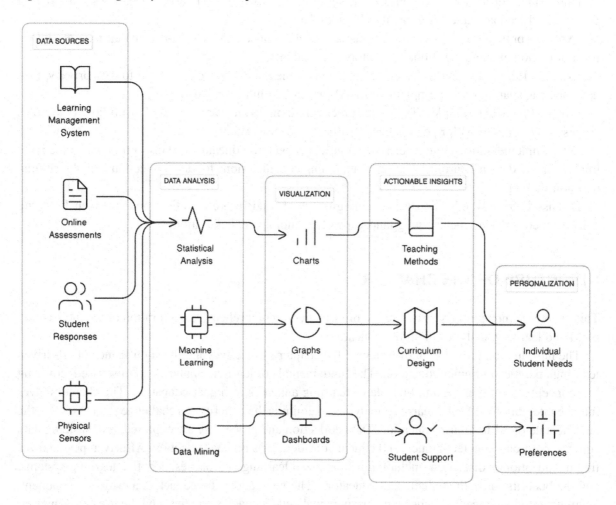

FUNDAMENTALS OF LEARNING ANALYTICS

What is Learning Analytics

Learning analytics is the process of collecting, analyzing, and interpreting data related to student learning and the contexts in which it occurs. It involves the measurement, collection, analysis, and reporting of data about learners and their contexts for understanding and optimizing learning and the environments in which it occurs.

In essence, learning analytics leverages data from various educational technologies and sources to gain insights into how students are engaging with educational content, identifying areas where they might be struggling, and offering personalized interventions or improvements to enhance their learning experiences.

Key components of learning analytics include:

Data Collection: Gathering data from various sources such as learning management systems, online assessments, student responses, and even physical sensors in some cases.

Data Analysis: Employing analytical techniques, including statistical analysis, machine learning, and data mining, to process and make sense of the collected data.

Visualization: Presenting data in visual formats such as charts, graphs, and dashboards to make it more accessible and understandable to educators and students.

Actionable Insights: Extracting actionable insights from the data this can be used to inform decisions related to teaching methods, curriculum design, and student support.

Personalization: Tailoring educational experiences to individual student needs and preferences based on the insights gained from data analysis.

Learning analytics has the potential to revolutionize education by enabling institutions and educators to make data-driven decisions, ultimately leading to more effective teaching and improved student outcomes. It plays a vital role in shaping the future of higher education by harnessing the power of data and technology to enhance the learning experience.

KEY CONCEPTS AND TERMINOLOGIES

Data Sources

Learning Management Systems (LMS): These are platforms used for delivering and managing educational courses. In learning analytics, data from LMS includes information on student access, interactions with course materials, quiz and assignment submissions, and grades.

Online Assessments: Data from quizzes, exams, and assignments conducted through digital platforms provide insights into student performance and learning behavior.

Clickstream Data: This refers to the data generated when students interact with online content, including which pages they visit, how long they stay on a page, and the sequence of their interactions.

Sensors and Wearables: Emerging technologies like Internet of Things (IoT) sensors and wearable devices can collect data related to students' physical activities, environmental factors, and health, which may be relevant in certain educational contexts.

Figure 4. Data sources technologies

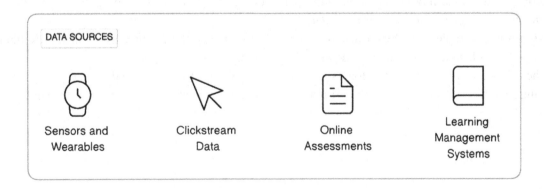

Data Analysis Techniques

Descriptive Analytics: This involves summarizing and visualizing data to provide insights into past events and trends, helping educators understand what has happened.

Predictive Analytics: Predictive analytics uses historical data to forecast future outcomes, such as predicting which students are at risk of failing a course.

Prescriptive Analytics: Building on predictive analytics, prescriptive analytics recommends specific actions to improve outcomes. For example, it might suggest interventions to help at-risk students succeed.

Learning Metrics

Key Performance Indicators (KPIs): These are specific metrics used to evaluate the success of educational programs or interventions. KPIs in learning analytics could include course completion rates, retention rates, and engagement levels.

Data Visualization and Dashboards

Data Visualization: This involves representing data graphically through charts, graphs, and other visual elements to make complex information more understandable.

Dashboards: Dashboards are user interfaces that provide a consolidated view of data. In learning analytics, dashboards are used to display key information and trends for educators and administrators.

Predictive Modeling

Machine Learning Models: Machine learning algorithms are used to build predictive models in learning analytics. These models analyze historical data to make predictions about future events or trends.

Student Success Predictions: Predictive models may be used to predict which students are likely to succeed or struggle in a course, allowing educators to provide targeted support.

Machine Learning in Learning Analytics

Role of Machine Learning: Machine learning plays a crucial role in uncovering patterns, trends, and insights within large datasets in learning analytics.

Algorithm Examples: Machine learning algorithms commonly applied in learning analytics include decision trees, clustering algorithms, and neural networks.

These key concepts and terminologies provide the foundation for understanding and implementing learning analytics, a field that uses data and analytics to enhance education and improve student outcomes.

Figure 5. Predictive modeling

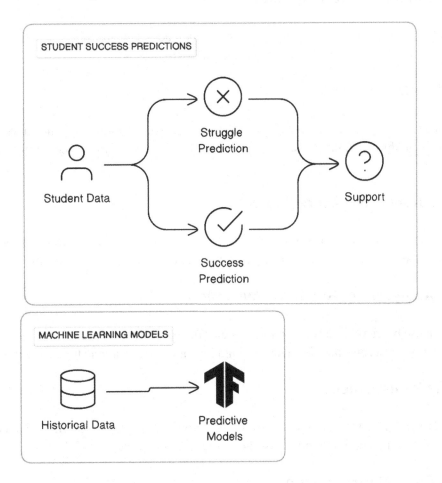

IMPORTANCE IN HIGHER EDUCATION

Data-Informed Decision Making

Learning analytics empowers educators and institutions with data-driven insights. It allows them to make informed decisions regarding curriculum design, teaching methods, and student support strategies. This data-driven approach enhances the quality of education.

Personalized Learning

Learning analytics enables personalized learning experiences. By analyzing students' performance and behavior, educators can tailor instruction to individual needs. This enhances engagement and the likelihood of student success.

Early Intervention for At-Risk Students

Learning analytics can identify at-risk students early in their academic journey. Educators can intervene with additional support, reducing dropout rates and improving retention.

Adaptive Learning Platforms

Higher education institutions are increasingly adopting adaptive learning platforms driven by learning analytics. These platforms adjust content and difficulty levels in real-time based on individual student performance.

Quality Assurance and Accreditation

Learning analytics aids in quality assurance efforts. It allows institutions to monitor and demonstrate the effectiveness of their educational programs, which is crucial for accreditation purposes.

Predictive Analytics for Resource Allocation

Institutions can use predictive analytics to forecast enrollment numbers and student needs. This helps in resource allocation, ensuring that adequate staff and resources are available to meet demand.

Continuous Improvement

Learning analytics supports a culture of continuous improvement. Educators can use data to assess the effectiveness of teaching methods and adjust their practices accordingly.

Enhanced Student Engagement

By understanding how students interact with course materials, educators can design more engaging content and activities. This leads to higher levels of student engagement.

Monitoring Student Progress

Learning analytics provides real-time insights into student progress. Educators can track how students are advancing through coursework and address any obstacles they encounter.

Data-Driven Research

Learning analytics generates a wealth of data that can be used for educational research. This research contributes to the broader field of educational science and informs pedagogical advancements.

In summary, learning analytics is a vital tool in higher education. It not only improves the learning experience for students but also assists educators and institutions in achieving better outcomes, ensuring data-driven decision-making, and continuously enhancing the quality of education provided.

THE ROLE OF AI IN LEARNING ANALYTICS

Integration of AI and Learning Analytics

AI-Powered Data Analysis: AI techniques, such as machine learning, natural language processing, and computer vision, can analyze vast amounts of educational data efficiently. This includes student interactions with online platforms, assessments, and learning materials.

Predictive Analytics: AI enhances predictive analytics in learning. Machine learning models can predict student performance, identify at-risk students, and recommend interventions for personalized learning experiences.

Smart Content Delivery: AI algorithms can personalize content delivery by recommending additional resources, quizzes, or activities based on individual student progress and learning preferences.

BENEFITS AND CHALLENGES

Benefits

Personalization: AI-driven learning analytics enables personalized learning paths, addressing the unique needs and abilities of each student.

Early Intervention: AI can flag students at risk of falling behind or dropping out, allowing educators to provide timely support.

Efficiency: AI automates data analysis, saving educators time and providing real-time insights.

Enhanced Engagement: AI can recommend engaging content and activities, increasing student motivation and participation.

Challenges

Data Privacy: Managing sensitive student data requires robust privacy protections and compliance with regulations like GDPR.

Data Quality: AI's effectiveness depends on the quality and accuracy of the data it analyzes, necessitating data cleaning and validation processes.

Ethical Considerations: Decisions made by AI algorithms, such as predicting student success or recommending interventions, raise ethical questions that require careful consideration.

Teacher-Technology Balance: Balancing AI-enhanced instruction with the role of educators can be a challenge, as AI is a tool to support rather than replace teachers.

CURRENT STATE OF AI IN HIGHER EDUCATION

Adaptive Learning Platforms: Many higher education institutions use AI-driven adaptive learning platforms that adjust course materials and difficulty based on student performance.

Chatbots and Virtual Assistants: AI-powered chatbots provide students with instant support for common queries, while virtual teaching assistants help educators manage administrative tasks.

Figure 6. Integration of AI and learning analytics

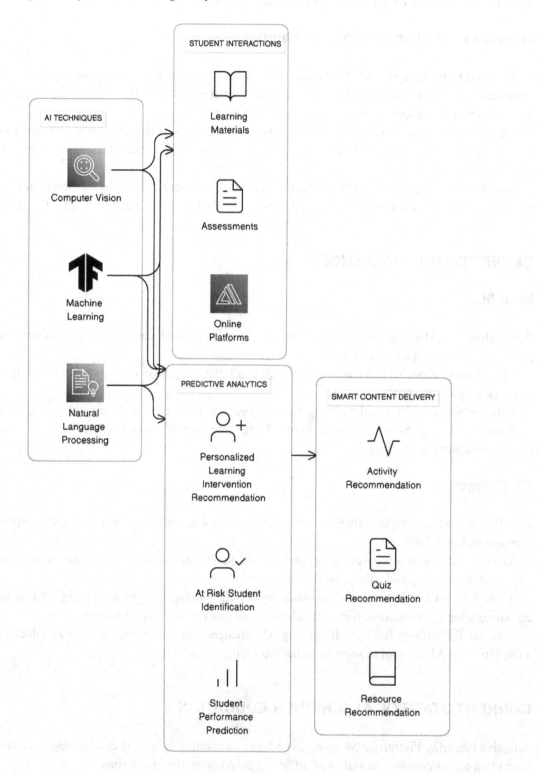

Learning Analytics Tools: AI-driven learning analytics tools are becoming more prevalent, offering educators insights into student performance and engagement.

AI for Content Creation: Some AI systems generate educational content, including quizzes, assessments, and even course materials.

AI in Assessments: AI can assess student-written essays and provide immediate feedback, saving educators time and offering student's constructive criticism.

The integration of AI and learning analytics has the potential to revolutionize higher education by providing personalized, data-driven learning experiences. While there are challenges to address, the benefits in terms of student success, engagement, and efficiency are substantial. The current state of AI in higher education is marked by ongoing innovation and adoption across various aspects of teaching and learning.

LITERATURE REVIEW

Berendt, Bettina, Allison Littlejohn, and Mike Blakemore (2020) examine the possibilities of AI and 'Big Data' in enhancing real-time monitoring of the education system while deliberating on their implications for the fundamental rights and freedoms of educators and learners alike.

Bozkurt et al. (2021) employ a systematic review approach spanning half a century (1970–2020) to investigate AI studies in education, incorporating social network analysis and text-mining methods for comprehensive insights.

Renz, André, Swathi Krishnaraja, and Elisa Gronau (2020) offer a concise overview of the current landscape of Learning Analytics and Artificial Intelligence in education in the initial section of their paper.

Rienties, Bart, Henrik Køhler Simonsen, and Christothea Herodotou (2020) deliver a succinct review encompassing four distinct research domains: Artificial Intelligence and Education (AIED), Computer-Supported Collaborative Learning (CSCL), Educational Data Mining (EDM), and Learning Analytics (LA).

Malcolm Tight (2019) reports on a systematic review of research pertaining to student retention and student engagement in higher education (HE).

Zawacki-Richter et al. (2020) provide an overview of research on AI applications in higher education through a systematic review.

Zhang, Liyin, Mian Wu, and Fan Ouyang (2023) propose a teaching and learning analytics (TLA) tool that integrates multiple data sources from the instructor and students during the educational process. They leverage various analytic methods to visualize results and offer supportive feedback, with the goal of providing data-driven evidence for academic improvement.

Escotet, Miguel Ángel (2023) discusses the rapid evolution of Artificial Intelligence, emphasizing its vast potential in education and higher education. The article takes an optimistic stance on the future of higher education with AI.

Ciolacu et al. (2018) introduce an innovative approach to promoting AI in Education 4.0.

Wang et al. (2023) investigate a range of AI applications, including personalized learning, adaptive testing, predictive analytics, and chatbots in the context of international student education. This research offers insights into how AI can enhance learning efficiency and provide tailored educational support.

Liu, Li, Rama Subbareddy, and C. G. Raghavendra (2022) introduce the Artificial Intelligence Based Inquiry Evaluation Student Learning System (AI-IESLS), designed to enhance interactive learning in a non-linear setting. The system employs concept mapping within a chatbot to enhance students' understanding of specific subjects, ultimately improving their learning outcomes.

Chen et al. (2020) evaluated of AI in Education (AIEd) definitions from both broad and narrow perspectives, providing clarity on the relationship between AIEd, Educational Data Mining, Computer-Based Education, and Learning Analytics.

Ungerer, Leona, and Sharon Slade's (2022) conclude by emphasizing the importance for higher education institutions to be mindful of the limitations and potential ethical issues surrounding AI solutions until formal ethical frameworks for their implementation are well-established.

Dogan, M. E., Goru Dogan, T., & Bozkurt, A. investigate the growing role of AI technologies in various aspects of life, with a specific focus on their impact on online distance education in their study.

Nazaretsky, T., Cukurova, M., & Alexandron, G. (2023) introduce a novel tool for assessing educators' trust in AI-based EdTech, demonstrating its internal structural validity. They utilize this instrument to depict the attitudes of secondary-level school teachers toward AI.

Henderson, M., Ryan, T., & Phillips, M (2022) provide insights into challenges unique to feedback, including the generation of constructive comments and the perceived obstacles in both student and educator attitudes and competencies.

Orsmond, P., & Merry, S. (2019) conducted interviews to explore the tutor's intentions when delivering precise feedback and to understand students' perceptions and utilization of that feedback.

Beaumont, Doherty & Shannon (2011) published an article presenting their research findings on the student assessment experience in school/college and higher education, including how the transition impacts student perceptions of feedback quality.

Xia et al. (2022) conducted a systematic review study to comprehend the opportunities and challenges in the emerging field of artificial intelligence in education (AIEd). They aimed to provide insights into this area by analyzing relevant literature.

In his article, Burke, D., (2009) delves into student strategies for responding to feedback brought from their previous educational experiences, particularly focusing on student perceptions of guidance received from teachers in school or college.

DATA COLLECTION AND PROCESSING

Sources of Educational Data

Learning Management Systems (LMS): LMS platforms generate rich data, including student logins, course access patterns, quiz scores, and forum interactions.

Online Platforms: Educational websites, forums, and e-learning platforms collect data on user behavior, such as which resources `students` access and for how long.

Assessment Tools: Data from quizzes, assignments, and exams provide insights into student performance and knowledge gaps.

Surveys and Feedback: Student surveys and feedback forms offer qualitative data on learning experiences.

IoT Devices: Smart classrooms and wearable devices can track physical and environmental data, like classroom attendance and ambient conditions.

Library Records: Data on which books and resources students borrow can indicate their areas of interest.

Data Preprocessing Techniques

Data Cleaning: Identifying and rectifying errors, inconsistencies, and missing values in the dataset to ensure accuracy.

Data Transformation: Converting data into a suitable format for analysis, including numerical encoding of categorical variables.

Feature Engineering: Creating new variables or features from existing data to enhance predictive models.

Normalization and Scaling: Ensuring that different data types or scales are comparable for analysis.

Dimensionality Reduction: Reducing the number of features while retaining relevant information to improve model efficiency.

Handling Imbalanced Data: Addressing situations where certain classes or outcomes are underrepresented in the dataset.

Data Splitting: Dividing the data into training, validation, and test sets for model development and evaluation.

Ethical Considerations in Data Collection

Informed Consent: Ensure that students and stakeholders are aware of data collection practices, the purpose of data usage, and their rights regarding their data.

Data Anonymization: Protect the identities of individuals by de-identifying or anonymizing data, especially when sharing or publishing research.

Data Security: Implement robust security measures to safeguard sensitive educational data from unauthorized access or breaches.

Bias and Fairness: Be mindful of biases in data that can lead to unfair or discriminatory outcomes, and take steps to mitigate them.

Transparency: Maintain transparency in data collection and processing practices, allowing stakeholders to understand how decisions are made based on the data.

Regulatory Compliance: Ensure compliance with data protection regulations, such as GDPR or FERPA, and relevant institutional policies.

Effective data collection and preprocessing are essential for deriving meaningful insights from educational data. Ethical considerations play a crucial role in responsible data handling, ensuring that student privacy and rights are respected throughout the process.

AI-DRIVEN PERSONALIZATION IN EDUCATION

Personalized Learning Approaches

Adaptive Learning: Adaptive learning systems use AI algorithms to tailor educational content and resources to individual students' needs. These systems continuously assess a student's performance and adjust the difficulty and type of content accordingly.

Differentiated Instruction: AI can help educators provide differentiated instruction by suggesting alternative resources, assignments, or learning paths based on each student's strengths and weaknesses.

Figure 7. Adaptive learning systems

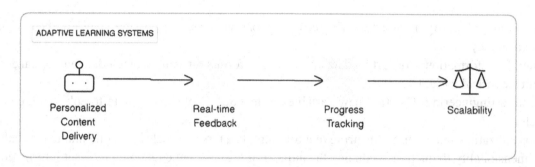

Learning Analytics: Learning analytics, powered by AI, track student progress and engagement to identify areas where individual students may require extra support or challenges.

Recommendation Systems: Similar to platforms like Netflix or Amazon, AI can recommend specific educational resources, books, or courses based on a student's past preferences and performance.

Adaptive Learning Systems

Personalized Content Delivery: AI-driven adaptive learning systems provide students with content that matches their skill level, learning pace, and style. For example, a student struggling with algebra might receive additional practice problems- while an advanced student moves on to more complex topics.

Real-time Feedback: These systems offer immediate feedback on assignments and quizzes, helping students understand their mistakes and improve.

Progress Tracking: Educators can use adaptive learning platforms to monitor individual students' progress, identifying those who may need extra assistance or enrichment.

Scalability: AI-driven adaptive learning can scale personalized education to larger student populations without overwhelming educators.

Benefits for Students and Educators

Improved Learning Outcomes: Personalized learning has been linked to improved student outcomes, including higher test scores, increased engagement, and better retention of material.

Time Efficiency: For educators, AI can automate routine tasks like grading, allowing more time for personalized instruction and mentoring.

Engagement: Personalized learning captures students' interest and keeps them engaged, as the material is more relevant to their abilities and interests.

Accessibility: AI can provide customized resources and learning paths for students with diverse learning needs, including those with disabilities.

Data-driven Insights: Educators can access data-driven insights from AI-powered learning analytics to inform their teaching strategies and identify areas of improvement in their courses.

AI-driven personalization in education has the potential to revolutionize the learning experience, making it more engaging, effective, and tailored to individual students' needs. These approaches benefit both students and educators by improving learning outcomes, saving time, and enhancing the overall quality of education.

FEEDBACK GENERATION

Automated Feedback Mechanisms

Instant Feedback: AI-driven systems can provide instant feedback to students on assignments, quizzes, and exams. This immediate feedback helps students identify errors and misconceptions while the material is fresh in their minds.

Consistency: Automated feedback ensures consistency in grading, reducing the potential for human bias or errors in assessments.

Efficiency: Grading and feedback generation can be time-consuming for educators. AI can automate these processes, freeing up educators to focus on more interactive and personalized aspects of teaching.

Scalability: As class sizes grow, automated feedback mechanisms can handle larger volumes of assignments and assessments efficiently.

Personalized Feedback Strategies

Targeted Suggestions: AI can provide targeted suggestions for improvement based on students' specific errors or areas of weakness. For instance, if a student struggles with algebraic equations, the system can recommend additional practice problems.

Progress Tracking: AI-driven systems track students' progress over time and provide feedback on their overall development, helping students set goals and work toward improvement.

Adaptive Challenges: Personalized feedback can include tailored challenges or tasks designed to stretch a student's abilities and encourage growth.

Goal Alignment: Feedback can be aligned with a student's individual learning goals, ensuring that it remains relevant and motivating.

Use of AI in Grading and Assessment

Automated Grading: AI can assess assignments, quizzes, and exams, providing scores and feedback instantly. This not only saves educators time but also ensures timely feedback for students.

Rubric Adherence: AI can evaluate student work against predefined rubrics, ensuring consistency in grading and feedback.

Content Analysis: In subjects like writing or language learning, AI can analyze the content of essays or responses and provide feedback on grammar, coherence, and clarity.

Adaptive Assessment: AI can generate adaptive assessments that adjust the difficulty of questions based on a student's performance, providing more accurate feedback on their knowledge and skills.

AI-driven feedback generation in education streamlines the assessment process, offers personalized guidance, and provides students with valuable insights into their performance. This approach enhances the learning experience by making feedback more accessible, timely, and tailored to individual needs.

Figure 8. AI in grading and assessment

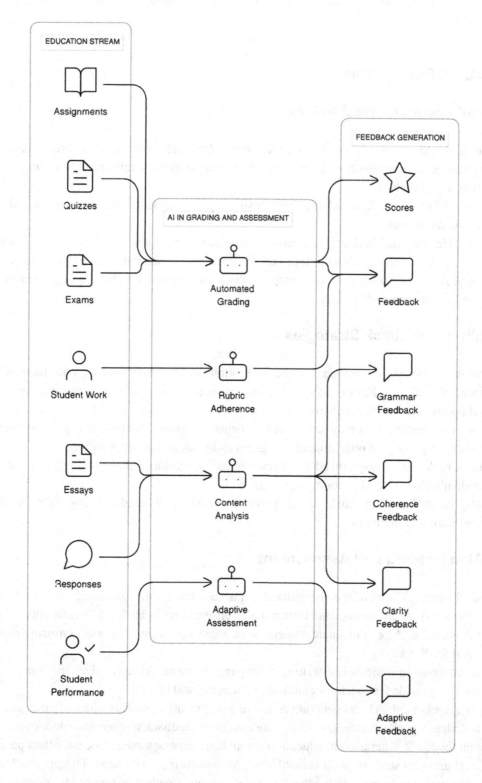

PREDICTIVE ANALYTICS FOR STUDENT SUCCESS

Early Warning Systems

Data Collection: Predictive analytics systems gather data from various sources, including student records, attendance, and engagement with course materials.

Identification of Patterns: These systems use machine learning algorithms to identify patterns and trends in student data. For example, they may notice that students who miss multiple classes tend to perform poorly.

Early Alerts: When certain patterns or indicators suggest that a student is at risk of falling behind or failing, early warning systems generate alerts for educators and advisors.

Timely Interventions: Early alerts allow educators and support staff to intervene promptly, offering additional assistance or resources to students who need it.

Identifying At-Risk Students

Risk Factors: Predictive analytics assess a range of risk factors, which may include attendance, grades, participation, and demographic information.

Machine Learning Models: Machine learning models are trained on historical data to recognize patterns associated with students who are likely to struggle academically or drop out.

Probability Scores: Each student is assigned a probability score indicating their risk level. Educators can prioritize their interventions based on these scores.

Continuous Monitoring: Predictive analytics systems continuously monitor students' progress, updating risk assessments as new data becomes available.

Intervention Strategies

Personalized Support: Predictive analytics help educators tailor their support to individual students' needs. For example, if a student is identified as at-risk due to poor attendance, the intervention might involve scheduling a meeting to discuss challenges and solutions.

Resource Allocation: Institutions can allocate resources more effectively by focusing support where it's most needed. This might involve hiring additional advisors or providing extra tutoring in specific subjects.

Proactive Measures: Rather than waiting for students to seek help, predictive analytics enable proactive measures. Educators can reach out to students who are at risk before problems escalate.

Continuous Improvement: Institutions can use feedback from predictive analytics to refine their intervention strategies and improve student success rates over time.

Predictive analytics for student success is a powerful tool for identifying at-risk students early in their academic journeys and providing targeted interventions. By harnessing the power of data and machine learning, educators and institutions can improve retention rates, boost academic achievement, and enhance the overall educational experience for students.

CASE STUDIES AND PRACTICAL APPLICATIONS

Real-World Examples of AI-Driven Learning Analytics

Georgia State University's Early Warning System: Georgia State University implemented an early warning system using predictive analytics to identify at-risk students. The system analyzes data such as grades, attendance, and course engagement to generate alerts for advisors. This approach resulted in a significant increase in student retention rates and timely interventions.

Arizona State University's Adaptive Learning Platforms: ASU employs AI-driven adaptive learning platforms that adjust course materials and assignments based on students' performance and learning pace. These systems provide personalized content and assessments, enhancing student engagement and success.

Carnegie Mellon's Open Learning Initiative (OLI): OLI uses data analytics to improve online course materials continually. By tracking student interactions with the content, OLI identifies areas where students struggle the most and updates the materials accordingly. This iterative approach has led to improved learning outcomes.

Table 1. Table summarizing real-world examples of AI-driven learning analytics

Learning Platform	Description	Data Collected	Analysis Techniques	Visualizations Used
Knewton	Adaptive learning platform that personalizes learning experiences.	Student interactions with learning content	Data mining, adaptive modeling	Individualized learning pathways
DreamBox	AI-powered mathematics program that provides personalized math lessons.	Student problem-solving data	Learning profiles, recommendations	Progress tracking, strength/weakness areas
Coursera	Online learning platform that offers courses from top universities.	Course engagement data	Engagement analytics	Completion rates, quiz scores
EdX	Online learning platform with a focus on interactive education.	Student interactions with course materials	Learning engagement metrics	Course activity, completion rates
Blackboard	Widely used learning management system in higher education.	Student activity within the LMS	Learning analytics	Course engagement, performance data
Cengage MindTap	Digital learning platform that offers personalized learning experiences.	Student interactions with textbooks, videos	Learning analytics	Class performance, assignment completion

This table provides a concise overview of various platforms that use AI-driven learning analytics, including a description of each platform, the type of data collected, the analysis techniques employed, and the visualizations used to provide insights to educators and students.

Success Stories From Higher Education Institutions

Purdue University Global: Purdue Global uses AI-driven analytics to predict student success. They have seen a significant increase in graduation rates and student satisfaction due to personalized interventions based on predictive data.

University of Maryland University College (UMUC): UMUC utilizes AI to analyze student behaviors and learning patterns in online courses. The insights gained from these analytics enable instructors to tailor their teaching methods to suit individual students better, resulting in improved course completion rates.

Stanford University: Stanford employs AI-driven algorithms to match students with appropriate courses. By considering students' backgrounds, interests, and academic strengths, they ensure that students are enrolled in courses most likely to lead to success.

Challenges Faced and Lessons Learned

Data Privacy and Ethics: Higher education institutions must navigate data privacy and ethical concerns when implementing AI-driven learning analytics. Ensuring that student data is used responsibly and securely is an ongoing challenge.

Faculty Training: Successfully integrating AI analytics into teaching requires faculty training. Institutions must invest in preparing educators to make the most of these tools.

Resource Allocation: Allocating resources effectively based on AI-driven insights can be challenging. Institutions need to balance their budgets to provide the necessary support for at-risk students.

Continuous Improvement: Institutions should view AI-driven learning analytics as a dynamic process. Continuously analyzing data, refining models, and adjusting interventions are crucial for long-term success.

AI-driven learning analytics has the potential to transform higher education by improving student success rates, enhancing personalized learning experiences, and optimizing resource allocation. However, it comes with challenges that institutions must address to fully harness its benefits while upholding ethical standards and data privacy.

ETHICAL AND PRIVACY CONSIDERATIONS

Data Security and Privacy Issues

Informed Consent: Institutions must obtain informed consent from students for collecting and using their data for analytics. Clear communication about data collection, storage, and usage is essential.

Data Security: Ensuring the security of student data is paramount. Robust encryption, access controls, and regular security audits should be in place to protect sensitive information from breaches.

Data Ownership: Clearly defining data ownership is crucial. Students should know who owns the data, how it will be used, and their rights regarding their educational data.

Ensuring Fairness and Transparency

Bias Mitigation: AI algorithms can inadvertently perpetuate biases present in historical data. Institutions must actively work to identify and mitigate bias in algorithms to ensure fair treatment of all students.

Transparency: Institutions should be transparent about the use of AI-driven analytics. Students should understand how data is collected, analyzed, and used to inform decisions about their education.

Explainability: AI models should be designed to provide explanations for their decisions. This helps students and educators understand why certain recommendations or interventions are made.

Compliance with Regulations

FERPA Compliance: Institutions must comply with the Family Educational Rights and Privacy Act (FERPA) in the United States, which governs the privacy of student records. This includes securing student data and providing students with access to their records.

GDPR Compliance: If serving students in the European Union, institutions need to comply with the General Data Protection Regulation (GDPR), which sets strict rules for data protection and privacy.

HIPAA Compliance: If dealing with health-related data, such as in medical education, institutions may need to adhere to the Health Insurance Portability and Accountability Act (HIPAA) regulations.

Local Regulations: Institutions should be aware of and comply with any local or national data protection laws that may apply.

Balancing the potential benefits of AI-driven learning analytics with ethical and privacy considerations is essential for maintaining trust among students, educators, and stakeholders. Institutions should establish clear policies and practices to ensure that data is used responsibly, fairly, and in compliance with relevant regulations.

CONCLUSION AND FUTURE STUDIES

Conclusion

Summary of Key Takeaways

In this chapter, we explored the transformative impact of AI-driven learning analytics in higher education. We began by defining learning analytics and highlighting its significance in modern education. We traced the evolution of AI in higher education, from early experiments to its current role as a powerful tool for enhancing student outcomes.

We delved into the fundamentals of learning analytics, discussing key concepts, terminologies, and their importance in understanding student behavior and performance. The chapter emphasized the ethical and privacy considerations necessary to ensure responsible use of student data.

The Future of AI-Driven Learning Analytics

The future of AI-driven learning analytics looks promising. Emerging technologies such as natural language processing and advanced machine learning will enable deeper insights into student learning. The potential impact on higher education is vast, from improving student retention and personalized learning to efficient resource allocation and data-driven decision-making.

Final Thoughts and Closing Remarks

As AI-driven learning analytics continues to evolve, educators, institutions, and policymakers need to collaborate in harnessing its full potential. The responsible use of AI in education, prioritizing ethical considerations, will be crucial in ensuring that AI-driven learning analytics benefit all students while upholding their privacy and maintaining fairness.

In closing, the chapter underscores the need for ongoing research, training, and interdisciplinary collaboration to unlock the future possibilities of AI-driven learning analytics in higher education. By embracing these opportunities and addressing challenges, the education sector can provide students with more personalized and effective learning experiences, ultimately shaping the future of education for the better.

Future Studies and Directions

Emerging Technologies in Learning Analytics

Natural Language Processing (NLP): NLP technologies will become more sophisticated in understanding and analyzing students' written and spoken language. This will enable deeper insights into student comprehension and communication skills.

Advanced Machine Learning: AI models will continue to advance, allowing for more accurate predictions of student performance and behavior. This will include improved recommendations for personalized learning pathways.

Explainable AI: There will be a growing emphasis on making AI-driven analytics more transparent and explainable. This will help educators and students better understand how decisions are made and build trust in the technology.

Ethical AI: The field of ethical AI will continue to develop, focusing on mitigating bias, ensuring fairness, and upholding privacy standards in learning analytics.

Potential Impact on Higher Education

Improved Student Retention: AI-driven learning analytics will play a vital role in identifying at-risk students and providing timely interventions, leading to higher retention rates.

Personalized Learning: The customization of educational content and pathways based on individual student needs and learning styles will become more prevalent, enhancing learning outcomes.

Efficient Resource Allocation: Institutions will optimize resource allocation by using data to target support and services where they are most needed, improving cost-effectiveness.

Data-Driven Decision-Making: Educators and administrators will increasingly rely on data-driven insights to make informed decisions about curriculum design, teaching methods, and institutional strategies.

Recommendations for Educators and Institutions

Invest in Training: Educators should receive training on using AI-driven learning analytics effectively, including interpreting data and implementing personalized interventions.

Data Governance: Establish clear data governance policies and practices to ensure data security, privacy, and compliance with regulations.

Interdisciplinary Collaboration: Encourage collaboration between data scientists, educators, and administrators to leverage the full potential of learning analytics.

Ethical Guidelines: Develop and adhere to ethical guidelines for the use of AI in education, emphasizing fairness, transparency, and privacy.

Continuous Improvement: Embrace a culture of continuous improvement in AI-driven learning analytics, regularly assessing the effectiveness of interventions and refining models.

AI-driven learning analytics holds significant promise for higher education. As emerging technologies continue to evolve and ethical considerations are prioritized, the field has the potential to transform how students learn and how institutions support their success. Educators and institutions that proactively embrace these trends and best practices are likely to lead the way in shaping the future of education.

REFERENCES

Beaumont, C., O'Doherty, M., & Shannon, L. (2011). Reconceptualising assessment feedback: A key to improving student learning? *Studies in Higher Education, 36*(6), 671–687. doi:10.1080/03075071003731135

Berendt, B., Littlejohn, A., & Blakemore, M. (2020). AI in education: Learner choice and fundamental rights. *Learning, Media and Technology, 45*(3), 312–324. doi:10.1080/17439884.2020.1786399

Bozkurt, A., Karadeniz, A., Baneres, D., Guerrero-Roldán, A. E., & Rodríguez, M. E. (2021). Artificial intelligence and reflections from educational landscape: A review of AI Studies in half a century. *Sustainability (Basel), 13*(2), 800. doi:10.3390u13020800

Burke, D. (2009). Strategies for using feedback students bring to higher education. *Assessment & Evaluation in Higher Education, 34*(1), 41–50. doi:10.1080/02602930801895711

Chen, X., Xie, H., Zou, D., & Hwang, G. J. (2020). Application and theory gaps during the rise of artificial intelligence in education. *Computers and Education: Artificial Intelligence, 1*, 100002. doi:10.1016/j.caeai.2020.100002

Ciolacu, M., Tehrani, A. F., Binder, L., & Svasta, P. M. (2018, October). Education 4.0-Artificial Intelligence assisted higher education: early recognition system with machine learning to support students' success. In *2018 IEEE 24th International Symposium for Design and Technology in Electronic Packaging(SIITME)* (pp. 23-30). IEEE. 10.1109/SIITME.2018.8599203

Dogan, M. E., Goru Dogan, T., & Bozkurt, A. (2023). The use of artificial intelligence (AI) in online learning and distance education processes: A systematic review of empirical studies. *Applied Sciences (Basel, Switzerland), 13*(5), 3056. doi:10.3390/app13053056

Escotet, M. Á. (2023). The optimistic future of Artificial Intelligence in higher education. *Prospects*, ●●●, 1–10. doi:10.100711125-023-09642-z

Henderson, M., Ryan, T., & Phillips, M. (2019). The challenges of feedback in higher education. *Assessment & Evaluation in Higher Education, 44*(8), 1237–1252. doi:10.1080/02602938.2019.1599815

Liu, L., Subbareddy, R., & Raghavendra, C. G. (2022). AI Intelligence Chatbot to Improve Students Learning in the Higher Education Platform. *Journal of Interconnection Networks, 22*(Supp02), 2143032. doi:10.1142/S0219265921430325

Nazaretsky, T., Cukurova, M., & Alexandron, G. (2022, March). An instrument for measuring `teachers` trust in AI-based educational technology. In *LAK22: 12th international learning analytics and knowledge conference* (pp. 56-66). 10.1145/3506860.3506866

Orsmond, P., & Merry, S. (2011). Feedback alignment: Effective and ineffective links between 'tutors' and 'students' understanding of coursework feedback. *Assessment & Evaluation in Higher Education, 36*(2), 125–136. doi:10.1080/02602930903201651

Renz, A., Krishnaraja, S., & Gronau, E. (2020). Demystification of Artificial Intelligence in Education–How much AI is really in the Educational Technology? [iJAI]. *International Journal of Learning Analytics and Artificial Intelligence for Education, 2*(1), 14. doi:10.3991/ijai.v2i1.12675

Rienties, B., Køhler Simonsen, H., & Herodotou, C. (2020, July). Defining the boundaries between artificial intelligence in education, computer-supported collaborative learning, educational data mining, and learning analytics: A need for coherence. In *frontiers in Education* (*Vol. 5,* p. 128). Frontiers Media SA.

Tight, M. (2020). Student retention and engagement in higher education. *Journal of Further and Higher Education, 44*(5), 689–704. doi:10.1080/0309877X.2019.1576860

Ungerer, L., & Slade, S. (2022). Ethical considerations of artificial intelligence in learning analytics in distance education contexts. In Learning Analytics in Open and Distributed Learning: Potential and Challenges (pp. 105-120). Singapore: Springer Nature Singapore. doi:10.1007/978-981-19-0786-9_8

Wang, T., Lund, B. D., Marengo, A., Pagano, A., Mannuru, N. R., Teel, Z. A., & Pange, J. (2023). Exploring the Potential Impact of Artificial Intelligence (AI) on International Students in Higher Education: Generative AI, Chatbots, Analytics, and International Student Success. *Applied Sciences (Basel, Switzerland), 13*(11), 6716. doi:10.3390/app13116716

Xia, Q., Chiu, T. K., Zhou, X., Chai, C. S., & Cheng, M. (2022). Systematic literature review on opportunities, challenges, and future research recommendations of artificial intelligence in education. *Computers and Education: Artificial Intelligence, 100118*. doi:10.1016/j.caeai.2022.100118

Zawacki-Richter, O., Marín, V. I., Bond, M., & Gouverneur, F. (2019). Systematic review of research on artificial intelligence applications in higher education–where are the educators? *International Journal of Educational Technology in Higher Education, 16*(1), 1–27. doi:10.118641239-019-0171-0

Zhang, L., Wu, M., & Ouyang, F. (2023). The design and implementation of a teaching and learning analytics tool in a face-to-face, small-sized course in China's higher education. *Education and Information Technologies*, 1–24. doi:10.100710639-023-11940-0

KEY TERMS AND DEFINITIONS

Artificial Intelligence (AI): refers to the development of computer systems and algorithms that can perform tasks typically requiring human intelligence, such as problem-solving, learning, and decision-making.

Internet of Things (IoT): is a network of interconnected physical devices and objects embedded with sensors, software, and connectivity, allowing them to collect and exchange data to perform various tasks and functions, often without direct human intervention.

Key Performance Indicators (KPIs): are measurable metrics or data points used to evaluate the performance, effectiveness, or success of an organization, project, or specific activity. They help in monitoring progress and making informed decisions.

Learning Management System (LMS): is a software platform designed to facilitate and manage online learning and training programs. It provides tools for course creation, content delivery, assessment, and learner tracking in a digital environment.

Machine Learning (ML): is a subset of artificial intelligence (AI) that involves the development of algorithms and statistical models that enable computer systems to improve their performance on a specific task through learning from data, without being explicitly programmed.

Chapter 10
Integrating Artificial Intelligence in Education for Sustainable Development

Oluwabunmi Dorcas Bakare-Fatungase

https://orcid.org/0000-0002-4665-3969

Lead City University, Nigeria

Feranmi Emmanuel Adejuwon

Lead City University, Nigeria

Temitope Oluwatofunmi Idowu-Davies

Emmanuel Alayande University of Education, Oyo, Nigeria

ABSTRACT

A promising technology that has the potential to change many facets of the educational ecosystem is artificial intelligence (AI) which is playing a significant role in the actualization of the sustainable development goals (SDGs). The present status of AI in education was examined and identified significant areas for emerging research initiatives. Unified theory of acceptance and use of technology (UTAUT) underpinned the study to showcase ways AI technologies can be adopted and used for teaching and learning for a sustainable future. The study recommended the need for Africa as a continent to have a holistic AI ecosystem that captures our African histories, perceptions, idiosyncrasies, languages, outlooks, nuances, non-westernizations, etc., in addition to Nigeria being proactive to be the AI hub of the continent. The study is significant to educational practice, society, and policy and is theoretically based on a developing country perspective.

INTRODUCTION

The 21st century has witnessed a swift and unprecedented transformation in the field of education, primarily attributable to the technological progress of Artificial Intelligence (AI). Using its capacities for

DOI: 10.4018/979-8-3693-0639-0.ch010

learning, reasoning, and decision-making, Artificial Intelligence (AI) has the potential to revolutionize the educational system for a sustainable future. One area where AI can have a big influence is personalized learning. AI-powered intelligent tutoring systems can adjust to the demands of each learner, providing individualized education and feedback. Meeting their specific learning needs raises student engagement and accomplishment which creates room for life-long learning that promotes sustainable development. Additionally, AI makes it possible for automatic grading and feedback, which lessens the workload on instructors and enables quicker and more accurate evaluation.

Asynchronous learning, in which students have more freedom to choose how they want to learn and can finish assignments at their own speed, has become more popular. This method can help students who have other obligations, disabilities or find it difficult to attend in-person classes because it lets them work when it is convenient for them. The digital gap, where students in low-income or rural locations might not have access to the technology or internet connectivity needed to fully participate in remote learning, has been brought to light by the transition to online learning. It also carried with it difficulties like a lack of motivation, accountability, and interaction (Baidoo-Anu and Ansah. 2023). In this wise, the application of AI to student learning has helped in assigning tasks based on individual competence, providing human–machine conversations, analyzing student work for feedback, and increasing adaptability and interactivity in digital environments. In teaching, it has helped in providing adaptive teaching strategies, enhancing teachers' ability to teach, and supporting teacher professional development. In administration, AI has helped in improving the performance of management platforms, providing convenient and personalized services, and supporting educational decision-making with evidence (Xia et al., 2023).

An intelligent virtual laboratory that meets the needs of students by assigning laboratory tasks at the appropriate level can be developed which provides an AI-based environment that can be used for personalised students learning. Similarly, an AI-integrated management system with augmented, virtual, and mixed reality technologies can be developed to monitor student learning progress for assigning adaptive tasks. Therefore, the interaction between humans and robots can make low-achieving pupils feel less ashamed and more capable, thus promoting an all-inclusive educational environment. Attendance and active engagement in class can also be measured by the facial recognition of each student; active participation can be enhanced by hearing each student's voice in the classroom or identifying each student's fingerprint at the door which is a veritable way of sensing, and detecting. In this instance, facial photos, fingerprints, and voice recognition can be used to feed data into machine algorithms to distinguish between teachers, pupils, and administrative staff. By including precise criteria, such as which students belong to which class and the stipulated session, the machine can determine whether a student is enrolled in that class or university. Depending on the specific academic activity allotted, the system demonstrates sufficient predictability on hourly, daily, or weekly basis.

Artificial Intelligence (AI) has enormous potential, but it also raises ethical issues and other fundamental issues that are core to the traditional pedagogical domain. Important factors to consider include protecting data privacy, mitigating algorithmic bias, and guaranteeing openness. To successfully integrate AI into teaching techniques, educators must get enough training and professional development which is lacking in most developing countries of which Nigeria is not an exception. Therefore, there is a need to examine these issues and build an enabling environment that leverages the advantages of AI in education, and cooperation among academics, policymakers, educators, developers, and the government to situate developing educational systems in contemporary AI discourse.

TRAJECTORIES OF ARTIFICIAL INTELLIGENCE (AI) IN HUMAN EXISTENCE

The intersection of history, science, and technology influenced the development of Artificial Intelligence (AI). Innovators like Alan Turing and John von Neumann laid the theoretical groundwork for intelligent machines in the middle of the 20th century which was a tech precedence of what is expected to usher in the 21st century, while the Dartmouth Workshop, organized by John McCarthy and others in 1956, marked the official start of AI as a field. Advances in computing made testing simpler, and early AI research concentrated on symbolic AI, logical reasoning, and machine learning. Despite early promise, the field experienced challenges throughout the AI winter of the 1970s and 1980s, which led to a drop in funding and interest.

However, the 1990s saw a resurgence as a result of the development of machine learning techniques, the advent of big data, and the introduction of cloud computing technologies. Artificial Intelligence (AI) applications like image identification and natural language processing have substantially improved due to the usage of neural networks in deep learning, a kind of machine learning. As AI advanced, it was extensively used across several industries, such as the educational sector which encouraged additional investment and innovation thus promoting the sustainable development of this sphere of human endeavour.

Artificial neural networks, massive data, cloud computing, and machine learning have made it possible to create a computer that can replicate human intellect. Research has shown that AI is an essential component of the Fourth Industrial Revolution (4thIR) and that it will eventually usher in innovation remodelling pedagogical revolution in the educational ecosystem (Bakare, 2023). Additionally, initiatives to integrate AI education into school curricula have started (Dai, et al. 2020; Knox, 2020) and there is a need for educators to embrace this paradigm shift. The knowledge and production of making smart computers or a mechanism that acts in a way that would be considered intellectual if it were a human being are two definitions of AI (McCarthy, 2007). John McCarthy first used the term AI in 1956 at the Dartmouth Artificial Intelligence Conference (AI). The discussion themes that gave birth to the idea of thinking machines included the link between creativity and randomness, how knowledge is produced from sensory inputs and others. The majority of participants thought that computers may someday outperform human intellect, but their main concerns were about when and how this would happen.

Artificial Intelligence (AI) is now evolving and spreading around the globe at a stunning rate and expanding swiftly. We must deal with the effects of technology since it affects so many facets of our lives. Our lives and civilizations are altering in innumerable ways as a result of the development and use of AI. The post-COVID-19 pandemic era is just speeding up these changes, which can frequently be difficult to comprehend and predict. Users may be exposed to hazards through the collection, usage, and exploitation of the data necessary to train and feed the algorithm as well as the algorithm itself (Borenstein and Howard, 2021). Although AI has advantages, there are problems that consumers might be oblivious to consumers. Artificial intelligence (AI) can change the educational system for a sustainable future by utilizing its capabilities for learning, reasoning, and decision-making. Personalized learning is one area where AI can have a significant impact. Intelligent teaching systems driven by AI can adapt to the needs of each learner, offering specialized advice and feedback. By addressing their specific learning requirements, teachers may assist students in feeling more motivated and effective. This paves the path for continuous improvement and lifetime learning. Automatic grading and comments are also made possible by AI, saving instructors' time and enabling a quicker, more precise evaluation. Although AI has a lot of potential, it also poses ethical dilemmas. Data privacy protection, algorithmic bias reduction, and openness assurance are crucial considerations. The majority of poor nations, including Nigeria, lack the professional training and development needed by teachers to integrate AI into their lesson plans successfully. It is necessary to address these issues and create a setting that makes use of AI's educational benefits to integrate the new educational system into the current AI debate. Collaboration between the government, lawmakers, educators, researchers, and developers is also crucial.

INCORPORATING AI TECHNOLOGIES IN EDUCATIONAL SETTINGS

Henry Ford used an analogy to demonstrate that technological advancements entails the society migrating from maintaining the status quo to thinking creatively and beyond the box. These ideas and approaches have been the driving forces behind the major technological improvements that have taken place over the years, notably in the realm of education. According to Chen, Chen, and Lin (2020), Dr. Potter in 1950, who is a university professor, trudged to a class with a massive stack of 40 marked submitted papers having read each one and assessing its language and content. When reviewing the papers, Dr. Potter suspected that some of them contained information that had been plagiarized from other sources, but he was unable to positively identify the source from which the student had gotten the data

In 2019, Dr. Potter walked into a class with very few papers, but after reading, finding plagiarism to be dealt with formally, and marking papers for many more students. When he is off campus, he can occasionally utilize technology to call in or video conference into the class and continue to fulfill his duties. Technology's advancement, diffusion, and introduction—particularly the development of AI have made it easier for teachers to carry out their duties more effectively and efficiently. These technological developments have also influenced other academic subjects, encouraging efficacy and efficiency. Before the advent of computers and other related technology, instructors and pupils carried out their duties manually or merely by exercising their own free will. According to Flamm (1988), the development of microcomputers and, subsequently personal computers in the 1970s marked a substantial shift toward electronic computers for the mass market.

The development of computer-aided instruction and learning (CAI/L) in classroom interactions, for example, was made possible by advancements in computers and related computing technologies that built on earlier research into programmed instructions from the mid-1900s. This use of computers in various departments within educational institutions and, more specifically, in the education sector was made possible. Thanks to more recent advancements in computer and computer-related technologies, including networking, the internet, the world wide web, increased processing, computing, and other capabilities, including various task-oriented programs and software packages, the use of computers in education has increased in a variety of ways.

Along with the adoption and use of new technologies, AI has been widely implemented in the educational sector. Devedžić (2004) pointed out, for example, that research and development into Web Intelligence (WI) and AI focuses on various aspects, such as machine learning to create distributed intelligence and striking a balance between Web technology and intelligent agent technology, agent self-organization, learning, and adaptation among other aspects of WI and AI that enable it to adapt to its environment and perform intelligent functions, which should be leveraged. Some divisions within educational institutions, as well as the education sector have embraced AI. A lot has changed as a result of the application of AI in education, including improved efficacy and efficiency in school administration, global learning, customized and adapted learning, smarter curriculum, and more. New educational applications are made feasible as AI develops.

Due to the ground-breaking advantages it provides, integrating AI technology into educational settings is crucial. By evaluating data and adjusting training to meet the individual requirements of each learner, AI enhances learning. It also simplifies administrative processes, giving teachers more time to devote to instructional design and individualized support, resulting in more effective and efficient teaching methods. Adopting AI's concept in education gives teachers more control, motivates students, and gets them ready for problems in the future. Academics, policymakers, and other interested parties must understand these developments and foster welcoming conditions that maximize AI's educational advantages instead of seeing these technologies as a displacer (Bakare, 2023).

ADVANTAGES OF AI IN CONTEMPORARY EDUCATIONAL SYSTEM

Artificial intelligence (AI), which has developed into a powerful force for change, is transforming many sectors as well as how people live, work, and learn. These technologies have the potential to improve current educational practices, potentially enhance pedagogical methods, give instructors greater control, and provide pupils with individualized and interesting learning opportunities. By adopting AI technology, academic institutions, and teachers may ensure that students receive tailored support and opportunities for academic success while also assisting them in realizing their full potential. AI may be used in education in a variety of ways, from personalised learning environments that adjust to the requirements of each student to sophisticated tutoring programs that offer prompt feedback and direction. Teachers are now able to spend more time on instructional design and student interactions because of automated grading and assessment systems. Students of all ages may study more easily and enjoyably thanks to Natural Language Processing (NLP) technologies' interactive and conversational interfaces.

There has been an increase in the use of AI in the education sector, expanding it beyond the traditional idea of AI as a supercomputer to include embedded computer systems. For instance, the incorporation of AI, computers, and other enabling technologies into robots may allow for the creation of robots that improve student learning, starting with the most fundamental kind of education, early childhood education. Robots are being used to teach kids fundamentals like spelling and pronunciation while adjusting to their learning methods, either with teachers or with other robots. In a similar vein, web-based and online education has advanced from simply making materials available online or on the web for students to simply download, study, and complete assignments to pass, to include intelligent and adaptive web-based systems that learn from instructor and learner behavior and adjust accordingly, enriching the educational experience, etc.

Additionally, AI makes it possible to develop immersive learning experiences through simulations and virtual reality, giving students the chance to investigate challenging topics in a secure and engaging setting. AI can assist in the early identification of at-risk youngsters through data analytics and insights, enabling swift interventions and customized support to enhance overall academic performance. While AI has enormous promise for improving education, its ethical problems are also brought up by its successful incorporation. For AI to be a useful addition to present teaching approaches rather than a replacement, problems with data privacy, algorithmic biases, and the value of human instructors must be resolved.

Generally speaking, AI in education has the power to alter teaching and learning, assist personalized learning, enhance administrative processes, and raise educational results. For instance, intelligent tutoring systems (ITS) that adapt instruction to each student's needs and increase engagement and achievement through personalized assistance and feedback employ AI algorithms to tailor learning. Additionally, customized learning refers to the customization of educational experiences based on unique student requirements, preferences, and learning styles. Artificial Intelligence (AI) technology may be used to provide tailored training, resources, and evaluations. Artificial intelligence (AI)-powered automated grading and feedback systems evaluate student assignments, examinations, and essays automatically to expedite the assessment process. Also, an automated grading and feedback systems free up instructors' time so they may concentrate on other things while still providing students with regular, timely feedback. These will all be examined in the context of current advancements in the field of artificial intelligence.

Artificial Intelligence (AI) may be used to handle repetitive administrative activities, sparing teachers and lecturers from spending a lot of time marking examinations and assigning homework. There is technology that can grade pupils on multiple-choice tests. However, there are significant issues with using automation to assign scores for tests that are essay-style. Software engineers are still investigating and developing methods for evaluating written responses and inquiries that take the form of essays. Similar to this, AI is used to process new students' entrance into educational institutions (Villegas-Ch et al., 2021)

There are several substantial benefits of incorporating Artificial Intelligence (AI) into modern schooling. By studying students' learning preferences and tendencies, Artificial Intelligence (AI) makes it possible to customize learning experiences for each learner. Because students may study at their own pace and in their own way, this method promotes more engagement and comprehension. With adaptive learning, algorithms change the level of difficulty and the nature of the information based on each student's success. With a dynamic approach, learning results are maximized while boredom or irritation are kept to a minimum and students are adequately challenged. Additionally, teachers may focus more on real teaching and student engagement since AI can handle administrative responsibilities like grading and attendance monitoring.

For educators, AI's data-driven insights are priceless. It can analyze enormous volumes of data to find learning patterns and areas that need improvement, allowing educated choices to be made concerning the creation of curricula and instruction strategies. Students who receive immediate feedback from AI-driven assessment systems are better able to understand their faults and areas for improvement, which improves learning and promotes self-directed learning. The use of tools like text-to-speech and translation services, which make education accessible to students with impairments, fosters inclusion. Artificial Intelligence (AI) also promotes international cooperation and provides 24/7 access to educational resources. Artificial intelligence (AI) helps to enhance learning outcomes by identifying at-risk pupils and implementing early intervention. In summary, incorporating AI into education might result in a more individualized, effective, and inclusive learning environment that better prepares students for the challenges of the digital era.

CHALLENGES AND LIMITATIONS OF AI IN EDUCATION

In as much as there are lots of advantages in the usage of AI in all facets of human existence, of which the educational ecosystem is not an exception, there are militating factors that are having negative effects. For instance, AI has a lot of potential to transform the healthcare industry as the technology could be able to read medical pictures more rapidly than a radiologist. To keep patients safe, however, algorithmic prejudice and other ethical issues must be resolved. For instance, it has previously been established that despite both groups having the same diagnosis, an AI system used to propose follow-up healthcare services failed black patients by referring them at a lower rate than their white counterparts (Borenstein and Howard, 2021)

Every topic has two sides, which is another reason why the difficulties facing current AI research in education will be highlighted. Privacy, security, and potential algorithmic biases are issues that are brought up by the gathering and analysis of sensitive student data. This poses difficulties for the use of AI in education and necessitates the development of strict moral principles and regulations to guarantee accountability, justice, and the protection of student rights in addition to upholding educators' professional dignity. Integration with existing educational systems and practices is hampered by the need for AI technology to be simple to integrate with current curricula, teaching methods, and systems of instruction. Librarians, whose role within the AI discourse is still at the infant stage in a developing country like Nigeria, even though these information managers offer a variety of products and services that support the accomplishment of all 17 Sustainable Development Goals, can embed user acceptance and trust into the fabric of the educational ecosystem (SDG).

Introducing artificial intelligence (AI) into the modern educational system has some difficulties and restrictions that need to be carefully considered. Due to the enormous volumes of student data that are gathered and processed by AI systems, worries regarding data security and privacy have been raised. To safeguard sensitive data from illegal access or breaches that might have far-reaching effects on both students and teachers, educational institutions must implement strong cybersecurity safeguards. More reason Chakroun et al. (2019, p. 7) affirmed the United Nations Educational, Scientific and Cultural Organization (UNESCO) ROAM principles could be a respite in this space which emphasized "Rights (addressing freedom of expression, access to information, media pluralism, and political participation); Openness (recognizing that some machine-learning approaches are an obstacle to transparency); Accessibility (access to research, to education human resources, data, connectivity, and hardware) and Multi-stakeholder governance (transparency, responsiveness, accountability, and collaboration)". If jointly harnessed, these principles can improve the ideals, standards, dogmas, conventions, codes, and principles that oversee the advancement and consumption of AI in the educational ecosystem.

An important worry is the possibility of bias in AI systems. If these algorithms are developed using biased data, they may worsen already existing educational disparities. AI systems may unintentionally favor specific socioeconomic groups, cultural backgrounds, or learning styles, for example, resulting in an unequal distribution of educational gains. To address prejudice in AI and assure justice and equity in educational outcomes, ongoing surveillance, data improvement, and algorithmic openness are required. Another difficulty is the possible dehumanization of the educational process. The empathy, emotional intelligence, and nuanced understanding that human educators bring to the table may not be present in AI, even while it may offer tailored learning routes and fast feedback. The development of social and emotional skills, which are essential for comprehensive human growth and successful communication, might be hampered in an educational environment that is solely AI-driven.

Furthermore, a large amount of technical know-how and financial resources are needed for the development and maintenance of AI systems. It may be difficult for smaller educational institutions to implement and maintain AI technology, which might exacerbate educational inequities. Additionally, the quick speed of technical development may make it challenging to maintain AI systems current, eventually rendering them ineffective or obsolete. Although AI has great potential to improve education, its difficulties must be carefully considered before use. These include issues with data security and privacy, the possibility of prejudice, the danger of dehumanizing the learning process, and resource constraints. Chakroun et al. (2019, p.24) went further to outline six challenges and "policy implications for AI within the educational domain which are developing a comprehensive public policy on AI for sustainable development; ensuring inclusion and equity in AI in education; preparing teachers for AI-powered education and preparing AI to understand education; developing quality and inclusive data systems; making research on AI in education significant; and ethics and transparency in data collection, use, and dissemination". To fully utilize AI for the benefit of students, teachers, and the larger educational system, these issues must be resolved.

ARTIFICIAL INTELLIGENCE (AI) AND SUSTAINABLE DEVELOPMENT

From its inception, artificial intelligence (AI) has become a potent tool for achieving sustainable development objectives. However, Singh et al. (2023) opined paucity of research on the analysis of AI research towards the SDGs. Artificial intelligence (AI) benefits several industries by analyzing data, forecasting results, and streamlining operations. In many crucial areas, AI is proving to be a revolutionary force in promoting the principles of sustainable development, and for AI to reach its full potential in addition to promoting SDGs, international cooperation is essential. Sustainable development's fundamental goal is to strike a balance between contemporary social advancement, environmental protection, and the welfare of coming generations without being compromised. Due to its special powers, AI can be essential in reaching these goals.

Environmental monitoring and conservation is one important area where AI excels. The technology is used in environmental conservation to monitor climatic indicators, forecast natural calamities, and support the preservation of biodiversity. The exponential rise of data gathered from sensors, satellites, and other sources necessitates the use of improved analytical tools, which AI is well-suited to supply. Using AI-driven algorithms, scientists and environmentalists can monitor ecosystem health, identify indications of climate change, and even forecast natural disasters by seeing trends and anomalies in this data. This capability enables informed decision-making and proactive solutions to environmental concerns.

By effectively managing resources and enhancing urban planning, AI increases precision agriculture, aids smart city projects, and optimizes renewable energy systems. The impact of AI also includes changing how we produce and manage energy. AI may improve the efficiency of solar, wind, and other sustainable energy systems, which is important given the growing emphasis on renewable energy sources. Artificial intelligence (AI) can optimize performance, guarantee dependability, and fine-tune operations through real-time analysis of energy production data. The smooth integration into current energy systems made possible by this optimization eventually speeds up the shift to a cleaner and more sustainable energy environment. In the same vein, the idea of smart cities has had a significant influence on AI, especially in urban environments. Urbanization offers sustainable development with both benefits and difficulties. Through the use of intelligent control systems, AI-driven solutions may improve energy efficiency in buildings while simultaneously optimizing traffic flow, and decreasing congestion and pollution. Additionally, by anticipating collection patterns, improving recycling procedures, and reducing environmental effects, AI can transform trash management.

Additionally, AI-powered healthcare systems improve diagnosis and treatment, and its use in disaster management speeds up response and recovery. AI has a huge potential to enable sustainable growth in the healthcare business. By analyzing vast medical data sets, AI may support medication discovery, individualize patient treatment plans, and early disease detection thus reducing the mortality rate. By aiding in the more efficient use of healthcare resources in addition to improving health outcomes, this addresses an important aspect of social well-being in human existence. In the educational sector, the place of AI within the discourse of SDG 4 cannot be over-emphasized as it is a veritable opportunity to promote an all-inclusive environment with unhindered accessibility to vocational training, lack of gender discrimination, digital divide or wealth disparity with the sole aim of achieving universal access to a quality higher education. Chakroun et al., (2019, p. 7) statement that "education powered by AI must be accessible for all, regardless of the individual's environment, nationality, culture, gender, disability status, sexuality, or age - if only to ensure that marginalized and disadvantaged groups are not excluded from AI-powered education" is consistent with this. Dorcas Bakare and Mike Bakare (2022) averred sustainability as core to the discipline of Library and Information Science (LIS) discipline and hinged on a curriculum that fits into the contemporary practice of sustainable environmental transformation which is core to SDG4. The study of Singh et al. (2023, p.12) revealed a bibliometric pattern of technological concepts such as AI, Natural Language Processing (NPL), learning environment, and higher education "was the most repeated problem area concept depicting the creation of an augmented learning approach with the help of AI" within the SDG4 ecosystem.

Although AI holds enormous potential, it is crucial to proceed with caution. For responsible AI applications, however, issues including privacy concerns and ethical issues must be resolved. It is important to address ethical issues related to algorithmic biases and the possibility of job displacement. It is crucial to strike a balance between social responsibility and technical growth. Global cooperation is necessary to realize AI's full potential for sustainable development. To make sure AI technologies are created and used with an emphasis on long-term societal and environmental advantages, organizations, and governments must collaborate.

INTEGRATING AI IN EDUCATION FOR SUSTAINABLE DEVELOPMENT

With Nigeria as a useful case study, integrating artificial intelligence (AI) in education for sustainable development has enormous promise. Nigeria, a developing nation, must overcome several obstacles to achieve sustainable development, from poor access to high-quality education to environmental issues and infrastructural issues to fit into the new order of AI-informed educational ecosystem. These issues can be solved and educational growth sustained in the education industry which can be promoted by utilizing AI.

Artificial Intelligence (AI) may be used in Nigeria to improve access to education by providing individualized and flexible learning opportunities. A huge and diverse population enables AI-driven systems to customize educational content to meet the requirements of each learner, enhancing engagement and understanding. This strategy can aid in closing the achievement gap and guarantee that all children, irrespective of their background, have access to high-quality learning resources. The Nigerian educational system struggles with difficulties including packed classrooms and insufficient teaching materials. This flexibility helps students understand things more clearly and increases engagement. More reason, Bakare and Jatto (2023) affirmed the importance of Chatbots for improved students' engagement and learning outcomes. By ensuring that instructional information resonates with students on a personal level, Artificial Intelligence (AI) may enhance educational outcomes, reduce dropout rates, and advance a more educated population. Additionally, there is a great chance for information specialists like librarians, who are regarded as the guardians of human knowledge, to use AI in the delivery of library and information services to support the realization of SDG4.

This technology may also help teachers by offering data-driven insights to improve lesson plans and curriculum creation. Artificial Intelligence (AI) can identify areas where pupils are having difficulty and recommend treatments by assessing student performance data. Teachers are better able to give timely assistance and modify their teaching tactics as a result of this targeted approach, which eventually improves learning results. Teachers have an equally important role. By offering insights into student performance trends and learning patterns, AI can help teachers. Teachers can use this data to improve their methods, spot areas for development, and create specialized interventions for students who need them. This data-driven strategy helps instructors provide high-quality instruction that meets the varied needs of students across the nation, fostering inclusion and fair access to information.

Environmental awareness is also a component of sustainable development. Artificial Intelligence (AI) can help with environmental education by offering real-time information about regional environmental problems and encouraging environmentally beneficial behavior. To integrate education with the concepts of sustainable living, AI-powered platforms may, for instance, provide interactive courses on renewable energy sources, trash reduction, and conservation. Artificial Intelligence (AI) may also be a catalyst for environmental education in the context of sustainable development. Nigeria has environmental issues such as resource depletion, pollution, and deforestation. Interactive education on conservation, renewable energy, and trash management may be delivered using platforms powered by AI. AI helps create a generation that values sustainable living habits by increasing knowledge of these concerns and fostering in pupils environmentally responsible attitudes.

Several issues must be resolved to incorporate AI into Nigerian education for sustainable growth properly. These include geographical limitations on access to technology, a lack of digital literacy, and possible biases in AI systems. The removal of these obstacles requires a multi-stakeholder strategy. To guarantee that all students and teachers have equitable access to AI-enabled educational technologies and that both groups receive the necessary training, the government, educational institutions, tech firms, and non-governmental organizations should work together. Obstacles must be overcome for AI to be successfully incorporated into the Nigerian education landscape. Particularly in rural places with limited access to technology and the internet, the digital divide continues to be a significant impediment. To narrow this gap, concerted efforts from all stakeholders will be required to make AI-enabled technology and training accessible to all sectors. It is crucial to carefully consider the ethical implications of AI, including potential biases in algorithms that might not take into account our Africanness, which accurately portrays who we are, and notably our indigenous identity, in order to achieve justice and fairness in educational outcomes. It is possible to build AI systems that speak our native languages using the richness of the Nigerian culture, thus overcoming the language gap that has long plagued the country's educational system.

To meet these issues, cooperation among diverse parties is crucial. By making investments in digital infrastructure and developing legislation that supports the inclusion of AI in education by taking into cognizance of language diversity, the Nigerian government can play a key role. Technology businesses and educational institutions may collaborate to create AI-driven platforms and train educators to fit into the new order of the AI-driven educational ecosystem. Non-Governmental Organizations (NGOs) may contribute by creating curricula that support sustainable development objectives and make sure that contextual relevance and nuances are taken into account while developing AI solutions.

The future of Nigeria's sustainable growth is bright thanks to the integration of AI in the classroom. AI can support educators, tailor learning experiences, and increase environmental awareness. The path to a more equitable and sustainable educational system that equips future generations with the means to support Nigeria's sustainable development goals may be paved, notwithstanding any barriers, by a concerted effort involving a variety of stakeholders. The teaching of sustainable development in Nigeria has the potential to change thanks to AI. This technology may alter educational experiences, support instructors, and foster environmental consciousness to help produce people who are knowledgeable, powerful, and concerned about the environment. By strategically collaborating and working to overcome barriers, Nigeria may use AI's revolutionary possibilities to further the achievement of its sustainable development goals.

THEORETICAL FRAMEWORK

A well-known theoretical basis for explaining user acceptance and adoption of new technologies is the Unified Theory of Acceptance and Use of Technology (UTAUT) model (Venkatesh, Thong, and Xu, 2016). This model's application to contextualize within a developing country's perspective, like Nigeria, can offer a conceptual framework for using AI technology as the cornerstone of contemporary education. The essential elements of the UTAUT model which are Performance Expectancy, Effort Expectancy, Social Influence, Facilitating Condition, and Behavioural Intention, will be broken down and related to the use of AI in education:

Performance Expectancy: This is operationalized as "The degree to which an educator believes that using AI will help his or her job performance in providing quality education to learners" and "The degree to which learners believe that using AI by educators will help his or her educational performance". The implication of this is that AI offers advantages in education such as tailored learning, greater access to high-quality information, and improved learning outcomes, which should be emphasized in underdeveloped nations. Stakeholders may foster favourable opinions about the capability of the technology to improve educational experiences by demonstrating how AI can handle certain difficulties in the educational system most especially for educators who have a mindset that the AI will displace them from their professional duties. Stakeholders in Nigeria should stress how AI can change education as well as its attendant consequences. This can involve demonstrating AI's capacity to offer customized educational experiences, adapt information to various learning preferences, and increase student engagement. Building a good view of AI's potential influence on education may be achieved by showcasing these advantages through pilot projects and success stories.

Effort Expectancy: This is operationalized as "The degree of ease associated with the use of AI by educators or learners for quality teaching and learning". It is critical to show that employing AI technologies in education is simple to use and intuitive to encourage AI adoption. To ensure that instructors and students feel comfortable and confident in using AI-powered platforms, training programs and seminars may acquaint them with them. Comprehensive training programs should be designed to combat any opposition to new technology, particularly among educators who might be less familiar with AI. Educators may become familiar with AI technologies through workshops, online tutorials, and peer-led training sessions, which will increase their comfort level and confidence when incorporating these tools into their lesson plans. This will provide a veritable opportunity for educators to be able to train learners in the ethical ways of using AI without compromising the professional standards of the educational domain.

Social Influence: This is operationalized as "The degree to which an educator or learner perceives that important others believe he/she should use AI for teaching and learning". The adoption of AI may be strongly impacted through cooperative efforts between governmental organizations, educational institutions, NGOs, and technological corporations. Aiming to instill faith and trust in the technology, leaders, and influencers should promote AI's potential to change education by showcasing successful case studies from other nations. It is essential to involve important influencers including elected officials, educators, and community leaders. The use of public people to promote AI integration can generate urgency and legitimacy. A successful adoption may also be ensured through cooperation between global organizations, regional NGOs, and IT businesses, which can offer resources and experience.

Facilitating Conditions: This is operationalized as "The degree to which an educator or learner believes that an organization and technical infrastructure exist to support the use AI for teaching and learning". For AI integration to be effective, it is crucial to provide the appropriate infrastructure, such as dependable internet connectivity and device access. Governments and organizations must make sure that teachers and students have the resources they require to easily access platforms with AI capabilities. It is critical to address infrastructural constraints within the Nigerian space as physical and digital infrastructure has always been left unattended within its technological discourse. Governments should make investments in dependable internet connectivity and give schools the equipment all that is to use platforms powered by AI. A digital divide that can impede the adoption of AI can be avoided by ensuring equal access in urban and rural regions.

Behavioral Intention to Use: This is operationalized as "Educator's intention to use AI for Teaching and learning". Stakeholders' desire to embrace the technology may be influenced by including them in decision-making and conversations about the advantages of AI. A favourable attitude toward AI integration may be fostered by creating a sense of ownership, engagement, and commitment on the part of the government to provide an enabling environment for the use of AI for teaching and learning. Engage in talks about the potential advantages of AI with educators, students, parents, and policymakers. Town hall meetings, workshops, and seminars that inform stakeholders about the possibilities of AI can increase interest in and the desire to use the technology.

The main constructs of UTAUT will go a long way in informing the use behaviour of AI within the Nigerian ecosystem if embraced holistically. This implies that concrete proof of the technology's efficacy may be obtained by measuring the use of AI technologies in education and their effects on learning outcomes. Regular feedback loops can assist in resolving any problems that may occur and optimizing AI solutions. Implementing trial programs in a few schools to highlight the real-world effects of AI might be essential. To demonstrate the effectiveness of AI, it is pertinent to gather information on student performance, engagement, and instructor satisfaction. The sharing of this success based on users' experience tales might inspire other institutions to imitate them. Therefore, for continued AI adoption for teaching and learning, a pleasant user experience is essential so users do not feel too overwhelmed or consumed by the new technological order. Feedback from educators and students may assist in identifying areas for improvement and enable systems powered by AI to be improved to better suit users seamlessly. This feedback loop may be used to pinpoint usability problems, pain points, grey areas, and potential improvement aspects. A favourable user experience is ensured and continued usage is promoted by adapting AI systems depending on user input.

The UTAUT model's application to the integration of AI in education in developing nations like Nigeria highlights the significance of addressing user perceptions, offering help, encouraging cooperation, and making sure that the user experience is without any hitch. By taking into account these elements, stakeholders may strategically use AI as the cornerstone of contemporary education, resulting in enhanced learning outcomes and sustainable development. Nigeria can foster an atmosphere that encourages the use of AI in education as exemplified by the Minister of Communications, Innovation and Digital Economy, 'Bosun Tijani who is presently seeking experts and researchers within the AI ecosystem and related fields that can collaborate in crafting a "National AI Strategy" which is expected to be the first of its kind within the African continent. This is a giant stride for the Nigerian state just like other countries such as the United Arab Emirates (UAE), Slovenia, Argentina, Palestine, etc. are at different stages of developing an AI ecosystem and policy framework. It places a strong emphasis on user-centricity, identifies potential difficulties, and promotes cooperation amongst many stakeholders. In the end, this strategy lays the way for AI to serve as the cornerstone of contemporary education, resulting in better learning outcomes, more access to high-quality education, and a workforce more prepared for the needs of the future.

FUTURE DIRECTIONS

With the help of AI-based virtual peers or intelligent tutoring systems, students can participate in collaborative problem-solving, knowledge-sharing, and group activities. This improves social interactions, teamwork, and the process of knowledge construction in educational settings. The integration of AI technology and collaborative learning strategies should be explored to promote Collaborative Learning (CL) and Social AI (SAI) that speaks to the African indigenous identity. Since the AI ecosystem is an emerging field within the African domain, research should equally be ongoing in pertinent areas for Special Education and Inclusive Learning Environments which should be to explore the potential of AI technology to serve children with varied needs in special education and inclusive learning settings. This will go a long way to creating AI tools and interventions that can adapt to the unique needs of each learner, offer individualized assistance, and encourage inclusive behaviours to ensure that all students have equal access to resources and opportunities.

CONCLUSION

Artificial Intelligence (AI) has the potential to change education by delivering personalized and engaging learning experiences, streamlining instructional strategies, and raising student achievement levels for a sustainable future. However, there are limitations and challenges associated with the use of AI in the educational ecosystem, including ethical issues, the requirement for seamless integration with current systems; the need for teacher preparation and professional development; equity and accessibility issues, and the significance of user acceptance and trust. This chapter has contributed significantly to the practice of contemporary educational landscape, society, policy and theoretically based on a developing country's perspectives.

RECOMMENDATION

There is a need for Africa as a continent to have a holistic AI ecosystem that captures our African histories, perceptions, idiosyncrasies, languages, outlook, nuances, etc., and not Westernized which implies the indoctrination of AI based on our Africanness. In this wise, it is sacrosanct for Nigeria to be proactive in the AI ecosystem by embracing its development, adoption, and policy framework within the educational space that will make the country the continent's AI hub. Also, educators within the Nigerian space should embrace AI with a positive disposition by seeing these technologies as enablers and not displacers of their professional duties. This will provide a channel of appropriately inculcating the requisite skillsets of knowing the pros and cons of using these technologies in students thus leading to an healthy AI ecosystem within the Nigerian educational landscape. Furthermore, the Nigerian Government should provide an enabling technological environment for academics by providing accessibility to grants or funding that will necessitate ground breaking AI research. Also, Librarians as the gatekeepers of human knowledge system should provide advocacy platforms that can be a veritable opportunity to broaden the horizon of educators and learners with the essential information on contemporary AI discourse.

ABBREVIATION

4thIR: Fourth Industrial Revolution
AI: Artificial Intelligence
CAI/L: Computer-Aided Instruction and Learning
CL: Collaborative Learning
NLP: Natural Language Processing Technologies
SAI: Social AI
SDG: Sustainable Development Goals
UNESCO: United Nations Educational, Scientific and Cultural Organization
WI: Web Intelligence

REFERENCES

Baidoo-Anu, D., & Ansah, L. O. (2023). Education in the era of generative artificial intelligence (AI): Understanding the potential benefits of ChatGPT in promoting teaching and learning. *Journal of AI*, *7*(1), 52–62. doi:10.61969/jai.1337500

Bakare, O., & Okuonghae, N. (2022). Information Managers as Change Agents in Achieving Sustainable Development in the 21st Century. *Journal of Environmental Science and Economics*, *1*(2), 58–66. doi:10.56556/jescae.v1i2.97

Bakare, O. D. (2023). Emerging Technologies as a Panacea for Sustainable Provision of Library Services in Nigeria. In *Global Perspectives on Sustainable Library Practices* (pp. 1–21). IGI Global.

Bakare, O. D., & Jatto, O. V. (2023). The Potential Impact of Chatbots on Student Engagement and Learning Outcomes. In *Creative AI Tools and Ethical Implications in Teaching and Learning* (pp. 212–229). IGI Global. doi:10.4018/979-8-3693-0205-7.ch012

Borenstein, J., & Howard, A. (2021). Emerging challenges in AI and the need for AI ethics education. *AI and Ethics*, *1*(1), 61–65. doi:10.100743681-020-00002-7

Chakroun, B., Miao, F., Mendes, V., Domiter, A., Fan, H., Kharkova, I., & Rodriguez, S. (2019). Artificial intelligence for sustainable development: synthesis report. *mobile learning week 2019*.

Chen, L., Chen, P., & Lin, Z. (2020). Artificial intelligence in education: A review. *IEEE Access : Practical Innovations, Open Solutions*, 8, 75264–75278. doi:10.1109/ACCESS.2020.2988510

Dai, Y., Chai, C. S., Lin, P. Y., Jong, M. S. Y., Guo, Y., & Qin, J. (2020). Promoting students' well-being by developing their readiness for the artificial intelligence age. *Sustainability (Basel)*, *12*(16), 6597. doi:10.3390u12166597

Devedžić, V. (2004). Web intelligence and artificial intelligence in education. *Journal of Educational Technology & Society*, *7*(4), 29–39.

Dorcas Bakare, O., & Mike Bakare, B. (2022). Redesigning Library and Information Science Curriculum for Sustainable Environmental Transformation Among Students of the Department of Library and Information Science, Lead City University. *Journal of Education for Library and Information Science*, 20210016. doi:10.3138/jelis-2021-0016

Flamm, K. (1988). *Creating the computer: government, industry, and high technology*. Brookings Institution Press.

Knox, J. (2020). Artificial intelligence and education in China. *Learning, Media and Technology*, *45*(3), 298–311. doi:10.1080/17439884.2020.1754236

McCarthy, J. (2007). From here to human-level AI. *Artificial Intelligence*, *171*(18), 1174–1182. doi:10.1016/j.artint.2007.10.009

Singh, A., Kanaujia, A., Singh, V. K., & Vinuesa, R. (2023). Artificial intelligence for Sustainable Development Goals: Bibliometric patterns and concept evolution trajectories. *Sustainable Development (Bradford)*, sd.2706. doi:10.1002d.2706

Venkatesh, V., Thong, J. Y., & Xu, X. (2016). Unified theory of acceptance and use of technology: A synthesis and the road ahead. *Journal of the Association for Information Systems*, *17*(5), 328–376. doi:10.17705/1jais.00428

Villegas-Ch, W., García-Ortiz, J., Mullo-Ca, K., Sánchez-Viteri, S., & Roman-Cañizares, M. (2021). Implementation of a virtual assistant for the academic management of a university with the use of artificial intelligence. *Future Internet*, *13*(4), 97. doi:10.3390/fi13040097

Xia, Q., Chiu, T. K., Zhou, X., Chai, C. S., & Cheng, M. (2022). Systematic literature review on opportunities, challenges, and future research recommendations of artificial intelligence in education. *Computers and Education: Artificial Intelligence*, *4*, 100118.

Chapter 11
AI–Driven Decision–Making Applications in Higher Education

Retno Lestari

https://orcid.org/0000-0003-4568-9596
Universitas Brawijaya, Indonesia

Heni Dwi Windarwati
Universitas Brawijaya, Indonesia

Ridhoyanti Hidayah
Universitas Brawijaya, Indonesia

ABSTRACT

Artificial intelligence (AI) systems have become ubiquitous daily, yet many are unaware of their presence. The advancements in artificial intelligence have contributed significantly to higher education by changing how we approach problem-solving. The transformative potential of AI technology in education and training cannot be overstated. Currently, educators are utilizing AI systems to identify individual learning needs and experiences, make data-driven decisions and allocate resources more effectively. This chapter aims to equip readers with a comprehensive knowledge of the application of AI-powered decision-making in higher education. With the valuable insights and resources provided, readers can confidently integrate and leverage the potential of AI in their decision-making processes. To fully realize the potential of AI, educators, and leaders must have a fundamental understanding of its capabilities and ethical considerations. This knowledge will enable them to engage confidently and critically with AI technology and maximize its benefits.

DOI: 10.4018/979-8-3693-0639-0.ch011

INTRODUCTION

Artificial Intelligence (AI) is the simulation of human intelligence in machines. It is a rapidly evolving field of computer science that involves the development of software systems that can perform tasks that typically require human cognitive abilities, such as learning, reasoning, and problem-solving. AI algorithms and statistical models enable machines to analyze large amounts of data, recognize patterns, and make predictions, among other things. The potential applications of AI are vast and span numerous industries, including healthcare, finance, and transportation. The development of AI requires expertise in fields such as computer science, mathematics, and engineering, as well as a deep understanding of human cognition. AI is a topic of great interest and importance in both academic and business settings, and it is expected to continue to drive innovation and change.. It utilizes various techniques and approaches, such as machine learning, natural language processing, and neural networks, to process and analyze complex data sets, recognize patterns, and make informed decisions based on the data. AI has become increasingly prevalent in various industries, such as healthcare, finance, and transportation, due to its ability to improve efficiency, accuracy, and productivity. Its applications range from predictive maintenance and fraud detection to autonomous vehicles and virtual assistants (Davenport & Kalakota, 2019). The education field is undergoing a massive transformation with the rise of Artificial Intelligence (AI). Innovative solutions are being developed using AI technology to enhance the teaching and learning experience for students, teachers, parents, and educational institutions worldwide. The aim of AI in education is not to replace human teachers with machines but to use computer intelligence to aid them in creating a more efficient and effective education system (JavaTPoint, 2021).

AI uses various techniques to generate predictions, content, recommendations, and decisions. It is important to note that the techniques consist of machine learning, including supervised, unsupervised, and reinforcement learning, logic and knowledge-based methods such as knowledge representation, expert systems, and inductive programming. Statistical approaches also form an integral part of these techniques (such as Bayesian estimation, search, and optimization methods). The software is specifically designed to achieve human-defined objectives and interacts with the environment accordingly (Xu, 2021; Sarker, 2022).

AI has the potential to improve teaching and learning practices significantly, as well as the organization and operation of higher education institutions. Despite the limited evidence-based research on the impact of AI in education, a critical and supervised approach is necessary to fully realize its potential (Zawacki-Richter *et al.*, 2019; Huang *et al.*, 2021). AI systems can be utilized in various ways to support teaching and learning, categorized as "student-facing," "teacher-facing," and "system-facing" AI systems. Through four use cases, including Student Teaching, Student Supporting, Teacher Supporting, and System Supporting, educators and learners can utilize AI systems to enhance the teaching, learning, and assessment process with confidence (Zawacki-Richter *et al.*, 2019). Implementing AI-powered decision-making in higher education is crucial for achieving better results. This chapter provides readers with the necessary guidance to accomplish this goal. A comprehensive study by Crompton and Burke in 2023 reveals that AI is increasingly utilized across higher education institutions for multiple purposes, including assessment and evaluation, prediction, AI assistance, intelligent tutoring systems (ITS), and managing student learning. The report also indicates that AI is primarily geared towards students, accounting for 72% of its usage, while instructors and managers follow at 17% and 11%, respectively.

BENEFITS OF INTEGRATING ARTIFICIAL INTELLIGENCE INTO HIGHER EDUCATION

As technology advances, AI-powered tools are becoming more prevalent in higher education. The benefits of these tools are numerous and varied. One significant advantage is the time they save instructors, allowing them to focus on other essential tasks. Additionally, AI-powered technology can cater to the unique needs of individual students, providing personalized and adaptive learning experiences. This technology can also provide real-time feedback, helping students to understand their progress and identify areas where they need additional support. Overall, the integration of AI-powered technology into higher education has the potential to enhance the learning experience for both students and instructors.

Assists in Generating Questions and Providing Feedback

AI-powered grading can analyze cultural and social nuances, thereby improving students' writing skills. Providing feedback in the form of text and/or pictures facilitates students' self-evaluation and promotes independent learning. Mousavi *et al.* (2020) have even developed an effective feedback system that considers student demographics, attributes, and academic status, making it a highly personalized tool for assessment. The value of AI's capacity to analyze data sets for group work feedback cannot be overstated (Ouatik *et al.*, 2021).

As an instructor, you can use AI to generate and create multiple test questions efficiently. Thanks to its natural language processing capabilities, AI produces incredibly realistic short-answer questions that can save you valuable time during tests. However, it is essential to thoroughly review the questions generated by AI to ensure they align precisely with the learning objectives, especially for high-scoring assessments. Furthermore, AI is critical in evaluating online activities through the Axial Code scoring and evaluation system. The assessment system thoroughly evaluates students' progress by analyzing their reflective practices, achievement goals, community identity, and higher-order thinking abilities, making it an indispensable tool for instructors rather than just a general resource and textbook (Huang *et al.*, 2021).

AI-powered solutions offer objective and efficient approaches to assess and provide feedback, allowing educators to focus on their core responsibilities and optimize the learning experience for their students. One of the most significant benefits of AI technology in education is automating administrative tasks, such as grading assignments, monitoring attendance, and maintaining records. These mundane tasks can be time-consuming and take away valuable time from educators that could be better spent on more critical tasks. By automating these tasks, educators can save considerable time, which can be utilized to enhance their teaching methods and engage with their students (Owan *et al.*, 2023).

AI-integrated grading systems are accurate and reliable and generate exam results promptly. The transparency of the process ensures that evaluations are fair and unbiased without the possibility of external manipulation. Furthermore, AI-powered curriculum offers educators valuable insights that can be used to adapt courses to enhance comprehension and retention. These insights can identify areas where students are struggling, and educators can modify their teaching methods to address these issues (Balla, 2023). AI-powered solutions can significantly contribute to the education system by streamlining processes and improving outcomes. By automating administrative tasks, providing objective assessments, and generating valuable insights, AI technology can help educators focus on their core responsibilities and optimize the learning experience for their students.

On the other hand, The incorporation of chatbots as AI assisting tools in educational evaluations has sparked apprehensions regarding possible academic dishonesty and the imperative to uphold the credibility of assessments. Additionally, ethical concerns are pertinent as it is paramount to guarantee that chatbots are impartial and equitable. Chatbots may present a risk of cheating, as students could employ them during exams or other evaluations, enabling them to obtain real-time responses. Such conduct undermines the integrity of assessments and confers an unjust advantage upon those who resort to chatbots (Kooli, 2023).

Predict Student Academic Performance

AI is being widely used in higher education to predict student academic performance. Predicting student performance using AI is an everyday occurrence. In a recent study conducted by Qian et al. (2021), an AI system was incorporated to predict future grades of students using various learning features, including past grades, in an artificial neural network. The study's significant finding is that AI can accurately predict student scores and identify those at risk of dropping out, a crucial issue in higher education. This powerful tool can prevent student failure in achieving their academic goals. Although there is often overlap in the possible axial codes, such as predicting at-risk students and predicting dropout, each provides different abilities. The exciting thing about this discovery is that AI can predict student scores and highlight students at risk of dropping out. This subject is sensitive, but student sensitivity is still essential in higher education settings. Furthermore, it can be a positive tool to prevent students from failing to achieve their goals. A recent study by Jiao *et al.* (2022) delved into using an artificial intelligence-powered prediction model to determine students' academic performance in online courses. The study highlighted the challenges of predicting academic performance in online courses due to the need for more usage of the learning process and summative data and the difficulty in precisely predicting the quantitative relations between variables and achievements. It then characterizes the learning data in an online engineering course, using an evolutionary computation technique to explore the best prediction model. The model is then validated using another online course with the same pedagogy and technology. The study found that the dominant variables in academic performance are knowledge acquisition, class participation, and summative performance, while prerequisite knowledge does not play a significant role. Based on these findings, the study provides pedagogical and analytical implications. Further, the genetic programming model is superior to other AI methods in terms of performance.

AI Assistant Tools in Higher Education

Assistants that leverage artificial intelligence (AI) to perform their tasks can be referred to by various names, such as virtual assistants, intelligent agents, intelligent helpers, intelligent tutors, or virtual agents. These terms reflect how users perceive AI technology. Chatbots are precious tools for students as they offer assistance and answer their questions. These assistants provide meaningful support and responses in four key areas, intending to motivate students to persist in their studies and degree programs while enhancing their academic performance. Thanks to the capabilities of AI, support is timely and does not require waiting for someone's availability. Moreover, the assistance provided considers students' academic abilities, preferences, and the most effective strategies for support (Crompton *et al.*, 2022). The potential of AI to revolutionize education is truly remarkable. By leveraging cutting-edge innovations such as artificial neural networks, machine learning, and Computer-Assisted Language Learning, students can experience personalized and collaborative learning in various settings. AI's advanced algorithms can help guide students on their educational journey, while automated assessment tools and facial recognition systems provide educators with valuable insights (Nguyen *et al.*, 2022). Some top AI-powered tools can help students improve their academic performances: 1) Open AI Playground: This feature-packed tool is designed to enhance your content creation skills, 2) Chat GPT-3/GPT-4: This AI tutor offers personalized assistance to help you excel in your studies, 3) Quillbot: This indispensable AI assistant is a must-have for writing tasks, 4) Fotor: This digital canvas is perfect for exploring your artistic pursuits, 5) Canva: This AI-powered design tool delivers intuitive, personalized design experiences, 6) Grammarly: This lifesaver tool helps student writers improve their grammar and writing skills, 7) Otter.ai: This lecture transcription tool keeps you on top of your notes and helps you stay organized, 8) Google Bard: This personal AI assistant helps you become more efficient and manage your time more effectively, 9) Slidesgo: This AI-powered tool helps you easily create stunning presentations, 10) 1Stepwise Math: This personalized learning tool helps you master math concepts and excel in coursework (AECC Study Abroad Consultants, 2023).

The rise of generative AI tools has made it easier for people to create and distribute manipulated media such as images, videos, and audio. This trend has brought about a significant risk of impersonation and deception, particularly for newsrooms and individuals who rely on accurate information. To address this issue, Meta has implemented a policy of removing synthetic media that has the potential to mislead viewers into believing that someone said or did something that they did not. Specifically, the platform eliminates videos that manipulate or merge content to appear genuine while allowing satire and parody. However, as deepfake technology continues to improve and become more prevalent, enforcing synthetic media policies will become increasingly challenging. Detection algorithms must continue to advance to ensure the safety and reliability of journalists and their audiences online. It is crucial to remain vigilant and implement measures against misinformation and disinformation (Chin, 2023).

ETHICAL FRAMEWORKS FOR THE USE OF AI IN HIGHER EDUCATION

Five Pillars of AI in Higher Education

As universities increasingly adopt artificial intelligence (AI) technologies in their operations, it is essential that they carefully consider the ethical implications of their use. AI ethics provides a framework for ensuring that AI systems are developed and deployed responsibly. Universities should be aware of five key pillars of AI ethics when implementing AI: accountability, reliability, explainability, security, and privacy (Gupta, 2022).

Accountability requires universities to take responsibility for the actions of their AI systems and ensure that they are used in a way that aligns with ethical values. Artificial Intelligence (AI) has the potential to revolutionize higher education and transform the university world. However, with great power comes great responsibility. Accountability ensures that AI is developed and used responsibly and truthfully. When AI is accountable, it can be relied upon to perform its intended functions accurately and reliably. This is crucial for businesses that rely on AI to automate processes and make decisions. To achieve accountability, university developers must design AI systems that are transparent, explainable, and auditable. This means that the AI system's workings and decision-making processes must be understandable to humans so that they can review and assess them. Additionally, AI systems must be auditable so their actions and decisions can be traced and checked. Accountability is the cornerstone of ethical AI. It ensures that AI is developed and used in a way that benefits humanity and the world at large. By embracing accountability, we can unlock the full potential of AI and create a better future for all.

The principle of accountability in regulating AIED must include explicit measures to ensure that each stakeholder involved in the design and use of AIED is held responsible and accountable for their actions. This consists of implementing auditability, minimization, and reporting procedures for any adverse side effects, trade-offs, or compensation related to using AIED. In other words, any negative impact of AIED must be identified, mitigated, and reported to ensure accountability and responsibility (Nguyen *et al.*, 2022).

The reliability of Artificial Intelligence (AI) is a critical aspect that requires attention. The data sources used by AI algorithms are continuously changing, and as new sources are added, the outputs from AI must be monitored and validated regularly. With the increasing deployment of AI across various industries, the reliability of algorithms becomes even more critical. AI algorithm errors can have significant consequences, leading to inaccurate or misleading information and poor decision-making. In higher education, standardized processes, data collection, and organization are essential to ensure that the technology managing this data, including AI, can run smoothly and without producing errors. Standardization ensures that the data AI algorithms consume is consistent, accurate, and reliable, leading to more accurate predictions and more reliable results.

Ensuring that the predictions made by AI models are explainable and can be understood across different departments is crucial. AI technology is only helpful if translated and used across the organization. If the technology cannot be understood, it can lead to confusion and siloed processes, ultimately rendering it irrelevant.

Explainability is critical in AI technology, especially in higher education institutions. The models used in these institutions must be explainable to ensure no inherent bias and that the technology generates actionable results. In other words, the predictions made by AI models must be readily interpretable, and the reasons behind them should be clear and transparent. This transparency is crucial in ensuring that the model's predictions are not biased based on race, gender, or other protected characteristics. Explainability is critical in ensuring that AI models used in higher education institutions are transparent and generate actionable results. By making AI technology explainable, universities can ensure that the models are trusted and the results help improve teaching, learning, and administrative processes.

The prevalence of ransomware attacks on organizations and protected data has underscored the importance of tech security. Given the increasing reliance on AI models, protecting them against such attacks is imperative. Therefore, the university must know the potential risks and their implications for the technology used.

Security breaches can have dire consequences, mainly when dealing with sensitive or confidential data. As such, ensuring that AI models are secure and impervious to malicious actors is critical. In this regard, attackers may target the model's parameters or inject malicious code, resulting in incorrect predictions or the theft of confidential data. Furthermore, the absence of privacy assurance in AI can lead to a loss of trust and reputational damage. In this case, the university may need help safeguarding its intellectual property and maintaining confidentiality of sensitive data. Consequently, it is imperative to have robust security measures in place to protect AI models against any potential risks.

Data privacy and security are fundamental concerns for leaders in higher education, particularly when utilizing AI. Cloud-based technologies have become the norm for business transactions and data storage in academia. Consequently, universities are now prioritizing the privacy and security of their data through technology. To maintain trust and safeguard assets, AI must ensure robust privacy measures. AI can streamline operations and minimize human error, making it an invaluable tool for universities. However, its effectiveness hinges on the institution's commitment to ethical standards and addressing its challenges. Continuous monitoring and improvement are essential to relying on AI and guaranteeing AI ethics. With AI's ever-changing nature, universities need to establish a foundation based on five ethical principles to ensure AI's reliability (Pastor-Escuredo *et al.*, 2022).

Nguyen *et al.* (2022) also added the principle of sustainability and proportionality in AIED that emphasize the need for justifiable design, development, and usage that avoids disruptions to the environment, world economy, and society, including the labour market, culture, and politics. The technical details in AIED must adhere to these principles to ensure a responsible and ethical approach towards its implementation. One fundamental idea when creating AIED is to ensure people of all backgrounds and abilities can use it. This is called the principle of inclusiveness in accessibility. It means that AIED must be designed to work for everyone, regardless of their technical skills, where they come from, or if they have any physical challenges. This way, anyone can use the technology and benefit from it. We must use fair, unbiased information and methods when creating and using Artificial Intelligence in Education (AIED). This is called the principle of inclusiveness in data and algorithms. This principle helps ensure that everyone, regardless of who they are or where they come from, has an equal chance to benefit from AIED. It is essential to follow this principle to ensure everyone is treated fairly and with respect when using AI in Education. The Principle of Human-Centred AIED states that AI education systems should be designed to help people learn better and faster while allowing them to make their own choices and control the process. It is essential to keep human needs and culture in mind when using AI in education.

Best Practices to Ensure the Safety and Integrity of the Data

Safety of Student Data Privacy

Maintaining security data involves a set of best practices that must be followed to ensure the safety and integrity of the data. These practices include but are not limited to regular backups, limiting access to only authorized personnel, using strong passwords and encryption for sensitive data, and monitoring for any suspicious activity. The following tips will help build a robust system for protecting student data privacy:

Firstly, review the data privacy policies of every app or third-party tool the school uses. Ensure that these policies align with the school's ethical and safety guidelines and that external parties keep their word. Sensitive information, such as emails or voice messages, should be encrypted. Several encryption services and tools can provide this extra layer of security. Unused files on the system, whether downloaded from the web or cloud, can potentially contain malware and should be regularly deleted.

Sharing student records should be restricted to only those with a legitimate educational need. Conduct realistic training sessions for educators, administrators, and students to prevent data breaches, treating them as real-life test cases. Users should log out or lock their computers and other learning platforms when not in use to ensure that no unauthorized access occurs.

Finally, the universities should educate students and staff members on online safety and data privacy. In addition, the universities should keep up to date with any student data privacy acts being passed. Incorporating these tips will help improve student data privacy and create a safer learning environment.

Challenges of Data Privacy Issues

Despite the significant progress made in safeguarding private information through student data privacy regulations, several challenges and issues require resolution to ensure the safety of all student data. One of the primary concerns is the risk of data breaches and security threats. Schools accumulate and maintain a wealth of information concerning their students, including sensitive data such as personal information, academic records, and medical histories. As a result, educational institutions have become an attractive target for hackers and unauthorized individuals seeking to exploit this information. Data breaches can result in the theft, misuse, or illicit access of student data, leading to identity theft, fraudulent practices, or other criminal activities.

Another issue is the need for more knowledge and adequate training among educators and staff regarding the best practices for handling student data safely. Inadvertent sharing of private information by teachers and trainers who need to be proficient in using digital tools or lack sufficient security measures is a significant risk. Implementing comprehensive training and awareness programs is essential to equip teachers with the necessary skills and knowledge to protect students' privacy.

Thirdly, companies that develop and sell educational technology services often gather and process student data as part of their offerings. Although many of these providers prioritize the safety of student information, there are instances when such data is shared with or sold to third parties without the appropriate permission or transparency. This lack of control over student data after it leaves the school presents a significant challenge to privacy protection.

In addition, student data privacy faces new challenges as online learning systems and digital tools for teaching become more popular. Remote learning environments often depend heavily on third-party applications and cloud services, raising concerns about data storage, encryption, and the potential for data leaks. It is crucial to implement robust security measures and carefully select technology partners to balance the advantages of digital learning and the need to protect students' privacy.

Lastly, collecting information about students can be used for profiling and targeted advertising, raising ethical questions. Using student data to generate profiles and send personalized advertisements raises concerns about privacy, informed consent, and potential abuse. Striking a balance between personalizing education and protecting students' privacy is a complex task that requires careful consideration.

Educating Students on Data Privacy

The subject of data privacy for students is of paramount importance. Educating students on data privacy is crucial to ensuring their personal information remains secure and protected. This can be achieved by imparting knowledge on password security, emphasizing the hazards of sharing personal information online, and highlighting the consequences of falling for cyber threats. Educators who are well-versed in the problem can teach students how to stay secure more effectively. The following are some tips that students must be prepared to enhance their privacy. Employing these guidelines in tandem can create a powerful shield against potential threats.

It is crucial to keep mobile devices and apps up to date. Students must avoid clicking on random links or visiting unknown websites. Suspicious emails should be deleted or reported to avoid granting access to accounts. Updating and protecting all home devices connected to the internet is also recommended.

Moreover, students should practice safe use of social media and avoid posting personal or sensitive information. Students should avoid using public and accessible Wi-Fi networks to prevent compromising sensitive information. Charging mobile devices in public spaces or charging stations should be avoided as it could lead to privileges being granted. Students must also protect home Wi-Fi networks and digital devices by changing the factory password.

Lastly, optimising operating systems, browsers, and security software is essential by installing recommended updates. Students following these guidelines can safeguard their privacy and remain protected from threats.

The Ethical Frameworks of AI in Higher Education

Artificial Intelligence (AI) has changed how people learn in higher education by providing personalized learning. AI-powered tools like exploratory learning, collaborative and automatic assessment systems, mobile game-based learning, and conversational chatbots have made education more focused on students. Although AI has created new education opportunities, many things still need to be researched. The impact of AI-driven tools on human thinking and learning a second language has yet to be fully understood. However, AI technology can improve students' learning and results while reducing the teacher's workload.

AI technology cannot replace the teaching work of teachers because it cannot understand which methods work best for each student. As AI technology grows, seeing how it transforms the education sector will be fascinating (Klimova *et al.*, 2023).

Holmes *et al.* (2022) stated that developing a comprehensive ethics of AI in higher education (AIED) is crucial. It should be more comprehensive than just six areas that are already identified, i.e., data, computational approaches, education, and their intersections. Many unknown ethical issues still need to be identified and addressed, especially at the intersection of data, computation, education, and the specific interaction between AI systems and human cognition (Figure 1). For a comprehensive framework for AIED ethics, conducting horizon-scanning interdisciplinary conversations and considering insights from the learning sciences, cognitive and educational neuroscience, and philosophical introspection is necessary. It is also essential to focus on the practical implementation of such a framework to provide genuine value for teachers, students, policymakers, and other stakeholders.

Figure 1. Ethical frameworks of AI in education
(Holmes et al., 2022)

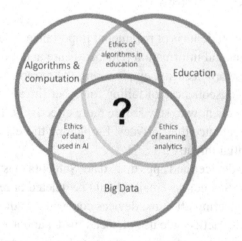

Moreover, while it is essential to prevent unethical activities, we should also consider the ethical cost of inaction and failure to innovate against the potential benefits of AIED innovation for learners, educators, educational institutions, and society. Therefore, AIED ethics should provide a proactive set of guidance to ground research and development, which is both protective and facilitative, to ensure the best outcomes for all stakeholders from the inevitable integration of AI into educational contexts.

Holmes *et al.* (2022) conducted a study revealing that some believe education inherently operates with ethical principles and good intentions. This perception is only partially accurate. Integrating e-learning or AIED systems into teaching does not guarantee ethical oversight. Good intentions are commendable but need to be improved. Respondents have emphasized identifying ethical risks and remaining vigilant against unintended consequences from incorporating pedagogical designs into AI systems. For instance, if an AIED system produces inaccurate assessments of an individual's learning progress, it can severely affect their well-being and advancement. Therefore, we must exercise great care in developing and deploying AI systems that can handle real-world scenarios and do not pose ethical threats.

Rutgers University-New Brunswick studied how artificial intelligence (AI) can help people. AI makes our lives easier and safer with things like Siri and Alexa. But AI also has some problems. The study talked about how facial recognition tech can help find lost children and identify rare diseases, but it can also worsen privacy and safety. We need to find ways to fix these problems (Derrow, 2022).

Using robust computer programs that predict outcomes, such as the likelihood of receiving a loan or a traffic ticket or even recognising faces, can have severe implications for one's privacy, health, well-being, and financial stability. In America, this can lead to unfairness, as the potential for misuse of these programs is high. There is a valid concern that these programs can become too sophisticated, leading to an abuse of power or manipulation of individuals, similar to the case with Facebook. The danger lies in the vast amounts of data fed into these programs, which can be used to make crucial decisions, such as approving a loan or implementing self-driving technology. However, it is essential to note that the creators of these programs may have their biases and opinions, which can lead to unfairness for everyone involved.

Regulation plays a crucial role in decision-making. However, transparency can only be achieved through proper education. To make algorithms transparent, they must be made available to anyone interested in examining them. This requires training people to document algorithms in an understandable language. AI's ability to explore permutations to a depth and degree that humans cannot is a significant advantage. Its advanced capabilities allow us to extend our intuition and find patterns beyond human capabilities. Nevertheless, it is crucial to ensure that our decisions are based on understandable data, whether a medical diagnosis or tax calculation. It's crucial to develop AI algorithms that are unbiased, transparent in their decision-making, and accountable for their outcomes, especially in higher education. This can prevent the perpetuation of existing inequalities and promote fairness. Prioritizing these principles safeguards against potential harm and upholds ethics and accountability in our work.

Ahmad *et al.* (2023) established ten guiding principles for the development of educational AI systems. These principles encompass a range of factors, from encouraging user participation in the learning process to promoting safe and collaborative human-machine interactions. Additionally, the principles aim to foster positive character traits, avoid information overload, create a curious and supportive learning environment, consider ergonomic features, respect the vital roles and skills of teachers, have respect for cultural values, accommodate student diversity, and never glorify the system at the expense of human potential for growth and learning.

Adherence to these principles ensures the ethical development of educational AI systems and enhances the quality of learning experiences for students. The principles emphasize the importance of creating a learning environment that is engaging, supportive, and accommodating to students' diverse needs while respecting cultural values and the vital roles of teachers. Furthermore, they underscore the necessity of avoiding information overload and glorifying the system, which could hinder students' potential for growth and learning. These principles provide invaluable guidance for developing educational AI systems that prioritize ethical considerations and enhance students' learning experiences.

An algorithm that treats people differently based on their group is unfair. In countries like the US or UK, groups that need extra protection include people of different ages, genders, colours, races, religions, nationalities, citizenships, veterans, those with specific genes, and people with other physical or mental abilities. But, the list of groups that need protection can change based on an algorithm's needs. Checking how well an algorithm works for different groups is essential for ensuring fairness. For example, Ocumpaugh *et al.* (2014) tested a system that detects student emotions to ensure it would work well for students in different areas. The focus was on groups of students who went to schools in other places, like cities, suburbs, and rural areas. The system was first made to work with data from mostly city students but was going to be used in many different places.

We call it discrimination when a system mistreats some people. Discrimination can happen on purpose or by accident. In America, some laws say certain types of discrimination are not allowed. For example, if a college only accepts students of one race and not others, that is not permitted. This is called "disparate treatment". But, if a college has a rule that does not use race but still accepts fewer students of one race than others, that is also not allowed. This is called "disparate impact". For instance, if a computer program is used to select who can attend college, the program looks at things like grades and how well they did in college. If this program selects fewer students of one race than others, that is also not allowed (Verma & Rubin, 2018).

Ethical Use of Artificial Intelligence in Teaching and Learning Process

The ethical use of AI in teaching and learning is the responsible and appropriate application of artificial intelligence technology in educational settings. The policies and considerations involves ensuring that AI is designed and used in ways that are fair, unbiased, and transparent, with a focus on enhancing learning outcomes for all students (Nguyen *et al.*, 2022). It also requires a commitment to protecting the privacy and security of student data, while promoting equity and inclusion in educational practices. Establishing ethical guidelines for AI systems in education is of utmost importance. These guidelines must prioritize the users' well-being, ensure a safe workplace, promote trustworthiness, maintain fairness, honour intellectual property rights, and uphold privacy and confidentiality. To attain these goals, adhering to the guidelines and principles outlined for developing ethical educational AI systems is crucial. This entails prioritizing the well-being and safety of users, maintaining trustworthiness and fairness, upholding privacy and confidentiality, and respecting cultural and individual differences. In addition, it is vital to stimulate user engagement, foster positive character traits, steer clear of information overload, cultivate an environment that promotes curiosity and learning, consider ergonomic features, and refrain from exalting the system at the expense of human potential for development and learning. By following these guidelines and principles, developers can create ethical and practical educational AI systems that promote the progress and development of their users (Nguyen *et al.*, 2022; Ahmad *et al.*, 2023).

Ethical use of AI and data in education is paramount. In order to attain this objective, it is imperative to consider four crucial factors. A human agency must be prioritized, enabling people to make informed decisions and take responsibility for their actions. Fairness is of the utmost importance, ensuring that everyone has equal access and treatment within the social organization. The well-being, safety, and dignity of all individuals must be taken into account to preserve humanity. Lastly, justified choice requires the use of knowledge, facts, and data to make collective decisions transparently and participatorily. Educators and school leaders must keep these ethical considerations in mind when deciding to implement AI systems in education. By guaranteeing the dependability of AI systems and addressing relevant concerns, we can establish a learning environment that is equitable and secure for all (European Commission, 2022).

The use of AI in collecting, examining, and disseminating data about people has ethical implications that cannot be ignored. For three decades, experts have been working to define ethical standards for information, but with the rise of data science, the focus has shifted to data ethics. While technology itself is not the issue, we must use software and data responsibly. By doing so, we can ensure that the benefits of technological advancements are enjoyed by all while minimizing any potential negative impacts (Dwivedi *et al.*, 2023).

Educational institutions have increasingly relied on automated learning algorithms to determine student acceptance and rejection. However, this approach poses significant concerns. Firstly, the lack of transparency is unacceptable when these programs fail to explain the reasons behind their decisions. Every student deserves the right to understand why they were accepted or rejected. Secondly, machine learning algorithms trained on specific data sets may lead to unfair discrimination when used on students from different regions. This could result in biased decision-making that cannot be tolerated (Akgun & Greenhow, 2022). Additionally, the use of large data sets to generate recommendations may not be suitable for students from different target groups. This issue can be avoided by basing recommendations on individual learning histories (European Commission, 2022).

Finally, the concentration of personal data on major educational platforms poses a severe risk to privacy. Cybercriminals may target large amounts of personal information from students and teachers. Moreover, dominant platforms may monopolize the market on the ability to develop the best algorithms, raising concerns about transparency in individual students' learning paths' decision-making. These issues must be addressed immediately to ensure fair and transparent decision-making in educational institutions (Khrisnan, 2022).

UNESCO (2019) has identified six significant challenges that must be addressed to achieve sustainable development of AI-powered education. These challenges include the need for comprehensive public policy, promoting inclusion and equity in education, preparing teachers for AI-powered education, educating AI to understand educational needs, developing quality and inclusive data systems, and ensuring ethical and transparent data collection, use, and dissemination. At the individual level, there are a variety of challenges that must be overcome. These challenges range from systemic issues such as bias, discrimination, and inequality for marginalized groups of students to ethical issues relating to privacy and bias in data collection and processing. Addressing these challenges is essential to ensure AI's equitable and ethical use in education.

The demand for higher education content and forms among university students is steadily increasing as society progresses. However, current teachings at universities and colleges are unable to meet these needs, prompting a much-needed reform process. To achieve this, it's essential to explore Higher Education learning approaches that conform to universities' and colleges' teaching experience and increase instructional impact (Coman *et al.*, 2020). Fortunately, improving technologies such as the augmented reality cloud platform, Artificial Intelligence Technology, mobile Internet, the Internet of Things Technology, and other information technology can be very helpful. The College of Higher Education offers a unique opportunity to build an Internet of Things and a cloud infrastructure for augmented reality services. The innovative network of Artificial Intelligence has revolutionized modern society. It comprises diverse technologies, including short-range wireless communication, sensor networks, mobile communication, real-time positioning, big data, intelligent information processing, and cloud computing. Students can now benefit from the Interactive Smart Educational System, which utilizes simulation AI technology and virtual reality to create an interactive environment, allowing for multiple perceptions, exploration, and other advantages (Alahi *et al.*, 2023). Thanks to this, users can have a virtual learning experience that offers rich sensory stimulations and natural interaction strategies.

BEST PRACTICES, STRATEGY AND ACTION PLAN FOR IMPLEMENTING ARTIFICIAL INTELLIGENCE TECHNOLOGY IN HIGHER EDUCATION

Action Plan for Implementing Artificial Intelligence Technology in Higher Education

The implementation of AI is poised to revolutionize higher education, and institutions must prepare accordingly. Adequate preparation will ensure that students are equipped with the skills and knowledge required to excel in a rapidly evolving technological landscape. As such, it is recommended that faculties begin exploring the potential applications of AI in the classroom and invest in the necessary infrastructure to support its integration. By doing so, they can remain at the forefront of innovation and provide students with an unparalleled educational experience.

Developing the System

The system's design is based on developing application software and constructing a sustainable educational system using artificial intelligence (AI) in higher education. To create a conducive learning environment with AI, the following guidelines must be followedProtection criteria: The learning education infrastructure is an essential aspect of higher education and is closely related to overhauling the curriculum. This infrastructure contains personal data, movement data, names, and more. The design of AI systems must take into account the protection of the system's data and ensure data security and user safety (Zhang *et al.*, 2021). To ensure that the incorporation of generative AI in teaching and learning is ethical and trustworthy, universities must take full accountability for their decisions related to it. This responsibility includes being open and transparent about the data collection and usage practices involved in implementing generative AI and being receptive to feedback and critiques from students and staff. By disclosing detailed information about the algorithms being utilized, their specific functions, and any potential biases or limitations, universities can create a culture of trust and confidence amongst their stakeholders in AI technology. When implementing generative AI technologies, educators must prioritize addressing ethical concerns, privacy, security, and other related matters. In doing so, universities can help ensure that their use of generative AI is effective but also responsible and ethical. This will help build a strong foundation for integrating AI into education while promoting greater awareness and understanding of these technologies' potential benefits and risks.Practical criteria: The system's construction cost should be minimized based on applicable system requirements and functions to make managing it more accessible and cheaper.

As AI becomes more prevalent in our society, a growing concern is that it may adversely affect our social consciousness and responsibility. It is essential to consider the potential negative consequences and take steps to mitigate them. How we tackle climate change will determine whether AI contributes to the downfall of a significant portion of society or advances the interests of those who thrive in chaos. The use of massive amounts of data by AI systems also raises legitimate concerns about privacy and security. Institutions need to prioritize data protection for generative AI technologies and implement proper security measures to prevent unauthorized access or use of the data. This includes ensuring that any data used for training or testing the technology is de-identified (Chan, 2023).

Modifiable criteria: The system design must meet the college's implementation needs, focus on system usability and upgradeability, and minimize the mix of modules to develop a potential core market model (Zhang *et al.*, 2021). For universities to effectively utilize AI in education, it's crucial to tailor advancements in AI technology to meet their specific needs. One way to achieve this is by providing financial support or resources to those developing AI tools and applications that address the educational requirements of their respective communities.

Furthermore, improving literacy education and fostering AI skills have significant implications, preparing the public to integrate AI technologies across various fields. By investing in AI technologies catering to universities' educational needs, we can ensure that the future workforce is well-equipped to handle the challenges and opportunities of rapid AI advancements.

Integrated quasi-criteria: The AI system design, data model structure, storage structure, and stored data must comply with college policy guidelines for long-term organizational utilization, starting with the total system design. Organizations utilizing AI should prioritize fostering inclusivity in the workplace. This can be accomplished by.assembling teams with diverse backgrounds and skill sets, hosting regular diversity workshops, and soliciting input from various stakeholders. At every step of the AI implementation process, it is crucial to encourage a variety of perspectives to ensure a comprehensive and inclusive result (Ryan & Stahl, 2021).

Open criteria: The higher education AI infrastructure in the college must be based on structured data interfaces to discuss and share knowledge and data with other information systems (*Jarrahi et al.*, 2023). Moreover, the AI network system and hardware computer models must be backed by the system (UNESCO, 2019). Infrastructural readiness, in the context of data and knowledge augmentation, refers to the availability and functionality of data and algorithmic systems. These systems work together to enhance and streamline knowledge processes, such as data analysis and decision-making. The data systems collect and store relevant information, while the algorithmic systems process and analyze this data to extract meaningful insights. When these systems function optimally, they can improve organizational efficiency and effectiveness (Jarrahi *et al.*, 2023).

Yang (2021) developed an AI system to assist schools in remote areas of China, especially those catering to minority groups, in utilizing multimedia network teaching resources provided by the state. The study resulted in the creation of a multimedia network teaching management system that aimed to enhance the overall level of multimedia network management. The system proved highly automated, enabling teaching staff to work more efficiently and accurately, improving the multimedia teaching of minority films and television. The multimedia teaching approach used in the system, which combined pictures, text, sound, image, and shadow, proved to be highly effective in demonstrating knowledge to students intuitively, making learning more relaxed and enjoyable and stimulating their desire to learn. In addition, AI involves an advanced teaching method that utilizes agent technology and information systems based on cognitive science theory. This method is known as the Browser/MultiAgent Server, which functions as a three-tier model. The multiagent layer connects the traditional Browser-Server structure, facilitating intelligent communication and teaching between the client and server. These agents possess independent learning and response abilities, which enable them to adapt and share tasks to complete the students' learning objectives. The system dynamically adjusts its teaching strategy based on the student's situation. The primary components of the databases are a student information database and a teaching content database, which complement each other (Li *et al.*, 2021).

Design AI Curriculum With the Expert Decision Support System

How we approach education is changing, and AI-powered systems are leading the way. These systems use machine learning algorithms to analyze each student's learning preferences, weaknesses, and progress, allowing for a more tailored and individualized approach to instruction. With AI constantly monitoring students' performance, educators can access rich data sets that inform their teaching strategies. AI algorithms can recommend appropriate resources, activities, and assessments based on predictive analysis of student performance, optimizing the learning journey and ensuring that students are appropriately challenged (Atalla *et al.*, 2023).

AI can quickly identify when a student is struggling and provide additional resources while adjusting the material to suit their difficulty level, improving their understanding. Conversely, if a student is advancing rapidly, AI can dynamically adjust the course pace to align with their learning speed and present more challenging tasks to keep them engaged. AI can also design customized learning journeys that cater to individual learner interests, preferences, and needs (Gray Group International, 2023).

Educators can use real-time progress monitoring and assessment to modify their pedagogical approaches and provide individualized instruction tailored to each student's needs. By utilizing the insights provided by AI-powered systems, educators can gain a deeper understanding of each student's learning profile, allowing them to provide targeted support and guidance specific to their unique requirements.

AI-powered systems can revolutionize education by providing a more personalized and individualized approach to instruction (Rayhan *et al.*, 2023; Seo *et al.*, 2021). By utilizing machine learning algorithms, educators can better understand each student's learning profile, enabling them to provide targeted support and guidance tailored to their unique needs and requirements.

Somasundaram *et al.* (2020) explained that designing a curriculum involves defining the outcomes a program aims to achieve and developing a course of study that aligns with those outcomes. This process encompasses the selection of core courses and the identification of supplementary ones that can enhance the learning experience. Integrating Artificial Intelligence (AI) technology is valuable in streamlining this process. By leveraging AI-powered platforms, educators can efficiently analyze data, identify patterns, and generate insights that can inform and optimize the design of a curriculum. Additionally, AI can assist in assessing and evaluating a curriculum, providing ongoing feedback that can help educators refine and improve their approach. Creating a well-structured curriculum can be daunting, but envisioning the design process as an Artificial Neural Network can make it more manageable. This approach offers a comprehensive view of the course sequence and the essential knowledge, skills, and competencies that must be imparted to the students. Each course should be outlined by its content, prerequisites, and projected outcomes to achieve this. Defining Program Outcomes (PO) and Course Outcomes (CO) clearly and precisely is essential. Program Outcomes (PO) describe the knowledge, skills, and competencies students should acquire from the program. On the other hand, course Outcomes (CO) define each course's objectives. By mapping courses and their respective COs to the POs, we can establish the graduate's role in the program and ensure that the program is aligned with the desired learning outcomes. This approach helps to ensure that each course builds on the knowledge and skills taught in the previous course, leading to a more coherent and practical curriculum.

The system uses an incremental tree to represent a newly created curriculum, which is then transformed into a concept map. This map contains all the components, their connections, and course tags. An overall evaluation is conducted by the curriculum evaluation component that computes a final score based on the strength of connections between different parts, such as speciality areas, work roles, and knowledge skill abilities. This score determines the quality of the curriculum design. Users receive overall feedback and recommendations for improvement, which may include adding or removing speciality areas and knowledge skill abilities. Users can apply the recommendations or maintain the original course design.

The output module gathers data from the created curriculum and sends it to CloudFront for optimal performance. Additionally, the module generates a PDF file for the finalized curriculum outline. A standout feature of the system is the ability to reuse existing curricula. By entering keywords, the curriculum evaluation component retrieves the highest matching curriculum, displaying it to the user. The nearest neighbour classification algorithm compares course tags and keywords the user enters. If the user modifies the curriculum, the incremental tree and concept map are updated, and the new curriculum can be saved under a new name (Hodhod *et al.*, 2018). Intelligent decision-making systems are widely utilized to aid decision-making in specific domains, employing expert techniques. They have proven successful in various fields, including medicine, engineering, and career guidance. Typically, expert systems are implemented to address a shortage of human and time resources. Expert systems have been developed to provide academic advice to students, assist novice users in navigating new software, and aid in making informed decisions regarding alternative public transportation options in specific cities (Sayed *et al.*, 2021).

Investigate the Usage of Artificial Intelligence in Higher Education

Integrating AI into higher education requires careful attention to various aspects, including AI platforms, AI-based internet applications, and private AI networks. These components aim to enhance university infrastructure, using the internet as a training framework to streamline business databases and store data uniformly in a single language and format. AI also provides advanced teaching methods and tools for accessing and querying historical business records. To obtain valuable insights from these records, they must be stored and maintained for an extended period and analyzed through statistical methods to transform raw data into actionable knowledge. Data administration is the primary focus of the physical education augmented reality environment, where new techniques can separate, clean, and combine original data to solve business problems. The physical storage structure is calculated in AI learning education, enabling system managers or individual users to obtain data from multiple sources, modify it, and store it to support the decision-making needs of the AI education environment in higher education and benefit the entire system (Zhang *et al.*, 2021).

Artificial Intelligence (AI) has become increasingly popular in the education sector due to its ability to enhance communication between teachers and students, provide personalized support to many learners, and create a sense of community among them. However, concerns have been raised regarding accountability, agency, and surveillance in using AI in education. These issues have highlighted the importance of transparency, human involvement, and comprehensive data collection and presentation in developing and implementing AI systems in education (Akgun & Greenhow, 2022).

It is crucial to ensure that AI systems are developed with transparency, which allows educators and learners to understand how the technology operates and how it affects their learning experience. Additionally, human involvement is necessary to ensure that AI systems are aligned with the values of education and that they promote the well-being of learners. This can be achieved through the active participation of teachers, students, and other stakeholders in designing and implementing AI systems (Seo *et al.*, 2021).

Furthermore, meticulous data collection and presentation are vital for the ethical use of AI in education. AI systems must collect data from learners clearly and transparently, and the data must be presented in a way that respects learners' privacy and rights. Additionally, data collection and presentation should be used to enhance the learning experience and support the personalization of education rather than to monitor and control learners (UNESCO, 2019).

The use of AI in education has the potential to revolutionize the sector, but it must be done responsibly and ethically. Transparency, human involvement, and comprehensive data collection and presentation are essential to ensure that AI systems are aligned with the values of education and that they promote the well-being of learners. Although AI in education systems has been positively recognized for improving the quantity and quality of communication between students and teachers, providing just-in-time, personalized support for large-scale settings, and enhancing the feeling of connection, there were concerns about responsibility, agency, and surveillance issues. These findings have implications for the design of AI systems to ensure explainability, human-in-the-loop, and careful data collection and presentation.

A study conducted by Crompton and Burke (2023) discovered that AI technology is predominantly used by undergraduate students, with 72% (99 out of 138 participants) of the users falling within this category. On the other hand, graduate students' usage of AI technology was only 9% (12 out of 138 participants). These results provide a clear and descriptive picture of the demographics of AI users, indicating that undergraduate students are the primary consumers of this technology. A recent survey was conducted among college students to gauge their opinion on AI-powered platforms like ChatGPT. The survey found that 51% of students believe using such platforms is cheating. Moreover, 60 per cent of the surveyed students reported that their university or instructor needed to provide adequate guidance on the ethical use of these platforms. However, 61 per cent of students believed that AI-powered platforms are the future of education. As the use of AI-powered platforms continues to grow, universities must establish clear policies to help students understand when it is appropriate to use them.

OpenAI, the company behind ChatGPT, cautions against penalizing students for using AI without understanding the expectations. Instead, OpenAI is working to provide students with the option to export their ChatGPT usage so they can share it with their professors. OpenAI also recommends that professors inform students if they use ChatGPT to create lessons. Conversations between students and lecturers are crucial in establishing guidelines for when AI can be used. Teachers also need to work with students to help them understand when they can use ChatGPT and when they should avoid it. AI has the potential to spread misinformation and pose real risks to humanity. The integration of chatbots in educational settings raises ethical concerns as they have the potential to supplant human interaction and expertise. This is especially crucial in counselling and mental health fields, where students require emotional support from trained professionals. The deployment of chatbots in such scenarios could lead to students depending on them as a substitute for human assistance. Nonetheless, it is noteworthy that while college students acknowledge the usefulness of chatbots in specific situations, they do not perceive them as a substitute for the guidance and care offered by human professionals (Kooli, 2023). Therefore, AI research and development must make advanced systems more accurate, secure, interpretable, transparent, robust, aligned, trustworthy, and loyal (Teal, 2023). In July of 2023, the White House made a groundbreaking announcement regarding using Artificial Intelligence (AI) to address society's most pressing challenges. The statement revealed that seven leading AI developers, including OpenAI, Google, and Meta, had voluntarily committed to investing in algorithms that would tackle social issues. This commitment was significant because it showed that these developers understood the potential power of AI and its ability to solve real-world problems. The generative AI industry must also be aware of data collection, risk assessment and mitigation, and internal accountability. Therefore, developers need to prioritize transparency and accountability to ensure that the use of AI remains ethical and beneficial to society (Chin, 2023).

Provides AI Security and Ethics Guidelines

The rapid advancements in artificial intelligence (AI) have sparked a productive dialogue about its integration into higher education. As AI continues to evolve, it is becoming increasingly clear that its potential benefits in the education sector are immense. AI technology can significantly enhance decision-making processes, lead to more efficient and effective outcomes, and help universities and colleges meet the needs of their students and faculty more effectively. However, there are also legitimate concerns about the security, privacy, and ethical considerations surrounding the use of AI in higher education. These risks must be navigated with proper guidance and protocols to ensure that AI is used responsibly and ethically. When using AI tools or services, the University should have a contract or agreement outlining the AI system's expectations, responsibilities, and limitations.

Furthermore, institutional IT systems and services should not rely solely on AI-generated code without human review. Human oversight and intervention are necessary to ensure that AI systems are used in a way that is consistent with the University's values and mission. Despite these challenges, the potential benefits of AI in higher education are significant. AI can help universities and colleges gain new insights into student behaviour and learning patterns, personalize learning experiences for individual students, and optimize administrative processes. If implemented responsibly, AI can lead to growth and innovation in higher education, helping institutions to remain competitive and provide the best possible education to their students. Weighing both AI's positive and negative impacts before deciding to implement it in higher education is crucial. With careful consideration, proper guidance, and protocols in place, the potential for growth and innovation is limitless (Zhao & Gómez Fariñas, 2023).

AI Risk Management Frameworks

The National Institute of Standards and Technology (NIST) (2023) has recently published AI Risk Management Framework intended to help organizations manage the risks associated with artificial intelligence (AI) deployment. The Framework provides a structured approach to identifying and mitigating AI risks, ensuring that AI systems are designed and implemented safely, securely, and trustworthy. The Framework is based on risk management principles and is designed to be scalable and flexible, enabling organizations of all sizes to use it. By adopting this Framework, organizations can ensure that the benefits of AI are maximized while minimizing the risks associated with its deployment. The Framework outlines the key attributes of trustworthy AI, which include:

- **Valid and Reliable:** Trustworthy AI should generate accurate results within expected timeframes. Independent auditors or third-party experts must validate the accuracy of the results to ensure that the results are reliable.

- **Safe:** Trustworthy AI should produce results that conform to safety expectations for the environment in which it is used. For example, AI should have safe and reliable diagnoses and treatment recommendations in healthcare. In transportation, AI should ensure safe and reliable navigation and control of vehicles.

- **Fair and Bias is Managed:** Bias can manifest in many ways, including data bias, algorithmic bias, and outcome bias. Standards and expectations for bias minimization should be defined before using AI to ensure fairness. Bias management should be an ongoing process, with regular monitoring and evaluation to ensure that the AI system is not perpetuating or reinforcing existing biases.

- **Secure and Resilient:** Security should be judged according to the standard confidentiality, integrity, and availability triad. The resilience of AI is the degree to which it can withstand and recover from attack. This includes protection against cyber-attacks, data breaches, and other malicious activities.

- **Transparent and Accountable:** Transparency refers to the ability to understand information about the AI system and when working with AI-generated information. Accountability is the shared responsibility of the creators/vendors of the AI as well as those who have chosen to implement it for a particular purpose. AI systems should be designed to be transparent and accountable, with clear documentation and audit trails that explain how the system works and how decisions are made.

- **Explainable and Interpretable:** These terms relate to the ability to explain how an output was generated and how to understand the meaning of the output. This is particularly important in healthcare, where AI systems may develop complex diagnoses and treatment recommendations. NIST provides examples related to rental applications and medical diagnosis in NISTIR 8367 Psychological Foundations of Explainability and Interpretability in Artificial Intelligence.

- **Privacy-enhanced:** This refers to privacy from a legal and ethical standpoint and may overlap with previously listed attributes. AI systems should be designed to ensure that personal data is protected and that privacy regulations and standards are followed. In conclusion, the AI Risk Management Framework is a comprehensive guide for organizations looking to ensure that AI is used, trustworthy and responsible. By following the guidelines outlined in the Framework, organizations can minimize the risks associated with AI and maximize its benefits.

AI systems are undoubtedly more efficient than humans when it comes to processing large amounts of data quickly. However, they can run into issues when dealing with complex situations requiring critical thinking and adapting to various contexts. This is where humans excel - they possess the cognitive and analytical skills to navigate complex problems quickly. To promote effective and meaningful learning for students, it is essential to integrate humans into the decision-making process of AI systems through the human-in-the-loop approach. This approach ensures that students feel in control of their online learning experience and can actively engage with the material (Seo *et al.*, 2021).

Achieving a balance between artificial and human intelligence is crucial for promoting student agency. By working together, AI and humans can leverage their strengths to create a more effective and engaging learning environment for students. Research in this area is essential to ensure that AI and human intelligence integration remains ethical, efficient, and effective.

CONCLUSION

Although several literature reviews have delved into the ethical implications of Artificial Intelligence (AI), there currently needs to be a consensus on the most suitable ethical theory to apply. This highlights the importance of considering the ethical dilemmas associated with AI. However, effectively and appropriately addressing these challenges may prove daunting due to the interdisciplinary nature of AI and the abstract nature of ethical principles. Additionally, the involvement of various stakeholders in educational discourse further complicates the application of ethical principles in a formal or deductive manner. As educators and leaders, it is crucial that we fully comprehend the impact of AI systems and digital data in education. By adopting the appropriate approach, we can unlock new opportunities to enhance teaching, learning, and assessment practices. However, it is equally imperative that we acknowledge potential obstacles and acquire new digital competencies to guarantee the successful implementation of these systems. Equipped with the right knowledge and skills, we can fully exploit the advantages of AI in education.

REFERENCES

AECC Study Abroad Consultants. (2023, June 30). *10 Best AI Tools for Students: A Comprehensive Guide*. Aecc INDONESIA. https://www.aeccglobal.co.id/blog/best-ai-tools-for-students

Ahmad, S. F., Han, H., Alam, M. M., Rehmat, M. K., Irshad, M., Arraño-Muñoz, M., & Ariza-Montes, A. (2023). Impact of artificial intelligence on human loss in decision making, laziness and safety in education. *Humanities & Social Sciences Communications*, *10*(1), 1. doi:10.105741599-023-01787-8 PMID:37325188

Akgun, S., & Greenhow, C. (2022). Artificial intelligence in education: Addressing ethical challenges in K-12 settings. *AI and Ethics*, *2*(3), 431–440. doi:10.100743681-021-00096-7 PMID:34790956

Alahi, M. E. E., Sukkuea, A., Tina, F. W., Nag, A., Kurdthongmee, W., Suwannarat, K., & Mukhopadhyay, S. C. (2023). Integration of IoT-Enabled Technologies and Artificial Intelligence (AI) for Smart City Scenario: Recent Advancements and Future Trends. *Sensors (Basel)*, *23*(11), 11. doi:10.339023115206 PMID:37299934

Atalla, S., Daradkeh, M., Gawanmeh, A., Khalil, H., Mansoor, W., Miniaoui, S., & Himeur, Y. (2023). An Intelligent Recommendation System for Automating Academic Advising Based on Curriculum Analysis and Performance Modeling. *Mathematics*, *11*(5), 5. doi:10.3390/math11051098

Balla, E. (2023). *Automated Grading Systems: How AI is Revolutionizing Exam Evaluation - DataScienceCentral.com*. Data Science Central. https://www.datasciencecentral.com/automated-grading-systems-how-ai-is-revolutionizing-exam-evaluation/

Chan, C. K. Y. (2023). A comprehensive AI policy education framework for university teaching and learning. *International Journal of Educational Technology in Higher Education*, *20*(1), 38. doi:10.118641239-023-00408-3

Chin, C. (2023). *Navigating the Risks of Artificial Intelligence on the Digital News Landscape*. CSIS. https://www.csis.org/analysis/navigating-risks-artificial-intelligence-digital-news-landscape

Coman, C., Țîru, L. G., Meseșan-Schmitz, L., Stanciu, C., & Bularca, M. C. (2020). Online Teaching and Learning in Higher Education during the Coronavirus Pandemic: Students' Perspective. *Sustainability (Basel)*, *12*(24), 24. doi:10.3390u122410367

Crompton, H., & Burke, D. (2023). Artificial intelligence in higher education: The state of the field. *International Journal of Educational Technology in Higher Education*, *20*(1), 22. doi:10.118641239-023-00392-8

Davenport, T., & Kalakota, R. (2019). The potential for artificial intelligence in healthcare. *Future Healthcare Journal*, *6*(2), 94–98. doi:10.7861/futurehosp.6-2-94 PMID:31363513

Derrow, P. (2022). *The Ethics of Algorithms*. Rutgers. https://www.rutgers.edu/magazine/winter-2022/ethics-algorithms

Dwivedi, Y. K., Kshetri, N., Hughes, L., Slade, E. L., Jeyaraj, A., Kar, A. K., Baabdullah, A. M., Koohang, A., Raghavan, V., Ahuja, M., Albanna, H., Albashrawi, M. A., Al-Busaidi, A. S., Balakrishnan, J., Barlette, Y., Basu, S., Bose, I., Brooks, L., Buhalis, D., & Wright, R. (2023). Opinion Paper: "So what if ChatGPT wrote it?" Multidisciplinary perspectives on opportunities, challenges and implications of generative conversational AI for research, practice and policy. *International Journal of Information Management*, *71*, 102642. doi:10.1016/j.ijinfomgt.2023.102642

European Commission. (2022). *Ethical guidelines on the use of artificial intelligence and data in teaching and learning for educators European Education Area*. EC. https://education.ec.europa.eu/news/ethical-guidelines-on-the-use-of-artificial-intelligence-and-data-in-teaching-and-learning-for-educators

Gray Group International. (2023). *Revolutionizing Personalized Learning: How Is AI Changing Education?* GGI. https://www.graygroupintl.com/blog/how-is-ai-changing-education

Gupta, V. (2022). *AI ethics: 5 key pillars*. The Enterprisers Project. https://enterprisersproject.com/article/2022/11/ai-ethics-5-key-pillars

Hodhod, R., Wang, S., & Khan, S. (2018). Cybersecurity Curriculum Development Using AI and Decision Support Expert System. *International Journal of Computer Theory and Engineering*, *10*(4), 111–115. doi:10.7763/IJCTE.2018.V10.1209

Holmes, W., Porayska-Pomsta, K., Holstein, K., Sutherland, E., Baker, T., Shum, S. B., Santos, O. C., Rodrigo, M. T., Cukurova, M., Bittencourt, I. I., & Koedinger, K. R. (2022). Ethics of AI in Education: Towards a Community-Wide Framework. *International Journal of Artificial Intelligence in Education*, *32*(3), 504–526. doi:10.100740593-021-00239-1

Huang, J., Saleh, S., & Liu, Y. (2021). A Review on Artificial Intelligence in Education. *Academic Journal of Interdisciplinary Studies*, *10*(3), 206. doi:10.36941/ajis-2021-0077

Jarrahi, M. H., Askay, D., Eshraghi, A., & Smith, P. (2023). Artificial intelligence and knowledge management: A partnership between human and AI. *Business Horizons*, *66*(1), 87–99. doi:10.1016/j.bushor.2022.03.002

JavaTPoint. (2021). *Artificial Intelligence in Education*. Javatpoint. https://www.javatpoint.com/artificial-intelligence-in-education

Jiao, P., Ouyang, F., Zhang, Q., & Alavi, A. H. (2022). Artificial intelligence-enabled prediction model of student academic performance in online engineering education. *Artificial Intelligence Review*, *55*(8), 6321–6344. doi:10.100710462-022-10155-y

Klimova, B., Pikhart, M., & Kacetl, J. (2023). Ethical issues of the use of AI-driven mobile apps for education. *Frontiers in Public Health*, *10*, 1118116. https://www.frontiersin.org/articles/10.3389/fpubh.2022.1118116. doi:10.3389/fpubh.2022.1118116 PMID:36711343

Kooli, C. (2023). Chatbots in Education and Research: A Critical Examination of Ethical Implications and Solutions. *Sustainability (Basel)*, *15*(7), 7. doi:10.3390u15075614

Krishnan, M. (2020). Against Interpretability: A Critical Examination of the Interpretability Problem in Machine Learning. *Philosophy & Technology*, *33*(3), 487–502. doi:10.100713347-019-00372-9

Li, J., Li, J., Yang, Y., & Ren, Z. (2021). Design of Higher Education System Based on Artificial Intelligence Technology. *Discrete Dynamics in Nature and Society*, *2021*, 1–11. doi:10.1155/2021/3303160

Mousavi, A., Schmidt, M., Squires, V., & Wilson, K. (2021). Assessing the Effectiveness of Student Advice Recommender Agent (SARA): The Case of Automated Personalized Feedback. *International Journal of Artificial Intelligence in Education*, *31*(3), 603–621. doi:10.100740593-020-00210-6

National Institute of Standards and Technology. (2023). *Artificial Intelligence Risk Management Framework (AI RMF 1.0)*. NIST. https://www.nist.gov/itl/ai-risk-management-framework

Nguyen, A., Ngo, H., Hong, Y., Dang, B., & Nguyen, B.-P. (2022). Ethical principles for artificial intelligence in education. *Education and Information Technologies*, *28*(4), 4221–4241. doi:10.100710639-022-11316-w PMID:36254344

Ocumpaugh, J., Baker, R., Gowda, S., Heffernan, N., & Heffernan, C. (2014). Population validity for educational data mining models: A case study in affect detection. *British Journal of Educational Technology*, *45*(3), 87–501. doi:10.1111/bjet.12156

Ouatik, F., Raoufi, M., Ouatik, F., & Skouri, M. (2021). E-Learning & decision making system for automate students assessment using remote laboratory and machine learning. *Journal of E-Learning and Knowledge Society*, *17*(1), 90–100. doi:10.20368/1971-8829/1135285

Owan, V., Abang, K., Idika, D., & Bassey, B. (2023). Exploring the potential of artificial intelligence tools in educational measurement and assessment. *Eurasia Journal of Mathematics, Science and Technology Education*, *19*(8), em2307. doi:10.29333/ejmste/13428

Pastor-Escuredo, D., Treleaven, P., & Vinuesa, R. (2022). An Ethical Framework for Artificial Intelligence and Sustainable Cities. *AI*, *3*(4), 961–974. doi:10.3390/ai3040057

Qian, Y., Li, C.-X., Zou, X.-G., Feng, X.-B., Xiao, M.-H., & Ding, Y.-Q. (2022). Research on predicting learning achievement in a flipped classroom based on MOOCs by big data analysis. *Computer Applications in Engineering Education*, *30*(1), 222–234. doi:10.1002/cae.22452

RayhanA.RayhanR.RayhanS. (2023*). Revolutionizing Education: The Power of Artificial Intelligence (AI)*. doi:10.13140/RG.2.2.10716.97924

Ryan, M., & Stahl, B. C. (2021). Artificial intelligence ethics guidelines for developers and users: Clarifying their content and normative implications. *Journal of Information. Communication and Ethics in Society, 19*(1), 61–86. doi:10.1108/JICES-12-2019-0138

Sarker, I. H. (2022). AI-Based Modeling: Techniques, Applications and Research Issues Towards Automation, Intelligent and Smart Systems. *SN Computer Science, 3*(2), 158. doi:10.100742979-022-01043-x PMID:35194580

Sayed, B. (2021). Application of expert systems or decision-making systems in the field of education. *Journal of Contemporary Issues in Business and Government, 27*(3), 2021. doi:10.47750/cibg.2021.27.03.159

Seo, K., Tang, J., Roll, I., Fels, S., & Yoon, D. (2021). The impact of artificial intelligence on learner–instructor interaction in online learning. *International Journal of Educational Technology in Higher Education, 18*(1), 54. doi:10.118641239-021-00292-9 PMID:34778540

Somasundaram, M., Latha, P., & Pandian, S. A. S. (2020). Curriculum Design Using Artificial Intelligence (AI) Back Propagation Method. *Procedia Computer Science, 172*, 134–138. doi:10.1016/j.procs.2020.05.020

Teal, M. (2023). *The Ethics of College Students Using ChatGPT - Ethics and Policy*. https://ethicspolicy.unc.edu/news/2023/04/17/the-ethics-of-college-students-using-chatgpt/

United Nations Educational, Scientific and Cultural Organization (UNESCO). (2019). *Artificial intelligence in education: Challenges and opportunities for sustainable development*. UNESCO. https://unesdoc.unesco.org/ark:/48223/pf0000366994

Verma, S., & Rubin, J. (2018). *Fairness definitions explained*. Proceedings of the International Workshop on Software Fairness - FairWare '18, 1–7. 10.1145/3194770.3194776

Xu, Y., Liu, X., Cao, X., Huang, C., Liu, E., Qian, S., Liu, X., Wu, Y., Dong, F., Qiu, C.-W., Qiu, J., Hua, K., Su, W., Wu, J., Xu, H., Han, Y., Fu, C., Yin, Z., Liu, M., & Zhang, J. (2021). Artificial intelligence: A powerful paradigm for scientific research. *Innovation (Cambridge (Mass.)), 2*(4), 100179. doi:10.1016/j.xinn.2021.100179 PMID:34877560

Yang, Y. (2021). Design and Implementation of Intelligent Learning System Based on Big Data and Artificial Intelligence. *Frontiers in Psychology, 12*, 726978. doi:10.3389/fpsyg.2021.726978 PMID:34858265

Zawacki-Richter, O., Marín, V. I., Bond, M., & Gouverneur, F. (2019). Systematic review of research on artificial intelligence applications in higher education – where are the educators? *International Journal of Educational Technology in Higher Education, 16*(1), 39. doi:10.118641239-019-0171-0

Zhang, Y., Qin, G., Cheng, L., Marimuthu, K., & Kumar, B. S. (2021). Interactive Smart Educational System Using AI for Students in the Higher Education Platform. *J. of Mult.-. Valued Logic & Soft Computing, 36*(1–3), 89–98.

Zhao, J., & Gómez Fariñas, B. (2023). Artificial Intelligence and Sustainable Decisions. *European Business Organization Law Review, 24*(1), 1–39. doi:10.100740804-022-00262-2

Chapter 12
AI–Driven Decision–Making and Optimization in Modern Agriculture Sectors

D. Joel Jebadurai
https://orcid.org/0000-0002-6947-8497
St. Joseph's College of Engineering, Chennai, India

Mary V. V. Sheela
Aarupadai Veedu Institute of Technology, Vinayaka Mission's Research Foundation, India

L. Rajeshkumar
https://orcid.org/0009-0007-8513-206X
St.Joseph's College of Engineering, India

M. Soundarya
https://orcid.org/0000-0001-7018-7972
Sathyabama Institute of Science and Technology, India

Rathi Meena
Dr. Umayal Ramanathan College for Women, India

Thirupathi Manickam
https://orcid.org/0000-0001-7976-6073
Christ University, India

Arul Vethamanikam G. Hudson
Ayya Nadar Janaki Ammal College, India

K. Dheenadhayalan
Mepco Schlenk Engineering College, India

M. Manikandan
SRM University, India

ABSTRACT

AI-driven decision-making tools have emerged as a novel technology poised to replace traditional agricultural practices. In this chapter, AI's pivotal role in steering the agricultural sector towards sustainability is highlighted, primarily through the utilization of AI techniques such as robotics, deep learning, the internet of things, image processing, and more. This chapter offers insights into the application of AI techniques in various functional areas of agriculture, including weed management, crop management, and soil management. Additionally, it underlines both the challenges and advantages presented by AI-driven applications in agriculture. In conclusion, the potential of AI in agriculture is vast, but it faces various impediments that, when properly identified and addressed, can expand its scope. This chapter serves as a valuable resource for government authorities, policymakers, and scientists seeking to explore the untapped potential of AI's significance in agriculture.

DOI: 10.4018/979-8-3693-0639-0.ch012

INTRODUCTION

Digital technologies have breathed new life into traditional sectors through innovative updates (Bhardwaj et al., 2021). This digital innovation not only enhances productivity but also minimizes adverse environmental impacts (Bacco et al., 2019). Digitalization encompasses a wide array of phenomena and technologies, including big data, the Internet of Things (IoT), augmented reality, robotics, sensors, 3D printing, system integration, ubiquitous connectivity, artificial intelligence, machine learning, digital twins, and blockchain, among others (Tilson et al., 2010). One of the swiftly advancing technologies making its mark in agriculture is Artificial Intelligence (AI). Through automation, predictive analysis, robotics, and optimization techniques, digital technology, especially AI, has breathed fresh vitality into the agriculture sector. Agriculture has become more cost-effective by embracing AI-associated tools. The journey of AI in agriculture began with its introduction in the 1960s to 1990s when it worked with limited data for decision-making. Then, from 2000 to 2010, precision agriculture emerged, solving agricultural issues such as diseases in the crops, soil fertility, and so on through AI-based Global Positioning System (GPS) and machine learning techniques. Subsequently, in the 2010s, satellites and drones were employed in agriculture to predict and address various agricultural challenges such as irrigation, pesticide spraying, weed identification, and so on by using predictive analysis. Presently, AI tools such as robotics, automation, big data, predictive analytics, and the Internet of Things (IoT) are applied in agriculture to effectively tackle complex problems such as harvesting, climate risks, and diseases in crops (Anyoha, 2017).

AI is of utmost importance in automating and optimizing farming operations. For instance, robots equipped with computer vision systems can perform tasks like selective harvesting or weed control with high precision and efficiency. AI-powered systems can monitor livestock health and behavior, detect diseases, and provide early warnings to farmers, leading to improved animal welfare. AI's integration into agriculture can transform the industry, making it more sustainable, productive, and resilient. By enabling farmers to make informed decisions, optimize resource allocation, and reduce environmental impact, AI can contribute to global food security and address the challenges faced by the agricultural sector in the 21st century.

With a predicted increase of 25.5% Compound Annual Growth Rate (CAGR) between 2020 and 2026, it is anticipated that the agriculture sector will see significant investments in AI in the upcoming years (marketsandmarkets.com 2021). AI has the potential to alter how agribusinesses are organized, compete, and participate in the food chain (Mhlanga, 2021). AI will also be able to address some of the most prominent societal issues, like workforce shortages and the urgent need to increase output while reducing damaging environmental emissions. This chapter is structured into five parts. The initial section covers the objectives and methodology. The second part delves into AI techniques applied in agriculture. The third part explores AI techniques as they relate to specific functional aspects of agriculture. The fourth part addresses both the advantages and hurdles associated with AI in this field. Lastly, the fifth part encompasses case studies, success stories, future trends, and concluding remarks regarding the role of AI in agriculture.

This chapter comes out with the following objectives. They are.

1. The first objectives of this study are to understand AI tools in agriculture such as Deep learning, Robots, Internet of Things (IoT), Image Processing, Artificial Neural Networks (ANN), Wireless Sensor Networks, Machine Learning (ML) Unmanned Aerial Vehicle/ Drones

2.   The second objective covered the AI applications in various functional areas of agriculture such as soil management, weed control, pest control, crop diseases management, crop management, pesticide spraying management, harvesting, weather forecasting, irrigation management, warehousing, agriculture supply chain management and livestock management presented.

3.   Benefits, challenges, case studies, and success stories of AI in agriculture are presented in the third objective.

METHODOLOGY

This book chapter is purely based on secondary data from published articles, case studies, government reports, etc. Secondary data was covered with a focus on AI techniques such as deep learning, robotics, Internet of Things (IoT), Image Processing, Artificial Neural Networks (ANN), Wireless Sensor Networks, Machine Learning (ML) Unmanned Aerial Vehicle/ Drones. Also, AI applied functional areas such as soil management, weed control, pest control, crop disease management, crop management, pesticide spraying management, harvesting, weather forecasting, irrigation management, warehousing, and agriculture supply chain management. Finally, the benefits and challenges of AI in agriculture are presented in addition to case studies and success stories.

AI-DRIVEN DECISION-MAKING TOOLS IN AGRICULTURE

Deep Learning

Deep learning, as an AI-based machine learning technology, finds application in predicting soil quality and recommending suitable crops for cultivation in specific soil types. Deep learning in agriculture is the use of cutting-edge machine learning methods, particularly deep neural networks, for a variety of applications in the agricultural industry. With the use of this technology, decision-making, and automation can be improved by processing and analyzing agricultural data using artificial neural networks with several layers. Deep learning is used in agriculture for a variety of tasks, including precision farming, disease diagnosis, weed identification, and animal monitoring (Zhu *et.al.* 2018). Through the provision of insights, optimization, and enhanced efficiency in different agricultural processes, it has the potential to transform farming operations.

Robots

Agricultural robots are machines specifically engineered for application in the field of agriculture, incorporating advanced AI techniques to autonomously make decisions. They are deployed in complex agricultural settings (Wakchaure *et.al.2023*). Here are various categories of robots utilized in agricultural contexts.

Field Robots

Field robots are often autonomous, mechatronic, mobile, decision-making machines that may perform a variety of semi-automated or fully automatic tasks related to crop production.

a. Tillage robots
b. Seeding robots
c. Crop protection robots
d. Field information collecting robots
e. Crop harvesting robots

Fruit and Vegetable Robots

These robots are mainly used for spraying, collecting, and harvesting fruits.

a. Transplanting robots
b. Fruit and Vegetable Patrolling Robots
c. Pesticide spraying robots
d. Gardening robots
e. Fruit and vegetable-picking robots

Animal Husbandry Robots

These robots are mainly used for taking care of the animal getting the yield from them. They are further classified into.

a. Breeding robots
b. Animal feeding robots
c. Milking robots
d. Egg-collecting robots

Internet of Things (IoT)

The Internet of Things (IoT) in agriculture pertains to the integration of interconnected devices, sensors, and systems within the agricultural sector to collect, transmit, and analyze data. This network of devices enables real-time monitoring, data-driven decision-making, and automation, enhancing various aspects of farming such as irrigation, precision farming, and weather monitoring. IoT is a sensor-based AI technology used for irrigating crops according to their water requirements (Farooq *et.al.*2019). By using this technology, farmers can automate the process of irrigation in agriculture.

Image Processing

Image processing in AI-driven agriculture involves the use of artificial intelligence and computer vision techniques to analyze images and visual data for various applications in the agricultural sector such as detecting diseases, yield prediction, pest and weed detection, grading, and classifying fruits and vegetables based on the pictures collected by the technology (Farhood *et.al* 2022).

Artificial Neural Networks

Neural networks, alternatively referred to as artificial neural networks (ANNs) or Simulated Neural Networks (SNNs), represent a subset of machine learning techniques that form the foundation of deep learning algorithms. These networks draw their name and structural inspiration from the human brain, emulating the intercommunication of biological neurons (Kujawa & Niedbała 2021). ANN is an AI-based technology that was used in agriculture to predict the yield of crops.

Wireless Sensor Networks (WSN)

WSN is an AI technology used to monitor the progress of the crops and suggest measures to improve the quality of the crops.

Machine Learning

Chatbot

The conversational virtual assistants that automate conversations with users are known as chatbots. With the use of machine learning and artificial intelligence-powered chatbots, we can now interpret natural language and communicate with users more individually (Jagtap *et.al* 2022). Agriculture has made use of this facility by supporting the farmers in receiving answers to their unanswered queries, offering them guidance, and giving them other recommendations as well.

Unmanned Aerial Vehicles (UAV)/Drones

Unmanned Aerial Vehicles, or UAVs, are aircraft that are operated remotely and equipped with Global Positioning System (GPS) technology, as well as specialized thermal and multispectral sensors. These sensors allow the UAVs to capture high-resolution images with precise geographic referencing, all while avoiding any disruptions caused by cloud cover. Unmanned Aerial Vehicles are known as drones. Due to its adaptability, drone technology has drawn the most interest and is predicted to have a significant future in the agricultural industry. Drones assist farmers in overcoming a range of additional challenges and gaining various advantages from precision agriculture, in addition to enhancing overall performance. The worldwide demand for agricultural drones is anticipated to reach $5.7 billion by 2025, rising at a 35.9 percent CAGR (Rehna & Inamdar 2022). They fill the gap left by human error and inefficiency in conventional farming operations. Utilizing drone technology aims to do away with all doubt and speculation in favor of precise and reliable data.

Table 1. Types of drones and their applications

S.No	Types of UAV/ Drones	Applications	Uses
1	Planting drones	Drones can launch seed-containing nutrient pods into the soil at optimal depths, contributing to cost and labor savings when it comes to large-scale tree-planting initiatives.	1. Reduce labour cost 2. High productivity 3. Seed protection (birds and rats, insects) 4. Accuracy of planting the seed (distance, depth)
2	Irrigation drones	Irrigation drones are applied to irrigate the water in scarce and desert/uncovered areas.	1, Irrigation scheduling 2. Identify the water deficiencies 3. Estimate crop water requirements 4. Avoids the wastage of water.
3	Soil analysis drones	Soil analysis drones using Augmented Reality and K-means clustering to understand the soil attributes such as Soil nutrition, Soil texture, Soil conditions, Soil moisture, and Soil temperature and communicate with the farmers for decision making.	1. Soil quality 2. Soil fertility 3. Soil conditions
4	Crop monitoring drones	Deep learning techniques were used to take a photo to understand the crop attributes. a. Crop scouting b. Crop health monitoring	1. Crop growth levels 2. Crop disease identification at the correct time 3. Assessments of crop nutritional requirements
5	Crop spraying drones	Drones possess the ability to survey the terrain and apply precise quantities of liquids. They achieve this by adjusting their distance from the ground and administering the liquid in real-time, ensuring uniform distribution. The application areas a. Weed detection b. Disease classification	1. Reduce labour cost 2. Pesticide and insect control 3. Work efficiency 4. Cover the uncovered areas
6	Health assessment drones	Health	1. Understand the crop health level.

AI APPLICATION AREAS IN AGRICULTURE

Soil Management

In traditional farming, farmers take measures to protect the various soil components, such as soil nutrition, moisture, texture, fertility, soil temperature, and so forth, by adding organic manure, such as cow dung, chicken manure, daily household wastes, and tree leaves. Due to the high level of human consumption and population explosion later in the 20th century, farmers turned to chemical-based insecticides and fertilizers to boost productivity (Aktar et.al.,). Consequently, activities such as soil acidification, excessive use of fertilizers and so on cause soils to gradually become unproductive. Soil quality and nutrition in the food were interrelated According to The Food and Agriculture Organization of the United Nations (FAO) (https://www.fao.org/soils-portal) over the last seventy years, the vitamins and nutrition in the food were drastically reduced. So, to rejuvenate soil fertility and its productivity, standard AI technologies such as Support Vector Machine (SVM), Decision Tree (DT), and Neural Network (NN) based models were used to develop sustainable soil management practices in modern agriculture. They are.

Table 2. AI applications areas in soil management of agriculture

Soil management of agriculture	AI techniques
Soil nutrition	ANN
Soil temperature	ANN
Soil moisture	ANN
Soil texture	ANN

a. Support Vector Machine (SVM)- It is an algorithm of machine learning models that predict the soil texture and its conditions for crop yield (Shi et.al 2012).
b. Decision Tree (DT)– A decision tree is an AI tool that takes qualitative data and converts it into quantitative data to predict soil quality and crop productivity in various aspects. (kalichkin 2021)
c. Artificial Neural Network (ANN)- It is a type of AI tool that provides a prediction about the soil quality for crop growth.

Weed Control

Biological hazards, including bacteria, viruses, weeds, fungi, and insects, can have a substantial impact on both the quantity and quality of crop production. Among these hazards, weeds stand out as a particularly significant issue, leading to substantial global yield losses. Weeds compete for vital resources such as light, water, space, and nutrients, resulting in a well-documented adverse effect on crop yields. When weeds go undetected and unmanaged, all aspects of a crop's nutrition are adversely affected (Gerhards *et.al* 2022). In the past, farmers relied on conventional methods to enhance agricultural productivity, but these approaches often fell short of effectively identifying and controlling weeds. To assist farmers, artificial intelligence (AI) technology has been harnessed in agriculture.

AI technologies such as Unmanned Aerial Vehicles (UAV), Digital Image Analysis (DIA), ANN, Optimization using Invasive Weed Optimization (IVO), Mechanical control of Weeds, Robotics, Sensor Machine Learning, Saloma expert system for evaluation prediction and weed management, Support Vector Machine (SVM), Learning Vector Quantization (LVQ) were used to control the weed among the crops.

Pest Control

According to FAO estimates in 2021, pests cause up to 40% of the world's crop yield to be lost each year. About $220 billion is lost annually to plant diseases and at least $70 billion to exotic insects in the global economy (https://www.fao.org/). Farmers have used a variety of insecticides extensively to improve the quality and storage life of crops. But over time, reckless usage of these pesticides led to environmental degradation, the development of potentially fatal diseases like cancer, severe respiratory and genetic conditions, and fetal demise. Sophisticated technical solutions are required in agriculture to identify plant pests early and prevent unintended herbicide consumption (Khan, 2022). For that, AI was adapted to pest control in agriculture. AI techniques such as deep learning, machine learning, drones, and thermal imaging technology were developing the algorithm to identify the pest in the initial stages and control it. AI techniques played the role of detection, classification, and recovery of plants from

Table 3. AI techniques in weed control

AI Techniques	Applications
Artificial Neural Network	Weed control
Robotics	Weed detection, weed control, weed management
Deep learning	Weed detection
Unmanned Aerial Vehicles (UAV)	It is an algorithm-based AI tool designed with the composition of cameras, sensors, and GPS technologies to identify, classify, and remove weeds.
Digital Image Analysis (DIA)	It includes image capturing, image processing, image filtering, and image classifications. It is used for the detection and separation of weeds
Optimization using Invasive Weed Optimization (IVO), ANN	Suggest a way to reduce the weeds
Mechanical control of Weeds, Robotics, Sensor Machine Learning,	Removal of resistant weeds
Saloma expert system for evaluation prediction and weed management	Prediction on the growth of weeds
Support Vector Machine (SVM),	Detects the stress of the crops
Learning Vector Quantization (LVQ).	It increases the weed recognition rate and reduces the processing time.

Table 4. AI techniques in pest control

AI Techniques	Applications
Unmanned Aerial Vehicles (UAV)	It is an algorithm-based AI tool designed with the composition of cameras, sensors, and GPS technologies to identify, classify, and remove weeds.
Artificial Neural Network (ANN)	Pest locator
Support Vector Machines (SVM)	Pest abolition
k-nearest neighbors (KNN)	Pest control
Naïve Bayes (NB) with a proposed CNN model	Pest identification
Satellite imagination linked to smartphones	Pest attack

diseases. With the aid of AI technology, timely treatment of pest attacks has a significant positive impact on the output of the crops.

Crop Disease Management

Crop diseases exert a range of detrimental effects on farmers, significantly compromising crop productivity. These diseases not only affect the quantity but also the quality of yields. In India, the combined impact of pathogens and pests results in a staggering 35% loss of field crops, translating into substantial financial losses for farmers (Dubey *et.al* 2019). Oftentimes, due to their lack of awareness and education, farmers fail to diagnose these diseases at an early stage, leading to the widespread proliferation of infections and the eventual loss of the entire harvest. Consequently, the application of AI technologies has been embraced to detect and diagnose diseases, ultimately enhancing crop productivity.

Table 5. AI applications in crop disease management

AI Techniques	Applications
Computer Vision System (CVS), Genetic Algorithm, ANN	It offers a multi-task to do remedial measures
Rule-Based Expert, Database	It identifies an area of the diseases for the crops
Fuzzy Logic (FL), Web GIS	Track the infected areas of crops
FL Web-Based, Web-Based Intelligent Disease Diagnosis System (WIDDS)	It suggests the remedial measures for crop diseases
FL & TTS converter	It is used for rapidly solving the pathological problems of plants
Expert system rule-base disease detection	It provides a preventive measure to diagnose the symptoms of plant diseases.
Fuzzy Xpest	High accuracy in forecasting the diseases of the crops
Web-Based Expert system	Gives an alternative suggestion to resolve the diseases of the crops.

AI techniques in disease management of agriculture include Computer Vision Systems (CVS), Genetic Algorithms, ANN, Rule-Based Experts, Data Base, Fuzzy Logic (FL), Web GIS, FL Web Based, Web-Based Intelligent Disease Diagnosis Systems (WIDDS), FL & TTS converter, Expert system rule-base disease detection, Fuzzy Xpest, Web-Based Expert system.

GoogleNet is a deep learning method popularly used worldwide to identify the diseases infected with the crops and suggest the medications to resolve them.

Crop Management

Crop management encompasses the comprehensive spectrum of activities associated with cultivating crops. This management cycle commences with the initial step of sowing, proceeds to encompass tasks like monitoring crop growth, harvesting, and storage, and culminates in distribution. At each stage of crop management, there exists a substantial risk of potential challenges, including pest infestations, disease outbreaks, and other issues (Rellier & Chédru 1992*).*). In response to these challenges, farmers have adapted traditional practices to mitigate the risks inherent in various facets of crop management while striving to make advancements in this domain. To aid these innovative approaches, AI techniques have been introduced.

AI techniques such as ANN CALEX, PROLOG, Robotics, and Fuzzy Cognitive Map were used in various dimensions of crop management such as harvesting, scheduling, and yielding of crops.

Table 6. AI in crop management

AI Techniques	Applications
ANN	Used for the crop yield, soil moisture, and salinity
CALEX	Scheduling of crop management activities
PROLOG	It removes the rarely used tools in farming activities
Robotics	It is used for harvesting crops
Fuzzy Cognitive Map	It improves crop yield and decision management

Pesticide Spraying Management

Spraying the pesticide on the crops followed the principles of right time, right zone, and right crop. Failed with the aforementioned principles, leads to the crop will be affected by diseases and pest attacks. So, farmers are spraying the pesticide for the crop's protection. Spraying pesticides on crops served a variety of reasons, including recovering the crops from diseases, controlling insects, reducing pest attacks, and giving the crops nutritious components, among others. Precision spraying technology reduces herbicides. Traditional farming methods require farmers to carry a sprayer and apply pesticides to the crops; however, this poses serious risks to the farmers' health and leaves very little coverage of the farmed areas. AI technology was applied to improve the management of spraying operations on crops (Katiyar 2022). AI algorithm-based tools fix the spraying zone, spray timer, and buffer zones to offer crop protection and nutrition.

Types of Sprayers

a.   Micro-spot spraying
b.   Variable rate technology
c.   Direct injection
d.   Sensor-based patch spraying
e.   Multi tank sprayers
f.   Spray robots
g.   Band spraying

Harvesting

Detecting crops, making excellent cuts, identifying damage, and selecting, and packaging them are difficult tasks in agriculture. One of the primary cost factors in agriculture production is the labor resources needed for harvesting. AI technologies were adapted to harvesting because of the high cost of laborers and the wastage/damage of the agricultural yield. The robot could automatically move along the rail, recognize, locate, and detect mature bunches, retain and separate the target, and gather harvested crops. A crucial harvesting robot technology is accurately identifying and detecting mature crops. A productive item detection and inspection method is required for the use of a robotic platform in harvesting (Kootstra *et.al* 2021). Different sensor technologies are used to discover and recognize crops in tree branches, assess their ripeness, map the geometry of their canopies, locate the trees in orchards, and eventually harvest the crops. The main focus of the harvesting robot is on five essential areas: detecting targets in

Table 7. AI in pesticide spraying management

AI Techniques	Applications
Robots	Spraying pesticides
Internet of Things (IoT)	Intelligent spraying
UAV or drones	Spraying pesticides and fertilizers

Table 8. AI applications in weather forecasting

AI Techniques	Applications
Machine learning	Predict the forthcoming storm impacts
Smart IoT Sensors	Predict rainfall rate
Deep learning	Weather patterns, climate conditions

complex backgrounds; separating soft crops; degree of energy consumption during harvest; adaptability of harvesting instruments; and conformation design to fit with irregular work fields. In addition, thermal imaging technology robots do the harvesting functions in low lighting conditions places also. An efficiently planned robotic system provides standard quality yield, avoids time-consuming, minimum damages, and high harvesting rate, and so on.

Weather Forecasting

Weather conditions are a prerequisite for agriculture to increase the quality of the agricultural produce. Farmers have been struggling a lot in recent days due to the unexpected climate change attack on agriculture which spoiled the agricultural yield tremendously. Consequently, to manage the climate evils attack on agriculture, AI technologies were used. AI predicts the climatic conditions based on the past weather date and provides feasible solutions to decide on crop sowing to harvesting.

In a recent collaboration with Karnataka, IBM's Watson platform (https://www.ibm.com/in-en/watson) was utilized to forecast tomato and maize prices. The Karnataka Agricultural Prices Commission benefited from an IBM-developed price prediction system with AI that forecasts market price trends for two weeks, while also analyzing tomato production patterns. This system leverages IBM's Watson Decision Platform and integrates satellite imagery and weather data for real-time monitoring of crop acreage and health. It can identify pest and disease infestations, estimate tomato production and yields, and provide price forecasts.

Irrigation Management

Conventional agricultural methods heavily rely on water for irrigation, especially in arid regions, where water is crucial for optimizing agricultural productivity. To address this, the "per drop more crop" approach has been recognized as a strategy to efficiently use limited water resources. Artificial intelligence (AI) has ushered in significant transformations in water management and irrigation practices. AI technologies can now accurately determine the specific water requirements of crops and provide irrigation precisely when the crops demand it.

ANN was used to identify the requirements of the water for the crops at various stages and do the irrigation by drip irrigation and sprinkler system (Valipour 2015). IoT is applied to do the smart irrigation system in agriculture by predicting the soil temperature moisture level and wind humidity. Deep learning helps farmers through irrigation scheduling in water scarcity areas.

Table 9. AI applications in irrigation management

AI Techniques	Applications
Artificial Neural Network Base Machine Learning	Identify crop water requirements in different cycles of growth and do the irrigation
Internet of Things	Smart irrigation system- Soil moisture, temperature, Wind speed
Deep learning	Irrigation scheduling
CNN based model	Image-based recognition of center pivot irrigation system

Warehousing

In the olden days, agriculture produced was stored in various formats. Farmers also felt happy with the techniques adopted by them. In traditional India, the majority of the farmers' houses were constructed like go-downs to store their agricultural produce and it is getting wasted due the environmental factors, animals, and pesticide attacks (Ramirez-Asis 2022). In AI-based agriculture assesses the storage requirements of the agricultural produce and lengthens the life of the agricultural yield.

Agriculture Food Supply Chain Management

In ancient times, the barter system facilitated the exchange of goods among individuals, but as cultures evolved and technology advanced, people began to transport their surplus products to assist those in need within their own country. AI technologies have opened up new opportunities for farmers to bring their agricultural produce to the global market and obtain profitable prices for their goods. The management of the agricultural food supply chain encompasses various phases, including pre-production, supply logistics, production processes, post-production logistics, processing, distribution logistics, sales logistics, and waste recycling. These tasks can be effectively executed with the assistance of AI techniques, such as machine learning, the Internet of Services, the Internet of Things, robots, industrial robots, sensors and drones, digital platforms, driverless vehicles, and machinery, as well as nanotechnology.

Livestock Management

Livestock is a pillar for the growth of the agriculture sector. People praise and celebrate the functions of the livestock because of their importance in agriculture. But in the modern days, tracking the status of the livestock and its health conditions becomes a complex job for the farmers. So, AI technologies provide alerts to the farmers about the Livestock growth and health conditions to the farmers to make the livestock better contribution to agriculture and farmers.

Machine learning can significantly improve predictive analytics, providing increased accuracy and timely information regarding areas such as animal health, productivity, and potential supply chain issues. The widespread integration of IoT devices has the potential to establish an extensive real-time tracking and monitoring system for livestock, making vital data easily accessible to both farmers and key industry stakeholders (Malhotra *et.al* 2023).

IoT-based Sensor technologies can be divided into two primary categories: wearable devices and environment-based sensors. Wearable sensors are affixed directly to the animal and are capable of tracking various parameters such as physiological data (e.g., heart rate, body temperature), behavioral patterns (e.g., feeding habits, movement), and other significant indicators of the animal's health and well-being. On the other hand, environment-based sensors are designed to monitor the conditions surrounding the animals. These sensors can encompass a range of technologies, including video cameras, thermal imaging sensors, accelerometers, load cells placed in feeding stations, and drones, among others. They yield valuable insights into the environment and how animals interact within it.

The JaguzaLivestock App (https://afrosoftug.com/) is a remote tracking application designed for monitoring livestock. Its primary purpose is to oversee the health of animals, encompassing aspects such as heart rate, respiratory rate, blood pressure, and digestion, thereby facilitating early detection of potential animal health issues. This artificial intelligence-driven tool is developed by a team of nine developers in Uganda and is closely integrated with a network of 49 veterinary doctors.

The application operates by affixing a tag or chip to individual animals. Data collected from these tags is transmitted to a reader, which stores the information using cloud technology. Subsequently, the necessary data is relayed to a mobile phone for appropriate action.

BENEFITS OF AI APPLICATIONS IN AGRICULTURE

The benefits of AI in agriculture as outlined by Oliveira & Silva in 2023 include:

Enhance Agricultural Efficiency

AI is a smart technology that enhances operational effectiveness across all agricultural activities. Starting with the preparation of the soil, the agricultural process' logistics operations are initiated. Utilizing technologies that are AI-enabled, promotes the health of the soil and plants. Large amounts of data were analyzed by AI technologies in the fields of crop production, harvesting, and sales decision-making.

Increases the Agricultural Profitability

The profitability of farmers grows as a result of AI-enabled technologies. Farmers face major dangers from pests. The productivity of all the crops will be harmed. Farmers are informed about the pest's initial landing place and can control it by employing AI-based solutions. By employing AI to maximize water use, farmers may grow more crops in locations with water shortages. Robots powered by AI have also taken the place of workers in agriculture. AI-enabled technologies evaluate the condition of the soil and advise on the best crops to plant for a higher yield.

Reduce the Problem of Food Shortage

AI helps the agriculture sectors to increase their productivity in terms of its applications in various fields of agriculture. Consequently, the food scarcity problems will be rectified.

Producing Quality Products

AI technology helps farmers to predict the capability of crop productivity and soil conditions before sowing the seeds. It helps the farmers to avoid the attack of crops from insects and a pest which leads to agricultural produce will be highly efficient.

Helps Farmers in Decision-Making

The World Bank estimates that 500 million smallholder farming households exist worldwide, making up a significant fraction of the impoverished who survive on less than $2 per day. Small-scale farmers lack access to markets and control over product prices, which causes them to undercut local retailers when selling their goods. AI-enabled solutions provide information about the past, present, and future movement of the relevant commodities process in the market, as well as the demand for the goods, to help farmers manage these challenges by making it easier for them to decide how much to charge for their agricultural commodities. Additionally, farmers can choose the crop to cultivate to enhance productivity despite environmental bad things happening thanks to AI technology that informs them about climatic conditions and can foresee them.

CHALLENGES OF AI APPLICATIONS IN AGRICULTURE

Sood et.al 2002 presented the challenges of AI in agriculture. They are:

Huge Investment

The substantial initial investment required for AI is primarily due to its technological components. For instance, implementing AI-driven robotics in agriculture necessitates a significant initial expenditure of $10,000, which places it beyond the financial means of marginal and small-scale farmers.

High Illiteracy Rate

In the Indian context, farmers exhibit a notably low literacy rate. To embrace AI technology in agriculture, farmers need to possess a fundamental understanding of this technology. Furthermore, transitioning from traditional farming to AI-driven farming represents a challenging and complex process that demands a readiness for transformation.

Fear of Technology Adoption

Becoming tech-savvy necessitates the confidence to effectively operate technology. Additionally, the adoption of technology is contingent on several factors, including one's confidence level, apprehensions, and the fear of potential failure. It's anticipated that the transition of farmers towards technology-driven agriculture will be a gradual process, and achieving a state of technology-oriented agriculture will require a significant amount of time.

Lack of Infrastructure

A robust infrastructure plays a crucial role in the successful integration of AI within the agricultural sector. In the Indian context, the technology infrastructure is still in its early stages of development and requires significant enhancements to facilitate the adoption of AI technology in agriculture.

Myth About Traditional Agriculture

Farmers hold the belief that traditional agricultural practices offer numerous advantages. There is a prevalent misconception that farmers must undergo education and transition toward technology-driven agriculture.

CASE STUDIES AND SUCCESS STORIES

In the United States, AI is widely used in precision agriculture, including autonomous tractors and drones for crop monitoring. Companies like John Deere employ AI for autonomous farming machinery. AI is also used in crop yield prediction, disease detection, and robotic harvesting.

In November 2022, DJI Agriculture (www.dji.com) introduced the Mavic 3 Multispectral, featuring a multispectral imaging system designed for the rapid acquisition of crop growth data. This innovation is poised to significantly enhance crop production efficiency in precision agriculture and environmental monitoring, offering global farmers the opportunity to elevate the quality of their yields while simultaneously reducing operational costs and boosting income.

In October 2022, Microsoft (https://www.microsoft.com/) made an important announcement, unveiling FarmVibes as an open-source initiative from Microsoft Research AI. FarmVibes.AI encompasses a comprehensive array of machine-learning models and technologies tailored for the field of sustainable agriculture. This resource empowers users with data processing techniques for amalgamating diverse spatiotemporal and geographical data sources, such as weather data, satellite imagery, and drone footage. This development promises to foster innovation and support the creation of advanced agricultural solutions by harnessing the power of data-driven and AI-driven approaches.

In the Indian context, M-Velanmai is a mobile app (https://agritech.tnau.ac.in/) designed by Tamil Nadu Agriculture University in September 2021 to support farmers in farming practices. M-Velanmai employs artificial intelligence and machine learning techniques to offer two categories of support services, namely, decision support and information support, to assist farmers within specific sub-basins of Tamil Nadu.

Under the decision support service, M-Velanmai is an AI-based visual diagnostic tool designed to help farmers identify issues like pests, diseases, and nutrient deficiencies in various crops. Machine learning models are created for individual crops to classify and diagnose crop problems from images. For each selected crop, a digital repository is established, comprising 300 to 500 images for different damage symptoms, along with recommended solutions. When a farmer encounters a problem, they can use their mobile camera to capture the symptoms and upload the image to the app's server. The app then employs machine learning models to compare the image with those in the cloud server. If the match is highly accurate (above 90% precision), the app provides instant advice in the form of text or voice messages to manage the issue. For cases with less than 90% accuracy, the farmer can request help from agricultural experts by sending a photo of the symptoms. These experts identify the problem and offer personalized advice in English or Tamil. The uploaded images are saved in the digital repository for future reference.

Under the information support service, the M-Velanmai app is a unified platform for delivering a range of information services to farmers, including weather forecasts, crop cultivation practices, and fertilizer recommendations. A database is created to store commonly asked queries from farmers. When a farmer seeks information support, they can input their query into the app. If the query matches one already stored in the database, the system retrieves advisory information from the cloud server and instantly sends it to the farmer. For new queries, the user is prompted to send it to experts. These experts respond with personalized advisories in text or voice messages, available in English or Tamil, as a reply to the farmers' queries.

In India, GramworkX has created a smart farm resource management tool that leverages IoT and AI technology. This tool assists farmers in efficiently managing their resources, particularly water usage. The device continuously collects essential farm data, including atmospheric temperature, pressure, humidity, rainfall, and soil moisture, at 10-minute intervals, transmitting this information to the cloud every hour. Subsequently, a machine learning algorithm generates predictions related to irrigation and other factors, which are accessible to farmers through a mobile application.

AI TRENDS IN AGRICULTURE

Artificial Intelligence (AI) holds tremendous promise for the agricultural sector. It has the potential to address numerous challenges, including climate-related risks, sustainability concerns, and the imperative to boost agricultural productivity. Although some farmers may initially be hesitant due to limited knowledge and education, over time, they are likely to embrace AI technologies in agriculture. AI has the power to revolutionize agriculture by reducing the need for human intervention and effectively meeting the increasing global demand for food.

Vantage Market Research (https://www.vantagemarketresearch.com/) has projected that Artificial Intelligence (AI) in the agriculture market is poised to attain a value of $4.2 billion by the year 2028, marking a substantial increase from the $1.1 billion it achieved in 2022. This growth is anticipated to occur at a Compound Annual Growth Rate (CAGR) of 25.1% over the forecast period at the global level. Consequently, the contribution of the agriculture sector shows progressive remarks of the economy at the global level.

CONCLUSION AND FUTURE DIRECTIONS OF RESEARCH

AI is a sophisticated technology that provides solutions to various unattended problems such as labor shortages, numerous crop diseases, and soil fertility in agriculture. So, AI is gaining attention and popularity among various stakeholders in the world. AI can only be a remedial technology to meet the growing food needs of the penetrated population in the world. It is necessary to research various functional areas of agriculture such as irrigation management, precision agriculture, and soil management.

AI holds a significant role in agriculture, although its full potential may not yet be fully harnessed by farmers. Very shortly, AI is poised to become a requisite tool in agriculture and an indispensable component of the industry. AI will become the most popular and cheapest technology to all farmers in the near future with the help of government subsidies for AI-based technologies such as robotics, drones, and so on. Farmers will also adapt themselves to AI-based technologies once they realize their benefits. Farmers needed to be educated and aware of the technologies to uplift the agriculture sector to the next level.

ABBREVIATION

AI Artificial Intelligence
IoT Internet of Things
CAGR Compound Annual Growth Rate
ANN Artificial Neural Networks
SNN Simulated Neural Networks
WSN Wireless Sensor Networks
UAV Unmanned Aerial Vehicles
ML Machine Learning
GPS Global Positioning System
FAO The Food and Agriculture Organization of the United Nations
SVM Support Vector Machine
DT Decision Tree
NN Neural Network
DIA Digital Image Analysis
IVO Invasive Weed Optimization
LVQ Learning Vector Quantization
CVS Computer Vision Systems
WIDDS Web-Based Intelligent Disease Diagnosis Systems

REFERENCES

Aktar, W., Sengupta, D., & Chowdhury, A. (2009). Impact of pesticides use in agriculture: Their benefits and hazards. *Interdisciplinary Toxicology*, 2(1), 1–12. doi:10.2478/v10102-009-0001-7 PMID:21217838

Anyoha, R. (2017). *The history of Artificial Intelligence*. Harvard Press. https://sitn.hms.harvard.edu/flash/2017/history-artificial-intelligence/

Bacco, M., Barsocchi, P., Ferro, E., Gotta, A., & Ruggeri, M. (2019). The digitization of agriculture: A survey of research activities on smart farming. *Array (New York, N.Y.)*, 3, 100009. doi:10.1016/j.array.2019.100009

Bhardwaj, H., Tomar, P., Sakalle, A., & Sharma, U. (2021). *Artificial Intelligence and IoT-Based Technologies for Sustainable Farming and Smart Agriculture*. P.15.IGI Publishers. . doi:10.4018/978-1-7998-1722-2.ch002

Cheng, C., Fu, J., Su, H., & Ren, L. (2023). Recent advancements in agriculture robots: Benefits and challenges. *Machines*, 11(1), 48. doi:10.3390/machines11010048

Demirel, M., & Kumral, N. A. (2021). Artificial intelligence in integrated pest management. In *Artificial Intelligence and IoT-Based Technologies for Sustainable Farming and Smart Agriculture* (pp. 289–313). IGI Global. doi:10.4018/978-1-7998-1722-2.ch018

Dharmaraj, V., & Vijayanand, C. (2018). Artificial intelligence (AI) in agriculture. *International Journal of Current Microbiology and Applied Sciences, 7*(12), 2122–2128. doi:10.20546/ijcmas.2018.712.241

Dubey, A. K., Rao, K. K., Kumar, S., Tamta, M., Dwivedi, S. K., Kumar, R., & Mishra, J. S. (2019). *Disease management in major field crops. Conservation Agriculture for Climate Resilient Farming & Doubling Farmers' Income.* ICAR Research Complex for Eastern Region, Patna Training Manual No.

Dulhare, U. N., & Gouse, S. (2022). *Automation of Rice Cultivation from Ploughing–Harvesting with Diseases, Pests, and Weeds to Increase the Yield Using AI.* Kumar. doi:10.1007/978-981-16-7985-8_51

Esposito, M., Crimaldi, M., Cirillo, V., Sarghini, F., & Maggio, A. (2021). Drone and sensor technology for sustainable weed management: A review. *Chemical and Biological Technologies in Agriculture, 8*(1), 18. doi:10.118640538-021-00217-8

Farhood, H., Bakhshayeshi, I., Pooshideh, M., Rezvani, N., & Beheshti, A. (2022). Recent advances in image processing techniques in agriculture. *Artificial Intelligence and Data Science in Environmental Sensing*, 129-153.

Farooq, M. S., Riaz, S., Abid, A., Abid, K., & Naeem, M. A. (2019). A Survey on the Role of IoT in Agriculture for the Implementation of Smart Farming. *IEEE Access : Practical Innovations, Open Solutions, 7*, 156237–156271. doi:10.1109/ACCESS.2019.2949703

Franzen, D., & Mulla, D. (2015). A history of precision agriculture. *Precision Agriculture Technology for Crop Farming*, 1–20.

Gerhards, R., Andujar Sanchez, D., Hamouz, P., Peteinatos, G. G., Christensen, S., & Fernandez-Quintanilla, C. (2022). Advances in site-specific weed management in agriculture—A review. *Weed Research, 62*(2), 123–133. doi:10.1111/wre.12526

Jagtap, S. T., Phasinam, K., Kassanuk, T., Jha, S. S., Ghosh, T., & Thakar, C. M. (2022). Towards application of various machine learning techniques in agriculture. *Materials Today: Proceedings, 51*, 793–797. doi:10.1016/j.matpr.2021.06.236

Javaid, M., Haleem, A., Khan, I. H., & Suman, R. (2023). Understanding the potential applications of Artificial Intelligence in the Agriculture Sector. *Advanced Agrochem, 2*(1), 15–30. doi:10.1016/j.aac.2022.10.001

Kalichkin, V. K., Alsova, O. K., & Maksimovich, K. Y. (2021, September). Application of the decision tree method for predicting the yield of spring wheat. []. IOP Publishing]. *IOP Conference Series. Earth and Environmental Science, 839*(3), 032042. doi:10.1088/1755-1315/839/3/032042

Katiyar, S. (2022). The use of pesticide management using artificial intelligence. In *Artificial Intelligence Applications in Agriculture and Food Quality Improvement* (pp. 74–94). IGI Global. doi:10.4018/978-1-6684-5141-0.ch005

Khan. (2022). Role of Artificial Intelligence in insect and pest management. *Just Agriculture*, pp.19-23.

Kootstra, G., Wang, X., Blok, P. M., Hemming, J., & Van Henten, E. (2021). Selective harvesting robotics: Current research, trends, and future directions. *Current Robotics Reports*, 2(1), 95–104. doi:10.100743154-020-00034-1

Kujawa, S., & Niedbała, G. (2021). Artificial neural networks in agriculture. *Agriculture*, 11(6), 497. doi:10.3390/agriculture11060497

Malhotra, M., Jaiswar, A., Shukla, A., Rai, N., Bedi, A., Iquebal, M. A., & Rai, A. (2023). Application of AI/ML Approaches for Livestock Improvement and Management. In *Biotechnological Interventions Augmenting Livestock Health and Production* (pp. 377–394). Springer Nature Singapore. doi:10.1007/978-981-99-2209-3_20

Mhlanga, D. (2021). Artificial intelligence in the industry 4.0, and its impact on poverty, innovation, infrastructure development, and the sustainable development goals: Lessons from emerging economies?'. *Sustainability (Basel)*, 13(11), 5788. doi:10.3390u13115788

Mozar, S. (2021). ICCCE. Lecture Notes in Electrical Engineering, 828. Springer, Singapore. doi:10.1007/978-981-16-7985-8_51

Navya, D. (2023). Artificial intelligence-based robot for harvesting, pesticide spraying and maintaining water management system in agriculture using IoT. *AIP Conference Proceedings*.

Neethirajan, S. (2023). Artificial Intelligence and Sensor Technologies in Dairy Livestock Export: Charting a Digital Transformation. *Sensors (Basel)*, 23(16), 7045. doi:10.339023167045 PMID:37631580

Oliveira, R. C. D., & Silva, R. D. D. S. E. (2023). Artificial Intelligence in Agriculture: Benefits, Challenges, and Trends. *Applied Sciences (Basel, Switzerland)*, 13(13), 7405. doi:10.3390/app13137405

Ramirez-Asis, E., Bhanot, A., Jagota, V., Chandra, B., Hossain, M. S., Pant, K., & Almashaqbeh, H. A. (2022). Smart logistic system for enhancing the farmer-customer corridor in the smart agriculture sector using artificial intelligence. *Journal of Food Quality*, 2022, 2022. doi:10.1155/2022/7486974

Rehna, V. J., & Inamdar, M. N. (2022). Impact of Autonomous Drone Pollination in Date Palms. *International Journal of Innovative Research and Scientific Studies*, 5(4), 297–305. doi:10.53894/ijirss.v5i4.732

Rellier, J. P., & Chédru, S. (1992). An artificial intelligence-based software for designing crop management plans. *Computers and Electronics in Agriculture*, 6(4), 273–294. doi:10.1016/0168-1699(92)90001-4

Shi, L., Duan, Q., Ma, X., & Weng, M. (2012). The Research of Support Vector Machine in Agricultural Data Classification. In D. Li & Y. Chen (Eds.), *Computer and Computing Technologies in Agriculture V. CCTA 2011. IFIP Advances in Information and Communication Technology* (Vol. 370). Springer. doi:10.1007/978-3-642-27275-2_29

Sood, A., Sharma, R. K., & Bhardwaj, A. K. (2022). Artificial intelligence research in agriculture: A review. *Online Information Review*, 46(6), 1054–1075. doi:10.1108/OIR-10-2020-0448

Tilson K. (2010). Lyytinen C. Sørensen Research commentary—digital infrastructures: the missing IS research agenda *Inf. Syst. Res., 21*.

Valipour, M. (2015). A comprehensive study on irrigation management in Asia and Oceania. *Archives of Agronomy and Soil Science, 61*(9), 1247–1271. doi:10.1080/03650340.2014.986471

Vilani Sachithra, L.D.C.S. (2020). How artificial intelligence uses to achieve the agriculture sustainability. *Systematic review*.

Wakchaure, M., Patel, B. K., & Mahindrakar, A. K. (2023). Application of AI techniques and robotics in agriculture: A review. *Artificial Intelligence in the Life Sciences, 3,* 100057. doi:10.1016/j.ailsci.2023.100057

Zhu, N., Liu, X., Liu, Z., Hu, K., Wang, Y., Tan, J., Huang, M., Zhu, Q., Ji, X., Jiang, Y., & Guo, Y. (2018). Deep learning for smart agriculture: Concepts, tools, applications, and opportunities. *International Journal of Agricultural and Biological Engineering, 11*(4), 32–44. doi:10.25165/j.ijabe.20181104.4475

Chapter 13
IoT–Integrated Machine Learning–Based Automated Precision Agriculture–Indoor Farming Techniques

Gowtham Rajendiran

https://orcid.org/0000-0002-7175-0576

Department of Computing Technologies, School of Computing, College of Engineering and Technology, SRM Institute of Science and Technology, Chengalpattu, India

Jebakumar Rethnaraj

Department of Computing Technologies, School of Computing, College of Engineering and Technology, SRM Institute of Science and Technology, Chengalpattu, India

ABSTRACT

Precision agriculture driven by the integration of the advanced technologies like internet of things (IoT) and machine learning (ML) is revolutionary precision agriculture, especially the indoor farming techniques. This chapter explores the comprehensive application of IoT and ML in automating indoor cultivation practices, examining their diverse benefits and practical uses in comparison with the traditional farming methodologies. IoT enables the indoor farmers to create controlled environments through interconnected sensors, monitoring crucial variables but not limited to temperature, humidity, and light intensity. Complemented by ML algorithms, data analysis becomes efficient, providing predictive models for crop growth, pest detection, and disease outbreaks. Automated environment climate control systems optimize resource utilization, while precision irrigation minimizes water usage. Real-time monitoring and early detection of plant health issues reduce crop losses, ensuring high-quality produce.

DOI: 10.4018/979-8-3693-0639-0.ch013

INTRODUCTION

Agriculture is one of the key sources that plays a significant part in the life of the country's economy. Traditional agriculture refers to the conventional farming methods that have been practiced for centuries, relying on manual labor and basic tools. In traditional agriculture, farmers often work in small plots of land using traditional seeds and farming practices passes down through the generations while traditional agriculture has played a crucial role in meeting food demands, it does have it disadvantages. One significant drawbacks is its relatively low efficiency and productivity. Manual labor-intensive tasks can be time-consuming and labor demanding, leading to potential wastage of water, fertilizers and pesticides. Moreover, traditional agriculture is more susceptible to the adverse effects of unpredictable weather conditions and environmental factors which can result in lower yields and economic losses. Meanwhile, food security is a global challenge and impacted by rapidly compounding effects of climate changes, population trends and supply chain shortcomings.

Agriculture's global impact cannot be overstated, as it remains the primary source of food for humanity. Despite the fact that the human population continues to grow, agricultural land remains static (Virk et al.2020). The authors (Mesgaran et al. 2017) also discovered that the ever-changing climatic conditions significantly reduce agricultural product output in conventional agricultural systems. As a result of the varying nature of farming resources and poor management, farmers continue to experience low agricultural output.

Drawbacks of Traditional Farming

Due to the low degree of automation in the farming area, the current state of the art in agriculture, particularly conventional agricultural systems, still confronts significant hurdles in terms of sustainability, labor-intensity, and energy efficiency needs. Also, the production level of the crops to be considered. Scalability problems also taken into account since the population explosion is the major cause.

Precision Agriculture and Smart Farming

In order to overcome the limitations and challenges faced in the conventional farming systems, the advent of the smart farming and precision agricultural sector to automate the farming processes towards achieving many goals towards sustainable agricultural systems. Some of them are listed below:

- High quantity of crop yield
- Better quality of the crops
- Efficient resource utilization
- Effective to handle climatic conditions
- Decision making in cropping patterns
- Environment and user-friendly
- Easy maintenance
- Minimized crop losses
- Easy to handle pests, diseases, weeds
- Minimize the crop growth time duration
- Early prediction on the crop loss or gain

Table 1. Evolution of smart farming techniques

Area of advancements	Description	Developed Year
Automated tractor for navigations and robots	Automated plowing of the circular fields based on the distance to the center	1941
Soil sampling	Recommendations to fertilize the soil	1967
Proximal sensing of soil and crops	Mapping of soil and crop properties	1973
Remote sensing	Diagnosing problems like soil erosion, drainage failures, weed growth, machinery malfunctioning, nutrient stress	1982
Variable rate fertilizer	Developed machineries for testing the cultivation fields	1985
Yield mapping	Spatial mapping of the crop yield before the availability of GPS	1987
Geo-statistics	Variability in soil moisture and soil hydraulic properties	1988
Global Positioning Systems (GPS)	Determining the location of the field for seedling and cultivation purpose	1991
Application of variable rate herbicide	Spraying of herbicides to prevent the growth of the weeds	1992
Variable rate irrigation	Identifying cultivation zones requiring different amounts of irrigation	1993
Profit finding of crops	Corn, soybean, wheat, barley, potato	1996
Embedding and deriving management zones and recommendations	Information analysis and decision support system in precision agriculture	2005
Spatial resolutions of the satellite data	Customized management recommendations for single plant growing in the field	2011

- Ensures and motivates organic way of crop cultivation
- Improves the growth of wide variety of crops
- Reduces the usage of pesticides, fungicides and other chemicals that are not good for health.
- Though huge amount for installations, less chances for failures and lasts for longer life-time.

Historical Evolution of Precision Farming

Precision farming is considered to be one of the top innovations in the field of agriculture. It has been evolved early in 20th centuries. The developments were from soil management, yield prediction to the disease handling. Table 1 showcases the dramatic changes in the fields of agriculture.

Smart farming, in particular, comprises the use of technology such as Artificial Intelligence (AI) in farm management to boost agricultural production quantity and quality (Adamides 2020). Drones and IoT sensors are two examples of smart farming instruments that are used to manage farms autonomously. Precision agriculture is the third method to the agricultural revolution that addresses the issues of what, when, and where resources should be applied or employed for maximum crop output (Balafoutis et al 2017). Agricultural mechanization utilizing tools and equipment was the first and second revolutions in agriculture, while the green revolution in agriculture deals with enhancing agricultural seeds and animal breeds (Abhinav et al. 2021). These ideas of smart farming and precision agriculture are similar but not identical, and the concepts have evolved as a useful tool in bridging the knowledge gap. Both are primarily focused with increasing agricultural yields.

John Deere is credited with the notion of digitizing agriculture in 1990, when intelligent instruments made planting and fertilizer application possible (Abhinav et al. 2021). The goal of this novel technique is to increase agricultural productivity and encourage farming. Prediction in smart farming is acquiring and evaluating data regarding agricultural aspects such as soil properties, fertilizer requirements, and atmospheric weather that are critical for crop performance. Smart farming models are constructed using this information to control and assure the accurate exploitation of farming resources autonomously (Abhinav et al. 2021, Mesgaran et al. 2017).

Precision agriculture is obviously significant, especially in developing nations such as Nigeria, where agriculture is largely performed traditionally, which means by the experience of the elderly.

Indoor Farming Practices

Also known as controlled environment agriculture (CEA) involves cultivating crops in controlled environments such as greenhouses or vertical farms. Through the integration of IoT and Machine learning (ML) (advanced technologies) indoor farming can achieve higher yields, precise climate control and sustainable agricultural practices.

Vertical Farming

Vertical farming is the cultivation of crops or plants in vertically stacked layers. It integrates soil-less farming technologies such as hydroponics, aeroponics, and aquaponics, as well as controlled environment agriculture approaches aimed at optimizing plant development (Vertical Farming – ATTRA – Sustainable Agriculture, 2023). In 2026, the area of high-tech greenhouses is predicted to increase from 50,000 to 80,000 hectares. At the same time, greenhouse horticulture is extremely labor-intensive, requiring an average of 7500 hours of labor per hectare each year (Smart Agriculture Market Size Worth $35.98 Billion by 2030: Grand View Research, Inc., 2022).

Table 2. Essential nutrients for efficient plant growth

Nutrients	Crop varieties
Plants in order to grow efficient crops, need nutrients to flourish and cannot function without them. All the growing systems use a different mixture of essential nutrients classified as micronutrients and macronutrients. Some of them are, <ul><li>Oxygen</li><li>Nitrogen</li><li>Sulfur</li><li>Potassium and phosphorus</li></ul>	One vital decision that makes a vertical farm successful is the type of crop to be grown. The most preferred crops for vertical farms include, <ul><li>Lettuce (all varieties)</li><li>Swiss chard</li><li>Tomatoes</li><li>Chilies</li><li>Straw berries</li><li>Spinach</li><li>Garlic and Cucumber</li></ul>

Figure 1. Classification of vertical farming techniques

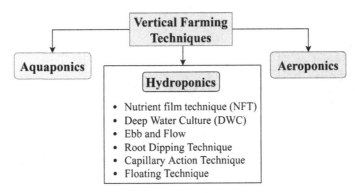

Nutrient Requirements and Crops That Can Be Grown in Vertical Farming Systems

Vertical farming uses vertically stacked layers to produce more food on the same land, often integrated into buildings, warehouses, or unfit spaces. It differs from traditional farming, which requires artificial temperature, light, water, and humidity control. If the delicate balance is not maintained, it's possible to lose the entire crop the way a traditional farm might in the event of a drought or flood (Eden Green Technology, 2023) (Bhatia, 2022).

Hydroponics System

Also known as soil-less farming system: the primary mechanism of growing plants in this system is simple; crops are suspended in a mixture of nutrients and water. This water mixture which could compare to the culture media, is recycled and circulated through the system multiple times. Although it is relatively a simple technique, it has many varieties as discussed below:

a) Nutrient Film Technique (NFT): This technique includes a titled hollow pipe with holes holding the plants and passing the nutrient solution to the roots. This hollow pipe system is connected to a water reservoir tank and a pump. A thin layer of nutrient water slowly passes from the titled pipe, and the roots can absorb the required nutrients while rest of the water will fall back into the reservoir tank because of the tilt.

b) Deep Water Culture (DWC): In this method, the plant roots are entirely immersed into the nutrient solution, which would be aerated continuously using an air stone and pump for roots to get sufficient oxygen.

c) Ebb and Flow: This technique is also known as "flood and drain" method which involves plants growing in an inert substrate such as perlite; the plots then sit on a grow tray. The nutrient reservoir beneath would intermittently flood the grow tray. One of the two holes in the grow tray acts as an inlet that brings the nutrient water into the grow tray using the pump and another as an outlet that drains the water back to the reservoir tank using gravity.

Figure 2. Advantages and challenges of vertical farming systems

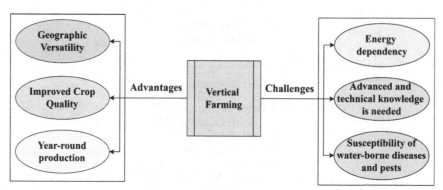

d) Root Dipping Method: The crops are cultivated in small plots fitted with growing materials such as gravel. The pots are half sub-merged in nutrient waters such as such that a portion of roots are in the water to absorb nutrients and the rest are exposed to the air for oxygen absorption.

Aquaponics System

Aquaponics is a closed-loop system that combines aquaculture and hydroponics. It involves a fish tank and plant growing bed, where ammonia-rich fish waste is fed to plants as bio-fertilizers. The roots filter the waste, returning clean water to the fish tank. Major fish species compatible with aquaponics include Tilapia, Trout, Perch, Arctic Char, and Bass. Fish selection depends on temperature, oxygen, and pH fluctuations. Aquaponics farms require round-the-clock monitoring for the first few weeks of establishment to prevent stress and dead fish. Advances in vertical farming and technology-driven cropping techniques promise a future of food availability and security despite limited natural resources.

Aeroponics System

Aeroponics is a technology also known as air-water cultivation system that allows the crop to grow in the air instead of soil or a growing medium inside a closed environment. According to the authors (Gowtham et al; 2023), the aeroponic vertical farming system offers numerous benefits, making it a promising option for future gardening. Data visualization tools can help quickly understand data distribution and relationships, identifying traits that may not be useful for predictions. The logistic regression model (LR) is highly efficient and accurate in complex algorithms. However, preprocessing the dataset is necessary for optimal performance. The logistic regression model has a mae of 2.92, indicating better accuracy and efficient crop yield prediction. This model is suitable for lettuce crop yield prediction in aeroponic systems.

Three Leading Advantages and Challenges Faced in the Indoor Vertical Farming Systems

Three Leading Advantages

Vertical farms generate more food per acre of land, utilize much less space and water resources, are ecologically sensitive, and can grow crops year-round despite poor weather conditions. Although these are the benefits of vertical farming, there are also the drawbacks that should be noted (Team Cultivatd, 2022).

a) Geographic Versatility: Vertical farming enables higher productivity in smaller areas, making it advantageous in areas with scarce land, challenging climates, or remote locations. Conventional farming requires long distances to reach consumers, making transportation to the consumer the most expensive part of the supply chain. By growing foods closer to consumers, such as operating vertical farms in urban or metropolitan areas, shipping time is significantly reduced, and CO2 emissions and food waste are reduced. This approach also results in fresher and more profitable produce.

"One acre of vertical farm is the equivalent of approximately twenty soil-based acres, depending on the type of crop grown."

b) Improved quality of Crops: Conventional farming faces significant crop losses due to diseases, pests, and weeds, affecting food security and safety. Vertical farming technologies can help control crop care and growth conditions, resulting in healthier and safer produce. These farms provide a natural barrier that keeps insects out and prevents fungal growth, reducing the need for pesticides. Vertical farms also offer predictable harvest times, improved volume, and repeatable production with consistent flavor and quality. This stable crop off-take allows vertical farms to meet consumer demands.

c) Potential for year-round production: Extreme weather conditions negatively impact crop production, yield, and quality. Indoor vertical farming, however, offers a solution by controlling the environment. This allows vertical farms to operate independently of external weather and light conditions, making them suitable for various regions, including those affected by catastrophic events like floods and droughts. Additionally, controlled environments do not affect seasonality, allowing farms to match production with demand year-round, providing consumers with locally-grown, fresh, and nutritious produce with better taste and quality.

Three Leading Challenges of Vertical Farming Systems

a) Energy dependency: Vertical farms are highly energy-dependent, requiring significant power to operate 24/7. Traditional farming relies on LED lighting, which consumes a significant amount of energy, accounting for up to 65% of a vertical farm's energy expenses. Technology and equipment are crucial for monitoring and maintaining the farm's environment, including humidity and temperature. Controlling these factors requires heating mechanisms, which are costly and energy-intensive, and ventilation and air-conditioning (HVAC) systems. If power is lost for an extended period, crop losses could be substantial. To address this dependency, backup systems can be introduced to ensure continuous operation during power disruptions and outages.

"There are systems that capture the extra energy generated by the LED lights and utilize it elsewhere on the farm or, in certain cases, transport it back to the national grids, thanks to ongoing improvements."

b) Advanced, technical knowledge is needed: Vertical farms require advanced technical knowledge to setup, monitor, and maintain, while minimizing human labor. Smart farming utilizes technologies like IoT, AI, Robotics, Machine learning, Deep Learning, imaging, and drones to increase crop production and optimize human labor efficiency. Fully-automated growing systems require advanced understanding to configure, supervise, and sustain them. Leadership, management experience, financial literacy, communication, and observation skills are also essential for a profitable vertical farming operation.

"A vertical will need to understand integrated pest control, plant nutrition, and plant science. Beyond that, having a rudimentary grasp of engineering, mechanics, and machinery will be essential; if a mobile tray, a pump, or another piece of equipment fails, you must be able to rapidly fix it."

c) Susceptibility to water-borne diseases/pests: Vertical farming systems are vulnerable to water-borne diseases and pests due to pathogen microbes entering the water network. While isolating plants from external environments provides protection, it's not comprehensive. Careful considerations must be given to crop inputs, packaging staff, and potential contamination risks, such as equipment operating near or above crops.

"Aspiration of water and inhalation of water aerosols, as well as indirect transmission from mist environment surfaces to hands, are some of the ways that water-borne diseases spread."

Vertical farming systems require proper hygiene practices and standard operating procedures for disciplined monitoring and cleaning.

"Within five minutes of contact, germs on plastic and stainless steel surfaces are reduced and effectively eliminated by nano-sized bubbles, which are 2500 times smaller than a grain of salt"

Vertical farming offers benefits over traditional plant production methods, allowing year-round indoor cultivation of regional or seasonal crops. However, it is resource-intensive, requiring energy and labor resources. Despite advancements in agriculture technology, the demand for energy and knowledgeable personnel remains standard.

INTERNET OF THINGS AND MACHINE LEARNING IN PRECISION AGRICULTURE

Digital agriculture refers to the widespread adoption of data-heavy techniques in crop and precision farming industries. With numerous sensors, farmers can obtain precise and timely data about their surroundings, operational atmosphere, and machinery data. The concept of "smartness" emerged from technological developments like IoT, Big Data, and Cloud Services. Artificial Intelligence plays a significant role in precision agriculture, as monitoring cameras and computers work together to help farmers perform their tasks more efficiently. Self-sufficient computers enable communication without human assistance, storing information about the current state and motivations for connecting to other parts of the system (Malchi et al; 2021) .

IoT design in smart farming improves farms' production capacity, global market competition, and employee efficiency. Smaller, advanced, and less expensive sensors are becoming more widely available due to technological advancements. Smart farming offers effective, easy-to-use, and all-inclusive solutions to industry issues, empowering agricultural growth. Mobile phones and Internet of Things devices provide farmers with access to data and information, enabling them to track their farms' progress (Natarajan et al; 2020)(Sreedhar et al 2020).

Traditional agricultural systems struggle to address food insufficiency and safety issues, leading to the development of vertical farming and aeroponics. Aeroponics is an emerging and resource-saving method for cultivating crops in limited areas with precise light, humidity, nutrients, and temperature. This method allows roots to dangle freely in the air, while essential nutrients are supplied through an atomization nozzle. Aeroponic crop cultivation is considered the most efficient, promising, significant, economic, and convenient soil-less plant-growing system. This paper proposes an automated Lettuce Crop Growth Monitoring System (LCGMS) that uses IoT and machine learning to automate the aeroponics system. The LGMS uses IoT sensors to capture parameters like pH, electrical conductivity, turbidity, temperature, and PPM, and uses a machine learning algorithm called support vector regression to process data from the IoT system. The proposed model achieves a higher prediction accuracy score of 82.07%, resulting in better yield prediction (Gowtham et al; 2023).

Everything in the web of Things will be used in smart farming computing in the future (IoT). It is crucial to the development of "Next Generations Everywhere Computing" which will replace the current methods of computing in the home and workplace. Researchers around the world, particulalrly in the field of high-speed wireless communications are increasingly focussing on the "Internet of Things".

Figure 3. Utilization of internet of things in various fields

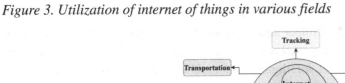

Figure 4. Layered IoT architecture for precision agriculture

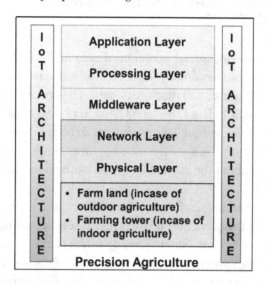

The Internet of Everything (IoE) can be found everywhere in everyday's life. It is helping to lay the groundwork for a wide range of products including dmart health services and education in schools as well as smart homes. The commercial use of IoT in numerous fields are illustrated in the following figure which includes production, public transport, agriculture and corporate management (Balaji et al; 2020)(Kumar et al 2019).

Agriculture is the area of IoT that has seen the most investigations. Given the world's ever increasing population, this is a vital subject for guaranteeing the global food security. In this discipline, researchers first began adopting ICT-based strategies, which were more effective in certain aspects but did not address our problems (Ganesh et al; 2021). IoT is being considered as an alternative to IoT for agriculture, as it is crucial for controlling the supply chain and infrastructure layer. Precision agriculture is expected to grow by 8 billion dollars by 2025. Data analytics from sensors can help farmers increase yields and address various agricultural problems with IoT-based smart farming. Farmers can access real-time data, as described in the study (Peneti et al; 2021)(Navulur et al; 2017).

IoT for Precision Agriculture

IoT, invented by Kevin Ashton in 1999, connects objects through the internet, enabling data transfer without human interaction. It includes devices, sensors, biochips, animals, and people with unique identifiers. Wireless sensor networks (WSN) collect and communicate environmental data, enabling quick responses or in-depth studies. IoT is widely used in precision agriculture, with the development of independent intellectual property rights sensors, intelligent tractors, UAVs, and robots. IoT frameworks can solve big data problems, and AI in IoT can process continuous data streams and identify patterns hidden by conventional gauges (Cai et al 2022, Shaik et al 2022, Xie et al 2022, Islam et al 2022). With the incorporation of all the aforementioned advancements, smart agriculture is possible.

IoT Architecture for Precision Agriculture

Due to the extensive usage of internet-connected devices in various applications, the researchers provided a variety of IoT topologies. The design of the IoT architecture will depend on the applications and problems to be solved.

The above figure showcase the traditional IoT design-based on the opinion of several researchers. This architecture has five different layers: physical, network, middleware, processing layer and application layer make up the precision agriculture IoT architecture. Each layer's responsibilities ate explained below in detail one by one:

a) Physical layer: The physical layer is the bottom layer of the IoT architecture. In most of the research papers, the physical layer is termed as the perception layer or device layer (Verma et al 2018). It consists of physical devices such as sensors, actuators, gateways, hubs, routers and other hardware devices which are connected to the microcontroller with the intent of real-time data collection. This layer os responsible for capturing data from the interconnected devices and transferring it to be the next layer.

b) Network layer: The network layer constitutes internet and communication technologies. The major role of this layer is to provide a connection between physical layer devices to the software and middleware layer. It ensures fast and reliable communication some of the common coomunication technologies used in the agricultural fields are LTE, GSM, Wi-Fi, Zigbee, RFID, NFC and Bluetooth.

c) Middleware layer: Middleware is software that interfaces with IoT components, enabling large-scale networking of devices. It supports device administration, discovery, interoperability, security, cloud services, portability, and context awareness. Examples include OpenIoT, Middlewhere, and Fiware. SMEPP and HYDRA are the best middleware for agriculture.

d) Processing layer: The layer stores, processes, and analyzes information from sensors and devices. It has two phases: data processing and data analytics. Data preparation involves storing and cleaning streaming data before feeding it into the analytics tool. Data analytics uses preprocessed data for mining operations, pattern analysis, and decision-making using machine learning and deep learning. It is used to estimate soil nutrients, crop output, fertilizer recommendations, sensed soil data, and growth environment data in both indoor and outdoor farming.

e) Application layer: The top layer of IoT architecture manages and uses data by end users, applications, or smart devices. Data can be managed on the cloud or in a data center, providing a user-friendly experience. In agriculture, this application layer offers farmers useful information like irrigation, water level, crop maturity, disease, and pest levels via message or phone call. Farmers can remotely control smart devices like UAVs for tasks like pesticide spraying and sowing.

Sensors Used in Smart Farming

Sensors are essential in IoT automation for gathering data from diverse fields like outdoor and indoor farming. These devices detect physical events and environmental changes, transmitting information to electrical systems. Sensors are primarily used in the IoT sector for data collection, generating measurable responses to changes in the environment. However, collecting real-time data in agriculture is challenging due to the constantly changing farming type and environment (Kour and Arora 2020).

Table 3. Description of different types of sensors utilized by the precision farming techniques

S. No	Sensor Type	Description
1	Optical Sensors	Sensors measure light intensity, temperature, pressure displacement, and other variables, primarily used in agriculture for evaluating soil attributes like pH, organic matter, and phenotyping. They also transform light beams into electrical output. (Kuska and Mahlein 2018).
2	Location Sensors	Precision agriculture relies on precise location, which is achieved through GPS satellite signals. These sensors map irregular landforms, uneven terrain, and water logging, enabling farmers to plan irrigation systems and spray fertilizer and pesticides precisely.
3	Electro-magnetic Sensors	Soil EC characteristics are crucial for crop development forecasting due to salinity and moisture content. Electromagnetic sensors measure soil particle conductivity and charge accumulation.
4	Electro-Chemical Sensors	Sensors in smart agriculture increasingly identify soil components using electrodes to measure ions concentration and detect voltage between sites, increasing their use in smart agriculture.
5	Airflow Sensors	These sensors will calculate the soil's air permeability. It is essential to measure the characteristics of the soil, including its kind, its structure, its humidity, and its wetness.
6	Acoustic Sensors	An acoustic sensor picks up noise and vibration from the environment. These sensors can be used to identify pests and disease-carrying insects in agriculture fields since they typically make sounds.

Selecting the right sensor for precision agriculture applications is crucial for low-cost, energy-saving, and real-time data collection. Key considerations include calibration, weather proofing, and wireless communication. Sensor classifications include optical, location, electromagnetic, electrochemical, airflow, and acoustic. Choosing the right sensor ensures optimal performance and minimizes cumbersome tasks.

Specific Sensor Details

Here are some of the listed sensors used in the farming methodologies in the tabular format.

ROLE OF ARTIFICIAL INTELLIGENCE IN SMART AGRICULTURE

Artificial Intelligence (AI) in agriculture refers to the integration of advanced technologies like Machine learning, computer vision and Internet of Things (IoT) to enhnace the agricultural practices and improve the overall efficiency and productivity in farming. AI-driven solutions in smart agriculture offer data driven insights, atomation and predictuve capabilities, transforming traditional farming into a more intelligent and sustainable process.

AI plays a significant role in precision agriculture field where six areas are focussed mainly and identified as key targets of application namely:

- Crop yield and price prediction
- Predictive insights
- Intelligent spraying
- Crop and environment monitoring
- Autonomous agriculture robots
- Crop disease diagnosis

Table 4. Description of different types of sensors utilized by the precision farming techniques with their specifications and applications

	Types of Environmental Sensors	
Sensor Type	*Measures*	*Applications*
Soil-moisture sensor (FC-28)	• Measures the mositure in the soil • Power consumption: 3.3-5V	• Automatic watering
Gro point profile sensor	• Measures multi-depth soil mositure • Power consumption: 6-18V	• Smart irrigation • Intelligent agriculture
Soil moisture sensor (EC-125)	• Measures the mositure in the soil • Power consumption: 3.3-5V	• Smart irrigation • Automatic watering system
4 in 1 soil meter	• Measures, pH level, sunlight intensity, soil mositure, soil temperature • Power consumption: 9V	• Smart agriculture
SHT 10 Soil temperature and humidity sensor	• Measures relative humidity and temperature • Power consumption: 3.3-5V	• Data logging for precision farming
Soil NPK sensor	• Measures the level of nitrogen, phosphorus and potassium • Power consumption: 9-24V	• Soil health monitoring for smart agriculture
	Types of Pest Sensors	
Sensor Type	*Measures*	*Applications*
Phero sensor SP	Measures pests, flies and insects	Pest data collection used for smart agriculture
Acoustic Sensors EC-0177	Measures pests based on the sounds	Pest level identification for smart agriculture
	Types of Leaf Sensors	
Sensor Type	*Measures*	*Applications*
PHYTOS 31 Leaf wetness sensor	Measures the mositure in the plant canopy and monitors crop foliar diseases.	• Automatic watering and monitoring • Data collection for recommended systems
Leaf temperature sensor	Measures the temperature of a leaf (specifically)	• Automatic yield growth prediction • Prediction of healthy plants for precision agriculture.

Figure 5. Applications of AI

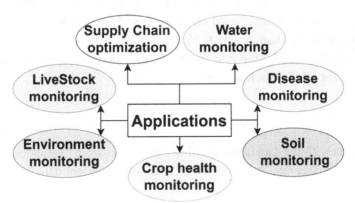

Figure 6. Types of Sensors

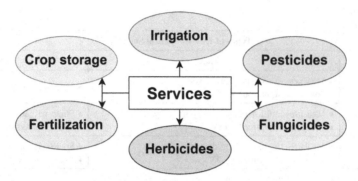

Figure 7. AI services in precision agriculture

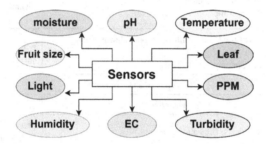

Applicability of IoT and ML Approaches for Smart Farming Applications

ML relates to the capability to learn from the previous experience. ML has emerged in line with the IoT technologies opening up new possibilities of unraveling, quantifying and comprehending data-intensive operations In agricultural operating contexts. ML is the brasnch of science that focusses on developing computer programs that can learn on their own how to react to the environment (Richardson et al; 2016). Bioinformatics, biochemistry, medicine, meteorology, economics, robotics, aquaculture, food security, climatology, supply chain logistics, smart home management are just few of the domains where ML is being used more and more each year (Sangamithra et al; 2017).

The algorithms that learn from input datasets using the predefined set of equations, train the sample and improve their performance. Authors in (Muang Prathub et al 2019) said that ML methods are more powerful in handling non-linear issues based on the sensor data or other sources. It helps real-world decision making with minimum human input. ML algorithms are being used in numerical contexts. However, accuracy is influenced by the information reliability. Consequently, the output format and variable play an important role in machine learning.

Agricultural Datasets

The agricultural datasets with the data from the IoT sensors either from the outdoor field or indoor farming land. Agricultural datasets may include various types of numerical data related to crops, weather, soil and other crop cultivation parameters in case of both indoor and outdoor farming practices.

a) *Crop yield data:* This dataset may contain information on the yield of different crops per acre or hectare. It can include numeric values representing the total yield

b) *Weather data:* Weather datasets may include numeric values such as temperature, humidity, precipitation, wind speed and solar radiation recorded at different time intervals (e.g., hourly, daily, monthly) for specific locations or weather stations.

c) *Soil Characteristics:* The soil properties numeric dataset such as pH level, organic matter content, nutrient levels (e.g., nitrogen, phosphorus, potassium) and soil moisture content.

d) *Pests and disease occurrences:* Numeric data related to the occurrence and severity of pests and diseases in crops can be part of the dataset which contains number of affected plants, pest population, disease incidence rate and intervention measures taken.

e) *Crop management practices:* Numeric data on crop management practices such as irrigation amounts, fertilizer applications and pesticide usage can be included in the datasets.

f) *Satellite Imagery and Remote Sensing data:* The datasets from satellite imagery and remote sensing such as the vegetation indices, land surface temperature and normalized difference water index (NDWI) are also considered to be the numerical datasets.

g) *Market prices and demand:* Data on crop process, demand, and market trends can aid farmers in making informed marketing and sales decisions. Indoor farming practices, particularly in CSV format, play a crucial role in machine learning model training. These numerical datasets are easy to understand and represent for both machines and humans.

h) Environmental Parameters:
   ○ Temperature: recorded at different intervals (hourly and daily basis) from the indoor environment.
   ○ Humidity: relative humidity levels measured to monitor the moisture content in the growing area.
   ○ Light intensity: measured in LUX or photosynthetic photon flux density (PPFD)

i) Plant growth data:
   ○ Plant Height: numeric values representing the height of individual plants at different growth stages.
   ○ Leaf area: measurements of the leaf area of the plants which can indicate their health and growth.
   ○ Biomass: weights of the plants or plant parts (i.e. leaves and stems) used to assess their growth and development.

j) Nutrient concentrations: Nutrient level concentrations of essential nutrients such as nitrogen, phosphorus and potassium (NPK) in the nutrient solution used for hydroponics, aquaponics, and aeroponics as well as in the advanced version of aeroponics system i.e. Fogponics vertical farming systems. pH level: numeric values representing the pH level of the nutrient solution to maintain the proper nutrient availability to the plants.

k) Irrigation and water management:
   ○ Water usage: quantities of water used for irrigation in hydroponics, measured at different levels even aquaponics, aeroponics and Fogponics system.
   ○ Irrigation schedule: time and duration of irrigation events to ensure optimal water delivery to the plants.

l) Pests and disease monitoring:

    ○   Pest population: numeric data on abundance of pests and their occurrences within the indoor farming environment.

    ○   Disease incidence: incidence rates of diseases affecting plants, measured at different intervals.

m)   Time series data: Time stamps: time and date information corresponding to each recorded data point in the dataset.

It is important to note that the specific content and structure of indoor farming dataset in CSV format will also depend on the data collection methodology and variables of interest. However, in this research part, the IoT sensors were used for data acquisition purposes.

STATE-OF-THE-ART REVIEW

The literature review on IoT and AI in the precision agriculture for indoor and outdoor farming provides an insightful analysis of the research and advancements in integrating IoT and AI technologies to optimize farming practices in controlled environments. It explores the current state of the field, identifies the key trends and highlights the potential benefits of using IoT and AI in smart farming practices.

The Scholars (Muang Prathub et al 2019) proposed an IoT-based system for managing farms using web applications on smart devices with network connectivity. This system offers intelligent services such as harvest estimation, determining cultivation issues, and providing recommendations for enhancements using context histories (Martini et al. 2021). (Helfer et al 2021) proposed a model for predicting soil clay quantity using multi-spectral imaging methods and Raspberry Pi tools, making it convenient for assessing soil chemical properties. (Abraham et al 2021) used IoT and machine learning to digitize agriculture, using sensors for remote monitoring and decision recommendations for yield enhancement. (Helfer et al 2020) developed a machine learning scheme for predicting soil chemical richness and yield efficiency using context history. These intelligent models and approaches reduce human involvement and improve productivity in agriculture by automating practices like fertilizer application and irrigation (Martini et al. 2021). They also minimize environmental pollution and ease of monitoring farms (Abhinav et al 2021).

Recent research on smart farming technologies, including robotics, IoT, and remote sensing (Adamides 2020) has reviewed crop, water, soil, and livestock management in agriculture (Liakos et al 2018). The authors (Adamides 2020), examined aspects of smart farming and identified shortcomings and future directions. They focused on models proposed to automate farming practices in Cyprus regions and control on crop, livestock, water, and soil management. Machine learning technologies can enhance farming by providing productive visions for farmers to make informed decisions. (Abhinav et al 2021) provided a systematic analysis of machine learning models in precision agriculture, focusing on soil constituents, yield analysis, and weed and disease recognition. These articles reveal how automated smart farming models can improve agricultural harvest for sustainable food supply.

Machine Learning Approaches Used in Smart Farming Models

Machine learning is a computer science discipline based on computational mathematics and statistics according the authors (Saud and Elfadil 2020). It uses datasets to train models for predictions. Machine learning models include supervised learning, unsupervised learning, and semi-supervised learning or reinforcement learning (Saud and Elfadil 2020, Suruliandi et al 2021). Each category has specific algorithms based on learning style and similarity (Saud and Elfadil 2020). These algorithms are used in smart farming for various purposes, including prediction, classification, clustering, and regression. However, unsupervised learning approaches like clustering are rarely applied to smart farming predictions (Bouighoulouden 2020).

Supervised Machine Learning Algorithms Used in Smart Farming

Supervised machine learning approaches are used to predict dependent variables from independent variables, using datasets as input data to train models (Siddique et al 2018). These algorithms are commonly used in farming predictions, with Naive Bayes and Random Forest (RF) being the most popular (Ayodele 2010), (Mupangwa et al 2020). Random forest algorithm plays a vital role in predicting various case applications including but not limited to, rainfall prediction, greenhouse yield prediction, diseases classification, health care applications, industrial production, waste water reduction, stock market prediction, plant growth and crop yield predictions. Predicting lettuce crop yields in aeroponics systems is a challenging task due to the influence of various growth factors like temperature, humidity, light, and nutrient levels. To tackle this challenge, the researchers (Gowtham Rajendiran and R. Jebakumar 2023) have explored the application of machine learning models, particularly the Random Forest (RF) algorithm, to forecast lettuce crop yields accurately. The study aimed to assess the potential of RF for precise lettuce crop yield prediction. The results of the research were promising. The RF model demonstrated remarkable accuracy, achieving a 92% prediction rate. This outperformed other regression algorithms commonly employed for lettuce crop yield forecasting. Notably, the RF model's predictions were considerably more accurate than those of other regression models, which exhibited a margin of error (measured by MAE) ranging from 0.098 to 3.76 concerning the average reported yield. These findings hold significant value for farmers who are interested in harnessing aeroponics technology to attain high-yield lettuce crops.

Naïve Bayes outperforms other models with 95% accuracy, while RF is recommended for crop suitability predictions. RF also performs well for crop yield prediction, with 95% accuracy, making it the best choice for crop yield prediction. In another study, RF was found to perform best for crop-soil prediction. Additionally, RF was used to estimate the early disparity of sugarcane output, with 95.45% and 79.21% accuracy achieved for classification and regression, respectively (Bondre and Mahagoankar 2019). These techniques are widely used in farming predictions, with Naive Bayes and RF being popular choices for crop suitability and yield prediction (Everingham et al 2016).

The authors (Gowtham et al; 2023) proposed a lettuce crop growth monitoring and yield prediction system using the LCGM-boost regression method, similar to the XGBoost algorithm. The model analyzes data from lettuce growth datasets, allowing for continuous monitoring and prediction of growth and yield. The LCGM-Boost regression model achieves better prediction accuracy of 95.86% and minimizes MSE, RMSE, and MAE scores for the chosen lettuce crop. This makes it suitable for automating lettuce crop growth environment and yield prediction without doubts.

Unsupervised Machine Learning Models for Smart Agriculture

Unsupervised learning is a machine learning algorithm that identifies patterns from unlabeled datasets without being monitored (Nasteski 2017). It can be categorized into various types, such as K-means, Principal component analysis (PCA), and hierarchical clustering. In this study, the author proposed a crop yield prediction model using K-means to provide farmers with automated crop to soil suitability management approaches for high crop yield. The model was tested using publicly available data from the Kaggle site, and the results showed a 67.875% accuracy. Although unsupervised machine learning algorithms are rarely used for smart farming, they are time-consuming and inefficient in terms of performance (Bouighoulouden 2020). The study's findings highlight the importance of considering the unique features and challenges of unsupervised learning in developing smart farming models.

Deep Learning Models Utilized by the Smart Farming

DL models are applicable in various problems such as the pattern recognition, classification, clustering, regression, predictive analysisn etc. there are several DL algorithms such as Feed-forward network (FNN), Recurrent Neural network (RNN), Radial Basis Function Neural Network (RBF-NN). However, Convolutional neural network (CNN) as well as the LSTM (Long Short Term Memory) were also used for smart farming predictions. Apart from all of these DL methodologies, ANN, stacked-sparse auto encoders were also utilized for better crop yield analysis (Khaki et al 2020, Agarwal and Tarar 2020, Ju et al 2020, Friday et al 2018).

Predicting diseases in crops is essential for yielding food crops and natural products. The proposed system, Disease detection with Auto-Spraying Mechanism (DD-ASM), uses a CNN model to classify plant diseases from the Plant Village dataset. This model predicts various plant diseases in the early stages and allows for the prevention of diseases using auto spraying mechanisms, which spray pesticides, fungicides, and insecticides on plant leaves (Gowtham et al; 2022).

Ensemble Machine Learning Models Utilized in Smart Farming

Ensemble learning is a machine learning model that combines the power of two or more learners to achieve better prediction results than individual models can achieve independently (Rajak et al 2019). In this study, the Bagging algorithm and the Gradient Boost Algorithm are observed ensemble learning models used in farming predictions. (Charoen-Ung and MittraPiyanurak; 2018) utilized the gradient boost ensemble-based framework for predicting sugarcane yield, achieving an overall accuracy of 71.64% higher than the benchmark model. Adaptive boost, or bagging, converts weak learners into strong learners. (Mishra et al. 2020) used Adaboost's efficient performance to improve crop yield analysis accuracy. They applied Adaptive Boost to several algorithms, such as Linear Regression (LR), Ridge Regression (RR), Lasso regression (Lr), and Support Vector Regression (SVR), to improve crop and climate recommendations. (Suruliandi et al; 2021) used Adaptive Bagging for crop prediction, which performs better when predictor bias is much greater than variance. The model used recursive feature elimination method of wrapper feature selection techniques.

The traditional farming methods have limitations such as decreasing productivity, increased use of herbicides and pesticides, and environmental health issues. These challenges are due to lack of technology, inept use, and outdated methods. To overcome these challenges, cutting-edge technology must be employed. The evolution of communication and analytics will bring about rapid changes in traditional farming (Adao et al 2017) (Talaviya et al 2020). AI in agriculture can mitigate these challenges by using Machine Learning (ML), Deep Learning (DL), and Internet of Things (IoT) (Khan et al 2022; Radoglou-Grammatikis et al 2020) (Akhter and Sofi et al 2022). This advanced technology helps farmers increase agricultural productivity sustainably without causing environmental hazards (Tripathi and Makedkar

2020, Yasmeen et al 2021; Khan et al 2022). By integrating cutting-edge technologies like AI, ML, DL, IoT, and cloud computing, smart agriculture is a management strategy that enables the agriculture sector to automatically track, monitor, intelligently control, and make decisions based on information and knowledge (Aishwarya et al 2022; Alrowais et al 2022; Abougreen and Chakraborthy, 2021).

MOTIVATION OF THE WORK

As a result of population growth, the world's food supply is increasing at an exponential rate. It is difficult to produce large amounts of food and other raw materials without changing farming techniques. The following are some of the issues associated with custom farming:

1. Traditional farming makes managing time and money tough.
2. If the same crop is planted repeatedly, vital nutrients will be lost.
3. Crops will be harmed and underperform as a result of inefficient early plant disease diagnosis, resulting in a large loss for farmers.
4. Improper pesticide application and pest identification will result in increased crop losses, poor outcomes, and impaired soil and crop nutrition.
5. Manual irrigation inefficiently delivers water to plant crops without regard for their demands. Furthermore, it is a poor method of managing the existing water supplies.
6. Manual weeding takes a lot of time and work, and employing herbicides may harm crops and the soil.

The only option to solve all of the aforementioned issues is to use contemporary agricultural technical developments. The benefits of AI and IoT in agriculture may be beneficial in rapidly and easily addressing problems that develop in this industry.

IMPLEMENTATION PROCEDURE

The implementation of the precision through the process of automation of indoor farming techniques using the IoT and ML involves the systematic and transformative approach. The execution procedure involves the crucial steps as provided below:

a. ***Problem definition and objective settings:*** Implementing an automated system requires clear goals and objectives, addressing key challenges like resource utilization, crop yield enhancement, and reducing environmental impacts.
b. ***Data collection and sensor deployment:*** Select and deploy the network of IoT sensors and devices within the indoor farming environment. These sensors should measure critical parameters such as temperature, humidity, light intensity, soil moisture, CO_2 levels and nutrient concentrations.
c. ***Data transmission and storage:*** Establish a reliable data transmission mechanism to ensure real-time communication between sensors and a centralized data storage system. Cloud-based platforms can be utilized for efficient data storage, processing and analysis.

d. ***Data pre-processing:*** Clean and pre-process the collected data to handle missing values, outliers and noise. Standardize and normalize the data to ensure consistent scales for accurate ML model training.

e. ***Feature Engineering:*** Identify the relevant features (input variables) for developing the machine learning models. These could include sensor readings, historical data and external factors like weather forecasts.

f. ***Algorithm selection and model development:*** Successful development of automated smart farming models relies on selecting suitable machine learning algorithms based on the problem's nature. Examples include regression or time-series models for yield prediction, classification models for disease classification and detection, and training models using historical data.

g. ***Real-time monitoring and decision making:*** Implement a real-time monitoring dashboard that displays data visualizations and insights from the IoT sensors and ML models. Farmers can utilize this dashboard to make the informed decisions about adjusting environmental conditions, irrigation and nutrient delivery.

h. ***Automated and control systems:*** Integrate the ML models with the automation and control systems that manage climate conditions, irrigation schedules and nutrient delivery. This ensures that the optimal conditions are maintained for crop growth based on the real-time data and predictive models.

i. ***Alerts and notifications:*** setting up an alerting mechanism that sends notifications to the farmers or agronomists when critical thresholds are exceeded or anomalies are detected. This enables prompt responses to potential issues.

j. ***Iterative improvements:*** Continuously collect data from IoT sensors and use it to refine and update the ML models over time. Regularly assess the model performance and adjust algorithms as needed to ensure the accuracy and reliability.

k. ***Training and adoption:*** Train farm personnel on how to use the IoT and ML-powered system effectively. Provide workshops or training sessions to ensure the proper utilization of the technology for optimal results.

l. ***Measuring and evaluating benefits:*** Regularly assess the benefits of the implemented systems, such as the increased crop yields, reduces resource usage and enhanced operational efficiency. Compare the outcomes with the traditional methods to quantify the advantages.

m. ***Scaling and expansion:*** Once the system proves successful, consider scaling up to larger farming areas or integrating it into a broader agricultural ecosystems. Explore the new opportunities for collaboration with other stakeholders in the agriculture industry.

n. ***Regulatory and Ethical considerations:*** Ensure regulatory standards and ethical guidelines related to the data privacy, environmental impact and technology usage in the agricultural field.

By following this comprehensive implementation plan, the integration of IoT and ML into the indoor farming practices can effectively automate and optimize agricultural techniques, leading to the increased productivity, sustainability and overall success in precision agriculture.

Accessibility and Adoption Barriers

A detailed exploration of the specific obstacles that hinder the widespread adoption of precision agriculture, the Internet of Things (IoT), and machine learning. To address this gap, a more comprehensive analysis of the factors that impede accessibility and adoption of these technologies is warranted.

- *Financial Hurdles:* Foremost among these obstacles is the cost associated with implementing advanced agricultural technologies. The adoption of precision agriculture, IoT, and machine learning systems often demands substantial initial investments. The chapter would benefit from a more thorough investigation of the financial challenges faced by farmers and potential strategies to mitigate or distribute these costs.
- *Skills and Training Gaps:* Another significant barrier relates to the lack of knowledge and skills required for the effective use of these technologies. Farmers and agricultural workers may lack the training necessary to operate IoT devices, interpret their data, or develop and maintain machine learning models. A more in-depth discussion within the chapter concerning the need for training programs and educational initiatives to bridge these skill gaps is essential.
- *Infrastructure Challenges:* The successful implementation of precision agriculture, IoT, and machine learning relies on dependable infrastructure, including access to high-speed internet and reliable power sources. However, in rural or remote farming areas, this infrastructure can be insufficient or unreliable, thereby limiting the adoption of these technologies. Therefore, it is crucial to delve into the constraints related to infrastructure and potential solutions.

Environmental and Sustainability Impact

While the chapter certainly offers valuable insights into the advantages of integrating precision agriculture, the Internet of Things (IoT), and machine learning into indoor farming, it is crucial to conduct a more in-depth examination of the substantial environmental and sustainability repercussions that arise from the application of these technologies. Beyond the immediate benefits, it's of paramount importance to explore the broader ecological consequences that underlie the transformation of agricultural practices.

- *Optimized Resource Deployment:* The adoption of precision agriculture, IoT, and machine learning leads to a significant reduction in resource consumption. By fine-tuning the allocation of water, nutrients, and other inputs in response to real-time data and the specific requirements of plants, these technologies effectively curtail resource wastage, promoting resource efficiency. This not only conserves invaluable resources like water but also diminishes the carbon footprint linked to the production and distribution of these resources.
- *Environmental Impact Mitigation:* Among the most compelling aspects of these technologies is their capacity to mitigate the environmental impact of agriculture. Precision agriculture, in particular, significantly reduces the use of chemicals and pesticides through accurate disease and pest detection, thus mitigating the environmental consequences associated with excessive chemical application. Additionally, the optimization of irrigation practices helps prevent overwatering, which can result in soil degradation and the contamination of nearby water sources.
- *Augmented Sustainability:* The convergence of precision agriculture, IoT, and machine learning inevitably contributes to enhanced sustainability in farming practices. Sustainability encompasses

not only the environmental dimension but also economic viability and social equity. Through more efficient resource utilization and reduced input costs, farmers can bolster the economic sustainability of their operations. Furthermore, the accessibility of data-driven insights empowers farmers to make well-informed decisions, thereby enhancing the overall resilience and longevity of their farming endeavors.

- *Mitigation of Climate Change:* The adoption of these technologies plays a pivotal role in mitigating climate change by curbing greenhouse gas emissions. Precision agriculture techniques aid in optimizing energy utilization and curtail emissions associated with unnecessary field operations. This aligns with broader initiatives aimed at combatting climate change by reducing the agricultural sector's contribution to greenhouse gas emissions.

CONCLUSION

The integration of precision agriculture with IoT and machine learning in indoor farming techniques is a significant advancement in modern agriculture. This innovative approach allows indoor farmers to navigate complex environments with unprecedented precision, fine-tuning variables and creating optimal growth conditions for crops. ML models enable early disease detection, accurate yield forecasts, and informed decision-making, allowing farmers to preempt challenges and capitalize on opportunities. The benefits of this synergy include enhanced resource efficiency, sustainable water and resource management, improved crop yields, and reduced chemical usage. However, challenges like data security, technology accessibility, and integration complexity require collaborative efforts among stakeholders across the agricultural spectrum. In conclusion, the integration of precision agriculture with IoT and ML in farming represents a pivotal shift that harmonizes centuries-old farming wisdom with cutting-edge technology, paving the way for a more sustainable, productive, and resilient future in indoor farming and global agriculture.

FUTURE SCOPE

The future direction of precision agriculture as augmented by the integration of IoT and Machine Learning into the indoor farming techniques, promise a landscape of continual innovation and transformative potential. This dynamic convergence is poised to shape the trajectory of agriculture in remarkable ways with several exciting unfolding:

- *Advanced Sensing and Data Fusion-as technology* are anticipated in IoT technology, capturing a broader spectrum of data including environmental factors, genetic information, metabolomics, and microbial dynamics. This fusion offers a holistic understanding of plant health, enabling accurate disease predictions and fine-tuned growth strategies.
- *Interoperability and standardization*: the establishment of industry-wide standards for data protocols and ML algorithms will foster interoperability and seamless integration of technologies. This standardization will dive widespread adoption, allowing diverse systems to communicate and collaborate effortlessly.
- *Edge computing and Real-time analytics:* The integration of edge computing with IoT systems will enable data processing and analytics at the source, reducing latency and facilitating real-time

decision –making. ML models will operate at the edge, providing instant insights and interventions, thus elevating the responsiveness and autonomy of indoor farming operations.

- *Explainable AI and Trustworthiness:* As ML models becomes more complex, the need for explainable AI becomes crucial. Future directions involving the development of models that not only provide accurate predictions but also offer insights into the rationale behind those predictions this will build trust among farmers and stakeholders, encouraging broader acceptance of AI-driven decisions.

- *AI-guided crop breeding:* ML algorithms will play an instrumental role in accelerating crop breeding processes. By analyzing genetic data and growth patterns, AI-driven breeding programs can create novel crop varieties optimized for specific indoor environments, climate conditions and consumer preferences.

- *Block chain and supply chain transparency:* Integration with the block chain technology will provide end-to-end transparency in the agricultural supply chain. Consumers will gain access to immutable records of a products journey from farm to table, ensuring food safety and authenticity.

- *Autonomous robotic farming:* Automation will reach new heights as autonomous robotic systems navigate indoor environments, handling tasks such as planting, pruning and harvesting. These robots will be guided by AI algorithms, optimizing efficiency and reducing labor-intensive processes.

- *Hybrid Ecosystems:* The integration of indoor and outdoor farming systems, with shared data and insights, will enable hybrid ecosystems that leverage the advantages of both approaches. AI models will assist in optimizing the allocation of resources between these systems, further enhancing sustainability.

- *Personalize nutrient delivery:* ML algorithms will enable the development of personalized nutrient delivery strategies based on the individual plant requirements. This level of precision will lead to enhanced nutrient uptake and minimized environmental impacts.

- *Global collaboration and knowledge sharing:* the agricultural community will witness increased collaboration among researchers, farmers and technology experts on global scale. Open-source platforms and data repositories will facilitate the exchange of knowledge, fostering innovation and driving the adoption of advanced technologies.

- *Data security concerns:* protecting the data from the attackers or intruders throughout the crop growth process is very much important as there is the possibility of stealing the data over the network while storing in the cloud or local servers and demanding the currency from the agripreneurs. Hence, high protection should be given for the plant growth data to avoid the data loss from the cyber-attacks. One solution may be employing high professional and skilled people in the field of data privacy and data security may be carried out. The other way of protecting the data is continuous monitoring over the network from attackers might be done.

In the midst of these exciting prospects, it is evident that the future of precision agriculture in indoor farming lies at the intersection of innovation, sustainability and data driven intelligence. The ongoing evolution of IoT and ML technologies will continue to reshape our understanding of agriculture paving the way for a more resilient, efficient and responsive food production system.

REFERENCES

Abougreen, A. N., & Chakraborty, C. (2021). Applications of machine learning and internet of things in agriculture. *Green Technological Innovation for Sustainable Smart Societies: Post Pandemic Era,* 257-279.

Abraham, G., Raksha, R., & Nithya, M. (2021, April). Smart agriculture based on IoT and machine learning. In *2021 5th International Conference on Computing Methodologies and Communication (IC-CMC)* (pp. 414-419). IEEE. 10.1109/ICCMC51019.2021.9418392

Adamides, G. (2020). A review of climate-smart agriculture applications in Cyprus. *Atmosphere (Basel),* *11*(9), 898. doi:10.3390/atmos11090898

Adão, T., Hruška, J., Pádua, L., Bessa, J., Peres, E., Morais, R., & Sousa, J. J. (2017). Hyperspectral imaging: A review on UAV-based sensors, data processing and applications for agriculture and forestry. *Remote Sensing (Basel),* *9*(11), 1110. doi:10.3390/rs9111110

Agarwal, S., & Tarar, S. (2021). A hybrid approach for crop yield prediction using machine learning and deep learning algorithms. [). IOP Publishing.]. *Journal of Physics: Conference Series,* *1714*(1), 012012. doi:10.1088/1742-6596/1714/1/012012

Aishwarya, R., Yogitha, R., Lakshmanan, L., Maheshwari, M., Suji Helen, L., & Nagarajan, G. (2022). Smart agriculture framework implemented using the internet of things and deep learning. In Biologically Inspired Techniques in Many Criteria Decision Making [Singapore: Springer Nature Singapore.]. *Proceedings of BITMDM,* *2021,* 639–648.

Akhter, R., & Sofi, S. A. (2022). Precision agriculture using IoT data analytics and machine learning. *Journal of King Saud University. Computer and Information Sciences,* *34*(8), 5602–5618. doi:10.1016/j.jksuci.2021.05.013

Alrowais, F., Asiri, M. M., Alabdan, R., Marzouk, R., Hilal, A. M., & Gupta, D. (2022). Hybrid leader based optimization with deep learning driven weed detection on internet of things enabled smart agriculture environment. *Computers & Electrical Engineering,* *104,* 108411. doi:10.1016/j.compeleceng.2022.108411

Ayodele, T. O. (2010). Types of machine learning algorithms. *New advances in machine learning,* *3,* 19-48.

Balafoutis, A. T., Beck, B., Fountas, S., Tsiropoulos, Z., Vangeyte, J., van der Wal, T., & Pedersen, S. M. (2017). Smart farming technologies–description, taxonomy and economic impact. *Precision agriculture: Technology and economic perspectives,* 21-77.

Balaji, K., Kiran, P. S., & Kumar, M. S. (2020). Resource aware virtual machine placement in IaaS cloud using bio-inspired firefly algorithm. *Journal of Green Engineering,* *10,* 9315–9327.

Bhatia, N. (2022, October 11). *Types of growing systems in Vertical Farming - Lab Associates.* Lab Associates. https://labassociates.com/types-of-growing-systems-in-vertical-farming

Bondre, D. A., & Mahagaonkar, S. (2019). Prediction of crop yield and fertilizer recommendation using machine learning algorithms. *International Journal of Engineering Applied Sciences and Technology,* *4*(5), 371–376. doi:10.33564/IJEAST.2019.v04i05.055

Bouighoulouden, A., & Kissani, I. (2020). Crop yield prediction using K-means clustering. School of Science and Engineering—Al Akhawayn University.

Cai, X., Fan, W., Wang, Y., & Qian, Y. (2022, October). Research and experiment on automatic navigation control technology of intelligent electric tractor. In *International Conference on Agri-Photonics and Smart Agricultural Sensing Technologies (ICASAST 2022)* (Vol. 12349, pp. 266-269). SPIE. 10.1117/12.2657209

Charoen-Ung, P., & Mittrapiyanuruk, P. (2018, July). Sugarcane yield grade prediction using random forest and gradient boosting tree techniques. In *2018 15th International Joint Conference on Computer Science and Software Engineering (JCSSE)* (pp. 1-6). IEEE. 10.1109/JCSSE.2018.8457391

Eden Green Technology. (2023, January 19). *What Is Vertical Farming? Everything You Should Know About This Innovation.* Eden Green; Eden Green Technology. https://www.edengreen.com/blog-collection/what-is-vertical-farming

Everingham, Y., Sexton, J., Skocaj, D., & Inman-Bamber, G. (2016). Accurate prediction of sugarcane yield using a random forest algorithm. *Agronomy for Sustainable Development, 36*(2), 1–9. doi:10.100713593-016-0364-z

Fahmida Islam, S., Uddin, M. S., & Bansal, J. C. (2022). Harvesting robots for smart agriculture. In *Computer Vision and Machine Learning in Agriculture* (Vol. 2, pp. 1–13). Springer Singapore. doi:10.1007/978-981-16-9991-7_1

Friday, N. H., Al-garadi, M. A., Mujtaba, G., Alo, U. R., & Waqas, A. (2018, March). Deep learning fusion conceptual frameworks for complex human activity recognition using mobile and wearable sensors. In *2018 International Conference on Computing, Mathematics and Engineering Technologies (iCoMET)* (pp. 1-7). IEEE. 10.1109/ICOMET.2018.8346364

Ganesh, D., Kumar, T. P., & Kumar, M. S. (2021). Optimised Levenshtein centroid cross-layer defence for multi-hop cognitive radio networks. *IET Communications, 15*(2), 245–256. doi:10.1049/cmu2.12050

Gowtham, R., & Jebakumar, R. (2022). AN IOT BASED PLANT LEAF DISEASE DETECTION USING MACHINE LEARNING AND AUTO SPRAYING MECHANISM. *Journal of Positive School Psychology*, 283–297.

Gowtham, R., & Jebakumar, R. (2023, February). A Machine Learning Approach for Aeroponic Lettuce Crop Growth Monitoring System. In *International Conference on Intelligent Sustainable Systems* (pp. 99-116). Singapore: Springer Nature Singapore. 10.1007/978-981-99-1726-6_9

Gowtham, R., & Jebakumar, R. (2023, March). Analysis and Prediction of Lettuce Crop Yield in Aeroponic Vertical Farming using Logistic Regression Method. In *2023 International Conference on Sustainable Computing and Data Communication Systems (ICSCDS)* (pp. 759-764). IEEE. 10.1109/ICSCDS56580.2023.10104763

Hegedűs, C., Frankó, A., Varga, P., Gindl, S., & Tauber, M. (2023, May). Enabling Scalable Smart Vertical Farming with IoT and Machine Learning Technologies. In *NOMS 2023-2023 IEEE/IFIP Network Operations and Management Symposium* (pp. 1-4). IEEE. 10.1109/NOMS56928.2023.10154269

Helfer, G. A., Barbosa, J. L. V., Alves, D., da Costa, A. B., Beko, M., & Leithardt, V. R. Q. (2021). Multispectral cameras and machine learning integrated into portable devices as clay prediction technology. *Journal of Sensor and Actuator Networks*, *10*(3), 40. doi:10.3390/jsan10030040

Helfer, G. A., Barbosa, J. L. V., dos Santos, R., & da Costa, A. B. (2020). A computational model for soil fertility prediction in ubiquitous agriculture. *Computers and Electronics in Agriculture*, *175*, 105602. doi:10.1016/j.compag.2020.105602

Islam, N., Rashid, M. M., Pasandideh, F., Ray, B., Moore, S., & Kadel, R. (2021). A review of applications and communication technologies for internet of things (Iot) and unmanned aerial vehicle (uav) based sustainable smart farming. *Sustainability (Basel)*, *13*(4), 1821. doi:10.3390u13041821

Ju, S., Lim, H., & Heo, J. (2020, January). Machine learning approaches for crop yield prediction with MODIS and weather data. In *40th Asian Conference on Remote Sensing: Progress of Remote Sensing Technology for Smart Future, ACRS 2019*.

Khaki, S., & Wang, L. (2019). Crop yield prediction using deep neural networks. *Frontiers in Plant Science*, *10*, 621. doi:10.3389/fpls.2019.00621 PMID:31191564

Khaki, S., Wang, L., & Archontoulis, S. V. (2020). A cnn-rnn framework for crop yield prediction. *Frontiers in Plant Science*, *10*, 1750. doi:10.3389/fpls.2019.01750 PMID:32038699

Khan, M. A., Alqahtani, A., Khan, A., Alsubai, S., Binbusayyis, A., Ch, M. M. I., Yong, H.-S., & Cha, J. (2022). Cucumber leaf diseases recognition using multi level deep entropy-ELM feature selection. *Applied Sciences (Basel, Switzerland)*, *12*(2), 593. doi:10.3390/app12020593

Kour, V. P., & Arora, S. (2020). Recent developments of the internet of things in agriculture: A survey. *IEEE Access: Practical Innovations, Open Solutions*, *8*, 129924–129957. doi:10.1109/ACCESS.2020.3009298

Kumar, M. S., & Harshitha, D. (2019). Process innovation methods on business process reengineering. *International Journal of Innovative Technology and Exploring Engineering*, *8*(11), 2766–2768. doi:10.35940/ijitee.K2244.0981119

Kuska, M. T., & Mahlein, A. K. (2018). Aiming at decision making in plant disease protection and phenotyping by the use of optical sensors. *European Journal of Plant Pathology*, *152*(4), 987–992. doi:10.100710658-018-1464-1

Liakos, K. G., Busato, P., Moshou, D., Pearson, S., & Bochtis, D. (2018). Machine learning in agriculture: A review. *Sensors (Basel)*, *18*(8), 2674. doi:10.339018082674 PMID:30110960

Malchi, S. K., Kallam, S., Al-Turjman, F., & Patan, R. (2021). A trust-based fuzzy neural network for smart data fusion in internet of things. *Computers & Electrical Engineering*, *89*, 106901. doi:10.1016/j.compeleceng.2020.106901

Martini, B. G., Helfer, G. A., Barbosa, J. L. V., Espinosa Modolo, R. C., da Silva, M. R., de Figueiredo, R. M., Mendes, A. S., Silva, L. A., & Leithardt, V. R. Q. (2021). IndoorPlant: A model for intelligent services in indoor agriculture based on context histories. *Sensors (Basel)*, *21*(5), 1631. doi:10.339021051631 PMID:33652603

Mesgaran, M. B., Madani, K., Hashemi, H., & Azadi, P. (2017). Iran's land suitability for agriculture. *Scientific Reports*, *7*(1), 7670. doi:10.103841598-017-08066-y PMID:28794520

Mishra, S., Mishra, D., & Santra, G. H. (2020). Adaptive boosting of weak regressors for forecasting of crop production considering climatic variability: An empirical assessment. *Journal of King Saud University. Computer and Information Sciences*, *32*(8), 949–964. doi:10.1016/j.jksuci.2017.12.004

Muangprathub, J., Boonnam, N., Kajornkasirat, S., Lekbangpong, N., Wanichsombat, A., & Nillaor, P. (2019). IoT and agriculture data analysis for smart farm. *Computers and Electronics in Agriculture*, *156*, 467–474. doi:10.1016/j.compag.2018.12.011

Mupangwa, W., Chipindu, L., Nyagumbo, I., Mkuhlani, S., & Sisito, G. (2020). Evaluating machine learning algorithms for predicting maize yield under conservation agriculture in Eastern and Southern Africa. *SN Applied Sciences*, *2*(5), 1–14. doi:10.100742452-020-2711-6

Nasteski, V. (2017). An overview of the supervised machine learning methods. *Horizons*, *4*, 51-62.

Natarajan, V. A., Kumar, M. S., Patan, R., Kallam, S., & Mohamed, M. Y. N. (2020, September). Segmentation of nuclei in histopathology images using fully convolutional deep neural architecture. In *2020 International Conference on computing and information technology (ICCIT-1441)* (pp. 1-7). IEEE. 10.1109/ICCIT-144147971.2020.9213817

Navulur, S., & Prasad, M. G. (2017). Agricultural management through wireless sensors and internet of things. *Iranian Journal of Electrical and Computer Engineering*, *7*(6), 3492. doi:10.11591/ijece.v7i6.pp3492-3499

Pathan, M., Patel, N., Yagnik, H., & Shah, M. (2020). Artificial cognition for applications in smart agriculture: A comprehensive review. *Artificial Intelligence in Agriculture*, *4*, 81–95. doi:10.1016/j.aiia.2020.06.001

Pawar, S., Dere, S., Akangire, A., Kamble, H., & Shrawne, S. (2021). *Smart farming using machine learning*. Smart Comput.

Peneti, S., Sunil Kumar, M., Kallam, S., Patan, R., Bhaskar, V., & Ramachandran, M. (2021). BDN-GWMNN: Internet of things (IoT) enabled secure smart city applications. *Wireless Personal Communications*, *119*(3), 2469–2485. doi:10.100711277-021-08339-w

Phasinam, K., Kassanuk, T., & Shabaz, M. (2022). Applicability of internet of things in smart farming. *Journal of Food Quality*, *2022*, 1–7. doi:10.1155/2022/7692922

Radoglou-Grammatikis, P., Sarigiannidis, P., Lagkas, T., & Moscholios, I. (2020). A compilation of UAV applications for precision agriculture. *Computer Networks*, *172*, 107148. doi:10.1016/j.comnet.2020.107148

Rajendiran, G., & Rethnaraj, J. (2023). Lettuce Crop Yield Prediction Analysis using Random Forest Regression Machine Learning Model in Aeroponics System. In *2023 Second International Conference on Augmented Intelligence and Sustainable Systems (ICAISS)* (pp. 565-572). IEEE. 10.1109/ICAISS58487.2023.10250535

Rajendiran, G., & Rethnaraj, J. (2023). Smart Aeroponic Farming System: Using IoT with LCGM-Boost Regression Model for Monitoring and Predicting Lettuce Crop Yield. *International Journal of Intelligent Engineering & Systems*, *16*(5).

Reddy, D. A., Dadore, B., & Watekar, A. (2019). Crop recommendation system to maximize crop yield in ramtek region using machine learning. *International Journal of Scientific Research in Science and Technology*, *6*(1), 485–489. doi:10.32628/IJSRST196172

Richardson, A., Signor, B. M., Lidbury, B. A., & Badrick, T. (2016). Clinical chemistry in higher dimensions: Machine-learning and enhanced prediction from routine clinical chemistry data. *Clinical Biochemistry*, *49*(16-17), 1213–1220. doi:10.1016/j.clinbiochem.2016.07.013 PMID:27452181

Sangamithra, B., Neelima, P., & Kumar, M. S. (2017, April). A memetic algorithm for multi objective vehicle routing problem with time windows. In *2017 IEEE International Conference on Electrical, Instrumentation and Communication Engineering (ICEICE)* (pp. 1-8). IEEE. 10.1109/ICEICE.2017.8191931

Saud, A., & Elfadil, N. (2020). Biometric authentication by using fingerprint recognition system. *Int J Sci Eng Sci*, *4*(5), 22–28.

Shaikh, F. K., Karim, S., Zeadally, S., & Nebhen, J. (2022). Recent trends in internet of things enabled sensor technologies for smart agriculture. *IEEE Internet of Things Journal*, *9*(23), 23583–23598. doi:10.1109/JIOT.2022.3210154

Sharma, A., Jain, A., Gupta, P., & Chowdary, V. (2020). Machine learning applications for precision agriculture: A comprehensive review. *IEEE Access : Practical Innovations, Open Solutions*, *9*, 4843–4873. doi:10.1109/ACCESS.2020.3048415

Shin, J. Y., Kim, K. R., & Ha, J. C. (2020). *Seasonal forecasting of daily mean air temperatures using a coupled global climate model and machine learning algorithm for field-scale agricultural management.*

Siddique, T., Barua, D., Ferdous, Z., & Chakrabarty, A. (2017, September). Automated farming prediction. In *2017 Intelligent systems conference (IntelliSys)* (pp. 757-763). IEEE.

Bloomberg. (2022, April 21). *Smart Agriculture Market Size Worth $35.98 Billion by 2030: Grand View Research, Inc.* Bloomberg.com. https://www.bloomberg.com/press-releases/2022-04-21/smart-agriculture-market-size-worth-35-98-billion-by-2030-grand-view-research-inc

Sreedhar, B. BE, M. S., & Kumar, M. S. (2020, October). A comparative study of melanoma skin cancer detection in traditional and current image processing techniques. In *2020 Fourth International Conference on I-SMAC (IoT in Social, Mobile, Analytics and Cloud)(I-SMAC)* (pp. 654-658). IEEE.

Suruliandi, A., Mariammal, G., & Raja, S. P. (2021). Crop prediction based on soil and environmental characteristics using feature selection techniques. *Mathematical and Computer Modelling of Dynamical Systems*, *27*(1), 117–140. doi:10.1080/13873954.2021.1882505

Talaviya, T., Shah, D., Patel, N., Yagnik, H., & Shah, M. (2020). Implementation of artificial intelligence in agriculture for optimisation of irrigation and application of pesticides and herbicides. *Artificial Intelligence in Agriculture*, *4*, 58–73. doi:10.1016/j.aiia.2020.04.002

Team Cultivatd. (2022, September 21). *3 Advantages and 3 Challenges of Vertical Farming*. Cultivatd. https://cultivatd.com/advantages-challenges-vertical-farming/

Tripathi, M. K., & Maktedar, D. D. (2020). A role of computer vision in fruits and vegetables among various horticulture products of agriculture fields: A survey. *Information Processing in Agriculture*, 7(2), 183–203. doi:10.1016/j.inpa.2019.07.003

Verma, S., Gala, R., Madhavan, S., Burkule, S., Chauhan, S., & Prakash, C. (2018, August). An internet of things (IoT) architecture for smart agriculture. In *2018 fourth international conference on computing communication control and automation (ICCUBEA)* (pp. 1-4). IEEE.

Virk, A. L., Noor, M. A., Fiaz, S., Hussain, S., Hussain, H. A., Rehman, M., & Ma, W. (2020). Smart farming: an overview. *Smart village technology: concepts and developments*, 191-201.

Xie, D., Chen, L., Liu, L., Chen, L., & Wang, H. (2022). Actuators and sensors for application in agricultural robots: A review. *Machines*, 10(10), 913. doi:10.3390/machines10100913

Yasmeen, U., Khan, M. A., Tariq, U., Khan, J. A., Yar, M. A. E., Hanif, C. A., & Nam, Y. (2021). Citrus diseases recognition using deep improved genetic algorithm. *Computers, Materials & Continua, 71*, 3667–3684. doi:10.32604/cmc.2022.022264

Chapter 14
Automated Plant Disease Detection Using Efficient Deep Ensemble Learning Model for Smart Agriculture

R. Karthick Manoj

Academy of Maritime Education and Training, India

Aasha Nandhini S.

SSN College of Engineering, India

T. Sasilatha

Academy of Maritime Education and Training, India

ABSTRACT

Early diagnosis of plant diseases is essential for successful plant disease prevention and control, as well as agricultural production management and decision-making. In this research, an efficient weighted average deep ensemble learning (EWADEL) model is used to detect plant diseases automatically. Transfer learning (TL) is a technique used to enhance existing algorithms. The performances of several pre-trained neural networks with DL such as ResNet152 DenseNet201, and InceptionV3, in addition to the usefulness of a weighted average ensemble models, are demonstrated for disease linked with leaf identification. To that aim, a EWADEL methodology is being researched in order to construct a robust network capable of predicting 12 different diseases of apple, Pomegranate, and tomato crops. Several convolutional neural network architectures were examined and ensemble to increase predictive performance using the EWADEL. In addition, the proposed approach included an examination of several deep learning models and developed EWADEL models.

DOI: 10.4018/979-8-3693-0639-0.ch014

INTRODUCTION

The effect of global warming has grown substantially in recent years. It is impacting all stages of cultivation and requiring farmers to adjust and adapt their agricultural practises through the use of new data-driven technology. As biotic and abiotic stressors are the limiting elements of agricultural output, disease of plants prediction has become a research focus. Instead of depending solely on an outside expert, technology instruments may now be used to assess whether a plant has a disease and what type of sickness it isAs the quality of picture collection by technological equipment increases, object identification, categorization, processing of images, and computational intelligence algorithms yield astoundingly good results Khan, R.U. (2021). Traditional optimisation and predictions approaches are outperformed by ML and DL. For starters, these systems can learn from vast volumes of data automatically, whereas older methods need human feature extraction and are restricted by data quantity. Second, unlike previous approaches, ML and DL models generalise effectively to new data. Third, ML and DL models, unlike previous approaches, can learn complicated, non-linear data connections. As a result, ML is superior at dealing with numerous variables, particularly complicated interactions. Artificial intelligence applications have been widely used in a wide range of fields. In this situation, precise and prompt identification and categorization of illnesses in plants is critical. Artificial intelligence advancements now allow for automated plant disease identification from raw images.

To categorise illnesses in plant leaves, this chapter investigates DL approaches, which are a subtype of ML techniques. Conventional ML approaches use human feature development to train classification algorithms, whereas DL techniques discover the features dynamically from the image itself. This chapter investigates a range of cutting-edge deep learning models for diagnosing and classifying diseases of plants using pictures from the Plant Village data set in addition to images collected individually (Domingues et al.2022). A database may be expanded using techniques like data augmentation, which employs rotation, flipping, and contrast. Three different and effective deep learning models, namely ResNet 152, Dense Net201, and InceptionNetv3, are evaluated and trained on these images. The performance study is conducted using accuracy metrics, and the top-performing deep learning model is ultimately selected. An efficient Weighted deep ensemble Learning (EWADEL) model which make it more efficient to achieve improved accuracy. Finally, the EWADEL model will be compared with its original version to prove the efficacy. The validation and results of the EWDEL model is also discussed in detail in this chapter.

LITERATURE SURVEY

This paper Javidan et.al (2023) provides a unique weighted majority voting ensemble strategy for detecting tomato leaves by distinguishing red, green, and blue pictures. As basic classifiers, six machine learning approaches were used. The proposed methods were then employed to improve sickness classification, with precision rates of 93.49% and 95.58%, correspondingly. The suggested technique's performance was compared to two well-known DL algorithms, which produced poor results. The suggested framework based on weighted majority voting beat the underlying ML, according to the study's findings. An infection identification method for crops has been developed employing either diseased and healthy leaves from different plant classes during this investigation Kondaveeti, et.al (2023). The fundamental models achieved accuracy levels below 90% based the crop illness data. The core algorithms now contain hard and soft voting categories to increase the system's accuracy. Soft voting entails examining the anticipated accuracy of each foundation methodology and selecting the way with the highest average weight as the final forecast.

In this field of study Saleem et al (2019), looks to provide enormous upside in terms of enhancing dependability. To discover and assess plant disease messages, many well-known designs and visualisation approaches are utilised. These architectures/techniques are also examined using a variety of efficiency measures. This research examines in depth the digitally produced models used to portray various plant ailments. Also, many research requirements are proposed in order to improve accessibility for identifying plant ailments. Convolutional neural network models were constructed in this paper employing DL techniques for recognising and diagnosing plant illnesses using basic leaf pictures of both healthy and sick crops. Ferentinos, K.P. (2018).The most successful prediction architecture had a success rating of 99.53% in determining a matched pair. Because of its high success rate, the algorithm might be expanded to enable for an entire plant sickness diagnosis method that operates in real-world production situations.

This article distinguishes between healthy and unhealthy leaves using Random Forest data sets. S. Ramesh and coworkers (2015). Our suggested paper covers implementation steps such as preparing the data, extraction of features and classification. The sets of ill and healthy leaves are mixed and trained using an algorithm based on random forests to identify damaged and healthy photos. Overall, training huge publically available data sets using machine learning provides us with a clear mechanism for identifying plant disease on a big scale.

The investigation Vishnoi (2021) backdrop for detection systems throughout different phases, including frequent illnesses, is highlighted. Modern feature extraction strategies are being explored in order to uncover ones that appear to work successfully across a wide range of crop species. In this study, Shrestha (2020) provides an overview of plant disease detection systems. This study proposes a CNN technique for identifying plant diseases. For example, simulation studies and assessments are carried out on photographs in terms of time difficulty and contaminated region area. It is accomplished through the use of computational image processing tools. The assessment's efficiency is 88.80%.

Portable systems and IoT interfaces are important in this design. They investigate innovative nanotechnology-based diagnostic methods, as well as new perspectives on technological relationship and knowledge in agriculture, with the aim of helping increase agricultural and rural development and transform the concept of precautionary measures that have an impact in the worldwide effort to fight against phytopathogens. The article presents a novel a web-based sickness detection system which employs compressed images to detect and categorise abnormalities in leaves. Nandhini, Aasha (2019). A statistically driven thresholding technique is proposed for ill leaf segmentation. The CS elements of the split leaves are transmitted to the World Wide Web to reduce storage complication. The tracking station provides the data, and the characteristics are taken from the rebuilt split image. The Support Vector Machine classifier is used for categorization and evaluation. The accuracy of the proposed method has been investigated and compared to current techniques. The proposed solution was also put through its paces in the lab with an older version of the Raspberry Pi 3 board. According to the statistics, the proposed approach has a 98.5% successful detection reliability.

Haridasan, A., (2023) described a system for proactively identifying and classifying illnesses from a provided image. The suggested method for diagnosing diseases of plants is based on artificial intelligence (AI) and incorporates numerous learning algorithms, minimising dependency on existing preventative measures in fields. After picture pre-processing, image segmentation is used to locate the sick area of the plant, with the illnesses mentioned above diagnosed just by their visual features. SVM classifiers and CNN are used in tandem to identify and categorise various paddy crop ailments. The proposed DL solution achieved the maximum validation accuracy of 0.9145. Li, L., and Zhang (2021) provide the most current advances in DL technology research in the context of agricultural illness identification. For this investigation, our team employs DL and sophisticated imaging methods to tackle existing successes and obstacles in diagnosing diseases of crop. They hope that the results of our research will be useful to experts tasked with diagnosing crop illnesses and problems with insects. We reviewed some of the current difficulties along with issues that must be addressed at the same timeframe.

Ahmed (2023) advocated utilising ML methods to construct models for identifying ailments in plants. The suggested plants disease danger evaluation model's performance is evaluated using objective criteria. According to the data, the integrated plant sickness model outperforms the previously suggested and built plant disease detection approaches. Sickness forecasting approaches developed and established attempted to foresee illness detection in its early phases, allowing for early preventative interventions and expected maintenance. The recommended hybrid technique was used in this work to diagnose Bacteria Spot illness in crops using plants photos, but it may be used for any crop condition. Bedi, P. (2021) used a publicly accessible dataset called Plant Village to capture images of peach harvest leaves for this study. In comparison to earlier research approaches, the proposed hybrid technique needs fewer parameters for training. As a consequence, the time required to train an algorithm for autonomous crop disease identification, as well as the time required to diagnose crop sickness using the learned model, is considerably reduced.

Nagaraju, (2020) analysed several of the existing neural network methods for interpreting visual data, with an emphasis on agricultural diagnosis of diseases. First, consider the information resources, computational models, and image processing techniques used for processing the presented pictures. Second, the study highlighted the outcomes of an analysis of numerous existing DL, which was followed by a discussion of the possibilities for hyperspectral processing of data in the years to come. The purpose of the survey is to assist potential investigators in learning about the capacity for DL while identifying plant illnesses by enhancing the system's effectiveness and accuracy. In this study, author Abbas (2021) describes a DL strategy for identifying tomato illness that uses the Conditional Evolutionary Adversarial Network to produce artificial pictures of tomatoes plant leaves. Then, utilising transferred learning, a Dense Net network is developed on simulated and actual information to classify leafy tomatoes into ten sickness categories. Using the publicly available PlantVillage data set, the suggested approach was thoroughly trained and verified. It is suggested had an accuracy of 99.51%. This technique outperforms the current techniques.

In the course of addressing the hyperspectral illness evaluation steps in the papers, Zhang, N (2020), the computations and methods from illness identification to qualitative as well as quantitative evaluation are subsequently detailed. Furthermore, it is suggested which different infectious agents proof of being a component of something, biotic and abiotic stress bias, disease of plants rapid detection, and satellite-based hyperspectral advances should be investigated after a review of the current major problems with recognising plant diseases in hyperspectral technological innovations..

Tiwari (2021) described a Dl method to perform plant illness identification and categorization utilising leaf images captured at different levels of resolution. A large collection of plant leaf images from several countries is utilised to train a dense convolutional neural network (CNN) architecture. Six plants from 27 distinct groups are tested in lab and on-field scenarios in the suggested study. This artificial neural network model was able to deal with a huge number of inter-class and intra-class differences in photos showing complex and difficult settings. The experimental findings reveal that the proposed DL technique can classify various types of plant leaves effectively and correctly. An average cross-validation efficiency, based on the experimental data.

In this work, an CNN algorithm based on TL has been created for the precise identification of plant illnesses. In the publication Mukti, (2019), we employed the ResNet, which network, which is a conventional CNN architecture, as our trained model in TL. In addition, many TL architectures were studied and compared to a few other regularly used pre-trained models. With an accuracy in training of 99.80%, the proposed model outperformed the others. Crop pictures were first utilised to diagnose plant diseases using traditional ML mining and image processing approaches, which resulted in a lack of accuracy and range. In detecting plant ailments, DL enhanced prediction accuracy while also expanding the number of diseases and plant species studied. Loey (2020) undertakes a study of research articles that illustrate the use of DL in the detection of crop illness as well as examines them in terms of data utilised, models employed, and the general outcome reached in the present paper.

Crop cultivation is critical in agriculture. Agriculture employs more than 70% of the population. At present, crop infection is ideal for inefficient food materials, where the production rate is lowered. Plant illnesses are caused by pesticides used in farming. This investigation Sankaran, K.S., (2020), investigates leaf detection and determines whether or not it is influenced by illnesses. This is the first step in preventing the illness from spread. Based on picture segmentation and green pixel masking, an upgraded k means clustering algorithm is proposed for crop early forecasting. Finally, it differentiates between normal and abnormal leaves.

However, crop leaf disease diagnosis and classification systems based on convolutional neural networks have made substantial progress in recent decades. The detection algorithms' efficacy is dependent on a huge volume and diversity of data. However, acquiring such a large amount of data is dependent on a variety of circumstances, including weather conditions, changing lighting, and the absence of disease at the time. Data augmentation strategies are critical for dealing with this problem. Several data augmentation approaches are used in this study by S. Talasila (2022).

In this paper, Chaudhary et al. (2016) proposed a novel hybrid ensemble approach that incorporates ML. Its goal is to increase ML algorithm performance in multiclass categorization settings. The efficacy of the new hybrid ensemble approach is evaluated using four typical agricultural multiclass datasets. It outperforms all of these datasets. It is used to a multiclass dataset of oilseed diseases. Logistic Regression and Nave Bayes are outperformed by the ensemble-Vote approach. The performance of the hybrid ensemble is compared to that of the ensemble-Vote.

This investigation aims to investigate the Optimisation with Ensemble Recurrent Neural Network for System Gopi and colleagues (2023). Because it adopts an ensemble learning technique that incorporates three DL models, the proposed model beats individual classifier models in prediction. The results of the trials revealed that the suggested model outperformed other techniques under various scenarios. By utilising a range of agro-factors, the proposed approach described here supports farmers in making decisions.

According to Shovon et al. (2023), the authors of this study suggested PlantDet, a strong new deep ensemble model built on various deep learning model. PlantDet has more dense layers than previous models and effective data augmentation, batch normalization layers. These characteristics make the model more resilient and enable it to handle under fitting and over fitting problems while retaining excellent performance. PlantDet performs better on the Rice Leaf dataset than the previous top model.

In order to assist farmers in need, this study Nagasubramanian et al., (2021) suggested a method that continuously checks crop development and leaf ailments. For agricultural regions, this system sends precise crop status signals to terminal IoT components to help with irrigation, dietary planning, and environmental compliance. In order to identify plant diseases early on, this work proposes ensemble classification and pattern recognition for crop monitoring systems. The suggested techniques use ensemble nonlinear SVM to identify leaf and crop diseases. This article also compares and examines a variety of ML techniques.

Yang et al. (2023) suggest a stacking-based continuous learning approach for the rapid and accurate diagnosis of rice leaf diseases in this study. For diverse categorization challenges, different improvement methodologies have varying implications on training and education processes. Several studies were conducted to look into the impact of alternatives enhancement techniques on the precision of rice leaf disease detection, including comparisons among single models and many stacking-based model arrangements, as well as comparison tests with diverse datasets. The model suggested in this paper was demonstrated to be greater in effectiveness than simple models and to yield useful results on an agricultural dataset, resulting in a more effective strategy for recognising plant illnesses.

Anwar et al. (2023) propose an ensemble-based technique based on transfer learning in this work. The experiment makes use of trained models as well as a voting classifier ensemble approach. These pre-trained models are employed in a parallel pipeline model to train the training dataset. The proposed ensemble model outperforms the current methodologies presented over the same selected dataset, with an accuracy of 82.5%, proving the methodology's usefulness.The fundamental purpose of this study Sreedevi et al., (2023) is to develop a one-of-a-kind system for identifying tomato leaf illnesses using deep learning methodologies, particularly for coping with low-resolution picture issues. The contrast enhancement approach is used for pre-processing, while DL is used to solve the low-resolution issue in pre-processed pictures. Controlling Parameter-based Artificial Gorilla Troops are used to maximise each classifier score. The proposed approach has a sensitivity of 93% and an accuracy of 92%. As a consequence, the efficacy of the proposed model has been evaluated using a variety of performance indicators in comparison to other recent methodologies.

METHODOLOGY

DL is employed in the current agricultural production to gauge the temperature and moisture content of plants. Growers may also keep an eye on their crops from anywhere on the planet. This sophisticated agriculture system powered by AI is incredibly effective.

Convolution Neural Networks Varior et al. (2016) are used often in human-computer interactions. Recently, it has also been applied in other situations. Compared to feed-forward networks, CNNs have an advantage since they can identify distinctive areas. The ability to extract attributes and actions may result from this. Both two-dimensional (2D) and three-dimensional (3D) data may be used by CNNs, and if appropriate, input data may be processed into matrices.

The traditional approaches Crespo, O., et.al (2017.) of diagnosing crop disease are based mostly on visual observations made in the field by experienced farmers or leaf specialists. This demands continual expert monitoring, which can be prohibitively expensive on large farms. In order to meet with agricultural specialists, farmers may have to travel a great distance, especially in developing nations. This is obviously time-consuming, expensive, and inherently slows, and it cannot be done for a wide range of crops. Nonetheless, due to significant advances in image processing and pattern recognition technologies, a new way for recognising and diagnosing plant diseases is now accessible. Since they can monitor enormous fields of crops and automatically identify disease signs as soon as they appear, image recognition and deep learning are the primary research topics Rothe,et.al (2015). Deep learning has lately displayed excellent performance in image processing and classification tasks, allowing for the speedy and precise prediction of an object's appearance in an image Sigaud, O et.al (2015). The visual properties required for deep learning-based object detection tasks are automatically learned by the object detector.

Dense Net

The feature maps of the current layer and all preceding levels comprise each layer of Huang et al. (2017)'s Dense Nets. As a result, these networks are computationally and memory-efficient, contain extensive representations of features for the input images, and are compact.If the connections among the layers nearest to the inputs and its layers nearest to the result are smaller, CNN can be taught quicker, deeper, and more precisely Too, E.C., et al (2019). A feed-forward connection connects each layer of the dense convolutional network to every other layer.

Inception Net

InceptionNet and other convolutional neural networks were developed for the Image Net with the intention of completing picture classification tasks The use of inception modules, which are layers meant to learn a combination of local and global properties from the input data, is a hallmark of InceptionNet.

Inception blocks use a modular design to solve this issue by letting the network learn various feature mappings at various scales. To create a more complete representation of the input data, these feature maps are then concatenated. This makes it possible for the network to gather a variety of information, both high-level and low-level, which can be helpful for tasks like image categorization. The Inception-Net design may learn a more extensive collection of characteristics from the input data by employing inception blocks, which can enhance the network's performance on tasks like image categorization Chen, J., et.al (2022).

ResNet

A residual neural network is a deep learning model where the weight layers use the inputs from the layer inputs to train residual functions. A network with skip connections that performs identity mappings and is appended to layer outputs is referred to as a residual network. With gates opened by very positive bias weights, it functions much like a highway network Murugan, et.al (2021,).

DL models with tens or hundreds of layers may now be trained simply and approach higher accuracy as they progress deeper . Identity skip connections, also known as "residual connections" in the 1997 LSTM networks, are also employed. The output of the last convolution block of a 152-layered deep residual network (ResNet-152) that has been pre-trained on ImageNet is used to extract deep residual features. The ResNet-152 is constructed from five convolutional blocks stacked on top of one another. ResNet's convolutional blocks differ from those of traditional CNNs by including a shortcut link between each block's input and output, leading to better optimisation and less complexity.

Transfer Learning

Transfer learning has been widely employed as a machine learning strategy in image identification. The goal of TL is to apply previous expertise to a novel or distinct activity. The more the similarities between the intended audience and source sectors, the simpler it is to communicate information. The primary issue it tries to address is the lack of trained samples in the area of interest, which makes learning features difficult for the DL algorithm Han, X, et al (2021). It is further classified as induced or unsupervised depending on whether the examples in the source and destination fields are labelled and whether the responsibilities are the same. Learning techniques are classified based on the contents of the transfer as representation of features, transfer, occurrence transfer, variable transfer, and association connection transfer.

Ensemble Learning

Classifier performance is improved via ensemble learning. AlSuwaidi et al (2018) describe the most frequent techniques as bagging, boosting, and stacking. An ensemble takes into account homogenous or heterogeneous groupings. In the first example, a single base classifier is trained on several datasets, but in the later situation, many classifiers are trained on the same dataset. The group of classifiers then forecasts the output based on the weighted average and votes on the basis classifiers' outputs. Ensemble learning is a ML approach that combines numerous models, known as base learners, to answer a single issue. Ensemble modelling techniques include bagging, boosting, and stacking. We used the Bagging strategy in our study, which consists of training various classifiers and compiling the final prediction. An efficient weighted average deep ensemble Learning model (EWADEL), such as ResNet152, DenseNet201, and InceptionV3, is used to identify plant diseases automatically and boost prediction accuracy using weighted averaging.

PROPOSED EFFICIENT WEIGHTED AVERAGE DEEP ENSEMBLE LEARNING (EWADEL) MODEL ARCHITECTURE

To fit in the model, photos are pre-processed and shrunk to 256*256 pixels in Deep Learning techniques. To begin, photos from the capture dataset as well as the publicly available dataset are utilised to train the model. The dataset is divided into 80% training 10% validation and 10% testing ratios at random. The training and testing photos are put into the proposed models, and the characteristics are extracted. Finally, the deep learning algorithms will recognise the images of diseased leaves. In the literature, efficient weighted average deep ensemble Learning (EWADEL) models like as ResNet152, DenseNet201, and InceptionNetv3 have been discovered for illness classification.

Figure 1 depicts the proposed framework. The multi crop leaf collection photographs were first pre-processed and resized. Pre-processing and data augmentation techniques were utilised to increase model generalisation. The data was divided into training, validation, and testing sets using data augmentation techniques. Using the training set photos, TL approaches were used to train several models, including InceptionV3, ResNet152, and DenseNet201. It imported these models without their final layers, allowing us to use our pooling and dense layers to generate the leaf species from the dataset. These models were developed during a 20-epoch period. Cross-validation validation accuracies of threefold and fivefold

Figure 1. Architecture of the proposed efficient deep ensemble learning (EWADEL) model

were also provided. The ensemble created on top of the component models uses the weighted average of the numerous models to generate the final forecast. The next sections go over component models, the concept of TL, and an efficient weighted average deep ensemble Learning (EWADEL) model.

IMAGE PROCESSING AND DATA AUGMENTATION

Deep learning models require a large dataset. Data augmentation approaches aid in the expansion of datasets, allowing them to be used with DL models (Shorten et al., 2019). A DL dataset is often divided into three sections: training, validation, and testing. The training set is used to train the model, whereas the validation set is usually utilised during training to modify hyperparameters. The test set consists of data that the DL model has never seen before and is used to evaluate the model's performance. The original dataset is typically split 80:10:10 for training, validation, and testing. The data must be pre-processed to

Figure 2. Data augmentation of sample images

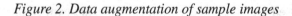

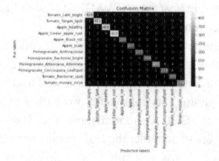

keep the algorithm constant and functioning smoothly. DL performs effectively and avoids overfitting when the input database is as large as feasible.

Convolution Neural Networks can learn more robust features by making tiny, imperceptible to the human sight adjustments to the input images, such as introducing noise and blur (Cygert and Czyżewski, 2020). In this work, Data augmentation techniques helps in increasing dataset making it suitable for deep learning models. The images are scaled randomly between 0.95 and 1.05 in both the horizontal and vertical dimensions, and they are randomly rotated between -30° and 30°. Here, the dataset has also been rotated and inverted. The image is rotated 45, 135, 225, and 315 degrees, as well as horizontally and vertically, by the position augmentation (Mikołajczyk et.al 2018).The purity or level of saturation of a color is represented by saturation. Blue, red, green, and other colors are represented by hue. Its possible values are 0 to 360. When assessing the contrast value of the color enhancement, the histogram is equalized. Accuracy is known to be increased by histogram equalization. The deep learning networks used in this task are ResNet152, Dense Net and Inception Net using transfer learning (Mzoughi et.al 2023).

For data augmentation, the standard open-access Plant Village dataset (Kaggle) of healthy and sick plant leaves is used. Figure 2 shows a sample of photos of leaves from the Plant Village databases. The collection contains 12 separate classes of three unique plant species, including photos of both healthy and disease-affected leaves for each class. After the dataset has been expanded, it may be utilised for training, validation, and testing. Data augmentation is a strategy for mitigating overfitting in which the size of the dataset is increased by creating fresh samples from the training set using a variety of modifications. In this research, we used common techniques like as rotation, shearing, zooming, cropping, flipping, and colour modification.

PERFORMANCE AND EVALUATION OF EWADELM

The deep learning model was initially evaluated using photos from the created dataset. To build the dataset from the publically accessible dataset, data augmentation methods such as picture scaling, filtering, and other methods such as clockwise and anticlockwise rotation, horizontal and vertical flipping, whitening, and shifting are employed. Figure 1 depicts an ensemble model that leverages the strengths of DenseNer201, ResNet152, and InceptionV3 to provide higher classification accuracy and resilience in Multi crop leaf disease detection. By using the capabilities of each individual model, we intend to increase the overall performance of our sickness detection system. The ensemble model is constructed in two phases. To begin, each model is trained separately using its own architecture and dataset. The training approach includes adjusting the essential parameters of each model, such as learning rate, batch size, and optimizer, to ensure optimal performance. Following the training of the different base models, their predictions on multi crop leaf pictures are integrated using a multi fusion approach to provide the final classification result. Weighted averaging computes the final forecast by multiplying each model's prediction by a weight and adding them together, to make the forecast, we used weighted averaging.

The selection of individual model weights and the fusion process, as well as hyper parameter tweaking, are critical for the ensemble model. Weights can be established based on each model's performance on a validation set or by employing approaches such as grid search. Individual hyperparameters of the underlying model, such as learning rate, batch size, and optimizer, were optimised. The ensemble model is trained by training each unique base model independently utilising their particular architectures and datasets. The forecasts from the fundamental models are merged using the fusion technique to get the final projection. The performance of the ensemble model is evaluated using typical evaluation metrics such as accuracy, precision, recall, F1-score, and confusion matrix.

This suggested ensemble model combines the capabilities of DenseNet201, ResNe152 and InceptionV3 to increase classification accuracy and resilience in multi crop leaf disease detection. We can produce more trustworthy and accurate forecasts by combining results from various models using a weighted average method and adequate hyper parameter tweaking. The ensemble model's performance is quantitatively assessed when it is evaluated using conventional metrics.

The detection and classification accuracy of the DL models are used to assess their performance. Based on the performance, the best performing DL model is picked, which is then improved by altering and fine adjusting the model's hyper parameters. ResNet-152's final convolution output 1st block (7 conv) Conv 7*7 Block 2 (28 commuters) Block 3 of Input (108 conv) Block 4 (7 convoluted) Layer that is completely interconnected Cascaded dense convolution layers with batch normalisation layers and parametric ReLU activation layers are used in the output block. Features were taken from the suggested fine-tuned model after this network had been trained, and they were then further flattened to categorise the data. A parametric ReLU activation layer and a hybrid loss function were used to achieve the fine-tuning. The problem of class inequality inspired the development of this loss function. Since Parametric ReLU adjusts the learning parameters depending on learning rate instead of using a Stochastic Gradient Descent Deep Learning Optimizer, it is utilised for fine-tuning models. The final EWADEL model is used for classifying the diseases and the performance is evaluated. The effectiveness of the EWADEL model is then compared with that of more established DL models as ResNet152, DenseNet201, and InceptionNet. The EWADEL model's performance is validated using metrics such as detection accuracy and classification accuracy using the supplemented dataset of apple, pomegranate, and tomato. This section goes over the experimental setup and analyses in depth.

Experimental Setup

In this work, the Jupyter notebook environment and Python 3.6 were used for all preprocessing, DL-based feature extraction, and classification. The model is built using the OpenCV-python3 package and the Keras library. A 3.40 GHz Intel(R) Core (TM) i5-6700 Central Processing Unit (CPU) and 16 GB of Random Access Memory (RAM) are used to perform the specified job. One of the most critical and vital aspects of the training process is hyperparameter selection. The attributes that regulate the whole training process are known as hyperparameters. Hyperparameters are variables that must be specified before the learning algorithm can be applied to the dataset. The number of classes determines how many unique labels in total are utilised in the collection. A network's learning rate determines how quickly it updates its parameters. A rapid learning rate speeds up learning even when a model may not converge. Although the network learning process is delayed because to the low learning rate, this allows the model to gradually converge. As a result, choosing the decaying learning rate is always preferred. The batch size specifies the number of subsamples of the dataset provided to the network after which parameter updates are performed. The batch size is set to 32 by default. It can, however, be 32, 64, 128, and so forth. The amount of training steps are necessary to train the model depends on the number of steps. Usually, it is calculated by dividing the dataset's total number of images by the batch size. The fundamental rule is to raise the deep learning model's training epoch count until training accuracy starts to outpace validation accuracy. An activation function aids the network in learning complicated data patterns. It takes the previous cell's output signal and changes it into a form that may be transmitted as the following cell's input. Softmax, Relu, Sigmoid, and other commonly used activation functions.

Performance Metrics

The effectiveness of the developed model was evaluated using a range of performance metrics, including accuracy, precision, recall, specificity, and F1-score. A number of indices are required to assess these metrics, including the four labels produced from the confusion matrix: False Positive (FP), True Negative (TN), True Positive (TP), and False Negative (FN). TP stands for images that were correctly classified within a certain category. The letters FP, TN, and FN stand for the quantity of incorrectly classified images from the relevant category, the quantity of incorrectly classified images from all other categories, and the quantity of misclassified images.

RESULT AND DISCUSSION

The experimental assessment for this research was carried out on a Google Colab using Python. To build DL models, the scikit-learning and Keras packages were used, accordingly. Grid-search with stratified crossvalidation, as well as the Keras Tuner utility, were used to optimize DL models. The scikit-learn and Keras packages were used to build the suggested model. The plant leaf images of various crops such as pomegranate, tomato, apple is taken from publicly available dataset for analysis. The dataset comprises of 1000 images of each disease for various crops such as apple, pomegranate and tomato. In order to expand the dataset, random flip, random rotation, and random contrast are used. For each illness, there are 2000 images in the enhanced dataset. 2000 photos from the crops dataset were used for training and validation of deep learning models for every disease.

Finally, in the Chapter research on Multi crop disease detection, the performance of DenseNet201, ResNet152, and InceptionV3 was tested by calculating loss and accuracy, as shown in figure4.Using a publicly available data set, the suggested EWADEL was fully examined. This assessment included measuring several performance measures such as accuracy, precision, recall, the F1-score and the confusion matrix. In compared to the individual models, the EWADEL model performed better, obtaining an amazing accuracy of 98.75%. In terms of accuracy and other key criteria, it beat the individual DenseNet201, ResNet152, and InceptionV3 models shown in Table 1.

The ensemble model dramatically increased overall accuracy, precision, recall, and F1-score by pooling predictions from various models, resulting in improved illness detection skills and robustness. Figure 3,4 and 5 depicts the confusion matrices for several deep learning algorithms. When compared to previous models, the EWADEL model clearly predicts a bigger number of testing photos with more accuracy. The findings indicate that the ensemble technique has the potential to be a viable tool for precise and robust Multi crop disease identification. Such developments have the potential to improve disease control practices and increase multi-crop yields.

Figures 6, 7, and 8 respectively, show the training loss, validation loss, training accuracy, and validation accuracy for the Inception Netv3, Dense Net 201, and ResNet 152 models. Further, the confusion matrix of the EWADEL is shown in Figure 9. The training and validation accuracy and training and validation loss is plotted against different epochs for EWADEL as shown in Figure 10.

Table 1. Comparison with proposed model

Model	Accuracy	Precision	Recall	F1-Score
DenseNet201	94.85%	95.73%	94.85%	95.87%
ResNet152	95.75%	95.71%	95.75%	95.75%
InceptionV3	92.95%	92.14%	92.95%	93.85%
Proposed Ensemble Model	98.75%	98.75%	98.75%	98.77%

Figure 3. Confusion matrix of DenseNet 201 model

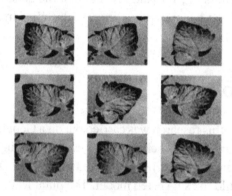

Figure 4. Confusion matrix of Inception Net V3 model

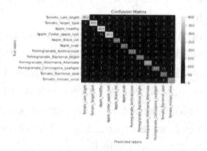

Figure 5. Confusion matrix of ResNet 152 model

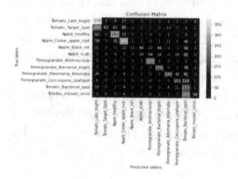

Figure 6. Accuracy and loss vs epochs for Inception Netv3

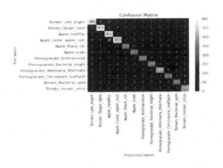

Figure 7. Accuracy and loss vs epochs for Dense Net201 model

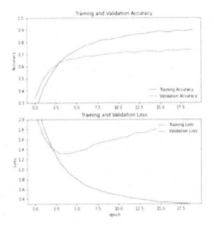

Figure 8. Accuracy and loss vs epochs for ResNet152 model

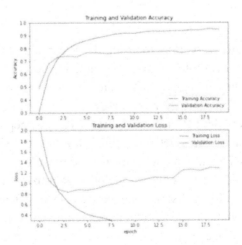

Figure 9. Accuracy and loss vs epochs for EWADEL model

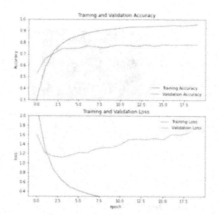

Figure 10. Confusion matrix of EWADEL model

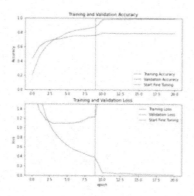

CONCLUSION

Plant diseases are a major threat to the world's food supply. The goal of this study was to identify multi crop leaf diseases using a combination technique that includes deep learning models DenseNet201, ResNet152, and InceptionV3. The findings revealed that the ensemble model, which incorporated the features of each individual model, performed remarkably well in correctly recognising multi crop leaf diseases. This chapter shows how the Efficient Weighted Average deep ensemble learning technique may be used to provide automated illness detection through image classification. A public dataset of multi crop leaf photos of sick and healthy plant leaves is used to train an EWADEL model to diagnose crop species and disease status of 12 distinct classes including 4 crop species, with an accuracy of 98.75 percent. The proposed model was able to discriminate between healthy leaves and several disorders that may be identified visually. The whole approach was presented, from collecting the pictures utilised for training and validation through image augmentation and, eventually, training and fine-tuning the deep CNN. It accomplishes classification by employing a grid search to find the optimal combination of weights, i.e., weight1, weight2, and weight3 for the various transfer learning models and CNN models with augmentation. At last summarised the final findings and concluded that the EWADEL model obtains the maximum accuracy, precision, recall, and F1 score.

REFERENCES

Aasha Nandhini, S., Hemalatha, R., Radha, S., & Indumathi, K. (2018). Web enabled plant disease detection system for agricultural applications using WMSN. *Wireless Personal Communications, 102*(2), 725–740. doi:10.100711277-017-5092-4

Abbas, A., Jain, S., Gour, M., & Vankudothu, S. (2021). Tomato plant disease detection using transfer learning with C-GAN synthetic images. *Computers and Electronics in Agriculture, 187*, 106279. doi:10.1016/j.compag.2021.106279

Ahmed, I., & Yadav, P. K. (2023). Plant disease detection using machine learning approaches. *Expert Systems: International Journal of Knowledge Engineering and Neural Networks, 40*(5), e13136. doi:10.1111/exsy.13136

AlSuwaidi, A., Grieve, B., & Yin, H. (2018). Feature-ensemble-based novelty detection for analyzing plant hyperspectral datasets. *IEEE Journal of Selected Topics in Applied Earth Observations and Remote Sensing, 11*(4), 1041–1055. doi:10.1109/JSTARS.2017.2788426

Anwar, Z., & Masood, S. (2023). Exploring Deep Ensemble Model for Insect and Pest Detection from Images. *Procedia Computer Science, 218*, 2328–2337. doi:10.1016/j.procs.2023.01.208

Bedi, P., & Gole, P. (2021). Plant disease detection using hybrid model based on convolutional autoencoder and convolutional neural network. *Artificial Intelligence in Agriculture, 5*, 90–101. doi:10.1016/j.aiia.2021.05.002

Buja, I., Sabella, E., Monteduro, A. G., Chiriacò, M. S., De Bellis, L., Luvisi, A., & Maruccio, G. (2021). Advances in plant disease detection and monitoring: From traditional assays to in-field diagnostics. *Sensors (Basel), 21*(6), 2129. doi:10.339021062129 PMID:33803614

Chaudhary, A., Kolhe, S., & Kamal, R. (2016). A hybrid ensemble for classification in multiclass datasets: An application to oilseed disease dataset. *Computers and Electronics in Agriculture, 124*, 65–72. doi:10.1016/j.compag.2016.03.026

Chen, J., Chen, W., Zeb, A., Yang, S., & Zhang, D. (2022). Lightweight inception networks for the recognition and detection of rice plant diseases. *IEEE Sensors Journal, 22*(14), 14628–14638. doi:10.1109/JSEN.2022.3182304

Crespo, O., Janssen, D., Garcia, C., & Ruiz, L. (2017). Biological and molecular diversity of Cucumber green mottle mosaic virus in Spain. *Plant Disease, 101*(6), 977–984. doi:10.1094/PDIS-09-16-1220-RE PMID:30682937

Cygert, S., & Czyżewski, A. (2020). Toward robust pedestrian detection with data augmentation. *IEEE Access: Practical Innovations, Open Solutions, 8*, 136674–136683. doi:10.1109/ACCESS.2020.3011356

Domingues, T., Brandão, T., & Ferreira, J. C. (2022). Machine learning for detection and prediction of crop diseases and pests: A comprehensive survey. *Agriculture, 12*(9), 1350. doi:10.3390/agriculture12091350

Ferentinos, K. P. (2018). Deep learning models for plant disease detection and diagnosis. *Computers and Electronics in Agriculture, 145*, 311–318. doi:10.1016/j.compag.2018.01.009

Gopi, P. S. S., & Karthikeyan, M. (2023). Red fox optimization with ensemble recurrent neural network for crop recommendation and yield prediction model. *Multimedia Tools and Applications*, 1–21. doi:10.100711042-023-16113-2

Han, X., Zhang, Z., Ding, N., Gu, Y., Liu, X., Huo, Y., Qiu, J., Yao, Y., Zhang, A., Zhang, L., Han, W., Huang, M., Jin, Q., Lan, Y., Liu, Y., Liu, Z., Lu, Z., Qiu, X., Song, R., & Zhu, J. (2021). Pre-trained models: Past, present and future. *AI Open*, *2*, 225–250. doi:10.1016/j.aiopen.2021.08.002

Haridasan, A., Thomas, J., & Raj, E. D. (2023). Deep learning system for paddy plant disease detection and classification. *Environmental Monitoring and Assessment*, *195*(1), 120. doi:10.100710661-022-10656-x PMID:36399232

Javidan, S. M., Banakar, A., Vakilian, K. A., & Ampatzidis, Y. (2023). Tomato leaf diseases classification using image processing and weighted ensemble learning. *Agronomy Journal*, agj2.21293. doi:10.1002/agj2.21293

Khan, R. U., Khan, K., Albattah, W., & Qamar, A. M. (2021). Image-based detection of plant diseases: From classical machine learning to deep learning journey. *Wireless Communications and Mobile Computing*, *2021*, 1–13. doi:10.1155/2021/5541859

Kondaveeti, H. K., Ujini, K. G., Pavankumar, B. V. V., Tarun, B. S., & Gopi, S. C. 2023, March. Plant Disease Detection Using Ensemble Learning. In *2023 2nd International Conference on Computational Systems and Communication (ICCSC)* (pp. 1-6). IEEE. 10.1109/ICCSC56913.2023.10142982

Li, L., Zhang, S., & Wang, B. (2021). Plant disease detection and classification by deep learning—A review. *IEEE Access : Practical Innovations, Open Solutions*, *9*, 56683–56698. doi:10.1109/ACCESS.2021.3069646

Loey, M., ElSawy, A., & Afify, M. (2020). Deep learning in plant diseases detection for agricultural crops: A survey. [IJSSMET]. *International Journal of Service Science, Management, Engineering, and Technology*, *11*(2), 41–58. doi:10.4018/IJSSMET.2020040103

Mikołajczyk, A., & Grochowski, M. (2018, May). *Data augmentation for improving deep learning in image classification problem. In 2018 international interdisciplinary PhD workshop (IIPhDW)*. IEEE.

Mukti, I. Z., & Biswas, D. 2019, December. Transfer learning based plant diseases detection using ResNet50. In *2019 4th International conference on electrical information and communication technology (EICT)* (pp. 1-6). IEEE. 10.1109/EICT48899.2019.9068805

Murugan, M. B., Rajagopal, M. K., & Roy, D. (2021, November). Iot based smart agriculture and plant disease prediction. *Journal of Physics: Conference Series*, *2115*(1), 012017. doi:10.1088/1742-6596/2115/1/012017

Nagaraju, M. & Chawla, P. (2020). Systematic review of deep learning techniques in plant disease detection. *International journal of system assurance engineering and management, 11*, 547-560.

Nagasubramanian, G., Sakthivel, R. K., Patan, R., Sankayya, M., Daneshmand, M., & Gandomi, A. H. (2021). Ensemble classification and IoT-based pattern recognition for crop disease monitoring system. *IEEE Internet of Things Journal*, *8*(16), 12847–12854. doi:10.1109/JIOT.2021.3072908

Ramesh, S., Hebbar, R., Niveditha, M., Pooja, R., Shashank, N., & Vinod, P. V. 2018, April. Plant disease detection using machine learning. In *2018 International conference on design innovations for 3Cs compute communicate control (ICDI3C)* (pp. 41-45). IEEE. 10.1109/ICDI3C.2018.00017

Rothe, P. R., & Kshirsagar, R. V. 2015, January. Cotton leaf disease identification using pattern recognition techniques. In *2015 International conference on pervasive computing (ICPC)* (pp. 1-6). IEEE. 10.1109/PERVASIVE.2015.7086983

Saleem, M. H., Potgieter, J., & Arif, K. M. (2019). Plant disease detection and classification by deep learning. *Plants*, 8(11), 468. doi:10.3390/plants8110468 PMID:31683734

Sankaran, K. S., Vasudevan, N., & Nagarajan, V. 2020, July. Plant disease detection and recognition using K means clustering. In *2020 International Conference on Communication and Signal Processing (ICCSP)* (pp. 1406-1409). IEEE. 10.1109/ICCSP48568.2020.9182095

Shorten, C., & Khoshgoftaar, T. M. (2019). A survey on image data augmentation for deep learning. *Journal of Big Data*, 6(1), 1–48. doi:10.118640537-019-0197-0

Shovon, M. S. H., Mozumder, S. J., Pal, O. K., Mridha, M. F., Asai, N., & Shin, J. (2023). PlantDet: A Robust Multi-Model Ensemble Method Based on Deep Learning for Plant Disease Detection. *IEEE Access : Practical Innovations, Open Solutions*, 11, 34846–34859. doi:10.1109/ACCESS.2023.3264835

Shrestha, G., Das, M. and Dey, N., 2020, October. Plant disease detection using CNN. In *2020 IEEE applied signal processing conference (ASPCON)* (pp. 109-113). IEEE.

Sigaud, O., & Droniou, A. (2015). Towards deep developmental learning. *IEEE Transactions on Cognitive and Developmental Systems*, 8(2), 99–114. doi:10.1109/TAMD.2015.2496248

Sreedevi, A., & Manike, C. (2023). Development of weighted ensemble transfer learning for tomato leaf disease classification solving low resolution problems. *Imaging Science Journal*, 71(2), 161–187. doi:10.1080/13682199.2023.2178605

Talasila, S., Rawal, K., & Sethi, G. (2022). Conventional data augmentation techniques for plant disease detection and classification systems. In *Intelligent Systems and Sustainable Computing* [Singapore: Springer Nature Singapore.]. *Proceedings of ICISSC*, 2021, 279–287.

Tiwari, V., Joshi, R. C., & Dutta, M. K. (2021). Dense convolutional neural networks based multiclass plant disease detection and classification using leaf images. *Ecological Informatics*, 63, 101289. doi:10.1016/j.ecoinf.2021.101289

Too, E. C., Yujian, L., Njuki, S., & Yingchun, L. (2019). A comparative study of fine-tuning deep learning models for plant disease identification. *Computers and Electronics in Agriculture*, 161, 272–279. doi:10.1016/j.compag.2018.03.032

Varior, R. R., Haloi, M., & Wang, G. (2016). *Gated siamese convolutional neural network architecture for human re-identification*. In Computer Vision–ECCV 2016: 14th European Conference, Amsterdam.

Vishnoi, V. K., Kumar, K., & Kumar, B. (2021). Plant disease detection using computational intelligence and image processing. *Journal of Plant Diseases and Protection*, 128(1), 19–53. doi:10.100741348-020-00368-0

Yang, L., Yu, X., Zhang, S., Zhang, H., Xu, S., Long, H., & Zhu, Y. (2023). Stacking-based and improved convolutional neural network: A new approach in rice leaf disease identification. *Frontiers in Plant Science, 14*, 1165940. doi:10.3389/fpls.2023.1165940 PMID:37346133

Zhang, N., Yang, G., Pan, Y., Yang, X., Chen, L., & Zhao, C. (2020). A review of advanced technologies and development for hyperspectral-based plant disease detection in the past three decades. *Remote Sensing (Basel), 12*(19), 3188. doi:10.3390/rs12193188

Chapter 15
Exploring the Power of AI–Driven Decision Making in the Judicial Domain:
Case Studies, Benefits, Challenges, and Solutions

Anu Thomas
 https://orcid.org/0000-0002-6606-3018
St. George's College. Aruvithura, India

ABSTRACT

Artificial intelligence (AI) has emerged as a promising technology capable of revolutionizing the judicial system by improving decision-making processes and reducing human biases. This manuscript explores the transformative potential of artificial intelligence (AI) in the judicial domain. It discusses the existing works in AI for predictive analytics, document analysis, and automated case management, in terms of methodologies and qualitative metrics used in each application. The manuscript also acknowledges the benefits, challenges, and solutions associated with incorporating AI into the judicial domain. These include the need for transparency and explainability in AI algorithms, and the ethical issues surrounding bias and privacy.

INTRODUCTION

Artificial Intelligence (AI) has emerged as a game-changing technology with immense potential in a variety of fields (Russell & Norvig, 2010). It includes a wide variety of techniques and methodologies that enable machines to emulate human cognitive functions, such as learning, reasoning, and decision-making. In sectors such as healthcare, finance, transportation, and entertainment, AI systems have made remarkable advances, demonstrating their ability to solve complex problems and generate valuable insights.

DOI: 10.4018/979-8-3693-0639-0.ch015

In recent years, the judicial domain has started recognising the transformative potential of AI. AI technologies can analyse vast amounts of judicial data, extracts key information, and provide valuable assistance to judges, attorneys, and legal professionals. They can contribute to more specific case outcome predictions, aid in legal research and document analysis, and simplify administrative tasks.

The prospective benefits of AI in the judicial domain are significant. AI can reduce the influence of human biases and increase the objectivity and impartiality of judicial decisions by augmenting human capabilities. It can facilitate quicker and more efficient case processing, resulting in less backlog and better access to justice. Moreover, AI systems can provide valuable insights and recommendations based on vast amounts of legal precedents and statutes, thereby assisting judges in making accurate decisions.

Nonetheless, the incorporation of AI into the judicial domain presents significant challenges and concerns that must be addressed with care. Providing transparency and explainability in AI algorithms is a significant obstacle. Maintaining public faith in the judicial system requires the capacity to comprehend and interpret the reasoning behind AI-generated decisions. Concerns regarding bias, privacy, and the possibility of unintended consequences raise ethical issues. To preserve accountability and ensure that AI systems operate within legal and ethical frameworks, it is crucial to strike a balance between human judgement and AI assistance.

This chapter aims to explore the potential of AI-driven decision making in the judicial domain by analyzing real-world case studies, evaluating its benefits, and addressing its implementation challenges. Grasping the potential of artificial intelligence and the considerations that accompany its adoption, pave the way for a future in which technology and human judgement coexist in harmony, ultimately resulting in a more effective and equitable judicial system. The sections that follow will delve deeper into specific case studies, benefits, and challenges, providing researchers, policymakers, and practitioners in the field of law and AI with valuable insights.

UNDERSTANDING AI IN THE JUDICIAL DOMAIN

Artificial Intelligence (AI) is a multidisciplinary discipline that incorporates a wide variety of technologies and methodologies designed to enable machines to mimic human cognitive functions such as learning, reasoning, and decision making (Russell et al.. AI-driven decision making in the judicial domain refers to the use of AI technologies and techniques to aid judges, attorneys, and legal professionals in their decision-making processes. It utilizes the power of computational algorithms, data analysis, and machine learning to augment human judgement and improve the efficiency and efficacy of the judicial system.

To understand the scope of AI applications in the judicial realm, it is critical to investigate the key AI technologies and methodologies relevant to this discipline. Predictive analytics is a key technology that uses past data and statistical models to predict future results. Predictive analytics can assist in predicting case outcomes, identify patterns and trends, and supporting judges in making well-informed decisions based on the likelihood of similar scenarios.

In the judicial domain, AI also demonstrates its capabilities in the area of document analysis. AI-powered document analysis tools analyze and extract relevant information from judicial documents, such as judgments, using natural language processing and machine learning algorithms (Raghav et al., 2016). These tools can assist legal professionals with legal research, case preparation, and information retrieval, saving time and effort.

Table 1. Overview of the applications of AI in the judicial domain

Applications	Description	Citation
Document Analysis & Legal Research	AI-powered tools employ natural language processing and machine learning algorithms to analyze and extract relevant information from legal documents, aiding in legal research, case preparation, and information retrieval.	(Thomas & Sangeetha, 2019); (Thomas & Sangeetha, 2021; Thomas & Sivanesan, 2022); (Raghav et al., 2016); (Zadgaonkar & Agrawal, 2023)
Predictive Analytics	Utilizes historical data and statistical models to predict case outcomes, identify patterns, and assist judges in making informed decisions.	(Russell & Norvig, 2010); (Aletras et al., 2016);(Haidar et al., 2022) (Shaikh et al., 2020);(Medvedeva et al., 2020); (Aissa et al., 2021);(Sharma et al., 2021);(Zahir, 2023);(Katz et al., 2017) ; (Strickson & De La Iglesia, 2020)
Case Management	Uses predefined rules and algorithms to automate routine tasks in the judicial process, such as case management, scheduling, and document analysis.	((Barysė & Sarel, 2023); (Gans-Combe, 2022)

In addition to predictive analytics, document analysis, and automated case management also contribute to the improvement of the judicial domain. Investigative assistance tools employ AI techniques to process and analyze large volumes of data, facilitating the identification of patterns, connections, and evidence in complex cases (European Commission, 2020). In order to ensure a seamless assimilation of AI into the judicial system, capacity development programmes equip judges and legal professionals with the necessary knowledge and skills to utilize AI technologies effectively in their work.

This section provides a solid foundation for the subsequent discussions on their specific applications, benefits, and challenges by explaining the various AI technologies and techniques relevant to the legal domain. It showcases a variety of AI tools that can be utilized to improve the effectiveness, accuracy, and fairness of judicial processes. In addition, it highlights the potential of AI-driven decision making to augment human judgement and enhance the overall functioning of the judiciary. In summary, this section serves as a comprehensive introduction to AI in the judicial domain. It elucidates the scope of AI-driven decision making, introduces key AI technologies and techniques relevant to the judicial system, and sets the stage for further exploration of case studies, benefits, challenges and solutions in the subsequent sections. The following Table 1 gives a summary of the applications of AI in the judicial domain.

CASE STUDIES ON AI IN THE JUDICIAL DOMAIN

Case Study One: Application of AI in Legal Research and Document Analysis

Overview of the Case Study

In the judicial domain, AI has found valuable applications in legal research and document analysis. These AI-driven technologies have the potential to revolutionize how legal professionals conduct research, analyze documents, and extract relevant information. Traditional legal research involves manually reading and analyzing numerous documents, which can be time-consuming and labor-intensive. AI tools can quickly scan and analyze vast amounts of legal texts, identifying relevant passages, extract key legal con-

Table 2. Overview of AI tools for legal research and document analysis

Tool	Description
RAVN ACE	RAVN ACE is an AI-powered platform that utilizes natural language processing and machine learning algorithms to extract key information from legal documents, including court judgments.
Kira Systems	Kira Systems is an AI-powered contract analysis platform that can also be used for extracting relevant information from court judgments.
Luminance	Luminance is an AI-based document analysis platform that utilizes machine learning to analyze legal documents, including court judgments, to extract important information.
ROSS Intelligence	ROSS Intelligence is an AI legal research platform that leverages natural language processing and machine learning to analyze legal documents, including court judgments, providing relevant insights.
iManage RAVN	iManage RAVN is an AI-powered platform that automates the analysis and extraction of relevant information from unstructured data within legal documents, including court judgments.
Casetext	Casetext is an AI-powered legal research platform that utilizes natural language processing to analyze legal documents, including court judgments, providing relevant case law and statutory information.
LexisNexis	LexisNexis offers AI-powered solutions for legal research and document analysis, providing access to comprehensive legal content, case law, and regulatory information, including court judgments.
Fastcase	Fastcase is an AI-powered legal research platform that provides access to a vast database of case law, statutes, and legal documents, including court judgments, facilitating efficient document analysis.
Judicata	Judicata is an AI-driven legal research platform that employs natural language processing to analyze legal documents, including court judgments, and provide comprehensive search results and insights.
Westlaw	Westlaw is an AI-enhanced legal research platform that leverages machine learning algorithms to analyze legal documents, including court judgments, assisting in legal research and document analysis tasks.
LegalMind Judgement Analyser	LegalMind Judgement Analyser is an AI tool specifically designed for the analysis and extraction of relevant information from court judgments, providing valuable insights and facilitating legal research.
Mleaptech	Mleaptech is an AI-powered platform that specializes in extracting relevant information from legal documents, including court judgments, using advanced natural language processing techniques.

cepts, precedents, legal arguments, and provide summaries or insights based on the analyzed documents (Thomas & Sangeetha, 2021; Thomas & Sangeetha, 2019; Thomas & Sivanesan, 2022). Table 2 depicts prominent tools in the market which helps in the extraction of judicial facts from court judgments. These AI-powered tools employ natural language processing and machine learning algorithms to analyze large volumes of legal documents, identify relevant case precedents, and extract key information.

Relevant Information in Court Decisions

In recent times, there has been a significant surge in the availability of court judgments, or case laws, in digital format. These electronic documents contain a wealth of knowledge in the form of judicial facts. For example, each judgment comprises certain facts (Thomas et al., 2021):

- Name of the appellate court, case number, date of decision;
- Parties, attorneys and judges involved;
- Final judgements, cases cited, rules referred to;
- Other people involved in the judgement (investigators, witnesses, accused, co-accused, etc.)

The above-mentioned facts serve as the backbone of various artificial intelligence systems such as Legal information retrieval systems[123], Legal question answering systems[45], and Case based reasoning (Ashley & Aleven, 1997; Rissland et al., 2005).

Methods Used in Extracting Key Information From Court Decisions

We infer from the existing literature that most studies in the legal domain use either rule-based, knowledge-based, machine-learning based or pure linguistic methods.

- Rule based systems: Rule-based systems for information extraction from judicial decisions are methods that use predefined rules or patterns to identify and extract relevant information from legal texts(Andrew, 2018, 2018; Cheng et al., 2009; Dozier et al., 2010; Zhuang et al., 2017).
- Ontology based systems: Ontology based judicial information extraction is a technique that uses domain knowledge in ontologies to extract relevant information from legal texts, such as court decisions. Some examples of information that can be extracted are legal events, facts, entities, and relations.(Buey et al., 2016; de Araujo et al., 2017)
- Machine learning based systems: (Zadgaonkar & Agrawal, 2023) suggested a framework using topic modeling techniques, an unsupervised machine learning technique, for legal information extraction from the Indian judicial system's unstructured legal judgments. (Thomas & Sangeetha, 2021) proposed a semi-supervised, knowledge-integrated pattern learning approach to extract domain-specific facts from judicial text. Also, (Thomas & Sivanesan, 2022) proposed an efficient RE system consisting of Knowledge-based and Semi-supervised learning systems, integrated with domain ontology. The proposed system is used to extract domain-specific relations from Indian judicial text.
- Deep learning based systems: In recent years, deep learning models have outperformed traditional methods in many natural language processing tasks, such as text classification, language modeling, information extraction, speech recognition, machine translation, etc. These models are able to learn the long-term dependencies and context information of text, and generate fluent and coherent text. One of the most widely used deep learning models for natural language processing is the recurrent neural network (RNN), which can capture the sequential and temporal dynamics of text. RNNs have achieved promising results in various applications, such as language modeling and machine translation. In the judicial domain, (Xi & Zhenxing, 2018) showed that hierarchical bidirectional LSTM, a type of RNN, is an effective tool for extracting information from real-life lawsuit documents.
- Hybrid models: (Poudyal & Quaresma, 2012) proposed a hybrid approach that used both statistical and rule-based techniques to extract key information from unstructured judicial documents. (Thomas & Sangeetha, 2019) used deep learning and clustering methods separately, along with a knowledge-based approach, to extract generic entity names (such as person, location, and organization names) from Indian judicial text.

Quality Measures Used in Evaluating Information Extraction from Court Judgments

Precision, recall and fscore are the qualitative metrics used in evaluating an Information Extraction (IE) system from court judgments. **Precision** measures the proportion of correctly identified entities out of all entities that the system identified. **Recall**, on the other hand, measures the proportion of correctly identified entities out of all actual entities in the text. The **F-score** is the harmonic mean of precision and recall, providing a single metric that balances both values. These metrics are crucial in determining the effectiveness of an IE system, as they provide insight into its accuracy and completeness. High precision indicates that the system is reliable and makes few mistakes, while high recall indicates that the system is comprehensive and misses few entities. The F-score provides a balance between these two aspects, making it a particularly useful metric when comparing different systems or configurations. It's important to note that these metrics are dependent on the quality and representativeness of the test data, and should be interpreted in light of this.

Benefits Achieved Through AI-Driven Document Analysis

AI-driven document analysis in the judicial domain has brought numerous benefits that have enhanced legal research, case preparation, and information retrieval processes. Some of the key benefits include:

- Time-saving and Efficiency: AI-powered document analysis tools can process vast volumes of legal documents, including court judgments, at a significantly faster pace than human researchers. This capability enables legal professionals to save time and increase their efficiency in reviewing and analyzing relevant information (source: Luminance).
- Enhanced Accuracy and Precision: By utilizing natural language processing (NLP) and machine learning algorithms, AI tools can extract relevant information from court judgments with a high degree of accuracy and precision. They can identify key legal concepts, case citations, statutes, and other important details, eliminating the need for manual extraction (source: ROSS Intelligence).
- Comprehensive Legal Research: AI-driven document analysis tools have access to extensive databases of legal content and case law. They can efficiently analyze court judgments to identify relevant precedents, legal arguments, and historical rulings, providing comprehensive and up-to-date research results (source: LexisNexis).
- Improved Information Retrieval: AI tools can facilitate efficient retrieval of specific information from court judgments. By categorizing and tagging legal documents based on relevant criteria, such as case type, jurisdiction, or legal concepts, AI-driven systems enable legal professionals to quickly locate and extract the information they need (source: Kira Systems).
- Identification of Patterns and Insights: AI-powered document analysis can identify patterns, correlations, and trends within court judgments that may not be readily apparent to human researchers. This ability can help legal professionals uncover valuable insights, such as emerging legal issues or judicial preferences, which can inform case strategy and decision-making (source: RAVN ACE).
- Cost Reduction: AI tools can significantly reduce costs associated with manual document analysis and research. By automating time-consuming tasks, legal professionals can allocate their resources more efficiently, resulting in cost savings for law firms, legal departments, and clients (source: Casetext).

Overall, the benefits of AI-driven document analysis in the judicial domain include time savings, improved accuracy, comprehensive research capabilities, efficient information retrieval, valuable insights, and cost reduction. These benefits contribute to more effective legal processes and better-informed decision-making in the legal profession.

Case Study Two: AI-Based Predictive Analytics in Judicial Domain

Overview of the Case Study

This section delves into the application of AI-based predictive analytics in judicial decision making. The study involves the implementation of advanced machine learning algorithms and predictive models to analyze extensive judicial data and forecast case outcomes(Katz et al., 2017) (Strickson & De La Iglesia, 2020). Researchers gather a wide range of data, including case details, legal precedents, judge rulings, and other pertinent factors from previous judgments either manually or by making use of document analysis methods. This data is then used to train the predictive analytics model, which can predict the probable outcome of future cases based on similar patterns and factors (Refer Figure 1). Regarding the documents, the languages used for the judicial decision prediction are English, German, Portuguese, Turkish, Chinese, Farsi, French, Iranian and Spanish. English is most used language in the literature.

Parameters Considered in ML Based Decision Prediction

In the context of predicting judicial outcomes using machine learning, several parameters or features are typically considered. These include:

a. Legal Precedents: Past court decisions on similar cases can provide valuable insights for predicting the outcome of a current case.
b. Judge's Ruling History: The past decisions made by the judge presiding over the case can also influence the outcome.
c. Appeal Origin Court and Sections: The court from which the case originated and the specific sections of law being invoked can play a role in the outcome.
d. Case Details: Specific details of the case, such as the nature of the crime, evidence presented, and arguments made, can significantly impact the decision.
e. Text Features: The language used in case documents can also be analyzed to predict outcomes. This includes the use of natural language processing (NLP) techniques to extract meaningful features from the text.

Steps Involved in the Creation of Predictive Models

Various steps involved in the creation of predictive models using machine learning are given below. Also, figure 1 illustrates the pictorial representation of the entire process.

1. The raw data, which consists of judgments from the court, is collected and processed to train the machine learning model.
2. Features are identified within the processed legal data.
3. A database is created using the processed data.
4. A predictive AI model is selected and trained on the processed data.

Figure 1. Research Methodology for developing predictive models
(Shaikh et al., 2020)

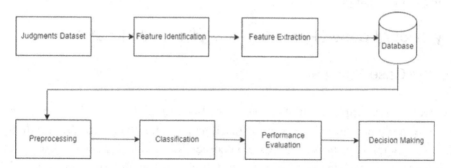

5. The machine adjusts the parameters of the AI model until it reaches a predetermined level of accuracy.

The following methods have been increasingly used for judgment prediction in the judicial domain.

Methods Used in Predicting Judicial Decisions

While both Machine Learning (ML) and Deep Learning (DL) are subsets of Artificial Intelligence (AI), they have distinct characteristics. Supervised ML leverages patterns from vectorized textual data for classification, thereby enhancing the user experience. On the other hand, DL, which is a subset of ML, employs complex, multi-layer neural networks. A significant advantage of DL networks, despite being under the AI umbrella like ML, is their ability to continually improve as the volume of data increases. The following section describes the most commonly used machine learning (ML) and deep learning (DL) algorithms in predicting judicial decisions.

Deep Learning Algorithms: Deep learning algorithms such as Convolutional Neural Networks (CNN), Long Short-Term Memory (LSTM), Deep Pyramid CNN (DPCNN), and Recurrent Convolutional Neural Networks (RCNN) have been used to predict judgments in judicial cases (Alghazzawi et al., 2022);(Wang et al., 2020);(Shang, 2022), (Sivaranjani et al., 2021). These algorithms are trained on a large number of text files of judicial cases using the pre-training language model Bidirectional Encoder Representations from Transformers (BERT)(Devlin et al., 2019). Furthermore, some authors proposed modifications to the BERT algorithm, such as ooBERT, LEGAL-BERT, and ft-BERT.

Support Vector Machines (SVM), k-nearest neighbors (KNN), and Naive Bayes (NB): These machine learning techniques have been used to anticipate court outcomes based on past judicial data(Shaikh et al., 2020; Zhong et al., 2018). Also, Table 3 provides an overview of commonly available tools used in AI driven predictive analytics.

Quality Measures Used in Validating Decision Prediction

The effectiveness of a prediction model is influenced by several factors, including the size of the corpora used, the specific application domain, and the machine learning (ML) or deep learning (DL) algorithm employed. Our review of the literature indicates that various quality measures are used to evaluate these

Table 3. Overview of AI tools for predictive analysis in judicial domain

Tool	Description
Lex Machina	Legal analytics platform that uses machine learning and natural language processing to extract insights from legal documents and court records. Provides case outcomes, judge behavior, and legal trends for data-driven decision-making.
Ravel Law	Legal research and analytics platform that utilizes machine learning algorithms to analyze and categorize case law. Offers visualizations, data analytics, and predictive tools to aid legal professionals in understanding legal precedents and predicting case outcomes.
Blue J Legal	AI-driven platform focused on tax law prediction. Analyzes tax legislation and historical case law data using machine learning techniques to provide predictions on how courts are likely to rule on specific tax issues.
Gavelytics	AI-powered legal analytics tool specializing in judicial behavior analysis. Analyzes judges' past rulings, motion outcomes, and other factors using machine learning algorithms to predict how judges are likely to rule on specific legal issues.
CaseText	Legal research platform leveraging machine learning to analyze and organize case law. Offers tools for searching and accessing relevant cases and statutes, along with features for predicting case outcomes based on legal arguments and precedents.

models. Accuracy, which quantifies the ratio of successful classifications, is the most frequently used measure. Other metrics include the F1 score, precision (Chou & Hsing, 2010), and Root Squared Error.

Benefits Achieved Through AI-Driven Predictive Analytics

AI-driven predictive analytics offers numerous benefits in judicial decision making. Firstly, it equips judges, attorneys, and legal professionals with valuable insights and predictions regarding case outcomes, enabling them to make more informed decisions. This has the potential to enhance the efficiency and accuracy of the judicial process. Predictive analytics can also help identify patterns and factors influencing case outcomes, shedding light on potential biases or inconsistencies within the legal system. By understanding these insights, proactive measures can be taken to address these issues and improve the fairness and objectivity of the judicial system.

Case Study Three: AI-Powered Automation in Case Processing and Management

Overview of the Case Study

AI-powered automation plays a crucial role in streamlining routine administrative tasks in case management, resulting in improved efficiency and reduced errors. For instance, AI systems can handle scheduling hearings, generating notifications, and managing documentation, which traditionally required significant manual effort .Furthermore, AI-powered case management systems are capable of tracking case progress, monitoring deadlines, and providing timely reminders (Vijayaraghavan, n.d.). This ensures that tasks are completed within the designated timeframes, reducing case delays and facilitating effective time management. Moreover, these systems enhance transparency by keeping all stakeholders, including judges, attorneys, and clients, well-informed about the status of each case. Real-time updates and notifications help establish clear communication channels, leading to better collaboration and increased trust in the judicial process.

Benefits of AI-Powered Automation in Case Processing and Management

AI-powered automation in case processing and management offers several benefits:

- Increased Efficiency: Automation reduces the need for manual and repetitive tasks, streamlining case processing and management workflows. It eliminates time-consuming administrative tasks, such as data entry, document handling, and scheduling, allowing legal professionals to focus on more complex and critical aspects of their work (Vijayaraghavan, n.d.).
- Improved Accuracy: AI-powered automation reduces the risk of human error in case processing and management. By leveraging machine learning algorithms and natural language processing, automation systems can accurately extract and analyze data, ensuring data integrity and minimizing mistakes (Federico et al., 2019).
- Enhanced Resource Allocation: AI-powered automation assists in optimizing resource allocation by providing insights into case priorities, workload distribution, and resource utilization. This ensures efficient allocation of personnel, time, and other resources, leading to improved productivity and cost-effectiveness (Ruan et al., 2018).
- Improved Transparency and Accountability: Automated case management systems maintain accurate and detailed records, facilitating transparency and accountability in the judicial process. They provide an audit trail of actions taken, decisions made, and the reasons behind them, enabling stakeholders to review and evaluate the case management process (Vijayaraghavan, n.d.).
- Enhanced Collaboration and Communication: Automation systems enable seamless collaboration among multiple stakeholders involved in case processing and management. They facilitate secure sharing and access to case-related information, allowing for efficient communication and coordination among judges, attorneys, clerks, and other relevant parties.

CHALLENGES IN AI-DRIVEN DECISION MAKING IN THE JUDICIAL DOMAIN

The adoption of AI in the judicial domain offers significant potential for improving predictive analytics, case management, and legal research & document analysis. However, there are several challenges must be addressed to ensure the successful integration of AI technologies in these areas. This section examines the challenges associated with using AI in predictive analytics, case management, and legal research & document analysis in the judicial domain.

First, data availability and quality pose significant challenges. Accessing comprehensive and reliable judicial data, considering privacy concerns and diverse data sources, is essential for training accurate AI models. Second, interpretability and explainability of AI algorithms are crucial in the judicial domain to ensure transparency and fairness(Rudin, 2019). Developing interpretable models and methods for explaining AI-driven decisions is a significant challenge.

Third, ethical and legal implications arise when using AI in the judicial domain. Avoiding biases, protecting privacy, and complying with legal and ethical standards are essential considerations(Jobin et al., 2019). Addressing potential biases, discrimination, and unintended consequences is necessary to maintain the integrity and trust in AI-driven systems. Fourth, integrating and adopting AI technologies in existing judicial processes can be challenging due to resistance to change, lack of awareness, and concerns about job displacement.

Finally, human-machine collaboration is critical. Balancing human expertise with AI assistance, maintaining human oversight and accountability, and preserving the central role of human judgment are important challenges. AI should augment human decision making while recognizing the limits of AI and upholding the ethical and legal responsibility of humans(Floridi et al., 2018).

Addressing these challenges requires collaboration among AI researchers, legal experts, policymakers, and stakeholders. It involves developing ethical guidelines, ensuring transparency and explainability of AI algorithms, addressing data quality and privacy concerns, promoting education and awareness, and fostering a culture of responsible AI adoption in the judicial domain. By addressing these challenges, AI can play a transformative role in improving predictive analytics, case management, and legal research & document analysis in the judicial domain.

PROPOSED SOLUTIONS

Addressing and mitigating potential biases and ethical concerns associated with the use of AI in the judicial domain is a complex task. Here are some strategies that can be employed:

- Bias Detection and Mitigation: Implementing bias detection methods, such as fairness metrics and auditing, can help identify and mitigate biases in AI algorithms1. Training AI agents using diverse and representative data sets can also help reduce the risk of bias.
- Transparency and Dialogue: Recognizing bias and minimizing manipulation by increasing transparency and opening a dialogue about the ethical challenges that AI presents is crucial.
- Policy and Organizational Responses: Policy-level proposals, organisational responses and guidance for individuals can be effective in addressing ethical issues of AI.
- Training and Awareness: Holding regular training sessions on diversity, equity, inclusion and ethics; establishing key performance indicators (KPIs); and recognizing employees for mitigating bias are effective ways to encourage teams to actively look for bias in AI systems.

These considerations can significantly impact the implementation and acceptance of AI-driven decision-making tools within the legal system. If biases and ethical concerns are not adequately addressed, it could lead to unfair outcomes and loss of trust in the system. On the other hand, if these issues are effectively managed, it could enhance the fairness, efficiency, and transparency of the legal system, thereby increasing its acceptance. However, it's important to note that the guarded deployment of AI technologies is recommended to prevent harm arising from AI systems' operations.

CONCLUSION

In conclusion, this book chapter has explored the potential of AI-driven decision making in the judicial domain through the examination of case studies and discussions on its methodologies, benefits, challenges, and solutions. The case studies have demonstrated the transformative impact of AI in areas such as predictive analytics, case management, legal research & document analysis, highlighting improved judicial information extraction, decision quality, efficiency, and access to justice as key benefits. However, challenges persist, including the need for transparency and explainability of AI algorithms, addressing ethical considerations such as bias and privacy, maintaining human oversight and accountability, and adapting legal and regulatory frameworks. To effectively harness AI-driven decision making in the pursuit of a fair and efficient judicial system, recommendations have been provided. These include promoting transparency and explainability, addressing ethical considerations, maintaining human oversight, and adapting legal frameworks. By implementing these recommendations, the judicial system can embrace the potential of AI while upholding the principles of fairness, justice, and individual rights.

REFERENCES

Aissa, H., Tarik, A., Zeroual, I., & Yousef, F. (2021). Using Machine Learning to Predict Outcomes of Accident Cases in Moroccan Courts. *Procedia Computer Science*, *184*, 829–834. doi:10.1016/j.procs.2021.03.103

Aletras, N., Tsarapatsanis, D., Preoţiuc-Pietro, D., & Lampos, V. (2016). Predicting judicial decisions of the European Court of Human Rights: A Natural Language Processing perspective. *PeerJ. Computer Science*, *2*, e93. doi:10.7717/peerj-cs.93

Alghazzawi, D., Bamasag, O., Albeshri, A., Sana, I., Ullah, H., & Asghar, M. Z. (2022). Efficient Prediction of Court Judgments Using an LSTM+CNN Neural Network Model with an Optimal Feature Set. *Mathematics*, *10*(5), 5. doi:10.3390/math10050683

Andrew, J. J. (2018). Automatic Extraction of Entities and Relation from Legal Documents. In N. Chen, R. E. Banchs, X. Duan, M. Zhang, & H. Li (Eds.), *Proceedings of the Seventh Named Entities Workshop* (pp. 1–8). Association for Computational Linguistics. 10.18653/v1/W18-2401

Ashley, K. D., & Aleven, V. (1997). Reasoning symbolically about partially matched cases. *Proceedings of the 15th International Joint Conference on Artifical Intelligence* - Volume 1, (pp. 335–341). ACL.

Barysė, D., & Sarel, R. (2023). Algorithms in the court: Does it matter which part of the judicial decision-making is automated? *Artificial Intelligence and Law*. Advance online publication. doi:10.100710506-022-09343-6 PMID:36643574

Buey, M. G., Garrido, A. L., Bobed, C., & Ilarri, S. (2016). The AIS Project: Boosting Information Extraction from Legal Documents by using Ontologies: *Proceedings of the 8th International Conference on Agents and Artificial Intelligence*, (pp. 438–445). ScitePress. 10.5220/0005757204380445

Cheng, T. T., Cua, J. L., Tan, M. D., Yao, K. G., & Roxas, R. E. (2009). Information extraction from legal documents. *2009 Eighth International Symposium on Natural Language Processing*, (pp. 157–162). IEEE. 10.1109/SNLP.2009.5340925

Chou, S., & Hsing, T.-P. (2010). Text Mining Technique for Chinese Written Judgment of Criminal Case. In H. Chen, M. Chau, S. Li, S. Urs, S. Srinivasa, & G. A. Wang (Eds.), *Intelligence and Security Informatics* (pp. 113–125). Springer. doi:10.1007/978-3-642-13601-6_14 de Araujo, D. A., Rigo, S. J., & Barbosa, J. L. V. (2017). Ontology-based information extraction for juridical events with case studies in Brazilian legal realm. *Artificial Intelligence and Law*, *25*(4), 379–396. doi:10.100710506-017-9203-z

Devlin, J., Chang, M.-W., Lee, K., & Toutanova, K. (2019). BERT: Pre-training of Deep Bidirectional Transformers for Language Understanding. In J. Burstein, C. Doran, & T. Solorio (Eds.), *Proceedings of the 2019 Conference of the North American Chapter of the Association for Computational Linguistics: Human Language Technologies,* Volume 1 *(Long and Short Papers)* (pp. 4171–4186). Association for Computational Linguistics. 10.18653/v1/N19-1423

Dozier, C., Kondadadi, R., Light, M., Vachher, A., Veeramachaneni, S., & Wudali, R. (2010). Named Entity Recognition and Resolution in Legal Text. In E. Francesconi, S. Montemagni, W. Peters, & D. Tiscornia (Eds.), Semantic Processing of Legal Texts (Vol. 6036, pp. 27–43). Springer Berlin Heidelberg. doi:10.1007/978-3-642-12837-0_2

Floridi, L., Cowls, J., Beltrametti, M., Chatila, R., Chazerand, P., Dignum, V., Luetge, C., Madelin, R., Pagallo, U., Rossi, F., Schafer, B., Valcke, P., & Vayena, E. (2018). AI4People—An Ethical Framework for a Good AI Society: Opportunities, Risks, Principles, and Recommendations. *Minds and Machines*, *28*(4), 689–707. doi:10.100711023-018-9482-5 PMID:30930541

Gans-Combe, C. (2022). Automated Justice: Issues, Benefits and Risks in the Use of Artificial Intelligence and Its Algorithms in Access to Justice and Law Enforcement. In D. O'Mathúna & R. Iphofen (Eds.), *Ethics, Integrity and Policymaking: The Value of the Case Study* (pp. 175–194). Springer International Publishing. doi:10.1007/978-3-031-15746-2_14

Haidar, A., Ahajjam, T., Zeroual, I., & Farhaoui, Y. (2022). Application of machine learning algorithms for predicting outcomes of accident cases in Moroccan courts. *Indonesian Journal of Electrical Engineering and Computer Science*, *26*(2), 2. doi:10.11591/ijeecs.v26.i2.pp1103-1108

Jobin, A., Ienca, M., & Vayena, E. (2019). The global landscape of AI ethics guidelines. *Nature Machine Intelligence*, *1*(9), 9. doi:10.103842256-019-0088-2

Katz, D. M., Bommarito, M. J., & Blackman, J. (2017). A general approach for predicting the behavior of the Supreme Court of the United States. *PLoS One*, *12*(4), e0174698. doi:10.1371/journal.pone.0174698 PMID:28403140

Medvedeva, M., Vols, M., & Wieling, M. (2020). Using machine learning to predict decisions of the European Court of Human Rights. *Artificial Intelligence and Law*, *28*(2), 237–266. doi:10.100710506-019-09255-y

Poudyal, P., & Quaresma, P. (2012). An hybrid approach for legal information extraction. In *Legal Knowledge and Information Systems* (pp. 115–118). IOS Press. doi:10.3233/978-1-61499-167-0-115

Raghav, K., Reddy, K., & Reddy, V. (2016). *Analyzing the Extraction of Relevant Legal Judgments using Paragraph-level and Citation Information*. Semantic Scholar. https://www.semanticscholar.org/paper/Analyzing-the-Extraction-of-Relevant-Legal-using-Raghav-Reddy/7453ba87fb9418c6e4f5609cc3ba3d99b9b34874

Rissland, E. L., Ashley, K. D., & Branting, L. K. (2005). Case-based reasoning and law. *The Knowledge Engineering Review*, *20*(3), 293–298. doi:10.1017/S0269888906000701

Rudin, C. (2019). *Stop Explaining Black Box Machine Learning Models for High Stakes Decisions and Use Interpretable Models Instead* (arXiv:1811.10154). arXiv. https://doi.org//arXiv.1811.10154 doi:10.48550

Russell, S. J., & Norvig, P. (2010). *Artificial intelligence a modern approach*. London. https://ds.amu.edu.et/xmlui/bitstream/handle/123456789/10406/artificial%20intelligence%20-%20a%20modern%20approach%20%283rd%2C%202009%29.pdf?sequence=1&isAllowed=y

Shaikh, R. A., Sahu, T. P., & Anand, V. (2020). Predicting Outcomes of Legal Cases based on Legal Factors using Classifiers. *Procedia Computer Science*, *167*, 2393–2402. doi:10.1016/j.procs.2020.03.292

Shang, X. (2022). A Computational Intelligence Model for Legal Prediction and Decision Support. *Computational Intelligence and Neuroscience*, *2022*, e5795189. doi:10.1155/2022/5795189 PMID:35785064

Sharma, S., Shandilya, R., & Sharma, S. (2021). *Predicting Indian Supreme Court Decisions* (SSRN Scholarly Paper 3917603). doi:10.2139/ssrn.3917603

Sivaranjani, N., Jayabharathy, J., & Teja, P. C. (2021). Predicting the supreme court decision on appeal cases using hierarchical convolutional neural network. *International Journal of Speech Technology*, *24*(3), 643–650. doi:10.100710772-021-09820-4

Strickson, B., & De La Iglesia, B. (2020). Legal Judgement Prediction for UK Courts. *Proceedings of the 2020 The 3rd International Conference on Information Science and System*, (pp. 204–209). ACM. 10.1145/3388176.3388183

Thomas, A., & Sangeetha, S. (2019). An innovative hybrid approach for extracting named entities from unstructured text data. *Computational Intelligence*, *35*(4), 799–826. doi:10.1111/coin.12214

Thomas, A., & Sangeetha, S. (2021). Semi-supervised, KNOWLEDGE-INTEGRATED pattern learning approach for fact extraction from judicial text. *Expert Systems: International Journal of Knowledge Engineering and Neural Networks*, *38*(3), e12656. doi:10.1111/exsy.12656

Thomas, A., & Sivanesan, S. (2022). An adaptable, high-performance relation extraction system for complex sentences. *Knowledge-Based Systems*, *251*(C), 108956. doi:10.1016/j.knosys.2022.108956

Vijayaraghavan, J. R. (n.d.). *Introduction of Artificial Intelligence in the Judicial system*.

Wang, Y., Gao, J., & Chen, J. (2020). Deep Learning Algorithm for Judicial Judgment Prediction Based on BERT. *2020 5th International Conference on Computing, Communication and Security (ICCCS)*, (pp. 1–6). IEEE. 10.1109/ICCCS49678.2020.9277068

Zadgaonkar, A., & Agrawal, A. J. (2023). An Approach for Analyzing Unstructured Text Data Using Topic Modeling Techniques for Efficient Information Extraction. *New Generation Computing*. doi:10.100700354-023-00230-5

Zahir, J. (2023). Prediction of court decision from Arabic documents using deep learning. *Expert Systems: International Journal of Knowledge Engineering and Neural Networks*, *40*(6), e13236. doi:10.1111/exsy.13236

Zhong, H., Guo, Z., Tu, C., Xiao, C., Liu, Z., & Sun, M. (2018). Legal Judgment Prediction via Topological Learning. In E. Riloff, D. Chiang, J. Hockenmaier, & J. Tsujii (Eds.), *Proceedings of the 2018 Conference on Empirical Methods in Natural Language Processing* (pp. 3540–3549). Association for Computational Linguistics. 10.18653/v1/D18-1390

Zhuang, C., Zhou, Y., Ge, J., Li, Z., Li, C., Zhou, X., & Luo, B. (2017). Information Extraction from Chinese Judgment Documents. *2017 14th Web Information Systems and Applications Conference (WISA)*, (pp. 240–244). ScitePress.

ENDNOTES

1 https://www.lexml.gov.br/
2 https://www.legislation.gov.uk/
3 https://www.lexisnexis.com/
4 https://www.findlaw.com/
5 https://legal.thomsonreuters.com/

Chapter 16
AI–Driven Decision Support System for Intuitionistic Fuzzy Assignment Problems

P. Senthil Kumar

(iD) https://orcid.org/0000-0003-4317-1021

Amity School of Engineering and Technology, Amity University, Bengaluru, India

ABSTRACT

The assignment problem (AP) is a well-known optimization problem that deals with the allocation of 'n' jobs to 'n' machines on a 1-to-1 basis. It minimizes the cost/time or maximizes the profit/production of the problem. Generally, the profit, sale, cost, and time are all called the parameters of the AP (in a traditional AP, out of these parameters, exactly one parameter will be considered a parameter of the problem). These are not at all crisp numbers due to several uncontrollable factors, which are in the form of uncertainty and hesitation. So, to solve the AP in this environment, the author proposes the software and ranking method-based PSK (P. Senthil Kumar) method. Here, plenty of theorems related to intuitionistic fuzzy assignment problems (IFAPs) are proposed and proved by the PSK. To show the superiority of his method, he presents 4 IFAPs. The computer programs for the proposed problems are presented precisely, and the results are verified with Matlab, RGui, etc. In addition, comparative results, discussion, merits and demerits of his method, and future studies are given.

DOI: 10.4018/979-8-3693-0639-0.ch016

INTRODUCTION AND LITERATURE SURVEY

There are several methods available to solve real-world problems. Mainly, assignment problems (AP) and its solving methods are used to solve real-life problems. An AP plays an important role in assigning the following effectively:

- drivers ↔ trucks
- trucks ↔ routes
- persons ↔ jobs
- operators ↔ machines
- problems ↔ research teams, etc.

The AP is a special case of the linear programming problem (LPP). In LPP, the plan of the decision maker (DM) is to assign 'n' no. of jobs to 'n' no. of machines at a minimum cost or time. In the management science literature, to find out the solutions to assignment problems (APs), many researchers presented different methods. Some of the methods are listed in Table 1.

To solve real-world problems by using uncertain parameters, Zadeh (1965) introduced the fuzzy set (FS) theory which is the extension of the crisp set. The crisp sets consider the values 0 and 1 whereas the fuzzy sets consider the values in [0, 1]. The values in [0, 1] are called membership values in FSs. So, there is no FS without the membership values. Due to the important feature of FS theory, it is widely used in many fields.

Therefore, the fuzzy set theory has helped many authors to solve the issues of assignment, transportation, and LPP under uncertainty. Some of the current publications related to these issues are presented in Table 2.

The FS theory deals only with the membership value, but it does not consider the non membership and hesitation index. To counter this issue, Atanassov (1983) introduced the intuitionistic fuzzy set (IFS) theory, which is the extension of both crisp and FSs. Due to this important feature of IFS theory, it is widely used in many fields, for example, transportation, assignment, decision-making, etc.

Due to the existence of uncertainty in the FAPs and FTPs, many authors studied APs and TPs with IFSs. Some of the current studies related to these studies are given in Table 3.

A ranking formula or ranking technique will be helpful to compare two IFNs, which is also used to solve real-world problems. Some of the current research publications related to ranking techniques are shown in Table 4.

The IFAP is one of the optimization problems. Recently, several authors have presented new techniques for optimization problems. To know more, the authors name and published years of some of the academic publications that related to optimization problems are mentioned here (Utami et al., 2019; Lebedeva and Poltavskaya, 2020; Beaula and Seetha, 2020; Khalifa, 2020; Hirata et al., 2020; Prifti et al., 2020; González et al., 2020; Lyapin et al., 2020; Ekanayake et al., 2020; Marelli et al., 2021; Tanneau et al., 2021; Zhang et al., 2021; Rizk-Allah et al., 2021; Chang et al., 2021; Kalhoro et al., 2021; Mohan et al., 2021; Khalifa et al., 2021; Herzel et al., 2021; Wang et al., 2021; Sangeetha et al., 2022; Kanagajothi and Kumar, 2022; Taillard, 2023; Kumar, 2024).

In this book chapter, we are examining the IFAP. Let $[\tilde{C}_{ij}^{I}]_{n \times n}$ be the squared intuitionistic fuzzy cost/time matrix and let $\tilde{c}_{ij}^{I}$ be the intuitionistic fuzzy cost/time of assigning the jth job to the ith machine.

Table 1. Some of the academic publications related to APs

Authors	Aim	Methods
Kuhn (1955)	To introduce and solve the AP	Hungarian
Dutta and Pal (2015)	To find out the optimal solution of AP	Modified Hungarian
Matsiy et al. (2015)	To solve the AP	Recurrent
Shah et al. (2015)	To solve the $m{\times}n$ AP	An alternate approach same as Hungarian
Lee (2015)	To solve the AP	Minimum cost moving
Betts and Vasko (2016)	To solve the unbalanced assignment problem	Hungarian
Porchelvi and Anitha (2018)	To find out the optimal solution for AP	Average total opportunity cost
Jamali et al. (2019)	To find out the IBFS using Modified Weighted Opportunity Cost based Least Cost Matrix (MWOC-LCM)	MWOC-LCM
Murugesan and Esakkiammal (2020a, b)	To find the optimal solution of AP	New Method (NM), Advanced Method (NS-AVSNM), Innovative Method (TVAM), New Methodology (MAP) and TERM
Nu'man et al. (2020)	To find out the suitable location with the help of assignment method	Assignment method
Munot and Ghadle (2020)	To obtain the optimal solution of AP with congruence modulo approach	New algorithm
Wang et al. (2020)	To solve the shortest time AP	Minimum adjustment
Hussein and Shiker (2020)	To find a solution to the AP	Al-Saeedi's 1st method and Al-Saeedi's 2nd method
Kaur et al. (2020)	To do the time-cost trade-off analysis of a priority based AP	Criteria based iterative algorithm
Jayalakshmi et al., (2020)	To solve the AP	Standard method
De Turck (2020)	To find the efficient resource allocation through ILPP	Integer linear programming
Hu and Liu (2021)	To solve the generalized AP	Network flow algorithm
Li et al. (2021)	To solve the multi-dimensional APs	A dual approach
Chandrakala (2021)	To find the optimal solution of a travelling salesman and AP	Enhanced zero suffix approach
Mondal and Tsourdos (2021)	To find the optimum task allocation	Genetic Algorithm
Sadiq et al. (2022)	To compare the solution of AP with three different approaches	Hungarian, Alternate and New Technique
Beirkdar and Ramesh (2022)	To find an optimal solution of APs in the complete interval	A new approach
Shanmugasundari and Aarthi (2022)	To solve the real-world problems	The modified approach of fuzzy measures
Gothi et al. (2023)	To find the optimal solution of AP	Median and Variable approaches
Arora and Sharma (2023)	To solve task AP	Branch and Bound method
Mohammed et al. (2023)	To compare the solution of AP with existing approaches	Penalty Approach

The methods mentioned in Table 1 are not all useful for solving AP with uncertain parameters.

Table 2. Current studies related to fuzzy assignment, fuzzy transportation and fuzzy LPP

Authors	Aim	Methods
Ingle and Ghadle (2019)	To find out the optimal solution for FAP	Novel
Santhi and Ananthanarayanan (2020)	To find out the optimal assignment for FAP	Standard deviation
Mohideen and Kumar (2010a, b)	To identify the best fuzzy transportation method	Zero point and MODI
Kumar (2010, 2017a)	To present the comparative study	Zero point and MODI
Kumar (2016a, b, 2018a)	To find out the optimal solution for FTP	PSK
Beaula and Saravanan (2020)	To find out the optimal solution for a fully fuzzy linear programming problem (FFLPP)	New
Dhanasekar et al. (2020)	To solve FAP and fuzzy traveling salesman problem	Improved Hungarian
Josephine et al. (2020)	To find a solution to FTP	Dynamic method
Valliathal and Revathi (2020)	To find the optimal solution for FAP	Penalty method
Pérez-Cañedo and Concepción-Morales (2020)	To solve the fuzzy linear assignment problem	Theory of algebraic and total ordering of fuzzy numbers
Muamer (2020)	To solve the FAP	Hungarian
Zaitseva et al. (2020)	To solve the AP with incomplete information	Game-theoretic approach
Ahmed (2021)	To solve a FTP	Linear programming and goal programming
Kar and Shaw (2020)	To obtain the optimal solution of AP with triangular fuzzy data	Hungarian
Gaspars-Wieloch (2021)	To solve the AP under uncertainty	Binary Programming
Prabha et al. (2021)	To find a solution to the Unbalanced FTP	Heuristic Method
Ahmed et al. (2021)	To solve a TP	Fuzzy multi-objective defuzzification method
Neelambari et al. (2023)	To develop a novel strategy for solving FAPs	SBD

Here, we need to assign the machines to jobs on a 1-to-1 basis. At the same time, we should find the optimal allocations which optimize the objective function. The proposed method in this book chapter is named the PSK method and it is based on the ranking method and software. Solving IFAPs using the PSK method with the help of Matlab and RGui is new in the literature. In addition, many useful theorems are stated and efficiently proved.

This book chapter discusses the AP and presents a software and ranking method-based PSK approach to solving the AP in an environment with uncertainty and hesitation. The author introduces IFAPs and provides several theorems related to these problems. The chapter includes computer programs for the proposed problems, their verification with Matlab and RGui, and a comparative analysis, discussion of merits and demerits of the proposed method, and suggestions for future studies. Overall, the chapter covers the relevant and specialized topic of the book title and presents a systematic approach to addressing it.

The rest of this book chapter is organized as follows. Section 2 presents the concepts of IFS, IFN and TIFN. Further, it provides arithmetic operations and ordering principles between two IFNs. Section 3 presents the mathematical model with tabular representation of IFAP. Further, it presents some useful

Table 3. Current studies related to IFAPs and IFTPs

Authors	Aim	Methods
Hussain and Kumar (2012a, b,c, 2013)	To solve the different types of IFTPs	VAM, MODI and zero point
Kumar and Hussain (2014a,b,c, 2016a, b)	To solve the balanced, unbalanced and mixed intuitionistic fuzzy assignment problem (MIFAP)	Hungarian, linear programming and a new algorithm
Kumar (2017b, 2023a,b,c)	To solve the TPs and APs with FNs and IFNs	PSK
Kumar and Hussain (2014d, 2015, 2016c)	To solve the different types of TPs with IFNs	Zero point, MODI and PSK
Narayanamoorthy et al. (2017)	To optimize both the fuzzy and IFAPs	Ones assignment
Kumar (2018b, c, 2020a)	To solve the IFTPs	Linear programming, MODI and intuitionistic fuzzy zero-point
Kumar (2018d, e, 2019a)	To optimize the intuitionistic fuzzy objective function	Min zero-min cost, linear programming and PSK
Taghaodi (2019)	To find the optimal solution for type-2 IFTP	North west corner, least cost, Vogel's approximation and MODI
Kumar (2019b, 2020b,c,d)	To optimize the objective function with IFNs	Software, PSK, linear programming and new algorithm
Abirami et al. (2020)	To solve the TP with a trapezoidal intuitionistic fuzzy number (TrIFN)	New approach
Soundararajan and Kumar (2020)	To find the optimal solution for UBIFTP and to avoid large number of iterations	Monalisha's approximation
Kar et al. (2020)	To find the optimal solution of AP with trapezoidal intuitionistic type-2 fuzzy data	Hungarian method
Selvakumari and Subasri (2020)	To compare fuzzy, intuitionistic and neutrosophic AP with nonagonal FN	Hungarian method
Kumar (2021, 2022)	To solve the optimization problem with IFNs	Software and the new algorithm
Stanojević and Stanojević (2021)	To solve the TP with trapezoidal fuzzy parameters and intuitionistic fuzzy parameters	Standard method
Rani et al. (2022)	To solve the interval-valued IFAP	Branch and bound approach

Table 4. Recent research publications related to intuitionistic fuzzy ranking

Authors	Method	Year
Varghese and Kuriakose	Centroid	2012
Velu et al.	New ranking	2017
Shakouri et al.	Parametric	2020
Qiang et al.	New ranking	2020
Mohan et al.	A new approach	2020
Bharati	New ranking	2021

definitions related to IFAP. Section 4 provides the PSK method and some useful theorems with corollary. Section 5 presents 4 examples to illustrate the proposed method. Section 6 provides concluding remarks with future studies.

DEFINITIONS AND NOTATIONS

Some key definitions used in this book chapter are given in this section.

Definition: Let X be a finite universal set. An IFS A in X is an object having the form:

$$A = \left\{ \left\langle x, \mu_A(x), \vartheta_A(x) \right\rangle s.t. x \in X \right\}. \tag{1}$$

where, the functions $\mu_A(x), \vartheta_A(x) : X \to [0,1]$ define, respectively, the degree of membership and degree of non-membership of the element $x \in X$ to the set A, which is a subset of X, and for every element $x \in X$,

$$0 \le \mu_A(x) + \vartheta_A(x) \le 1. \tag{2}$$

IFS A and the total of its membership and non-membership values can be represented symbolically by Equations (1) and (2), respectively.

Definition: The function

$$\pi_A(x) = 1 - \mu_A(x) - \vartheta_A(x) \tag{3}$$

is called the IFS index/hesitation margin of x in A. $\pi_A(x)$ is the degree of indeterminacy of x∈X to the IFS A and $\pi_A(x) \in [0,1]$.

That is, $\pi_A(x)$: X→[0,1] and $0 \le \pi_A(x) \le 1$ for every x∈X. $\pi_A(x)$ expresses the lack of knowledge of whether x belongs to IFS A or not.

Equation (3) can be used to symbolically depict the hesitation value of IFS A.

Example: Let A be an IFS with μ_A(x)=0.1 and ϑ_A(x)=0.3

$$\Rightarrow \pi_A(x) = 1 - 0.1 - 0.3$$

=0.6

It can be interpreted as "the degree that the object $x \in A$ is 0.1, the degree that the object $x \notin A$ is 0.3 and the degree of hesitancy is 0.6".

Definition: An Intuitionistic fuzzy subset A = {<x, μ_A(x), ϑ_A (x)>s.t. x∈X} of the real line 'R' is called an intuitionistic fuzzy number (IFN) if the following holds:

1. ∃ m ∈ R s.t. μ_A(m) = 1 & ϑ_A(m) = 0, where m is the average of A.

2. The function 'μA' is a continuous mapping from $R \to [0, 1]$ and $\forall x \in R$, *t*he mathematical relation $0 \le \mu_A(x) + \vartheta_A(x) \le 1$ holds.

The membership and non-membership function of 'A' are of the following form:

$$\mu_A(x) = \begin{cases} 0 & for -\infty < x \le m - a \\ f_1(x) & for\ x \in [m - a, m] \\ 1 & for\ x = m \\ h_1(x) & for\ x \in [m, m + b] \\ 0 & for\ m + \beta \le x < \infty \end{cases}$$

Where '$f_1(x)$' and '$h_1(x)$' are strictly increasing ($\uparrow$) and decreasing ($\downarrow$) functions in $[m-\alpha, m]$ and $[m.m+\beta]$ respectively.

$$\vartheta_A(x) = \begin{cases} 0 & for -\infty < x \le m - a' \\ f_2(x) & for\ x \in [m - a', m]; 0 \le f_1(x) + f_2(x) \le 1 \\ 1 & for\ x = m \\ h_2(x) & for\ x \in [m, m + \beta']; 0 \le h_1(x) + h_2(x) \le 1 \\ 0 & for\ m + \beta' \le x < \infty \end{cases}$$

Here 'm' is the average of A.

The letters 'α', 'β' are called the left and right spreads of $\mu_A(x)$, respectively.

The letters 'α'', 'β''' are called the left and right spreads of $\vartheta_A(x)$, respectively.

Symbolically, the IFN $\tilde{A}^I$ is represented as $A_{IFN} = (m; \alpha, \beta)$.

Definition: A TIFN 'A' is IFS in 'R' with the membership function $\mu_A(x)$ & non-membership function $\vartheta_A(x)$. Where,

$$\mu_A(x) = \begin{cases} 0, & for\ x < a_1 \\ \dfrac{x - a_1}{a_2 - a_1}, & for\ a_1 \le x \le a_2 \\ 1, & for\ x = a_2 \\ \dfrac{a_3 - x}{a_3 - a_2}, & for\ a_2 \le x \le a_3 \\ 0, & for\ x > a_3 \end{cases} \quad \& \quad \vartheta_A(x) = \begin{cases} 1, & for\ x < a_1 \\ \dfrac{a_2 - x}{a_2 - a_1'}, & for\ a_1' \le x \le a_2 \\ 0, & for\ x = a_2 \\ \dfrac{x - a_2}{a_3' - a_2}, & for\ a_2 \le x \le a_3' \\ 1, & for\ x > a_3' \end{cases}$$

Where $a_1' \le a_1 \le a_2 \le a_3 \le a_3'$ and $\mu_A(x)$, $\vartheta_A(x)$ less than or equal to 0.5 for $\mu_A(x)$ equal to $\vartheta_A(x)$ for all, x belongs to R. It is denoted by $\tilde{A}^I = \left(a_1, a_2, a_3; a_1', a_2, a_3' \right)$.

Definition: The arithmetic operations ($\oplus$ and $\ominus$) between $\tilde{A}^I = \left(a_1, a_2, a_3; a_1^{'}, a_2, a_3^{'}\right)$ and $\tilde{B}^I = \left(b_1, b_2, b_3; b_1^{'}, b_2, b_3^{'}\right)$ are defined as follows.

1. $\tilde{A}^I \oplus \tilde{B}^I = \left(a_1 + b_1, a_2 + b_2, a_3 + b_3; a_1^{'} + b_1^{'}, a_2 + b_2, a_3^{'} + b_3^{'}\right)$
2. $\tilde{A}^I \ominus \tilde{B}^I = \left(a_1 - b_3, a_2 - b_2, a_3 - b_1; a_1^{'} - b_3^{'}, a_2 - b_2, a_3^{'} - b_1^{'}\right)$

Definition: From $\tilde{A}^I = \left(a_1, a_2, a_3; a_1^{'}, a_2, a_3^{'}\right)$ and $\tilde{B}^I = \left(b_1, b_2, b_3; b_1^{'}, b_2, b_3^{'}\right)$, we can define the set of TIFNs is as follows.

1. $\Re\left(\tilde{A}^I\right) > \Re\left(\tilde{B}^I\right) \Leftrightarrow \tilde{A}^I \succ \tilde{B}^I$
2. $\Re\left(\tilde{A}^I\right) < \Re\left(\tilde{B}^I\right) \Leftrightarrow \tilde{A}^I \prec \tilde{B}^I$
3. $\Re\left(\tilde{A}^I\right) = \Re\left(\tilde{B}^I\right) \Leftrightarrow \tilde{A}^I \approx \tilde{B}^I$

Where,

$$\left(\tilde{A}^I\right) = \frac{1}{3}\left[\frac{\left(a_3^{'} - a_1^{'}\right)\left(a_2 - 2a_3^{'} - 2a_1^{'}\right) + \left(a_3 - a_1\right)\left(a_1 + a_2 + a_3\right) + 3\left(a_3^{'2} - a_1^{'2}\right)}{a_3^{'} - a_1^{'} + a_3 - a_1}\right]$$

If the above formula is not suitable to compute the ranking for TIFNs, then we can use the following accuracy function.

$$f\left(\tilde{A}^I\right) = \frac{\left(a_1 + 2a_2 + a_3\right) + \left(a_1^{'} + 2a_2 + a_3^{'}\right)}{8} . \Rightarrow$$

1. $f(\tilde{A}^I) > f(\tilde{B}^I)$ if and only if $\tilde{A}^I \succ \tilde{B}^I$.
2. $f(\tilde{A}^I) < f(\tilde{B}^I)$ if $\tilde{A}^I \prec \tilde{B}^I$.
3. $f(\tilde{A}^I) = f(\tilde{B}^I) \Leftrightarrow \tilde{A}^I \approx \tilde{B}^I$.

Definition: The ordering $\succeq$ and $\preceq$ between $\tilde{A}^I$ and $\tilde{B}^I$ are defined as follows.

1. $\tilde{A}^I \succeq \tilde{B}^I \Longleftrightarrow$ (if and only if) $\tilde{A}^I \succ \tilde{B}^I$ or $\tilde{A}^I \approx \tilde{B}^I$.
2. $\tilde{A}^I \preceq \tilde{B}^I \Leftrightarrow$ (iff) $\tilde{A}^I \prec \tilde{B}^I$ or $\tilde{A}^I \approx \tilde{B}^I$.

Definition: Let $\{\tilde{\Psi}_i^I, i = 1, 2, \ldots, n\}$ be a set of TIFNs. Then, we can define the following.

1. If $(\tilde{\Psi}_k^I) \leq (\tilde{\Psi}_i^I) \forall i$, then the TIFN $\tilde{\Psi}_k^I$ is the min. of $\{\tilde{\Psi}_i^I, i = 1, 2, \ldots, n\}$.

2. If $(\tilde{\Psi}_t^I) \geq (\tilde{\Psi}_i^I)$ $\forall i$, then the TIFN $\tilde{\Psi}_t^I$ is the max. of $\{\tilde{\Psi}_i^I, i = 1, 2, \ldots, n\}$.

THE PROPOSED MODEL AND KEY DEFINITIONS OF IFAP

In this section, mathematical formulation, tabular representation and key definitions of IFAP are all presented.

Consider the assignment of 'n' jobs to 'n' machines and consider each machine is capable of doing any job at different costs. Let c_{ij} be the cost of assigning the job 'j' to the machine 'i'. Let y_{ij} be the decision variable (DV). It is denoted by the assignment of ith machine to j^{th} job. The aim of solving this problem is to minimize the total cost of the job assignment subject to assigning of all the jobs to the available machines. This problem is called AP.

The mathematical model of AP is given below.

Model One

(Objective function) Minimize $Z = \sum_{i=1}^{n} \sum_{j=1}^{n} c_{ij} y_{ij}$

$$s.t. \begin{cases} \sum_{j=1}^{n} y_{ij} = 1, & i = 1, 2, \ldots, n \\ \sum_{i=1}^{n} y_{ij} = 1, & j = 1, 2, \ldots, n \\ y_{ij} \in \{0, 1\} \end{cases}$$

Where $y_{ij}=1$, if i^{th} machine is assigned to j^{th} job

$=0$, if i^{th} machine is not assigned to j^{th} job

Consider model 1 with intuitionistic fuzzy costs instead of crisp costs and say it is model 2. Then, it is known as BIFAP (Balanced IFAP).

Model Two

(Objective function) Minimize $\tilde{Z}^I = \sum_{i=1}^{n} \sum_{j=1}^{n} \tilde{c}_{ij}^I y_{ij}$

Subject to the constraints (4) to (6) (see, Equations (4) to (6)).

We could not minimize model 2 directly because intuitionistic fuzzy costs (IFCs) are involved in the objective function. Therefore, model 2 is converted into model 1, and then it is solved by regular method(s) or software (e.g., Matlab, RGui, etc.).

The tabular form of IFAP is presented in Table 5.

The equivalent transportation model to the given IFAP is presented in Table 6.

We should be aware of the following definitions before studying IFAPs:

Definition: If an AP has the intuitionistic fuzzy parameter, then it is called IFAP.

Table 5. BIFAP

	1	2	...	n
1	$\tilde{c}_{11}^{I}$	$\tilde{c}_{12}^{I}$	...	$\tilde{c}_{1n}^{I}$
2	$\tilde{c}_{21}^{I}$	$\tilde{c}_{22}^{I}$	...	$\tilde{c}_{2n}^{I}$
⋮	⋮	⋮		⋮
n	$\tilde{c}_{n1}^{I}$	$\tilde{c}_{n2}^{I}$	...	$\tilde{c}_{nn}^{I}$

Note: Rows represent machines, and columns represent jobs.

Definition: If an AP has a mixture of crisp, fuzzy, and intuitionistic fuzzy parameters, then it is called MIFAP.

Definition: If an IFAP has an equal number of rows and columns, then the problem is called BIFAP.

Definition: If an IFAP has an unequal number of rows and columns, then the problem is called an unbalanced intuitionistic fuzzy assignment problem (UBIFAP).

The upcoming section presents the PSK method, newly stated theorems and corollary, and their proofs.

THE PSK METHOD

The PSK technique includes the following phases.

1. Form an IFAP for the given data with rows (machines) and columns (jobs).
2. By using the suitable ranking procedure, transform IFAP into CAP.
3. To find out the optimum assignment and its relevant objective value either with the help of the Hungarian method or with the help of software (e.g., RGui, Lingo, Matlab and Tora) to the CAP.
4. Let us assume that the assigned cells costs are $\tilde{0}^{I}$'s and the remaining cells costs are their original cost. Say it is a new IFAP or new IFAT. Now, subtract each column's entries for the current table

Table 6. Tabular representation of BIFAP in the form of TP

	1	2	...	n	Supply
1	$\tilde{c}_{11}^{I}$	$\tilde{c}_{12}^{I}$	...	$\tilde{c}_{1n}^{I}$	1
2	$\tilde{c}_{21}^{I}$	$\tilde{c}_{22}^{I}$	...	$\tilde{c}_{2n}^{I}$	1
⋮	⋮	⋮		⋮	⋮
n	$\tilde{c}_{n1}^{I}$	$\tilde{c}_{n2}^{I}$	...	$\tilde{c}_{nn}^{I}$	1
Demand	1	1	...	1	n

Note: Rows represent factories, and columns represent warehouses.

from the column min. and subtract each row's entries of the reduced table from the row min. Clearly, each column and each row of the resulting table has exactly one $\tilde{0}^I$. Thus, the current resulting table is called the optimum or optimal table.

5. Assign the ith machine to j^{th} job if the intersection of the cost, i.e., the occupied cell cost of the cell (i,j) is $\tilde{0}^I$. Also, let us take the value of the DV in this occupied cell is $y_{ij}=1$ ($i=1,2,\ldots,n$ and $j=1,2,\ldots,n$). Next, we put $y_{ij}=0$ ($i=1,2,\ldots,n$ and $j=1,2,\ldots,n$) for all unoccupied cells (i.e., see [$\tilde{c}_{ij}^{I\sim}$ $\tilde{u}_i^{I\sim}$ $\tilde{v}_j^I$] $\succ \tilde{0}^I$) in such a way that assigns all the jobs to all the machines. Lastly, compute the optimum (i.e., minimum) assignment cost by using the mathematical relation $\tilde{Z}_{Min}^I \approx \sum_{i=1}^{n}\sum_{j=1}^{n}[\tilde{c}_{ij}^I y_{ij}]$.

The following theorems are proved to ensure that the assignment obtained by the PSK method to the IFAP is always optimal.

Theorem: Any optimum assignment to the IFAP (S_1), where (S_1) Minimize $\tilde{Z}^{I*} \approx \sum_{i=1}^{n}\sum_{j=1}^{n}[\tilde{c}_{ij}^{I\sim}$ $\tilde{u}_i^{I\sim}$ $\tilde{v}_j^I]y_{ij}$ subject to (4) to (6) are satisfied, where $\tilde{u}_i^I$ (min. of ith row of the newly constructed cost matrix $\left[\tilde{c}_{ij}^I\right]$) and $\tilde{v}_j^I$ (min. of jth column of the resulting cost matrix $[\tilde{c}_{ij}^{I\sim}$ $\tilde{u}_i^I]$) are some real TIFNs, is an optimum assignment to the problem (S), where (S) Minimize $\tilde{Z}^I \approx \sum_{i=1}^{n}\sum_{j=1}^{n}[\tilde{c}_{ij}^I \otimes y_{ij}]$ subject to (4) to (6) are satisfied.

Proof

Let $\tilde{u}_i^I$ be the min. of ith row of the newly constructed cost matrix $[\tilde{c}_{ij}^I]$. Now, we subtract $\tilde{u}_i^I$ from the ith row entries so that the resulting cost matrix is $[\tilde{c}_{ij}^{I\sim}$ $\tilde{u}_i^I]$. Let $\tilde{v}_j^I$ be the min. of jth column of the resulting cost matrix $[\tilde{c}_{ij}^{I\sim}$ $\tilde{u}_i^I]$. Now, we subtract $\tilde{v}_j^I$ from the jth column entries so that the resulting cost matrix is $\left[\tilde{c}_{ij}^{I\sim}$ $\tilde{u}_i^{I\sim}$ $\tilde{v}_j^I\right]$. It may be noted that $\left[\tilde{c}_{ij}^{I\sim}$ $\tilde{u}_i^{I\sim}$ $\tilde{v}_j^I\right] \succeq \tilde{0}^I$, $\forall i,j$. Additionally, we have each row and each column exactly one $\tilde{0}^I$.

Now,

$$\tilde{Z}^{I*} \approx \left[\sum_{i=1}^{n}\sum_{j=1}^{n}(\tilde{c}_{ij}^{I\sim}$ $\tilde{u}_i^{I\sim}$ $\tilde{v}_j^I)y_{ij}\right]$$

$$\approx \left[\left(\sum_{i=1}^{n}\sum_{j=1}^{n}\tilde{c}_{ij}^I \otimes y_{ij}\right)\Theta\left(\sum_{i=1}^{n}\sum_{j=1}^{n}\tilde{u}_i^I \otimes y_{ij}\right)\Theta\left(\sum_{i=1}^{n}\sum_{j=1}^{n}\tilde{v}_j^I \otimes y_{ij}\right)\right]$$

$$\approx \left[\tilde{Z}^{I\sim}\sum_{i=1}^{n}\tilde{u}_i^I\left(\sum_{j=1}^{n}y_{ij}\right)\sim\sum_{j=1}^{n}\tilde{v}_j^I\left(\sum_{i=1}^{n}y_{ij}\right)\right]$$

$$\tilde{Z}^{I*} \approx [\tilde{Z}^{I\sim} \left(\sum_{i=1}^{n} \tilde{u}_i^I \right)^\sim \left(\sum_{j=1}^{n} \tilde{v}_j^I \right)]$$

$\because \sum_{i=1}^{n} \tilde{u}_i^I$ and $\sum_{j=1}^{n} \tilde{v}_j^I$ are independent of y_{ij}, $\forall i,j$, we can conclude that any optimum assignment to the problem (S_1) is also an optimum assignment to the problem (S).

Corollary: If y_{ij}^{ol}, $i=1,2,\ldots,n$ and $j=1,2,\ldots,n$ is a feasible solution to the problem (S) and $\left(\tilde{c}_{ij}^{I\sim} \tilde{u}_i^{I\sim} v_j^I \right) \succeq \tilde{0}^I$, $\forall i,j$, where $\tilde{u}_i^I$ and $\tilde{v}_j^I$ are some real TIFNs, such that the min. $\sum_{i=1}^{n}\sum_{j=1}^{n}(\tilde{c}_{ij}^{I\sim} \tilde{u}_i^{I\sim} \tilde{v}_j^I)y_{ij}$ subject to (4) to (6) are satisfied, is $\tilde{0}^I$, then y_{ij}^{ol}, $i=1,2,\ldots,n$ and $j=1,2,\ldots,n$ is an optimal solution to the problem (S).

Proof

Let y_{ij}^{ol}, $i=1,2,\ldots,n$ and $j=1,2,\ldots,n$ be the feasible solution to the problem (S). Now, consider the problem (S) with $\left(\tilde{c}_{ij}^{I}\ominus\tilde{u}_i^{I}\ominus\tilde{v}_j^{I} \right) \succeq \tilde{0}^I$, $\forall i,j$, denoted by problem (S_1). From the above-stated theorem, clearly, (S) is the original problem and (S_1) is the reduced problem of the problem (S). Furthermore, in a problem (S_1) there is no possibility of minimizing the cost below $\tilde{0}^I$. Hence, if y_{ij}^{ol}, $i=1,2,\ldots,n$ and $j=1,2,\ldots,n$ is a feasible solution to the problem (S) and $\left(\tilde{c}_{ij}^{I}\ominus\tilde{u}_i^{I}\ominus v_j^I \right) \succeq \tilde{0}^I$, $\forall i,j$, where $\tilde{u}_i^I$ and $\tilde{v}_j^I$ are some real TIFNs, such that the min. $\sum_{i=1}^{n}\sum_{j=1}^{n}(\tilde{c}_{ij}^{I\sim} \tilde{u}_i^{I\sim} \tilde{v}_j^I)y_{ij}$ subject to (4) to (6) are satisfied, is $\tilde{0}^I$, then y_{ij}^{ol}, $i=1,2,\ldots,n$ and $j=1,2,\ldots,n$ is an optimal solution to the problem (S).

Theorem: Let S be an IFAP. Then, the assignment obtained by the PSK method for 'S' is an optimal assignment for 'S' (named as PSK Theorem).

Proof

Now, we are going to describe the proposed method in detail.

First, form an IFAP for the given data with rows (machines) and columns (jobs). Next, by using the suitable ranking procedure, transform IFAP into CAP. Now, solve the CAP using the software (e.g., RGui, Lingo, Matlab and Tora) or any theoretical methods (e.g., Hungarian method). This will yield the optimum assignment and objective value for the CAP. The optimum assigned cells in the crisp cost matrix are referred as assigned cells. The total number of cells minus assigned cells is equal to the remaining cells and are called unassigned cells. In $n \times n$ CAP, the total number of assigned cells are n which are all have 0 costs. |||^{ly}, IFAP also will have the same n number of assigned cells but their corresponding costs are $\tilde{0}^I$. Moreover, the CAP has exactly one assigned cell in each column and row. |||^{ly}, the IFAP has exactly one assigned cell in each column and row.

Now, construct the new cost matrix whose assigned cells cost are $\tilde{0}^I$ and the remaining cells cost are its original cost. Let $\tilde{u}_i^I$ be the min. of ith row of the current cost matrix $[\tilde{c}_{ij}^I]$. Now, we subtract $\tilde{u}_i^I$

from the ith row entries so that the reduced cost matrix is $[\tilde{c}_{ij}^{I^{\sim}} \ \tilde{u}_i^I]$. Let $\tilde{v}_j^I$ be the min. of jth column of the reduced cost matrix $[\tilde{c}_{ij}^{I^{\sim}} \ \tilde{u}_i^I]$. Now, we subtract $\tilde{v}_j^I$ from the jth column entries so that the reduced cost matrix is $\left[\tilde{c}_{ij}^I \ominus \tilde{u}_i^I \ominus \tilde{v}_j^I\right]$. It may be noted that $\left[\tilde{c}_{ij}^I \ominus \tilde{u}_i^I \ominus \tilde{v}_j^I\right] \succeq \tilde{0}^I$, $\forall i,j$. Clearly, we have each row and each column exactly one $\tilde{0}^I$. This reduced cost matrix is referred as optimum assignment cost matrix.

Ultimately, we have a solution y_{ij}, $i=1,2,...,n$ and $j=1,2,...,n$ for the IFAP whose cost matrix is [$\tilde{c}_{ij}^{I^{\sim}} \ \tilde{u}_i^{I^{\sim}} \ \tilde{v}_j^I$] such that $y_{ij}=0$ for $[\tilde{c}_{ij}^{I^{\sim}} \ \tilde{u}_i^{I^{\sim}} \ \tilde{v}_j^I] \succ \tilde{0}^I$ and $y_{ij}=1$ for $[\tilde{c}_{ij}^{I^{\sim}} \ \tilde{u}_i^{I^{\sim}} \ \tilde{v}_j^I] \approx \tilde{0}^I$. So, the min. $\sum_{i=1}^{n}\sum_{j=1}^{n}[\tilde{c}_{ij}^{I^{\sim}} \ \tilde{u}_i^{I^{\sim}} \ \tilde{v}_j^I]y_{ij}$ subject to (4) to (6) are satisfied, is $\tilde{0}^I$. Thus, by the Corollary, the solution y_{ij}, $i=1,2,...,n$ and $j=1,2,...,n$ is obtained by the PSK method for the IFAP (S) is an optimal solution for the IFAP (S).

Theorem: If equivalent TIFNs replace some (or all) of the TIFNs in the IFAPs, then the new IFAPs will have the same set of optimum solutions.

Proof

In general, IFAPs are APs in which only the assignment costs (or profits) are represented in terms of TIFNs or IFNs. We can see that, in the IFAPs, the decision variables (DVs) are all in CNs. In the IFAPs, the DVs always depend on their constraints. But the constraints are all having the crisp decision variables (CDVs). From this argument, the optimal solution is always CNs. The optimal solution remains unchanged if all the costs of the AP remain unchanged. Also, our assumption is to replace equivalent TIFNs in the IFAPs. Hence, the costs are unchanged in the new IFAPs and only the existing assignment costs are replaced by their equivalent TIFNs. $\Rightarrow$ If equivalent TIFNs replace some (or all) of the TIFNs in the IFAPs, then the new IFAPs will have the same set of optimum solutions.

Theorem: Any solution of FAP is also the solution of its equivalent CAP.

Proof

The proof is similar to the previous theorem.

Theorem: Any solution of mixed fuzzy assignment problem (MFAP) is also the solution of its equivalent CAP.

Proof

The proof is similar to the previous theorem.

Theorem: Any solution of IFAP is also the solution of its equivalent CAP.

Proof

The proof is similar to the previous theorem.

Theorem: Any solution of MIFAP is also the solution of its equivalent CAP.

Proof

The proof is similar to the previous theorem.

EXAMPLES

In this section, 4 examples are given to illustrate the PSK method.

Example One

A mobile phone manufacturing company named Vasikaran has 3 jobs- Assembling, Testing and Packing. These 3 jobs can be done by 3 employees- Kavya, Bhavya and Navya. These 3 employees are capable of doing these 3 jobs but a single employee can undertake only 1 job at a time (this is the general assumption of AP). The performing time of each job is not known exactly due to the following reasons: lack of experience, interest, capacity and understanding. So, the time consumption for all the jobs is given in terms of IFNs. From the past experience, the time (in hrs) that each employee takes to do each job is presented in Table 7.

Table 7. BIFAP

	Assembling (A)	Testing (T)	Packing (P)
Kavya (X)	(7, 21, 29; 2, 21, 34)	(7, 20, 57; 3, 20, 61)	(12, 25, 56; 8, 25, 60)
Bhavya (Y)	(8, 9, 16; 2, 9, 22)	(4, 12, 35; 1, 12, 38)	(6, 14, 28; 3, 14, 31)
Navya (Z)	(5, 9, 22; 2, 9, 25)	(10, 15, 20; 5, 15, 25)	(4, 16, 19; 1, 16, 22)

Find the assignment of Women to jobs that will minimize the total time taken.

Solution:

Assume that $y_{11}, y_{12}, y_{13}, y_{21}, y_{22}, y_{23}, y_{31}, y_{32}$ and y_{33} are DVs. Now, solve the following mathematical program to find out the values of $y_{11}, y_{12}, y_{13}, y_{21}, y_{22}, y_{23}, y_{31}, y_{32}$ and y_{33}.

To solve the following mathematical programming, now transform the BFIFAP into its relevant, crisp AP using step 2 of the proposed method.

(Objective function) Min $\tilde{Z}^I$ [$\Re$(7, 21, 29; 2, 21, 34) y_{11}+$\Re$(7, 20, 57; 3, 20, 61) y_{12}+ $\Re$(12, 25, 56; 8, 25, 60) y_{13}+$\Re$(8, 9, 16; 2, 9, 22) y_{21}+$\Re$(4, 12, 35; 1, 12, 38) y_{22}+$\Re$(6, 14, 28; 3, 14, 31) y_{23}+ $\Re$(5, 9, 22; 2, 9, 25) y_{31}+$\Re$(10, 15, 20; 5, 15, 25) y_{32}+$\Re$(4, 16, 19; 1, 16, 22) y_{33}]

$$\text{s.t.} \begin{cases} \begin{cases} x_{11} + x_{12} + x_{13} = 1, \\ x_{21} + x_{22} + x_{23} = 1, \\ x_{31} + x_{32} + x_{33} = 1, \\ x_{41} + x_{42} + x_{43} = 1, \end{cases} \text{Women(X,Y,Z)/Machines constraints} \\ \begin{cases} x_{11} + x_{21} + x_{31} = 1, \\ x_{12} + x_{22} + x_{32} = 1, \\ x_{13} + x_{23} + x_{33} = 1, \\ x_{14} + x_{24} + x_{34} = 1, \end{cases} \text{Jobs(Assembling, Testing, Packing) constraints} \\ x_{ij} \in \{0,1\} \quad \text{Feasibility restriction} \end{cases}$$

Using the ranking procedure, this intuitionistic fuzzy mathematical programming problem (IFMPP) can be transformed into the CAP (crisp assignment problem) and it is presented in Table 8.

Table 8. The crisp form of the given BIFAP

	Assembling (A)	Testing (T)	Packing (P)
Kavya (X)	19	28	31
Bhavya (Y)	11	17	16
Navya (Z)	12	15	13

The problem in Table 8 can be written as a mathematical programming, which is as follows:

Min Z [(19×y_{11}) + (28×y_{12}) + (31×y_{13}) + (11×y_{21}) + (17×y_{22}) + (16×y_{23}) + (12×y_{31}) + (15×y_{32}) + (13×y_{33})]

$$\text{s.t.} \begin{cases} \begin{cases} x_{11} + x_{12} + x_{13} = 1, \\ x_{21} + x_{22} + x_{23} = 1, \\ x_{31} + x_{32} + x_{33} = 1, \\ x_{41} + x_{42} + x_{43} = 1, \end{cases} \text{Women(X,Y,Z)/Machines constraints} \\ \begin{cases} x_{11} + x_{21} + x_{31} = 1, \\ x_{12} + x_{22} + x_{32} = 1, \\ x_{13} + x_{23} + x_{33} = 1, \\ x_{14} + x_{24} + x_{34} = 1, \end{cases} \text{Jobs(Assembling, Testing, Packing) constraints} \\ x_{ij} \in \{0,1\} \quad \text{Feasibility restriction} \end{cases}$$

From step 3, we now obtain the following optimum solution and objective value (for the CAP).

$y_{11} = y_{22} = y_{33} = 1$, $y_{12} = y_{13} = y_{21} = y_{23} = y_{31} = y_{32} = 0$, and $\left(\tilde{Z}^I \right) = 49$ (in hrs).

$\Rightarrow$ Kavya $(X) \rightarrow$ Assembling,
Bhavya $(Y) \rightarrow$ Testing,
Navya $(Z) \rightarrow$ Packing.

$$\Rightarrow \tilde{Z}^I_{Min} = \tilde{c}^I_{11} \oplus \tilde{c}^I_{22} \oplus \tilde{c}^I_{33}$$

$$= (7, 21, 29; 2, 21, 34) \oplus (4, 12, 35; 1, 12, 38) \oplus (4, 16, 19; 1, 16, 22)$$

$$\tilde{Z}^I_{Min} = (15, 49, 83; 4, 49, 94) \tag{7}$$

$$\left(\tilde{Z}^I_{Min} \right) = 49 \text{ (in hrs)}$$

Equation (7) represents the most accurate optimal value of example number 1.

Solution by Lingo:

The problem in Table 8 can be written as a pure integer linear programming problem (PILPP) and it is given below.

Min Z $[(19 \times y_{11}) + (28 \times y_{12}) + (31 \times y_{13}) + (11 \times y_{21}) + (17 \times y_{22}) + (16 \times y_{23}) + (12 \times y_{31}) + (15 \times y_{32}) + (13 \times y_{33})]$

$$s.t. \begin{cases} x_{11} + x_{12} + x_{13} = 1, \\ x_{21} + x_{22} + x_{23} = 1, \\ x_{31} + x_{32} + x_{33} = 1, \\ x_{11} + x_{21} + x_{31} = 1, \\ x_{12} + x_{22} + x_{32} = 1, \\ x_{13} + x_{23} + x_{33} = 1, \\ x_{ij} \in \{0,1\}. \end{cases}$$

The Lingo computer programming for this problem is given below.

```
MODEL:

!Objective function;
```

```
[_1] MIN= 19 * Y11 + 28 * Y12 + 31 * Y13 + 11 * Y21 + 17 * Y22 + 16 * Y23 + 12
* Y31 + 15 * Y32 + 13 * Y33;
!S.t the constraints;
 [_2] Y11 + Y12 + Y13 = 1;
 [_3] Y21 + Y22 + Y23 = 1;
 [_4] Y31 + Y32 + Y33 = 1;
 [_5] Y11 + Y21 + Y31 = 1;
 [_6] Y12 + Y22 + Y32 = 1;
 [_7] Y13 + Y23 + Y33 = 1;
@BIN(Y11); @BIN(Y12); @BIN(Y13); @BIN(Y21); @BIN(Y22); @BIN(Y23);
@BIN(Y31); @BIN(Y32); @BIN(Y33);
END
```

The lingo input and its model statistics for the crisp version of problem 1 are given in Figures 1 and 2.

Figure 1. The lingo input for the crisp version of problem one

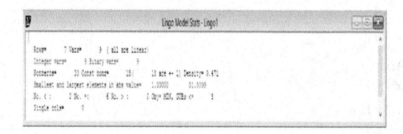

Figure 2. The lingo model statistics for the crisp version of problem one

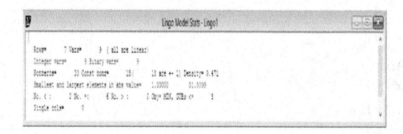

Different types of lingo matrix pictures are presented in Figures 3 to 6.

Figure 3. Unpermuted lingo matrix picture, for example-one

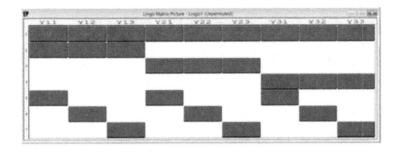

Figure 4. Lower triangular lingo matrix picture, for example-one

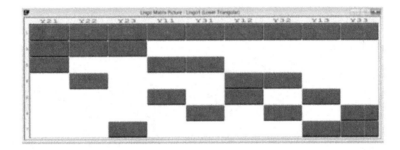

Figure 5. Block triangular lingo matrix picture (GP1-3 blocks), for example-one

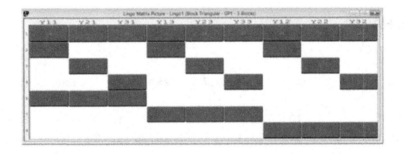

Figure 6. Block triangular lingo matrix picture (GP2-2 blocks), for example-one

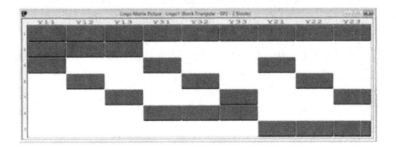

By applying the Lingo software to this problem, we obtain the following.

$$y_{11} = y_{22} = y_{33} = 1, \ y_{12} = y_{13} = y_{21} = y_{23} = y_{31} = y_{32} = 0 \text{ and } Z_{min} = 49 \text{ (in hrs)}.$$

$$\Rightarrow \tilde{Z}^I_{Min} = (15,49,83; \ 4,49,94)$$

$$\Rightarrow \left(\tilde{Z}^I_{Min} \right) = 49.$$

The lingo solution report for the crisp version of problem 1 is presented in Figure 7.

Figure 7. The lingo solution report for the crisp version of problem one

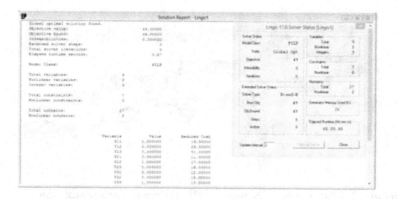

Solution by TORA:

	x1	x2	x3	x4	x5	x6	x7	x8	x9	Enter <, >, or = R.H.S.
Var. Name	Y11	Y12	Y13	Y21	Y22	Y23	Y31	Y32	Y33	
Minimize	19.00	28.00	31.00	11.00	17.00	16.00	12.00	15.00	13.00	
Constr 1	1.00	1.00	1.00	0.00	0.00	0.00	0.00	0.00	0.00	=1.00
Constr 2	0.00	0.00	0.00	1.00	1.00	1.00	0.00	0.00	0.00	=1.00
Constr 3	0.00	0.00	0.00	0.00	0.00	0.00	1.00	1.00	1.00	=1.00
Constr 4	1.00	0.00	0.00	1.00	0.00	0.00	1.00	0.00	0.00	=1.00
Constr 5	0.00	1.00	0.00	0.00	1.00	0.00	0.00	1.00	0.00	=1.00
Constr 6	0.00	0.00	1.00	0.00	0.00	1.00	0.00	0.00	1.00	=1.00
Lower Bound	0.00	0.00	0.00	0.00	0.00	0.00	0.00	0.00	0.00	
Upper Bound	∞	∞	∞	∞	∞	∞	∞	∞	∞	
Unrestr'd (y/n)?	n	n	n	n	n	n	n	n	n	
Integer (y/n)?	y	y	y	y	y	y	y	y	y	

By applying the Tora software to this problem, we obtain the following.

$y_{11} = y_{22} = y_{33} = 1$, $y_{12} = y_{13} = y_{21} = y_{23} = y_{31} = y_{32} = 0$ and $Z_{min} = 49$ (in hrs).

$$\Rightarrow \tilde{Z}^I_{\text{Min}} = (15,49,83; 4,49,94)$$

$$\Rightarrow \left(\tilde{Z}^I_{\text{Min}}\right) = 49.$$

Figures 8 and 9 show the Tora solution report for the crisp version of problem 1.

Figure 8. The Tora solution report for the crisp version of problem one (Automated B&B)

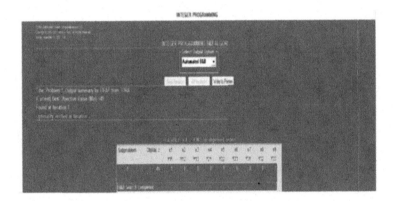

Figure 9. The Tora solution report for the crisp version of problem one (User-guided B&B)

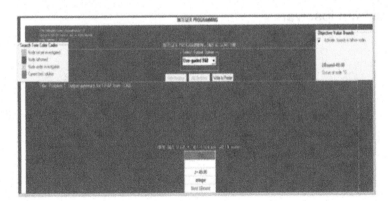

Solution by MATLAB

```
>> clc;
>> clear all;
>> f=[19 28 31 11 17 16 12 15 13];
>> A=[];
>> b=[];
>> Aeq= [1 1 1 0 0 0 0 0 0; 0 0 0 1 1 1 0 0 0; 0 0 0 0 0 0 1 1 1; 1 0 0 1 0 0
1 0 0; 0 1 0 0 1 0 0 1 0; 0 0 1 0 0 1 0 0 1];
>> beq= [1 1 1 1 1 1];
>> [y,f]= bintprog(f,A,b,Aeq,beq);
Optimization terminated.
>> disp(y);
     1
     0
     0
     0
     1
     0
     0
     0
     1

>> disp(f);
    49
```

Solution by RGui With lpsolver

```
>Ctrl+L
> library(lpSolve)
> assign.costs <- matrix (c(19, 11, 12, 28, 17, 15, 31, 16, 13), 3, 3)
> assign.costs
     [,1] [,2] [,3]
[1,]   19   28   31
[2,]   11   17   16
[3,]   12   15   13
> lp.assign (assign.costs)
Success: the objective function is 49
> lp.assign (assign.costs)$solution
     [,1] [,2] [,3]
[1,]    1    0    0
```

```
[2,]    0    1    0
[3,]    0    0    1
```

Example Two

Consider an IFAP with 4 machines (see rows)- M_1, M_2, M_3, M_4 and 4 jobs (see columns)- J_1, J_2, J_3, J_4. The profit matrix $\left[\tilde{c}_{ij}^I \right]_{4 \times 4}$ is presented in Table 9 and its elements are IFN.

Table 9. BIFAP relevant to example two

		Jobs →			
		J_1	J_2	J_3	J_4
Machines ↓	M_1	(27, 50, 109; 13, 50, 123)	(56, 67, 111; 40, 67, 127)	(8, 22, 120; 4, 22, 124)	(75, 100, 128; 62, 100, 141)
	M_2	(52, 68, 93; 44, 68, 101)	(43, 90, 119; 35, 90, 127)	(34, 56, 93; 18, 56, 109)	(60, 70, 89; 50, 70, 99)
	M_3	(72, 80, 109; 58, 80, 123)	(78, 90, 108; 65, 90, 121)	(85, 98, 150; 76, 98, 159)	(52, 68, 93; 44, 68, 101)
	M_4	(23, 40, 81; 17, 40, 87)	(44, 58, 90; 38, 58, 96)	(63, 89, 109; 49, 89, 123)	(64, 72, 95; 51, 72, 108)

To determine the optimum assignment so that the total profit of the job assignment becomes maximum.

Solution

Assume that y_{11}, y_{12}, y_{13}, y_{14}, y_{21}, y_{22}, y_{23}, y_{24}, y_{31}, y_{32}, y_{33}, y_{34}, y_{41}, y_{42}, y_{43} and y_{44} are DVs. Now, solve the following IFMPP to find out the values of y_{11}, y_{12}, y_{13}, y_{14}, y_{21}, y_{22}, y_{23}, y_{24}, y_{31}, y_{32}, y_{33}, y_{34}, y_{41}, y_{42}, y_{43} and y_{44}.

From Model (2), the given IFAP can be written in the following mathematical programming form:

(Objective function) Max $\tilde{Z}^I$ $\Re(27,50,109; 13,50,123) y_{11} + \Re(56,67,111; 40,67,127) y_{12} + \Re(8,22,120; 4,22,124) y_{13} + \Re(75,100,128; 62,100,141) y_{14} + \Re(52,68,93; 44,68,101) y_{21} + \Re(43,90,119; 35,90,127) y_{22} + \Re(34,56,93; 18,56,109) y_{23} + \Re(60,70,89; 50,70,99) y_{24} + \Re(72,80,109; 58,80,123) y_{31} + \Re(78,90,108; 65,90,121) y_{32} + \Re(85,98,150; 76,98,159) y_{33} + \Re(52,68,93; 44,68,101) y_{34} + \Re(23,40,81; 17,40,87) y_{41} + \Re(44,58,90; 38,58,96) y_{42} + \Re(63,89,109; 49,89,123) y_{43} + \Re(64,72,95; 51,72,108) y_{44}$

$$
s.t. \begin{cases}
\begin{cases}
y_{11} + y_{12} + y_{13} + y_{14} = 1, \\
y_{21} + y_{22} + y_{23} + y_{24} = 1, \\
y_{31} + y_{32} + y_{33} + y_{34} = 1, \\
y_{41} + y_{42} + y_{43} + y_{44} = 1, \\
\end{cases} & \text{Machines } (M_1, M_2, M_3, M_4) \text{ constraints} \\
\begin{cases}
y_{11} + y_{21} + y_{31} + y_{41} = 1, \\
y_{12} + y_{22} + y_{32} + y_{42} = 1, \\
y_{13} + y_{23} + y_{33} + y_{43} = 1, \\
y_{14} + y_{24} + y_{34} + y_{44} = 1, \\
\end{cases} & \text{Jobs}(J_1, J_2, J_3, J_4) \text{ constraints} \\
y_{ij} \in \{0,1\} & \text{Feasibility restriction}
\end{cases}
$$

By applying a suitable ranking method, we obtain the following CAP (see Table 10).

Table 10. The crisp form of BIFAP relevant to example two

		Jobs →			
		J_1	J_2	J_3	J_4
Machines ↓	M_1	62	78	50	101
	M_2	71	85	61	73
	M_3	87	92	111	71
	M_4	48	64	87	77

(Objective function) Max Z [$(62 \times y_{11}) + (78 \times y_{12}) + (50 \times y_{13}) + (101 \times y_{14}) + (71 \times y_{21}) + (84 \times y_{22}) + (61 \times y_{23}) + (73 \times y_{24}) + (87 \times y_{31}) + (92 \times y_{32}) + (111 \times y_{33}) + (71 \times y_{34}) + (48 \times y_{41}) + (64 \times y_{42}) + (87 \times y_{43}) + (77 \times y_{44})$]

$$
s.t. \begin{cases}
\begin{cases}
y_{11} + y_{12} + y_{13} + y_{14} = 1, \\
y_{21} + y_{22} + y_{23} + y_{24} = 1, \\
y_{31} + y_{32} + y_{33} + y_{34} = 1, \\
y_{41} + y_{42} + y_{43} + y_{44} = 1, \\
\end{cases} \\
\begin{cases}
y_{11} + y_{21} + y_{31} + y_{41} = 1, \\
y_{12} + y_{22} + y_{32} + y_{42} = 1, \\
y_{13} + y_{23} + y_{33} + y_{43} = 1, \\
y_{14} + y_{24} + y_{34} + y_{44} = 1 \\
\end{cases} \\
\quad y_{ij} \in \{0,1\}
\end{cases}
$$

From the Hungarian method, we obtain,

$$y_{14} = y_{22} = y_{31} = y_{43} = 1,$$

$$y_{11} = y_{12} = y_{13} = y_{21} = y_{23} = y_{24} = y_{32} = y_{33} = y_{34} = y_{41} = y_{42} = y_{44} = 0, \text{ and}$$

$$\left(\tilde{Z}^I\right) = Rs.359 \approx 360.$$

$$\Rightarrow M_1 \to J_4,$$

$$M_2 \to J_2,$$

$$M_3 \to J_1,$$

$$M_4 \to j_3.$$

$$\Rightarrow \tilde{Z}^I = \tilde{c}_{14}^I \oplus \tilde{c}_{22}^I \oplus \tilde{c}_{31}^I \oplus \tilde{c}_{33}^I$$

$$= (75,100,128; 62,100,141) \oplus (43,90,119; 35,90,127) \oplus (72,80,109; 58,80,123) \oplus$$

$$(63, 89, 109; 49, 89, 123)$$

$$\tilde{Z}_{Max}^I = (253, 359, 465; 204, 359, 514) \tag{8}$$

$$\Rightarrow \left(\tilde{Z}_{Max}^I\right) = Rs.359 \approx \Delta 360$$

Equation (8) represents the most accurate optimal value of example number 2.

Also, we can write the Lingo computer programming for this problem. In addition, we can solve this problem both by Lingo and Tora.

Solution by MATLAB

```
>> clc;
>> clear all;
>> f=-[62 78 50 101 71 85 61 73 87 92 111 71 48 64 87 77];
>> A=[];
>> b=[];
>> Aeq= [1 1 1 1 0 0 0 0 0 0 0 0 0 0 0 0; 0 0 0 0 1 1 1 1 0 0 0 0 0 0 0 0; 0 0
0 0 0 0 0 1 1 1 1 0 0 0 0; 0 0 0 0 0 0 0 0 0 0 0 0 1 1 1 1; 1 0 0 0 1 0 0 0
1 0 0 0 1 0 0 0; 0 1 0 0 0 1 0 0 0 1 0 0 0 1 0 0; 0 0 1 0 0 0 1 0 0 0 1 0 0 0
1 0; 0 0 0 1 0 0 0 1 0 0 0 1 0 0 0 1];
```

```
>> beq= [1 1 1 1 1 1 1 1];
>> [y,f]= bintprog(f,A,b,Aeq,beq);
Optimization terminated.
>> disp(y);
     0
     0
     0
     1
     0
     1
     0
     0
     1
     0
     0
     0
     0
     0
     1
     0
>> disp(f);
  -360
```

The given problem is a maximization problem. Therefore, the maximum objective value is Max Z=-f=-(-360)=Rs.360 (in other words, ₹ 360).

Solution by RGui With lpsolver

```
>Ctrl+L
> library(lpSolve)
> assign.costs <- matrix (-c(62, 71, 87, 48, 78, 85, 92, 64, 50, 61, 111, 87,
101, 73, 71, 77), 4, 4)
> assign.costs
     [,1] [,2] [,3] [,4]
[1,]  -62  -78  -50 -101
[2,]  -71  -85  -61  -73
[3,]  -87  -92 -111  -71
[4,]  -48  -64  -87  -77
> lp.assign (assign.costs)
Success: the objective function is -360
> lp.assign (assign.costs)$solution
     [,1] [,2] [,3] [,4]
[1,]    0    0    0    1
```

```
[2,]    0     1     0     0
[3,]    1     0     0     0
[4,]    0     0     1     0
```

The given problem is a maximization problem. Therefore, the maximum objective value is Max Z=-f=-(-360)=Rs.360 (in other words, ₹ 360).

Example Three

Minimize the UBIFAP shown in Table 11.

Table 11. 3×2 IFAP

		Jobs	
		J_1	J_2
Machines	M_1	(12, 25, 56; 8, 25, 60)	(5, 9, 22; 2, 9, 25)
	M_2	(4, 16, 19; 1, 16, 22)	(8, 9, 16; 2, 9, 22)
	M_3	(6, 14, 28; 3, 14, 31)	(7, 21, 29; 2, 21, 34)

Solution: Assume that y_{11}, y_{12}, y_{13}, y_{21}, y_{22}, y_{23}, y_{31}, y_{32} and y_{33} are DVs. Now, solve the UBIFAP given in Table 11 to find out the values of y_{11}, y_{12}, y_{13}, y_{21}, y_{22}, y_{23}, y_{31}, y_{32} and y_{33}. $\Rightarrow y_{12} = y_{21} = y_{33} = 1$, $y_{11} = y_{13} = y_{22} = y_{23} = y_{31} = y_{32} = 0$, and $Z_{Min} = 25$.

$$\Rightarrow M_1 \to J_2,$$

$$M_2 \to J_1,$$

$$M_3 \to J_3.$$

$$\Rightarrow \tilde{Z}^I_{Min} = \tilde{c}^I_{11} \oplus \tilde{c}^I_{22} \oplus \tilde{c}^I_{33}$$

$$= (5,9,22; 2,9,25) \oplus (4,16,19; 1,16,22) \oplus (0,0,0; 0,0,0)$$

$$\tilde{Z}^I_{Min} = (9,25,41; 3,25,47). \tag{9}$$

$$\left(\tilde{Z}^I_{Min}\right) = 25.$$

Equation (9) represents the most accurate optimal value of example number 3.
Solution by Lingo: By applying a suitable ranking method, we obtain the following CAP.

Table 12. The crisp form of 3×2 IFAP relevant to example three

		Jobs	
		J_1	J_2
Machines	M_1	31	12
	M_2	13	11
	M_3	16	19

The balanced assignment problem (BAP) relevant to Table 12 is presented in Table 13.

Table 13. The crisp form of BIFAP relevant to example three

		Jobs		
		J_1	J_2	J_3
Machines	M_1	31	12	0
	M_2	13	11	0
	M_3	16	19	0

The problem in Table 13 can be written as a PILPP, and it is given below.

(Objective function) Min Z $[(31 \times y_{11}) + (12 \times y_{12}) + (0 \times y_{13}) + (13 \times y_{21}) + (11 \times y_{22}) + (0 \times y_{23}) + (16 \times y_{31}) + (19 \times y_{32}) + (0 \times y_{33})]$.

$$s.t. \begin{cases} \begin{cases} y_{11} + y_{12} + y_{13} = 1, \\ y_{21} + y_{22} + y_{23} = 1, \\ y_{31} + y_{32} + y_{33} = 1, \end{cases} \\ \begin{cases} y_{11} + y_{21} + y_{31} = 1, \\ y_{12} + y_{22} + y_{32} = 1, \\ y_{13} + y_{23} + y_{33} = 1, \end{cases} \\ \quad y_{ij} \in \{0,1\} \end{cases}$$

Machines (M_1, M_2, M_3) constraints, Jobs (J_1, J_2, J_3) constraints and feasibility restrictions.

The Lingo computer programming for this problem is as follows.

```
MODEL:

!Objective function;
  [_1] MIN= 31 * Y11 + 12 * Y12 + 13 * Y21 + 11 * Y22 + 16 * Y31 + 19 * Y32;

!S.t the following constraints;
```

```
[_2]  Y11 + Y12 + Y13 = 1;
[_3]  Y21 + Y22 + Y23 = 1;
[_4]  Y31 + Y32 + Y33 = 1;
[_5]  Y11 + Y21 + Y31 = 1;
[_6]  Y12 + Y22 + Y32 = 1;
[_7]  Y13 + Y23 + Y33 = 1;
@BIN(Y11); @BIN(Y12); @BIN(Y13); @BIN(Y21); @BIN(Y22);
@BIN(Y23);@BIN(Y31); @BIN(Y32); @BIN(Y33);
END
```

The lingo input and its model statistics for the crisp version of problem 3 are given in Figures 10 and 11.

Figure 10. The lingo input for the crisp version of problem three

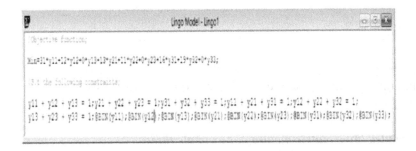

Figure 11. The lingo model statistics for the crisp version of problem three

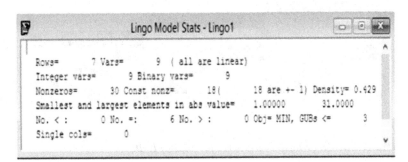

By applying Lingo to Table 13, we obtain the following.

$$y_{12} = y_{21} = y_{33} = 1, y_{11} = y_{13} = y_{22} = y_{23} = y_{31} = y_{32} = 0, \text{ and } Z_{Min} = 25.$$

$$\Rightarrow \tilde{Z}_{Min}^{I} = (9, 25, 41; 3, 25, 47).$$

$$\Rightarrow \left(\tilde{Z}^I_{Min} \right) = 25.$$

The solution report for the crisp version of problem 3 is presented in Figure 12.

Figure 12. The solution report for the crisp version of problem three

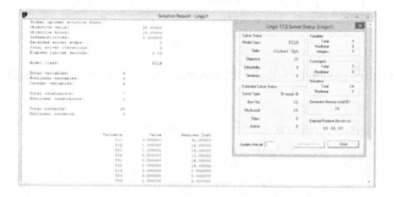

Different types of lingo matrix pictures are presented in Figures 13 to 16.

Figure 13. Unpermuted lingo matrix picture, for example three

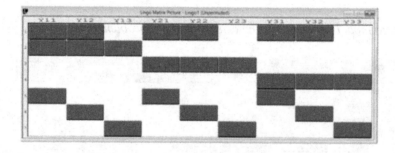

Figure 14. Lower triangular lingo matrix picture, for example three

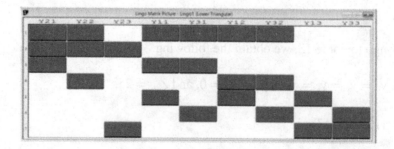

Figure 15. Block triangular lingo matrix picture (GP1-3 blocks), for example three

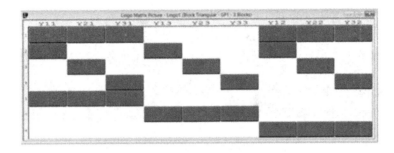

Figure 16. Block triangular lingo matrix picture (GP2-2 blocks), for example three

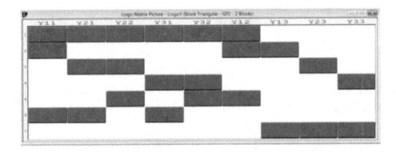

Solution by Tora

By applying Tora to Table 11, we obtain the following.

$y_{12} = y_{21} = y_{33} = 1, y_{11} = y_{13} = y_{22} = y_{23} = y_{31} = y_{32} = 0$ and $Z_{Min} = 25$.

$\Rightarrow \tilde{Z}_{Min}^{I} = (9, 25, 41; 3, 25, 47)$.

$\Rightarrow \left(\tilde{Z}_{Min}^{I} \right) = 25$.

Figures 17 and 18 show the Tora solution report for the crisp version of problem 3.

Figure 17. The Tora solution report for the crisp version of problem three (Automated B&B)

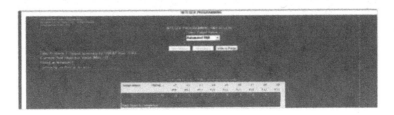

Figure 18. The Tora solution report for the crisp version of problem three (User-guided B&B)

Solution by MATLAB

```
>> clc;
>> clear all;
>> f=[31 12 0 13 11 0 16 19 0];
>> A=[];
>> b=[];
>> Aeq= [1 1 1 0 0 0 0 0 0; 0 0 0 1 1 1 0 0 0; 0 0 0 0 0 0 1 1 1; 1 0 0 1 0 0
1 0 0; 0 1 0 0 1 0 0 1 0; 0 0 1 0 0 1 0 0 1];
>> beq= [1 1 1 1 1 1];
>> [y,f]= bintprog(f,A,b,Aeq,beq);

Optimization terminated.

>> disp(y);
     0
     1
     0
     1
     0
     0
     0
     0
     1

>> disp(f);
    25
```

Solution by RGui with lpsolver:

```
>Ctrl+L
> library(lpSolve)
> assign.costs <- matrix (c(31, 13, 16, 12, 11, 19, 0, 0, 0), 3, 3)
> assign.costs
     [,1] [,2] [,3]
[1,]   31   12    0
[2,]   13   11    0
[3,]   16   19    0
> lp.assign (assign.costs)
Success: the objective function is 25
> lp.assign (assign.costs)$solution
     [,1] [,2] [,3]
[1,]    0    1    0
[2,]    1    0    0
[3,]    0    0    1
```

Example Four

Maximize the UBIFAP shown in Table 14.

Table 14. 3×4 IFAP

		Tasks			
		T_1	T_2	T_3	T_4
Workers	W_1	(64, 72, 95; 51, 72, 108)	(63, 89, 109; 49, 89, 123)	(44, 58, 90; 38, 58, 96)	(23, 40, 81; 17, 40, 87)
	W_2	(52, 68, 93; 44, 68, 101)	(75, 100, 128; 62, 100, 141)	(78, 90, 108; 65, 90, 121)	(72, 80, 109; 58, 80, 123)
	W_3	(60, 70, 89; 50, 70, 99)	(34, 56, 93; 18, 56, 109)	(43, 90, 119; 35, 90, 127)	(52, 68, 93; 44, 68, 101)

Solution: Assume that y_{11}, y_{12}, y_{13}, y_{14}, y_{21}, y_{22}, y_{23}, y_{24}, y_{31}, y_{32}, y_{33}, y_{34}, y_{41}, y_{42}, y_{43} and y_{44} are DVs. Now, solve the IFAP given in Table 14 to find out the values of y_{11}, y_{12}, y_{13}, y_{14}, y_{21}, y_{22}, y_{23}, y_{24}, y_{31}, y_{32}, y_{33}, y_{34}, y_{41}, y_{42}, y_{43} and y_{44}.

$\Rightarrow y_{11} = y_{22} = y_{33} = y_{44} = 1$, $y_{12} = y_{13} = y_{14} = y_{21} = y_{23} = y_{24} = y_{31} = y_{32} = y_{34} = y_{41} = y_{42} = y_{43} = 0$, and $Z_{Max} = 263$.

$\Rightarrow T_1 \rightarrow W_1$,

$T_2 \rightarrow W_2,$

$T_3 \rightarrow W_3,$

$T_4 \rightarrow W_4.$

$\Rightarrow \tilde{Z}^I_{Max} = \tilde{c}^I_{14} \oplus \tilde{c}^I_{22} \oplus \tilde{c}^I_{31} \oplus \tilde{c}^I_{33}$

$= (64, 72, 95; 51, 72, 108) + (75, 100, 128; 62, 100, 141) + (43, 90,119; 35, 90,127) + (0, 0, 0; 0, 0, 0).$

$$\tilde{Z}^I_{Max} = (182, 262, 342; 148, 262, 376). \tag{10}$$

Equation (10) represents the most accurate optimal value of example number 4.

Also, we can write the Lingo computer programming for this problem. In addition, we can solve this problem both by Lingo and Tora.

Solution by MATLAB

```
>> clc;
>> clear all;
>> f=-[77 87 64 48 71 101 92 87 73 61 85 71 0 0 0 0];
>> A=[];
>> b=[];
>> Aeq= [1 1 1 1 0 0 0 0 0 0 0 0 0 0 0 0; 0 0 0 0 1 1 1 1 0 0 0 0 0 0 0 0; 0 0
0 0 0 0 0 1 1 1 1 0 0 0 0; 0 0 0 0 0 0 0 0 0 0 0 0 1 1 1 1; 1 0 0 0 1 0 0 0
1 0 0 0 1 0 0 0; 0 1 0 0 0 1 0 0 0 1 0 0 0 1 0 0; 0 0 1 0 0 0 1 0 0 0 1 0 0 0
1 0; 0 0 0 1 0 0 0 1 0 0 0 1 0 0 0 1];
>> beq= [1 1 1 1 1 1 1 1];
>> [y,f]= bintprog(f,A,b,Aeq,beq);
Optimization terminated.
>> disp(y);
     1
     0
     0
     0
     0
     1
     0
     0
     0
     0
```

```
    1
    0
    0
    0
    0
    1
>> disp(f);
  -263
```

The given problem is a maximization problem. Therefore, the maximum objective value is Max Z=-f=-(-263)=Rs.263 (in other words, ₹ 263).

Solution by RGui With lpsolver

```
>Ctrl+L
> library(lpSolve)
> assign.costs <- matrix (-c(77, 71, 73, 0, 87, 101, 61, 0, 64, 92, 85, 0, 48,
87, 71, 0), 4, 4)
> assign.costs
      [,1] [,2] [,3] [,4]
[1,]  -77  -87  -64  -48
[2,]  -71 -101  -92  -87
[3,]  -73  -61  -85  -71
[4,]    0    0    0    0
> lp.assign (assign.costs)
Success: the objective function is -263
> lp.assign (assign.costs)$solution
      [,1] [,2] [,3] [,4]
[1,]    1    0    0    0
[2,]    0    1    0    0
[3,]    0    0    1    0
[4,]    0    0    0    1
```

The given problem is a maximization problem. Therefore, the maximum objective value is Max Z=-f=-(-263)=Rs.263 (in other words, ₹ 263).

Results and Discussion

A comparative analysis between PSK method and already existing methods is presented in Table 15. From Table 15, this chapter author concludes that the assignments obtained by the PSK method are same as that of the assignments obtained by the existing methods. Further, he has presented the intuitionistic fuzzy assignment time by Figure 19.

From (7), the optimum i.e., minimum total intuitionistic fuzzy assignment time is:

$$\tilde{Z}^{I}_{Min} = (15, 49, 83; 4, 49, 94) \tag{7}$$

Table 15. A comparative analysis between the PSK method and already existing methods

Ranking method	Problem No.	Solution Methods					
		PSK Method	**IFHM**	**Matlab**	**RGui**	**Lingo**	**Tora**
Varghese and Kuriakose	I	(15, 49, 83; 4, 49, 94) 49 (in hrs)	(15, 49, 83; 4, 49, 94) 49 (in hrs)	(15, 49, 83; 4, 49, 94) 49 (in hrs)	(15, 49, 83; 4, 49, 94) 49 (in hrs)	(15, 49, 83; 4, 49, 94) 49 (in hrs)	(15, 49, 83; 4, 49, 94) 49 (in hrs)
	II	(253,359,465; 204,359,514) ₹359	(253,359,465; 204,359,514) ₹359	(253,359,465; 204,359,514) ₹359	(253,359,465; 204,359,514) ₹359	(253,359,465; 204,359,514) ₹359	(253,359,465; 204,359,514) ₹359
	III	(9, 25, 41; 3, 25, 47) 25	(9, 25, 41; 3, 25, 47) 25	(9, 25, 41; 3, 25, 47) 25	(9, 25, 41; 3, 25, 47) 25	(9, 25, 41; 3, 25, 47) 25	(9, 25, 41; 3, 25, 47) 25
	IV	(182,262,342; 148,262,376) ~263	(182,262,342; 148,262,376) ~263	(182,262,342; 148,262,376) ~263	(182,262,342; 148,262,376) ~263	(182,262,342; 148,262,376) ~263	(182,262,342; 148,262,376) ~263

Figure 19. Graphical representation of IFAT

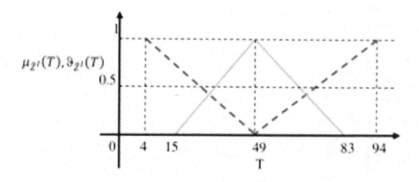

With the help of Figure 19, the equation (7) can be explained as follows: The level of acceptance of the performing time (T) for the DM increases (↑) if T increases (↑) from $4 \to 15$ hrs; while it decreases (↓)if T increases (↑) from $4 \to 49$ hrs. Beyond (4, 49), the degree of acceptance/the degree of satisfaction for the DM is 0. The DM is totally satisfied/T is totally acceptable if T is 49 hrs. The degree of non-acceptance of T for the DM decreases (↓) if T increases (↑) from $4 \to 49$ hrs while it increases (↑) if T increases (↑) from $49 \to 94$ hrs. Beyond (4, 94), T is totally un-acceptable (see Figure 19). Assuming that $\mu_{\tilde{Z}^I}(T)$ is membership value and $\vartheta_{\tilde{Z}^I}(T)$ is non-membership value of T (in hrs). Then, the degree of acceptance of T is $100\mu_{\tilde{Z}^I}(T)\%$ for the DM and the degree of non-acceptance is $100\vartheta_{\tilde{Z}^I}(T)\%$ for the DM. DM is not sure by $100\left(1 - \mu_{\tilde{Z}^I}(T) - \vartheta_{\tilde{Z}^I}(T)\right)\%$ that she/he should accept T or not. Values of $\mu_{\tilde{z}^I}(T)$ and $\vartheta_{\tilde{z}^I}(T)$ at different values of T can be determined by using the following equations (11) and (12).

$$\mu_{\tilde{z}^I}(T) = \begin{cases} 0, & for \quad T < 15 \\ \dfrac{T-15}{34}, & for \quad 15 \leq T \leq 49 \\ 1, & for \quad T = 49 \\ \dfrac{83-T}{34}, & for \quad 49 \leq T \leq 83 \\ 0, & for \quad T > 83 \end{cases} \tag{11}$$

$$\vartheta_{\tilde{z}^I}(T) = \begin{cases} 1, & for \quad T < 4 \\ \dfrac{49-T}{45}, & for \quad 4 \leq T \leq 49 \\ 0, & for \quad T = 49 \\ \dfrac{T-49}{45}, & for \quad 49 \leq T \leq 94 \\ 1, & for \quad T > 94 \end{cases} \tag{12}$$

PSK method- advantages:

- It is simple and easy to understand.
- The assignments obtained by this method are always optimal. Additionally, it gives a chance to solve all the types of IFAPs.
- It provides an alternative idea to solve the variety of optimization problems with IFSs.
- It always reduces the DM's computation time.
- It has been used to solve both the maximization and minimization of IFAPs.
- It is a systematic approach.
- It is always reliable and efficient. Generally, its solutions are always feasible, appropriate, and optimal.
- Its number of steps is very low. So, it is also called a student-friendly method.
- It is very useful to solve real-life related APs.
- It has very little computation when compared to other recent methodologies.
- By this method, we can verify whether the obtained solutions are optimal or not since the solutions of this method are always based on theoretical methods or software (e.g., RGui, Lingo, Tora and Matlab).
- It is used to solve UBIFAP also. So, there is no need of any new method/algorithm to solve UBIFAP.

- If Ph.D. scholars, scientists, students, and managers/practitioners study this method, they will get vast knowledge in IFSs.
- Those who need to solve the operations research or management science-related problems can study this method.
- It acts as a brain for studying IFSAPs. The extension of IFAP is called IFSAP.
- It is a cost-effective method since it is independent of copyrighted software.

PSK method- disadvantages:

- Without knowing the software (e.g., RGui, Lingo, Tora and Matlab) or Hungarian method, we can't solve IFAPs.
- We can't solve IFAPs when the software meets any issues.
- Knowing the software or Hungarian method is most important before we study the PSK method. We can't solve IFAPs without knowing these.
- It provides efficient solutions when we use efficient software. Alternatively, if the software is not efficient, then it will give inappropriate solutions.

Basically, the AP is one of the optimization problems where the objective function is either maximized or minimized, subject to a given set of constraints. If the problem has a number of feasible alternative solutions, then we apply the optimization technique to determine the most accurate solution. In this book chapter, the author has used the optimization technique to minimize the time and maximize the profit of job assignments. We can use multi-criteria decision-making (MCDM) if the AP has more than one parameter (i.e., multi-objective optimization problems).

General Discussion: How can the proposed PSK method be further validated and compared to existing methods in solving intuitionistic fuzzy assignment problems, and what performance metrics should be employed to provide a comprehensive analysis? By using Python programming, we can further validate the PSK method and compare the existing results by using different ranking methods in IFAPs. We can compare the computer's execution or running time for the proposed computer code. From the Tora software, we can also present the sensitivity analysis for the given problems.

The following are the reviewers' comments on this book chapter: The chapter discusses the AP and presents a software and ranking method-based PSK approach to solve the AP in an environment with uncertainty and hesitation. The author introduces IFAPs and provides several theorems related to these problems. The chapter includes computer programs for the proposed problems, their verification with Matlab and RGui, and a comparative analysis, discussion of merits and demerits of the proposed method, and suggestions for future studies. Overall, the manuscript covers a relevant and specialized topic and presents a systematic approach to address it.

In the discussion of the merits and demerits of the PSK method, can the manuscript delve deeper into specific real-world applications or scenarios where the proposed approach could offer significant advantages or face practical challenges, providing more context for the reader? In the numerical examples, the manuscript delves deeper into specific real-world applications or scenarios where the proposed approach could offer significant advantages or face practical challenges. So, the author omitted it here. Otherwise, it will increase the length of the chapter unnecessarily.

Strengths relate to the application of some very recent developments in the development of algorithms for optimizing IFAPs, particularly the PSK method. The author has presented 4 examples to illustrate the proposed methodology in slightly different settings in this book chapter. From this, the author would like to share his ideas with the Ph. D scholars, scientists, students, and managers/practitioners interested in this aspect of Operations Research through the proposed book chapter. Because it will be helpful to learn about some recent developments in APs.

CONCLUSION AND FUTURE WORK

This chapter started with a good introduction and literature review. Some recent academic publications have been reviewed in this chapter. This chapter mainly focuses on applying the PSK method for optimizing IFAPs. It has many theorems and one result. It has 4 examples to illustrate the superiority of the PSK method. It has different computer programs for each example. Also, it has comparative results, discussion, advantages and disadvantages of the PSK method, and future studies.

In this book chapter, an innovative method called the PSK method (alternative to IFHM) has been proposed to find out both the optimal assignment and objective value in IFAP. This novel method provides the optimal accurate value directly for IFAPs. The presented results have been verified with software solutions such as RGui, Lingo, Matlab and Tora. From the proposed theorems and result, we can conclude that any IFAPs that can be solved by the existing methods ((Kumar and Hussain (2014), Jayalakshmi (2016)) can also be solved by the PSK method. The key findings and contributions of the research are that the author developed the RGui and Matlab coding to solve IFAPs with the method of PSK, successfully achieved the optimal solution, and verified it with some other software and theoretical methods. The author's future work is to develop the software for the PSK method and extend this method to solve 3D IFAPs. Python programming is one of the most popular computer programming languages. In the future, interested researchers can develop Python code for the problems discussed in this chapter.

ACKNOWLEDGMENT

The author would like to thank his teachers because, without them, he couldn't have come to this position. The author would also like to acknowledge his family members for their motivation and kind support.

REFERENCES

Abirami, B., Vamitha, V., & Rajaram, S. (2020). A new approach for solving trapezoidal intuitionistic fuzzy transportation problem. [AMSJ]. *Advances in Mathematics: Scientific Journal, 9*(11), 9149–9159. doi:10.37418/amsj.9.11.20

Ahmed, H. H. (2021). Solving the problem of fuzzy transportation using linear programming and goal programming. *Further Advances in Internet of Things in Biomedical and Cyber Physical Systems, 193*, 313–330. doi:10.1007/978-3-030-57835-0_23

Ahmed, J. S., Mohammed, H. J., & Chaloob, I. Z. (2021). Application of a fuzzy multi-objective de-fuzzification method to solve a transportation problem. *Materials Today: Proceedings.* doi:10.1016/j.matpr.2020.12.1062

Arora, J., & Sharma, S. (2023). Solving task assignment problem using branch and bound method. *Journal of Applied Mathematics and Statistical Analysis, 4*(1), 14–20.

Atanassov, K. T. (1983). Intuitionistic Fuzzy Sets. *Int J Bioautomation, 20*(S1), S1-S6.

Beaula, T., & Saravanan, S. (2020). A new method for solving fully fuzzy linear programming problems. *Malaya Journal of Matematik, S*(1), 397–401. doi:10.26637/MJM0S20/0076

Beaula, T., & Seetha, R. (2020). Nonlinear programming with Trapezoidal intuitionistic fuzzy parameters. *Malaya Journal of Matematik, 8*(4), 2088–2091. doi:10.26637/MJM0804/0129

Beirkdar, R., & Ramesh, G. (2022, November). A new approach for finding an optimal solution of assignment problems in complete interval. In. AIP Conference Proceedings: Vol. 2516. *No. 1* (p. 320003). AIP Publishing LLC. doi:10.1063/5.0109470

Betts, N., & Vasko, F. J. (2016). Solving the unbalanced assignment problem: Simpler is better. *American Journal of Operations Research, 06*(04), 296–299. doi:10.4236/ajor.2016.64028

Bharati, S. K. (2021). Transportation problem with interval-valued intuitionistic fuzzy sets: impact of a new ranking. *Progress in Artificial Intelligence*, 1-17. doi:10.1007/s13748-020-00228-w

Chandrakala, P. (2021). Enhanced zero suffix approach for the optimal solution of a travelling salesman and assignment problem: A summary. [IRJASH]. *International Research Journal on Advanced Science Hub, 03*(Special Issue ICOST 2S, 02S), 1–5. doi:10.47392/irjash.2021.031

Chang, J. F., Lai, C. J., Wang, C. N., Hsueh, M. H., & Nguyen, V. T. (2021). Fuzzy optimization model for decision-making in supply chain management. [MATH]. *Mathematics, 9*(4), 312. doi:10.3390/math9040312

De la Torre, R., Corlu, C. G., Faulin, J., Onggo, B. S., & Juan, A. A. (2021). Simulation, optimization, and machine learning in sustainable transportation systems: Models and applications. *Sustainability (Basel), 13*(3), 1551. doi:10.3390u13031551

De Turck, F. (2020). Efficient resource allocation through integer linear programming: a detailed example. *arXiv preprint arXiv:2009.13178.*

Dhanasekar, S., Parthiban, V., & David Maxim Gururaj, A. (2020). Improved Hungarian method to solve fuzzy assignment problem and fuzzy traveling salesman problem. *Advances in Mathematics: Scientific Journal, 9*(11), 9417–9427. doi:10.37418/amsj.9.11.46

Dutta, J., & Pal, S. C. (2015). A note on Hungarian method for solving assignment problem. *Journal of Information and Optimization Sciences, 36*(5), 451–459. doi:10.1080/02522667.2014.926711

Ekanayake, E. M. U. S. B., Perera, S. P. C., Daundasekara, W. B., & Juman, Z. A. M. S. (2020). A modified ant colony optimization algorithm for solving a transportation problem. *Journal of Advances in Mathematics and Computer Science, 35*(5), 83–101. doi:10.9734/jamcs/2020/v35i530284

Gaspars-Wieloch, H. (2021). The assignment problem in human resource project management under uncertainty. *Risks, 9*(1), 1–17. doi:10.3390/risks9010025

González, D. P., Borda, D. C., Mele, F. D., Sarmiento, A. B., & Santiago, M. D. (2020). An optimization approach for the design and planning of the oil palm supply chain in Colombia. *Computers & Chemical Engineering, 107208.* doi:10.1016/j.compchemeng.2020.107208

Gothi, M., Patel, R. G., & Patel, B. S. (2023). Optimal solution to the assignment problem. *Annals of Mathematics and Computer Science, 16,* 112–122. https://annalsmcs.org/index.php/amcs/article/view/183

Herzel, A., Ruzika, S., & Thielen, C. (2021). Approximation Methods for Multiobjective Optimization Problems: A Survey. *INFORMS Journal on Computing,* ijoc.2020.1028. Advance online publication. doi:10.1287/ijoc.2020.1028

Hirata, A., Oda, T., Saito, N., Kanahara, K., Hirota, M., & Katayama, K. (2020, October). Approach of a solution construction method for mesh router placement optimization problem. In *2020 IEEE 9th Global Conference on Consumer Electronics (GCCE) (pp. 467-468).* IEEE. 10.1109/GCCE50665.2020.9291943

Hu, Y., & Liu, Q. (2021). A network flow algorithm for solving generalized assignment problem. *Mathematical Problems in Engineering, 2021,* 1–8. doi:10.1155/2021/5803092

Hussain, R. J., & Kumar, P. S. (2012a). The transportation problem in an intuitionistic fuzzy environment. *International Journal of Mathematics Research, 4*(4), 411–420.

Hussain, R. J., & Kumar, P. S. (2012b). Algorithmic approach for solving intuitionistic fuzzy transportation problem. *Applied Mathematical Sciences, 6*(77-80), 3981–3989.

Hussain, R. J., & Kumar, P. S. (2012c, July). The transportation problem with the aid of triangular intuitionistic fuzzy numbers. In *International Conference on MMASC Conf. Vol. 1* (pp. 819-825). Shanga Verlag.

Hussain, R. J., & Kumar, P. S. (2013). An optimal more-for-less solution of mixed constraints intuitionistic fuzzy transportation problems. *International Journal of Contemporary Mathematical Sciences, 8*(12), 565–576. doi:10.12988/ijcms.2013.13056

Hussein, H. A., & Shiker, M. A. K. (2020). Two new effective methods to find the optimal solution for the assignment problems. *Jour of Adv Research in Dynamical & Control Systems, 12*(7), 49–54. doi:10.5373/JARDCS/V12I7/20201983

Ingle, S. M., & Ghadle, K. P. (2019). Optimal solution for fuzzy assignment problem and applications. *Computing in Engineering and Technology,* 155–164. doi:10.1007/978-981-32-9515-5_15

Jamali, A. J. U., Mondal, R. R., & Reza, A. S. (2019). *Weighted cost opportunity based algorithm for unbalanced transportation problem.* Proceedings of the 5th International Conference on Engineering Research, Innovation and Education, Sylhet, Bangladesh.

Jayalakshmi, M. (2016). A new approach for solving balanced and/or unbalanced intuitionistic fuzzy assignment problems. *Research Journal of Pharmacy and Technology, 9*(12), 2382–2388. doi:10.5958/0974-360X.2016.00477.7

Jayalakshmi, M., Anuradha, D., Kavitha, K., Sobana, V. E., & Kaspar, S. (2020). Study on assignment problem. *Journal of Critical Reviews, 7*(19), 4764–4768. doi:10.31838/jcr.07.19.557

Josephine, F. S., Saranya, A., & Nishandhi, I. F. (2020). A dynamic method for solving intuitionistic fuzzy transportation problem. *European Journal of Molecular and Clinical Medicine*, 7(11), 5843–5854.

Kalhoro, H. B., Abdulrehman, H., Shaikh, M. M., & Soomro, A. S. (2021). The maximum range column method – going beyond the traditional initial basic feasible solution methods for the transportation problems. [JMCMS]. *Journal of Mechanics of Continua and Mathematical Sciences*, 16(1), 74–86. doi:10.26782/jmcms.2021.01.00006

Kanagajothi, D., & Kumar, B. R. (2022, November). Reduce the optimal cost on single valued neutrosophic transportation model. In. AIP Conference Proceedings: Vol. 2516. *No. 1* (p. 200004). AIP Publishing LLC. doi:10.1063/5.0108862

Kar, R., & Shaw, A. K. (2020). A new approach to find optimal solution of assignment problem using Hungarian method by triangular fuzzy data. *Mathematics in Engineering, Science and Aerospace*, 11(4), 1059–1074.

Kar, R., Shaw, A. K., & Das, B. (2020). Alternative approach to find optimal solution of assignment problem using Hungarian method by trapezoidal intuitionistic type-2 fuzzy data. *Annals of Optimization Theory and Practice*, 3(3), 155–173. doi:10.22121/AOTP.2020.257124.1055

Kaur, P., Dahiya, K., & Verma, V. (2020). *Time-cost trade-off analysis of a priority based assignment problem* OPSEARCH. doi:10.100712597-020-00483-4

Khalifa, H. (2020). A novel approach for optimization of transportation problem in chaos environment. [IJTE]. *International Journal of Transportation Engineering*, 8(1), 107–114.

Khalifa, H., Elhenawy, M., Masoud, M., Bhuiyan, H., & Sabar, N. R. (2021). On Multi-Objective Multi-Item Solid Transportation Problem in Fuzzy Environment. [JACM]. *International Journal of Applied and Computational Mathematics*, 7(1), 1–16. doi:10.100740819-021-00961-3

Kuhn, H. W. (1955). The Hungarian method for the assignment problem. [NRL]. *Naval Research Logistics Quarterly*, 2(1-2), 83–97. doi:10.1002/nav.3800020109

Kumar, P. S. (2010). *A comparative study on transportation problem in fuzzy environment* [M.Phil thesis, Jamal Mohamed College, Tiruchirappalli, India].

Kumar, P. S. (2016a). A Simple Method for Solving Type-2 and Type-4 Fuzzy Transportation Problems. *The International Journal of Fuzzy Logic and Intelligent Systems*, 16(4), 225–237. doi:10.5391/IJFIS.2016.16.4.225

Kumar, P. S. (2016b). PSK Method for Solving Type-1 and Type-3 Fuzzy Transportation Problems. *International Journal of Fuzzy System Applications*, 5(4), 121–146. doi:10.4018/IJFSA.2016100106

Kumar, P. S. (2017a). PSK Method for Solving Type-1 and Type-3 Fuzzy Transportation Problems. *Fuzzy Systems*, 367–392. doi:10.4018/978-1-5225-1908-9.ch017

Kumar, P. S. (2017b). *Algorithmic approach for solving allocation problems under intuitionistic fuzzy environment Jamal Mohamed College, Tiruchirappalli, India.*

Kumar, P. S. (2018a). Search for an Optimal Solution to Vague Traffic Problems Using the PSK Method. *Advances in Computational Intelligence and Robotics*, 219–257. doi:10.4018/978-1-5225-5396-0.ch011

Kumar, P. S. (2018b). Linear Programming Approach for Solving Balanced and Unbalanced Intuitionistic Fuzzy Transportation Problems. *International Journal of Operations Research and Information Systems*, *9*(2), 73–100. doi:10.4018/IJORIS.2018040104

Kumar, P. S. (2018c). A note on 'a new approach for solving intuitionistic fuzzy transportation problem of type-2'. *International Journal of Logistics Systems and Management*, *29*(1), 102–129. doi:10.1504/IJLSM.2018.088586

Kumar, P. S. (2018d). A Simple and Efficient Algorithm for Solving Type-1 Intuitionistic Fuzzy Solid Transportation Problems. *International Journal of Operations Research and Information Systems*, *9*(3), 90–122. doi:10.4018/IJORIS.2018070105

Kumar, P. S. (2018e). PSK Method for Solving Intuitionistic Fuzzy Solid Transportation Problems. *International Journal of Fuzzy System Applications*, *7*(4), 62–99. doi:10.4018/IJFSA.2018100104

Kumar, P. S. (2019a). PSK method for solving mixed and type-4 intuitionistic fuzzy solid transportation problems. *International Journal of Operations Research and Information Systems*, *10*(2), 20–53. doi:10.4018/IJORIS.2019040102

Kumar, P. S. (2019b). Intuitionistic fuzzy solid assignment problems: A software-based approach. *International Journal of System Assurance Engineering and Management*, *10*(4), 661–675. doi:10.100713198-019-00794-w

Kumar, P. S. (2020a). Intuitionistic fuzzy zero point method for solving type-2 intuitionistic fuzzy transportation problem. *International Journal of Operational Research*, *37*(3), 418–451. doi:10.1504/IJOR.2020.105446

Kumar, P. S. (2020b). The PSK Method for Solving Fully Intuitionistic Fuzzy Assignment Problems With Some Software Tools. *Advances in Business Strategy and Competitive Advantage*, 149–202. doi:10.4018/978-1-5225-8458-2.ch009

Kumar, P. S. (2020c). Algorithms for solving the optimization problems using fuzzy and intuitionistic fuzzy set. *International Journal of System Assurance Engineering and Management*, *11*(1), 189–222. doi:10.100713198-019-00941-3

Kumar, P. S. (2020d). Developing a new approach to solve solid assignment problems under intuitionistic fuzzy environment. *International Journal of Fuzzy System Applications*, *9*(1), 1–34. doi:10.4018/IJFSA.2020010101

Kumar, P. S. (2021). Finding the Solution of Balanced and Unbalanced Intuitionistic Fuzzy Transportation Problems by Using Different Methods With Some Software Packages. Handbook of Research on Applied AI for International Business and Marketing Applications, 278–320. IGI Global. doi:10.4018/978-1-7998-5077-9.ch015

Kumar, P. S. (2022). Computationally simple and efficient method for solving real-life mixed intuitionistic fuzzy 3D assignment problems. *International Journal of Software Science and Computational Intelligence*. doi:10.4018/IJSSCI.291715

Kumar, P. S. (2023a). The PSK method: A new and efficient approach to solving fuzzy transportation problems. In *Transport and Logistics Planning and Optimization* (pp. 149–197). IGI Global. doi:10.4018/978-1-6684-8474-6.ch007

Kumar, P. S. (2023b). The theory and applications of the software-based PSK method for solving intuitionistic fuzzy solid transportation problems. In *Perspectives and Considerations on the Evolution of Smart Systems* (pp. 137–186). IGI Global. doi:10.4018/978-1-6684-7684-0.ch007

Kumar, P. S. (2023c). Algorithms and software packages for solving transportation problems with intuitionistic fuzzy numbers. In *Operational Research for Renewable Energy and Sustainable Environments*. IGI Global.

Kumar, P. S. (2024). Theory and applications of the software-based PSK method for solving intuitionistic fuzzy solid assignment problems. In *Applications of New Technology in Operations and Supply Chain Management*. IGI Global.

Kumar, P. S., & Hussain, R. J. (2014a). New algorithm for solving mixed intuitionistic fuzzy assignment problem. *Elixir Appl. Math*, *73*, 25971–25977.

Kumar, P. S., & Hussain, R. J. (2014b, July). A method for finding an optimal solution of an assignment problem under mixed intuitionistic fuzzy environment. In *ICMS Conf.* (pp. 417-421). Elsevier.

Kumar, P. S., & Hussain, R. J. (2014c). A method for solving balanced intuitionistic fuzzy assignment problem. *International Journal of Engineering Research and Applications*, *4*(3), 897–903.

Kumar, P. S., & Hussain, R. J. (2014d). A systematic approach for solving mixed intuitionistic fuzzy transportation problems. *International Journal of Pure and Applied Mathematics*, *92*(2), 181–190. doi:10.12732/ijpam.v92i2.4

Kumar, P. S., & Hussain, R. J. (2015). A method for solving unbalanced intuitionistic fuzzy transportation problems. *Notes on Intuitionistic Fuzzy Sets*, *21*(3), 54–65.

Kumar, P. S., & Hussain, R. J. (2016a). An algorithm for solving unbalanced intuitionistic fuzzy assignment problem using triangular intuitionistic fuzzy number. *The Journal of Fuzzy Mathematics*, *24*(2), 289–302.

Kumar, P. S., & Hussain, R. J. (2016b). A simple method for solving fully intuitionistic fuzzy real life assignment problem. *International Journal of Operations Research and Information Systems*, *7*(2), 39–61. doi:10.4018/IJORIS.2016040103

Kumar, P. S., & Hussain, R. J. (2016c). Computationally simple approach for solving fully intuitionistic fuzzy real life transportation problems. *International Journal of System Assurance Engineering and Management*, *7*(S1, Suppl 1), 90–101. doi:10.100713198-014-0334-2

Lebedeva, O. A., & Poltavskaya, J. O. (2020, December). Cost optimization of intermodal freight transportation in the transport network. In Journal of Physics: Conference Series (Vol. 1680, No. 1, p. 012033). IOP Publishing. doi:10.1088/1742-6596/1680/1/012033

Lee, S. U. (2015). An Assignment Problem Algorithm Using Minimum Cost Moving Method. *Journal of the Korea Society of Computer and Information, 20*(8), 105–112. doi:10.9708/jksci.2015.20.8.105

Li, J., Kirubarajan, T., Tharmarasa, R., Brown, D., & Pattipati, K. R. (2021). A dual approach to multidimensional assignment problems. *Journal of Global Optimization, 81*(3), 1–26. doi:10.100710898-020-00988-8

Lyapin, S., Rizaeva, Y., Kadasev, D., & Kadaseva, I. (2020, November). Models for Ensuring the Minimum Arrival Time of Accident Response Services in Intelligent Transportation and Logistics System. In *2020 2nd International Conference on Control Systems, Mathematical Modeling, Automation and Energy Efficiency (SUMMA) (pp. 766-771)*. IEEE. 10.1109/SUMMA50634.2020.9280810

Marelli, D., Xu, Y., Fu, M., & Huang, Z. (2021). Distributed Newton optimization with maximized convergence rate. *arXiv preprint arXiv:2102.08726*

Matsiy, O. B., Morozov, A. V., & Panishev, A. V. (2015). The Recurrent Method to Solve the Assignment Problem. *Cybernetics and Systems Analysis, 51*(6), 939–946. doi:10.100710559-015-9786-x

Mohammed, H., Oduro, F. T., & Appiah, S. K. (2023). Alternate approach (Penalty Approach) to assignment problem solving and comparison to existing approaches. *Journal of Advances in Mathematics and Computer Science, 38*(8), 6–15. doi:10.9734/jamcs/2023/v38i81785

Mohan, S., Kannusamy, A., & Samiappan, V. (2020). A new approach for ranking of intuitionistic fuzzy numbers. *Journal of Fuzzy Extension and Applications, 1*(1), 15–26. doi:10.22105/jfea.2020.247301.1003

Mohan, S., Kannusamy, A. P., & Sidhu, S. K. (2021). Solution of intuitionistic fuzzy linear programming problem by dual simplex algorithm and sensitivity analysis. *Computational Intelligence*, 1– 21. doi:10.1111/coin.12435

Mohideen, S. I., & Kumar, P. S. (2010a). A comparative study on transportation problem in fuzzy environment. In *International Conference on Emerging Trends in Mathematics and Computer Applications (ICETMCA2010)*. MEPCO Schlenk Engineering College.

Mohideen, S. I., & Kumar, P. S. (2010b). A comparative study on transportation problem in fuzzy environment. *International Journal of Mathematics Research, 2*(1), 151–158.

Mondal, S., & Tsourdos, A. (2021). Two-Dimensional Quantum Genetic Algorithm: Application to Task Allocation Problem. *Sensors (Basel), 21*(4), 1251. doi:10.339021041251 PMID:33578712

Muamer, M. (2020). Fuzzy Assignment problems. *Journal of Science, 10*, 40–47. https://www.misuratau.edu.ly/journal/sci/upload/file/R-1263-ISSUE-10%20PAGES%2040-47.pdf

Munot, D. A., & Ghadle, K. P. (2020). A new approach to solve assignment problem using congruence modulo and its coding in matlab. *Advances in Mathematics: Scientific Journal, 9*(11), 9551–9557. doi:10.37418/amsj.9.11.58

Murugesan, R., & Esakkiammal, T. (2020a). Direct Methods for Finding Optimal Solution of Assignment Problems Are Not Always Dependable. *Applied Mathematical Sciences (Ruse)*, *14*(17), 823–830. doi:10.12988/ams.2020.914284

Murugesan, R., & Esakkiammal, T. (2020b). TERM – a very simple and efficient method to solve assignment problems. *Applied Mathematical Sciences (Ruse)*, *14*(17), 801–809. doi:10.12988/ams.2020.914275

Narayanamoorthy, S., Annapoorani, V., & Santhiya, M. (2017). A Method for Solving Fuzzy and Intuitionistic Fuzzy Assignment Problem using Ones Assignment Method with Fuzzy Numbers. *International Journal of Pure and Applied Mathematics*, *117*(14), 91–99.

Neelambari, R., Anupriya, S., Revathi, S., & Venkatesh, S. (2023). A novel method for the fuzzy assignment problem using SBD. *Eur. Chem. Bull.*, *12*(Special Issue 9), 601-611. DOI: doi:10.48047/ecb/2023.12.9.56

Nu'man, A. H., Nurwandi, L., Orgianus, Y., & Abdullah, A. G. (2020). Location determination with assignment method in design seaweed supply chain. *Journal of Engineering Science and Technology*, *15*(6), 3920–3934.

Pérez-Cañedo, B., & Concepción-Morales, E. R. (2020). A lexicographic approach to fuzzy linear assignment problems with different types of fuzzy numbers. *International Journal of Uncertainty, Fuzziness and Knowledge-based Systems*, *28*(03), 421–441. doi:10.1142/S0218488520500178

Porchelvi, R. S., & Anitha, M. (2018). Optimal Solution for Assignment Problem by Average Total Opportunity Cost Method. *Journal of Mathematics and Informatics*, *13*, 21–27. doi:10.22457/jmi.v13a3

Prabha, S. K., Hema, P., Sangeetha, S., Sreedevi, S., Guhan, T., & Pillai, M. V. J. (2021). Unbalanced FTP with Circumcenter of Centroids and Heuristic Method. *Annals of the Romanian Society for Cell Biology*, *25*(1), 5672–5684. http://annalsofrscb.ro/index.php/journal/article/view/726

Prifti, V., Dervishi, I., Dhoska, K., Markja, I., & Pramono, A. (2020, December). Minimization of transport costs in an industrial company through linear programming. In IOP Conference Series: Materials Science and Engineering (Vol. 909, No. 1, p. 012040). IOP Publishing. doi:10.1088/1757-899X/909/1/012040

Qiang, Z., JunHua, H., An, L., GuoMing, C., & QiMin, Y. (2020, August). New ranking methods of intuitionistic fuzzy numbers and Pythagorean fuzzy numbers. In *2020 Chinese Control And Decision Conference (CCDC)* (pp. 4661-4666). IEEE. 10.1109/CCDC49329.2020.9164633

Rani, J. J., Manivannan, A., & Dhanasekar, S. (2022, November). A branch and bound approach for solving interval valued intuitionistic fuzzy assignment problem. In. AIP Conference Proceedings: Vol. 2516. *No. 1* (p. 200021). AIP Publishing LLC. doi:10.1063/5.0108972

Rizk-Allah, R. M., Abo-Sinna, M. A., & Hassanien, A. E. (2021). Intuitionistic fuzzy sets and dynamic programming for multi-objective non-linear programming problems. *International Journal of Fuzzy Systems*, *23*(2), 1–19. doi:10.100740815-020-00973-z

Sadiq, F., Mohammedali, M., & Sabri, R. (2022). A new application of assignment problems using three techniques with it comparison. *Journal of Al-Qadisiyah for Computer Science and Mathematics*, *14*(4), 19–28. doi:10.29304/jqcm.2022.14.4.1098

Sangeetha, V., Vijayarangam, J., & Elumalai, P. (2022, November). Mid-range technique and fuzzy Big-M method based solution for fuzzy transportation problem. In. AIP Conference Proceedings: Vol. 2516. *No. 1* (p. 200008). AIP Publishing LLC. doi:10.1063/5.0109704

Santhi, G., & Ananthanarayanan, M. (2020). Standard deviation method for solving fuzzy assignment problem. *IMPACT: International Journal of Research in Humanities, Arts and Literature, 8*(4), 25–30.

Selvakumari, K., & Subasri, S. (2020). Comparative analysis of fuzzy, intuitionistic and neutrosophic assignment problem using nonagonal fuzzy number. *European Journal of Molecular and Clinical Medicine, 7*(2), 5099–5109.

Shah, K., Reddy, P., & Vairamuthu, S. (2015). Improvement in hungarian algorithm for assignment problem. In *Artificial Intelligence and Evolutionary Algorithms in Engineering Systems* (pp. 1–8). Springer. doi:10.1007/978-81-322-2126-5_1

Shakouri, B., Abbasi Shureshjani, R., Daneshian, B., & Hosseinzadeh Lotfi, F. (2020). A Parametric Method for Ranking Intuitionistic Fuzzy Numbers and Its Application to Solve Intuitionistic Fuzzy Network Data Envelopment Analysis Models. *Complexity, 2020*, 1–25. doi:10.1155/2020/6408613

Shanmugasundari, M., & Aarthi, S. (2022, November). Modified approach of fuzzy measures using trapezoidal fuzzy numbers to solve the real world problems under fuzzy environment. In AIP Conference Proceedings (Vol. 2516, No. 1, p. 200001). AIP Publishing LLC. doi:10.1063/5.0108541

Soundararajan, S., & Kumar, M. S. (2020). Solving unbalanced intuitionistic fuzzy transportation problem. *Journal of Computational Mathematics, 4*(1), 1–8. doi:10.26524/cm61

Stanojević, B., & Stanojević, M. (2021). Approximate membership function shapes of solutions to intuitionistic fuzzy transportation problems. *International Journal of Computers, Communications & Control, 16*(1), 1–15.

Taghaodi, R. (2019). A novel solution approach for solving intuitionistic fuzzy transportation problem of type-2. *Annals of Optimization Theory and Practice, 2*(2), 11–24. doi:10.22121/AOTP.2019.198947.1022

Taillard, É. D. (2023). *Design of heuristic algorithms for hard optimization with python codes for the travelling salesman problem.* Springer Nature. doi:10.1007/978-3-031-13714-3

Tanneau, M., Anjos, M. F., & Lodi, A. (2021). Design and implementation of a modular interior-point solver for linear optimization. *Mathematical Programming Computation, 13*(3), 1–43. doi:10.100712532-020-00200-8

Utami, W. S., Diwandari, S., & Hermawan, A. (2019). Transportation problem optimization systems using the algorithm of allocation table method. *International Journal of Applied Business and Information Systems, 3*(2), 45–52.

Valliathal, M., & Revathi, M. (2020). A new approach to find optimal solution of fuzzy assignment problem using penalty method for hendecagonal fuzzy number. *International Journal of Fuzzy Computation and Modelling, 3*(1), 61. doi:10.1504/IJFCM.2020.106101

Varghese, A., & Kuriakose, S. (2012). Centroid of an intuitionistic fuzzy number. *Notes on Intuitionistic Fuzzy Sets, 18*(1), 19–24.

Velu, L. G. N., Selvaraj, J., & Ponnialagan, D. (2017). A new ranking principle for ordering trapezoidal intuitionistic fuzzy numbers. *Complexity*, *2017*, 1–24. doi:10.1155/2017/3049041

Wang, S., Huang, X., Yin, C., & Richel, A. (2021). A critical review on the key issues and optimization of agricultural residue transportation. *Biomass and Bioenergy*, *146*, 105979. doi:10.1016/j.biombioe.2021.105979

Wang, Y., Zhou, C., & Zhou, Z. (2020, October). The shortest time assignment problem and its improved algorithm. In *International Conference on Computer Engineering and Networks (pp.* 583-588*)*. Springer, Singapore. 10.1007/978-981-15-8462-6_65

Yu, Z., & Khan, S. A. R. (2021). Green supply chain network optimization under random and fuzzy environment. *International Journal of Fuzzy Systems*, 1–12. doi:10.100740815-020-00979-7

Zadeh, L. A. (1965). Fuzzy sets. *Information and Control*, *8*(3), 338–353. doi:10.1016/S0019-9958(65)90241-X

Zaitseva, I., Malafeyev, O., Konopko, E., Taran, V., & Durakova, A. (2020, November). Simulation of optimal solutions for assignment problems in the context of incomplete information. In AIP Conference Proceedings (Vol. 2293, No. 1, p. 420012). AIP Publishing LLC. doi:10.1063/5.0026848

Zhang, K., Zhu, J., Zhang, Y., & Huang, Q. (2021). Optimization method for linear constraint problems. *Journal of Computational Science*, *51*, 101315. doi:10.1016/j.jocs.2021.101315

Chapter 17
Enhanced YOLO Algorithm for Robust Object Detection in Challenging Nighttime and Blurry, Low Vision

S. Prince Sahaya Brighty

https://orcid.org/0000-0002-4683-0013
Sri Ramakrishna Engineering College, India

R. Anuradha
Sri Ramakrishna Engineering College, India

M. Brindha
Sri Ramakrishna Engineering College, India

ABSTRACT

In today's computer vision systems, the spread of object detection has been booming. Object detection in challenging conditions such as low-illumination or misty nights remains a difficult task, especially for one-stage detectors, which have limited improved solutions available. This approach improves upon existing one-stage models and excels in detecting objects in partially visible, and night environments. It segments objects using bounding boxes and tracks them in motion pictures. To detect an object in low-light environment we employ an RGB camera to generate a properly lighted image from an unilluminated image using dehazing and grayscale conversion methods. Secondly, low-illuminated images undergo dehazing and gray-scale conversion techniques to obtain a better-lighted image using the popular one-stage object detection algorithm YOLOv8. Video inputs are also taken for fast-moving vehicles; rates ranging from 5 frames per second to 160 frames per second could be efficiently predicted by YOLO-ODDT. All renowned object detectors are overshadowed in terms of speed and accuracy.

DOI: 10.4018/979-8-3693-0639-0.ch017

INTRODUCTION

The advancement of object detection in computer vision systems owes much to the development of convolutional neural networks (CNNs). The integration of object detection techniques into computer vision research necessitates accurate object detection. However, challenges persist in detecting objects under low-light, dark, and adverse weather conditions for most detection models. In such conditions, images often appear blurry and dark.

Two primary models categorize object detectors: one-stage and two-stage models. One-stage models, exemplified by YOLOv4, Mobile Net SSD, and Squeeznet, balance efficiency and accuracy through a straightforward structure and swift operation, combining classification and regression tasks. On the other hand, two-stage models like R-CNN, Mask, and Mask Refined R-CNN prioritize accuracy at the expense of processing speed. YOLOv8, the latest addition to the YOLO series, introduces a decoupled head architecture that separates regression and classification, enhancing the balance between detection accuracy and efficiency compared to previous models.

Despite CNNs advancing object detection, challenges persist, especially in challenging conditions. One-stage models offer a compromise between efficiency and accuracy, while two-stage models prioritize accuracy but sacrifice processing speed. YOLOv8, with its Decoupled Head architecture, seeks to optimize this balance.

This study focuses on refining the stem layer of YOLOv8 to address challenges in accurately detecting objects under blurry lighting conditions, resulting in the proposed YOLO-ODDT architecture. The modified stem layer architecture, as illustrated in Figure 1, aims to mitigate difficulties posed by unclear lighting conditions in object detection tasks.

The main contributions of the proposed method are as follows:

1. Precision enhancement of object segmentation within bounding boxes, particularly those with significant overlap. The model's efficacy has been evaluated across various datasets, including Nightjars, MS COCO, and ImageNet, demonstrating promising outcomes in detecting objects in low-light and blurred conditions.

2. In the subsequent algorithmic phase, the system computes object distances and estimates real-time object counts through segmentation masks. The approach leverages segmentation masks to precisely recognize objects and promptly gauge their proximity to the observer, holding significant potential for applications ranging from object tracking to autonomous navigation systems.

3. Moving to the third phase, the algorithm employs a specialized variant of Non-Maximum Suppression (NMS) known as Diag-NMS. This method utilizes the diagonal length of bounding boxes to determine box similarity and control intersection over union (IoU). This tailored NMS modification offers heightened resilience, resulting in improved differentiation and retention of bounding boxes for targets with substantial overlap. Through Diag-NMS, a more precise and efficient object detection mechanism is achieved, particularly beneficial in scenarios where multiple targets closely coexist.

Figure 1. Object detection model overview

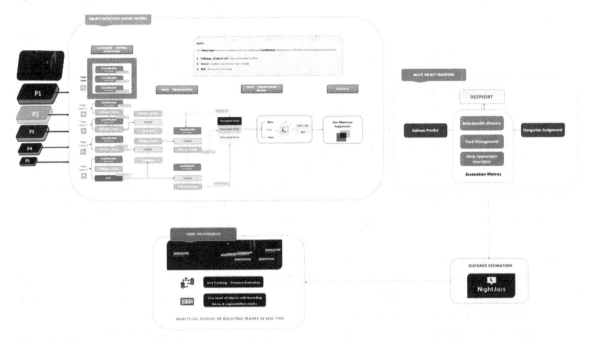

RELATED WORKS

The study work focused on methodologies that detect objects in dark, blurred, low-illuminated scenes and foggy, misty climates. Current research utilizes different one-phase and two-phase detectors with equipment establishment cameras and high-figuring frameworks to further develop the identification precision. Most of these methodologies are only applicable for image enhancement in dark conditions. Rishi Mehta et al. performed object detection using the YOLO model (Mehta, 2019). YOLO, a single-stage object detector, goes through one phase, whereas two-stage detectors go through two phases; thus, they are less precise than two-stage finders but significantly quicker. The COCO dataset, which has 80 labels, was used to train the model (Sik-Ho Tsang, 2018). Object detection is treated as a regression issue in these techniques (Keita,). To achieve better results, the author advised using a combination of lidar and low-light object identification (Lin et al., 2015; Zhou et al., 2021). Qingyang Tao et al. introduced a low-light item recognition strategy because of pyramid organizations (Tao et al., 2020). The fundamental goal was to add a preprocessing module before the location network to distinguish low-light objects. A low-goal pyramid enlarging light organization is utilized to save the handling of images and memory. The efficiency of the recommended method has been demonstrated by experiments on a 10K RAW-RGB low-light image dataset.

Hongli Liu et al., to avoid the sluggish speed of object detection (Liu et al., 2019), introduced a station pruning methodology that can limit the model size of an article recognition organization. Pruning techniques of two sorts were used in the item location organization: global pruning and neighborhood pruning. The pruning plans were tested on the customary receptive field block net (RFBNet). The global pruning plan packed the model size to 60%, and the neighborhood pruning plan compacted the model size to 35%. This technique diminished the size of the model. Yukihiro Sasagawa et al. suggested a strategy for integrating different models rather than establishing a new dataset (Sasagawa & Nagahara, 2020). In this technique, preprepared models from various spaces are consolidated utilizing glue layers and a generative model, which takes care of the dormant properties of the paste layers to prepare them without an extra dataset. The proposed model utilized less computational power than the regular technique.

Tejal Palwankar et al. used cutting-edge technology for object identification to achieve excellent accuracy and real-time performance (Palwankar & Kothari, 2022). The cutting-edge approaches are classified into two groups. The first class of techniques is one-stage methods that favor inference speed. The second category includes two-stage approaches that favor detection accuracy. Faster-RCNN and SSD (Liu, 2016; Sabina, et al., 2022) had the highest accuracy of all. The resulting system is quick and precise, making it useful for applications that need object detection.

Gupta et al. conducts a comprehensive survey of diverse object detections utilizing YOLO, with the primary objective of enhancing the accuracy of current systems. Additionally, the author introduces various modifications applied to the fundamental YOLO method, providing a detailed analysis of their impact on detection performance () . Object detection stands as a pivotal facet within computer vision, aiming to precisely locate and categorize objects embedded in images. The adoption of deep convolutional neural networks (CNNs) as the primary architecture for object detection has proven highly efficient, surpassing traditional models reliant on manual feature extraction. The emergence of Transformers, enriched with potent self-attention mechanisms, has further propelled performance to unprecedented levels.

Wei Chen et al. addressing real-world vision tasks, the need for acquiring 3D information encompassing spatial coordinates, orientation, and velocity of objects has intensified research in 3D scene object detection. Despite the stellar performance of LiDAR-based 3D object detection algorithms, their widespread adoption in practical applications remains challenging due to prohibitive costs () .This paper provides a comprehensive overview of the developmental trajectory, varied frameworks, contributions, advantages, disadvantages, and emerging trends in both image-based 2D and 3D object detection algorithms in recent years. The synthesis encompasses representative datasets, evaluation metrics, associated techniques, and applications.

METHODOLOGY

Object Detection Model

Our approach introduces a single-stage detection system designed to proficiently recognize objects in scenarios involving blurriness and low-light conditions. This system consists of three fundamental components: an object detection model, a distance tracking module, and Diag-NMS processing. These components are depicted in Figure 2. For model training, we leveraged the extensively used MS Coco Dataset in conjunction with the CSP Darknet architecture. Additionally, we integrated real-world low-light images sourced from CCTV surveillance camera recordings. The Yolo-ODDT algorithm is responsible for data processing, followed by enhancement through the Deepsort distance tracking algorithm. This combined approach ensures an accurate determination of an object's distance from the observer and facilitates the precise monitoring of its motion.

Several modifications have been implemented in the evolution from YOLOv8 to YOLO-ODDT, as illustrated in Figure 3:

Figure 2. Process workflow

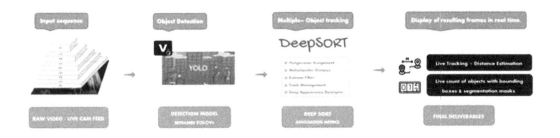

Figure 3. Object detection model

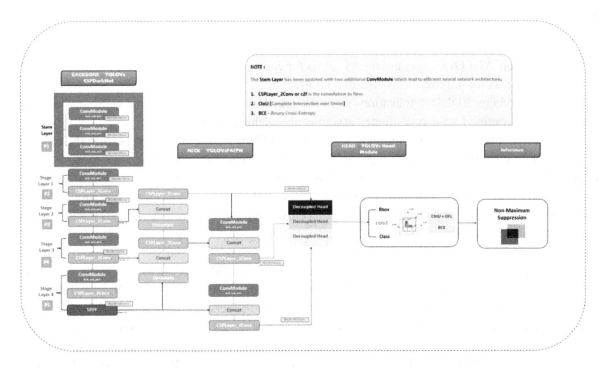

Backbone: The CSP Darknet remains the backbone, although in YOLO-ODDT, the C3 module of YOLOv5 has been substituted with the C2f module. This replacement enhances the model's lightweight design. Additionally, YOLOv8 adopts the SPPF module from YOLOv5 and other architectures. Notably, the stem layer has been augmented by incorporating two extra convolution modules, thereby contributing to an even more efficient neural network structure.

PAN-FPN: While YOLOv8 retains the PAN concept, a comparison of the structural schematics of YOLOv5 and YOLOv8 highlights that YOLOv8 omits the convolutional structure within the PAN-FPN up sampling stage seen in YOLOv5. Additionally, the C3 module in this context has been replaced by the C2f module.

Anchor-Free: YOLOv8 departs from the previous anchor-based approach and adopts the anchor-free concept instead.

Figure 4. Comparison of YOLO-ODDT with YOLO V8 and various YOLO object detectors V7, YOLO X, V5, and YOLO R

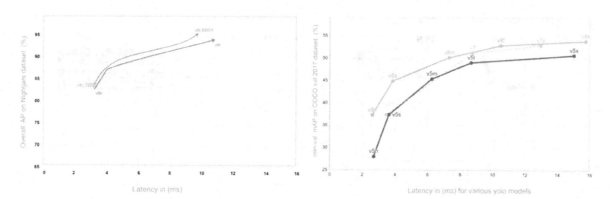

Loss Function: YOLOv8 integrates the VFL loss for classification purposes, complemented by DFL loss and CIOU loss for improved classification accuracy.

Sample Matching: YOLOv8 transitions from the previous methods of IOU matching or unilateral ratio allocation, opting for the task-aligned assignment matching methodology.

These alterations collectively culminate in the YOLO-ODDT architecture, enhancing the model's ability to effectively detect objects under challenging conditions. The more recent versions of YOLO have exceptional inference speed and mean average accuracy and precision in contrast to SSD (mAP) (Bochkovskiy et al., 2020). Additionally, SSD is still one of the quickest object detection models, while YOLO's performance is only slightly faster due to YOLO's accuracy (Menon et al., 2021), which is due in large part to SSD's ability to distinguish objects of varying sizes (Wang et al., 2022). The YOLOv8 model can accurately anticipate video inputs with frame rates between 5 and 160 per second. YOLOv8 performs better than both transformer-based and convolution-based object detectors, with an average accuracy of 56.8%. YOLOv7 outperformed certain object detectors, including YOLOv4 (Purwar & Verma, 2022; Ren et al., 2017), YOLOv5 (Ahmad et al., 2019; Jocher et al., 2020), YOLOv3 (Jiang et al., 2020; Menon et al., 2021; Purwar & Verma, 2022; Ren et al., 2017), and YOLOv5.

Figure 4 depicts a comparison between the mean average precision performance and latency of the modified YOLOv8-ODDT and other YOLO versions on the Nightjars and MS-Coco datasets. The results demonstrate that the YOLO-ODDT exhibits superior latency and accuracy compared to its predecessors while maintaining an impressive inference speed. This is attributed to the novel architectural modifications, such as the use of the anchor-free approach and the replacement of the C3 module with the C2f module.

Object Tracking Model

Figure 5 indicates that the DeepSORT algorithm is linked with three different association metrics:

Mahalanobis distance: This is a statistical measure that is used to calculate the distance between two points in a multivariate space. In the context of object tracking, the Mahalanobis distance is used to measure the similarity between the appearance of a detected object and the appearance of a tracked object.

Figure 5. Object tracking model

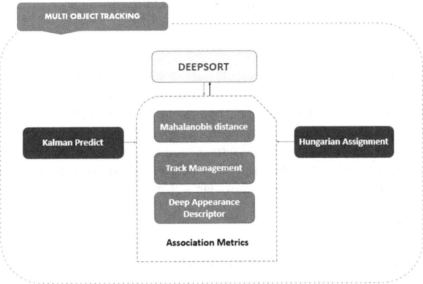

Track management: This refers to the process of managing the tracks of detected objects over time. In the context of the DeepSORT algorithm, track management involves keeping track of the position, velocity, and other characteristics of each object over time.

Deep appearance descriptor: This is a method of representing the appearance of objects using a deep neural network. In the context of the DeepSORT algorithm, deep appearance descriptors are used to calculate the similarity between the appearance of a detected object and the appearance of a tracked object.

Figure 5 indicates that the DeepSORT algorithm is linked with two other processes:

Kalman predicts: This refers to the Kalman filter, which is a mathematical algorithm used to estimate the state of a system based on a series of measurements. In the context of object tracking, the Kalman filter is used to predict the future position of an object based on its current position and velocity.

Hungarian assignment: This is a method of assigning detected objects to existing tracks based on the calculated association metrics. The Hungarian algorithm is a combinatorial optimization algorithm that is commonly used for this task in object-tracking applications. These processes and metrics are used to calculate the similarity between detected objects and tracked objects, predict the future position of objects, and assign objects to existing tracks based on the calculated similarities.

Diag-NMS

Diag-NMS (diagonal nonmaximum suppression) is an algorithm used to reduce the number of duplicate bounding boxes that are generated during object detection. It is commonly used in computer vision applications where multiple bounding boxes may be generated for the same object.

Sorting: The algorithm sorts the detected bounding boxes by their confidence scores, with the highest confidence scores placed at the top of the list.

Diagonal suppression: The algorithm then iterates through the sorted list of bounding boxes and removes any boxes that have a high degree of overlap with other boxes. Specifically, it removes any box that intersects with another box at an angle greater than a certain threshold. This threshold is typically set to 45 degrees. The formula for diagonal suppression is as follows:

$$\text{If } (x2 - x1) * (y4 - y3) - (x4 - x3) * (y2 - y1) > 0 \tag{1}$$

then remove the bounding box. In eqn.1. $(x1, y1)$ and $(x2, y2)$ represent the coordinates of the top-left and bottom-right corners of the first bounding box, respectively, while $(x3, y3)$ and $(x4, y4)$ represent the coordinates of the top-left and bottom-right corners of the second bounding box, respectively. If the value of the formula is greater than zero, then the second bounding box is removed.

Final suppression: Finally, the algorithm performs nonmaximum suppression (NMS) on the remaining bounding boxes to remove any duplicates. This step involves comparing the remaining boxes and removing any boxes that have a high degree of overlap with other boxes.

Distance Estimation

Distance from any referral boundary could be measured by

$$\text{Focal length} = (w * Distance)/W \tag{2}$$

$$\text{Distance} = (W * Focal\ length)/w \tag{3}$$

where $w \rightarrow$ width in pixels

$W \rightarrow$ width in inches

In eqn.2 and eqn.3 We measure the distance of an object from the reference boundary, which can be assigned

Depending on the surveillance camera placement.

MobileNet SSD

The SSD comprises two sections: an SSD head and a spine/backbone model. The spine model principally comprises a pretrained picture characterization organization, for example, ResNet or VGG16, which satisfies the occupation of an element extractor yet without the final grouping layer. The SSD head, which is made out of at least one convolutional layer that gives multiscale highlight mappings, produces the bounding box and class expectations. The head is also responsible for the algorithm's capacity to detect objects of all sizes while remaining spatially invariant. Like YOLO (Sabina, et al., 2022), the initial stage of SSD is to divide the picture into a grid of cells, with each cell being in charge of determining whether an object is present and, if so, what its coordinates are.

Each bounding box forecast is treated by the MobileNet SSD as a regression problem, starting with the anchor box with the most noteworthy IoU and bit by bit reverting to the fundamental truth jumping box by registering. YOLO predicts many bounding boxes for everything it finds and then runs NMS to wipe out the undesirable bounding boxes while retaining the final box coordinates.

Figure 6. Object distance calculation

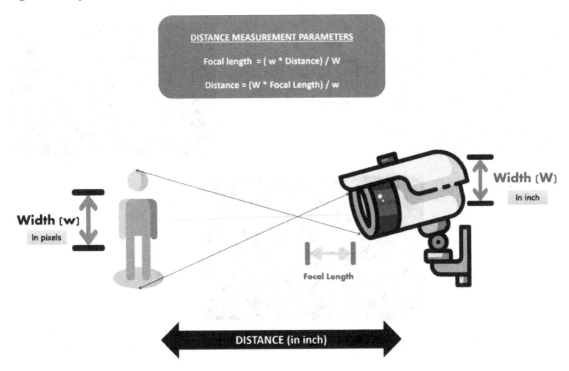

MobileNet SSD vs. ImageNet Dataset

ImageNet, the largest object picture dataset, is used to train the MobileNet SSD model. The community has given ImageNet much attention (Sabina, et al., 2022; Tripathi et al., 2022). Its library of more than a million photos and 1,000 image-level item classes permitted models to be improved and set another norm for the object image classification task to be established.

The COCO dataset has an edge in the fulfillment of the picture comments with 80 object types, although the quantity of photographs given is not identical to that of ImageNet.

IMAGE ENHANCEMENT THROUGH DEHAZING AND GRAYSCALE CONVERSION

The grayscale conversion of the image obtains better clarity of the image, and the processing time of the grayscale image consumes less file size. Image dehazing is a method for dealing with the deterioration of photos of the natural world caused by low visibility weather, dust, and other causes.

The results show that the modified YOLO-ODDT model improves the mAP by 1.9%, indicating that the model can detect and track objects in low-light conditions. This performance improvement is likely to have practical implications for applications such as surveillance, autonomous driving, and robotics, where detection and tracking object are important.

The modified YOLO-ODDT model had lower training losses than the original model. Training loss is a measure of how well the model can learn from the training data, and a lower training loss indicates

Figure 7. Dehazing and Grayscale conversion

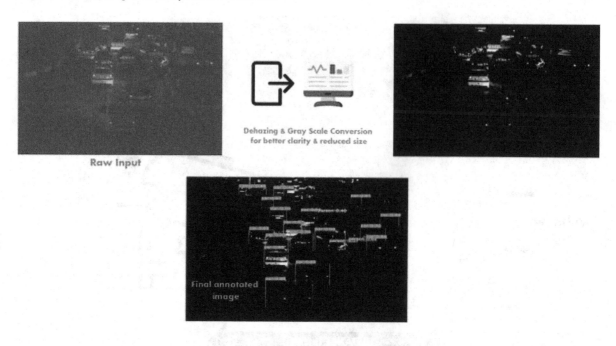

Figure 8. Overlapping bounding box detection

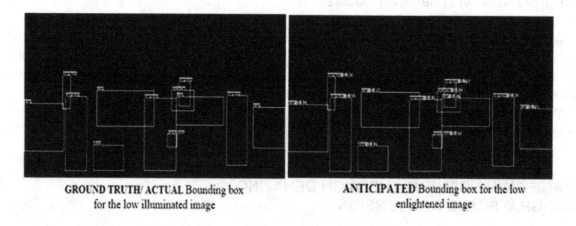

Table 1. Comparison of traditional YoloV8 with the distance-influenced Yolo-object detection and tracking model

Model	Epochs	Train/box_loss	Train/obj_loss	Train/cls_loss	Metrics/precision	Metrics/recall	Metrics/mAP
YoloV8	50	0.03089	0.017924	0.0032889	0.921	0.937	0.957
Improved Yolo ODDT	50	0.02792	0.016306	0.0030128	0.973	0.981	0.976

Figure 9. Original image with low illumination scene; b) Improvisation of low illuminated scene using dehazed and grayscale conversion; c) Final annotated image with distance estimation

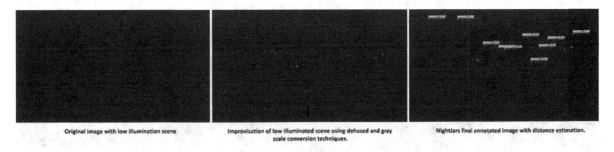

that the model is learning more efficiently and effectively. This indicates that the modifications made to the YOLO-ODDT model have improved its overall performance and effectiveness.

RESULT VISUALIZATION

Results on the NightJars Dataset

The night jars dataset is a combination of Microsoft COCO 2017, argoverse, Pascal VOC (), and random custom dark images (approx. 2000 images). Using these combinations of data can improve the accuracy and efficiency of the model, as we will use the pretrained images as a starting point.

Results on MS-COCO Dataset

Microsoft COCO is the most current of the well-known object datasets, which include lakhs of images divided into 80 object classes (Chen et al., 2023; Pacal et al., 2022). The PASCAL VOC image dataset contains 26,305 photos, which are divided into 20 object types, including segmentations and labels for object regions of interest (Redmon et al., 2016). The Argoverse Dataset is possibly one of the largest lidar datasets in autonomous driving cars and includes millions of lidar frames with 8 object classes (Redmon & Farhadi, 2018). The proposed model uses PyTorch, a rapid prototyping framework for research that even runs on CPUs.

Figure 10. Original image with low illumination scene; b) Dehazed and grayscale converted image; c) YOLO ODDT with a count of objects, tracking, and distance estimation

Figure 11. Custom dark dataset-YOLO ODDT results for various dark, low light, and blurred images

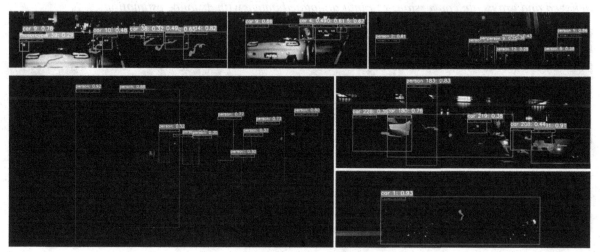

Results of NightJars for various scenarios

Evaluation Metrics

Evaluation metrics are used to measure the performance of machine learning models and algorithms. The choice of evaluation metric depends on the specific task at hand and the nature of the data being analyzed. We use the accuracy metric in classification tasks. Accuracy measures the percentage of correctly classified instances in the test data. Precision measures the percentage of true positives among all predicted positives, while recall measures the percentage of true positives among all actual positives. These metrics are commonly used in tasks where false positives or false negatives have different implications. mAP measures the average precision across all object classes and detection thresholds, providing a more comprehensive evaluation of the model's performance.

For our training and validation sets, the comparison of YOLOv8 and YOLO-ODDT plots of box loss, object loss, classification loss, accuracy, and mean-average precision (mAP) over the training epochs are displayed in Fig. 11. (a) and Fig. 11.(b). It shows good accuracy over YOLOv8.

Object detection is not only carried out for images but also applicable for videos and real-time detections using webcams and cameras with more accurate detections and compatibility with all devices since our model is trained using PyTorch.

- Precise boundary boxes and graphical implementations of detection are also included.
- It can run both on CPU and GPU devices.
- The object is detected in partially dark, extent dull, and even thermal condition images.
- Our discovery frameworks will do their best to detect the presence of objects to potentially keep a safe distance from a collision.

Figure 12. Performance of YOLOv8 on the custom nightjar dataset

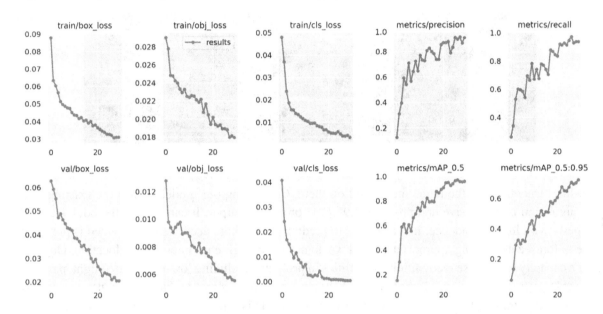

CONCLUSION

In this model, we focused on detecting the objects in low illuminated, dark, blurry, foggy, and misty climatic conditions to ensure security at night, especially for foot pilgrimages, security surveillance of defense agencies, and whoever wants to detect the objects at night. If people scan anything in front of them during the night using their mobile devices, they will easily recognize the objects inside the

Figure 13. Performance of the YOLO-ODDT on the custom nightjar dataset

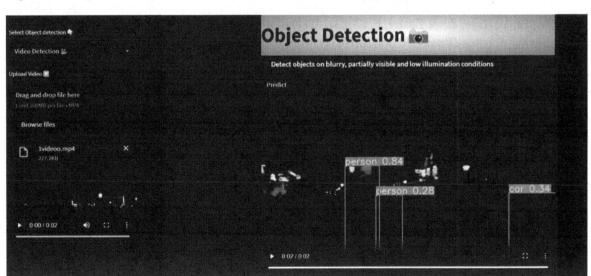

Figure 14. Detected objects with class names on videos and webcams

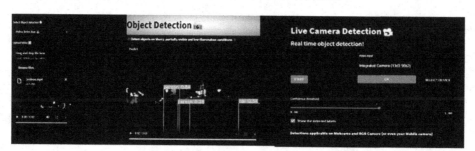

box-like structures and the name mentioned on them. Comparing our model against the existing one, our algorithm is impressive and provides 0.95-0.97 precision output. It can predict the bounding box properly with high confidence. It is also able to predict videos more accurately. The video is presently able to foresee everything appropriately, and we do not see any glitches in our video location. Our system's capacity to increase recognition capabilities in problems including low-illuminated light, partially viewable pictures, and thermal images. The key benefit of this project is that it computes the precise rectangular bounding box of the object with its distance. This will make the users easily understand the object with its name and distance tracking. Our approach is expected to engage the viewpoint and projection of growth changes in low-light domain studies across different domains.

REFERENCES

Ahmad, M., Ahmed, I., & Adnan, A. (2019). Overhead view person detection using YOLO. In 2019 IEEE 10th annual ubiquitous computing, electronics & mobile communication conference (UEMCON) (pp. 0627–0633). IEEE. doi:10.1109/UEMCON47517.2019.8992980

Bochkovskiy, A., Wang, C. Y., & Liao, H. Y. M. (2020). *Yolov4: optimal object detection speed and accuracy.* arXiv preprint arXiv:2004.10934

Chen, W., Li, Y., Tian, Z., & Zhang, F. (2023). 2D and 3D object detection algorithms from images: A Survey. *Array-Science Direct, 19*. doi:10.1016/j.array.2023.100305

JiangZ.ZhaoL.LiS.JiaY. (2020). Real-time object detection method based on improved YOLOv4-tiny. arXiv:2011.04244

JocherG.ChangyuL.HoganA.YuL.RaiP.SullivanT. (2020). Ultralytics/yolov5: Initial Release (v1.0). Zenodo. doi:10.5281/zenodo.3908560

Keita, Z. (2022). *YOLO object detection, its benefits.* DataCamp. https://www.datacamp.com/blog/yolo-object-detection-explained

Lin T.Y., Maire, M, Belongie, S, Bourdev, L, Girshick, R, Hays, J, Perona, P, Ramanan, D, Zitnick, C. L. & Dollár, P. (2015). Microsoft COCO: common objects in Context. *Computer Vision and Pattern Recognition,* 2–8.

Liu, H., Bai, H., Jie, F., & Zhang, M. (2019). *Channel pruning for object detection network.* IET 8th International Conference on Wireless, Mobile & Multimedia Networks, Beijing, China. 10.1049/cp.2019.1157

Liu, W. (2016) *SSD: Single Shot MultiBox Detector.* arXiv. https://arxiv.org/abs/1512.02325

Mahto, P., Garg, P., Seth, P., & Panda, J. (2020). Refining yolov4 for vehicle detection. [IJARET]. *Int J Adv Res Eng Technol, 11*(5), 409–419.

Mehta, R. (2019). Turning Object Detection into Low Light Object Detection, 2019. *Medium.* https://rishi30-mehta.medium.com/turning-object-detection-into-low-light-object-detection-b5973efffdd7

Menon, A., Omman, B., & Asha, S. (2021). Pedestrian Counting Using Yolo V3. In *2021 International Conference on Innovative Trends in Information Technology (ICITIIT)* (pp. 1–9). IEEE.

Pacal, I., Karaman, A., Karaboga, D., Akay, B., Basturk, A., Nalbantoglu, U., & Coskun, S. (2022). An efficient real-time colonic polyp detection with YOLO algorithms trained by using negative samples and large datasets. *Comput. Biol. Med., 141*, 105031.

Palwankar, T., & Kothari, K. (2022). *Real Time Object Detection using SSD and MobileNet.* Ijraset Journal For Research in Applied Science and Engineering Technology. doi:10.22214/ijraset.2022.40755

Purwar, R. K., & Verma, S. (2022). Analytical study of YOLO and its various versions in crowd counting. In *Intelligent data communication technologies and Internet of things* (pp. 975–989). Springer.

Redmon, J., Divvala, S., Girshick, R., & Farhadi, A. (2016). You only look once: Unified, real-time object detection. *Proceedings of the IEEE conference on computer vision and pattern recognition*, (pp. 779–788). IEEE. 10.1109/CVPR.2016.91

Redmon, J., & Farhadi, A. (2018). *Yolov3: An incremental improvement.* arXiv preprint arXiv:1804.02767

Ren, P., Fang, W., & Djahel, S. (2017). *A novel YOLO-Based real-time people counting approach, In 2017 international smart cities conference (ISC2).* IEEE.

Sabina, N., Aneesa, M. P., & Haseena, P. V. (2022). Object Detection using YOLO And Mobilenet SSD: A Comparative Study. Inter*national Journal Of Engineering Research. & Technology (Ijert), 11*(6).

Sasagawa, Y., & Nagahara, H. (2020, November). YOLO in the Dark - Domain Adaptation Method for Merging Multiple Models. *Lecture Notes in Computer Science, 12366*, 345–359. doi:10.1007/978-3-030-58589-1_21

Sik-Ho Tsang. (2018). *Review: SSD — Single Shot Detector.* Object Detection.

Tao, Q., Ren, K., Feng, B., & Xuejin, G. (October 2020). An accurate low-light object detection method based on pyramid networks. *Optoelectronic Imaging and Multimedia Technology.*

Tripathi, G., Manish, S., Chaynika, D., & Pallavi, P. (2022). Object Detection using YOLO: A Survey. *5th International Conference on Contemporary Computing and Informatics.* IEEE. 10.1109/IC3I56241.2022.10073281

WangC.-Y.BochkovskiyA.LiaoH.-Y. M. (6 Jul 2022). YOLOv7: Trainable bag-of-freebies sets new state-of-the-art for real-time object detectors. https://arxiv.org/abs/2207.02696

Zhou, F., Zhao, H., & Nie, Z. (2021). Safety helmet detection based on YOLOv5. *2021 IEEE International Conference on Power Electronics, Computer Applications (ICPECA),* (pp. 6–11). IEEE. 10.1109/ICPECA51329.2021.9362711

Chapter 18
Smart Speakers:
A New Normal Lifestyle

Asi Lakshmi Priyanka

https://orcid.org/0000-0002-1958-0813

Satya Institute of Technology and Management, India

ABSTRACT

Smart speakers have taken the world by storm and have become an essential part of many households. As the use of smart speakers becomes more prevalent, the role of artificial intelligence (AI) in buying behavior has become increasingly important. With smart speakers becoming more intelligent and better integrated with AI, they have the potential to revolutionize the way consumers shop. This chapter will explore the impact of smart speakers on AI in buying behavior, the benefits and challenges of adopting this technology, and the future outlook of smart speakers and AI in commerce.

INTRODUCTION

The rise of smart speakers and AI in decision-making:

The rapid advancement of technology has paved the way for innovative solutions to everyday challenges, including decision-making. In recent years, smart speakers and artificial intelligence (AI) have emerged as powerful tools in enhancing our ability to make informed choices.

Smart speakers are voice-activated devices that use natural language processing (NLP) and artificial intelligence (AI) technologies to interact with users. These devices are integrated with virtual assistants such as Amazon Alexa, Google Assistant, Apple Siri, or Microsoft Cortana, enabling users to control their smart homes, play music, order food, or shop online using voice commands.

A smart speaker is a device that uses voice recognition technology to interact with users. They are designed to provide a seamless experience for consumers who want to access music, news, weather, and other information, as well as control their smart home devices, all with the sound of their voice. Smart speakers are hands-free and require minimal effort on the part of the user to operate.

DOI: 10.4018/979-8-3693-0639-0.ch018

Figure 1. Smart speakers

The Evolution of Smart Speakers and AI Technology

In recent years, we have witnessed a remarkable evolution in technology, with smart speakers becoming an integral part of our homes. These voice-activated devices, such as Amazon Echo or Google Home, have revolutionized the way we interact with technology. Alongside smart speakers, artificial intelligence (AI) has also made significant advancements, enabling these devices to understand and respond to our commands.

Impact of Smart Speakers and AI on Decision-Making

The integration of AI technology into smart speakers has transformed them into decision support systems. These systems have the ability to provide information, guidance, and recommendations to aid in making informed decisions. From choosing the right recipe for dinner to managing personal finances, smart speakers equipped with AI can offer valuable insights and assistance.

UNDERSTANDING DECISION SUPPORT SYSTEMS: DEFINITION AND COMPONENTS

Definition and Concept of Decision Support Systems (DSS)

Decision Support Systems, or DSS, are software applications that assist individuals or organizations in making decisions by analyzing relevant data, providing insights, and offering recommendations. These systems leverage advanced algorithms, AI, and other technologies to facilitate decision-making processes.

Key Components and Functionalities of DSS

DSS consist of various components that work together to provide decision support. These include data management, model management, knowledge base, user interface, and decision analysis tools. Data management handles the collection, storage, and retrieval of relevant information, while model management deals with the creation and implementation of decision models. The knowledge base stores expertise and rules, and the user interface allows users to interact with the system. Decision analysis tools help in analyzing data and generating insights.

SMART SPEAKERS AND AI: REVOLUTIONIZING DECISION-MAKING IN THE NEW NORMAL

The Role of Smart Speakers in Enhancing Decision-Making

Smart speakers have become invaluable tools for decision-making, especially in the new normal where our lifestyles have shifted significantly. From managing daily routines and schedules to seeking advice on various matters, smart speakers can provide real-time information, recommendations, and reminders, ultimately streamlining our decision-making processes. AI is at the core of smart speakers and allows them to understand human speech, recognize accents, and respond intelligently to user requests. AI also powers voice search technology, enabling users to find information, locate products, and make purchases using their voice. The more users interact with smart speakers, the more intelligent and personalized they become, thanks to the machine learning algorithms. The role of AI in smart speakers has significantly transformed the way people interact with technology. AI-powered virtual assistants such as Amazon's Alexa, Google Home, and Apple's Siri have become more intuitive and responsive through machine learning algorithms that enable them to understand natural language queries and provide accurate responses. They can handle routine tasks such as setting alarms, ordering groceries, controlling smart home devices, answering general knowledge questions and playing music. Even more impressive is their growing ability to learn user preferences and adapt accordingly. With the integration of AI in smart speakers, users can now engage in multistep conversations that allow for intricate commands and more personalized experiences overall. The potential of AI-powered speakers to improve everyday living experiences is enormous as advancements continue to be made, leading to increasingly sophisticated features while becoming more accessible to a wider audience.

Leveraging AI for personalized decision support: AI plays a crucial role in enhancing decision-making through personalized support. Smart speakers equipped with AI algorithms can learn and understand user preferences, behaviors, and patterns over time. This allows them to offer tailored recommendations and suggestions based on individual needs and preferences, further empowering users to make informed decisions that align with their unique circumstances.

ARTIFICIAL INTELLIGENCE

Definition

"The science and engineering of creating intelligent machineries, where intelligence is the computational part of the ability to achieve goals in the world" John McCarthy (1955).

"The science of making machines do things that would require intelligence if done by men" Marvin Minsky (1968).

"AI is the field of computer science that enables machines to perform tasks requiring human-like intelligence. It involves creating intelligent agents that can sense, comprehend, learn, and act in a way that extends human capabilities" Jair Ribeiro.

"Intelligence demonstrated by a machine or by software. [Where] intelligence measures an agent's general ability to achieve goals in a wide range of environments" Calum Chase.

"A constellation of technologies that extend human capabilities by sensing, comprehending, acting and learning allowing people to do much more" Accenture.

"Anything that makes machines act more intelligently" IBM.

"Defining artificial intelligence is not just difficult; it is impossible, not the least because we do not understand human intelligence. Paradoxically, advances in AI will help more to define what human intelligence is not than what artificial intelligence is" OReilly.

"A field of computer science that focuses on creating machines that can learn, recognize, predict, plan, and recommend --plus understand and respond to images and language" Sales Force.

"The ability of a digital computer or computer-controlled robot to perform tasks commonly associated with intelligent beings" B.J. Copeland defined in Encyclopaedia of Britannica.

"It is the science and engineering of making intelligent machines, especially intelligent computer programs. It is related to the similar task of using computers to understand human intelligence, but AI does not have to confine itself to methods that are biologically observable" University of Stanford.

AI is an interdisciplinary field of study that concerns itself with the creation of computing systems capable of performing tasks that typically require human intelligence. Our evolving understanding of how the human mind works has enabled the development of computational models that mimic, or even surpass, human intelligence in certain domains. The field of AI holds vast potential to solve a multitude of problems in various disciplines, including computer science, psychology, philosophy, and more.

Key Features of Smart Speakers

Voice Recognition Technology

The most important feature of a smart speaker is its voice recognition technology. This technology allows the device to recognize and respond to individual voices, enabling personalized experiences for each user. Voice recognition also makes it possible for users to operate the device hands-free, making it a convenient and easy-to-use tool.

Smart Home Integration

Smart speakers can be integrated with other smart home devices, such as lighting, thermostats, and security systems. This allows users to control their entire smart home ecosystem with the sound of their voice. With smart home integration, users can turn on lights, adjust the temperature, and even lock doors, all without getting up from their seat.

Sound Quality and Audio Performance

Smart speakers are designed to provide high-quality sound and audio performance. Many smart speakers come equipped with surrounding sound, noise cancellation, and other features that deliver superior sound quality. Some smart speakers can also be paired with other speakers to create a more immersive audio experience.

TOP SMART SPEAKERS IN THE MARKET

Amazon Echo

The Amazon Echo is one of the most popular smart speakers in the market. It offers voice recognition technology, smart home integration, and superior sound quality. It also has a wide range of features, including music streaming, news updates, and weather forecasts.

Google Home

Google Home is another popular smart speaker that offers voice recognition technology, smart home integration, and excellent sound quality. It also offers access to Google Assistant, making it easy to access information, check your calendar, and even make phone calls.

Apple HomePod

The Apple HomePod offers a high-end audio experience, delivering excellent sound quality and audio performance. It also offers smart home integration and can be used to access Siri, Apple's voice assistant.

Sonos One

Sonos One is a versatile smart speaker that offers voice recognition technology, smart home integration, and excellent sound quality. It also supports a wide range of music streaming services, making it a great option for music lovers.

SMART SPEAKERS AND HOME AUTOMATION

Smart speakers have revolutionized home automation by providing voice control of smart home devices. No more fumbling with remotes or smartphone apps - simply speak to your smart speaker and you can turn off lights, adjust the temperature, or even order groceries. Integration with other smart home systems is another way that smart speakers have transformed home automation. With integration capabilities, smart speakers can work seamlessly with other devices, such as door locks, security cameras, and entertainment systems. This integration allows for a more cohesive and streamlined user experience. The increased convenience and efficiency that smart speakers provide cannot be understated. They allow for hands-free control of multiple devices, freeing up time and energy for other tasks. This can be particularly helpful for those with mobility or accessibility needs.

Evolution of Smart Speaker

The device included a higher-fidelity speaker and a 7-inch display. This marked an important moment in which smart speakers began to move beyond just voice control, allowing for visual content delivery.

In 2018, Google introduced Google Home Hub, which was a significant departure from the original smart speaker model. The device featured a 7-inch touchscreen, which allowed for visual information delivery beyond what was available with just voice control. Google Home Hub also implemented home automation, allowing users to control smart home devices with their voice or touch. This was a critical step in integrating smart speakers into the larger trend of smart homes.

Amazon responded to the Google Home Hub by introducing the Echo Show. The echo show was a direct response to the Google Home Hub with a similarly sized screen, home automation capabilities, and visual information display. The echo show allowed for video conferencing and could even display video feeds from home security cameras. The Echo Show was an important moment in the broader technological trend of smart homes, in which devices could be easily controlled and monitored by homeowners.

As smart speakers continued to evolve, the focus shifted toward improving their intelligence and understanding. Apple's HomePod, introduced in 2018, represented a significant breakthrough in this area. The device implemented Apple's Siri virtual assistant, which was designed to be more responsive and understand natural language. The HomePod also provided a high-fidelity sound, making it an attractive option for music lovers.

Smart speakers also began to incorporate machine learning algorithms, allowing them to "learn" user preferences and adapt accordingly. For example, Amazon Echo could learn your music preferences over time and create personalized playlists based on those preferences.

In recent years, smart speakers have begun to integrate with other devices, creating a more interconnected ecosystem. For instance, Amazon Echo can connect with other devices, such as lights or thermostats, allowing for voice or touch control over these devices. The Amazon Echo even features an "Alexa Guard" feature, which uses machine learning to detect suspicious behavior and alert homeowners of potential intrusions.

In an effort to compete with Amazon and Google, Facebook introduced Portal, a smart speaker designed for video calling. The portal was heavily criticized for its lack of privacy protections and sparked a broader conversation around privacy protections for smart speaker devices.

Figure 2. The decade of voice assistant revolution

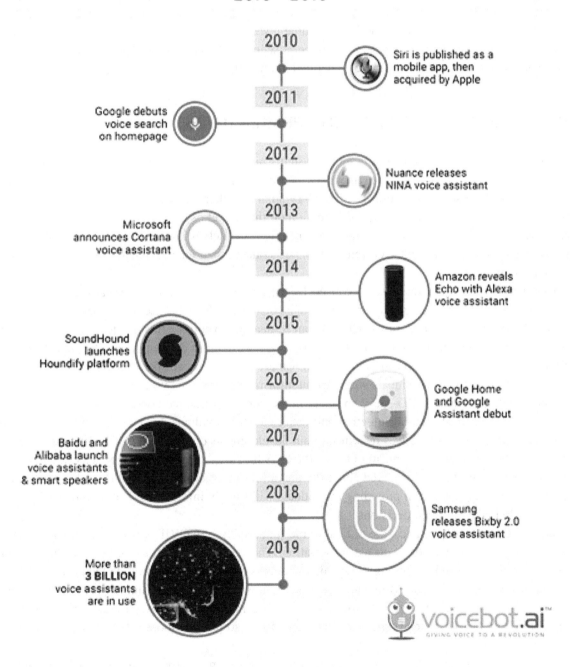

Finally, smart speakers have begun to integrate with smart assistants on mobile devices, such as Siri or Google Assistant. This integration allows for a more seamless experience across devices, with users being able to access their smart assistant in a variety of settings beyond the home.

Smart speakers have undergone remarkable evolution in their short history. What began as a simple device to answer basic questions has transformed into a sophisticated ecosystem of interconnected devices capable of learning and adapting to user preferences. Smart speakers are now a critical component of the trend toward smart homes and have become invaluable to many users with an interest in home automation. As technology continues to advance, it seems certain that smart speakers will continue to evolve and adapt, becoming even more embedded in our daily lives.

HOW COVID-19 IMPACTED SMART SPEAKER USAGE

COVID-19 has disrupted economies, social systems, and politics worldwide. Consequently, several economies, such as the United States, have invested in technological innovations to curb the spread of the pandemic. One such innovation is COVID-19 smart speakers. Essentially, these speakers are designed to provide users with real-time information on the spread of the virus, health advice, and news on relevant COVID-related issues. In light of this, this essay delves into the concept of COVID-smart speakers, their significance in the current COVID-19 context, their technological aspects, and potential future developments.

COVID-19 is an infectious disease caused by the coronavirus. The virus spreads mainly through respiratory droplets when an infected person coughs or sneezes. The disease often presents with symptoms of flu or pneumonia and, in some cases, can be deadly. To combat this pandemic, doctors, public health officials, and information technology experts are working to develop means to limit the spread of the disease. One such approach is the COVID-smart speaker. These speakers are devices that have been developed to equip individuals with current information about the virus.

The significance of COVID-smart speakers in the current pandemic context cannot be overstated. With the ever-increasing rate of infection and death cases, individuals, businesses, and organizations seek measures to keep themselves informed about developments during the COVID-19 crisis. Considering the role of online communication today, the COVID-smart speaker has become a critical tool for individuals who want to stay updated about the prevailing virus situation in real time. In other words, these speakers are essential in providing individuals with timely information and data-driven insights that can help make informed decisions.

Several technological aspects are critical to the functioning of COVID-smart speakers. First, these devices use voice commands to access information. The speech recognition software in the speakers converts voice commands, enabling the speaker to access the internet and provide the necessary information. Second, speakers use AI technology to learn how different people interact with them. Learning from user engagement is vital to speakers becoming more effective over time. Consequently, AI technology in COVID-19 smart speakers has learned how to provide more relevant and personalized information to users.

Third, COVID-smart speakers use machine learning algorithms to process and analyze large volumes of data. By analyzing various data on the virus's spread, speakers can provide users with relevant and timely data-driven insights. In this way, COVID-smart speakers empower individuals to make informed decisions about their health, social interactions, and travel plans. Fourth, COVID-smart speakers have robust natural NLP capabilities. NLP helps speakers better understand and interpret the user's commands, leading to improved interaction and engagement.

There are several potential future developments for COVID-smart speakers. First, COVID-smart speakers could find applications in contact tracing. Contact tracing is the process of identifying and monitoring people who might have been infected with the virus. With the use of Bluetooth and Wi-Fi, these speakers can detect users' locations, making it easier to track and monitor their contacts. Second, COVID-smart speakers could be used to monitor individuals' compliance with safety protocols and guidelines. Such compliance could be monitored using speech and facial recognition software to help public health officials enforce fraud regulations.

Moreover, COVID-smart speakers could be used to monitor individuals' vital signs, including temperature and heart rate. By providing users with a measure of their physical well-being, individuals could respond early to changes in their health and seek timely medical attention. Finally, COVID-smart speakers could be integrated with virtual reality platforms to provide immersive training experiences to medical professionals. Such experiences could be used to train medical professionals on best practices in dealing with COVID-19 patients.

COVID-19 smart speakers are a breakthrough technology designed to provide users with real-time information on the spread and management of COVID-19. With the pandemic situation worsening in many countries, these speakers provide a convenient and practical solution for individuals seeking current information on the virus. The technological aspects that make these devices function include speech recognition software, AI technology, machine learning algorithms, and natural processing language capabilities. Future developments could see COVID-smart speakers integrated with contact tracing, compliance monitoring, vital sign monitoring, and virtual reality experiences. In the end, COVID-smart speakers offer a relevant solution that could help individuals, organizations, and governments navigate the pandemic and create a viable future.

SMART HOME-SMART SPEAKER

Smart home devices control various systems in the home. This means one can use your voice to turn on your lights, adjust your thermostat, and even lock your doors. Smart speakers act as a central hub for your smart home, allowing you to control everything from one central location.

Security is a critical concern for many homeowners, and smart speakers can help address this issue. Smart speakers can connect to smart cameras and allow you to view the footage from your camera on your phone or tablet. This allows you to monitor your home from anywhere, giving you peace of mind when you're away from home. Smart speakers can also be used to control smart locks, allowing you to secure your home with the sound of your voice.

In addition to their many functional benefits, smart speakers can also be used for entertainment purposes. They can play music, podcasts, and even audiobooks with a simple voice command. They can also be used to control smart TVs, allowing you to change channels and adjust the volume without having to pick up a remote control.

One of the main benefits of using a smart speaker in your smart home is its ability to learn your habits and preferences. Smart speakers can learn from past commands and interactions, allowing them to provide more personalized responses and suggestions. This helps make your smart home more intuitive and efficient over time.

As smart speakers continue to evolve and improve, they will likely become even more intelligent and capable. Smart speakers are already being used in healthcare to help patients manage chronic conditions and monitor their health. They can also be used in classrooms to aid in learning and education. The possibilities are endless, and as technology continues to advance, we can expect to see even more exciting developments in the world of smart speakers and smart homes.

The smart speaker is an essential component of any smart home. It allows homeowners to automate and control their home's various systems and appliances using their voice, making their lives more convenient and efficient. The intelligence and comprehension of smart speakers have made them a popular and essential tool for homeowners.

EARLIER STUDY

A voice partner called a brilliant speaker alludes to conversational specialists who perform errands with or for an individual (Mari et al. 2020). The demonstration of putting orders web-based utilizing a voice collaborator goes under the name of "voice shopping" or "voice trade". Currently, significant tech organizations are progressively commercializing voice partner items and fostering their shopping capacities, which uncovers voice partners' problematic potential for showcasing (Dawa and Bendle 2018).

A smart speaker is a sort of remote speaker equipped for detecting its neighborhood climate and collaborating keenly with its client through voice colleagues (O'Keeffe, 2018). The most famous shrewd speakers being used today are Amazon speakers and Google Home. They are each outfitted with manmade intelligence-based voice colleagues called Alexa and Google Associate individually. Surviving examinations recognize that exploration on the reception and utilization of savvy speakers is extremely scant yet vital given the rising notoriety and the rising number of administrations given through these gadgets. Voice shopping is one of the administrations currently being given through shrewd speakers.

Buyers now embrace it as an option internet shopping channel. Rzepka, Berger, and Hess (2020) utilized meetings to show that while purchasers see it to expand proficiency, comfort, and happiness, they regret its security holes and low specialized development of savvy speakers for voice shopping. This frequently drives buyers to need to exchange security for comfort, which impacts the manner in which they take on brilliant speakers (Lau, Zimmerman, and Schaub, 2018).

Despite the fact that specialists stand up to the ascent of voice shopping, the investigation of how voice right hand, as another shopping medium, influences utilization remains significantly uninvestigated. Existing writing is to a great extent elucidating, hypothetical, or trial based. Kumar et al. (2016) provide a system to grasp smart specialist innovation applications and utilize a grounded hypothesis approach. Jones (2018) gives a contextual investigation to investigate the ramifications, application, and open doors for voice artificial intelligence in showcasing. Smith (2020) inspects what sort of promotional message is satisfactory to shoppers on voice man-made intelligence through an overview. Ba et al. (2020) create hypothetical models of deal strategies through a voice partner.

Munz and Morwitz (2020) lead fifteen lab examinations and find that data introduced by voice are harder for shoppers to process than similar data introduced and recorded as a hard copy. Luo et al. (2019) exploit Refered to from https://www.reuters.com/article/us-amazon-com-marriott-intnl /amazons-alexa-will-now-steward at Marriott-inns idUSKBN1JF16P field try information to concentrate on how the revelation of man-made intelligence helped monetary chatbot would influence client buy choices. Luo et al. (2020) demonstrate the way that organizations can profit from recruiting an artificial intelligence mentor over human chiefs while preparing deals specialists. Notwithstanding these surviving investigations, the subject of whether and what the reception of a voice collaborator means for utilization in a certifiable setting remains obscure.

Ghose et al. (2013) investigate how buyers' web-based perusing conduct fluctuates between PCs and portable channels. They show that more modest screen sizes on cell phones increment clients' expense to peruse for data. Wang et al. (2015) concentrate on what cell phones mean for customer buy conduct and show that buy likelihood and the typical request esteem increment as clients become acclimated with portable shopping. Xu et al. (2014) inspect purchasers' news utilization conduct because of the presentation of the portable channel and find that the presentation of a versatile application prompts an enormous expansion popular at the relating portable news site.

Tan and Netessine (2020) concentrate on the effect of tabletop innovation on eatery execution and observe that tabletop innovation is probably going to further develop normal deals per check and decrease the feast span by further developing assistance quality. What is absent in the writing, other than the fundamental impact of voice colleague reception on utilization, is the way voice right hand as a new channel of shopping influences conventional buy channels. The current review adds to this strand of writing by investigating the overflow impact of voice collaborator reception on deals through versatile channels.

SMART SPEAKERS AND THE CONSUMER BUYING PROCESS

Exploring the Consumer Buying Process

The consumer buying process encompasses a series of stages that a buyer goes through while making a purchase decision. These stages include problem recognition, information search, evaluation of alternatives, purchase decision, and postpurchase evaluation. The consumer buying process is influenced by several factors, such as personal, social, cultural, and psychological factors. Smart speakers have revolutionized the way consumers make purchases by offering a convenient, voice-activated method of shopping from the comfort of their homes. The buying process through these smart devices involves various stages, starting with awareness and discovery of products or services through search queries spoken to the device. Next comes information gathering, where consumers utilize smart speakers to learn about product features, price comparisons, and reviews.

This is followed by evaluation and consideration, where consumers weigh the pros and cons before making a purchase decision. Finally, postpurchase behavior includes feedback sharing, future purchase intent, and loyalty building. Overall, exploring consumer buying behavior through smart speakers can provide valuable insights for businesses to optimize their marketing strategies to deliver better customer experiences, particularly in an age where digital interactions are becoming more prevalent.

How Smart Speakers Change the Buying Process

Smart speakers disrupt the traditional consumer buying process by providing a new channel for product discovery, research, and purchasing. Unlike traditional methods such as browsing online catalogs or visiting physical stores, smart speakers enable users to make purchases using their voice without needing to use a screen or a keyboard. This convenience and ease of use are changing the way consumers shop and are leading to impulse purchases, especially for low-cost items. Smart speakers have revolutionized the way in which consumers purchase products and services. These devices allow for convenient voice-activated shopping, eliminating the need for physical browsing or typing on a keyboard. For retailers, this means that they must prioritize their online presence and ensure that their products are easily discoverable through voice commands.

Smart speakers are voice-activated virtual assistants that can perform a variety of tasks, including playing music, controlling various home devices such as lights and thermostats, and answering a wide range of questions. Smart speakers have gained immense popularity among consumers due to their convenience and ease of use. It is essential to understand consumer behavior regarding the adoption, usage, and purchasing of smart speakers to analyze the factors that can affect their growth in the market.

Factors Affecting Consumer Behavior

Consumer behavior is affected by several factors, such as demographic, psychographic, social, cultural, and personal factors. Demographic factors such as age, gender, income, and education level can have a significant effect on the adoption of smart speakers. For example, younger consumers are generally more likely to adopt new technology, whereas older consumers may be more hesitant in doing so.

Psychographic factors such as personality traits, interests, and values can also play a role in consumer behavior. Consumers who enjoy technology and are early adopters of new innovations are more likely to purchase smart speakers.

Social and cultural trends can also affect consumer behavior. The increasing prevalence of smart homes and the desire for convenience and automation in household tasks have contributed to the growth of smart speaker adoption. Furthermore, broader technological advancements such as 5G and IoT have enabled the development of smart home devices, making them more accessible and affordable to consumers.

Another significant factor is **flexibility,** which can affect the decision-making process. Consumers, who place a high value on convenience, ease of use, and time-saving benefits are more likely to purchase smart speakers. The device's ability to integrate with other devices and services can also play a role in purchasing decisions.

Motivations and Benefits for Consumers

Motivations for purchasing smart speakers can vary among consumers. The most common benefits associated with smart speakers include convenience, efficiency, and ease of use. The ability to control multiple home devices through voice commands is a significant advantage.

Smart speakers are also perfect for **hands –free operations** such as cooking or completing household tasks, which require manual dexterity. The device's ability to answer questions accurately and provide real-time information leads to their widespread adoption, particularly for people with visual impairments.

Additionally, music enthusiasts and audiophiles have been drawn to the high-quality sound output offered by smart speakers. The integration of virtual assistants such as Alexa and Google Home has also been a significant selling point, paired with the opportunity to link to various other services and devices.

Consumer Adoption Process

The consumer adoption process includes five stages, namely, awareness, interest, evaluation, trial, and adoption. In the awareness stage, consumers become familiar with the smart speaker device through marketing, word-of-mouth, or product reviews.

The interest stage is when consumers show interest in the device and begin actively researching and seeking more information. In the evaluation stage, consumers assess the features, benefits, and drawbacks of each device to make an informed decision regarding purchasing.

The trial stage involves physically testing the device and experiencing it first-hand, either through in-store demos or the purchase and trial period. Finally, the adoption stage involves the actual purchase of the device, giving rise to post-purchase activities such as usage, satisfaction and loyalty.

Consumer Behaviors After Adoption

Post-purchase behavior includes usage, satisfaction, and loyalty. Consumers who are satisfied with their device usage are more likely to become loyal to the brand. In contrast, unsatisfied consumers are more likely to switch to a different brand or device.

Usage behavior regarding smart speakers can vary widely depending on individual preferences. Some users leverage the device for home automation tasks such as adjusting lighting and temperature, while others prefer educational questions or listening to music.

The ability of smart speakers to interact with other virtual assistants and devices has also become an increasingly critical feature. The integration of virtual assistants has enabled much more extensive options, such as the ability to order groceries or control smart home devices through voice commands.

Consumer Perception

Consumer perception is crucial in determining the success of a brand. Consumers have a positive perception that the device helps in brand recognition and recommends it to others. Conversely, consumers who have a negative perception will have adverse effects on the brand that can lead to a decline in revenue and sales.

Consumer perception can be influenced by various factors, such as personal experience, brand reputation, marketing campaigns, and word-of-mouth. The level of satisfaction achieved by the device also heavily impacts the perception of the brand by consumers.

Consumers Tend to Remain Loyal to a Specific Brand

Smart speakers also provide an opportunity for personalized recommendations, as these devices track user activity and preferences to deliver tailored suggestions. With the addition of payment capabilities in smart speakers, consumers can easily make purchases with just a few words spoken aloud. This ease of use is particularly beneficial to customers who may have mobility or vision impairments that make traditional shopping methods challenging. As smart speaker technology continues to advance, it is likely that more industries will adapt to this new buying process to meet consumer demand for simplicity and convenience.

THE IMPACT OF AI ON CONSUMER BEHAVIOR

Role of AI in Understanding Consumer Preferences

AI is revolutionizing the way retailers understand consumer preferences and behavior. By analyzing vast amounts of data about consumer behavior, AI algorithms can identify patterns, trends, and preferences that were previously unknown or hard to detect. This enables retailers to provide personalized recommendations, tailor marketing messages, and create hypertargeted advertising campaigns. Smart speakers powered by AI have revolutionized the way consumers interact with technology. These devices, such as Amazon Echo and Google Home, are equipped to understand voice commands from individuals and provide personalized recommendations for music, movies, and other entertainment. In addition to offering convenience, smart speakers have become a powerful tool for understanding consumer preferences. AI algorithms can analyze user interactions with the device to deliver tailored recommendations based on their preferences and behaviors. These data can be used by companies to improve marketing strategies, develop new products that better suit market demands, and meet evolving consumer needs. As AI technology continues to advance, smart speakers will increasingly play a critical role in helping businesses gain valuable insights into customer behavior, thereby boosting competitiveness and profitability in an ever-changing marketplace.

How AI is Changing the Way Consumers Shop

AI is also changing the way consumers shop by providing a more personalized and seamless shopping experience. By using data such as past purchases, search queries, and browsing behavior, AI can recommend products that are more likely to be of interest to a particular user. This personalization can lead to higher customer satisfaction and loyalty, as well as increased sales and revenue for retailers. AI smart speakers are revolutionizing the way consumers approach their daily routines. With advanced voice recognition technology, these devices can carry out complex tasks and provide information at rapid speed. As a result, consumers have access to an unprecedented level of convenience and efficiency. Such devices allow users to control connected appliances, order groceries, play music, and even order food delivery – all with just a simple voice command. Additionally, AI smart speakers are making it easier for individuals to keep up with news and current events and manage their schedules seamlessly. The integration of these devices into the home is transforming the way people interact with technology and has wide-reaching implications for various industries, including e-commerce and advertising. As these devices become more sophisticated, they will continue altering consumers' behaviors in profound ways, including providing personalized recommendations based on individual usage patterns.

BENEFITS OF SMART SPEAKERS FOR CONSUMERS AND RETAILERS

Convenience and Time-Saving Benefits for Consumers

The primary benefit of smart speakers for consumers is the convenience and time-saving aspects of using voice commands to perform tasks. Whether it is ordering groceries online, listening to music, or turning off lights, smart speakers enable users to perform tasks without needing to use a screen or a keyboard. This hands-free and screen-less experience can be particularly useful for people with disabilities or mobility issues. Smart speakers have revolutionized the way consumers interact with technology, providing them with a new level of convenience and time-saving benefits. With voice recognition capabilities, users can control various aspects of their home, such as lighting, temperature, and security systems, without lifting a finger. They can also use smart speakers to save significant amounts of time on tasks such as shopping, setting reminders or creating shopping lists. The ability to access a wealth of information without having to scroll through countless websites is yet another advantage provided by smart speakers. By integrating applications such as calendars and news services directly into the device's interface, convenience is significantly enhanced while saving valuable time for busy consumers. Overall, this cutting-edge technology has enormous potential in simplifying day-to-day life for consumers in an increasingly fast-paced world.

Advantages of Smart Speakers for Retailers

For retailers, the benefits of smart speakers include the ability to reach new customers, increase sales, and collect valuable data about consumer behavior. Smart speakers also provide an additional channel for customer service and support, as well as a way to promote new products and services. As AI technology continues to improve, retailers will be able to provide even more personalized and targeted experiences through smart speakers. The introduction of smart speakers has transformed the retail industry, providing retailers with new opportunities for sales and customer engagement. Smart speakers enable retailers to create personalized shopping experiences for customers by providing relevant recommendations and suggestions based on their purchase history. In addition, smart speakers allow retailers to leverage voice technology to interact with customers in real time through virtual assistants that can answer questions, provide product information and guide customers through the buying process. Retailers can further use smart speakers to collect data about their customers' shopping habits and preferences, enabling them to improve their marketing strategies and better meet consumer needs. Overall, smart speakers offer many advantages for retailers, such as improved sales revenue, enhanced customer experience and access to valuable data insights.

VOICE-EMPOWERED GADGETS

- Savvy speakers arrived at a record high (150 million units) in 2020. In spite of the coronavirus flare-up, there was a critical flood popular for shrewd speakers in 2019 — especially throughout the Christmas season (Q4). (Business Wire)
- By 2022, 55% of nuclear families are projected to have shrewd speaker gadgets. That will be a 42% climb from the family possession numbers today (OC&C Methodology Specialists)
- The deals of worldwide clever speakers are supposed to surpass 30 billion bucks by 2024. Before long, brilliant speakers will be among the top-selling client electronic items (Worldwide Market Experiences)
- Thirty-four percent of the people who do not have a voice collaborator need to buy one. Late adopters will develop the market of savvy speakers (Worldwide Web File)

VOICE-EMPOWERED ASSOCIATION

- Sixty-five percent of people matured 25 to 49 converses with their voice-empowered gadgets once daily. This 25- to 49-year-old segment is apparently to direct voice look through every day, followed barely by clients matured 18 to 24 and 50 or more year-advanced age gatherings, individually. Despite the fact that the 25- to 49-year-advanced age bunch is a seriously dynamic voice searcher bunch, the 18-24 segment is licensed with helping to move early acknowledgment of the headways.
- Wearable gadget proprietors (71%) figure they will perform more voice look-through in the distance. However, wearable gadget clients are truly hopeful, and speaker and tablet clients are not a long way behind.
- Sixty-one percent of the 25- to 64-year-old bunch favors utilizing their voice gadgets more. The 18- to 24-year-advanced age bunch mirrors this pattern, with 57% expressing that they will expand the utilization of voice gadgets in the impending years.
- Ninety-three percent of the clients are happy with voice associates. The enormous benefits clients refer to for utilizing voice speakers are the capacity to find moment solutions to their inquiries, make their lives peaceful, and perform multiple tasks.
- Thirty percent of the sites perusing meetings were screen-less in 2020. This impelled a change in the ways in which clients collaborate with brands on the web.
- Sixty-five percent of Google Home and Amazon Reverberation clients cannot envision returning to earlier strategies when they had astute speakers. For the majority, brilliant speakers are not only gadgets but also a fundamental piece of their daily schedule.
- In 2020, voice shopping produced more than $2 billion bucks in deals. In addition, voice shopping income was projected to soar in 2021. In particular, in view of the new measurements, the voice shopping market is projected to reach $40 billion bucks by 2022.
- Approximately 20% of the all-out questions with voice search are incited by 25 catchphrases set. These include fundamentally of inquiry words, for example, "what" or "how" and modifiers, for example, "simple" or "best. "For watchwords and content.

VOICE SHOPPING BUYS

- Approximately 43% of voice-empowered gadget clients influence their contraptions to shop. Clients across different age bunches are utilizing their gadgets to assist with buying on the web — a 41% ascent in 2018 as it were.
- By 2022, voice is projected to be an enormous channel with 40 billion bucks. Today, voice shopping contributes approximately $2 billion bucks in customer spending. Thus, to make use and make the majority of this income creating a learning experience, advertisers today should appreciate their shopper's voices.
- Brilliant speaker (11.5%) gadget proprietors buy through voice shopping month to month. This compares to approximately 5.5 million American adults buying through their shrewd speaker day to day (Voicebot)

- Brilliant speaker proprietors (52%) are keen on obtaining data about brand advancements, deals, and deals. Customers are available to make significant associations with brands through voice shopping channels.
- 51% of clients who shop through voice influence it to track down items. Additionally, 22% of those clients make purchases through voice straightforwardly, while 17% have utilized it to reorder products.
- In 2021, approximately one of every three (32%) US clients will have wise speakers. This shows an 8% increment from 2020.
- Approximately 7 out of 10 clients (71%) inclined toward utilizing voice look for an inquiry over the regular technique for entering.
- In 2022, the most recent examination numbers show that 2 million clients in the US are expected to buy utilizing the voice search usefulness of their savvy speakers.
- Seventy-two percent of US clients draw in with voice search by means of advanced partners such as Alexa, Siri, Cortana and Google Right hand.
- In spite of being available all around, 62% of the clients would use their voice aides while performing various tasks.

The consistent improvement of the internet business shows that clients' inclinations for web-based shopping are fundamental to consider. While clients love to investigate their chances on the web and buy what they need without visiting an actual store, voice shopping has completely reimagined the internet-based client experience. Additionally, voice search insights show that voice shopping is staying put and is setting down deep roots. More creative and high-level gadgets will continue to strike the market and make voice searches more available. Subsequently, more clients will utilize useful highlights and impact this innovation's development.

CHALLENGES AND CONCERNS WITH SMART SPEAKER ADOPTION

Security and Privacy Issues

One of the primary concerns with smart speaker and AI technology is the potential for security and privacy breaches. Smart speakers are always listening and collecting data, which can be a cause for concern for some consumers. There have also been instances where third-party developers have accessed user data without consent. As technology continues to evolve, it will be vital for companies to address and resolve these concerns to gain consumer trust. Smart speakers are becoming increasingly popular in households around the world, mostly due to their convenience and functionality. However, while these devices may be useful, they also present numerous security and privacy concerns. One of the most significant issues with smart speakers is that they are always listening, which poses a risk of conversations being recorded or inadvertently activated by third-party applications. Hackers can gain access to stored information via unsecured internet connections, leaving users vulnerable to identify theft and fraudulent activities. Additionally, many smart speaker companies collect vast amounts of user data for targeted advertising purposes. As smart speaker technology continues to advance — with more services added every day — it is imperative that manufacturers take necessary steps to ensure security and privacy measures are strong enough to protect their users' sensitive information from malicious actors.

Learning Curve for Consumers

Another challenge with smart speaker adoption is the learning curve for the technology. While smart speakers have become more user-friendly, there is still a learning curve for some consumers, particularly older generations and those who may be less tech-savvy. The learning curve for consumers of smart speakers can vary depending on their level of experience with technology, as well as the specific features and capabilities of the device they are using. However, even those who are new to devices such as Amazon Echo or Google Home can quickly adapt to their user-friendly interfaces and begin using them effectively for various tasks such as playing music, setting reminders and alarms, and accessing news or weather updates. The key challenge for users may be navigating more advanced features such as integrating with smart home devices or setting up routines that execute multiple commands at once. As these devices continue to evolve in complexity, manufacturers will need to strike a balance between offering sophisticated functionality while maintaining ease of use to ensure a positive consumer experience. Overall, while there may be some initial challenges in mastering all functions of smart speakers, most consumers should find the overall learning process relatively smooth and intuitive.

FUTURE OUTLOOK FOR SMART SPEAKERS AND AI IN COMMERCE

Predictions for Smart Speaker and AI Growth

Industry experts predict that smart speaker and AI technology will continue to grow and become even more integrated into our daily lives. In fact, it is predicted that over half of households in the U.S. will have a smart speaker by the year 2022. As the technology continues to evolve, there will be even more opportunities for companies to use smart speakers and AI to enhance the customer experience and drive sales. The rapid rise of smart speaker technology and AI has been a game changer in the realm of voice-enabled computing. In addition, AI-driven advancements are set to continue on an unprecedented scale, revolutionizing industries such as healthcare and education while creating new opportunities for businesses through personalized customer experiences and enhanced efficiency. As this technology continues to improve and become more widely adopted, we can expect to see further integration into everyday life via smart homes and connected devices. However, concerns around data privacy remain paramount in discussions surrounding growth, as industries strive to maintain trust among consumers by developing secure solutions for sensitive information sharing through these emerging technologies.

Future Applications for Smart Speakers and AI

In the future, smart speakers and AI technology could be used for a variety of applications in commerce. One potential application is using voice-activated technology to make purchases. Additionally, smart speakers and AI could be used to personalize the shopping experience by offering personalized recommendations and product suggestions based on previous purchases or user data. The future of smart speakers and AI is limitless, with potential applications spanning across industries and sectors. In healthcare, it is envisioned that smart speakers will be able to monitor patients remotely, track vital signs and even administer medication or remind them to take their pills.

In retail, personalized shopping experiences are becoming increasingly popular - imagine a smart speaker that can suggest products based on your previous purchases or preferences. In education, AI-powered virtual assistants could revolutionize the way students learn by providing individualized support and interactive learning experiences. Furthermore, in the home automation sector, intelligent homes powered by AI would allow for seamless control of various devices such as security systems, lighting and temperature across all platforms without having to lift a finger. As the technology continues to evolve at an astonishing pace, the possibilities of what we can achieve with smart speakers and AI are quite promising.

First, smart speakers and AI are expected to create more personalized experiences for consumers. As more businesses integrate smart speakers in their operations, they will be able to collect customer data and analyze it more effectively. With these data, businesses can tailor their marketing strategies to individual customer preferences, leading to a more customized experience. Additionally, as smart devices become more advanced and have access to more data, AI will become increasingly capable of anticipating customer needs before they even know what they want.

Second, smart speakers and AI are expected to drive a more conversational commerce experience among businesses and consumers. Conversational commerce refers to utilizing chatbots and voice assistants to communicate with consumers, providing them with a more interactive shopping experience. With the help of AI, smart speakers can automatically provide a list of recommended products based on consumers' interests and preferences, making the shopping experience more conversational.

Third, smart speakers and AI are expected to revolutionize the retail industry by introducing virtual commerce stores. Virtual commerce stores enable consumers to shop without any physical limitations using augmented reality (AR) and virtual reality (VR) technologies. Customers can use their smart speakers to navigate these virtual stores and interact with virtual assistants to have a more immersive shopping experience.

Fourth, smart speakers and AI are expected to improve logistics management significantly. With the use of smart speakers, businesses can automate supply chains and streamline fulfillment processes, thus improving inventory management processes. Additionally, the use of AI-powered chatbots can provide consumers with real-time updates on their order delivery status and minimize the number of calls customer service will receive related to delivery inquiries.

Fifth, smart speakers and AI are expected to enhance product recommendations. By collecting data from consumers, AI can help businesses customize recommendations based on the customer's purchasing history, browsing behavior, and demographics. As a result, customers can receive more relevant and personalized recommendations, leading to increased customer satisfaction and sales.

Sixth, smart speakers and AI are expected to revolutionize payments. The integration of AI-powered assistants in payment processes can prevent payment delays and provide quick access to product information, hence reducing friction in the payment process. The incorporation of voice recognition can also help secure payments, reducing the risk of fraud.

Seventh, smart speakers and AI are expected to transform business intelligence and data analytics. Businesses can use AI-powered chatbots to monitor, collect and interpret data, allowing them to gain insight into customer trends, feedback and preferences. With improved analytics tools, businesses can make more informed decisions and respond promptly to market changes.

Eighth, smart speakers and AI are expected to integrate with the Internet of Things (IoT). As an increasing number of devices become IoT-compatible, AI-powered voice assistants can integrate these devices to provide a more seamless home shopping experience. Consumers can use their smart speakers to control other household devices, such as thermostats, lighting systems, and security systems, enhancing the overall experience.

Ninth, smart speakers and AI are expected to improve customer service significantly. Chatbots powered by AI can take over the bulk of customer inquiries, thereby freeing customer service representatives to focus on complex queries and tasks that require empathy and human intervention.

Tenth, smart speakers and AI are expected to create new opportunities for growth for businesses. As consumers become more reliant on voice assistants and chatbots to make purchases and acquire information, businesses that have invested in these technologies are likely to benefit the most. Businesses can also use AI-powered analytics to gain insights into market trends, identify new business opportunities, and stay ahead of competitors.

The future outlook of smart speakers and AI in commerce is incredibly positive. The technology will continue revolutionizing the commerce industry, enhancing customer experiences, optimizing logistics, improving business intelligence and analytics, and creating new opportunities for growth. As AI technology continues to evolve, it is anticipated that the application of smart speakers and AI in commerce will become even more sophisticated, allowing businesses to stay competitive in the ever-evolving commerce landscape.

CASE STUDIES ON SUCCESSFUL INTEGRATION OF SMART SPEAKER IN DIFFERENT INDUSTRIES

Examples of Retailers Using Smart Speakers and AI

Several retailers have already integrated smart speakers and AI technology into their businesses with great success. Smart speakers are a rising technological trend that has taken off in the last few years. The proliferation of this technology has created new opportunities for businesses, particularly in the context of the Internet of Things (IoT). The integration of smart speakers into businesses has proven to be a lucrative and innovative strategy that has helped them engage customers, automate tasks, and improve efficiency. This essay will explore case studies on how businesses have integrated smart speakers into their operations.

Walmart Case Study

Walmart partnered with Google Assistant to allow customers to make purchases through their smart speakers. One noteworthy example is Amazon, which has integrated its Echo line of smart speakers with its e-commerce platform. By speaking to their device, customers can order products from Amazon and have them delivered straight to their door.

Another example is Walmart, who partnered with Google Home to allow customers to use voice commands for grocery shopping lists and manage their orders through the Google Express platform. While these developments may be significant for consumer convenience, they also provide valuable data for retailers on purchasing patterns and preferences, allowing them to work toward providing a more personalized shopping experience in the future. Expert analysis predicts that the impact of smart speakers on retail will only increase as advancements in AI technology continue to improve the accuracy of personalization algorithms.

Sephora Case Study

Another example is Sephora, who launched a virtual assistant on their app and integrated it with Google Assistant to offer personalized makeup tutorials and product recommendations. Smart speakers and AI are revolutionizing the way retailers interact with their customers.

Sodaclick Voice AI technology

Sodaclick Voice AI technology is a game-changer. It's like having a superpower that lets you talk to devices without any frustration. They use this super cool microphone called the multi array element microphone. It has this special patented noise reduction feature. So, it cancels out all the noise that's not coming from the direction it wants to listen to. That means it can focus only the customer. It works at high noise environments such as coffee shops, malls and airports.

Capital One Case Study

Capital One is a US-based financial services company that has integrated smart speaker technology into its operations, allowing customers to check their account balance, make payments, and perform other financial transactions through Amazon's Alexa. This integration has proven to be a useful way to enhance customers' experience and improve banks' efficiency. Capital One's integration with Amazon's Alexa is a good example of how financial institutions can benefit from adopting smart speaker technology.

Audio Burst Case Study

An audio burst is an AI-powered audio search and delivery platform that has integrated smart speakers into its operations. The company has created an app that allows users to search and play audio content through smart speakers. The app also allows users to share audio content and discover new content that aligns with their interests. Audio burst integration with smart speakers is an excellent way to make audio content more accessible and personalized, making it easy for users to access audio content using smart speakers.

Domino's Pizza Case Study

Domino's Pizza is a well-known pizza chain that has integrated smart speaker technology into its operations. Domino launched a smart speaker app that allows customers to order pizza through Alexa without having to interact with a physical person. This innovative approach has made the ordering process more convenient and efficient for customers, especially during peak hours. Domino's Pizza's integration with Alexa is another example of how the hospitality industry can utilize smart speakers to improve customer service.

LG Electronics Case Study

LG Electronics is a South Korean electronics company that has integrated smart speakers into its operations. LG has developed smart speakers that integrate with its home appliances, allowing users to control appliances such as air conditioners and refrigerators using voice commands. This integration has made the use of appliances more convenient and efficient for users, allowing them to control their home environment with ease. This example provides a glimpse into how smart speakers can be utilized in the home appliance industry.

BMW Case Study

BMW is a German luxury car manufacturer that has integrated smart speaker technology into its vehicles. BMW's cars come equipped with Amazon's Alexa, allowing drivers to perform voice commands such as changing the radio station, setting the temperature, and finding directions. This integration has made it easier for drivers to focus on the road while still performing important functions in the car. This example highlights the potential that smart speakers have in the automobile industry.

Ford Case Study

Ford is an American multinational automaker that has integrated smart speaker technology into its cars. Ford's cars come equipped with Amazon's Alexa, allowing drivers to perform voice commands. Ford has also integrated Alexa into its SYNC 3 Infotainment system, allowing users to control the car's features using voice commands. The integration of smart speaker technology into cars is an excellent way to improve the driving experience for users and streamline the operation of vehicles.

Smart speakers have proven to be an innovative and useful technology that has been integrated into the operations of many businesses across a range of industries.

Benefits and Results of Implementing Smart Speaker Technology

Retailers who have implemented smart speaker technology have seen numerous benefits, including increased customer engagement, higher conversion rates, and increased sales. Companies report that using smart speakers and AI has led to a more personalized shopping experience for consumers, leading to increased customer satisfaction and loyalty. With the rapid technological advancement of smart speaker technology, businesses can benefit significantly from their implementation. Smart speakers offer streamlined communication and task management, making them ideal for professional settings. They allow for hands-free operation, enabling employees to multitask without interruption. Their voice recognition feature simplifies scheduling appointments, sending messages, and even conducting research on specific topics. Moreover, using smart speakers can enhance team collaboration by allowing real-time access to information and increasing productivity levels. With modern advancements in AI, smart speakers can also interpret data and provide feedback on complex problems within seconds. The integration of a smart speaker into a business' day-to-day operations has been shown to improve work efficiency while reducing operational costs, resulting in higher profitability overall.

CONCLUSION AND FINAL THOUGHTS ON THE FUTURE OF SMART SPEAKERS AND AI IN BUYING BEHAVIOR

Summary of Findings

Overall, smart speakers and AI technology have had a significant impact on buying behavior. These technologies have allowed companies to personalize the shopping experience, enhance customer engagement, and drive sales. However, there are also challenges that need to be addressed regarding security and privacy concerns and the learning curve for some consumers. Smart speakers and AI have revolutionized the way consumers interact with brands and make purchasing decisions. With more advanced technologies emerging constantly, it is expected that smart speakers will become even more personalized and offer greater control to consumers in directing their purchases. However, while the advantages of smart speaker technology are undeniable, concerns around data privacy and security must be effectively addressed by companies to maintain consumer trust. Ultimately, the successful adoption of smart speakers in buying behavior will depend on whether they can provide a seamless and frictionless experience for consumers, integrating seamlessly with existing online stores and channels. It is clear that there is a bright future for this emerging technology as long as companies continue leveraging its advantages while also enhancing user privacy protection and delivering seamless experiences to customers.

Final Thoughts on the Future of Smart Speakers and AI in Commerce

As smart speaker and AI technology continue to evolve and become more integrated into our daily lives, there will be even more opportunities for companies to use these technologies to enhance the customer experience and drive sales. However, it will be essential for companies to address and resolve any challenges and concerns to gain consumer trust and loyalty. In conclusion, the impact of smart speakers on AI in buying behavior is substantial, and we can expect to see more retailers utilizing this technology to improve the shopping experience. While there are concerns surrounding privacy and security, the benefits of adopting smart speakers and AI in commerce cannot be ignored. As technology advances and consumer behavior continues to evolve, the future of smart speakers and AI in buying behavior looks promising. As the adoption of smart speakers and AI technology in commerce continues to grow, it is clear that these devices will become increasingly important for businesses looking to streamline their operations and improve customer service.

However, it is important to remember that there are still significant challenges ahead. One major issue is the risk of data privacy violations when using these devices to collect and store personal information about customers. To avoid this risk, companies must be transparent with their users about what information they are collecting and how it will be used. Additionally, as the technology becomes more sophisticated, we may see increased competition from other players in the market. Ultimately, although smart speakers and AI have already proven themselves to be powerful tools for commerce, and as long as companies make thoughtful decisions about how they implement these technologies, there is no reason to doubt that they will continue to play an ever-growing role in our daily lives.

FUTURE PERSPECTIVES: THE ROLE OF TRADITIONAL DESIGN METHODS IN AI-DRIVEN DECISION MAKING

Advancements and Innovations in AI-Driven Decision Making

AI-driven decision making is an ever-evolving field with boundless potential. Advancements and innovations in AI algorithms promise to bring even smarter decision-making capabilities, like having a personal assistant who can predict your thoughts before you even think them (well, almost).

As AI continues to advance, traditional design methods will play a vital role in harnessing its potential. Design thinking principles, efficiency considerations, and ethical frameworks will guide AI development towards creating systems that truly benefit users, making us wonder how we ever survived without their AI-powered wisdom.

Potential Challenges and Opportunities for Traditional Design Methods

Of course, challenges and opportunities lie in the path of integrating traditional design methods with AI-driven decision making. Designers and developers will need to strike a balance between pushing the boundaries of innovation and ensuring that AI systems remain trustworthy and user-friendly.

As AI becomes more integrated into our daily lives, the responsibility lies with designers and developers to ensure that the human touch and user-centered approaches remain at the core. While AI might be encroaching on decision-making territory, traditional design methods will keep it in check, allowing us to coexist harmoniously and prevent any world-domination mishaps.

In conclusion, traditional design methods bring a dose of humanity, empathy, and user-centeredness into the world of AI-driven decision making. By embracing design thinking, balancing efficiency and ethics, integrating user feedback, and considering the future perspectives, we can unlock the full potential of AI as our trusty companion in making better decisions. After all, who doesn't want a smart speaker that not only tells jokes but also helps us navigate life's perplexities?In conclusion, traditional design methods have a significant role to play in enhancing AI-driven decision making, particularly in the context of smart speakers. By incorporating user-centric design principles, considering ethical considerations, and leveraging design thinking, we can create more intuitive and efficient systems. It is crucial to continuously integrate user feedback and stay updated with advancements in AI technology to ensure the continual improvement and evolution of AI-driven decision-making systems. By embracing the potential of traditional design methods, we can unlock the full potential of AI in making informed decisions, ultimately improving the overall user experience and transforming the way we interact with technology.

REFERENCES

Adjerid, I., Peer, E., & Acquisti, A. (2018). Beyond the privacy paradox: Objective versus relative risk in privacy decision making. MIS Quarterly: Management. *Management Information Systems Quarterly*, 42(2), 465–488. doi:10.25300/MISQ/2018/14316

Ba, W., Mendelson, H., & Zhu, M. (2020). *Sales Policies for a Virtual Assistant.* ArXiv preprint arXiv: 2009.03719..

Bronnenberg B, Dubé JP, Mela C (2010) Do digital video recorders influence sales? *Journal of Marketing Research, 47*(6), 998–1010.

Bansal, G., Zahedi, F. M., & Gefen, D. (2016). Do context and personality matter? Trust and privacy concerns in disclosing private information online. *Information & Management, 53*(1), 1–21. doi:10.1016/j. im.2015.08.001

Bawack, R. E., Wamba, S. F., & Carillo, K. (2019). Where Information Systems Research Meets Artificial Intelligence Practice: Toward the Development of an AI Capability Framework. *DIGIT 2019 Proceedings,* (5). https://aisel.aisnet.org/digit2019/5

Behrenbeck, K., Peter, B., Peter, C., Rugholm, J., Frank, S., Wachinger, T., & Zocchi, A. (2015). *Perspectives on retail and consumer goods. In Perspectives on retail and consumer goods.* McKinsey. https://www.mckinsey.com/~/media/McKinsey/Industries/Retail/Our Insights/Perspectives on retail and consumer goods Number 7/Perspectives-on-Retail-and-Consumer-Goods_Issue-7.ashx

Bohm, A. S., George, E. J., Cyphers, B., & Lu, S. (2017). Privacy and Liberty in an Always-On, Always-Listening World. *The Columbia Science and Technology Law Review, 19*, 1–45.

Borning, M., & Kesdogan, D. (2001). Privacy in e-commerce. *Communications of the ACM, 48*(4), 229–235. doi:10.1145/1053291.1053295

Bringula, R. P. (2016). Factors Affecting Web Portal Information Services Usability: A Canonical Correlation Analysis. *International Journal of Human-Computer Interaction, 32*(10), 814–826. doi:10.10 80/10447318.2016.1199180

Brito, P. Q., & Stoyanova, J. (2018). Marker versus Markerless Augmented Reality. Which Has More Impact on Users? *International Journal of Human-Computer Interaction, 34*(9), 819–833. doi:10.108 0/10447318.2017.1393974

Chae, M., & Kim, J. (2004). Do size and structure matter to mobile users? An empirical study of the effects of screen size, information structure, and task complexity on user activities with standard web phones. *Behaviour & Information Technology, 23*(3), 165–181. doi:10.1080/01449290410001669923

Chevalier, J., & Goolsbee, A. (2003). Measuring prices and price competition online: Amazon. com and BarnesandNoble. com. *Quantitative Marketing and Economics, 1*(2), 203–222. doi:10.1023/A:1024634613982

Cruz, A., & Karatzas, S. (2019). Book highlight—Developing an effective digital presence. *Global Business and Organizational Excellence, 38*(2), 64–74. doi:10.1002/joe.21911

Datta, H., Knox, G., & Bronnenberg, B. J. (2018). Changing their tune: How consumers' adoption of online streaming affects music consumption and discovery. *Marketing Science, 37*(1), 5–21. doi:10.1287/ mksc.2017.1051

Dawar, N., & Bendle, N. (2018). Marketing in the age of Alexa. Harvard Business Review, 96(3), 80-86. Ghose A (2018) TAP: Unlocking the mobile economy. MIT Press. Ghose A, Goldfarb A, Han SP (2013) How is the mobile Internet different? Search costs and local activities. *Information Systems Research, 24*(3), 613–631.

Deng, X. N., & Joshi, K. D. (2016). Why individuals participate in micro-task crowdsourcing work environment: Revealing crowdworkers' perceptions. *Journal of the Association for Information Systems, 17*(10), 648–673. doi:10.17705/1jais.00441

Jones, V.K. (2018). Voice-activated change: Marketing in the age of artificial intelligence and virtual assistants. *Journal of Brand Strategy, 7*(3), 233-245.

Kumar V, Dixit A, Javalgi RRG, Dass M (2016) Research framework, strategies, and applications of intelligent agent technologies (IATs) in marketing. *Journal of the Academy of Marketing Science, 44*(1), 24-45.

Lee, R.S. (2013). Vertical integration and exclusivity in platform and two-sided markets. *American Economic Review, 103*(7), 2960-3000.

Leslie, P. (2004). (forthcoming). Price Discrimination in Broadway Theatres, RAND Journal of Economics, 35, 3, 520-41.

Luini, L. & Sabbatini P. (2010) *Demand cross elasticity without substitutability: Evidence from an experiment.* Available at SSRN 1617337.

Luo, X., Qin, M.S., Fang, Z., & Qu, Z. (2020) Artificial Intelligence Coaches for Sales Agents: Caveats and Solutions. *Journal of Marketing.*

Compilation of References

Aasha Nandhini, S., Hemalatha, R., Radha, S., & Indumathi, K. (2018). Web enabled plant disease detection system for agricultural applications using WMSN. *Wireless Personal Communications*, *102*(2), 725–740. doi:10.100711277-017-5092-4

Aayula. (2022). Design and Implementation of sensor and IoT based Remembrance system for closed one. *Telematique*, *21*(1), 2769–2778.

Abate, C., Decherchi, S., & Cavalli, A. (2023). Graph neural networks for conditional de novo drug design. *Wiley Interdisciplinary Reviews. Computational Molecular Science*, *13*(4), e1651. doi:10.1002/wcms.1651

Abbas, A., Jain, S., Gour, M., & Vankudothu, S. (2021). Tomato plant disease detection using transfer learning with C-GAN synthetic images. *Computers and Electronics in Agriculture*, *187*, 106279. doi:10.1016/j.compag.2021.106279

Abdalla, Y., Elbadawi, M., Ji, M., Alkahtani, M., Awad, A., Orlu, M., Gaisford, S., & Basit, A. W. (2023). Machine learning using multimodal data predicts the production of selective laser sintered 3D printed drug products. *International Journal of Pharmaceutics*, *633*, 122628. doi:10.1016/j.ijpharm.2023.122628 PMID:36682506

Abedi Gheshlaghi, H., Feizizadeh, B., & Blaschke, T. (2019). GIS-based forest fire risk mapping using the analytical networkprocess and fuzzy logic. *Journal of Environmental Planning and Management*, *63*(3), 481–499. doi:10.1080/09640568.2019.1594726

Abirami, B., Vamitha, V., & Rajaram, S. (2020). A new approach for solving trapezoidal intuitionistic fuzzy transportation problem. [AMSJ]. *Advances in Mathematics: Scientific Journal*, *9*(11), 9149–9159. doi:10.37418/amsj.9.11.20

Abnoosian, K., Farnoosh, R., & Behzadi, M. H. (2023). Prediction of diabetes disease using an ensemble of machine learning multi-classifier models. *BMC Bioinformatics*, *24*(1), 337. doi:10.118612859-023-05465-z PMID:37697283

Abood, M. J. K., & Abdul-Majeed, G. H. (2023). Classification of network slicing threats based on slicing enablers: A survey. *International Journal of Intelligent Networks*, *4*(April), 103–112. doi:10.1016/j.ijin.2023.04.002

Abougreen, A. N., & Chakraborty, C. (2021). Applications of machine learning and internet of things in agriculture. *Green Technological Innovation for Sustainable Smart Societies: Post Pandemic Era*, 257-279.

Abraham, G., Raksha, R., & Nithya, M. (2021, April). Smart agriculture based on IoT and machine learning. In *2021 5th International Conference on Computing Methodologies and Communication (ICCMC)* (pp. 414-419). IEEE. 10.1109/ICCMC51019.2021.9418392

Ackley, D., Birkebak, J., Blumel, J., Bourcier, T., de Zafra, C., Goodwin, A., Halpern, W., Herzyk, D., Kronenberg, S., Mauthe, R., Shenton, J., Shuey, D., & Wange, R. L. (2023). FDA and industry collaboration: Identifying opportunities to further reduce reliance on nonhuman primates for nonclinical safety evaluations. *Regulatory Toxicology and Pharmacology*, *138*, 105327. doi:10.1016/j.yrtph.2022.105327 PMID:36586472

Adamides, G. (2020). A review of climate-smart agriculture applications in Cyprus. *Atmosphere (Basel)*, *11*(9), 898. doi:10.3390/atmos11090898

Adão, T., Hruška, J., Pádua, L., Bessa, J., Peres, E., Morais, R., & Sousa, J. J. (2017). Hyperspectral imaging: A review on UAV-based sensors, data processing and applications for agriculture and forestry. *Remote Sensing (Basel)*, *9*(11), 1110. doi:10.3390/rs9111110

Adjerid, I., Peer, E., & Acquisti, A. (2018). Beyond the privacy paradox: Objective versus relative risk in privacy decision making. MIS Quarterly: Management. *Management Information Systems Quarterly*, *42*(2), 465–488. doi:10.25300/MISQ/2018/14316

AECC Study Abroad Consultants. (2023, June 30). *10 Best AI Tools for Students: A Comprehensive Guide*. Aecc INDONESIA. https://www.aeccglobal.co.id/blog/best-ai-tools-for-students

Agarwal, S., & Tarar, S. (2021). A hybrid approach for crop yield prediction using machine learning and deep learning algorithms. []. IOP Publishing.]. *Journal of Physics: Conference Series*, *1714*(1), 012012. doi:10.1088/1742-6596/1714/1/012012

Ahamad, S., Veeraiah, V., Ramesh, J. V. N., Rajadevi, R., Reeja, S. R., Pramanik, S., & Gupta, A. (2023). Deep Learning based Cancer Detection Technique. Thrust Technologies' Effect on Image Processing. IGI Global.

Ahamad, S., Veeraiah, V., Ramesh, J. V. N., Rajadevi, R., Reeja, S. R., Pramanik, S., & Gupta, A. (2023). *Deep Learning based Cancer Detection Technique, Thrust Technologies' Effect on Image Processing*. IGI Global.

Ahmad, M., Ahmed, I., & Adnan, A. (2019). Overhead view person detection using YOLO. In 2019 IEEE 10th annual ubiquitous computing, electronics & mobile communication conference (UEMCON) (pp. 0627–0633). IEEE. doi:10.1109/UEMCON47517.2019.8992980

Ahmad, S. F., Han, H., Alam, M. M., Rehmat, M. K., Irshad, M., Arraño-Muñoz, M., & Ariza-Montes, A. (2023). Impact of artificial intelligence on human loss in decision making, laziness and safety in education. *Humanities & Social Sciences Communications*, *10*(1), 1. doi:10.105741599-023-01787-8 PMID:37325188

Ahmed, H. H. (2021). Solving the problem of fuzzy transportation using linear programming and goal programming. *Further Advances in Internet of Things in Biomedical and Cyber Physical Systems*, *193*, 313–330. doi:10.1007/978-3-030-57835-0_23

Ahmed, I., & Yadav, P. K. (2023). Plant disease detection using machine learning approaches. *Expert Systems: International Journal of Knowledge Engineering and Neural Networks*, *40*(5), e13136. doi:10.1111/exsy.13136

Ahmed, J. S., Mohammed, H. J., & Chaloob, I. Z. (2021). Application of a fuzzy multi-objective defuzzification method to solve a transportation problem. *Materials Today: Proceedings*. doi:10.1016/j.matpr.2020.12.1062

Aishwarya, R., Yogitha, R., Lakshmanan, L., Maheshwari, M., Suji Helen, L., & Nagarajan, G. (2022). Smart agriculture framework implemented using the internet of things and deep learning. In Biologically Inspired Techniques in Many Criteria Decision Making [Singapore: Springer Nature Singapore.]. *Proceedings of BITMDM*, *2021*, 639–648.

Aissa, H., Tarik, A., Zeroual, I., & Yousef, F. (2021). Using Machine Learning to Predict Outcomes of Accident Cases in Moroccan Courts. *Procedia Computer Science*, *184*, 829–834. doi:10.1016/j.procs.2021.03.103

Ai, W., Patel, N. D., Roop, P. S., Malik, A., & Trew, M. L. (2020, June). Closing the Loop: Validation of Implantable Cardiac Devices With Computational Heart Models. *IEEE Journal of Biomedical and Health Informatics*, *24*(6), 1579–1588. doi:10.1109/JBHI.2019.2947007 PMID:31613786

Akansha, K. (2022). Email Security. *Journal of Image Processing and Intelligent remote sensing*, *2*(6).

Akgun, S., & Greenhow, C. (2022). Artificial intelligence in education: Addressing ethical challenges in K-12 settings. *AI and Ethics*, *2*(3), 431–440. doi:10.100743681-021-00096-7 PMID:34790956

Akhter, R., & Sofi, S. A. (2022). Precision agriculture using IoT data analytics and machine learning. *Journal of King Saud University. Computer and Information Sciences*, *34*(8), 5602–5618. doi:10.1016/j.jksuci.2021.05.013

Aktar, W., Sengupta, D., & Chowdhury, A. (2009). Impact of pesticides use in agriculture: Their benefits and hazards. *Interdisciplinary Toxicology*, *2*(1), 1–12. doi:10.2478/v10102-009-0001-7 PMID:21217838

Alahi, M. E. E., Sukkuea, A., Tina, F. W., Nag, A., Kurdthongmee, W., Suwannarat, K., & Mukhopadhyay, S. C. (2023). Integration of IoT-Enabled Technologies and Artificial Intelligence (AI) for Smart City Scenario: Recent Advancements and Future Trends. *Sensors (Basel)*, *23*(11), 11. doi:10.339023115206 PMID:37299934

Albahli, S. (2020). Type 2 machine learning: An effective hybrid prediction model for early type 2 diabetes detection. *Journal of Medical Imaging and Health Informatics*, *10*(5), 1069–1075. doi:10.1166/jmihi.2020.3000

Albahra, S., Gorbett, T., Robertson, S., D'Aleo, G., Kumar, S. V. S., Ockunzzi, S., Lallo, D., Hu, B., & Rashidi, H. H. (2023). Artificial intelligence and machine learning overview in pathology & laboratory medicine: A general review of data preprocessing and basic supervised concepts. *Seminars in Diagnostic Pathology*, *40*(2), 71–87. doi:10.1053/j.semdp.2023.02.002 PMID:36870825

Albahri, O. S. (2019). Fault-Tolerant mHealth Framework in the Context of IoT-Based Real-Time Wearable Health Data Sensors. *IEEE Access : Practical Innovations, Open Solutions*, *7*, 50052–50080. doi:10.1109/ACCESS.2019.2910411

Aletras, N., Tsarapatsanis, D., Preoţiuc-Pietro, D., & Lampos, V. (2016). Predicting judicial decisions of the European Court of Human Rights: A Natural Language Processing perspective. *PeerJ. Computer Science*, *2*, e93. doi:10.7717/peerj-cs.93

Alexander, M., Solomon, B., Ball, D. L., Sheerin, M., Dankwa-Mullan, I., Preininger, A. M., Jackson, G. P., & Herath, D. M. (2020). Evaluation of an artificial intelligence clinical trial matching system in Australian lung cancer patients. *JAMIA Open*, *3*(2), 209–215. doi:10.1093/jamiaopen/ooaa002 PMID:32734161

Alghazzawi, D., Bamasag, O., Albeshri, A., Sana, I., Ullah, H., & Asghar, M. Z. (2022). Efficient Prediction of Court Judgments Using an LSTM+CNN Neural Network Model with an Optimal Feature Set. *Mathematics*, *10*(5), 5. doi:10.3390/math10050683

Aliper, A., Kudrin, R., Polykovskiy, D., Kamya, P., Tutubalina, E., Chen, S., Ren, F., & Zhavoronkov, A. (2023). Prediction of clinical trials outcomes based on target choice and clinical trial design with multimodal artificial intelligence. *Clinical Pharmacology and Therapeutics*, *114*(5), 972–980. doi:10.1002/cpt.3008 PMID:37483175

Almotiri. S. (2016). Mobile health system in the context of IoT. *2016 IEEE 4th International Conference on Future Internet of Things and Cloud Workshops*. IEEE. doi:10.1109/W-FiCloud.2016.24

Alrowais, F., Asiri, M. M., Alabdan, R., Marzouk, R., Hilal, A. M., & Gupta, D. (2022). Hybrid leader based optimization with deep learning driven weed detection on internet of things enabled smart agriculture environment. *Computers & Electrical Engineering*, *104*, 108411. doi:10.1016/j.compeleceng.2022.108411

AlSuwaidi, A., Grieve, B., & Yin, H. (2018). Feature-ensemble-based novelty detection for analyzing plant hyperspectral datasets. *IEEE Journal of Selected Topics in Applied Earth Observations and Remote Sensing*, *11*(4), 1041–1055. doi:10.1109/JSTARS.2017.2788426

Ammour, A., Aouraghe, I., Khaissidi, G., Mrabti, M., Aboulem, G., & Belahsen, F. (2020). A new semi-supervised approach for characterizing the Arabic on-line handwriting of Parkinson's disease patients. *Computer Methods and Programs in Biomedicine, 183*, 104979. doi:10.1016/j.cmpb.2019.07.007 PMID:31542687

Anand, R., Singh, J., Pandey, D. K., Pandey, B., Nassa, V. K., & Pramanik, S. (2022). Modern Technique for Interactive Communication in LEACH-Based Ad Hoc Wireless Sensor Network. In M. M. Ghonge, S. Pramanik, & A. D. Potgantwar (Eds.), *Software Defined Networking for Ad Hoc Networks*. Springer., doi:10.1007/978-3-030-91149-2_3

Anderson, T. M., White, S., Davis, B., Erhardt, R., Palmer, M., Swanson, A., Kosmala, M., & Packer, C. (2016). The spatial distribution of African savannah herbivores: Species associations and habitat occupancy in a landscape context. *Philosophical Transactions of the Royal Society of London. Series B, Biological Sciences, 371*(1703), 20150314. doi:10.1098/rstb.2015.0314 PMID:27502379

Andrew, J. J. (2018). Automatic Extraction of Entities and Relation from Legal Documents. In N. Chen, R. E. Banchs, X. Duan, M. Zhang, & H. Li (Eds.), *Proceedings of the Seventh Named Entities Workshop* (pp. 1–8). Association for Computational Linguistics. 10.18653/v1/W18-2401

Andrianov, A. M., Shuldau, M. A., Furs, K. V., Yushkevich, A. M., & Tuzikov, A. V. (2023). AI-driven de novo design and molecular modeling for discovery of small-molecule compounds as potential drug candidates targeting SARS-CoV-2 main protease. *International Journal of Molecular Sciences, 24*(9), 8083. doi:10.3390/ijms24098083 PMID:37175788

Andrushia, A. D., Neebha, T. M., Patricia, A. T., Sagayam, K. M., & Pramanik, S. (2023). Capsule Network based Disease Classification for VitisVinifera Leaves. *Neural Computing & Applications*. doi:10.100700521-023-09058-y

Anwar, Z., & Masood, S. (2023). Exploring Deep Ensemble Model for Insect and Pest Detection from Images. *Procedia Computer Science, 218*, 2328–2337. doi:10.1016/j.procs.2023.01.208

Anyoha, R. (2017). *The history of Artificial Intelligence*. Harvard Press. https://sitn.hms.harvard.edu/flash/2017/history-artificial-intelligence/

Apostolopoulos, I. D., & Mpesiana, T. A. (2020). Covid-19: Automatic detection from X-ray images utilizing transfer learning with convolutional neural networks. *Physical and Engineering Sciences in Medicine, 43*(2), 635–640. doi:10.100713246-020-00865-4 PMID:32524445

Arora, J., & Sharma, S. (2023). Solving task assignment problem using branch and bound method. [JAMSA]. *Journal of Applied Mathematics and Statistical Analysis, 4*(1), 14–20.

Arrowsmith, J. (2011). Trial watch: Phase II failures: 2008-2010. *Nature Reviews. Drug Discovery, 10*(5), 328–329. doi:10.1038/nrd3439 PMID:21532551

Ashley, K. D., & Aleven, V. (1997). Reasoning symbolically about partially matched cases. *Proceedings of the 15th International Joint Conference on Artifical Intelligence* - Volume 1, (pp. 335–341). ACL.

Askr, H., Elgeldawi, E., Aboul Ella, H., Elshaier, Y. A. M. M., Gomaa, M. M., & Hassanien, A. E. (2023). Deep learning in drug discovery: An integrative review and future challenges. *Artificial Intelligence Review, 56*(7), 5975–6037. doi:10.100710462-022-10306-1 PMID:36415536

Atalla, S., Daradkeh, M., Gawanmeh, A., Khalil, H., Mansoor, W., Miniaoui, S., & Himeur, Y. (2023). An Intelligent Recommendation System for Automating Academic Advising Based on Curriculum Analysis and Performance Modeling. *Mathematics, 11*(5), 5. doi:10.3390/math11051098

Atanassov, K. T. (1983). Intuitionistic Fuzzy Sets. *Int J Bioautomation, 20*(S1), S1-S6.

Aydin, H. E., & Iban, M. C. (2023). Predicting and analyzing flood susceptibility using boosting-based ensemble machine learning algorithms with SHapley Additive exPlanations. *Natural Hazards, 116*(3), 2957–2991. doi:10.100711069-022-05793-y

Ayodele, T. O. (2010). Types of machine learning algorithms. *New advances in machine learning, 3,* 19-48.

Ba, W., Mendelson, H., & Zhu, M. (2020). *Sales Policies for a Virtual Assistant.* ArXiv preprint arXiv: 2009.03719..

Babitha, M. (2022). Trends of Artificial Intelligence for online exams in education. *International journal of Early Childhood special. Education, 14*(01), 2457–2463.

Bacco, M., Barsocchi, P., Ferro, E., Gotta, A., & Ruggeri, M. (2019). The digitization of agriculture: A survey of research activities on smart farming. *Array (New York, N.Y.), 3,* 100009. doi:10.1016/j.array.2019.100009

Badwan, B. A., Liaropoulos, G., Kyrodimos, E., Skaltsas, D., Tsirigos, A., & Gorgoulis, V. G. (2023). Machine learning approaches to predict drug efficacy and toxicity in oncology. *Cell Reports Methods, 3*(2), 100413. doi:10.1016/j.crmeth.2023.100413 PMID:36936080

Bagde, A., Dev, S., Madhavi, K., Sriram, L., Spencer, S. D., Kalvala, A., Nathani, A., & Singh, M. (2023). Biphasic burst and sustained transdermal delivery in vivo using an AI-optimized 3D-printed MN patch. *International Journal of Pharmaceutics, 636,* 122647. doi:10.1016/j.ijpharm.2023.122647 PMID:36754185

Baidoo-Anu, D., & Ansah, L. O. (2023). Education in the era of generative artificial intelligence (AI): Understanding the potential benefits of ChatGPT in promoting teaching and learning. *Journal of AI, 7*(1), 52–62. doi:10.61969/jai.1337500

Bakare, O. D. (2023). Emerging Technologies as a Panacea for Sustainable Provision of Library Services in Nigeria. In *Global Perspectives on Sustainable Library Practices* (pp. 1–21). IGI Global.

Bakare, O. D., & Jatto, O. V. (2023). The Potential Impact of Chatbots on Student Engagement and Learning Outcomes. In *Creative AI Tools and Ethical Implications in Teaching and Learning* (pp. 212–229). IGI Global. doi:10.4018/979-8-3693-0205-7.ch012

Bakare, O., & Okuonghae, N. (2022). Information Managers as Change Agents in Achieving Sustainable Development in the 21st Century. *Journal of Environmental Science and Economics, 1*(2), 58–66. doi:10.56556/jescae.v1i2.97

Balafoutis, A. T., Beck, B., Fountas, S., Tsiropoulos, Z., Vangeyte, J., van der Wal, T., & Pedersen, S. M. (2017). Smart farming technologies–description, taxonomy and economic impact. *Precision agriculture: Technology and economic perspectives,* 21-77.

Balaji, K., Kiran, P. S., & Kumar, M. S. (2020). Resource aware virtual machine placement in IaaS cloud using bio-inspired firefly algorithm. *Journal of Green Engineering, 10,* 9315–9327.

Balla, E. (2023). *Automated Grading Systems: How AI is Revolutionizing Exam Evaluation - DataScienceCentral.com.* Data Science Central. https://www.datasciencecentral.com/automated-grading-systems-how-ai-is-revolutionizing-exam-evaluation/

Bannigan, P., Bao, Z., Hickman, R. J., Aldeghi, M., Häse, F., Aspuru-Guzik, A., & Allen, C. (2023). Machine learning models to accelerate the design of polymeric long-acting injectables. *Nature Communications, 14*(1), 35. doi:10.103841467-022-35343-w PMID:36627280

Bansal, G., Zahedi, F. M., & Gefen, D. (2016). Do context and personality matter? Trust and privacy concerns in disclosing private information online. *Information & Management, 53*(1), 1–21. doi:10.1016/j.im.2015.08.001

Ban, Y., Zhang, P., Nascetti, A., Bevington, A. R., & Wulder, M. A. (2020). Near Real-Time Wildfire Progression Monitoring with Sentinel-1 SAR Time Series and Deep Learning. *Scientific Reports*, *10*(1), 1322. doi:10.103841598-019-56967-x PMID:31992723

Bao, Z., Bufton, J., Hickman, R. J., Aspuru-Guzik, A., Bannigan, P., & Allen, C. (2023). Revolutionizing drug formulation development: The increasing impact of machine learning. *Advanced Drug Delivery Reviews*, *202*, 115108. doi:10.1016/j.addr.2023.115108 PMID:37774977

Barysė, D., & Sarel, R. (2023). Algorithms in the court: Does it matter which part of the judicial decision-making is automated? *Artificial Intelligence and Law*. Advance online publication. doi:10.100710506-022-09343-6 PMID:36643574

Batanova, E., Birmpa, I., & Meisser, G. (2023). Use of Machine Learning to classify clinical research to identify applicable compliance requirements. *Informatics in Medicine Unlocked*, *39*, 101255. doi:10.1016/j.imu.2023.101255

Baviskar, K., Bedse, A., Raut, S., & Darapaneni, N. (2023). Artificial intelligence and machine learning-based manufacturing and drug product marketing. In Bioinformatics Tools for Pharmaceutical Drug Product Development (pp. 197-231). Wiley. doi:10.1002/9781119865728.ch10

Bawack, R. E., Wamba, S. F., & Carillo, K. (2019). Where Information Systems Research Meets Artificial Intelligence Practice: Toward the Development of an AI Capability Framework. *DIGIT 2019 Proceedings*, (5). https://aisel.aisnet.org/digit2019/5

Beaula, T., & Saravanan, S. (2020). A new method for solving fully fuzzy linear programming problems. [MJM]. *Malaya Journal of Matematik*, *S*(1), 397–401. doi:10.26637/MJM0S20/0076

Beaula, T., & Seetha, R. (2020). Nonlinear programming with Trapezoidal intuitionistic fuzzy parameters. [MJM]. *Malaya Journal of Matematik*, *8*(4), 2088–2091. doi:10.26637/MJM0804/0129

Beaumont, C., O'Doherty, M., & Shannon, L. (2011). Reconceptualising assessment feedback: A key to improving student learning? *Studies in Higher Education*, *36*(6), 671–687. doi:10.1080/03075071003731135

Bedi, P., & Gole, P. (2021). Plant disease detection using hybrid model based on convolutional autoencoder and convolutional neural network. *Artificial Intelligence in Agriculture*, *5*, 90–101. doi:10.1016/j.aiia.2021.05.002

Behrenbeck, K., Peter, B., Peter, C., Rugholm, J., Frank, S., Wachinger, T., & Zocchi, A. (2015). *Perspectives on retail and consumer goods. In Perspectives on retail and consumer goods*. McKinsey. https://www.mckinsey.com/~/media/McKinsey/Industries/Retail/Our Insights/Perspectives on retail and consumer goods Number 7/Perspectives-on-Retail-and-Consumer-Goods_Issue-7.ashx

Beirkdar, R., & Ramesh, G. (2022, November). A new approach for finding an optimal solution of assignment problems in complete interval. In. AIP Conference Proceedings: Vol. 2516. *No. 1* (p. 320003). AIP Publishing LLC. doi:10.1063/5.0109470

Belgherbi, B., Benabdeli, K., & Mostefai, K. (2018). Mapping the riskforest fires in Algeria: Application of the forest of Guetarnia in Western Algeria. *Ekologia (Bratislava)*, *37*(3), 289–300. doi:10.2478/eko-2018-0022

Berendt, B., Littlejohn, A., & Blakemore, M. (2020). AI in education: Learner choice and fundamental rights. *Learning, Media and Technology*, *45*(3), 312–324. doi:10.1080/17439884.2020.1786399

Betts, N., & Vasko, F. J. (2016). Solving the unbalanced assignment problem: Simpler is better. [AJOR]. *American Journal of Operations Research*, *06*(04), 296–299. doi:10.4236/ajor.2016.64028

Bharati, S. K. (2021). Transportation problem with interval-valued intuitionistic fuzzy sets: impact of a new ranking. *Progress in Artificial Intelligence*, 1-17. doi:10.1007/s13748-020-00228-w

Bhardwaj, H., Tomar, P., Sakalle, A., & Sharma, U. (2021). *Artificial Intelligence and IoT-Based Technologies for Sustainable Farming and Smart Agriculture.* P.15.IGI Publishers. . doi:10.4018/978-1-7998-1722-2.ch002

Bhatia, N. (2022, October 11). *Types of growing systems in Vertical Farming - Lab Associates.* Lab Associates. https://labassociates.com/types-of-growing-systems-in-vertic al-farming

Bhattacharya, A., Ghosal, A., Obaid, A. J., Krit, S., Shukla, V. K., Mandal, K., & Pramanik, S. (2021). Unsupervised Summarization Approach with Computational Statistics of Microblog Data. In D. Samanta, R. R. Althar, S. Pramanik, & S. Dutta (Eds.), *Methodologies and Applications of Computational Statistics for Machine Learning* (pp. 23–37). IGI Global. doi:10.4018/978-1-7998-7701-1.ch002

Biswas, Simões-Capela, Van Hoof, & Van Helleputte. (2019). Heart Rate Estimation From Wrist-Worn Photoplethysmography: A Review. *IEEE Sensors Journal, 19*(16), 6560-6570. . doi:10.1109/JSEN.2019.2914166

Bloomberg. (2022, April 21). *Smart Agriculture Market Size Worth $35.98 Billion by 2030: Grand View Research, Inc.* Bloomberg.com. https://www.bloomberg.com/press-releases/2022-04-21/smart-ag riculture-market-size-worth-35-98-billion-by-2030-grand-view -research-inc

Bochkovskiy, A., Wang, C. Y., & Liao, H. Y. M. (2020). *Yolov4: optimal object detection speed and accuracy.* arXiv preprint arXiv:2004.10934

Bohm, A. S., George, E. J., Cyphers, B., & Lu, S. (2017). Privacy and Liberty in an Always-On, Always-Listening World. *The Columbia Science and Technology Law Review, 19*, 1–45.

Bondre, D. A., & Mahagaonkar, S. (2019). Prediction of crop yield and fertilizer recommendation using machine learning algorithms. *International Journal of Engineering Applied Sciences and Technology, 4*(5), 371–376. doi:10.33564/IJEAST.2019.v04i05.055

Borenstein, J., & Howard, A. (2021). Emerging challenges in AI and the need for AI ethics education. *AI and Ethics, 1*(1), 61–65. doi:10.100743681-020-00002-7

Borjigin, T., Zhan, X., Li, J., Meda, A., & Tran, K. K. (2023). Predicting mini-tablet dissolution performance utilizing X-ray computed tomography. *European Journal of Pharmaceutical Sciences, 181*, 106346. doi:10.1016/j.ejps.2022.106346 PMID:36494000

Borning, M., & Kesdogan, D. (2001). Privacy in e-commerce. *Communications of the ACM, 48*(4), 229–235. doi:10.1145/1053291.1053295

Boschetti, E., D'Amato, A., Candiano, G., & Righetti, P. G. (2018). Protein biomarkers for early detection of diseases: The decisive contribution of combinatorial peptide ligand libraries. *Journal of Proteomics, 188*, 1–14. doi:10.1016/j.jprot.2017.08.009 PMID:28882677

Bouighoulouden, A., & Kissani, I. (2020). Crop yield prediction using K-means clustering. School of Science and Engineering—Al Akhawayn University.

Bournez, C., Riool, M., de Boer, L., Cordfunke, R. A., de Best, L., van Leeuwen, R., Drijfhout, J. W., Zaat, S. A. J., & van Westen, G. J. P. (2023). CalcAMP: A new machine learning model for the accurate prediction of antimicrobial activity of peptides. *Antibiotics (Basel, Switzerland), 12*(4), 725. doi:10.3390/antibiotics12040725 PMID:37107088

Boussouf, S., Fernández, T., & Hart, A. B. (2023). Landslide susceptibility mapping using maximum entropy (MaxEnt) and geographically weighted logistic regression (GWLR) models in the Río Aguas catchment (Almería, SE Spain). *Natural Hazards, 117*(1), 207–235. doi:10.100711069-023-05857-7

Bozkurt, A., Karadeniz, A., Baneres, D., Guerrero-Roldán, A. E., & Rodríguez, M. E. (2021). Artificial intelligence and reflections from educational landscape: A review of AI Studies in half a century. *Sustainability (Basel), 13*(2), 800. doi:10.3390u13020800

Bringula, R. P. (2016). Factors Affecting Web Portal Information Services Usability: A Canonical Correlation Analysis. *International Journal of Human-Computer Interaction, 32*(10), 814–826. doi:10.1080/10447318.2016.1199180

Brito, P. Q., & Stoyanova, J. (2018). Marker versus Markerless Augmented Reality. Which Has More Impact on Users? *International Journal of Human-Computer Interaction, 34*(9), 819–833. doi:10.1080/10447318.2017.1393974

Bronnenberg B, Dubé JP, Mela C (2010) Do digital video recorders influence sales? *Journal of Marketing Research, 47*(6), 998–1010.

Brophy, E., Hennelly, B., De Vos, M., Boylan, G., & Ward, T. (2022). Improved Electrode Motion Artefact Denoising in ECG Using Convolutional Neural Networks and a Custom Loss Function. *IEEE Access : Practical Innovations, Open Solutions, 10*, 54891–54898. doi:10.1109/ACCESS.2022.3176971

Buey, M. G., Garrido, A. L., Bobed, C., & Ilarri, S. (2016). The AIS Project: Boosting Information Extraction from Legal Documents by using Ontologies: *Proceedings of the 8th International Conference on Agents and Artificial Intelligence*, (pp. 438–445). ScitePress. 10.5220/0005757204380445

Buja, I., Sabella, E., Monteduro, A. G., Chiriacò, M. S., De Bellis, L., Luvisi, A., & Maruccio, G. (2021). Advances in plant disease detection and monitoring: From traditional assays to in-field diagnostics. *Sensors (Basel), 21*(6), 2129. doi:10.339021062129 PMID:33803614

Burke, D. (2009). Strategies for using feedback students bring to higher education. *Assessment & Evaluation in Higher Education, 34*(1), 41–50. doi:10.1080/02602930801895711

Businessware. (2023, October 15). Life image and mendel.ai partner to bring the power of ai to accelerate clinical trial process for life sciences and academic medical facilities. *BuisnessWire*. https://www.businesswire.com/news/home/20181106005630/en/life-image-and-mendel.ai-partner-to-bring-the-power-of-ai-to-accelerate-clinical-trial-process-for-life-sciences-and-academic-medical-facilities

Cacciamani, G. E., Chen, A., Gill, I. S., & Hung, A. J. (2023). Artificial intelligence and urology: Ethical considerations for urologists and patients. *Nature Reviews. Urology.* doi:10.103841585-023-00796-1 PMID:37524914

Cai, X., Fan, W., Wang, Y., & Qian, Y. (2022, October). Research and experiment on automatic navigation control technology of intelligent electric tractor. In *International Conference on Agri-Photonics and Smart Agricultural Sensing Technologies (ICASAST 2022)* (Vol. 12349, pp. 266-269). SPIE. 10.1117/12.2657209

Cardille, J. A., & Ventura, S. J. (2001). Occurrence of wildfire in thenorthern Great Lakes Region: Effects of land cover and landownership assessed at multiple scales. *International Journal of Wildland Fire, 10*(2), 145–154. doi:10.1071/WF01010

Carou-Senra, P., Ong, J. J., Castro, B. M., Seoane-Viaño, I., Rodríguez-Pombo, L., Cabalar, P., Alvarez-Lorenzo, C., Basit, A. W., Pérez, G., & Goyanes, A. (2023). Predicting pharmaceutical inkjet printing outcomes using machine learning. *International Journal of Pharmaceutics: X, 5*, 100181. doi:10.1016/j.ijpx.2023.100181 PMID:37143957

Čartolovni, A., Tomičić, A., & Lazić Mosler, E. (2022). Ethical, legal, and social considerations of AI-based medical decision-support tools: A scoping review. *International Journal of Medical Informatics*, *161*, 104738. doi:10.1016/j.ijmedinf.2022.104738 PMID:35299098

Cascini, F., Beccia, F., Causio, F. A., Melnyk, A., Zaino, A., & Ricciardi, W. (2022). Scoping review of the current landscape of AI-based applications in clinical trials. *Frontiers in Public Health*, *10*, 949377. doi:10.3389/fpubh.2022.949377 PMID:36033816

Chae, M., & Kim, J. (2004). Do size and structure matter to mobile users? An empirical study of the effects of screen size, information structure, and task complexity on user activities with standard web phones. *Behaviour & Information Technology*, *23*(3), 165–181. doi:10.1080/01449290410001669923

Chakraborty, C., & Kishor, A. (2022, December). Real-Time Cloud-Based Patient-Centric Monitoring Using Computational Health Systems. *IEEE Transactions on Computational Social Systems*, *9*(6), 1613–1623. doi:10.1109/TCSS.2022.3170375

Chakroun, B., Miao, F., Mendes, V., Domiter, A., Fan, H., Kharkova, I., & Rodriguez, S. (2019). Artificial intelligence for sustainable development: synthesis report. *mobile learning week 2019*.

Chan, C. K. Y. (2023). A comprehensive AI policy education framework for university teaching and learning. *International Journal of Educational Technology in Higher Education*, *20*(1), 38. doi:10.118641239-023-00408-3

Chandan, R. R., Soni, S., Raj, A., Veeraiah, V., Dhabliya, D., Pramanik, S., & Gupta, A. (2023). Genetic Algorithm and Machine Learning. Advanced Bioinspiration Methods for Healthcare Standards, Policies, and Reform. IGI Global. doi:10.4018/978-1-6684-5656-9

Chandra, B. S., Sastry, C. S., & Jana, S. (2019, March). Robust Heartbeat Detection From Multimodal Data via CNN-Based Generalizable Information Fusion. *IEEE Transactions on Biomedical Engineering*, *66*(3), 710–717. doi:10.1109/TBME.2018.2854899 PMID:30004868

Chandrakala, P. (2021). Enhanced zero suffix approach for the optimal solution of a travelling salesman and assignment problem: A summary. [IRJASH]. *International Research Journal on Advanced Science Hub*, *03*(Special Issue ICOST 2S, 02S), 1–5. doi:10.47392/irjash.2021.031

Chandrasekar, V., Ansari, M. Y., Singh, A. V., Uddin, S., Prabhu, K. S., Dash, S., Khodor, S. A., Terranegra, A., Avella, M., & Dakua, S. P. (2023). Investigating the use of machine learning models to understand the drugs permeability across placenta. *IEEE Access : Practical Innovations, Open Solutions*, *11*, 52726–52739. doi:10.1109/ACCESS.2023.3272987

Chang, J. F., Lai, C. J., Wang, C. N., Hsueh, M. H., & Nguyen, V. T. (2021). Fuzzy optimization model for decision-making in supply chain management. [MATH]. *Mathematics*, *9*(4), 312. doi:10.3390/math9040312

Charles, V., Emrouznejad, A., & Gherman, T. (2023). A critical analysis of the integration of blockchain and artificial intelligence for supply chain. *Annals of Operations Research*, *327*(1), 7–47. doi:10.100710479-023-05169-w PMID:36718465

Charoen-Ung, P., & Mittrapiyanuruk, P. (2018, July). Sugarcane yield grade prediction using random forest and gradient boosting tree techniques. In *2018 15th International Joint Conference on Computer Science and Software Engineering (JCSSE)* (pp. 1-6). IEEE. 10.1109/JCSSE.2018.8457391

Chatterjee, A., Walters, R., Shafi, Z., Ahmed, O. S., Sebek, M., Gysi, D., Yu, R., Eliassi-Rad, T., Barabási, A.-L., & Menichetti, G. (2023). Improving the generalizability of protein–ligand binding predictions with AI-Bind. *Nature Communications*, *14*(1), 1989. doi:10.103841467-023-37572-z PMID:37031187

Chaudhary, A., Kolhe, S., & Kamal, R. (2016). A hybrid ensemble for classification in multiclass datasets: An application to oilseed disease dataset. *Computers and Electronics in Agriculture*, *124*, 65–72. doi:10.1016/j.compag.2016.03.026

Chaudhary, S., Muthudoss, P., Madheswaran, T., Paudel, A., & Gaikwad, V. (2023). Artificial intelligence (AI) in drug product designing, development, and manufacturing. In A. Philip, A. Shahiwala, M. Rashid, & M. Faiyazuddin (Eds.), *A Handbook of Artificial Intelligence in Drug Delivery* (pp. 395–442). Academic Press. doi:10.1016/B978-0-323-89925-3.00015-0

Cheikhrouhou, O., Mahmud, R., Zouari, R., Ibrahim, M., Zaguia, A., & Gia, T. N. (2021). One-Dimensional CNN Approach for ECG Arrhythmia Analysis in Fog-Cloud Environments. *IEEE Access : Practical Innovations, Open Solutions*, 9, 103513–103523. doi:10.1109/ACCESS.2021.3097751

Chen, W., Li, Y., Tian, Z., & Zhang, F. (2023). 2D and 3D object detection algorithms from images: A Survey. *Array-Science Direct, 19*. doi:10.1016/j.array.2023.100305

Cheng, C., Fu, J., Su, H., & Ren, L. (2023). Recent advancements in agriculture robots: Benefits and challenges. *Machines, 11*(1), 48. doi:10.3390/machines11010048

Cheng, T. T., Cua, J. L., Tan, M. D., Yao, K. G., & Roxas, R. E. (2009). Information extraction from legal documents. *2009 Eighth International Symposium on Natural Language Processing*, (pp. 157–162). IEEE. 10.1109/SNLP.2009.5340925

Chen, J., Chen, W., Zeb, A., Yang, S., & Zhang, D. (2022). Lightweight inception networks for the recognition and detection of rice plant diseases. *IEEE Sensors Journal, 22*(14), 14628–14638. doi:10.1109/JSEN.2022.3182304

Chen, J., Valehi, A., & Razi, A. (2019). Smart Heart Monitoring: Early Prediction of Heart Problems Through Predictive Analysis of ECG Signals. *IEEE Access : Practical Innovations, Open Solutions*, 7, 120831–120839. doi:10.1109/ACCESS.2019.2937875

Chen, L., Chen, P., & Lin, Z. (2020). Artificial intelligence in education: A review. *IEEE Access : Practical Innovations, Open Solutions*, 8, 75264–75278. doi:10.1109/ACCESS.2020.2988510

Chen, R., Cai, N., Luo, Z., Wang, H., Liu, X., & Li, J. (2023). Multi-task banded regression model: A novel individual survival analysis model for breast cancer. *Computers in Biology and Medicine, 162*(April), 107080. doi:10.1016/j.compbiomed.2023.107080 PMID:37271111

Chen, S., Gao, J., Chen, J., Xie, Y., Shen, Z., Xu, L., Che, J., Wu, J., & Dong, X. (2023a). ClusterX: A novel representation learning-based deep clustering framework for accurate visual inspection in virtual screening. *Briefings in Bioinformatics, 24*(3), bbad126. Advance online publication. doi:10.1093/bib/bbad126 PMID:37020333

Chen, W., Liu, X., Zhang, S., & Chen, S. (2023b). Artificial intelligence for drug discovery: Resources, methods, and applications. *Molecular Therapy. Nucleic Acids, 31*, 691–702. doi:10.1016/j.omtn.2023.02.019 PMID:36923950

Chen, X., Xie, H., Zou, D., & Hwang, G. J. (2020). Application and theory gaps during the rise of artificial intelligence in education. *Computers and Education: Artificial Intelligence, 1*, 100002. doi:10.1016/j.caeai.2020.100002

Chen, Y. (2017). Integrated and intelligent manufacturing: Perspectives and enablers. *Engineering (Beijing), 3*(5), 588–595. doi:10.1016/J.ENG.2017.04.009

Chen, Y., Jia, J., Wu, C., Ramirez-Granada, L., & Li, G. (2023). Estimation on total phosphorus of agriculture soil in China: A new sight with comparison of model learning methods. *Journal of Soils and Sediments, 23*(2), 998–1007. doi:10.100711368-022-03374-x

Chevalier, J., & Goolsbee, A. (2003). Measuring prices and price competition online: Amazon. com and BarnesandNoble. com. *Quantitative Marketing and Economics, 1*(2), 203–222. doi:10.1023/A:1024634613982

Chin, C. (2023). *Navigating the Risks of Artificial Intelligence on the Digital News Landscape*. CSIS. https://www.csis.org/analysis/navigating-risks-artificial-intelligence-digital-news-landscape

Chinthamu. (2023). Self-Secure firmware model for Blockchain-Enabled IOT environment to Embedded system. *European Chemical Bulletin*, *12*(S3), 653–660. 10.31838/ecb/2023.12.s3.075

Choudhary, S., Narayan, V., Faiz, M., & Pramanik, S. (2022). Fuzzy Approach-Based Stable Energy-Efficient AODV Routing Protocol in Mobile Ad hoc Networks. In M. M. Ghonge, S. Pramanik, & A. D. Potgantwar (Eds.), *Software Defined Networking for Ad Hoc Networks*. Springer. doi:10.1007/978-3-030-91149-2_6

Chou, S., & Hsing, T.-P. (2010). Text Mining Technique for Chinese Written Judgment of Criminal Case. In H. Chen, M. Chau, S. Li, S. Urs, S. Srinivasa, & G. A. Wang (Eds.), *Intelligence and Security Informatics* (pp. 113–125). Springer. doi:10.1007/978-3-642-13601-6_14

Ciolacu, M., Tehrani, A. F., Binder, L., & Svasta, P. M. (2018, October). Education 4.0-Artificial Intelligence assisted higher education: early recognition system with machine learning to support students' success. In *2018 IEEE 24th International Symposium for Design and Technology in Electronic Packaging(SIITME)* (pp. 23-30). IEEE. 10.1109/SIITME.2018.8599203

Clyde, A., Liu, X., Brettin, T., Yoo, H., Partin, A., Babuji, Y., Blaiszik, B., Mohd-Yusof, J., Merzky, A., Turilli, M., Jha, S., Ramanathan, A., & Stevens, R. (2023). AI-accelerated protein–ligand docking for SARS-CoV-2 is 100-fold faster with no significant change in detection. *Scientific Reports*, *13*(1), 2105. doi:10.103841598-023-28785-9 PMID:36747041

Collaborations Pharmaceuticals. (2023, June 3). Collaborations Pharmaceuticals, Inc. Collaborations Pharmaceuticals, Inc. and Atomwise Try to Beat Parkinson's Disease Using Artificial Intelligence. *PR Newswire*. https://www.prnewswire.com/news-releases/collaborations-pharmaceuticals-inc-and-atomwise-try-to-beat-parkinsons-disease-using-artificial-intelligence-300724633.html

Cook, D., Brown, D., Alexander, R., March, R., Morgan, P., Satterthwaite, G., & Pangalos, M. N. (2014). Lessons learned from the fate of AstraZeneca's drug pipeline: A five-dimensional framework. *Nature Reviews. Drug Discovery*, *13*(6), 419–431. doi:10.1038/nrd4309 PMID:24833294

Crespo, O., Janssen, D., Garcia, C., & Ruiz, L. (2017). Biological and molecular diversity of Cucumber green mottle mosaic virus in Spain. *Plant Disease*, *101*(6), 977–984. doi:10.1094/PDIS-09-16-1220-RE PMID:30682937

Crompton, H., & Burke, D. (2023). Artificial intelligence in higher education: The state of the field. *International Journal of Educational Technology in Higher Education*, *20*(1), 22. doi:10.118641239-023-00392-8

Cruz, A., & Karatzas, S. (2019). Book highlight—Developing an effective digital presence. *Global Business and Organizational Excellence*, *38*(2), 64–74. doi:10.1002/joe.21911

Cygert, S., & Czyżewski, A. (2020). Toward robust pedestrian detection with data augmentation. *IEEE Access : Practical Innovations, Open Solutions*, *8*, 136674–136683. doi:10.1109/ACCESS.2020.3011356

Czub, N., Szlęk, J., Pacławski, A., Klimończyk, K., Puccetti, M., & Mendyk, A. (2023). Artificial intelligence-based quantitative structure-property relationship model for predicting human intestinal absorption of compounds with serotonergic activity. *Molecular Pharmaceutics*, *20*(5), 2545–2555. doi:10.1021/acs.molpharmaceut.2c01117 PMID:37070956

Dai, Y., Chai, C. S., Lin, P. Y., Jong, M. S. Y., Guo, Y., & Qin, J. (2020). Promoting students' well-being by developing their readiness for the artificial intelligence age. *Sustainability (Basel)*, *12*(16), 6597. doi:10.3390u12166597

Dandolo, D., Masiero, C., Carletti, M., Dalle Pezze, D., & Susto, G. A. (2023). AcME—Accelerated model-agnostic explanations: Fast whitening of the machine-learning black box. *Expert Systems with Applications*, *214*, 119115. doi:10.1016/j.eswa.2022.119115

Datta, H., Knox, G., & Bronnenberg, B. J. (2018). Changing their tune: How consumers' adoption of online streaming affects music consumption and discovery. *Marketing Science*, *37*(1), 5–21. doi:10.1287/mksc.2017.1051

Davenport, T., & Kalakota, R. (2019). The potential for artificial intelligence in healthcare. *Future Healthcare Journal*, *6*(2), 94–98. doi:10.7861/futurehosp.6-2-94 PMID:31363513

Dawar, N., & Bendle, N. (2018). Marketing in the age of Alexa. Harvard Business Review, 96(3), 80-86. Ghose A (2018) TAP: Unlocking the mobile economy. MIT Press. Ghose A, Goldfarb A, Han SP (2013) How is the mobile Internet different? Search costs and local activities. *Information Systems Research*, *24*(3), 613–631.

de Araujo, D. A., Rigo, S. J., & Barbosa, J. L. V. (2017). Ontology-based information extraction for juridical events with case studies in Brazilian legal realm. *Artificial Intelligence and Law*, *25*(4), 379–396. doi:10.100710506-017-9203-z

De la Torre, R., Corlu, C. G., Faulin, J., Onggo, B. S., & Juan, A. A. (2021). Simulation, optimization, and machine learning in sustainable transportation systems: Models and applications. [SU]. *Sustainability (Basel)*, *13*(3), 1551. doi:10.3390u13031551

De Turck, F. (2020). Efficient resource allocation through integer linear programming: a detailed example. *arXiv preprint arXiv:2009.13178*.

Dedeloudi, A., Weaver, E., & Lamprou, D. A. (2023). Machine learning in additive manufacturing & Microfluidics for smarter and safer drug delivery systems. *International Journal of Pharmaceutics*, *636*, 122818. doi:10.1016/j.ijpharm.2023.122818 PMID:36907280

DeGroat, W., Venkat, V., Pierre-Louis, W., Abdelhalim, H., & Ahmed, Z. (2023). Hygieia: AI/ML pipeline integrating healthcare and genomics data to investigate genes associated with targeted disorders and predict disease. *Software Impacts*, *16*, 100493. doi:10.1016/j.simpa.2023.100493

Delso, G., Cirillo, D., Kaggie, J. D., Valencia, A., Metser, U., & Veit-Haibach, P. (2021). How to Design AI-Driven Clinical Trials in Nuclear Medicine. *Seminars in Nuclear Medicine*, *51*(2), 112–119. doi:10.1053/j.semnuclmed.2020.09.003 PMID:33509367

Demirel, M., & Kumral, N. A. (2021). Artificial intelligence in integrated pest management. In *Artificial Intelligence and IoT-Based Technologies for Sustainable Farming and Smart Agriculture* (pp. 289–313). IGI Global. doi:10.4018/978-1-7998-1722-2.ch018

Deng, J., Ye, Z., Zheng, W., Chen, J., Gao, H., Wu, Z., Chan, G., Wang, Y., Cao, D., Wang, Y., Lee, S. M.-Y., & Ouyang, D. (2023). Machine learning in accelerating microsphere formulation development. *Drug Delivery and Translational Research*, *13*(4), 966–982. doi:10.100713346-022-01253-z PMID:36454434

Deng, X. N., & Joshi, K. D. (2016). Why individuals participate in micro-task crowdsourcing work environment: Revealing crowdworkers' perceptions. *Journal of the Association for Information Systems*, *17*(10), 648–673. doi:10.17705/1jais.00441

Derrow, P. (2022). *The Ethics of Algorithms*. Rutgers. https://www.rutgers.edu/magazine/winter-2022/ethics-algorithms

Destro, F., Nagy, Z. K., & Barolo, M. (2022). A benchmark simulator for quality-by-design and quality-by-control studies in continuous pharmaceutical manufacturing – Intensified filtration-drying of crystallization slurries. *Computers & Chemical Engineering*, *163*, 107809. doi:10.1016/j.compchemeng.2022.107809

Devedžić, V. (2004). Web intelligence and artificial intelligence in education. *Journal of Educational Technology & Society*, *7*(4), 29–39.

Devi, S. (2022). A path towards child-centric Artificial Intelligence based Education. *International Journal of Early Childhood special. Education*, *14*(03), 9915–9922.

Devlin, J., Chang, M.-W., Lee, K., & Toutanova, K. (2019). BERT: Pre-training of Deep Bidirectional Transformers for Language Understanding. In J. Burstein, C. Doran, & T. Solorio (Eds.), *Proceedings of the 2019 Conference of the North American Chapter of the Association for Computational Linguistics: Human Language Technologies,* Volume 1 *(Long and Short Papers)* (pp. 4171–4186). Association for Computational Linguistics. 10.18653/v1/N19-1423

Dhamodaran, S., Ahamad, S., Ramesh, J. V. N., Muthugurunathan, G., Manikandan, K., Pramanik, S., & Pandey, D. (2023). Food Quality Assessment using Image Processing Technique. Thrust Technologies' Effect on Image Processing. IGI Global.

Dhamodaran, S., Ahamad, S., Ramesh, J. V. N., Sathappan, S., Namdev, A., Kanse, R. R., & Pramanik, S. (2023). *Fire Detection System Utilizing an Aggregate Technique in UAV and Cloud Computing, Thrust Technologies' Effect on Image Processing*. IGI Global.

Dhanasekar, S., Parthiban, V., & David Maxim Gururaj, A. (2020). Improved Hungarian method to solve fuzzy assignment problem and fuzzy traveling salesman problem. [AMSJ]. *Advances in Mathematics: Scientific Journal, 9*(11), 9417–9427. doi:10.37418/amsj.9.11.46

Dharmaraj, V., & Vijayanand, C. (2018). Artificial intelligence (AI) in agriculture. *International Journal of Current Microbiology and Applied Sciences, 7*(12), 2122–2128. doi:10.20546/ijcmas.2018.712.241

Di Lascio, E., Gerebtzoff, G., & Rodríguez-Pérez, R. (2023). Systematic evaluation of local and global machine learning models for the prediction of adme properties. *Molecular Pharmaceutics, 20*(3), 1758–1767. doi:10.1021/acs.molpharmaceut.2c00962 PMID:36745394

Dixit. (2014). A Review paper on Iris Recognition. *Journal GSD International society for green. Sustainable Engineering and Management, 1*(14), 71–81.

Dixit. (2015). Iris Recognition by Daugman's Algorithm – an Efficient Approach. *Journal of applied Research and Social Sciences, 2*(14), 1 - 4.

Dogan, M. E., Goru Dogan, T., & Bozkurt, A. (2023). The use of artificial intelligence (AI) in online learning and distance education processes: A systematic review of empirical studies. *Applied Sciences (Basel, Switzerland), 13*(5), 3056. doi:10.3390/app13053056

Domingues, T., Brandão, T., & Ferreira, J. C. (2022). Machine learning for detection and prediction of crop diseases and pests: A comprehensive survey. *Agriculture, 12*(9), 1350. doi:10.3390/agriculture12091350

Dorcas Bakare, O., & Mike Bakare, B. (2022). Redesigning Library and Information Science Curriculum for Sustainable Environmental Transformation Among Students of the Department of Library and Information Science, Lead City University. *Journal of Education for Library and Information Science*, 20210016. doi:10.3138/jelis-2021-0016

Dozier, C., Kondadadi, R., Light, M., Vachher, A., Veeramachaneni, S., & Wudali, R. (2010). Named Entity Recognition and Resolution in Legal Text. In E. Francesconi, S. Montemagni, W. Peters, & D. Tiscornia (Eds.), Semantic Processing of Legal Texts (Vol. 6036, pp. 27–43). Springer Berlin Heidelberg. doi:10.1007/978-3-642-12837-0_2

Drüke, M., Sakschewski, B., von Bloh, W., Billing, M., Lucht, W., & Thonicke, K. (2023). Fire may prevent future Amazon forest recovery after large-scale deforestation. *Communications Earth & Environment, 4*(1), 248. doi:10.103843247-023-00911-5

Dubey, A. K., Rao, K. K., Kumar, S., Tamta, M., Dwivedi, S. K., Kumar, R., & Mishra, J. S. (2019). *Disease management in major field crops. Conservation Agriculture for Climate Resilient Farming & Doubling Farmers' Income*. ICAR Research Complex for Eastern Region, Patna Training Manual No.

Dulhare, U. N., & Gouse, S. (2022). *Automation of Rice Cultivation from Ploughing–Harvesting with Diseases, Pests, and Weeds to Increase the Yield Using AI*. Kumar. doi:10.1007/978-981-16-7985-8_51

Dushyant, K., Muskan, G., Gupta, A., & Pramanik, S. (2022). Utilizing Machine Learning and Deep Learning in Cyber security: An Innovative Approach. In M. M. Ghonge, S. Pramanik, R. Mangrulkar, & D. N. Le (Eds.), *Cyber security and Digital Forensics*. Wiley. doi:10.1002/9781119795667.ch12

Dutta, J., & Pal, S. C. (2015). A note on Hungarian method for solving assignment problem. [JIOS]. *Journal of Information and Optimization Sciences*, *36*(5), 451–459. doi:10.1080/02522667.2014.926711

Dutta, S., Pramanik, S., & Bandyopadhyay, S. K. (2021). Prediction of Weight Gain during COVID-19 for Avoiding Complication in Health. *International Journal of Medical Science and Current Research*, *4*(3), 1042–1052.

Dwivedi, Y. K., Kshetri, N., Hughes, L., Slade, E. L., Jeyaraj, A., Kar, A. K., Baabdullah, A. M., Koohang, A., Raghavan, V., Ahuja, M., Albanna, H., Albashrawi, M. A., Al-Busaidi, A. S., Balakrishnan, J., Barlette, Y., Basu, S., Bose, I., Brooks, L., Buhalis, D., & Wright, R. (2023). Opinion Paper: "So what if ChatGPT wrote it?" Multidisciplinary perspectives on opportunities, challenges and implications of generative conversational AI for research, practice and policy. *International Journal of Information Management*, *71*, 102642. doi:10.1016/j.ijinfomgt.2023.102642

Dziak, D. (2017). IoT-based information system for healthcare application: design methodology approach. *mdpi.com*. doi:10.3390/app7060596

Eden Green Technology. (2023, January 19). *What Is Vertical Farming? Everything You Should Know About This Innovation*. Eden Green; Eden Green Technology. https://www.edengreen.com/blog-collection/what-is-vertical-farming

Ekanayake, E. M. U. S. B., Perera, S. P. C., Daundasekara, W. B., & Juman, Z. A. M. S. (2020). A modified ant colony optimization algorithm for solving a transportation problem. [JAMCS]. *Journal of Advances in Mathematics and Computer Science*, *35*(5), 83–101. doi:10.9734/jamcs/2020/v35i530284

El-Naggar, N. E.-A., Dalal, S. R., Zweil, A. M., & Eltarahony, M. (2023). Artificial intelligence-based optimization for chitosan nanoparticles biosynthesis, characterization and in-vitro assessment of its anti-biofilm potentiality. *Scientific Reports*, *13*(1), 4401. doi:10.103841598-023-30911-6 PMID:36928367

El-Sappagh, S., Elmogy, M., Ali, F., Abuhmed, T., Islam, S. R., & Kwak, K. S. (2019). A comprehensive medical decision–support framework based on a heterogeneous ensemble classifier for diabetes prediction. *Electronics (Basel)*, *8*(6), 635. doi:10.3390/electronics8060635

EMA. (2021). *Guidelines on Good Manufacturing Practice specific to Advanced Therapy Medicinal Products*. EMA.

Escotet, M. Á. (2023). The optimistic future of Artificial Intelligence in higher education. *Prospects*, •••, 1–10. doi:10.100711125-023-09642-z

Esposito, M., Crimaldi, M., Cirillo, V., Sarghini, F., & Maggio, A. (2021). Drone and sensor technology for sustainable weed management: A review. *Chemical and Biological Technologies in Agriculture*, *8*(1), 18. doi:10.118640538-021-00217-8

European Commission. (2022). *Ethical guidelines on the use of artificial intelligence and data in teaching and learning for educators European Education Area*. EC. https://education.ec.europa.eu/news/ethical-guidelines-on-the-use-of-artificial-intelligence-and-data-in-teaching-and-learning-for-educators

Everingham, Y., Sexton, J., Skocaj, D., & Inman-Bamber, G. (2016). Accurate prediction of sugarcane yield using a random forest algorithm. *Agronomy for Sustainable Development*, *36*(2), 1–9. doi:10.100713593-016-0364-z

Exscientia. (2023, June 3). *World-first as AI-designed drug for OCD proceeds to clinical trials.* Excientia. https://www.exscientia.ai/news-insights/world-first-as-ai-designed-drug-for-ocd-proceeds-to-clinical-trials

Fagerholm, U., Hellberg, S., Alvarsson, J., & Spjuth, O. (2023). In silico prediction of human clinical pharmacokinetics with ANDROMEDA by prosilico: Predictions for an established benchmarking dataset, a modern small drug dataset, and a comparison with laboratory methods. *Alternatives to Laboratory Animals, 51*(1), 39–54. doi:10.1177/02611929221148447 PMID:36572567

Fahmida Islam, S., Uddin, M. S., & Bansal, J. C. (2022). Harvesting robots for smart agriculture. In *Computer Vision and Machine Learning in Agriculture* (Vol. 2, pp. 1–13). Springer Singapore. doi:10.1007/978-981-16-9991-7_1

Fallani, A., Sandonas, L. M., & Tkatchenko, A. (2023). Enabling inverse design in chemical compound space: Mapping quantum properties to structures for small organic molecules. *arXiv preprint arXiv:2309.00506.* doi:/arXiv.2309.00506 doi:10.48550

Fang, C., Wang, Y., Grater, R., Kapadnis, S., Black, C., Trapa, P., & Sciabola, S. (2023). Prospective validation of machine learning algorithms for absorption, distribution, metabolism, and excretion prediction: An industrial perspective. *Journal of Chemical Information and Modeling, 63*(11), 3263–3274. doi:10.1021/acs.jcim.3c00160 PMID:37216672

Fanourgakis, S., Synacheri, A. C., Lavigne, M. D., Konstantopoulos, D., & Fousteri, M. (2023). Histone H2Bub dynamics in the 5′ region of active genes are tightly linked to the UV-induced transcriptional response. *Computational and Structural Biotechnology Journal, 21,* 614–629. doi:10.1016/j.csbj.2022.12.013 PMID:36659919

Farhood, H., Bakhshayeshi, I., Pooshideh, M., Rezvani, N., & Beheshti, A. (2022). Recent advances in image processing techniques in agriculture. *Artificial Intelligence and Data Science in Environmental Sensing,* 129-153.

Farooq, M. S., Riaz, S., Abid, A., Abid, K., & Naeem, M. A. (2019). A Survey on the Role of IoT in Agriculture for the Implementation of Smart Farming. *IEEE Access : Practical Innovations, Open Solutions, 7,* 156237–156271. doi:10.1109/ACCESS.2019.2949703

Feng, H., & Wei, G. W. (2023). Virtual screening of DrugBank database for hERG blockers using topological Laplacian-assisted AI models. *Computers in Biology and Medicine, 153,* 106491. doi:10.1016/j.compbiomed.2022.106491 PMID:36599209

Ferentinos, K. P. (2018). Deep learning models for plant disease detection and diagnosis. *Computers and Electronics in Agriculture, 145,* 311–318. doi:10.1016/j.compag.2018.01.009

Fernández-Quintero, M. L., Ljungars, A., Waibl, F., Greiff, V., Andersen, J. T., Gjølberg, T. T., Jenkins, T. P., Voldborg, B. G., Grav, L. M., Kumar, S., Georges, G., Kettenberger, H., Liedl, K. R., Tessier, P. M., McCafferty, J., & Laustsen, A. H. (2023). Assessing developability early in the discovery process for novel biologics. *mAbs, 15*(1), 2171248. doi:10.1080/19420862.2023.2171248 PMID:36823021

Ficzere, M., Mészáros, L. A., Kállai-Szabó, N., Kovács, A., Antal, I., Nagy, Z. K., & Galata, D. L. (2022). Real-time coating thickness measurement and defect recognition of film coated tablets with machine vision and deep learning. *International Journal of Pharmaceutics, 623,* 121957. doi:10.1016/j.ijpharm.2022.121957 PMID:35760260

Finney, C. A., Delerue, F., Gold, W. A., Brown, D. A., & Shvetcov, A. (2023). Artificial intelligence-driven meta-analysis of brain gene expression identifies novel gene candidates and a role for mitochondria in Alzheimer's disease. *Computational and Structural Biotechnology Journal, 21,* 388–400. doi:10.1016/j.csbj.2022.12.018 PMID:36618979

Fisher, A. C., Liu, W., Schick, A., Ramanadham, M., Chatterjee, S., Brykman, R., Lee, S. L., Kozlowski, S., Boam, A. B., Tsinontides, S. C., & Kopcha, M. (2022). An audit of pharmaceutical continuous manufacturing regulatory submissions and outcomes in the US. *International Journal of Pharmaceutics*, *622*, 121778. doi:10.1016/j.ijpharm.2022.121778 PMID:35500688

Flamm, K. (1988). *Creating the computer: government, industry, and high technology*. Brookings Institution Press.

Floridi, L., Cowls, J., Beltrametti, M., Chatila, R., Chazerand, P., Dignum, V., Luetge, C., Madelin, R., Pagallo, U., Rossi, F., Schafer, B., Valcke, P., & Vayena, E. (2018). AI4People—An Ethical Framework for a Good AI Society: Opportunities, Risks, Principles, and Recommendations. *Minds and Machines*, *28*(4), 689–707. doi:10.100711023-018-9482-5 PMID:30930541

Franzen, D., & Mulla, D. (2015). A history of precision agriculture. *Precision Agriculture Technology for Crop Farming*, 1–20.

Fregoso-Aparicio, L., Noguez, J., Montesinos, L., & García-García, J. A. (2021). Machine learning and deep learning predictive models for type 2 diabetes: A systematic review. *Diabetology & Metabolic Syndrome*, *13*(1), 1–22. doi:10.118613098-021-00767-9 PMID:34930452

Friday, N. H., Al-garadi, M. A., Mujtaba, G., Alo, U. R., & Waqas, A. (2018, March). Deep learning fusion conceptual frameworks for complex human activity recognition using mobile and wearable sensors. In *2018 International Conference on Computing, Mathematics and Engineering Technologies (iCoMET)* (pp. 1-7). IEEE. 10.1109/ICOMET.2018.8346364

G. M., V., Ravi, S., V., G. E. A. & S., K.P. (2023, August). Explainable Deep Learning-Based Approach for Multilabel Classification of Electrocardiogram. *IEEE Transactions on Engineering Management*, *70*(8), 2787–2799. doi:10.1109/TEM.2021.3104751

Ganesh, D., Kumar, T. P., & Kumar, M. S. (2021). Optimised Levenshtein centroid cross-layer defence for multi-hop cognitive radio networks. *IET Communications*, *15*(2), 245–256. doi:10.1049/cmu2.12050

Ganie, S. M., & Malik, M. B. (2022). An ensemble machine learning approach for predicting type-II diabetes mellitus based on lifestyle indicators. *Healthcare Analytics*, *2*, 100092. doi:10.1016/j.health.2022.100092

Gans-Combe, C. (2022). Automated Justice: Issues, Benefits and Risks in the Use of Artificial Intelligence and Its Algorithms in Access to Justice and Law Enforcement. In D. O'Mathúna & R. Iphofen (Eds.), *Ethics, Integrity and Policymaking: The Value of the Case Study* (pp. 175–194). Springer International Publishing. doi:10.1007/978-3-031-15746-2_14

García-Garví, A., Layana-Castro, P. E., & Sánchez-Salmerón, A. J. (2023). Analysis of a C. elegans lifespan prediction method based on a bimodal neural network and uncertainty estimation. *Computational and Structural Biotechnology Journal*, *21*, 655–664. doi:10.1016/j.csbj.2022.12.033 PMID:36659931

Garreau, D. (2023). Theoretical analysis of LIME. In J. Benois-Pineau, R. Bourqui, D. Petkovic, & G. Quénot (Eds.), *Explainable Deep Learning AI* (pp. 293–316). Academic Press. doi:10.1016/B978-0-32-396098-4.00020-X

Gaspars-Wieloch, H. (2021). The assignment problem in human resource project management under uncertainty. *Risks*, *9*(1), 1–17. doi:10.3390/risks9010025

Gautam, V., Gaurav, A., Masand, N., Lee, V. S., & Patil, V. M. (2023). Artificial intelligence and machine-learning approaches in structure and ligand-based discovery of drugs affecting central nervous system. *Molecular Diversity*, *27*(2), 959–985. doi:10.100711030-022-10489-3 PMID:35819579

Gerhards, R., Andujar Sanchez, D., Hamouz, P., Peteinatos, G. G., Christensen, S., & Fernandez-Quintanilla, C. (2022). Advances in site-specific weed management in agriculture—A review. *Weed Research*, *62*(2), 123–133. doi:10.1111/wre.12526

González, D. P., Borda, D. C., Mele, F. D., Sarmiento, A. B., & Santiago, M. D. (2020). An optimization approach for the design and planning of the oil palm supply chain in Colombia. *Computers & Chemical Engineering*, *107208*. doi:10.1016/j.compchemeng.2020.107208

Goparaju, L., Prasad, R. C. P., Babu Suresh, K. V., & Tecimen, H. B. (2023). Editorial: Forest fire emissions and their impact on global climate change. *Frontiers in Forests and Global Change*, *6*, 1188632. doi:10.3389/ffgc.2023.1188632

Gopi, P. S. S., & Karthikeyan, M. (2023). Red fox optimization with ensemble recurrent neural network for crop recommendation and yield prediction model. *Multimedia Tools and Applications*, 1–21. doi:10.100711042-023-16113-2

Gothi, M., Patel, R. G., & Patel, B. S. (2023). Optimal solution to the assignment problem. *Annals of Mathematics and Computer Science*, *16*, 112–122. https://annalsmcs.org/index.php/amcs/article/view/183

Gowtham, R., & Jebakumar, R. (2023, February). A Machine Learning Approach for Aeroponic Lettuce Crop Growth Monitoring System. In *International Conference on Intelligent Sustainable Systems* (pp. 99-116). Singapore: Springer Nature Singapore. 10.1007/978-981-99-1726-6_9

Gowtham, R., & Jebakumar, R. (2022). AN IOT BASED PLANT LEAF DISEASE DETECTION USING MACHINE LEARNING AND AUTO SPRAYING MECHANISM. *Journal of Positive School Psychology*, 283–297.

Gowtham, R., & Jebakumar, R. (2023, March). Analysis and Prediction of Lettuce Crop Yield in Aeroponic Vertical Farming using Logistic Regression Method. In *2023 International Conference on Sustainable Computing and Data Communication Systems (ICSCDS)* (pp. 759-764). IEEE. 10.1109/ICSCDS56580.2023.10104763

Gray Group International. (2023). *Revolutionizing Personalized Learning: How Is AI Changing Education?* GGI. https://www.graygroupintl.com/blog/how-is-ai-changing-education

Greden, J. F., Parikh, S. V., Rothschild, A. J., Thase, M. E., Dunlop, B. W., DeBattista, C., Conway, C. R., Forester, B. P., Mondimore, F. M., Shelton, R. C., Macaluso, M., Li, J., Brown, K., Gilbert, A., Burns, L., Jablonski, M. R., & Dechairo, B. (2019). Impact of pharmacogenomics on clinical outcomes in major depressive disorder in the GUIDED trial: A large, patient- and rater-blinded, randomized, controlled study. *Journal of Psychiatric Research*, *111*, 59–67. doi:10.1016/j.jpsychires.2019.01.003 PMID:30677646

Grisoni, F. (2023). Chemical language models for de novo drug design: Challenges and opportunities. *Current Opinion in Structural Biology*, *79*, 102527. doi:10.1016/j.sbi.2023.102527 PMID:36738564

Guardieiro, V., Raimundo, M. M., & Poco, J. (2023). Enforcing fairness using ensemble of diverse Pareto-optimal models. *Data Mining and Knowledge Discovery*, *37*(5), 1930–1958. doi:10.100710618-023-00922-y

Gugliette, D., Conedera, M., Mazzoleni, S., & Ricotta, C. (2011). Mapping fire ignition risk in a complex anthropogenic landscape. *Remote Sensing Letters*, *2*(3), 213–219. doi:10.1080/01431161.2010.512927

Gupta, V. (2022). *AI ethics: 5 key pillars*. The Enterprisers Project. https://enterprisersproject.com/article/2022/11/ai-ethics-5-key-pillars

Gupta, A., Verma, A., & Pramanik, S. (2022). Security Aspects in Advanced Image Processing Techniques for COVID-19. In S. Pramanik, A. Sharma, S. Bhatia, & D. N. Le (Eds.), *An Interdisciplinary Approach to Modern Network Security*. CRC Press.

Gupta, N. S., & Kumar, P. (2023). Perspective of artificial intelligence in healthcare data management: A journey towards precision medicine. *Computers in Biology and Medicine, 162*(April), 107051. doi:10.1016/j.compbiomed.2023.107051 PMID:37271113

Hadap, A., Pandey, A., Jain, B., & Rawat, R. (2023). Theories methods and the parameters of quantitative structure–activity relationships and artificial neural network. In D. K. Verma, C. Verma, & J. Aslam (Eds.), *Computational Modeling and Simulations for Designing of Corrosion Inhibitors* (pp. 319–335)., doi:10.1016/B978-0-323-95161-6.00019-9

Haidar, A., Ahajjam, T., Zeroual, I., & Farhaoui, Y. (2022). Application of machine learning algorithms for predicting outcomes of accident cases in Moroccan courts. *Indonesian Journal of Electrical Engineering and Computer Science, 26*(2), 2. doi:10.11591/ijeecs.v26.i2.pp1103-1108

Han, R., Xiong, H., Ye, Z., Yang, Y., Huang, T., Jing, Q., Lu, J., Pan, H., Ren, F., & Ouyang, D. (2019). Predicting physical stability of solid dispersions by machine learning techniques. *Journal of Controlled Release, 311-312*, 16–25. doi:10.1016/j.jconrel.2019.08.030 PMID:31465824

Hansen, M. C., Potapov, P. V., Moore, R., Hancher, M., Turubanova, S. A., Tyukavina, A., Thau, D., Stehman, S. V., Goetz, S. J., Loveland, T. R., Kommareddy, A., Egorov, A., Chini, L., Justice, C. O., & Townshend, J. R. G. (2013). High-Resolution Global Maps of 21st-Century Forest Cover Change. *Science, 342*(6160), 850–853. doi:10.1126cience.1244693 PMID:24233722

Han, X., Zhang, Z., Ding, N., Gu, Y., Liu, X., Huo, Y., Qiu, J., Yao, Y., Zhang, A., Zhang, L., Han, W., Huang, M., Jin, Q., Lan, Y., Liu, Y., Liu, Z., Lu, Z., Qiu, X., Song, R., & Zhu, J. (2021). Pre-trained models: Past, present and future. *AI Open, 2*, 225–250. doi:10.1016/j.aiopen.2021.08.002

Haridasan, A., Thomas, J., & Raj, E. D. (2023). Deep learning system for paddy plant disease detection and classification. *Environmental Monitoring and Assessment, 195*(1), 120. doi:10.100710661-022-10656-x PMID:36399232

Hegedűs, C., Frankó, A., Varga, P., Gindl, S., & Tauber, M. (2023, May). Enabling Scalable Smart Vertical Farming with IoT and Machine Learning Technologies. In *NOMS 2023-2023 IEEE/IFIP Network Operations and Management Symposium* (pp. 1-4). IEEE. 10.1109/NOMS56928.2023.10154269

Helfer, G. A., Barbosa, J. L. V., Alves, D., da Costa, A. B., Beko, M., & Leithardt, V. R. Q. (2021). Multispectral cameras and machine learning integrated into portable devices as clay prediction technology. *Journal of Sensor and Actuator Networks, 10*(3), 40. doi:10.3390/jsan10030040

Helfer, G. A., Barbosa, J. L. V., dos Santos, R., & da Costa, A. B. (2020). A computational model for soil fertility prediction in ubiquitous agriculture. *Computers and Electronics in Agriculture, 175*, 105602. doi:10.1016/j.compag.2020.105602

Henderson, M., Ryan, T., & Phillips, M. (2019). The challenges of feedback in higher education. *Assessment & Evaluation in Higher Education, 44*(8), 1237–1252. doi:10.1080/02602938.2019.1599815

Hernández-Morcillo, M., Torralba, M., Baiges, T., Bernasconi, A., Bottaro, G., Brogaard, S., Bussola, F., Díaz-Varela, E., Geneletti, D., Grossmann, C. M., Kister, J., Klingler, M., Loft, L., Lovric, M., Mann, C., Pipart, N., Roces-Díaz, J. V., Sorge, S., Tiebel, M., & Plieninger, T. (2022). Scanning the solutions for the sustainable supply of forest ecosystem services in Europe. *Sustainability Science, 17*(5), 2013–2029. doi:10.100711625-022-01111-4 PMID:35340343

Herzel, A., Ruzika, S., & Thielen, C. (2021). Approximation Methods for Multiobjective Optimization Problems: A Survey. [IJOC]. *INFORMS Journal on Computing*, ijoc.2020.1028. Advance online publication. doi:10.1287/ijoc.2020.1028

He, S., Leanse, L. G., & Feng, Y. (2021). Artificial intelligence and machine learning assisted drug delivery for effective treatment of infectious diseases. *Advanced Drug Delivery Reviews, 178*, 113922. doi:10.1016/j.addr.2021.113922 PMID:34461198

Hirata, A., Oda, T., Saito, N., Kanahara, K., Hirota, M., & Katayama, K. (2020, October). Approach of a solution construction method for mesh router placement optimization problem. In *2020 IEEE 9th Global Conference on Consumer Electronics (GCCE) (pp. 467-468)*. IEEE. 10.1109/GCCE50665.2020.9291943

Hodhod, R., Wang, S., & Khan, S. (2018). Cybersecurity Curriculum Development Using AI and Decision Support Expert System. *International Journal of Computer Theory and Engineering, 10*(4), 111–115. doi:10.7763/IJCTE.2018.V10.1209

Holmes, W., Porayska-Pomsta, K., Holstein, K., Sutherland, E., Baker, T., Shum, S. B., Santos, O. C., Rodrigo, M. T., Cukurova, M., Bittencourt, I. I., & Koedinger, K. R. (2022). Ethics of AI in Education: Towards a Community-Wide Framework. *International Journal of Artificial Intelligence in Education, 32*(3), 504–526. doi:10.100740593-021-00239-1

Huang, J., Saleh, S., & Liu, Y. (2021). A Review on Artificial Intelligence in Education. *Academic Journal of Interdisciplinary Studies, 10*(3), 206. doi:10.36941/ajis-2021-0077

Hussain, R. J., & Kumar, P. S. (2012c, July). The transportation problem with the aid of triangular intuitionistic fuzzy numbers. In *International Conference on MMASC Conf. Vol. 1* (pp. 819-825). Shanga Verlag.

Hussain, R. J., & Kumar, P. S. (2012a). The transportation problem in an intuitionistic fuzzy environment. [IJMR]. *International Journal of Mathematics Research, 4*(4), 411–420.

Hussain, R. J., & Kumar, P. S. (2012b). Algorithmic approach for solving intuitionistic fuzzy transportation problem. [AMS]. *Applied Mathematical Sciences, 6*(77-80), 3981–3989.

Hussain, R. J., & Kumar, P. S. (2013). An optimal more-for-less solution of mixed constraints intuitionistic fuzzy transportation problems. [IJCMS]. *International Journal of Contemporary Mathematical Sciences, 8*(12), 565–576. doi:10.12988/ijcms.2013.13056

Hussein, H. A., & Shiker, M. A. K. (2020). Two new effective methods to find the optimal solution for the assignment problems. [JARDCS]. *Jour of Adv Research in Dynamical & Control Systems, 12*(7), 49–54. doi:10.5373/JARDCS/V12I7/20201983

Hu, Y., & Liu, Q. (2021). A network flow algorithm for solving generalized assignment problem. *Mathematical Problems in Engineering, 2021*, 1–8. doi:10.1155/2021/5803092

Ihnaini, B., Khan, M. A., Khan, T. A., Abbas, S., Daoud, M. S., Ahmad, M., & Khan, M. A. (2021). A smart healthcare recommendation system for multidisciplinary diabetes patients with data fusion based on deep ensemble learning. *Computational Intelligence and Neuroscience, 2021*, 2021. doi:10.1155/2021/4243700 PMID:34567101

Ingle, S. M., & Ghadle, K. P. (2019). Optimal solution for fuzzy assignment problem and applications. *Computing in Engineering and Technology*, 155–164. doi:10.1007/978-981-32-9515-5_15

Islam, N., Rashid, M. M., Pasandideh, F., Ray, B., Moore, S., & Kadel, R. (2021). A review of applications and communication technologies for internet of things (Iot) and unmanned aerial vehicle (uav) based sustainable smart farming. *Sustainability (Basel), 13*(4), 1821. doi:10.3390u13041821

Jagtap, S. T., Phasinam, K., Kassanuk, T., Jha, S. S., Ghosh, T., & Thakar, C. M. (2022). Towards application of various machine learning techniques in agriculture. *Materials Today: Proceedings, 51*, 793–797. doi:10.1016/j.matpr.2021.06.236

Jain, I., Jain, V. K., & Jain, R. (2018). Correlation feature selection based improved-Binary Particle Swarm Optimization for gene selection and cancer classification. *Applied Soft Computing, 62*, 203–215. doi:10.1016/j.asoc.2017.09.038

Jamali, A. J. U., Mondal, R. R., & Reza, A. S. (2019). *Weighted cost opportunity based algorithm for unbalanced transportation problem*. Proceedings of the 5th International Conference on Engineering Research, Innovation and Education, Sylhet, Bangladesh.

Jariwala, N., Putta, C. L., Gatade, K., Umarji, M., Ruhina Rahman, S. N., Pawde, D. M., Sree, A., Kamble, A. S., Goswami, A., Chakraborty, P., & Shunmugaperumal, T. (2023). Intriguing of pharmaceutical product development processes with the help of artificial intelligence and deep/machine learning or artificial neural network. *Journal of Drug Delivery Science and Technology*, *87*, 104751. doi:10.1016/j.jddst.2023.104751

Jarrahi, M. H., Askay, D., Eshraghi, A., & Smith, P. (2023). Artificial intelligence and knowledge management: A partnership between human and AI. *Business Horizons*, *66*(1), 87–99. doi:10.1016/j.bushor.2022.03.002

Javaid, M., Haleem, A., Khan, I. H., & Suman, R. (2023). Understanding the potential applications of Artificial Intelligence in the Agriculture Sector. *Advanced Agrochem*, *2*(1), 15–30. doi:10.1016/j.aac.2022.10.001

Javaid, M., & Khan, I. H. (2021). Internet of Things (IoT) enabled healthcare helps to take the challenges of COVID-19 Pandemic. *Journal of Oral Biology and Craniofacial Research*, *11*(2), 209–214. doi:10.1016/j.jobcr.2021.01.015 PMID:33665069

JavaTPoint. (2021). *Artificial Intelligence in Education*. Javatpoint. https://www.javatpoint.com/artificial-intelligence-in-education

Javidan, S. M., Banakar, A., Vakilian, K. A., & Ampatzidis, Y. (2023). Tomato leaf diseases classification using image processing and weighted ensemble learning. *Agronomy Journal*, agj2.21293. doi:10.1002/agj2.21293

Jayalakshmi, M. (2016). A new approach for solving balanced and/or unbalanced intuitionistic fuzzy assignment problems. [RJPT]. *Research Journal of Pharmacy and Technology*, *9*(12), 2382–2388. doi:10.5958/0974-360X.2016.00477.7

Jayalakshmi, M., Anuradha, D., Kavitha, K., Sobana, V. E., & Kaspar, S. (2020). Study on assignment problem. [JCR]. *Journal of Critical Reviews*, *7*(19), 4764–4768. doi:10.31838/jcr.07.19.557

Jayasingh, R. (2022). Speckle noise removal by SORAMA segmentation in Digital Image Processing to facilitate precise robotic surgery. *International Journal of Reliable and Quality E-Healthcare*, *11*(1), 1–19. doi:10.4018/IJRQEH.295083

Jiang Y. (2023). IEMS: An IoT-Empowered Wearable Multimodal Monitoring System in Neurocritical Care. *IEEE Internet of Things Journal, 10*(2), 1860-1875. . doi:10.1109/JIOT.2022.3210930

Jiang, J., Lu, A., Ma, X., Ouyang, D., & Williams, R. O. III. (2023). The applications of machine learning to predict the forming of chemically stable amorphous solid dispersions prepared by hot-melt extrusion. *International Journal of Pharmaceutics: X*, *5*, 100164. doi:10.1016/j.ijpx.2023.100164 PMID:36798832

Jiang, W., Majumder, S., Kumar, S., Subramaniam, S., Li, X., Khedri, R., Mondal, T., Abolghasemian, M., Satia, I., & Deen, M. J. (2022). A Wearable Tele-Health System towards Monitoring COVID-19 and Chronic Diseases. *IEEE Reviews in Biomedical Engineering*, *15*, 61–84. doi:10.1109/RBME.2021.3069815 PMID:33784625

JiangZ.ZhaoL.LiS.JiaY. (2020). Real-time object detection method based on improved YOLOv4-tiny. arXiv:2011.04244

Jian, Y., Pasquier, M., Sagahyroon, A., & Aloul, F. (2021, December). A machine learning approach to predicting diabetes complications. []. MDPI.]. *Health Care*, *9*(12), 1712. PMID:34946438

Jiao, P., Ouyang, F., Zhang, Q., & Alavi, A. H. (2022). Artificial intelligence-enabled prediction model of student academic performance in online engineering education. *Artificial Intelligence Review*, *55*(8), 6321–6344. doi:10.100710462-022-10155-y

Jobin, A., Ienca, M., & Vayena, E. (2019). The global landscape of AI ethics guidelines. *Nature Machine Intelligence*, *1*(9), 9. doi:10.103842256-019-0088-2

JocherG.ChangyuL.HoganA.YuL.RaiP.SullivanT. (2020). Ultralytics/yolov5: Initial Release (v1.0). Zenodo. doi:10.5281/zenodo.3908560

Johannsen, S., Gierse, R. M., Olshanova, A., Smerznak, E., Laggner, C., Eschweiler, L., & Reiling, N. (2023). Not every hit-identification technique works on 1-deoxy-d-xylulose 5-phosphate synthase (DXPS): Making the most of a virtual screening campaign. *ChemMedChem*, 202200590(11), e202200590. doi:10.1002/cmdc.202200590 PMID:36896721

Jones, V.K. (2018). Voice-activated change: Marketing in the age of artificial intelligence and virtual assistants. *Journal of Brand Strategy, 7*(3), 233-245.

Josephine, F. S., Saranya, A., & Nishandhi, I. F. (2020). A dynamic method for solving intuitionistic fuzzy transportation problem. [EJMCM]. *European Journal of Molecular and Clinical Medicine, 7*(11), 5843–5854.

Joy, S. I., Kumar, K. S., Palanivelan, M., & Lakshmi, D. (2023). Review on Advent of Artificial Intelligence in Electro-cardiogram for the Detection of Extra-Cardiac and Cardiovascular Disease. *Canadian Journal of Electrical and Computer Engineering, 46*(2), 99–106. doi:10.1109/ICJECE.2022.3228588

Ju, S., Lim, H., & Heo, J. (2020, January). Machine learning approaches for crop yield prediction with MODIS and weather data. In *40th Asian Conference on Remote Sensing: Progress of Remote Sensing Technology for Smart Future, ACRS 2019*.

K. Kazi. Lassar Methodology for Network Intrusion Detection. *Scholarly Research Journal for Humanity science and English Language*, 2017, Vol 4, Issue 24, pp.6853 - 6861.

Kaku, K., Nakayama, Y., Yabuuchi, J., Naito, Y., & Kanasaki, K. (2023). Safety and effectiveness of empagliflozin in clinical practice as monotherapy or with other glucose-lowering drugs in Japanese patients with type 2 diabetes: Subgroup analysis of a 3-year postmarketing surveillance study. *Expert Opinion on Drug Safety, 22*(9), 819–832. doi:10.1080/14740338.2023.2213477 PMID:37194266

Kalhoro, H. B., Abdulrehman, H., Shaikh, M. M., & Soomro, A. S. (2021). The maximum range column method – going beyond the traditional initial basic feasible solution methods for the transportation problems. [JMCMS]. *Journal of Mechanics of Continua and Mathematical Sciences, 16*(1), 74–86. doi:10.26782/jmcms.2021.01.00006

Kalichkin, V. K., Alsova, O. K., & Maksimovich, K. Y. (2021, September). Application of the decision tree method for predicting the yield of spring wheat. []. IOP Publishing]. *IOP Conference Series. Earth and Environmental Science, 839*(3), 032042. doi:10.1088/1755-1315/839/3/032042

Kalmkar, S., Mujawar, A., & Liyakat, D. K. K. S. (2022). 3D E-Commers using AR. *International Journal of Information Technology & Computer Engineering, 2*(6), 18–27. doi:10.55529/ijitc.26.18.27

Kamuni. (2022). Fruit Quality Detection using Thermometer. *Journal of Image Processing and Intelligent Remote Sensing, 2*(5).

Kanagajothi, D., & Kumar, B. R. (2022, November). Reduce the optimal cost on single valued neutrosophic transportation model. In. AIP Conference Proceedings: Vol. 2516. *No. 1* (p. 200004). AIP Publishing LLC. doi:10.1063/5.0108862

Karabulut, M., Karakoc, A., Gurbuz, M., & Kizilelma, Y. (2013). Determination of forest fire risk areas using geo-graphicalinformation systems in Baskonus Mountain (Kahramanmaras). *The Journal of International Social Research, 6*(24), 171–179.

Karboub, K., Tabaa, M., Monteiro, F., Dellagi, S., Moutaouakkil, F., & Dandache, A. (2021). Automated Diagnosis System for Outpatients and Inpatients with Cardiovascular Diseases. *IEEE Sensors Journal, 21*(2), 1935-1946. . doi:10.1109/JSEN.2020.3019668

Kar, R., & Shaw, A. K. (2020). A new approach to find optimal solution of assignment problem using Hungarian method by triangular fuzzy data. [MESA]. *Mathematics in Engineering. Science and Aerospace, 11*(4), 1059–1074.

Kar, R., Shaw, A. K., & Das, B. (2020). Alternative approach to find optimal solution of assignment problem using Hungarian method by trapezoidal intuitionistic type-2 fuzzy data. [AOTP]. *Annals of Optimization Theory and Practice, 3*(3), 155–173. doi:10.22121/AOTP.2020.257124.1055

Kasture, K., & Shende, P. (2023). Amalgamation of artificial intelligence with nanoscience for biomedical applications. *Archives of Computational Methods in Engineering, 30*(8), 4667–4685. doi:10.100711831-023-09948-3

Katiyar, S. (2022). The use of pesticide management using artificial intelligence. In *Artificial Intelligence Applications in Agriculture and Food Quality Improvement* (pp. 74–94). IGI Global. doi:10.4018/978-1-6684-5141-0.ch005

Katz, D. M., Bommarito, M. J., & Blackman, J. (2017). A general approach for predicting the behavior of the Supreme Court of the United States. *PLoS One, 12*(4), e0174698. doi:10.1371/journal.pone.0174698 PMID:28403140

Kaur, P., Dahiya, K., & Verma, V. (2020). *Time-cost trade-off analysis of a priority based assignment problem* [OPSE]. OPSEARCH. doi:10.100712597-020-00483-4

Kazemi, Z., Safavi, A. A., Pouresmaeeli, S., & Naseri, F. (2019). A practical framework for implementing multivariate monitoring techniques into distributed control system. *Control Engineering Practice, 82*, 118–129. doi:10.1016/j.conengprac.2018.10.003

Kazi. Model for Agricultural Information system to improve crop yield using IoT. *Journal of open Source Development,* 2022, Vol 9, Issue 2, pp. 16 – 24.

Kazi, K. (2022). Smart Grid energy saving technique using Machine Learning. *Journal of Instrumentation Technology and Innovations, 12*(3), 1–10.

Kazi, K. (2022). *Systematic Survey on Alzheimer (AD).* Diseases Detection.

Kazi, K. S. (2023). IoT based Healthcare system for Home Quarantine People. *Journal of Instrumentation and Innovation Sciences, 8*(1), 1–8.

Kazi, S. L. (2018). Significance of Projection and Rotation of Image in Color Matching for High-Quality Panoramic Images used for Aquatic study. *International Journal of Aquatic Science, 09*(02), 130–145.

Keita, Z. (2022). *YOLO object detection, its benefits.* DataCamp. https://www.datacamp.com/blog/yolo-object-detection-explained

Kelly, B. S., Kirwan, A., Quinn, M. S., Kelly, A. M., Mathur, P., Lawlor, A., & Killeen, R. P. (2023). The ethical matrix as a method for involving people living with disease and the wider public (PPI) in near-term artificial intelligence research. *Radiography, 29*, S103–S111. doi:10.1016/j.radi.2023.03.009 PMID:37062673

Khadela, A., Popat, S., Ajabiya, J., Valu, D., Savale, S., & Chavda, V. P. (2023). AI, ML and other bioinformatics tools for preclinical and clinical development of drug products. In Bioinformatics Tools for Pharmaceutical Drug Product Development (pp. 255-284). Wiley. doi:10.1002/9781119865728.ch12

Khaki, S., & Wang, L. (2019). Crop yield prediction using deep neural networks. *Frontiers in Plant Science, 10*, 621. doi:10.3389/fpls.2019.00621 PMID:31191564

Khaki, S., Wang, L., & Archontoulis, S. V. (2020). A cnn-rnn framework for crop yield prediction. *Frontiers in Plant Science, 10*, 1750. doi:10.3389/fpls.2019.01750 PMID:32038699

Khalifa, H. (2020). A novel approach for optimization of transportation problem in chaos environment. [IJTE]. *International Journal of Transportation Engineering, 8*(1), 107–114.

Khalifa, H., Elhenawy, M., Masoud, M., Bhuiyan, H., & Sabar, N. R. (2021). On Multi-Objective Multi-Item Solid Transportation Problem in Fuzzy Environment. [JACM]. *International Journal of Applied and Computational Mathematics, 7*(1), 1–16. doi:10.100740819-021-00961-3

Khan. (2022). Role of Artificial Intelligence in insect and pest management. *Just Agriculture*, pp.19-23.

Khan, M. A., Alqahtani, A., Khan, A., Alsubai, S., Binbusayyis, A., Ch, M. M. I., Yong, H.-S., & Cha, J. (2022). Cucumber leaf diseases recognition using multi level deep entropy-ELM feature selection. *Applied Sciences (Basel, Switzerland), 12*(2), 593. doi:10.3390/app12020593

Khan, M. A., Iqbal, N., Jamil, H., & Kim, D. H. (2023). An optimized ensemble prediction model using AutoML based on soft voting classifier for network intrusion detection. *Journal of Network and Computer Applications, 212*, 103560. doi:10.1016/j.jnca.2022.103560

Khan, R. U., Khan, K., Albattah, W., & Qamar, A. M. (2021). Image-based detection of plant diseases: From classical machine learning to deep learning journey. *Wireless Communications and Mobile Computing, 2021*, 1–13. doi:10.1155/2021/5541859

Khan, S. R., Al Rijjal, D., Piro, A., & Wheeler, M. B. (2021). Integration of AI and traditional medicine in drug discovery. *Drug Discovery Today, 26*(4), 982–992. doi:10.1016/j.drudis.2021.01.008 PMID:33476566

Khojaste-Sarakhsi, M., Haghighi, S. S., Ghomi, S. M. T. F., & Marchiori, E. (2022). Deep learning for Alzheimer's disease diagnosis: A survey. *Artificial Intelligence in Medicine, 130*(June), 102332. doi:10.1016/j.artmed.2022.102332 PMID:35809971

Kibria, H. B., Nahiduzzaman, M., Goni, M. O. F., Ahsan, M., & Haider, J. (2022). An ensemble approach for the prediction of diabetes mellitus using a soft voting classifier with an explainable AI. *Sensors (Basel), 22*(19), 7268. doi:10.339022197268 PMID:36236367

Klimova, B., Pikhart, M., & Kacetl, J. (2023). Ethical issues of the use of AI-driven mobile apps for education. *Frontiers in Public Health, 10*, 1118116. https://www.frontiersin.org/articles/10.3389/fpubh.2022.1118116. doi:10.3389/fpubh.2022.1118116 PMID:36711343

Knox, J. (2020). Artificial intelligence and education in China. *Learning, Media and Technology, 45*(3), 298–311. doi:10.1080/17439884.2020.1754236

Kondaveeti, H. K., Ujini, K. G., Pavankumar, B. V. V., Tarun, B. S., & Gopi, S. C. 2023, March. Plant Disease Detection Using Ensemble Learning. In *2023 2nd International Conference on Computational Systems and Communication (ICCSC)* (pp. 1-6). IEEE. 10.1109/ICCSC56913.2023.10142982

Kooli, C. (2023). Chatbots in Education and Research: A Critical Examination of Ethical Implications and Solutions. *Sustainability (Basel), 15*(7), 7. doi:10.3390u15075614

Kootstra, G., Wang, X., Blok, P. M., Hemming, J., & Van Henten, E. (2021). Selective harvesting robotics: Current research, trends, and future directions. *Current Robotics Reports, 2*(1), 95–104. doi:10.100743154-020-00034-1

Kour, V. P., & Arora, S. (2020). Recent developments of the internet of things in agriculture: A survey. *IEEE Access : Practical Innovations, Open Solutions, 8*, 129924–129957. doi:10.1109/ACCESS.2020.3009298

Krishnan, M. (2020). Against Interpretability: A Critical Examination of the Interpretability Problem in Machine Learning. *Philosophy & Technology, 33*(3), 487–502. doi:10.100713347-019-00372-9

Kuhn, H. W. (1955). The Hungarian method for the assignment problem. [NRL]. *Naval Research Logistics Quarterly*, *2*(1-2), 83–97. doi:10.1002/nav.3800020109

Kujawa, S., & Niedbała, G. (2021). Artificial neural networks in agriculture. *Agriculture*, *11*(6), 497. doi:10.3390/agriculture11060497

Kulkov, I. (2021). The role of artificial intelligence in business transformation: A case of pharmaceutical companies. *Technology in Society*, *66*, 101629. doi:10.1016/j.techsoc.2021.101629

Kumar V, Dixit A, Javalgi RRG, Dass M (2016) Research framework, strategies, and applications of intelligent agent technologies (IATs) in marketing. *Journal of the Academy of Marketing Science, 44*(1), 24-45.

Kumar, P. S. (2010). *A comparative study on transportation problem in fuzzy environment* [M.Phil thesis, Jamal Mohamed College, Tiruchirappalli, India].

Kumar, P. S. (2017a). PSK Method for Solving Type-1 and Type-3 Fuzzy Transportation Problems. *Fuzzy Systems*, 367–392. doi:10.4018/978-1-5225-1908-9.ch017

Kumar, P. S. (2017b). *Algorithmic approach for solving allocation problems under intuitionistic fuzzy environment* [PhD thesis]. *Jamal Mohamed College, Tiruchirappalli, India.*

Kumar, P. S. (2021). Finding the Solution of Balanced and Unbalanced Intuitionistic Fuzzy Transportation Problems by Using Different Methods With Some Software Packages. Handbook of Research on Applied AI for International Business and Marketing Applications, 278–320. IGI Global. doi:10.4018/978-1-7998-5077-9.ch015

Kumari, B., & Pandey, A. C. (2020). MODIS based forest fire hotspot analysis and its relationship with climatic variables. *Spatial Information Research*, *28*(1), 87–99. doi:10.100741324-019-00275-z

Kumar, M. S., & Harshitha, D. (2019). Process innovation methods on business process reengineering. *International Journal of Innovative Technology and Exploring Engineering*, *8*(11), 2766–2768. doi:10.35940/ijitee.K2244.0981119

Kumar, P. S. (2016a). A Simple Method for Solving Type-2 and Type-4 Fuzzy Transportation Problems. [IJFIS]. *The International Journal of Fuzzy Logic and Intelligent Systems*, *16*(4), 225–237. doi:10.5391/IJFIS.2016.16.4.225

Kumar, P. S. (2016b). PSK Method for Solving Type-1 and Type-3 Fuzzy Transportation Problems. [IJFSA]. *International Journal of Fuzzy System Applications*, *5*(4), 121–146. doi:10.4018/IJFSA.2016100106

Kumar, P. S. (2018a). Search for an Optimal Solution to Vague Traffic Problems Using the PSK Method. *Advances in Computational Intelligence and Robotics*, 219–257. doi:10.4018/978-1-5225-5396-0.ch011

Kumar, P. S. (2018b). Linear Programming Approach for Solving Balanced and Unbalanced Intuitionistic Fuzzy Transportation Problems. [IJORIS]. *International Journal of Operations Research and Information Systems*, *9*(2), 73–100. doi:10.4018/IJORIS.2018040104

Kumar, P. S. (2018c). A note on 'a new approach for solving intuitionistic fuzzy transportation problem of type-2'. [IJLSM]. *International Journal of Logistics Systems and Management, 29*(1), 102–129. doi:10.1504/IJLSM.2018.088586

Kumar, P. S. (2018d). A Simple and Efficient Algorithm for Solving Type-1 Intuitionistic Fuzzy Solid Transportation Problems. [IJORIS]. *International Journal of Operations Research and Information Systems*, *9*(3), 90–122. doi:10.4018/IJORIS.2018070105

Kumar, P. S. (2018e). PSK Method for Solving Intuitionistic Fuzzy Solid Transportation Problems. [IJFSA]. *International Journal of Fuzzy System Applications*, *7*(4), 62–99. doi:10.4018/IJFSA.2018100104

Kumar, P. S. (2019a). PSK method for solving mixed and type-4 intuitionistic fuzzy solid transportation problems. [IJORIS]. *International Journal of Operations Research and Information Systems*, *10*(2), 20–53. doi:10.4018/IJORIS.2019040102

Kumar, P. S. (2019b). Intuitionistic fuzzy solid assignment problems: A software-based approach. [IJSA]. *International Journal of System Assurance Engineering and Management*, *10*(4), 661–675. doi:10.100713198-019-00794-w

Kumar, P. S. (2020a). Intuitionistic fuzzy zero point method for solving type-2 intuitionistic fuzzy transportation problem. [IJOR]. *International Journal of Operational Research*, *37*(3), 418–451. doi:10.1504/IJOR.2020.105446

Kumar, P. S. (2020b). The PSK Method for Solving Fully Intuitionistic Fuzzy Assignment Problems With Some Software Tools. *Advances in Business Strategy and Competitive Advantage*, 149–202. doi:10.4018/978-1-5225-8458-2.ch009

Kumar, P. S. (2020c). Algorithms for solving the optimization problems using fuzzy and intuitionistic fuzzy set. [IJSA]. *International Journal of System Assurance Engineering and Management*, *11*(1), 189–222. doi:10.100713198-019-00941-3

Kumar, P. S. (2020d). Developing a new approach to solve solid assignment problems under intuitionistic fuzzy environment. [IJFSA]. *International Journal of Fuzzy System Applications*, *9*(1), 1–34. doi:10.4018/IJFSA.2020010101

Kumar, P. S. (2022). Computationally simple and efficient method for solving real-life mixed intuitionistic fuzzy 3D assignment problems. [IJSSCI]. *International Journal of Software Science and Computational Intelligence*. doi:10.4018/IJSSCI.291715

Kumar, P. S. (2023a). The PSK method: A new and efficient approach to solving fuzzy transportation problems. In *Transport and Logistics Planning and Optimization* (pp. 149–197). IGI Global. doi:10.4018/978-1-6684-8474-6.ch007

Kumar, P. S. (2023b). The theory and applications of the software-based PSK method for solving intuitionistic fuzzy solid transportation problems. In *Perspectives and Considerations on the Evolution of Smart Systems* (pp. 137–186). IGI Global. doi:10.4018/978-1-6684-7684-0.ch007

Kumar, P. S. (2023c). Algorithms and software packages for solving transportation problems with intuitionistic fuzzy numbers. In *Operational Research for Renewable Energy and Sustainable Environments*. IGI Global.

Kumar, P. S. (2024). Theory and applications of the software-based PSK method for solving intuitionistic fuzzy solid assignment problems. In *Applications of New Technology in Operations and Supply Chain Management*. IGI Global.

Kumar, P. S., & Hussain, R. J. (2014a). New algorithm for solving mixed intuitionistic fuzzy assignment problem. *Elixir Appl. Math*, *73*, 25971–25977.

Kumar, P. S., & Hussain, R. J. (2014b, July). A method for finding an optimal solution of an assignment problem under mixed intuitionistic fuzzy environment. In *ICMS Conf.* (pp. 417-421). Elsevier.

Kumar, P. S., & Hussain, R. J. (2014c). A method for solving balanced intuitionistic fuzzy assignment problem. [IJERA]. *International Journal of Engineering Research and Applications*, *4*(3), 897–903.

Kumar, P. S., & Hussain, R. J. (2014d). A systematic approach for solving mixed intuitionistic fuzzy transportation problems. [IJPAM]. *International Journal of Pure and Applied Mathematics*, *92*(2), 181–190. doi:10.12732/ijpam.v92i2.4

Kumar, P. S., & Hussain, R. J. (2015). A method for solving unbalanced intuitionistic fuzzy transportation problems. [NIFS]. *Notes on Intuitionistic Fuzzy Sets*, *21*(3), 54–65.

Kumar, P. S., & Hussain, R. J. (2016a). An algorithm for solving unbalanced intuitionistic fuzzy assignment problem using triangular intuitionistic fuzzy number. *The Journal of Fuzzy Mathematics*, *24*(2), 289–302.

Kumar, P. S., & Hussain, R. J. (2016b). A simple method for solving fully intuitionistic fuzzy real life assignment problem. [IJORIS]. *International Journal of Operations Research and Information Systems, 7*(2), 39–61. doi:10.4018/IJORIS.2016040103

Kumar, P. S., & Hussain, R. J. (2016c). Computationally simple approach for solving fully intuitionistic fuzzy real life transportation problems. [IJSA]. *International Journal of System Assurance Engineering and Management, 7*(S1, Suppl 1), 90–101. doi:10.100713198-014-0334-2

Kumtole, S. (2022). Automatic wall painting robot Automatic wall painting robot. *Journal of Image Processing and Intelligent remote sensing, 2*(6).

Kuska, M. T., & Mahlein, A. K. (2018). Aiming at decision making in plant disease protection and phenotyping by the use of optical sensors. *European Journal of Plant Pathology, 152*(4), 987–992. doi:10.100710658-018-1464-1

Kuter, S., Usul, N., & Kuter, N. (2011). Bandwidth determination forkernel density analysis of wildfire events at forest sub-districtscale. *Ecological Modelling, 222*(17), 3033–3040. doi:10.1016/j.ecolmodel.2011.06.006

Kyro, G. W., Brent, R. I., & Batista, V. S. (2023). HAC-Net: A hybrid attention-based convolutional neural network for highly accurate protein–ligand binding affinity prediction. *Journal of Chemical Information and Modeling, 63*(7), 1947–1960. doi:10.1021/acs.jcim.3c00251 PMID:36988912

Lagare, R. B., Huang, Y. S., Bush, C. O. J., Young, K. L., Rosario, A. C. A., Gonzalez, M., Mort, P., Nagy, Z. K., & Reklaitis, G. V. (2023). Developing a virtual flowability sensor for monitoring a pharmaceutical dry granulation line. *Journal of Pharmaceutical Sciences, 112*(5), 1427–1439. doi:10.1016/j.xphs.2023.01.009 PMID:36649791

Lebedeva, O. A., & Poltavskaya, J. O. (2020, December). Cost optimization of intermodal freight transportation in the transport network. In Journal of Physics: Conference Series (Vol. 1680, No. 1, p. 012033). IOP Publishing. doi:10.1088/1742-6596/1680/1/012033

Lee, R.S. (2013). Vertical integration and exclusivity in platform and two-sided markets. *American Economic Review, 103*(7), 2960-3000.

Lee, J., Yoon, H., Lee, Y. J., Kim, T. Y., Bahn, G., Kim, Y. H., Lim, J.-M., Park, S.-W., Song, Y.-S., Kim, M.-S., & Beck, B. R. (2023). Drug–target interaction deep learning-based model identifies the flavonoid troxerutin as a candidate TRPV1 antagonist. *Applied Sciences (Basel, Switzerland), 13*(9), 5617. doi:10.3390/app13095617

Leela, M., Helenprabha, K., & Sharmila, L. (2023). Prediction and classification of Alzheimer Disease categories using Integrated Deep Transfer Learning Approach. *Measurement. Sensors, 27*(March), 100749. doi:10.1016/j.measen.2023.100749

Lee, S. U. (2015). An Assignment Problem Algorithm Using Minimum Cost Moving Method. [JKSCI]. *Journal of the Korea Society of Computer and Information, 20*(8), 105–112. doi:10.9708/jksci.2015.20.8.105

Lee, S.-Y., Huang, P.-W., Chiou, J.-R., Tsou, C., Liao, Y.-Y., & Chen, J.-Y. (2019, December). Electrocardiogram and Phonocardiogram Monitoring System for Cardiac Auscultation. *IEEE Transactions on Biomedical Circuits and Systems, 13*(6), 1471–1482. doi:10.1109/TBCAS.2019.2947694 PMID:31634841

Leslie, P. (2004). (forthcoming). Price Discrimination in Broadway Theatres, RAND Journal of Economics, 35, 3, 520-41.

Li, Y. (2023). Hybrid D1DCnet Using Forehead iPPG for Continuous and Noncontact Blood Pressure Measurement. *IEEE Sensors Journal, 23*(3), 2727-2736. . doi:10.1109/JSEN.2022.3230210

Liakos, K. G., Busato, P., Moshou, D., Pearson, S., & Bochtis, D. (2018). Machine learning in agriculture: A review. *Sensors (Basel), 18*(8), 2674. doi:10.339018082674 PMID:30110960

Li, J., Kirubarajan, T., Tharmarasa, R., Brown, D., & Pattipati, K. R. (2021). A dual approach to multi-dimensional assignment problems. *Journal of Global Optimization*, *81*(3), 1–26. doi:10.100710898-020-00988-8

Li, J., Li, J., Yang, Y., & Ren, Z. (2021). Design of Higher Education System Based on Artificial Intelligence Technology. *Discrete Dynamics in Nature and Society*, *2021*, 1–11. doi:10.1155/2021/3303160

Li, L., Zhang, S., & Wang, B. (2021). Plant disease detection and classification by deep learning—A review. *IEEE Access : Practical Innovations, Open Solutions*, *9*, 56683–56698. doi:10.1109/ACCESS.2021.3069646

Lin T.Y., Maire, M, Belongie, S, Bourdev, L, Girshick, R, Hays, J, Perona, P, Ramanan, D, Zitnick, C. L. & Dollár, P. (2015). Microsoft COCO: common objects in Context. *Computer Vision and Pattern Recognition, 2–8.*

Lin, Y., Zhang, Y., Wang, D., Yang, B., & Shen, Y.-Q. (2022). Computer especially AI-assisted drug virtual screening and design in traditional Chinese medicine. *Phytomedicine*, *107*, 154481. doi:10.1016/j.phymed.2022.154481 PMID:36215788

Liu, H., Bai, H., Jie, F., & Zhang, M. (2019). *Channel pruning for object detection network.* IET 8th International Conference on Wireless, Mobile & Multimedia Networks, Beijing, China. 10.1049/cp.2019.1157

Liu, W. (2016) *SSD: Single Shot MultiBox Detector.* arXiv. https://arxiv.org/abs/1512.02325

Liu, C., Zhang, X., Zhao, L., Liu, F., Chen, X., Yao, Y., & Li, J. (2019, April). Signal Quality Assessment and Lightweight QRS Detection for Wearable ECG SmartVest System. *IEEE Internet of Things Journal*, *6*(2), 1363–1374. doi:10.1109/JIOT.2018.2844090

Liu, J. Y. H., & Rudd, J. A. (2023). Predicting drug adverse effects using a new gastro-intestinal pacemaker activity drug database (GIPADD). *Scientific Reports*, *13*(1), 6935. doi:10.103841598-023-33655-5 PMID:37117211

Liu, J., Jia, H., Mei, M., Wang, T., Chen, S., & Li, J. (2022). Efficient degradation of diclofenac by digestate-derived biochar catalyzed peroxymonosulfate oxidation: Performance, machine learning prediction, and mechanism. *Process Safety and Environmental Protection*, *167*, 77–88. doi:10.1016/j.psep.2022.09.007

Liu, L., Subbareddy, R., & Raghavendra, C. G. (2022). AI Intelligence Chatbot to Improve Students Learning in the Higher Education Platform. *Journal of Interconnection Networks*, *22*(Supp02), 2143032. doi:10.1142/S0219265921430325

Liu, Q., Gao, C., Zhao, Y., Huang, S., Zhang, Y., Dong, X., & Lu, Z. (2023). Health warning based on 3R ECG Sample's combined features and LSTM. *Computers in Biology and Medicine*, *162*(April), 107082. doi:10.1016/j.compbiomed.2023.107082 PMID:37290388

Liu, X., Zhang, W., Tong, X., Zhong, F., Li, Z., Xiong, Z., Xiong, J., Wu, X., Fu, Z., Tan, X., Liu, Z., Zhang, S., Jiang, H., Li, X., & Zheng, M. (2023). MolFilterGAN: A progressively augmented generative adversarial network for triaging AI-designed molecules. *Journal of Cheminformatics*, *15*(1), 42. doi:10.118613321-023-00711-1 PMID:37031191

Loey, M., ElSawy, A., & Afify, M. (2020). Deep learning in plant diseases detection for agricultural crops: A survey. [IJSSMET]. *International Journal of Service Science, Management, Engineering, and Technology*, *11*(2), 41–58. doi:10.4018/IJSSMET.2020040103

Lu, A., Zhang, J., Jiang, J., Zhang, Y., Giri, B. R., Kulkarni, V. R., Aghda, N. H., Wang, J., & Maniruzzaman, M. (2022). Novel 3d printed modular tablets containing multiple anti-viral drugs: A case of high precision drop-on-demand drug deposition. *Pharmaceutical Research*, *39*(11), 2905–2918. doi:10.100711095-022-03378-9 PMID:36109460

Luini, L. & Sabbatini P. (2010) *Demand cross elasticity without substitutability: Evidence from an experiment.* Available at SSRN 1617337.

Lu, M., Yin, J., Zhu, Q., Lin, G., Mou, M., Liu, F., Pan, Z., You, N., Lian, X., Li, F., Zhang, H., Zheng, L., Zhang, W., Zhang, H., Shen, Z., Gu, Z., Li, H., & Zhu, F. (2023). Artificial Intelligence in Pharmaceutical Sciences. *Engineering (Beijing)*. Advance online publication. doi:10.1016/j.eng.2023.01.014

Luo, X., Qin, M.S., Fang, Z., & Qu, Z. (2020) Artificial Intelligence Coaches for Sales Agents: Caveats and Solutions. *Journal of Marketing*.

Lv, Q., Zhou, F., Liu, X., & Zhi, L. (2023). Artificial intelligence in small molecule drug discovery from 2018 to 2023: Does it really work? *Bioorganic Chemistry*, *141*, 106894. doi:10.1016/j.bioorg.2023.106894 PMID:37776682

Lyapin, S., Rizaeva, Y., Kadasev, D., & Kadaseva, I. (2020, November). Models for Ensuring the Minimum Arrival Time of Accident Response Services in Intelligent Transportation and Logistics System. In *2020 2nd International Conference on Control Systems, Mathematical Modeling, Automation and Energy Efficiency (SUMMA) (pp. 766-771)*. IEEE. 10.1109/SUMMA50634.2020.9280810

MacMath, D., Chen, M., & Khoury, P. (2023). Artificial Intelligence: Exploring the Future of Innovation in Allergy Immunology. *Current Allergy and Asthma Reports*, *23*(6), 351–362. doi:10.100711882-023-01084-z PMID:37160554

Macri, R., & Roberts, S. L. (2023). The use of artificial intelligence in clinical care: A values-based guide for shared decision making. *Current Oncology (Toronto, Ont.)*, *30*(2), 2178–2186. doi:10.3390/curroncol30020168 PMID:36826129

Madarász, L., Mészáros, L. A., Köte, Á., Farkas, A., & Nagy, Z. K. (2023). AI-based analysis of in-line process endoscope images for real-time particle size measurement in a continuous pharmaceutical milling process. *International Journal of Pharmaceutics*, *641*, 123060. doi:10.1016/j.ijpharm.2023.123060 PMID:37209791

Mahto, P., Garg, P., Seth, P., & Panda, J. (2020). Refining yolov4 for vehicle detection. [IJARET]. *Int J Adv Res Eng Technol*, *11*(5), 409–419.

Ma, L., Zhang, J., Lin, L., Wang, T., Ma, C., Wang, X., Li, M., Qiao, Y., Wang, Y., Zhang, G., & Wu, Z. (2023). Data-driven engineering framework with AI algorithm of Ginkgo Folium tablets manufacturing. *Acta Pharmaceutica Sinica. B*, *13*(5), 2188–2201. doi:10.1016/j.apsb.2022.08.011 PMID:37250167

Malchi, S. K., Kallam, S., Al-Turjman, F., & Patan, R. (2021). A trust-based fuzzy neural network for smart data fusion in internet of things. *Computers & Electrical Engineering*, *89*, 106901. doi:10.1016/j.compeleceng.2020.106901

Malhotra, M., Jaiswar, A., Shukla, A., Rai, N., Bedi, A., Iquebal, M. A., & Rai, A. (2023). Application of AI/ML Approaches for Livestock Improvement and Management. In *Biotechnological Interventions Augmenting Livestock Health and Production* (pp. 377–394). Springer Nature Singapore. doi:10.1007/978-981-99-2209-3_20

Malik, S., Harous, S., & El-Sayed, H. (2020, September). Comparative analysis of machine learning algorithms for early prediction of diabetes mellitus in women. In *International Symposium on Modelling and Implementation of Complex Systems* (pp. 95-106). Cham: Springer International Publishing.

Malik, T., Rabbani, G., & Farooq, M. (2013). Forest fire risk zonation using remote sensing and GIS technology in Kansrao ForestRange of Rajaji National Park, Uttarakhand, India. India. *International Journal of Advanced RS and GIS*, *2*(1), 86–95.

Malviya, N., Malviya, S., & Dhere, M. (2023). Transformation of pharma curriculum as per the anticipation of pharma industries-need to empower fresh breeds with globally accepted pharma syllabus, soft skills, ai and hands-on training. *Indian Journal of Pharmaceutical Education and Research*, *57*(2), 320–328. doi:10.5530/ijper.57.2.41

Mansour, R. F., Amraoui, A. E., Nouaouri, I., Díaz, V. G., Gupta, D., & Kumar, S. (2021). Artificial Intelligence and Internet of Things Enabled Disease Diagnosis Model for Smart Healthcare Systems. *IEEE Access : Practical Innovations, Open Solutions, 9*, 45137–45146. doi:10.1109/ACCESS.2021.3066365

Manzano, T., Fernàndez, C., Ruiz, T., & Richard, H. (2021). Artificial Intelligence Algorithm Qualification: A Quality by Design Approach to Apply Artificial Intelligence in Pharma. *PDA Journal of Pharmaceutical Science and Technology, 75*(1), 100–118. doi:10.5731/pdajpst.2019.011338 PMID:32817323

Marelli, D., Xu, Y., Fu, M., & Huang, Z. (2021). Distributed Newton optimization with maximized convergence rate. *arXiv preprint arXiv:2102.08726.*

Martin, C., DeStefano, K., Haran, H., Zink, S., Dai, J., Ahmed, D., Razzak, A., Lin, K., Kogler, A., Waller, J., Kazmi, K., & Umair, M. (2022). The ethical considerations including inclusion and biases, data protection, and proper implementation among AI in radiology and potential implications. *Intelligence-Based Medicine, 6*, 100073. doi:10.1016/j.ibmed.2022.100073

Martínez-Fernández, J., Chuvieco, E., & Koutsias, N. (2013). Modelling long-term fire occurrence factors in Spain byaccounting for local variations with geographically weightedregression. *Natural Hazards and Earth System Sciences, 13*(2), 311–327. doi:10.5194/nhess-13-311-2013

Martini, B. G., Helfer, G. A., Barbosa, J. L. V., Espinosa Modolo, R. C., da Silva, M. R., de Figueiredo, R. M., Mendes, A. S., Silva, L. A., & Leithardt, V. R. Q. (2021). IndoorPlant: A model for intelligent services in indoor agriculture based on context histories. *Sensors (Basel), 21*(5), 1631. doi:10.339021051631 PMID:33652603

Matsiy, O. B., Morozov, A. V., & Panishev, A. V. (2015). The Recurrent Method to Solve the Assignment Problem. *Cybernetics and Systems Analysis, 51*(6), 939–946. doi:10.100710559-015-9786-x

Mazin. (2022). IoT and artificial intelligence implementations for remote healthcare monitoring systems: A survey. *Computer and Information Sciences, 34*(8), 4687-4701

McCarthy, J. (2007). From here to human-level AI. *Artificial Intelligence, 171*(18), 1174–1182. doi:10.1016/j.artint.2007.10.009

Medvedeva, M., Vols, M., & Wieling, M. (2020). Using machine learning to predict decisions of the European Court of Human Rights. *Artificial Intelligence and Law, 28*(2), 237–266. doi:10.100710506-019-09255-y

Mehta, R. (2019). Turning Object Detection into Low Light Object Detection, 2019. *Medium.* https://rishi30-mehta.medium.com/turning-object-detection-into-low-light-object-detection-b5973efffdd7

Menon, A., Omman, B., & Asha, S. (2021). Pedestrian Counting Using Yolo V3. In *2021 International Conference on Innovative Trends in Information Technology (ICITIIT)* (pp. 1–9). IEEE.

Mesgaran, M. B., Madani, K., Hashemi, H., & Azadi, P. (2017). Iran's land suitability for agriculture. *Scientific Reports, 7*(1), 7670. doi:10.103841598-017-08066-y PMID:28794520

Mhlanga, D. (2021). Artificial intelligence in the industry 4.0, and its impact on poverty, innovation, infrastructure development, and the sustainable development goals: Lessons from emerging economies?'. *Sustainability (Basel), 13*(11), 5788. doi:10.3390u13115788

Miao, Z., Gaynor, K. M., Wang, J., Liu, Z., Muellerklein, O., Norouzzadeh, M. S., McInturff, A., Bowie, R. C. K., Nathan, R., Yu, S. X., & Getz, W. M. (2019). Insights and approaches using deep learning to classify wildlife. *Scientific Reports, 9*(1), 8137. doi:10.103841598-019-44565-w PMID:31148564

Microsoft. (2023). *Novartis empowers scientists with AI to speed the discovery and development of breakthrough medicines.* Microsoft. https://news.microsoft.com/source/features/digital-transformation/novartis-empowers-scientists-ai-speed-discovery-development-breakthrough-medicines/

Mikołajczyk, A., & Grochowski, M. (2018, May). *Data augmentation for improving deep learning in image classification problem. In 2018 international interdisciplinary PhD workshop (IIPhDW).* IEEE.

Mishra, S., Mishra, D., & Santra, G. H. (2020). Adaptive boosting of weak regressors for forecasting of crop production considering climatic variability: An empirical assessment. *Journal of King Saud University. Computer and Information Sciences, 32*(8), 949–964. doi:10.1016/j.jksuci.2017.12.004

Mohammed, H., Oduro, F. T., & Appiah, S. K. (2023). Alternate approach (Penalty Approach) to assignment problem solving and comparison to existing approaches. [JAMCS]. *Journal of Advances in Mathematics and Computer Science, 38*(8), 6–15. doi:10.9734/jamcs/2023/v38i81785

Mohan, S., Kannusamy, A. P., & Sidhu, S. K. (2021). Solution of intuitionistic fuzzy linear programming problem by dual simplex algorithm and sensitivity analysis. *Computational Intelligence,* 1–21. doi:10.1111/coin.12435

Mohan, S., Kannusamy, A., & Samiappan, V. (2020). A new approach for ranking of intuitionistic fuzzy numbers. [JFEA]. *Journal of Fuzzy Extension and Applications, 1*(1), 15–26. doi:10.22105/jfea.2020.247301.1003

Mohideen, S. I., & Kumar, P. S. (2010a). A comparative study on transportation problem in fuzzy environment. In *International Conference on Emerging Trends in Mathematics and Computer Applications (ICETMCA2010).* MEPCO Schlenk Engineering College.

Mohideen, S. I., & Kumar, P. S. (2010b). A comparative study on transportation problem in fuzzy environment. [IJMR]. *International Journal of Mathematics Research, 2*(1), 151–158.

Mondal, D., Ratnaparkhi, A., Deshpande, A., Deshpande, V., Kshirsagar, A. P., & Pramanik, S. (2023). Applications, Modern Trends and Challenges of Multiscale Modelling in Smart Cities. In *Data-Driven Mathematical Modeling in Smart Cities.* IGI Global., doi:10.4018/978-1-6684-6408-3.ch001

Mondal, S., & Tsourdos, A. (2021). Two-Dimensional Quantum Genetic Algorithm: Application to Task Allocation Problem. *Sensors (Basel), 21*(4), 1251. doi:10.339021041251 PMID:33578712

Monteith, S., Glenn, T., Geddes, J. R., Achtyes, E. D., Whybrow, P. C., & Bauer, M. (2023). Challenges and ethical considerations to successfully implement artificial intelligence in clinical medicine and neuroscience: A narrative review. *Pharmacopsychiatry, 56*(6), 209–213. doi:10.1055/a-2142-9325 PMID:37643732

Mo, Q., Zhang, T., Wu, J., Wang, L., & Luo, J. (2023). Identification of thrombopoiesis inducer based on a hybrid deep neural network model. *Thrombosis Research, 226,* 36–50. doi:10.1016/j.thromres.2023.04.011 PMID:37119555

Morales, J., Moeyersons, J., Armanac, P., Orini, M., Faes, L., Overeem, S., Van Gilst, M., Van Dijk, J., Van Huffel, S., Bailon, R., & Varon, C. (2021, June). Model-Based Evaluation of Methods for Respiratory Sinus Arrhythmia Estimation. *IEEE Transactions on Biomedical Engineering, 68*(6), 1882–1893. doi:10.1109/TBME.2020.3028204 PMID:33001798

Mourtzis, D., Angelopoulos, J., & Panopoulos, N. (2020). Intelligent predictive maintenance and remote monitoring framework for industrial equipment based on mixed reality. *Frontiers of Mechanical Engineering, 6,* 578379. doi:10.3389/fmech.2020.578379

Mousavi, A., Schmidt, M., Squires, V., & Wilson, K. (2021). Assessing the Effectiveness of Student Advice Recommender Agent (SARA): The Case of Automated Personalized Feedback. *International Journal of Artificial Intelligence in Education*, *31*(3), 603–621. doi:10.100740593-020-00210-6

Muamer, M. (2020). Fuzzy Assignment problems. *Journal of Science*, *10*, 40–47. https://www.misuratau.edu.ly/journal/sci/upload/file/R-1263-ISSUE-10%20PAGES%2040-47.pdf

Muangprathub, J., Boonnam, N., Kajornkasirat, S., Lekbangpong, N., Wanichsombat, A., & Nillaor, P. (2019). IoT and agriculture data analysis for smart farm. *Computers and Electronics in Agriculture*, *156*, 467–474. doi:10.1016/j.compag.2018.12.011

Muhammed Niyas, K. P., & Thiyagarajan, P. (2023). A systematic review on early prediction of Mild cognitive impairment to alzheimers using machine learning algorithms. *International Journal of Intelligent Networks*, *4*(April), 74–88. doi:10.1016/j.ijin.2023.03.004

Mujumdar, A., & Vaidehi, V. (2019). Diabetes prediction using machine learning algorithms. *Procedia Computer Science*, *165*, 292–299. doi:10.1016/j.procs.2020.01.047

Mukti, I. Z., & Biswas, D. 2019, December. Transfer learning based plant diseases detection using ResNet50. In *2019 4th International conference on electrical information and communication technology (EICT)* (pp. 1-6). IEEE. 10.1109/EICT48899.2019.9068805

Muniraj, P., Sabarmathi, K. R., Leelavathi, R., & Balaji, B. S. (2023). HNTSumm: Hybrid text summarization of transliterated news articles. *International Journal of Intelligent Networks*, *4*(March), 53–61. doi:10.1016/j.ijin.2023.03.001

Munot, D. A., & Ghadle, K. P. (2020). A new approach to solve assignment problem using congruence modulo and its coding in matlab. [AMSJ]. *Advances in Mathematics: Scientific Journal*, *9*(11), 9551–9557. doi:10.37418/amsj.9.11.58

Mupangwa, W., Chipindu, L., Nyagumbo, I., Mkuhlani, S., & Sisito, G. (2020). Evaluating machine learning algorithms for predicting maize yield under conservation agriculture in Eastern and Southern Africa. *SN Applied Sciences*, *2*(5), 1–14. doi:10.100742452-020-2711-6

Murali, P., & Karuppasamy, R. (2023). Imidazole and biphenyl derivatives as anticancer agents for glioma therapeutics: Computational drug repurposing strategy. *Anti-cancer Agents in Medicinal Chemistry*, *23*(9), 1085–1101. doi:10.2174/1871520623666230125090815 PMID:36698225

Murugan, M. B., Rajagopal, M. K., & Roy, D. (2021, November). Iot based smart agriculture and plant disease prediction. *Journal of Physics: Conference Series*, *2115*(1), 012017. doi:10.1088/1742-6596/2115/1/012017

Murugesan, R., & Esakkiammal, T. (2020a). Direct Methods for Finding Optimal Solution of Assignment Problems Are Not Always Dependable. [AMS]. *Applied Mathematical Sciences (Ruse)*, *14*(17), 823–830. doi:10.12988/ams.2020.914284

Murugesan, R., & Esakkiammal, T. (2020b). TERM – a very simple and efficient method to solve assignment problems. [AMS]. *Applied Mathematical Sciences (Ruse)*, *14*(17), 801–809. doi:10.12988/ams.2020.914275

Nadda, R., Repaka, R., & Sahani, A. K. (2023). Honeybee stinger-based biopsy needle and influence of the barbs on needle forces during insertion/extraction into the iliac crest: A multilayer finite element approach. *Computers in Biology and Medicine*, *162*(May), 107125. doi:10.1016/j.compbiomed.2023.107125 PMID:37290393

Nagaraju, M. & Chawla, P. (2020). Systematic review of deep learning techniques in plant disease detection. *International journal of system assurance engineering and management, 11*, 547-560.

Nagare, S. (2015). An Efficient Algorithm brain tumor detection based on Segmentation and Thresholding. Journal of Management in Manufacturing and services, 2.

Nagare, S. (2014). Different Segmentation Techniques for brain tumor detection: A Survey. *MM- International society for green. Sustainable Engineering and Management, 1*(14), 29–35.

Nagasubramanian, G., Sakthivel, R. K., Patan, R., Sankayya, M., Daneshmand, M., & Gandomi, A. H. (2021). Ensemble classification and IoT-based pattern recognition for crop disease monitoring system. *IEEE Internet of Things Journal, 8*(16), 12847–12854. doi:10.1109/JIOT.2021.3072908

Narayanamoorthy, S., Annapoorani, V., & Santhiya, M. (2017). A Method for Solving Fuzzy and Intuitionistic Fuzzy Assignment Problem using Ones Assignment Method with Fuzzy Numbers. [IJPAM]. *International Journal of Pure and Applied Mathematics, 117*(14), 91–99.

Nasteski, V. (2017). An overview of the supervised machine learning methods. *Horizons, 4*, 51-62.

Natarajan, V. A., Kumar, M. S., Patan, R., Kallam, S., & Mohamed, M. Y. N. (2020, September). Segmentation of nuclei in histopathology images using fully convolutional deep neural architecture. In *2020 International Conference on computing and information technology (ICCIT-1441)* (pp. 1-7). IEEE. 10.1109/ICCIT-144147971.2020.9213817

National Institute of Standards and Technology. (2023). *Artificial Intelligence Risk Management Framework (AI RMF 1.0).* NIST. https://www.nist.gov/itl/ai-risk-management-framework

Navabhatra, A., Brantner, A., & Yingngam, B. (2022). Artificial neural network modeling of nanostructured lipid carriers containing 5-*O*-caffeoylquinic acid-rich cratoxylum formosum leaf extract for skin application. *Advanced Pharmaceutical Bulletin, 12*(4), 801–817. doi:10.34172/apb.2022.082 PMID:36415630

Navulur, S., & Prasad, M. G. (2017). Agricultural management through wireless sensors and internet of things. *Iranian Journal of Electrical and Computer Engineering, 7*(6), 3492. doi:10.11591/ijece.v7i6.pp3492-3499

Navya, D. (2023). Artificial intelligence-based robot for harvesting, pesticide spraying and maintaining water management system in agriculture using IoT. *AIP Conference Proceedings.*

Nazaretsky, T., Cukurova, M., & Alexandron, G. (2022, March). An instrument for measuring `teachers` trust in AI-based educational technology. In *LAK22: 12th international learning analytics and knowledge conference* (pp. 56-66). 10.1145/3506860.3506866

Neelakandan, A. R., & Rajanikant, G. K. (2023). A deep learning and docking simulation-based virtual screening strategy enables the rapid identification of HIF-1α pathway activators from a marine natural product database. *Journal of Biomolecular Structure & Dynamics.* doi:10.1080/07391102.2023.2194997

Neelambari, R., Anupriya, S., Revathi, S., & Venkatesh, S. (2023). A novel method for the fuzzy assignment problem using SBD. [ECB]. *Eur. Chem. Bull., 12*(Special Issue 9), 601-611. 10.48047/ecb/2023.12.9.56

Neethirajan, S. (2023). Artificial Intelligence and Sensor Technologies in Dairy Livestock Export: Charting a Digital Transformation. *Sensors (Basel), 23*(16), 7045. doi:10.339023167045 PMID:37631580

Ngoc, T. T. H., Pramanik, S., & Khanh, P. T. (2023). The Relationship between Gender and Climate Change in Vietnam. *The Seybold Report.* 10.17605/OSF.IO/KJBPT

Nguyen, A., Ngo, H., Hong, Y., Dang, B., & Nguyen, B.-P. (2022). Ethical principles for artificial intelligence in education. *Education and Information Technologies, 28*(4), 4221–4241. doi:10.100710639-022-11316-w PMID:36254344

Nguyen, H. N. B., & Patuwo, M. Y. (2023). Quantitative structure-activity relationship (QSAR) modeling of the activity of anti-colorectal cancer agents featuring quantum chemical predictors and interaction terms. *Results in Chemistry, 5,* 100888. doi:10.1016/j.rechem.2023.100888

Nikita, S. (2022). Announcement system in Bus. *Journal of Image Processing and Intelligent remote sensing, 2*(6).

Nikita, K. (2020). Design of Vehicle system using CAN Protocol. *International Journal for Research in Applied Science and Engineering Technology, 8*(V), 1978–1983. doi:10.22214/ijraset.2020.5321

Noaro, G., Zhu, T., Cappon, G., Facchinetti, A., & Georgiou, P. (2023). A personalized and adaptive insulin bolus calculator based on double deep q- learning to improve type 1 diabetes management. *IEEE Journal of Biomedical and Health Informatics, 27*(5), 2536–2544. doi:10.1109/JBHI.2023.3249571 PMID:37027579

Norouzzadeh, M. S., Nguyen, A., Kosmala, M., Swanson, A., Palmer, M. S., Packer, C., & Clune, J. (2018). Automatically identifying, counting, and describing wild animals in camera-trap images with deep learning. *Proceedings of the National Academy of Sciences of the United States of America, 115*(25), E5716–E5725. doi:10.1073/pnas.1719367115 PMID:29871948

Novartis. (2023, October 15). *Novartis Institutes for Biomedical Research, AI predicts heart cell damage.* Novartis. https://www.novartis.com/stories/discovery/ai-predicts-heart-cell-damage

Nu'man, A. H., Nurwandi, L., Orgianus, Y., & Abdullah, A. G. (2020). Location determination with assignment method in design seaweed supply chain. *Journal of Engineering Science and Technology, 15*(6), 3920–3934.

Obeid, S., Madžarević, M., Krkobabić, M., & Ibrić, S. (2021). Predicting drug release from diazepam FDM printed tablets using deep learning approach: Influence of process parameters and tablet surface/volume ratio. *International Journal of Pharmaceutics, 601,* 120507. doi:10.1016/j.ijpharm.2021.120507 PMID:33766640

Ocumpaugh, J., Baker, R., Gowda, S., Heffernan, N., & Heffernan, C. (2014). Population validity for educational data mining models: A case study in affect detection. *British Journal of Educational Technology, 45*(3), 87–501. doi:10.1111/bjet.12156

Oh, T. H., Park, H. M., Kim, J. W., & Lee, J. M. (2022). Integration of reinforcement learning and model predictive control to optimize semi-batch bioreactor. *AIChE Journal. American Institute of Chemical Engineers, 68*(6), e17658. doi:10.1002/aic.17658

Oliveira, R. C. D., & Silva, R. D. D. S. E. (2023). Artificial Intelligence in Agriculture: Benefits, Challenges, and Trends. *Applied Sciences (Basel, Switzerland), 13*(13), 7405. doi:10.3390/app13137405

Opoku Agyeman, M., Guerrero, A. F., & Vien, Q.-T. (2022). Classification Techniques for Arrhythmia Patterns Using Convolutional Neural Networks and Internet of Things (IoT) Devices. *IEEE Access : Practical Innovations, Open Solutions, 10,* 87387–87403. doi:10.1109/ACCESS.2022.3192390

Orsmond, P., & Merry, S. (2011). Feedback alignment: Effective and ineffective links between 'tutors' and 'students' understanding of coursework feedback. *Assessment & Evaluation in Higher Education, 36*(2), 125–136. doi:10.1080/02602930903201651

Osman, A. H., & Aljahdali, H. M. (2017). Diabetes disease diagnosis method based on feature extraction using K-SVM. *International Journal of Advanced Computer Science and Applications, 8*(1).

Ouatik, F., Raoufi, M., Ouatik, F., & Skouri, M. (2021). E-Learning & decision making system for automate students assessment using remote laboratory and machine learning. *Journal of E-Learning and Knowledge Society, 17*(1), 90–100. doi:10.20368/1971-8829/1135285

Owan, V., Abang, K., Idika, D., & Bassey, B. (2023). Exploring the potential of artificial intelligence tools in educational measurement and assessment. *Eurasia Journal of Mathematics, Science and Technology Education, 19*(8), em2307. doi:10.29333/ejmste/13428

Pacal, I., Karaman, A., Karaboga, D., Akay, B., Basturk, A., Nalbantoglu, U., & Coskun, S. (2022). An efficient real-time colonic polyp detection with YOLO algorithms trained by using negative samples and large datasets. *Comput. Biol. Med., 141*, 105031.

Palwankar, T., & Kothari, K. (2022). *Real Time Object Detection using SSD and MobileNet*. Ijraset Journal For Research in Applied Science and Engineering Technology. doi:10.22214/ijraset.2022.40755

Pandey, B. K., Pandey, D., Nassa, V. K., George, A. S., Pramanik, S., & Dadheech, P. (2023). Applications for the Text Extraction Method of Complex Degraded Images. The Impact of Thrust Technologies on Image Processing. Nova Publishers.

Pandey, B. K., Pandey, D., Wairya, S., Agarwal, G., Dadeech, P., Dogiwal, S. R., & Pramanik, S. (2022). Application of Integrated Steganography and Image Compressing Techniques for Confidential Information Transmission. Cyber Security and Network Security. Wiley. . doi:10.1002/9781119812555.ch8

Pandey, B. K., Pandey, D., Nassa, V. K., Hameed, A. S., George, A. S., Dadheech, P., & Pramanik, S. (2023). A Review of Various Text Extraction Algorithms for Images. In *The Impact of Thrust Technologies on Image Processing*. Nova Publishers. doi:10.52305/ATJL4552

Pardeshi. (2022). Development of Machine Learning based Epileptic Seizureprediction using Web of Things (WoT). *NeuroQuantology : An Interdisciplinary Journal of Neuroscience and Quantum Physics, 20*(8), 9394–9409.

Pardeshi. (2022). Implementation of Fault Detection Framework for Healthcare Monitoring System Using IoT, Sensors in Wireless Environment. *Telematique, 21*(1), 5451–5460.

Parimbelli, E., Wilk, S., Cornet, R., Sniatala, P., Sniatala, K., Glaser, S. L. C., Fraterman, I., Boekhout, A. H., Ottaviano, M., & Peleg, M. (2021). A review of AI and Data Science support for cancer management. *Artificial Intelligence in Medicine, 117*(August 2020), 102111. doi:10.1016/j.artmed.2021.102111

Pastor-Escuredo, D., Treleaven, P., & Vinuesa, R. (2022). An Ethical Framework for Artificial Intelligence and Sustainable Cities. *AI, 3*(4), 961–974. doi:10.3390/ai3040057

Patel, C. N., Mall, R., & Bensmail, H. (2023). AI-driven drug repurposing and binding pose meta dynamics identifies novel targets for monkeypox virus. *Journal of Infection and Public Health, 16*(5), 799–807. doi:10.1016/j.jiph.2023.03.007 PMID:36966703

Patel, S., Patel, M., Kulkarni, M., & Patel, M. S. (2023). DE-INTERACT: A machine-learning-based predictive tool for the drug-excipient interaction study during product development—Validation through paracetamol and vanillin as a case study. *International Journal of Pharmaceutics, 637*, 122839. doi:10.1016/j.ijpharm.2023.122839 PMID:36931538

Pathan, M., Patel, N., Yagnik, H., & Shah, M. (2020). Artificial cognition for applications in smart agriculture: A comprehensive review. *Artificial Intelligence in Agriculture, 4*, 81–95. doi:10.1016/j.aiia.2020.06.001

Patil, R. S., Kulkarni, S. B., & Gaikwad, V. L. (2023). Artificial intelligence in pharmaceutical regulatory affairs. *Drug Discovery Today, 28*(9), 103700. doi:/ doi:10.1016/j.drudis.2023.103700

Pawar, S., Dere, S., Akangire, A., Kamble, H., & Shrawne, S. (2021). *Smart farming using machine learning*. Smart Comput.

Peña. (2014). *Ontology agents and their applications in the web-based education systems: towards an adaptive and intelligent service artificial intelligence on education view project*. Springer. doi:10.1007/978-3-540-88071-4_11

Peneti, S., Sunil Kumar, M., Kallam, S., Patan, R., Bhaskar, V., & Ramachandran, M. (2021). BDN-GWMNN: Internet of things (IoT) enabled secure smart city applications. *Wireless Personal Communications, 119*(3), 2469–2485. doi:10.100711277-021-08339-w

Pereira, C. R., Pereira, D. R., Weber, S. A. T., Hook, C., de Albuquerque, V. H. C., & Papa, J. P. (2019). A survey on computer-assisted Parkinson's Disease diagnosis. *Artificial Intelligence in Medicine, 95*(August 2018), 48–63. doi:10.1016/j.artmed.2018.08.007

Pérez-Cañedo, B., & Concepción-Morales, E. R. (2020). A lexicographic approach to fuzzy linear assignment problems with different types of fuzzy numbers. *International Journal of Uncertainty, Fuzziness and Knowledge-based Systems, 28*(03), 421–441. doi:10.1142/S0218488520500178

Phasinam, K., Kassanuk, T., & Shabaz, M. (2022). Applicability of internet of things in smart farming. *Journal of Food Quality, 2022*, 1–7. doi:10.1155/2022/7692922

Ponzoni, I., Páez Prosper, J. A., & Campillo, N. E. (2023). Explainable artificial intelligence: A taxonomy and guidelines for its application to drug discovery. *Wiley Interdisciplinary Reviews. Computational Molecular Science, 13*(6), e1681. doi:10.1002/wcms.1681

Porchelvi, R. S., & Anitha, M. (2018). Optimal Solution for Assignment Problem by Average Total Opportunity Cost Method. *Journal of Mathematics and Informatics, 13*, 21–27. doi:10.22457/jmi.v13a3

Pornaroontham, P., Kim, K., Kulprathipanja, S., & Rangsunvigit, P. (2023). Water-soluble organic former selection for methane hydrates by supervised machine learning. *Energy Reports, 9*, 2935–2946. doi:10.1016/j.egyr.2023.01.118

Poudyal, P., & Quaresma, P. (2012). An hybrid approach for legal information extraction. In *Legal Knowledge and Information Systems* (pp. 115–118). IOS Press. doi:10.3233/978-1-61499-167-0-115

Prabha, S. K., Hema, P., Sangeetha, S., Sreedevi, S., Guhan, T., & Pillai, M. V. J. (2021). Unbalanced FTP with Circumcenter of Centroids and Heuristic Method. *Annals of the Romanian Society for Cell Biology, 25*(1), 5672–5684. http://annalsofrscb.ro/index.php/journal/article/view/726

Pradeepa, M. (2022). Student Health Detection using a Machine Learning Approach and IoT. *2022 IEEE 2nd Mysore sub section International Conference (MysuruCon)*. IEEE.

Pramanik, S. (2023). An Adaptive Image Steganography Approach depending on Integer Wavelet Transform and Genetic Algorithm. *Multimedia Tools and Applications, 82*(22), 34287–34319. Advance online publication. doi:10.100711042-023-14505-y

Pramanik, S. (2023). Intelligent Farming Utilizing a Soil Tracking Device. In A. K. Sharma, N. Chanderwal, R. Khan, & I. G. I. Global (Eds.), *Convergence of Cloud Computing, AI and Agricultural Science*. doi:10.4018/979-8-3693-0200-2.ch009

Pramanik, S., & Bandyopadhyay, S. (2023). Identifying Disease and Diagnosis in Females using Machine Learning. In I. G. I. John Wang (Ed.), *Encyclopedia of Data Science and Machine Learning*. Global., doi:10.4018/978-1-7998-9220-5.ch187

Pratihast, A. K., De Vries, B., Avitabile, V., De Bruin, S., Herold, M., & Bergsma, A. (2016). Design and implementation of an interactive web-based near real-time forest monitoring system. *PLoS One, 11*(3), e0150935. doi:10.1371/journal.pone.0150935 PMID:27031694

Praveenkumar, S., Veeraiah, V., Pramanik, S., Basha, S. M., Lira Neto, A. V., De Albuquerque, V. H. C., & Gupta, A. (2023). *Prediction of Patients' Incurable Diseases Utilizing Deep Learning Approaches, ICICC 2023*. Springer. doi:10.1007/978-981-99-3315-0_4

Prifti, V., Dervishi, I., Dhoska, K., Markja, I., & Pramono, A. (2020, December). Minimization of transport costs in an industrial company through linear programming. In IOP Conference Series: Materials Science and Engineering (Vol. 909, No. 1, p. 012040). IOP Publishing. doi:10.1088/1757-899X/909/1/012040

Puranik, A., Dandekar, P., & Jain, R. (2022). Exploring the potential of machine learning for more efficient development and production of biopharmaceuticals. *Biotechnology Progress*, *38*(6), e3291. doi:10.1002/btpr.3291 PMID:35918873

Purwar, R. K., & Verma, S. (2022). Analytical study of YOLO and its various versions in crowd counting. In *Intelligent data communication technologies and Internet of things* (pp. 975–989). Springer.

Qiang, Z., JunHua, H., An, L., GuoMing, C., & QiMin, Y. (2020, August). New ranking methods of intuitionistic fuzzy numbers and Pythagorean fuzzy numbers. In *2020 Chinese Control And Decision Conference (CCDC)* (pp. 4661-4666). IEEE. 10.1109/CCDC49329.2020.9164633

Qian, Y., Li, C.-X., Zou, X.-G., Feng, X.-B., Xiao, M.-H., & Ding, Y.-Q. (2022). Research on predicting learning achievement in a flipped classroom based on MOOCs by big data analysis. *Computer Applications in Engineering Education*, *30*(1), 222–234. doi:10.1002/cae.22452

Radoglou-Grammatikis, P., Sarigiannidis, P., Lagkas, T., & Moscholios, I. (2020). A compilation of UAV applications for precision agriculture. *Computer Networks*, *172*, 107148. doi:10.1016/j.comnet.2020.107148

Raghav, K., Reddy, K., & Reddy, V. (2016). *Analyzing the Extraction of Relevant Legal Judgments using Paragraph-level and Citation Information*. Semantic Scholar. https://www.semanticscholar.org/paper/Analyzing-the-Extraction-of-Relevant-Legal-using-Raghav-Reddy/7453ba87fb9418c6e4f5609cc3ba3d99b9b34874

Rahman. (2020). Intelligent waste management system using deep learning with IoT. *Journal of King Saud University. Computer and Information Sciences*. doi:10.1016/j.jksuci.2020.08.016

Rajendiran, G., & Rethnaraj, J. (2023). Lettuce Crop Yield Prediction Analysis using Random Forest Regression Machine Learning Model in Aeroponics System. In *2023 Second International Conference on Augmented Intelligence and Sustainable Systems (ICAISS)* (pp. 565-572). IEEE. 10.1109/ICAISS58487.2023.10250535

Rajendiran, G., & Rethnaraj, J. (2023). Smart Aeroponic Farming System: Using IoT with LCGM-Boost Regression Model for Monitoring and Predicting Lettuce Crop Yield. *International Journal of Intelligent Engineering & Systems*, *16*(5).

Ramesh, S., Hebbar, R., Niveditha, M., Pooja, R., Shashank, N., & Vinod, P. V. 2018, April. Plant disease detection using machine learning. In *2018 International conference on design innovations for 3Cs compute communicate control (ICDI3C)* (pp. 41-45). IEEE. 10.1109/ICDI3C.2018.00017

Ramirez-Asis, E., Bhanot, A., Jagota, V., Chandra, B., Hossain, M. S., Pant, K., & Almashaqbeh, H. A. (2022). Smart logistic system for enhancing the farmer-customer corridor in the smart agriculture sector using artificial intelligence. *Journal of Food Quality*, *2022*, 2022. doi:10.1155/2022/7486974

Rangelov, D., Boerger, M., Tcholtchev, N., Lämmel, P., & Hauswirth, M. (2023). Design and Development of a Short-Term Photovoltaic Power Output Forecasting Method Based on Random Forest, Deep Neural Network and LSTM Using Readily Available Weather Features. *IEEE Access : Practical Innovations, Open Solutions*, *11*, 41578–41595. doi:10.1109/ACCESS.2023.3270714

Rani, J. J., Manivannan, A., & Dhanasekar, S. (2022, November). A branch and bound approach for solving interval valued intuitionistic fuzzy assignment problem. In. AIP Conference Proceedings: Vol. 2516. *No. 1* (p. 200021). AIP Publishing LLC. doi:10.1063/5.0108972

Rani, K. J. (2020). Diabetes prediction using machine learning. *International Journal of Scientific Research in Computer Science Engineering and Information Technology, 6*, 294–305. doi:10.32628/CSEIT206463

Ranjan, A., Kumar, H., Kumari, D., Anand, A., & Misra, R. (2023). Molecule generation toward target protein (SARS-CoV-2) using reinforcement learning-based graph neural network via knowledge graph. *Network Modeling and Analysis in Health Informatics and Bioinformatics, 12*(1), 13. doi:10.100713721-023-00409-2 PMID:36627927

Ranson, J. M., Bucholc, M., Lyall, D., Newby, D., Winchester, L., Oxtoby, N. P., Veldsman, M., Rittman, T., Marzi, S., Skene, N., Al Khleifat, A., Foote, I. F., Orgeta, V., Kormilitzin, A., Lourida, I., & Llewellyn, D. J. (2023). Harnessing the potential of machine learning and artificial intelligence for dementia research. *Brain Informatics, 10*(1), 6. doi:10.118640708-022-00183-3 PMID:36829050

Rashid, M. M., Askari, M. R., Chen, C., Liang, Y., Shu, K., & Cinar, A. (2022). Artificial intelligence algorithms for treatment of diabetes. *Algorithms, 15*(9), 299. doi:10.3390/a15090299

Rathee, S., MacMahon, M., Liu, A., Katritsis, N. M., Youssef, G., Hwang, W., Wollman, L., & Han, N. (2022). DILI C: An AI-based classifier to search for drug-induced liver injury literature. *Frontiers in Genetics, 13*, 867946. doi:10.3389/fgene.2022.867946 PMID:35846129

Rathore, A. S., Nikita, S., Thakur, G., & Mishra, S. (2023). Artificial intelligence and machine learning applications in biopharmaceutical manufacturing. *Trends in Biotechnology, 41*(4), 497–510. doi:10.1016/j.tibtech.2022.08.007 PMID:36117026

Ravi. (2012). *Pattern Recognition- An Approach towards Machine Learning*. Lambert Publications.

Rawat, S., & Sah, A. (2012). An approach to Enhance the software and services of Health care centre. *AHA Journals, 3*(7), 126–137.

Rawat, S., & Kumar, R. (2020). Direct-Indirect Link Matrix: A Black Box Testing Technique for Component-Based Software. *International Journal of Information Technology Project Management, 11*(4), 56–69. doi:10.4018/IJITPM.2020100105

Rawat, S., & Sah, A. (2013). An Approach to Integrate Heterogeneous Web Applications. *International Journal of Computer Applications, 70*(23), 7–12. doi:10.5120/12205-7639

RayhanA.RayhanR.RayhanS. (2023*). Revolutionizing Education: The Power of Artificial Intelligence (AI)*. doi:10.13140/RG.2.2.10716.97924

Raza, U., Kulkarni, P., & Sooriyabandara, M. (2017). Low power wide area networks: An overview. *IEEE Communications Surveys and Tutorials, 19*(2), 855–873. doi:10.1109/COMST.2017.2652320

Reddy, D. A., Dadore, B., & Watekar, A. (2019). Crop recommendation system to maximize crop yield in ramtek region using machine learning. *International Journal of Scientific Research in Science and Technology, 6*(1), 485–489. doi:10.32628/IJSRST196172

Redmon, J., & Farhadi, A. (2018). *Yolov3: An incremental improvement*. arXiv preprint arXiv:1804.02767

Redmon, J., Divvala, S., Girshick, R., & Farhadi, A. (2016). You only look once: Unified, real-time object detection. *Proceedings of the IEEE conference on computer vision and pattern recognition*, (pp. 779–788). IEEE. 10.1109/CVPR.2016.91

Reepu, K. S., Chaudhary, M. G., Gupta, K. G., Pramanik, S. & Gupta, A. (2023). Information Security and Privacy in IoT. Handbook of Research in Advancements in AI and IoT Convergence Technologies. IGI Global.

Reepu, S. Kumar, Chaudhary, M. G., Gupta, K. G., Pramanik, S., & Gupta, A. (2023). Information Security and Privacy in IoT. J. Zhao, V. V. Kumar, R. Natarajan and T. R. Mahesh, (eds.) Handbook of Research in Advancements in AI and IoT Convergence Technologies. IGI Global.

Rehna, V. J., & Inamdar, M. N. (2022). Impact of Autonomous Drone Pollination in Date Palms. *International Journal of Innovative Research and Scientific Studies*, 5(4), 297–305. doi:10.53894/ijirss.v5i4.732

Rellier, J. P., & Chédru, S. (1992). An artificial intelligence-based software for designing crop management plans. *Computers and Electronics in Agriculture*, 6(4), 273–294. doi:10.1016/0168-1699(92)90001-4

Ren, F., Ding, X., Zheng, M., Korzinkin, M., Cai, X., Zhu, W., Mantsyzov, A., Aliper, A., Aladinskiy, V., Cao, Z., Kong, S., Long, X., Man Liu, B. H., Liu, Y., Naumov, V., Shneyderman, A., Ozerov, I. V., Wang, J., Pun, F. W., & Zhavoronkov, A. (2023). AlphaFold accelerates artificial intelligence powered drug discovery: Efficient discovery of a novel CDK20 small molecule inhibitor. *Chemical Science (Cambridge)*, 14(6), 1443–1452. doi:10.1039/D2SC05709C PMID:36794205

Ren, P., Fang, W., & Djahel, S. (2017). *A novel YOLO-Based real-time people counting approach, In 2017 international smart cities conference (ISC2).* IEEE.

Renz, A., Krishnaraja, S., & Gronau, E. (2020). Demystification of Artificial Intelligence in Education–How much AI is really in the Educational Technology? [iJAI]. *International Journal of Learning Analytics and Artificial Intelligence for Education*, 2(1), 14. doi:10.3991/ijai.v2i1.12675

Richardson, A., Signor, B. M., Lidbury, B. A., & Badrick, T. (2016). Clinical chemistry in higher dimensions: Machine-learning and enhanced prediction from routine clinical chemistry data. *Clinical Biochemistry*, 49(16-17), 1213–1220. doi:10.1016/j.clinbiochem.2016.07.013 PMID:27452181

Richardson, P., Griffin, I., Tucker, C., Smith, D., Oechsle, O., Phelan, A., & Stebbing, J. (2020). Baricitinib as potential treatment for 2019-nCoV acute respiratory disease. *Lancet*, 395(10223), e30–e31. doi:10.1016/S0140-6736(20)30304-4 PMID:32032529

Rienties, B., Køhler Simonsen, H., & Herodotou, C. (2020, July). Defining the boundaries between artificial intelligence in education, computer-supported collaborative learning, educational data mining, and learning analytics: A need for coherence. In *frontiers in Education (Vol. 5,* p. 128). Frontiers Media SA.

Rissland, E. L., Ashley, K. D., & Branting, L. K. (2005). Case-based reasoning and law. *The Knowledge Engineering Review*, 20(3), 293–298. doi:10.1017/S0269888906000701

Rizk-Allah, R. M., Abo-Sinna, M. A., & Hassanien, A. E. (2021). Intuitionistic fuzzy sets and dynamic programming for multi-objective non-linear programming problems. [IJFS]. *International Journal of Fuzzy Systems*, 23(2), 1–19. doi:10.100740815-020-00973-z

Roshini, A., & Kiran, K. V.D. (2023). Hierarchical energy efficient secure routing protocol for optimal route selection in wireless body area networks. *International Journal of Intelligent Networks, 4*, 19–28. doi:10.1016/j.ijin.2022.11.006

Rothe, P. R., & Kshirsagar, R. V. 2015, January. Cotton leaf disease identification using pattern recognition techniques. In *2015 International conference on pervasive computing (ICPC)* (pp. 1-6). IEEE. 10.1109/PERVASIVE.2015.7086983

Roy, P.S. (2003). Forest fire and degradation assessment using satellite remote sensing and geographic information system. *Satellite Remote Sensing and GIS Applications in Agricultural Meteorology*, 361-400.

Roy, A., & Pramanik, S. (2023). A Review of the Hydrogen Fuel Path to Emission Reduction in the Surface Transport Industry. *International Journal of Hydrogen Energy*.

Russell, S. J., & Norvig, P. (2010). *Artificial intel-ligence a modern approach.* London. https://ds.amu.edu.et/xmlui/bitstream/handle/123456789/10406 /artificial%20intelligence%20-%20a%20modern%20approach%20%28 3rd%2C%202009%29.pdf?sequence=1&isAllowed=y

Ryan, M., & Stahl, B. C. (2021). Artificial intelligence ethics guidelines for developers and users: Clarifying their content and normative implications. *Journal of Information. Communication and Ethics in Society, 19*(1), 61–86. doi:10.1108/ JICES-12-2019-0138

Sabina, N., Aneesa, M. P., & Haseena, P. V. (2022). Object Detection using YOLO And Mobilenet SSD: A Comparative Study. Inter*national Journal Of Engineering Research. & Technology (Ijert), 11*(6).

Sadiq, F., Mohammedali, M., & Sabri, R. (2022). A new application of assignment problems using three techniques with it comparison. [JQCM]. *Journal of Al-Qadisiyah for Computer Science and Mathematics, 14*(4), 19–28. doi:10.29304/ jqcm.2022.14.4.1098

Sadri, A. (2023). Is target-based drug discovery efficient? Discovery and "off-target" mechanisms of all drugs. *Journal of Medicinal Chemistry, 66*(18), 12651–12677. doi:10.1021/acs.jmedchem.2c01737 PMID:37672650

Sadybekov, A. V., & Katritch, V. (2023). Computational approaches streamlining drug discovery. *Nature, 616*(7958), 673–685. doi:10.103841586-023-05905-z PMID:37100941

Sah, A., Bhadula, S. J., Dumka, A., & Rawat, S. (2018). A software engineering perspective for development of enterprise applications. Handbook of Research on Contemporary Perspectives on Web-Based Systems, (pp. 1–23). IGI Global. doi:10.4018/978-1-5225-5384-7.ch001

Sah, A., Dumka, A., & Rawat, S. (2018). Web technology systems integration using SOA and web services. Handbook of Research on Contemporary Perspectives on Web-Based Systems, (pp. 24–45). IGI Global. doi:10.4018/978-1-5225- 5384-7.ch002

Sah, A., Studies, E., Rawat, S., Choudhury, T., Studies, E., Dewangan, B. K., & Studies, E. (2021). An extensive Review of Web-Based Multi Granularity Service Composition. *International Journal of Web-Based Learning and Teaching Technologies, 17*(4), 0–0. doi:10.4018/IJWLTT.285570

Sah, A., Choudhury, T., Rawat, S., & Tripathi, A. (2020). A Proposed Gene Selection Approach for Disease Detection. *Advances in Intelligent Systems and Computing, 1120,* 199–206. doi:10.1007/978-981-15-2449-3_16

Saha, E., Rathore, P., Parida, R., & Rana, N. P. (2022). The interplay of emerging technologies in pharmaceutical supply chain performance: An empirical investigation for the rise of Pharma 4.0. *Technological Forecasting and Social Change, 181,* 121768. doi:10.1016/j.techfore.2022.121768

Saleem, M. H., Potgieter, J., & Arif, K. M. (2019). Plant disease detection and classification by deep learning. *Plants, 8*(11), 468. doi:10.3390/plants8110468 PMID:31683734

Samanta, D., Dutta, S., Galety, M. G., & Pramanik, S. (2021). A Novel Approach for Web Mining Taxonomy for High-Performance Computing. *The 4th International Conference of Computer Science and Renewable Energies (ICCSRE'2021).* IEEE. 10.1051/e3sconf/202129701073

Sangamithra, B., Neelima, P., & Kumar, M. S. (2017, April). A memetic algorithm for multi objective vehicle routing problem with time windows. In *2017 IEEE International Conference on Electrical, Instrumentation and Communication Engineering (ICEICE)* (pp. 1-8). IEEE. 10.1109/ICEICE.2017.8191931

Sangeetha, V., Vijayarangam, J., & Elumalai, P. (2022, November). Mid-range technique and fuzzy Big-M method based solution for fuzzy transportation problem. In. AIP Conference Proceedings: Vol. 2516. *No. 1* (p. 200008). AIP Publishing LLC. doi:10.1063/5.0109704

Sankaran, K. S., Vasudevan, N., & Nagarajan, V. 2020, July. Plant disease detection and recognition using K means clustering. In *2020 International Conference on Communication and Signal Processing (ICCSP)* (pp. 1406-1409). IEEE. 10.1109/ICCSP48568.2020.9182095

Santhi, G., & Ananthanarayanan, M. (2020). Standard deviation method for solving fuzzy assignment problem. [Impact: IJRHAL]. *IMPACT: International Journal of Research in Humanities. Arts and Literature*, 8(4), 25–30.

Sarkar, C., Das, B., Rawat, V. S., Wahlang, J. B., Nongpiur, A., Tiewsoh, I., Lyngdoh, N. M., Das, D., Bidarolli, M., & Sony, H. T. (2023). Artificial intelligence and machine learning technology driven modern drug discovery and development. *International Journal of Molecular Sciences*, 24(3), 2026. doi:10.3390/ijms24032026 PMID:36768346

Sarker, I. H. (2022). AI-Based Modeling: Techniques, Applications and Research Issues Towards Automation, Intelligent and Smart Systems. *SN Computer Science*, 3(2), 158. doi:10.100742979-022-01043-x PMID:35194580

Sasagawa, Y., & Nagahara, H. (2020, November). YOLO in the Dark - Domain Adaptation Method for Merging Multiple Models. *Lecture Notes in Computer Science*, 12366, 345–359. doi:10.1007/978-3-030-58589-1_21

Saud, A., & Elfadil, N. (2020). Biometric authentication by using fingerprint recognition system. *Int J Sci Eng Sci*, 4(5), 22–28.

Sayed, B. (2021). Application of expert systems or decision-making systems in the field of education. *Journal of Contemporary Issues in Business and Government*, 27(3), 2021. doi:10.47750/cibg.2021.27.03.159

Selvakumari, K., & Subasri, S. (2020). Comparative analysis of fuzzy, intuitionistic and neutrosophic assignment problem using nonagonal fuzzy number. *European Journal of Molecular and Clinical Medicine*, 7(2), 5099–5109.

Seo, K., Tang, J., Roll, I., Fels, S., & Yoon, D. (2021). The impact of artificial intelligence on learner–instructor interaction in online learning. *International Journal of Educational Technology in Higher Education*, 18(1), 54. doi:10.118641239-021-00292-9 PMID:34778540

Shafi, S., & Ansari, G. A. (2021, May). Early prediction of diabetes disease & classification of algorithms using machine learning approach. In *Proceedings of the International Conference on Smart Data Intelligence (ICSMDI 2021)*. SSRN. 10.2139srn.3852590

Shah, K., Reddy, P., & Vairamuthu, S. (2015). Improvement in hungarian algorithm for assignment problem. In *Artificial Intelligence and Evolutionary Algorithms in Engineering Systems* (pp. 1–8). Springer. doi:10.1007/978-81-322-2126-5_1

Shah, S., Töreyin, H., Güngör, C. B., & Hasler, J. (2019, December). A Real-Time Vital-Sign Monitoring in the Physical Domain on a Mixed-Signal Reconfigurable Platform. *IEEE Transactions on Biomedical Circuits and Systems*, 13(6), 1690–1699. doi:10.1109/TBCAS.2019.2949778 PMID:31670678

Shaikh, F. K., Karim, S., Zeadally, S., & Nebhen, J. (2022). Recent trends in internet of things enabled sensor technologies for smart agriculture. *IEEE Internet of Things Journal*, 9(23), 23583–23598. doi:10.1109/JIOT.2022.3210154

Shaikh, R. A., Sahu, T. P., & Anand, V. (2020). Predicting Outcomes of Legal Cases based on Legal Factors using Classifiers. *Procedia Computer Science*, 167, 2393–2402. doi:10.1016/j.procs.2020.03.292

Shakouri, B., Abbasi Shureshjani, R., Daneshian, B., & Hosseinzadeh Lotfi, F. (2020). A Parametric Method for Ranking Intuitionistic Fuzzy Numbers and Its Application to Solve Intuitionistic Fuzzy Network Data Envelopment Analysis Models. *Complexity*, 2020, 1–25. doi:10.1155/2020/6408613

Shamreen Ahamed, B., Arya, M. S., & Nancy, A. O. (2022). Diabetes Mellitus Disease Prediction Using Machine Learning Classifiers and Techniques Using the Concept of Data Augmentation and Sampling. In *ICT Systems and Sustainability: Proceedings of ICT4SD 2022* (pp. 401–413). Springer Nature Singapore.

Shang, X. (2022). A Computational Intelligence Model for Legal Prediction and Decision Support. *Computational Intelligence and Neuroscience*, *2022*, e5795189. doi:10.1155/2022/5795189 PMID:35785064

Shanmugasundari, M., & Aarthi, S. (2022, November). Modified approach of fuzzy measures using trapezoidal fuzzy numbers to solve the real world problems under fuzzy environment. In AIP Conference Proceedings (Vol. 2516, No. 1, p. 200001). AIP Publishing LLC. doi:10.1063/5.0108541

Sharma, S., Shandilya, R., & Sharma, S. (2021). *Predicting Indian Supreme Court Decisions* (SSRN Scholarly Paper 3917603). doi:10.2139/ssrn.3917603

Sharma, A., Jain, A., Gupta, P., & Chowdary, V. (2020). Machine learning applications for precision agriculture: A comprehensive review. *IEEE Access: Practical Innovations, Open Solutions*, *9*, 4843–4873. doi:10.1109/ACCESS.2020.3048415

Shi, L., Duan, Q., Ma, X., & Weng, M. (2012). The Research of Support Vector Machine in Agricultural Data Classification. In D. Li & Y. Chen (Eds.), *Computer and Computing Technologies in Agriculture V. CCTA 2011. IFIP Advances in Information and Communication Technology* (Vol. 370). Springer. doi:10.1007/978-3-642-27275-2_29

Shi, L., Yan, F., & Liu, H. (2023). Screening model of candidate drugs for breast cancer based on ensemble learning algorithm and molecular descriptor. *Expert Systems with Applications*, *213*, 119185. doi:10.1016/j.eswa.2022.119185

Shin, J. Y., Kim, K. R., & Ha, J. C. (2020). *Seasonal forecasting of daily mean air temperatures using a coupled global climate model and machine learning algorithm for field-scale agricultural management.*

Shirbandi, K., Khalafi, M., Mirza-Aghazadeh-Attari, M., Tahmasbi, M., Kiani Shahvandi, H., Javanmardi, P., & Rahim, F. (2021). Accuracy of deep learning model-assisted amyloid positron emission tomography scan in predicting Alzheimer's disease: A Systematic Review and meta-analysis. *Informatics in Medicine Unlocked*, *25*(August), 100710. doi:10.1016/j.imu.2021.100710

Shirgan. (2010). Face Recognition based on Principal Component Analysis and Feed Forward Neural Network. *National Conference on Emerging trends in Engineering, Technology, Architecture*. IEEE.

Shivaprakash, K. N., Swami, N., Mysorekar, S., Arora, R., Gangadharan, A., Vohra, K., Jadeyegowda, M., & Kiesecker, J. M. (2022). Potential for Artificial Intelligence (AI) and Machine Learning (ML) Applications in Biodiversity Conservation, Managing Forests, and Related Services in India. *Sustainability (Basel)*, *14*(12), 7154. doi:10.3390u14127154

Shorten, C., & Khoshgoftaar, T. M. (2019). A survey on image data augmentation for deep learning. *Journal of Big Data*, *6*(1), 1–48. doi:10.118640537-019-0197-0

Shovon, M. S. H., Mozumder, S. J., Pal, O. K., Mridha, M. F., Asai, N., & Shin, J. (2023). PlantDet: A Robust Multi-Model Ensemble Method Based on Deep Learning for Plant Disease Detection. *IEEE Access: Practical Innovations, Open Solutions*, *11*, 34846–34859. doi:10.1109/ACCESS.2023.3264835

Shrestha, G., Das, M. and Dey, N., 2020, October. Plant disease detection using CNN. In *2020 IEEE applied signal processing conference (ASPCON)* (pp. 109-113). IEEE.

Siddique, T., Barua, D., Ferdous, Z., & Chakrabarty, A. (2017, September). Automated farming prediction. In *2017 Intelligent systems conference (IntelliSys)* (pp. 757-763). IEEE.

Sigaud, O., & Droniou, A. (2015). Towards deep developmental learning. *IEEE Transactions on Cognitive and Developmental Systems*, *8*(2), 99–114. doi:10.1109/TAMD.2015.2496248

Sik-Ho Tsang. (2018). *Review: SSD — Single Shot Detector*. Object Detection.

Singh Sharma, K. (2023). Artificial intelligence assisted fabrication of 3D, 4D and 5D printed formulations or devices for drug delivery. *Current Drug Delivery*, 20(6), 752–769. doi:10.2174/1567201820666221207140956 PMID:36503474

Singh, A., Kanaujia, A., Singh, V. K., & Vinuesa, R. (2023). Artificial intelligence for Sustainable Development Goals: Bibliometric patterns and concept evolution trajectories. *Sustainable Development (Bradford)*, sd.2706. doi:10.1002d.2706

Singh, G., Vadera, M., Samavedham, L., & Lim, E. C. H. (2016). Machine Learning-Based Framework for Multi-Class Diagnosis of Neurodegenerative Diseases: A Study on Parkinson's Disease. *IFAC-PapersOnLine*, 49(7), 990–995. doi:10.1016/j.ifacol.2016.07.331

Sinha, M., Chacko, E., Makhija, P., & Pramanik, S. (2021). Energy Efficient Smart Cities with Green IoT. In C. Chakrabarty (Ed.), *Green Technological Innovation for Sustainable Smart Societies: Post Pandemic Era*. Springer. doi:10.1007/978-3-030-73295-0_16

Sivaranjani, N., Jayabharathy, J., & Teja, P. C. (2021). Predicting the supreme court decision on appeal cases using hierarchical convolutional neural network. *International Journal of Speech Technology*, 24(3), 643–650. doi:10.100710772-021-09820-4

Sobhia, M. E., Kumar, H., & Kumari, S. (2023). Bifunctional robots inducing targeted protein degradation. *European Journal of Medicinal Chemistry*, 255, 115384. doi:10.1016/j.ejmech.2023.115384 PMID:37119667

Somasundaram, M., Latha, P., & Pandian, S. A. S. (2020). Curriculum Design Using Artificial Intelligence (AI) Back Propagation Method. *Procedia Computer Science*, 172, 134–138. doi:10.1016/j.procs.2020.05.020

Soni, M., & Varma, S. (2020). *Diabetes prediction using machine learning techniques. International Journal of Engineering Research & Technology* (Vol. 9). Ijert.

Sood, A., Sharma, R. K., & Bhardwaj, A. K. (2022). Artificial intelligence research in agriculture: A review. *Online Information Review*, 46(6), 1054–1075. doi:10.1108/OIR-10-2020-0448

Soundararajan, S., & Kumar, M. S. (2020). Solving unbalanced intuitionistic fuzzy transportation problem. *Journal of Computational Mathematics*, 4(1), 1–8. doi:10.26524/cm61

Sowmya, S. V., & Somashekar, R. K. (2010). Application of remotesensing and geographical information system in mapping forestfire risk zone at Bhadra wildlife sanctuary, India. *Journal of Environmental Biology*, 31(6), 969. PMID:21506484

Sreedevi, A., & Manike, C. (2023). Development of weighted ensemble transfer learning for tomato leaf disease classification solving low resolution problems. *Imaging Science Journal*, 71(2), 161–187. doi:10.1080/13682199.2023.2178605

Sreedhar, B. BE, M. S., & Kumar, M. S. (2020, October). A comparative study of melanoma skin cancer detection in traditional and current image processing techniques. In *2020 Fourth International Conference on I-SMAC (IoT in Social, Mobile, Analytics and Cloud)(I-SMAC)* (pp. 654-658). IEEE.

Sreenivasulu. (2022). Implementation of Latest machine learning approaches for students Grade Prediction. *International Journal of Early Childhood special. Education*, 14(03), 9887–9894.

Ståhl, N., Falkman, G., Karlsson, A., Mathiason, G., & Boström, J. (2019). Deep reinforcement learning for multiparameter optimization in de novo drug design. *Journal of Chemical Information and Modeling*, 59(7), 3166–3176. doi:10.1021/acs.jcim.9b00325 PMID:31273995

Stanojević, B., & Stanojević, M. (2021). Approximate membership function shapes of solutions to intuitionistic fuzzy transportation problems. [IJCCC]. *International Journal of Computers, Communications & Control*, 16(1), 1–15.

Stokes, J. M., Yang, K., Swanson, K., Jin, W., Cubillos-Ruiz, A., Donghia, N. M., MacNair, C. R., French, S., Carfrae, L. A., Bloom-Ackermann, Z., Tran, V. M., Chiappino-Pepe, A., Badran, A. H., Andrews, I. W., Chory, E. J., Church, G. M., Brown, E. D., Jaakkola, T. S., Barzilay, R., & Collins, J. J. (2020). A deep learning approach to antibiotic discovery. *Cell*, *180*(4), 688–702.e613. doi:10.1016/j.cell.2020.01.021 PMID:32084340

Strickson, B., & De La Iglesia, B. (2020). Legal Judgement Prediction for UK Courts. *Proceedings of the 2020 The 3rd International Conference on Information Science and System*, (pp. 204–209). ACM. 10.1145/3388176.3388183

Suhartono, D., Majiid, M. R. N., Handoyo, A. T., Wicaksono, P., & Lucky, H. (2023). Toward a more general drug target interaction prediction model using transfer learning. *Procedia Computer Science*, *216*, 370–376. doi:10.1016/j.procs.2022.12.148 PMID:36643181

Sun, Wang, Qu, & Xiong. (2022). BeatClass: A Sustainable ECG Classification System in IoT-Based eHealth. *IEEE Internet of Things Journal, 9*(10), 7178-7195. . doi:10.1109/JIOT.2021.3108792

Suruliandi, A., Mariammal, G., & Raja, S. P. (2021). Crop prediction based on soil and environmental characteristics using feature selection techniques. *Mathematical and Computer Modelling of Dynamical Systems*, *27*(1), 117–140. doi:10.1080/13873954.2021.1882505

Szlęk, J., Khalid, M. H., Pacławski, A., Czub, N., & Mendyk, A. (2022). Puzzle Out Machine Learning Model-Explaining Disintegration Process in ODTs. *Pharmaceutics*, *14*(4), 859. doi:10.3390/pharmaceutics14040859 PMID:35456693

Tadlagi. (2022). Depression Detection. [JHMIB]. *Journal of Mental Health Issues and Behavior*, *2*(6), 1–7.

Taghaodi, R. (2019). A novel solution approach for solving intuitionistic fuzzy transportation problem of type-2. *Annals of Optimization Theory and Practice*, *2*(2), 11–24. doi:10.22121/AOTP.2019.198947.1022

Taillard, É. D. (2023). *Design of heuristic algorithms for hard optimization with python codes for the travelling salesman problem*. Springer Nature. doi:10.1007/978-3-031-13714-3

Tai, P., Wu, F., Chen, R., Zhu, J., Wang, X., & Zhang, M. (2023). Effect of herbaceous plants on the response of loose silty sand slope under rainfall. *Bulletin of Engineering Geology and the Environment*, *82*(1), 42. doi:10.100710064-023-03066-x

Talasila, S., Rawal, K., & Sethi, G. (2022). Conventional data augmentation techniques for plant disease detection and classification systems. In *Intelligent Systems and Sustainable Computing* [Singapore: Springer Nature Singapore.]. *Proceedings of ICISSC*, *2021*, 279–287.

Talaviya, T., Shah, D., Patel, N., Yagnik, H., & Shah, M. (2020). Implementation of artificial intelligence in agriculture for optimisation of irrigation and application of pesticides and herbicides. *Artificial Intelligence in Agriculture*, *4*, 58–73. doi:10.1016/j.aiia.2020.04.002

Tanaka, Y., Minet, P., & Watteyne, T. (2019). Tanaka. 6LoWPAN fragment forwarding. *IEEE Commun. Stand. Mag*, *3*(1), 35–39. doi:10.1109/MCOMSTD.2019.1800029

Tanneau, M., Anjos, M. F., & Lodi, A. (2021). Design and implementation of a modular interior-point solver for linear optimization. [MPC]. *Mathematical Programming Computation*, *13*(3), 1–43. doi:10.100712532-020-00200-8

Tao, Q., Ren, K., Feng, B., & Xuejin, G. (October 2020). An accurate low-light object detection method based on pyramid networks. *Optoelectronic Imaging and Multimedia Technology*.

Tăuţan, A. M., Ionescu, B., & Santarnecchi, E. (2021). Artificial intelligence in neurodegenerative diseases: A review of available tools with a focus on machine learning techniques. *Artificial Intelligence in Medicine, 117*(July 2020). doi:10.1016/j.artmed.2021.102081

Teal, M. (2023). *The Ethics of College Students Using ChatGPT - Ethics and Policy.* https://ethicspolicy.unc.edu/news/2023/04/17/the-ethics-of-college-students-using-chatgpt/

Team Cultivatd. (2022, September 21). *3 Advantages and 3 Challenges of Vertical Farming.* Cultivatd. https://cultivatd.com/advantages-challenges-vertical-farming/

TEMPUS. (2023, October 15). *Tempus Announces Real-World Data-Driven Program to Accelerate Precision Oncology Research.* TEMPUS. https://www.tempus.com/news/tempus-announces-real-world-data-driven-program-to-accelerate-precision-oncology-research/

Thakkar, S., Slikker, W. Jr, Yiannas, F., Silva, P., Blais, B., Chng, K. R., Liu, Z., Adholeya, A., Pappalardo, F., Soares, M. L. C., Beeler, P. E., Whelan, M., Roberts, R., Borlak, J., Hugas, M., Torrecilla-Salinas, C., Girard, P., Diamond, M. C., Verloo, D., & Tong, W. (2023). Artificial intelligence and real-world data for drug and food safety – A regulatory science perspective. *Regulatory Toxicology and Pharmacology, 140,* 105388. doi:10.1016/j.yrtph.2023.105388 PMID:37061083

Thomas, A., & Sangeetha, S. (2019). An innovative hybrid approach for extracting named entities from unstructured text data. *Computational Intelligence, 35*(4), 799–826. doi:10.1111/coin.12214

Thomas, A., & Sangeetha, S. (2021). Semi-supervised, KNOWLEDGE-INTEGRATED pattern learning approach for fact extraction from judicial text. *Expert Systems: International Journal of Knowledge Engineering and Neural Networks, 38*(3), e12656. doi:10.1111/exsy.12656

Thomas, A., & Sivanesan, S. (2022). An adaptable, high-performance relation extraction system for complex sentences. *Knowledge-Based Systems, 251*(C), 108956. doi:10.1016/j.knosys.2022.108956

Tight, M. (2020). Student retention and engagement in higher education. *Journal of Further and Higher Education, 44*(5), 689–704. doi:10.1080/0309877X.2019.1576860

Tilson K. (2010). Lyytinen C. Sørensen Research commentary—digital infrastructures: the missing IS research agenda *Inf. Syst. Res., 21.*

Tiwari, V., Joshi, R. C., & Dutta, M. K. (2021). Dense convolutional neural networks based multiclass plant disease detection and classification using leaf images. *Ecological Informatics, 63,* 101289. doi:10.1016/j.ecoinf.2021.101289

Too, E. C., Yujian, L., Njuki, S., & Yingchun, L. (2019). A comparative study of fine-tuning deep learning models for plant disease identification. *Computers and Electronics in Agriculture, 161,* 272–279. doi:10.1016/j.compag.2018.03.032

Tran, T. T. V., Tayara, H., & Chong, K. T. (2023). Recent studies of artificial intelligence on in silico drug distribution prediction. *International Journal of Molecular Sciences, 24*(3), 1815. doi:10.3390/ijms24031815 PMID:36768139

Tripathi, G., Manish, S., Chaynika, D., & Pallavi, P. (2022). Object Detection using YOLO: A Survey. *5th International Conference on Contemporary Computing and Informatics.* IEEE. 10.1109/IC3I56241.2022.10073281

Tripathi, M. K., & Maktedar, D. D. (2020). A role of computer vision in fruits and vegetables among various horticulture products of agriculture fields: A survey. *Information Processing in Agriculture, 7*(2), 183–203. doi:10.1016/j.inpa.2019.07.003

Tuppad, A., & Patil, S. D. (2022). Machine learning for diabetes clinical decision support: A review. *Advances in Computational Intelligence, 2*(2), 22. doi:10.100743674-022-00034-y PMID:35434723

U.S. Food and Drug Administration (U.S. FDA). (2019). *Proposed regulatory framework for modifications to artificial intelligence/machine learning (ai/ml)-based software as a medical device (SAMD) - discussion paper and request for feedback.* US FDA.

Ungerer, L., & Slade, S. (2022). Ethical considerations of artificial intelligence in learning analytics in distance education contexts. In Learning Analytics in Open and Distributed Learning: Potential and Challenges (pp. 105-120). Singapore: Springer Nature Singapore. doi:10.1007/978-981-19-0786-9_8

United Nations Educational, Scientific and Cultural Organization (UNESCO). (2019). *Artificial intelligence in education: Challenges and opportunities for sustainable development.* UNESCO. https://unesdoc.unesco.org/ark:/48223/pf0000366994

Utami, W. S., Diwandari, S., & Hermawan, A. (2019). Transportation problem optimization systems using the algorithm of allocation table method. *International Journal of Applied Business and Information Systems, 3*(2), 45–52.

Vahida. (2023). Deep Learning, YOLO and RFID based smart Billing Handcart. *Journal of Communication Engineering & Systems, 13*(1), 1–8.

Valipour, M. (2015). A comprehensive study on irrigation management in Asia and Oceania. *Archives of Agronomy and Soil Science, 61*(9), 1247–1271. doi:10.1080/03650340.2014.986471

Valliathal, M., & Revathi, M. (2020). A new approach to find optimal solution of fuzzy assignment problem using penalty method for hendecagonal fuzzy number. [IJFCM]. *International Journal of Fuzzy Computation and Modelling, 3*(1), 61. doi:10.1504/IJFCM.2020.106101

Varghese, A., & Kuriakose, S. (2012). Centroid of an intuitionistic fuzzy number. [NIFS]. *Notes on Intuitionistic Fuzzy Sets, 18*(1), 19–24.

Varior, R. R., Haloi, M., & Wang, G. (2016). *Gated siamese convolutional neural network architecture for human re-identification.* In Computer Vision–ECCV 2016: 14th European Conference, Amsterdam.

Veenis, J. F., & Brugts, J. J. (2020). Remote monitoring of chronic heart failure patients: Invasive versus non-invasive tools for optimising patient management. Netherlands. *The Hearing Journal, 28*(1), 3–13. doi:10.100712471-019-01342-8 PMID:31745814

Veeraiah, V., Shiju, D. J., Ramesh, J. V. N., Ganesh, K. R., Pramanik, S., & Pandey, D. (2023). *A, Gupta, Healthcare Cloud Services in Image Processing, Thrust Technologies' Effect on Image Processing.* IGI Global.

Velu, L. G. N., Selvaraj, J., & Ponnialagan, D. (2017). A new ranking principle for ordering trapezoidal intuitionistic fuzzy numbers. *Complexity, 2017*, 1–24. doi:10.1155/2017/3049041

Venkatesh, V., Thong, J. Y., & Xu, X. (2016). Unified theory of acceptance and use of technology: A synthesis and the road ahead. *Journal of the Association for Information Systems, 17*(5), 328–376. doi:10.17705/1jais.00428

Verma, S., & Rubin, J. (2018). *Fairness definitions explained.* Proceedings of the International Workshop on Software Fairness - FairWare '18, 1–7. 10.1145/3194770.3194776

Verma, S., Gala, R., Madhavan, S., Burkule, S., Chauhan, S., & Prakash, C. (2018, August). An internet of things (IoT) architecture for smart agriculture. In *2018 fourth international conference on computing communication control and automation (ICCUBEA)* (pp. 1-4). IEEE.

Veverka, P., Brom, T., Janovič, T., Stojaspal, M., Pinkas, M., Nováček, J., & Hofr, C. (2023). Electron microscopy reveals toroidal shape of master neuronal cell differentiator REST – RE1-silencing transcription factor. *Computational and Structural Biotechnology Journal, 21*, 731–741. doi:10.1016/j.csbj.2022.12.026 PMID:36698979

Vidya Chellam, V., Veeraiah, V., Khanna, A., Sheikh, T. H., Pramanik, S., & Dhabliya, D. (2023). *A Machine Vision-based Approach for Tuberculosis Identification in Chest X-Rays Images of Patients, ICICC 2023*. Springer. doi:10.1007/978-981-99-3315-0_3

Vijayan, V. V., & Anjali, C. (2015, December). Prediction and diagnosis of diabetes mellitus—A machine learning approach. In 2015 IEEE Recent Advances in Intelligent Computational Systems (RAICS) (pp. 122-127). IEEE.

Vijayaraghavan, J. R. (n.d.). *Introduction of Artificial Intelligence in the Judicial system*.

Vilani Sachithra, L.D.C.S. (2020). How artificial intelligence uses to achieve the agriculture sustainability. *Systematic review*.

Villegas-Ch, W., García-Ortiz, J., Mullo-Ca, K., Sánchez-Viteri, S., & Roman-Cañizares, M. (2021). Implementation of a virtual assistant for the academic management of a university with the use of artificial intelligence. *Future Internet*, *13*(4), 97. doi:10.3390/fi13040097

Vinay. (2022). *Multiple object detection and classification based on Pruning using YOLO*. Lambart Publications.

Virk, A. L., Noor, M. A., Fiaz, S., Hussain, S., Hussain, H. A., Rehman, M., & Ma, W. (2020). Smart farming: an overview. *Smart village technology: concepts and developments*, 191-201.

Vishnoi, V. K., Kumar, K., & Kumar, B. (2021). Plant disease detection using computational intelligence and image processing. *Journal of Plant Diseases and Protection*, *128*(1), 19–53. doi:10.100741348-020-00368-0

Vogt, M. (2023). Exploring chemical space — Generative models and their evaluation. *Artificial Intelligence in the Life Sciences*, *3*, 100064. doi:10.1016/j.ailsci.2023.100064

Vora, L. K., Gholap, A. D., Jetha, K., Thakur, R. R. S., Solanki, H. K., & Chavda, V. P. (2023). Artificial intelligence in pharmaceutical technology and drug delivery design. *Pharmaceutics*, *15*(7), 1916. doi:10.3390/pharmaceutics15071916 PMID:37514102

Waghmare. (2022). Smart watch system. [IJITC]. *International Journal of Information Technology and Computer Engineering*, *2*(6), 1–9.

Wakchaure, M., Patel, B. K., & Mahindrakar, A. K. (2023). Application of AI techniques and robotics in agriculture: A review. *Artificial Intelligence in the Life Sciences*, *3*, 100057. doi:10.1016/j.ailsci.2023.100057

Wale. (2019). Smart Agriculture System using IoT. *International Journal of Innovative Research In Technology*, *5*(10), 493–497.

Walsh, D., Schuler, A. M., Hall, D., Walsh, J. R., & Fisher, C. K. (2021). Using digital twins to reduce sample sizes while maintaining power and statistical accuracy. *Alzheimer's & Dementia*, *17*(S9), e054657. doi:10.1002/alz.054657

Wang, Y., Gao, J., & Chen, J. (2020). Deep Learning Algorithm for Judicial Judgment Prediction Based on BERT. *2020 5th International Conference on Computing, Communication and Security (ICCCS)*, (pp. 1–6). IEEE. 10.1109/ICCCS49678.2020.9277068

Wang C.-Y. Bochkovskiy A. Liao H.-Y. M. (6 Jul 2022). YOLOv7: Trainable bag-of-freebies sets new state-of-the-art for real-time object detectors. https://arxiv.org/abs/2207.02696

Wang, F., Sangfuang, N., McCoubrey, L. E., Yadav, V., Elbadawi, M., Orlu, M., Gaisford, S., & Basit, A. W. (2023). Advancing oral delivery of biologics: Machine learning predicts peptide stability in the gastrointestinal tract. *International Journal of Pharmaceutics*, *634*, 122643. doi:10.1016/j.ijpharm.2023.122643 PMID:36709014

Wang, G., Zhang, S., Dong, S., Lou, D., Ma, L., Pei, X., Xu, H., Farooq, U., Guo, W., & Luo, J. (2019, April). Stretchable Optical Sensing Patch System Integrated Heart Rate, Pulse Oxygen Saturation, and Sweat pH Detection. *IEEE Transactions on Biomedical Engineering*, *66*(4), 1000–1005. doi:10.1109/TBME.2018.2866151 PMID:30130170

Wang, L., Yu, Z., Wang, S., Guo, Z., Sun, Q., & Lai, L. (2022). Discovery of novel SARS-CoV-2 3CL protease covalent inhibitors using deep learning-based screen. *European Journal of Medicinal Chemistry*, *244*, 114803. doi:10.1016/j. ejmech.2022.114803 PMID:36209629

Wang, S., Huang, X., Yin, C., & Richel, A. (2021). A critical review on the key issues and optimization of agricultural residue transportation. *Biomass and Bioenergy*, *146*, 105979. doi:10.1016/j.biombioe.2021.105979

Wang, S., Yang, J., Chen, H., Chu, K., Yu, X., Wei, Y., Zhang, H., Rui, M., & Feng, C. (2022). A strategy for the effective optimization of pharmaceutical formulations based on parameter-optimized support vector machine model. *AAPS PharmSciTech*, *23*(1), 66. doi:10.120812249-022-02210-2 PMID:35102463

Wang, T., Lund, B. D., Marengo, A., Pagano, A., Mannuru, N. R., Teel, Z. A., & Pange, J. (2023). Exploring the Potential Impact of Artificial Intelligence (AI) on International Students in Higher Education: Generative AI, Chatbots, Analytics, and International Student Success. *Applied Sciences (Basel, Switzerland)*, *13*(11), 6716. doi:10.3390/app13116716

Wang, Y., Zhou, C., & Zhou, Z. (2020, October). The shortest time assignment problem and its improved algorithm. In *International Conference on Computer Engineering and Networks (pp. 583-588)*. Springer, Singapore. 10.1007/978-981-15-8462-6_65

Wang, Z., Ong, C. L. J., & Fu, Z. (2022). AI models to assist vancomycin dosage titration. *Frontiers in Pharmacology*, *13*, 801928. doi:10.3389/fphar.2022.801928 PMID:35211014

Weiskirchen, R., & Penning, L. C. (2021). COMMD1, a multipotent intracellular protein involved in copper homeostasis, protein trafficking, inflammation, and cancer. *Journal of Trace Elements in Medicine and Biology*, *65*, 126712. doi:10.1016/j.jtemb.2021.126712 PMID:33482423

Wong, C. H., Siah, K. W., & Lo, A. W. (2019). Corrigendum: Estimation of clinical trial success rates and related parameters. *Biostatistics (Oxford, England)*, *20*(2), 366. doi:10.1093/biostatistics/kxy072 PMID:30445524

Xia, Q., Chiu, T. K., Zhou, X., Chai, C. S., & Cheng, M. (2022). Systematic literature review on opportunities, challenges, and future research recommendations of artificial intelligence in education. *Computers and Education: Artificial Intelligence*, *100118*. doi:10.1016/j.caeai.2022.100118

Xie, D., Chen, L., Liu, L., Chen, L., & Wang, H. (2022). Actuators and sensors for application in agricultural robots: A review. *Machines*, *10*(10), 913. doi:10.3390/machines10100913

Xu, J., Wang, Y., Zhang, J., Abdelmoneim, A. A., Liang, Z., Wang, L., Jin, J., Dai, Q., & Ye, F. (2023). Elastic network models and molecular dynamic simulations reveal the molecular basis of allosteric regulation in ubiquitin-specific protease 7 (USP7). *Computers in Biology and Medicine*, *162*(March), 107068. doi:10.1016/j.compbiomed.2023.107068 PMID:37290391

Xu, Y., Liu, X., Cao, X., Huang, C., Liu, E., Qian, S., Liu, X., Wu, Y., Dong, F., Qiu, C.-W., Qiu, J., Hua, K., Su, W., Wu, J., Xu, H., Han, Y., Fu, C., Yin, Z., Liu, M., & Zhang, J. (2021). Artificial intelligence: A powerful paradigm for scientific research. *Innovation (Cambridge (Mass.))*, *2*(4), 100179. doi:10.1016/j.xinn.2021.100179 PMID:34877560

Yacoub, A. S., Ammar, H. O., Ibrahim, M., Mansour, S. M., & El Hoffy, N. M. (2022). Artificial intelligence-assisted development of in situ forming nanoparticles for arthritis therapy via intra-articular delivery. *Drug Delivery*, *29*(1), 1423–1436. doi:10.1080/10717544.2022.2069882 PMID:35532141

Yang, G., Pang, G., Pang, Z., Gu, Y., Mäntysalo, M., & Yang, H. (2019). Non-Invasive Flexible and Stretchable Wearable Sensors With Nano-Based Enhancement for Chronic Disease Care. *IEEE Reviews in Biomedical Engineering, 12,* 34–71. doi:10.1109/RBME.2018.2887301 PMID:30571646

Yang, L., Yu, X., Zhang, S., Zhang, H., Xu, S., Long, H., & Zhu, Y. (2023). Stacking-based and improved convolutional neural network: A new approach in rice leaf disease identification. *Frontiers in Plant Science, 14,* 1165940. doi:10.3389/fpls.2023.1165940 PMID:37346133

Yang, M. J., Song, H., Shi, P., Liang, J., Hu, Z., Zhou, C., Hu, P. P., Yu, Z. L., & Zhang, T. (2023). Integrated mRNA and miRNA transcriptomic analysis reveals the response of Rapana venosa to the metamorphic inducer (juvenile oysters). *Computational and Structural Biotechnology Journal, 21,* 702–715. doi:10.1016/j.csbj.2022.12.047 PMID:36659925

Yang, Y. (2021). Design and Implementation of Intelligent Learning System Based on Big Data and Artificial Intelligence. *Frontiers in Psychology, 12,* 726978. doi:10.3389/fpsyg.2021.726978 PMID:34858265

Yasmeen, U., Khan, M. A., Tariq, U., Khan, J. A., Yar, M. A. E., Hanif, C. A., & Nam, Y. (2021). Citrus diseases recognition using deep improved genetic algorithm. *Computers, Materials & Continua, 71,* 3667–3684. doi:10.32604/cmc.2022.022264

Yin, B. K., Lázaro, D., & Wang, Z. Q. (2023). TRRAP-mediated acetylation on Sp1 regulates adult neurogenesis. *Computational and Structural Biotechnology Journal, 21,* 472–484. doi:10.1016/j.csbj.2022.12.024 PMID:36618986

Yingngam, B. (2023). New drug discovery. In Multidisciplinary Applications of Natural Science for Drug Discovery and Integrative Medicine (pp. 134-184). IGI Global. doi:10.4018/978-1-6684-9463-9.ch005

Yingngam, B., Navabhatra, A., Rungseevijitprapa, W., Prasitpuriprecha, C., & Brantner, A. (2021). Comparative study of response surface methodology and artificial neural network in the optimization of the ultrasound-assisted extraction of diarylheptanoid phytoestrogens from *Curcuma comosa* rhizomes. *Chemical Engineering and Processing, 165,* 108461. doi:10.1016/j.cep.2021.108461

Yoo, J., Kim, T. Y., Joung, I., & Song, S. O. (2023). Industrializing AI/ML during the end-to-end drug discovery process. *Current Opinion in Structural Biology, 79,* 102528. doi:10.1016/j.sbi.2023.102528 PMID:36736243

Yu, H., Liu, C., Zhang, L., Wu, C., Liang, G., Escorcia-Gutierrez, J., & Ghoneim, O. A. (2023). An intent classification method for questions in "Treatise on Febrile diseases" based on TinyBERT-CNN fusion model. *Computers in Biology and Medicine, 162*(May), 107075. doi:10.1016/j.compbiomed.2023.107075 PMID:37276755

Yu, Z., & Khan, S. A. R. (2021). Green supply chain network optimization under random and fuzzy environment. *International Journal of Fuzzy Systems,* 1–12. doi:10.100740815-020-00979-7

Zadeh, L. A. (1965). Fuzzy sets. *Information and Control, 8*(3), 338–353. doi:10.1016/S0019-9958(65)90241-X

Zadgaonkar, A., & Agrawal, A. J. (2023). An Approach for Analyzing Unstructured Text Data Using Topic Modeling Techniques for Efficient Information Extraction. *New Generation Computing.* doi:10.100700354-023-00230-5

Zahir, J. (2023). Prediction of court decision from Arabic documents using deep learning. *Expert Systems: International Journal of Knowledge Engineering and Neural Networks, 40*(6), e13236. doi:10.1111/exsy.13236

Zaitseva, I., Malafeyev, O., Konopko, E., Taran, V., & Durakova, A. (2020, November). Simulation of optimal solutions for assignment problems in the context of incomplete information. In AIP Conference Proceedings (Vol. 2293, No. 1, p. 420012). AIP Publishing LLC. doi:10.1063/5.0026848

Zawacki-Richter, O., Marín, V. I., Bond, M., & Gouverneur, F. (2019). Systematic review of research on artificial intelligence applications in higher education–where are the educators? *International Journal of Educational Technology in Higher Education*, *16*(1), 1–27. doi:10.118641239-019-0171-0

Zhang, B. (2022). A Framework for Remote Interaction and Management of Home Care Elderly Adults. IEEE Sensors Journal, 22(11). . doi:10.1109/JSEN.2022.3170295

Zhang, K., Zhu, J., Zhang, Y., & Huang, Q. (2021). Optimization method for linear constraint problems. *Journal of Computational Science*, *51*, 101315. doi:10.1016/j.jocs.2021.101315

Zhang, L., Wu, M., & Ouyang, F. (2023). The design and implementation of a teaching and learning analytics tool in a face-to-face, small-sized course in China's higher education. *Education and Information Technologies*, 1–24. doi:10.100710639-023-11940-0

Zhang, N., Yang, G., Pan, Y., Yang, X., Chen, L., & Zhao, C. (2020). A review of advanced technologies and development for hyperspectral-based plant disease detection in the past three decades. *Remote Sensing (Basel)*, *12*(19), 3188. doi:10.3390/rs12193188

Zhang, S., Lei, H., Zhou, Z., Wang, G., & Qiu, B. (2023). Fatigue life analysis of high-strength bolts based on machine learning method and SHapley Additive exPlanations (SHAP) approach. *Structures*, *51*, 275–287. doi:10.1016/j.istruc.2023.03.060

Zhang, S., Zhang, X., Du, J., Wang, W., & Pi, X. (2023). Multitarget meridians classification based on the topological structure of anticancer phytochemicals using deep learning. *Journal of Ethnopharmacology*, *117244*. doi:10.1016/j.jep.2023.117244 PMID:37777031

Zhang, Y., Qin, G., Cheng, L., Marimuthu, K., & Kumar, B. S. (2021). Interactive Smart Educational System Using AI for Students in the Higher Education Platform. *J. of Mult.-. Valued Logic & Soft Computing*, *36*(1–3), 89–98.

Zhao, J., & Gómez Fariñas, B. (2023). Artificial Intelligence and Sustainable Decisions. *European Business Organization Law Review*, *24*(1), 1–39. doi:10.100740804-022-00262-2

Zhavoronkov, A., Ivanenkov, Y. A., Aliper, A., Veselov, M. S., Aladinskiy, V. A., Aladinskaya, A. V., Terentiev, V. A., Polykovskiy, D. A., Kuznetsov, M. D., Asadulaev, A., Volkov, Y., Zholus, A., Shayakhmetov, R. R., Zhebrak, A., Minaeva, L. I., Zagribelnyy, B. A., Lee, L. H., Soll, R., Madge, D., & Aspuru-Guzik, A. (2019). Deep learning enables rapid identification of potent DDR1 kinase inhibitors. *Nature Biotechnology*, *37*(9), 1038–1040. doi:10.103841587-019-0224-x PMID:31477924

Zhong, H., Guo, Z., Tu, C., Xiao, C., Liu, Z., & Sun, M. (2018). Legal Judgment Prediction via Topological Learning. In E. Riloff, D. Chiang, J. Hockenmaier, & J. Tsujii (Eds.), *Proceedings of the 2018 Conference on Empirical Methods in Natural Language Processing* (pp. 3540–3549). Association for Computational Linguistics. 10.18653/v1/D18-1390

Zhou, F., Zhao, H., & Nie, Z. (2021). Safety helmet detection based on YOLOv5. *2021 IEEE International Conference on Power Electronics, Computer Applications (ICPECA)*, (pp. 6–11). IEEE. 10.1109/ICPECA51329.2021.9362711

Zhou, S. K., Greenspan, H., Davatzikos, C., Duncan, J. S., Van Ginneken, B., Madabhushi, A., Prince, J. L., Rueckert, D., & Summers, R. M. (2021, May). A Review of Deep Learning in Medical Imaging: Imaging Traits, Technology Trends, Case Studies With Progress Highlights, and Future Promises. *Proceedings of the IEEE*, *109*(5), 820–838. doi:10.1109/JPROC.2021.3054390 PMID:37786449

Zhu, M., Wang, J., Yang, X., Zhang, Y., Zhang, L., Ren, H., Wu, B., & Ye, L. (2022). A review of the application of machine learning in water quality evaluation. *Eco-Environment & Health, 1*(2). doi:10.1016/j.eehl.2022.06.001

Zhuang, C., Zhou, Y., Ge, J., Li, Z., Li, C., Zhou, X., & Luo, B. (2017). Information Extraction from Chinese Judgment Documents. *2017 14th Web Information Systems and Applications Conference (WISA)*, (pp. 240–244). ScitePress.

Zhu, N., Liu, X., Liu, Z., Hu, K., Wang, Y., Tan, J., Huang, M., Zhu, Q., Ji, X., Jiang, Y., & Guo, Y. (2018). Deep learning for smart agriculture: Concepts, tools, applications, and opportunities. *International Journal of Agricultural and Biological Engineering*, *11*(4), 32–44. doi:10.25165/j.ijabe.20181104.4475

Zou, Y., Shi, Y., Sun, F., Liu, J., Guo, Y., Zhang, H., Lu, X., Gong, Y., & Xia, S. (2022). Extreme gradient boosting model to assess risk of central cervical lymph node metastasis in patients with papillary thyroid carcinoma: Individual prediction using SHapley Additive exPlanations. *Computer Methods and Programs in Biomedicine*, *225*, 107038. doi:10.1016/j.cmpb.2022.107038 PMID:35930861

About the Contributors

Van Thanh Tien Nguyen received his master's degrees in both mechanical engineering and linguistics from Viet Nam National University Ho Chi Minh City, Bach Khoa University, and HCMC University of Social Sciences and Humanities in 2012 and 2020, respectively. He holds a Ph.D. degree in Industrial Engineering and Management from the National Kaohsiung University of Science and Technology, Taiwan. He has published over 61 journal papers and conference papers, served as a reviewer for more than 75 SCI/Scopus Journals with over 1010 review reports, and handled as an Academic Editor for several Q1 Journals with over 65 scientific manuscripts. He has experience studying and working in labs as a researcher/professional in many countries, such as Korea, Thailand, Russia, and Taiwan. He is currently working as a lecturer for the Industrial University of Ho Chi Minh City, Vietnam. His areas of interest are machine learning (AI), compliant mechanisms optimization design, numerical computation, MCDM, and Supply chain management. The concentration studies conducted by this individual have significantly influenced his field, as evidenced by his Scopus H-index of 16 and 553 citations (updated as of December 31, 2023).

Thi Minh Nhut Vo received her M.Sc degree at National Kaohsiung University of Science and Technology (NKUST), Taiwan. She is currently pursuing the Ph.D. program in Industrial Engineering and Management at National Kaohsiung University of Science and Technology, Taiwan. Prior to coming to NKUST, she worked in the banking sector, jewelry industry, Information Technology, and E-commerce. She is now working as a self-publishing author with many books about lean management and other fields. Her areas of interest are the Internet of Things, Blockchain, cloud computing, machine learning (AI), green energy, logistics, E-Commerce, and numerical computation.

***

Feranmi Adejuwon is a computer educator and researcher at Lead City University's Faculty of Education's Department of Science Education. His research interests include things like instructional technology, cybersecurity education, and the usage and security of information. He is excited about highlighting the significant contributions that cybersecurity education can make in order to establish a safe and secure online presence.

Bhuvaneswari Amma N.G. received the Ph.D. Degree from the National Institute of Technology, Tiruchirappalli, Tamil Nadu, India in 2020. Currently she is an Assistant Professor in the School of

Computer Science and Engineering, Vellore Institute of Technology, Chennai, Tamil Nadu, India. Her areas of interest include network security, machine learning, data analytics, and statistical methods.

Oluwabunmi Bakare-Fatungase is an Information Professional/Researcher in the Department of Information Management, Faculty of Communication & Information Sciences, Lead City University. Her research interest covers emerging technologies, digital & virtual libraries, information use and user communities, bullying and mobile bullying, etc. She is passionate about emphasizing the significant roles of Librarians in solving different societal issues with the arsenal of information at their disposal. She is a fellow of the Council for the Development of Social Science Research in Africa and a Queen Elizabeth Scholar in the Advanced Scholars West Africa (QES-AS-WA) program, Carleton University, Canada.

S. Prince Sahaya Brighty has over 17 years of teaching experience and currently working as an Assistant Professor (Selection Grade) in the Department of Computer Science and Engineering at Sri Ramakrishna Engineering College. She completed her B.E(with Distinction) in Computer Science and Engineering from Noorul Islam College of Engineering, Nagercoil (Anna University,Chennai) in 2005. She completed her Masters' (with Distinction) in Computer Science and Engineering from Kumaraguru College of Technology,Coimbatore(Anna University,Chennai) in the year 2013. Her research area includes AI & Machine Learning, Data Science and Wireless sensor networks,.She has published two patents with grant and received two copyrights. She has published 18 papers in reputed International Journals such as Springer, IEEE etc. She has also published papers in 16 International and National conferences. She has received the Best paper award in a Springer and IEEE International Conferences. She has guided around 30 UG projects . She is a lifetime member of CSI, IRACST and IAENG.

M. Brindha currently pursuing Bachelors programme in Computer Science and Engineering at Sri Ramakrishna Engineering College. As a fan of artificial intelligence;i have worked on a number of projects involving the deployment of neural network models.

Sachin Chaudhary completed his Graduation from MJPRU, and Post Graduation from AKTU, Moradabad, U.P. Currently Pursuing his Ph.D. in Computer Science and Engineering from Govt. Recognized University. Presently, he is working as an Assistant Professor in the Department of Computer Science and Applications, IIMT University, Meerut, U.P, India. He has been awarded as Excellence in teaching award 2019. He is the reviewer member of some reputed journals. He has published several book chapters and research papers of national and international reputed journals.

Joel Jebadurai Devapitchai serving as Assistant Professor in Department of MBA, St.Joseph's College of Engineering, OMR, Chennai, He has published more than 40 research articles in various peer reviewed journals. He has published two books. He has been awarded with Major Research Project Sponsored by Indian Council of Social Sciences Research, New Delhi.

E. Poovammal is the Professor in the Department of Computer Science and Engineering at SRM Institute of Science and Technology. She joined in SRM in the year 1996. Before joining SRM, Dr. Poovammal has held a number of positions including M/S. Masseys Engineering, where she worked as an Estimation Engineer; I.T.I Computer Center and Tuticorin Port Trust. Dr. Poovammal obtained her B.E. Degree in Electrical and Electronics Engineering from Madurai Kamaraj University in the year

1990, M.E degree in Computer Science and Engineering from Madras University in the year 2002 and Ph.D. degree in Computer Science and Engineering from SRM University in 2011. Her research interests include Association Rule Mining, Web Mining, Text Mining, Image and Video mining, Privacy and of software Research, Privacy and Security in the Cloud as well as Big Data Analytics. She currently guides six research scholars. Since last 4 years she is certified as Adjunct Faculty for the two courses, by Institute of software Research, Carnegie Mellon University, Pittsburgh, USA. She has published in more than 30 referred journals and presented in various international and national conferences. She is the Recipient of "Best Academic Dean award", by Association of Scientists, Developers and Faculties (ASDF), 2015 and Recipient of "Women Engineer award", by IET-CLN, 2013. She is the life member of ISTE and Indian Science Congress. She is also the member of other professional bodies like IET, IEEE, ACM and CSI.

Hudson Arul Vethamanikam G. working as an Assistsant Professor in Department of Business Administration, Ayya Nadar Janaki Ammal College,Sivakasi Tamilnadu. He has received various awards for his research contribution.

Ridhoyanti Hidayah is a lecturer in the Nursing Department, Faculty of Health Sciences, Universitas Brawijaya, Indonesia. Her specialty is in mental health nursing. She received her bachelor of nursing in the School of Nursing, Faculty of Medicine, Universitas Brawijaya in 2009. Her master of nursing was achieved from Faculty of Nursing, Universitas Airlangga in 2015. She also provides mental health counselling in community integrated village in East Java.

Tran Thi Hong Ngoc, Head Department of Environmental Management, Faculty of Engineering - Technology - Environment, An Giang University, Vietnam. Her research area at Ph.D. level is "Evaluation of hydrological models for water resources management planning and estimating of sediment load on the floodplain of Long Xuyen Quadrangle An Giang, Vietnam". It involves analyzing various factors such as precipitation patterns, soil properties, vegetation cover, land use to simulate the movement of water through the hydrological cycle as well as calculating evapotranspiration for crops to solve the problem of water balance and a little my hydraulic knowledge being applied in some small projects such as water resources management, flood forecasting, environmental impact assessment, climate change and infrastructure design.

Temitope Oluwatofunmi Idowu-Davies is an educational expert who is passionate about instilling core religious and theological values in learners in addition to promoting equity within the gender ecosystem which is fundamental in the SDGs. She is presently working on contemporary technological trends that scholars should toe in order to be able to effectively discharge their duties to learners.

Dheenadhayalan K. working as an Assistant Professor in Department of MBA, Mepco schlenk Engineering college, Sivakasi. He had a rich experience in the field of teaching.

Phan Truong Khanh - Vice Dean, Faculty of Engineering-Technology-Environment, An Giang University. He has 15 years of experience in environmental and natural resource management such as: Identify vegetation structure, biomass and carbon stocks of wetlands, building of vegetation cover maps by using remote sensing and GIS. Moreover, He also has done researches on water balance for floodplains, calculating water needs for agriculture, interpreting remote sensing images to estimate evapotranspiration for crops. Determining the flooded area for the delta or the area of land was affected by saltwater intrusion to serve crop planning, towards smart and sustainable agriculture.

Bhupendra Kumar completed his Graduation and Post Graduation from Chaudhary Charan Singh University, Meerut, U.P. and Ph.D. in Computer Science and Engineering from Mewar University, Hapur. Presently, he is working as a Professor in the Department of Computer Science and Applications, IIMT University, Meerut, U.P. He has been a huge teaching experience of 19 years. He is the reviewer member of some reputed journals. He has published several book chapters and research papers of national and international reputed journals.

P. Senthil Kumar is an Associate Professor (Mathematics) at the Amity School of Engineering and Technology of Amity University, Bengaluru, Karnataka, India. He received BSc, MSc, and MPhil degrees from Jamal Mohamed College (JMC), Tiruchirappalli, in 2006, 2008, and 2010, respectively. Furthermore, he received a B.Ed. degree from the Jamal Mohamed College of Teacher Education in 2009. Additionally, he completed PGDCA in 2011 at Bharathidasan University and PGDAOR in 2012 at Annamalai University, Tamil Nadu, India. He completed his PhD at JMC in 2017. He has published many research papers in peer-reviewed journals. He has also presented research papers at various conferences. He has introduced the PSK (P. Senthil Kumar) method and PSK theorem for solving assignment problems (APs) in uncertain environments. And also, he has proved the supporting theorem, which states that the assignment obtained by the PSK method for solving fuzzy APs is always optimal. Its relevant articles have been published in Springer and IGI Global Journals, which are indexed in Scopus and WoS. His areas of research interest include operations research and fuzzy and intuitionistic fuzzy optimization.

L.Rajeshkumar, Assistant Professor in the Department of MBA. He has graduated BBA from Aditanar College of Arts and Sciences, MBA, and M.Phil from Manonmaniam Sundarnar University in Tirunelveli. In December 2012, he qualified for the UGC-NET examination. Then 2018, he received his Ph.D with a marketing specialization especially in FMCG. He started his career at Manonmaniam Sundaranar University College, Govindaperi, in September, 2012. After that, he moved to DMI. St. Eugune University, Zambia, for one year in the 2014–15 academic year. In 2015, he began his Ph.D. studies at Manonmaniam Sundarnar University in Tirunelveli. In July 2018, he submitted his thesis and started his journey at the Aarupadai Veedu Institute of Technology, Chennai, in February 2018. Then, in February 2020, he shifted his work to TNJFU - Fisheries Business School, Tamilnadu Dr.J. Jayalalithaa Fisheries University, OMR Campus, Chennai. After that, in October 2022, he joined as an assistant professor in the department of MBA at St.Joseph's College of Engineering, Chennai. Overall, he has 11 years of experience, including 3 years of research and 8 years of teaching. He has specialized in Marketing and Finance. He has published many research papers in National and International journals. He has participated in many FDPs, workshops, and seminars at the national and international levels. He received numerous awards, including the Best NSS Volunteer Award at the University level, the Young Citizen Award, and the Yuva Shri Kala Bharathi Award. He also has a volunteer who enjoys organising programmes and social activities such as blood donations. He is more interested in sports.

Retno Lestari, an esteemed nursing lecturer at Brawijaya University's Faculty of Health Sciences. Her impressive academic background includes earning her bachelor's degree from the prestigious University of Indonesia's Faculty of Nursing in 2003 and a master's degree in nursing education from Monash University, Australia, in 2009. In 2020, she completed her doctoral degree at Airlangga University's Faculty of Public Health.

Rathi Meena M has been rich experience in the field of research and teaching.

Manikandan Working as an Assistant Professor, SRM college of management, SRM University. He had a very good experience in the field of research and teaching.

M. Soundarya, acted as an assistant professor in the School of management studies Sathyabama Institute of science and Technology. She had a lot research papers to her credit.

Thirupathi Manickam, M.Com, M.Phil, B.Ed, TN-SET, KSET, Ph.D., works as an Assistant professor in the Department of Professional Studies at Christ University, Bangalore. It is one of the leading institutions in Bangalore, Karnataka, and the institution is Accredited by NIRF, NBA and NAAC Accredited university. He has more than seven years of teaching and Research experience. He has 52 citations and three h-Index. He has published 26 research papers in Scopus, Web of Science, UGC-CARE, and UGC-approved and leading International journals and 11 presented papers in national and international conferences. He has also participated in over 50 seminars, conferences, FDP & workshops at the National and International Levels. His areas of expertise are Financial Accounting, Corporate Accounting, Financial Management, Management Accounting, Taxation, Digital Marketing and Technology Management.

R. Karthickmanoj received B.E (Electronics and Communication Engineering) from Syed Ammal Engineering College in 2007, M.E (VLSI Design) from SRM Eswari Engineering College, Chennai in 2012 and the Pursuing Doctoral degree from Academy of Maritime Education and Training, Deemed to be University, Chennai from 2019. Having 9 Plus years experience in both teaching and Industry. Currently, working as Assistant Professor in Academy of Maritime Education and Training, Deemed to be University, Chennai. He has published 03 national, 04international journals and nearly 10 National and international conferences Proceedings. He has Received certificate of Appreciation for contributing a chapter in the event Asia book of records. He is a life Member in 6 Professional Bodies, and acting as reviewer for reputed journals. His areas of interest are VLSI, Signal Processing, Robotics and Artificial Intelligence.

S. Aasha Nandhini is working as Assistant Professor, Department of ECE, SSN College of Engineering. She has received her B.E. degree in Electronics and Communication Engineering from Anna University and M.E. degree in Communication Systems from Anna University, Chennai. She obtained her Ph.D. degree from Anna University for her research work on Video compressive sensing. Her research interests include Wireless Multimedia Sensor Networks, Compressed Sensing, IoT, and Artificial Intelligence. She has 9 research publications in international journals, 9 research publications in national and international conferences, 2 book chapters, and one book.

Abhiruj Navabhatra is an assistant professor at Rangsit University in Thailand, specializing in pharmaceutical sciences and technology. His journey in academia began in 2005 when he earned a bachelor's degree in pharmacy. His deep interest in pharmacology and toxicology led him to further his education, culminating in a Ph.D. from Chulalongkorn University in 2016. During his research fellowship and internship from 2014 to 2016, he worked at the Toxicogenomics Laboratory within the Department of Clinical Pharmacology at Nagoya University's Graduate School of Medicine, located in Nagoya, Aichi, Japan. Here, he broadened his research horizons to encompass the study of enzymes' mechanisms, specifically cytochrome P450 (CYP), with a focus on drug-drug and drug-herb interactions (DDIs). Dr. Navabhatra's concentrated research has significantly impacted his field, earning him a Scopus H-index of 5. Over his career, he has published more than ten scholarly articles and conference papers. His research predominantly examines pharmacology and toxicology, optimization algorithms, and the integration of machine learning in the realm of pharmaceutical sciences. His research, recognized and published in several esteemed journals, has enriched numerous pivotal publications within his field. Through his dedicated efforts in research and education, Dr. Navabhatra continues to be a progressive force within the field of pharmaceutical sciences and technology.

Rajneesh Panwar Graduated and Post Graduated in Mathematics and Computer Application from Ch. Charan Singh University, Meerut (U.P.) and received his M. Tech. in Computer Science from Shobhit University, Meerut. Presently, he is working as an Assistant Professor in the School of Computer Science and Application IIMT University, Meerut, U.P. He qualifies GATE 2021 and UGC-NET June 2020 and December 2020. He has published several book chapters and research papers of national and international repute.

Sabyasachi Pramanik is a professional IEEE member. He obtained a Ph.D. in Computer Science and Engineering from Sri Satya Sai University of Technology and Medical Sciences, Bhopal, India. Presently, he is an Associate Professor, Department of Computer Science and Engineering, Haldia Institute of Technology, India. He has many publications in various reputed international conferences, journals, and book chapters (Indexed by SCIE, Scopus, ESCI, etc). He is doing research in the fields of Artificial Intelligence, Data Privacy, Cybersecurity, Network Security, and Machine Learning. He also serves on the editorial boards of several international journals. He is a reviewer of journal articles from IEEE, Springer, Elsevier, Inderscience, IET and IGI Global. He has reviewed many conference papers, has been a keynote speaker, session chair, and technical program committee member at many international conferences. He has authored a book on Wireless Sensor Network. He has edited 8 books from IGI Global, CRC Press, Springer and Wiley Publications.

Asi Lakshmi Priyanka is an Assistant Professor, author, guide from the Department of Management Studies at Satya Institute of Technology and Management, Vizianagaram, Andhra Pradesh. MBA., Ph.D. (pursuing) in the Department of Commerce and Management Studies from Andhra University, Visakhapatnam. She has 10 years of teaching experience in the field of management studies. She has published several papers and book chapters in peer-reviewed journals and books. She has guided more than 40 projects for management students. She is a passionate educator and is committed to helping students learn and understand the management studies subjects. She is one of the reviewers for the International Journal of Emerging technologies and Innovative Research. Mrs. Lakshmi Priyanka is a valuable asset to the Satya institute of Technology and Management and in the field of management studies. She is a dedicated educator and researcher.

Anuradha Radhakrishnan has 19 years of Experience in Teaching, currently working as an Associate Professor in the Department of Computer Science and Engineering at Sri Ramakrishna Engineering College. Have completed Ph.D. in the Research Area Data Mining (Fuzzy logic) and has a Master's degree in Computer Science Engineering and a Bachelor's degree in Computer Hardware and Software Engineering. SPOC of the Artificial Intelligence-Research Group and guided projects in the areas of Artificial Intelligence, Machine Learning, Cryptography and Data Analytics. Life member of ISTE, IEANG, & CSI and published Research papers in Scopus indexed Journals and Conferences. Awarded Silver Partner faculty under Inspire -The Campus Connect, Faculty Partnership Model, Infosys. Worked on consultancy projects with G.E Healthcare & LTTS (L&T technology) in the domain of medical image processing and deep learning. Convener of Artificial Intelligence Research Group at SREC and Lead person representing SREC at Leadingindia.ai, a nationwide initiative for artificial intelligence skilling and research-Bennett University, Noida. Currently working on TNSCST Funded project that involves Women Health with Brain Computer Interface and Yoga therapy.

Gowtham Rajendiran is a Full-Time Research Scholar in the Department of Computing Technologies, SRM Institute of Science and Technology, Kattankulathur Campus, Tamil Nadu, India. He completed his UG and PG degrees in the stream of Computer Science and Engineering with good academic records. Currently, he is carrying out his research work in the agriculture field with the help of IoT and Machine Learning Technologies. He has published many articles, one in an International journal and the other three papers in International Conferences which are indexed by the Scopus Database.

Saurabh Rawat is conscientious and self motivated individual with great enthusiasm and determination to succeed through his pupils. He is highly experienced professional with more than 20 years in the field of computers and Mathematics. An alumnus of IIT, specializes in Vedic Mathematics, believes in concept based learning along with innovative techniques. Every year he guides many students through on and off campus recruitment in various multinational companies like Infosys, Accenture, TCS, Wipro and many more. Author has also assisted aspirants in various examinations like GRE, GMAT, CAT, MAT, SSC and many more. He has appeared in CAT examinations many times himself. He has several research papers and conference proceeding in reputed journals.

Jebakumar Rethnaraj is working as an Associate Professor in the Department of Computing Technologies, SRM Institute of Science and Technology, Kattankulathur Campus, Tamil Nadu, India. He has more than 18 years of teaching experience with good academic knowledge. He has guided more than five research scholars under his Ph. D guidance. Currently, he is guiding two full-time research scholars with domain expertise. Coming to his publications, he has published more than forty-five articles that include International Journals and Conferences which are indexed by Scopus database.

Anushree Sah is highly experienced IT professional having an experience of more than 18 years in the field of IT industry and education. The author has worked with the renowned companies like Oracle Financial Services & Software Ltd., Western Union, Dencare Ltd., DIT University, UPES etc. The author has completed her bachelor's in Computer Science and Engineering and has Master's degree from University of Greenwich, London, U.K. She holds various academic and administrative responsibilities in her current working place. The author specializes in Programming Languages, Web Technologies,

Blockchain, Building Enterprise Application, Service Oriented Computing and Cloud Computing. She has several research papers, conference proceedings, Book Chapters and Project.

Kewal Krishan Sharma is a professor in computer sc. in IIMT University, Meerut, U.P, India. He did his Ph.D. in computer network with this he has MCA, MBA and Law degree also. He did variously certification courses also. He has an overall experience of around 33 year in academic, business and industry. He wrote a number of research papers and books.

Vikas Sharma completed his Graduation and Post Graduation from Chaudhary Charan Singh University, Meerut, U.P. Currently Pursuing his Ph.D. in Computer Science and Engineering from Govt. Recognized University. Presently, he is working as an Assistant Professor in the Department of Computer Science and Applications, IIMT University, Meerut, U.P. He has been awarded as Excellence in teaching award 2019. He is the reviewer member of some reputed journals. He has published several book chapters and research papers of national and international reputed journals.

Polpan Sillapapibool is a lecturer at the Faculty of Pharmaceutical Sciences, Ubon Ratchathani University, Thailand. Having earned his Doctor of Pharmacy degree in 2023, he embarked on a rewarding academic journey. His specialized knowledge spans across three key areas of pharmaceutical sciences: pharmaceutical chemistry, pharmaceutical analysis, and quality control of pharmaceutical products. As an academic, he is dedicated to educating future generations of pharmacists, continually enriching the field with his research and insights.

Sasilatha T., Professor and Dean, Department of Electrical and Electronics Engineering has 26 years of experience in teaching, research and administration. She received her B.E Degree from Manonmaniam Sundaranar University, ME and Ph.D. Degrees from Anna University, Chennai. She has received CMI Level 5 Certificate in Management and Leadership from UK. She has published more than 100 articles in refereed International Journals and Conferences. Prior to joining AMET in 2017, she had served as a Faculty and elevated as various academic positions in St. Joseph's group of Institutions from 1996 to 2013. She served as Vice Principal in affiliated colleges. She has performed funded research projects and has participated in industry collaborated projects. She is a member of IEEE professional society, Life member of Indian Society for Technical Education (ISTE) and IAENG. She has guided 5 Ph.D. scholars and guiding 08 research scholars in the area of VLSI Design, Artificial Intelligence, Signal Processing and Wireless Sensor Networks. She has received certificate of appreciation from the International Association of Maritime Universities (IAMU) in 2019. Recently she has organized AICTE funded National conference and AICTE funded Short term training Program.

Anu Thomas is an accomplished academic with a Ph.D. in Computer Applications from the prestigious National Institute of Technology, Tiruchirappalli. She brings a wealth of expertise to the field of Computer Science and is currently serving as an Assistant Professor in the Department of Computer Applications at St. George's College, Aruvithura. Dr. Thomas specializes in several areas including Computational Linguistics, Information Extraction, Knowledge Graphs, Ontology, and Semantic Similarity. Her expertise extends to a range of cutting-edge technologies such as Python, Natural Language Processing, Machine Learning, IoT, and Deep Learning, making her a sought-after resource person in these fields. Above all, Dr. Thomas is a dedicated and innovative professional with a passion for advancing the field of computer science. Her commitment is evident in her groundbreaking research and teaching, which aim to push the boundaries of knowledge and innovation in the field. Her contributions to the academic community and her impact on her students undoubtedly make her a valuable asset in the realm of computer science education and research.

V. Sheela Mary working as a Professor in Department of Management, Aarupadai Veedu Institute of Technology, Paiyanoor, Vinayaka Mission's Research Foundation (Deemed to be University). She has a rich experience in the field of teaching and research. She is a motivating and talented person driven to inspire students to pursue academic excellence. She is having a teaching experience of around 21 years and 11 months. Since 2004, she has been involved in Management education at Aarupadai Veedu Institute of Technology, teaching Management & HR related subjects. She is consistently striving to create a challenging and engaging learning environment in which students become good learners. She has acquired many awards such as Excellence in Organisation Award, Best Women Teacher Award, Best Faculty award twice in different academic years, Best Paper Award (First Prize) twice for presentation of papers in International Conferences and Best Paper Award for publishing a journal in International Journal She has attended and participated in many workshops, seminars, webinars and presented papers in National conferences and International conferences. She has published Book Chapter Publications, Scopus Journal Publications, UGC Care List Journals and International Journals.

Tarun Kumar Vashishth is an active academician and researcher in the field of computer science with 21 years of experience. He earned Ph.D. Mathematics degree specialized in Operations Research; served several academic positions such as HoD, Dy. Director, Academic Coordinator, Member Secretary of Department Research Committee, Assistant Center superintendent and Head Examiner in university examinations. He is involved in academic development and scholarly activities. He is member of International Association of Engineers, The Society of Digital Information and Wireless Communications, Global Professors Welfare Association, International Association of Academic plus Corporate (IAAC), Computer Science Teachers Association and Internet Society. His research interest includes Cloud Computing, Artificial Intelligence, Machine Learning and Operations Research; published more than 20 research articles with 1 book and 10 book chapters in edited books. He is contributing as member of editorial and reviewers boards in conferences and various computer journals published by CRC Press, Taylor and Francis, Springer, IGI global and other universities.

Heni Dwi Windarwati is an esteemed nursing lecturer at the Faculty of Health Sciences of Universitas Brawijaya. She has an impressive educational background, having completed her undergraduate nursing program, nursing program, master's program specializing in psychiatric nursing, psychiatric nursing specialist program, and doctoral nursing program at the prestigious University of Indonesia.

Ayush Yadav, a driven B.Tech student immersing myself in the dynamic world of Computer Science and Engineering, with a keen focus on Artificial Intelligence and Machine Learning. My academic pursuits reflect not just a curriculum but a passion for pushing the boundaries of technology. During my academic journey, I have actively engaged in groundbreaking research projects that delve into the forefront of AI and ML. My dedication to innovation is evident in my authored and co-authored papers, shedding light on topics like "Smart Healthcare". Beyond the code, I am committed to understanding the societal implications of AI and ML, striving for ethical and responsible innovation. In essence, my journey in the world of AI and ML is fueled by a passion for innovation and a commitment to pushing the boundaries of technology. I invite you to explore more about my work and join me on this exciting journey of discovery.

Bancha Yingngam, an Associate Professor at Ubon Ratchathani University in Thailand, brings a wealth of knowledge and experience in Pharmaceutical Sciences and Technology. His academic path started in 2005, when he graduated with a bachelor's degree in pharmacy, receiving second-class honors. Driven by his passion for phytomedicines and community pharmacy, he furthered his studies, obtaining a Ph.D. in 2011 from the same university. Between 2013 and 2021, during his postdoctoral fellowship at Karl-Franzens-Universität Graz, Austria, he extended his research focus to include optimization and machine learning algorithms in the development of pharmaceutical, cosmetic, perfume, and nutraceutical products. This focus has significantly influenced his field, as exemplified by his Scopus H-index of 9. Throughout his career, Dr. Yingngam has written over twenty scholarly articles, book chapters, and conference papers. His research largely explores optimization algorithms and the integration of machine learning in healthcare product development. His research has been acknowledged and published in various esteemed journals, and his contributions have enriched several key publications in his field.

Index

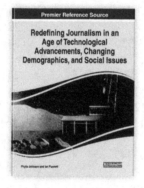

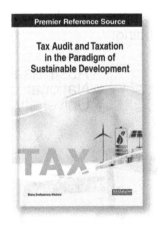

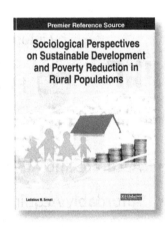

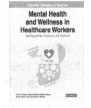

Printed in the United States
by Baker & Taylor Publisher Services